An Intimate

Portrait of

Larry Ellison

and Oracle

SOFTWAR

MATTHEW SYMONDS

with Commentary

by Larry Ellison

Simon & Schuster
New York London Toronto Sydney Singapore

SIMON & SCHUSTER
Rockefeller Center
1230 Avenue of the Americas
New York, NY 10020

For information regarding special discounts for bulk purchases,
please contact Simon & Schuster Special Sales at 1-800-456-6798 or
business@simonandschuster.com

Designed by Karolina Harris

Manufactured in the United States of America

10 9 8 7 6 5 4 3 2 1

Library of Congress Cataloging-in-Publication Data

Symonds, Matthew.
   Softwar : an intimate portrait of Larry Ellison and Oracle / Matthew Symonds with
commentary by Larry Ellison.
      p.   cm.
   1. Ellison, Larry.   2. Oracle Corporation—History.   3. Computer software
industry—United States—History.   4. Businessmen—United States—Biography.
I. Ellison, Larry.   II. Title.

HD9696.63.U62E4478   2003
338.7'610053'0973—dc22   2003058989

ISBN 0-7432-2504-X

To Alison and the children with all my love

ACKNOWLEDGMENTS

There are many people without whose help and advice this book could not have been written. Above all, I'm grateful to Larry Ellison, whose enthusiasm and commitment never wavered even after it became clear that the story would not only have its share of twists and turns but would have a conclusion somewhat less clear cut than he had hoped. My thanks also to Melanie Craft, who bore with fortitude my invasion of her and Larry's privacy. Very many Oracle executives, both past and present, gave freely of their time and thoughts. It's not possible to mention everyone; they know who they are, and they are quoted in the book. But with Mark Jarvis, Jeff Henley, Safra Catz, Mark Barrenechea, Jay Nussbaum, and Ron Wohl I enjoyed a kind of extended conversation over a period getting on for two years. I was continually struck by the frankness and openness of those working for Oracle today, even when it came to talking about their boss. I would also like to record my thanks to Ray Lane. He understood that my relationship with Ellison was collaborative, but he still consented to be interviewed on two occasions, each time for several hours. He may not realize it, but he still has some good friends at Oracle. I also want to mention Joshua Lederberg, Steve Jobs, Jimmy Linn, Jon Bannenberg, and Laura Seccombe, who, in their different ways, gave me insights into Ellison's life that were unique. I must thank, too, those who helped me in practical ways, in particular Joyce Higashi, Carolyn Balkenhol, and Judy Sim. Without them there really would have been no book. I should pay tribute to my literary agent, Andrew Wylie, and my editor at Simon & Schuster, Geoff Kloske. From the outset, Andrew helped shape and define the project and continually buoyed me with his confidence and support; Geoff honed, tightened, and, where necessary, discreetly made me intelligible to Americans. Finally, my thanks to Bill Emmott, the editor of *The Economist*, who graciously allowed me a year's leave to pursue this project and whose imaginative suggestion in 1997 that I should write about the unfolding drama of the Internet led directly to my meeting Larry Ellison.

CONTENTS

AUTHOR'S NOTE

In March 2000, I received a telephone call from Larry Ellison. He had an idea for doing a book about e-business and globalization and wanted to know if I would be interested in coauthorship. I was flattered, but it wasn't something I wanted to do for a number of reasons. In the first place, a relationship with Ellison of that kind would mean I would have to give up writing about the technology business for *The Economist* because of the potential for conflict of interest. Second, I had no desire to add to the torrent of indifferent books about the e-business phenomenon that were then flooding the business publishing market. Third, although we shared many views and I had grown to like Ellison and enjoy his company in the brief time I had known him, I thought that coauthoring a book with him would be a nightmare.

But while we were talking, a much more appealing proposition began to form in my mind: what I would be interested in doing was writing an intimate portrait of Ellison and his company on the basis of having a very high degree of access to both him and Oracle. I explained that I would have to have complete editorial control and that it might be some time before I could take leave of absence from *The Economist*. Ellison's answer was immediate: he'd love me to do it, and he was prepared to wait until I was ready.

Nine months later, in December 2000, accompanied by my New York–based literary agent, Andrew Wylie, I met with Ellison at his Japanese-style villa in Atherton, a leafy and very expensive suburb some twenty miles to the southwest of San Francisco that is home to much of the Silicon Valley establishment. The meeting had three purposes. First, I needed to establish the basis of my working relationship with Ellison: Wylie had concluded that there should be a formal collaboration agreement between us. Second, although Ellison and I had recently discussed the book over dinner at my house in London, I did not yet have a settled idea of what it should be, although I had already ruled out doing a conventional biography. I knew that if the project was to engage Ellison it would have to be relevant to his current concerns. Most of all, I wanted to test Ellison's claim that Oracle was poised for true greatness.

One of the things I had noticed while covering the technology business was that many of its key players had extraordinarily little interest in even the recent past. It was as much as most of them could do to remember what it was that Microsoft had done to end up in court. Even Marc Andreessen was much keener to talk about the new businesses he was investing in than his epic struggle against Bill Gates while at Netscape. His attitude was: been there; done that; move on. When Microsoft's witnesses were confronted with damning e-mails they'd written only a couple of years before, it is just possible their surprise and struggle to guess what they might have meant at the time wasn't completely phony. Ellison doesn't suffer from that kind of amnesia, but even though he reads history voraciously and tries to learn from it, what really interests him is not the last five years but the next five. To Ellison, the present and the near future elide so gracefully as to be almost indistinguishable. And when talking about software, last year is another country.

A collaboration agreement that gave me everything I would need was quickly reached. An innovative twist, devised by Andrew Wylie, was that Ellison would have a kind of right of reply or commentary within the book, which he could use either to express a counterpoint to any of my conclusions that he disagreed with or to amplify things that he thought important. Neither of us would be able to alter the words of the other. It is a unique form of joint copyright. I think it has worked.

There is one other thing I would like to say about my relationship with Ellison. In the course of my research, I met, somewhat to my surprise, a number of people who assumed that Ellison was paying me to write what he hoped would be a sympathetic account of his life. This is not the case. My compensation and expenses have been covered in full by the advance from my publisher. That said, I have stayed as his guest during my many visits to Oracle and have traveled with him on his private planes. I have also spent time with Ellison on his boats, recording extensive interviews during his vacations and, most recently, joining him in Auckland to report at first hand on his America's Cup campaign. Has this degree of intimacy undermined my ability to be objective about Ellison? It is hard for me to say, but I don't believe so. I like Ellison and there is much about him that I admire, but I am frequently critical of him. Most of us, I think, are able to reach reasonably objective judgments about even our closest friends. Liking them does not mean being oblivious to their faults. I have written the truth about Ellison as I have found it and reported faithfully, for better or ill, the words of the many people who know him whom I have interviewed. When Ellison's version of events appears questionable or his behavior less than admirable, I have said so. But to a great extent, the picture of Ellison that emerges is one formed by his own words during innumerable, at times brutally frank, conversations conducted over a period of two years. Ellison is, more often than not, his own harshest and most unrelenting critic.

SOFTWAR

1

LARRY AND ME

I first met Larry Ellison in his office at Oracle's Redwood Shores head-quarters on December 8, 1997. I had recently become *The Economist*'s technology and communications editor, and this was the first of what became regular visits to Silicon Valley. I had just completed two days of meetings at Microsoft's campus at Redmond, Washington, 800 miles to the north, where an array of impressively on-message executives had been wheeled out for my benefit—though unfortunately not Bill Gates himself. I would see him on my next visit, I was assured. But there was a strong hint that "face time with Bill" was conditional on *The Economist*'s taking a more sympathetic line toward Microsoft in the antitrust case that the Department of Justice was preparing against it. After a similar turn involving Oracle's most senior managers, I had been promised time with Ellison himself.

It turned out I'd picked a bad afternoon. I didn't know it at the time, but Oracle was about to issue its first earnings warning since the firm had nearly gone under in 1990. The economic crisis in Asia had taken its toll, and in North America, slowing license sales of Oracle's most important product, its all-conquering database, seemed to support the argument of some analysts that Oracle was dominating a market that was getting close to saturation. The following day, the stock lost 30 percent of its value.

As I waited, I could see Ellison through the glass doors of the eleventh-floor boardroom, huddled in conversation. He was already an hour and a half late for his interview with me and I knew he had to fly to New York later in the day to deliver a keynote speech at an Internet conference. I had heard stories about Ellison's lateness and didn't believe the press flak's distracted excuses about an "emergency" being the cause of the delay. Let's leave it for another time, I suggested grumpily. But at that moment, I was suddenly ushered into Ellison's handsome office with its expensive Japanese artifacts and panoramic views across the bay.

Despite the strain he must have been under, Ellison was courtesy itself. After apologizing profusely for his lateness, he began to talk about technology. His theme was the failure of the prevailing computer architecture of the day, known as client/server (because the job of running software was shared between server computers in corporate data centers and their desktop PC "clients"). He believed client/server was an "evolutionary dead end" that was "distributing complexity" with disastrous consequences. The answer was a new model of computing based on the Internet, in which the complexity and the computing would be hidden in the network. Users would be able to access everything they needed through a web browser that could be run by a machine much less expensive and cantankerous than a PC—a network computer.

There was nothing unexpected in this. It was a drum that Ellison had been beating for some time, and conceptually it was little different from Sun Microsystems's famous slogan that "the network is the computer." Ellison had first declared the PC "a ridiculous device" at a technology conference in Paris more than two years earlier. The speech, at the height of the hoopla surrounding the release of Windows 95 and in front of an audience that included Bill Gates, caused a minor sensation.*

Ellison ran through a well-rehearsed routine, but there was nonetheless something extraordinarily compelling about his argument. He seemed to be speaking directly to the problems that anyone who depended on computers at work knew all too well: the crash-prone PC with its incomprehensible error messages; the incredible effort of maintaining thousands of PCs across a company; the apparently insurmountable difficulties of getting reasonable performance and scalability across wide-area networks. The arguments seemed utterly rational and commonsensical, while Ellison himself was passionate and funny.

---

*LE writes: The arrival of Windows 95 received more media attention than the Middle East peace accords, which were signed that same week. But that wasn't the only thing I found odd. While everyone applauded Microsoft's increasingly complex desktop software, I was convinced that every application that could be moved off the PC should be moved off the PC. To me the entire industry was headed in the wrong direction.

• • •

Over the next three years, Ellison was proved to be far more right than wrong. The network computer itself proved to be a dazzling digression: Ellison had been right about how the Internet would change the way computers were used, but most people still reckoned that the best way of getting to the Internet was through a PC. A few network computers were made by Oracle and a loosely knit coalition of Microsoft's enemies, such as IBM and Sun Microsystems, but tumbling PC prices and the limitations imposed by slow dial-up connections quickly condemned them to irrelevance. Microsoft crowed; Ellison was made to look a bit foolish. But the PC versus the NC was a sideshow that stole attention from the real struggle for the future of computing. What mattered was that Ellison had understood better than anyone the potential impact of the Internet on enterprise computing in general and on Oracle in particular.*

While the technology analysts in the investment banks and the consultancies confidently predicted the maturing of the database market, Ellison realized that the Internet would exponentially increase both the number of database transactions and the number of people who would interact with Oracle's databases. That would mean more license growth than the analysts had dreamed of. Every time someone looked for a book on Amazon.com, bought stock through E*TRADE, or put something up for auction on eBay, that person was using an Oracle database. Ellison believed that the database would be the essential platform for Internet computing, effectively displacing the once all-important operating system.

Within companies, the same thing would happen. Instead of business software being used by only a handful of specialists, Internet-based applications could be extended to anyone with authorization and a

---

*LE writes: The primary message in Oracle's Internet computing announcement was that complex application software should move off desktop PCs and be embedded in the network on server computers. Users would then access these applications via an Internet browser. To demonstrate our new approach to computing, we built a simple $500 desktop computer that ran one and only one program: an Internet browser. The easily explained NC captured much more media attention than the more complex concept of an Internet computing architecture. In marketing, simple messages always win. The market itself has a different set of dynamics. PC prices dropped from $2,500 to $500, rendering the NC unnecessary. But at the same time, every other enterprise software company copied the fundamental structure of our Internet computing architecture.

browser. Every time one of those applications was used, there was a good chance that it would query the database that the application ran on. When the networking giant Cisco Systems talked of having a "URL for everything we do," it was another way of saying that everybody they employed was constantly using the firm's Oracle database. In a client/server world, less sophisticated databases, such as Microsoft's SQL Server, might have become "good enough" for many businesses, but with Internet computing came the need for databases that could support millions of users at once. With the coming of e-business, Oracle's databases became at least as much an essential element of infrastructure as Cisco's routers or the big server computers made by the likes of Sun that were also back in fashion. It was no coincidence that in early 2000 those three companies—the three superstars of the Internet—had a combined market value of nearly a trillion dollars.

If that was a stroke of luck for Oracle, what wasn't was Ellison's decision, to the horror of many colleagues and customers, to abandon all further development of client/server-based applications and concentrate the firm's entire engineering effort on building for the new computing architecture of the Internet. While rivals in the apps business, such as the German powerhouse SAP and PeopleSoft, talked up the Internet and put a web front-end on some of their products, Ellison went much further. Oracle was the first established software firm to risk everything on the new paradigm.

His rationale was simple: Oracle could never hope to be number one in enterprise applications as long as client/server prevailed—it was fated always to play second fiddle to SAP, whose strength in the enterprise apps market almost matched Oracle's dominance in databases. By getting to the Internet first, assuming that the software could be made to work, Ellison would force Oracle's competitors to become followers, gaining vital time-to-market over them. And, crucially in an industry in which perception is as important as reality, if Ellison's bet came off, it would make Oracle appear very cool.

The strategy of harnessing Internet hype and turning Oracle from stodgy to hip—Ellison's mantra had become "the Internet changes everything"—helped drive Oracle's market cap in 2000 to within touching distance of a Microsoft brought low by the government's antitrust case. Ellison even briefly overtook Bill Gates as the world's richest man, with a net worth of more than $50 billion. If newspaper and magazine articles about Ellison still found plenty of space to describe in loving detail his high-rolling ways, they were also forced to concede that there was substance too. Even though Ellison refused to conform to their idea of what an *Über*-geek should look and sound like—Gates had that one sewn up—there was a growing willingness to concede that, although as arrogant and addicted to hyperbole as ever, Ellison probably was an authentic business and technology visionary.

• • •

In December 2000, when I was thinking about writing this book, Ellison told me that he was preparing to bet the company all over again in a do-or-die attempt to make Oracle not just the biggest software company, but the world's most influential corporation. To Ellison, that meant not so much passing Microsoft in revenues, although that would be nice, but Oracle having become the successor to industrial icons such as Ford and IBM, whose products and vision had changed the way the world works. He couldn't bear to include Microsoft in that pantheon. At first it sounded like a characteristic piece of Ellisonian exaggeration. With Ellison, you never quite knew whether he was being provocative for the sake of it or whether he really meant it.

Before deciding to do the book, I went to see him at his home in Atherton. I needed to gauge how serious he really was. After talking through the day and well into the night, I concluded that he was very serious indeed.

His logic went like this: The arrival of the Internet meant we were now living at the beginning of the information age—"it's the information age, not the fucking operating system age"—and Oracle, it just so happened, was the leading company for helping people to manage their information. Software was the product that made the world go round, and the software business, according to Ellison, is and always has been based on the principle of winner take all. IBM and Microsoft, in their heydays, had demonstrated that. But now the rules of the game had shifted in Oracle's favor, and it was its turn to become the dominant force in computing. IBM and Microsoft had both bestrode their respective eras—eras that had been defined by the prevailing computer architectures of the day, the mainframe followed by client/server.

Ellison was convinced that Oracle was now poised to claim the mantle that Microsoft had snatched from IBM. But while these two companies' reigns had been temporary, Ellison reckoned Oracle could be on top for a very long time. He believed that the world was inexorably moving toward "one network [the Internet], one database [from Oracle]."He says: "I really don't think there will be another paradigm shift. This is it."

But the database alone could not bring Oracle the degree of success that Ellison was after. For that, he needed Oracle's applications to become the enterprising computing equivalent of Microsoft's ubiquitous Office. In other words, Oracle's Release 11i, or the E-Business Suite as Ellison preferred to call it, would need to become the standard package of applications for automating the world's businesses. Release 11i had shipped some six months earlier at the beginning of June and Ellison was convinced it was going to turn the economy of business computing on its head. Engineered for the Internet from scratch, it was one of the biggest and most complex pieces of software ever created. It brought together traditional enterprise resource planning (ERP) applications for running all of a company's back-office functions with the much newer customer relationship management (CRM) programs, which were designed to deal with every outward-facing task from sales automation to choreographing a sophisticated marketing campaign. It was, Ellison boasted, the only integrated suite that could do everything that most business customers would ever need it to do.

The consequence, Ellison argued, was that it was no longer necessary to hire expensive systems integrators from IBM or Accenture to glue together market-leading applications from different software vendors—the practice known as bringing together best-of-breed. "Building an integrated system out of several different software products that were never designed to work together is a very difficult task. At Oracle, we used to sell and deliver these best-of-breed systems; selling was easy, delivery was hard. IBM has thousands of consultants eager to help you make it work. The more complex the integration project the more likely it will be late and over budget. It may even fail completely. And in the end it's the customer who assumes the financial risk for the success or failure of these projects. This best-of-breed software product assembly approach is absolutely unique to the computer industry. If Detroit ran like Silicon Valley, nobody would sell cars—just parts. Customers would have to figure out which were the 'best' parts—a Honda engine, a Ford transmission, a BMW chassis, GM electrical system—and buy them and try to assemble them into a working car. Good luck. I know it sounds crazy, but that's how companies put together business systems today."

But not for much longer, if Ellison had anything to do with it. Ellison was betting that companies with the bitter experience of lengthy software implementations that never fully delivered or returned their investment would be willing to break with the past and buy nearly everything from Oracle. He was also betting that among software vendors only Oracle was big and powerful enough to put together a complete "soup-to-nuts" package of e-business applications, tightly integrated with the database, that would work reliably straight out of the box. And finally, he was betting that the giant systems integration and consulting firms, who recommended to clients what software they should buy, would not turn against Oracle for trying to destroy a large and lucrative part of their business. Ellison leaned back in his chair, grinning: "I feel slightly dizzy when I think about it. We have this one chance to win, and I know that unless we screw up, it's going to happen."

Ellison was, in effect, going to war with nearly the whole of the computing business. Mooning Microsoft was one thing, but challenging so much of the industry's conventional wisdom and vested interests at one time and with few allies seemed unnecessarily foolhardy. I wondered whether Ellison would have the stamina for such a grueling challenge. He was fifty-six years old and, thanks to the 24 percent stake in Oracle that he had clung to through thick and thin since the initial public offering in 1985, he was wealthy beyond even his own understanding.

Although he always talked about technology and Oracle with passion and intensity, he didn't have the methodical relentlessness that made Bill Gates so formidable and feared. By his own admission, Ellison was not an obsessive grinder like Gates: "I am a sprinter. I rest, I sprint, I rest, I sprint again." Ellison had a reputation for being easily bored by the process of running a business and often took time off, leaving the shop to senior colleagues. One of the reasons often trotted out for Oracle's success in the 1990s was Ellison's decision to hire Ray Lane, a senior executive credited with bringing order and discipline to the business, allowing Ellison just to do the vision thing and bunk off to sail his boats whenever he felt like it. But Lane had left Oracle nearly eighteen months before after falling out with Ellison. Since then, Ellison had taken full control of the company—how likely was it that he would he stay the course?

One reason to be skeptical was that Ellison just seemed to have too many things going on in his life besides Oracle. During the afternoon, we took a break from discussing the future of computing to take a tour of what would be his new home—nearly a decade in the making, and at that time, still nearly three years from completion. In the hills of Woodside, California, framing a five-acre artificial lake, six wooden Japanese houses, perfect replicas of the fifteenth- and sixteenth-century originals in Kyoto, were under construction. The site also contained two full-size ornamental bridges, hundreds of boulders trucked in from the high Sierras and arranged according to Zen principles and an equal number of cherry trees jostling for attention next to towering redwoods. Ellison re-marked: "If I'm remembered for anything, it's more likely to be for this than Oracle." *

In the evening, I noticed in Ellison's dining room a scale model of what would become his second home: a graceful-looking 450-foot motor-yacht capable of circumnavigating the globe. Already the owner of two mega-yachts, bought secondhand and extensively modified (the 192-foot *Ronin* based in Sausalito and the 244-foot *Katana,* which was kept at Antibes in the South of France), Ellison wanted to create the perfect yacht. The key to achieving this had been his successful courtship of a seventy-two-year-old Englishman, Jon Bannenberg, recognized as the greatest designer of very big, privately-owned yachts. With a budget of $200 million—about the same as that for the Japanese imperial village in Woodside—it would be Bannenberg's masterpiece. Bannenberg had committed himself to "handing over the keys" to Ellison in time for his summer holiday in 2003.

Then there was Ellison's flirtation with biotechnology. He had often said to me that when he finally left Oracle (yes, a life after Oracle was something that he contemplated), he would like to work in biotech, even describing it as a new career. He already owned an intellectually formi-dable Israeli company called Quark Biotech, a pioneer in applied genomics-based drug development, which develops therapeutic products that treat diseases such as cancer and osteoporosis by attacking their causes rather than their symptoms. Ellison's main philanthropic effort, through the Ellison Medical Foundation, was funding essential research into the diseases of aging. His detractors alleged that he was praying that his foundation would come up with an elixir of youth. It was a good joke given Ellison's distaste for mortality.

If Ellison could devote as much or as little time as he felt able to his two mammoth construction projects, the same could not be said of the America's Cup. After winning four maxi-class world championships in his 80-foot sloop *Sayonara* and narrowly escaping death in the lethal 1998 Sydney-to-Hobart race, Ellison had turned his attention to winning yachting's most prestigious prize. Although the races (in Auckland) to de-cide who would challenge Team New Zealand for the "auld mug" would not begin until the fall of 2002, in common with the other major syndi-

---

*LE writes: Gardens last for hundreds of years, companies don't. That's be-cause people love and take care of gardens.

cates, Ellison's team, Oracle Racing, was already in training on the water. Would Ellison be happy just to pay the bills—he had agreed to provide a budget for the team of $80 million—or was he planning a more active involvement?

If Ellison decided to take the helm, he would be up against the best professional "drivers" in the world and he already employed one of them: *Sayonara* veteran Chris Dickson from New Zealand. When I asked him, he looked sheepish: "It depends how fast our boat is. If it's fast enough, maybe. But I'm not telling anyone yet. I don't want to have a mutiny on my hands." I wasn't sure whether he was talking about the America's Cup team or his colleagues at Oracle. I was sure, however, that Ellison had no intention of standing in the background obediently signing checks. And if he was planning on driving in some of the races as he had hinted, what sort of commitment in terms of preparation and weeks spent away from Oracle did that imply?

Finally, although I didn't know then, there was even the possibility that Ellison might start a new family. Although Ellison's views on monogamy would never make him a standard-bearer for the moral majority, his five-year relationship with Melanie Craft, a writer twenty-five years his junior, had evolved into a deep mutual commitment. After three failed marriages, one other long-term relationship, and a string of less serious girlfriends, Ellison had pretty much convinced himself that being a husband was just something he was not very good at (although he gave himself higher marks as a father to his two teenage children). As his children by his third marriage were reaching young adulthood—David was eighteen and Megan fifteen—the idea of having more was growing on him. It wasn't something that he talked about, and he was sensitive enough not to want to put any pressure on Melanie, but it was there all the same.

• • •

I had been swept along by Ellison's arguments and exhilarated by his recklessness and the sheer grandeur of his optimism. As usual, everything he was saying made perfect sense and was intellectually compelling. Part of me thought: "He's right. If the E-Business Suite is all he says it is, why shouldn't he succeed with this? And if it does, why shouldn't Oracle become the most important company on earth."

However, Oracle's aggressive and sometimes arrogant style had made it plenty of enemies, and with the launch of the E-Business Suite it seemed that Ellison was intent on making a great many more. Critics had accused

Ellison and Oracle of overclaiming and hyping products that sometimes failed to live up to their billing (not exactly a unique crime in the software business, but one that was persistently pinned on Oracle). And although Oracle had the second biggest enterprise applications business in the world, the history of its applications had been, to put it mildly, torrid. If the software didn't deliver on Ellison's promise, there would be plenty of people more than happy to see him crash and burn.

Ellison was desperate for Oracle to fulfill what he saw as its true potential, but was he prepared to do what might be required in terms of sheer grinding slog for that to happen? Ellison had become used to having never to do anything he didn't want to. Was he ready to make the sacrifices that would likely be demanded of him? The progress of this campaign—certainly his most important and possibly his last—would have profound consequences both for Oracle and the reputation of its founder. I very much wanted to know how it would turn out.

2

ON THE ROAD

March 2001

It's a cold, gray dawn, and we're waiting for Larry Ellison, drinking bad coffee in a bleak "VIP" lounge tucked into a remote corner of Hong Kong's new Lantau Airport reserved for private jets. The welcoming committee consists of Judy Sim, a tall Chinese American who is Oracle's senior events manager, George and Rich, the two middle-aged, gun-toting ex-cops who take care of Ellison's personal security, and me. Two black S-Class Mercedes are ready to whisk Ellison the twenty miles to his suite in the Grand Hyatt Hotel overlooking the harbor. At 7 A.M. prompt, the elegant shape of Ellison's $35 million Gulfstream V, eleven hours out of San Jose, slips into view and taxis towards the terminal. The cabin door opens, and the two pilots bring out the bags and suit carriers to the waiting cars. But of Ellison there's no sign.

A good ten minutes later he emerges, looking distracted and worried. Two weeks ago, a year after the dot coms and the telcos first started taking a market hammering, the tech downturn finally caught up with Oracle. Big software deals suddenly evaporated in the few days before the close of Oracle's third quarter, forcing the world's biggest business software company to make an embarrassing earnings warning. For Ellison, who only a few weeks earlier had been confidently arguing that Oracle might yet prove immune to the forces wreaking havoc with the stock prices of rival technology firms, it was a dismaying moment, and this trip to China to drum up business for Oracle's ambitious new software package, the E-Business Suite, has taken on a new urgency.

Before getting into the backseat of the lead car, Judy Sim, who has

been out in Hong Kong for several days preparing the ground, hands Ellison a sheaf of briefing papers profiling the customers he will soon be
meeting and summarizing the points that the local sales team wants him
to focus on. But he's not looking at them. He stares bleakly out of the car
window as the convoy pulls away, his eyes filling with tears. It's an awkward moment. He takes a big gulp of air and mumbles, "It's been a hor-
rible weekend."

In the terminal he had made a cell phone call to Melanie Craft, his
thirty-two-year-old fiancée and partner for the last five years, at home in
California. He asked her to fly out to Hong Kong later in the day; it's
clear that something terrible has happened. "Maggie just died. Cancer.
She was ten years old. Damn, fuck. Sorry. She was my favorite cat.
Watching her die—I've been a complete basket case for the last three
days." Another prolonged pause, and he seems to pull himself together.
"You know, it's times like this that I wonder about doing deals with the
Devil. Sad thing is, even if you're ready to sell your soul, you usually find
that nobody's buying." Ellison doesn't like death. He resents it. How can
it be that one moment you're here and the next moment you're not? The
fate of Maggie, whose rapidly advancing cancer has so distressed him,
prompts a story about a time when he made a donation to the Ronald
McDonald House at Stanford. As a result, Ellison was expected to pay
visits to children's oncology wards. It was a nightmare. "Even the nurses
and doctors on those wards couldn't handle the emotional pain," he says.
"After six months, they either left or became numb to the point of losing
their ability to feel anything. I just couldn't go back into those wards."

Railing against the unfairness of death and confessing to his own emotional squeamishness seems to have made him feel a little better. For the
remainder of the ride to the hotel, he rifles through the briefing papers
that Sim has given him. He has half an hour before meeting Xiao-Chu
Wang, the chairman of China Mobile, the fast-growing wireless operator.
Straight after that he is to host a meeting with the bosses of nine local
firms.

• • •

The CEO roundtable at the Grand Hyatt is the first that Ellison has held
in Asia. The roundtable format has become one of Ellison's favorite ways
of selling Oracle's vision: self-important CEOs, who would not dream of
opening their door to even the most senior Oracle sales executive, are curious to meet Ellison, not least because of his often controversial
celebrity.

These events already have an established pattern. Ellison usually starts by describing Oracle's own experience of "transforming" itself into an e-business and saving a billion dollars' worth of cost along the way. In particular, he likes to paint a lurid picture of the inefficiency of Oracle's information systems before the Internet made a different model of computing possible. It's a riff designed to put the guests at ease—if Oracle, the leading provider of management information systems to most of the world's biggest companies, couldn't handle its own data properly, it's okay for others to admit that they're having problems. Ellison had told me that in America, the occasion often took on the flavor of a confessional—a kind of CEOs Anonymous—in which the leaders of household name companies would compete with one another to tell horror stories about expensive computer systems that had taken forever to install and never delivered. It didn't seem to worry Ellison that at least some of these nightmare experiences involved Oracle software and consultants—it was all the fault of the so-called client/server model of computing that Microsoft had helped to foist on the world. "We're all in the same boat," he would say, "paying top dollar for systems that tell us almost nothing about our businesses." Before we go into the room, Derek Williams, Oracle's top executive in Asia, warns Ellison that, this being the inscrutable East, he may find his audience less responsive than he's used to.

And so it is. The executives who have turned up are a pretty good cross section of local business: a couple of trading companies, two manufacturers, a telephone firm from the Philippines, a big e-business exchange and online marketplace, a clothing group, and the chief operating officer of Richard Li's once megahyped Pacific Century CyberWorks. The public sector is also there in the form of Jack So, chairman of the MTR rail system, and Nancy Tse, the deputy director of the hospital authority. But there is no buzz in the room. It's as if the guests are overawed by Ellison's presence and are not quite sure what's expected of them.

Ellison starts the meeting with his well-honed account of what it means to be an e-business and Oracle's own epiphany and redemption. The story is rambling and funny, but the message is clear. By streamlining its processes and using its own software and the Internet to automate them, Oracle not only saved $1 billion in annual costs but became an organization that was far more responsive to the needs of its customers. What's more, as all this had been achieved by centralizing information and going from literally thousands of server computers to just a handful, it meant being prepared to spend less, not more, on information technology. The obstacle to realizing such gains was no longer technological, it was whether the people within a company were prepared to embrace change, and that wouldn't happen unless senior management was ready to think how the business should operate for the next twenty-five years in the light of the Internet. Ellison ends with the challenge "Are you willing to pay less? That really is the question."

Perhaps the guests think the question is rhetorical, but after an uncomfortable pause Ellison cranks himself up again with an amplification of why spending less can result in better information. It's a bit repetitive, but it gives Williams the chance to add that you don't need to be a software firm like Oracle to do these things. GE Power Systems—Oracle's top reference *du jour*—is a classic bricks-and-mortar company, and many other customers were also proving what could be accomplished in a short time. That seems to get them going. From then on, it's a competition to show how switched on they all are. They want to know about the future of e-commerce after the dot-com crash, how to train their people to use the new technology, and what should be done to bring trading partners with them into e-business networks, especially small firms with limited IT resources and skepticism about what's in it for them.

Ellison has an answer for each of them. His line on e-commerce is that the Internet can make good companies better, but it won't turn bad businesses into good ones. He reckons that there won't turn out to be that many brand-new companies created by the Internet; mostly it's a question of existing firms getting smarter and more efficient. "Dot-com mania," he says, "was a fantasy, the world had gone a little bit crazy." On the training issue, he says, "When we say there's a training problem, it's usually because a product is too difficult to use. If you can use Yahoo! or Amazon without any training, you should be able to use most business software with little or no training. Unfortunately, our engineers usually stop short of making our products as easy to use as possible. The best and most leveraged approach is to make our software as easy to use as eBay, where seventy-year-old first-time computer users manage to buy and sell antiques."

The key to encouraging business partners to join online procurement exchanges and marketplaces is to convince them that it would make life easier for them, by giving them the opportunity to increase sales through better and faster information about market trends and to cut the cost of inventory and transaction processing. Patrick Wang, the very on-message chairman of Johnson Electric, a fast-growing $700 million manufacturer of microelectric motors, asks Ellison about Covisint, the giant auto industry exchange that Oracle is involved with. Covisint is a sore subject with Ellison—it was one of the last big deals brought in by Ray Lane, the powerful second in command at Oracle with whom Ellison, to a chorus of disapproval from Wall Street, had abruptly parted company nine months earlier. "Actually," Ellison says, "competitor collaboration is quite difficult; nothing quite like this has ever been tried before. Getting the Covisint partners [which include all the big three U.S. automakers] to cooperate over the long term will just not work, in my opinion." He reckons that it will go back to being a Ford-only exchange. The model for business-to-business (B2B) exchanges, he argues, is the one that Oracle has built for Sony—you need an exchange to be built around one "nucleating" company, strong enough both to drive and to provide liquidity, he says.

Mr. Wang looks a little taken aback. Ellison repeats his mantra that the watchwords of e-business are "automate and monitor," and the meeting breaks up. Although the guests seem happy enough and are making all the right noises about wanting to work with Oracle on their e-business plans, it's hard to gauge whether it's been a success. After the long flight and the distress over the cat, Ellison's performance has been, by his normal standards, a little flat. And without much coming back across the table to stimulate him, he's been mostly on autopilot.

• • •

The next day Ellison visits China Resources, one of the largest mainland enterprises in Hong Kong. With a spread of businesses similar to the giant Jardine Matheson, it provides about 40 percent of Hong Kong's food staples, trades in oil and gas, and has interests in supermarkets, hotels, and port developments. China Resources' president is Frank Ning, a tough, forty-something Chinese national who spent some time at a university in America. Ning comes over as a pragmatist, relieved that the dot-com fever has passed and interested in the practical ways the Internet can improve his sprawling $5 billion business. He uses the example of how his grandfather, as the boss of a trading company in Guangzhou during the 1920s, had approached the coming of the telephone. "He used it to improve his business, not set up a telephone trading company." Ning also points out that with capital markets in headlong retreat, everybody is slowing down their IT investments, and that might not be such a bad thing.

Ellison has been happy to agree with most of what Ning has said up to then, but he bridles at the idea that anyone should delay getting their business onto the Internet. "Yes, but the Internet is a tremendous efficiency tool. We can deliver a very rapid return on your investment. We focus on rapid, low-cost implementations—our CRM [customer relationship management] and distribution software can go in very quickly. You should use the Internet not because it's new and cool, but because it will save you money." Ning changes gear. "We used to be a trading monopoly with China, although now we're a public company. Use us as an example for Chinese companies on the mainland, many of whom we do business with, of how Oracle software can help them. We're doing okay now, but we're determined to deliver more of the trading process online in a practical manner—we're moving online because it makes it better for our customers."

Ellison spots the opportunity. He suggests that China Resources could become the center of an online trading network, hosting e-business "hub" software and extending a new level of service to trading partners. That way, China Resources could, for example, link silk makers in China directly to designers in Italy; local manufacturers would know what to produce almost as soon as the fashions are penned. In other words, there may be advantages for Ning that he hasn't even thought of yet. It's a subtle way of deflecting Ning's hint that Oracle should give him a special deal because of his connections with businesses on the mainland.

The last meeting in Hong Kong is in the paneled boardroom of the powerful Wharf Group with its owner, Peter Wu. Wu is expected to be the next chief executive of the Hong Kong "special administrative region" when C. H. Tung's five-year term runs out in 2002. He's a hybrid businessman/politician—smooth and fluent in a way that Frank Ning was not and keen to brag about the economic prowess of Hong Kong in particular and northeast Asia in general. Both private- and public-sector finances are in good shape, he boasts, and Hong Kong, which was already doing 40 percent of its trade with China, would gain hugely from China's forthcoming membership in the World Trade Organization. The key to understanding the dynamism of the economy, not just in Hong Kong but elsewhere in Asia, Wu claims, is the role of SMEs (small and medium-sized enterprises) as the driving force. Ellison remarks that SMEs have also become the main engine of Oracle's own growth and points out that if you can't automate the SMEs, the Sonys and the Hutchinsons that do business with them won't be automated either, no matter what they spend on IT.

But Wu is doubtful whether Oracle makes the kind of simple and affordable software that these people would buy. "They are not like dot coms," he says. "They have never heard the words 'burn rate,' and they can't afford to spend millions on complicated and interminable systems implementations." This is just the opening that Ellison wants. A big part of his message is that Oracle's customers should install the software in "plain vanilla" form and avoid expensive modifications. But he suddenly makes the extraordinary claim that Oracle is intending to get the initial purchase price of the applications suite for small businesses down to $20,000 and get the software up and running almost before the ink dries on the contract—in other words, in just a few hours. Williams looks astonished, but it's quintessential Ellison; because he's already worked out in his own mind how something like this could, in theory, be done, it follows that all the practical difficulties have already been overcome.*

It's also an opportunity to expound on a core Ellison theme: "the war against complexity." Software has to be made much more simple. Computing has become so complex that customers have to hire experts just to explain the industry's products. Everyone has been trying to make their products more powerful and in the process they have become more difficult to use. Oracle, by contrast, with its E-Business Suite has delivered an integrated closed loop that delivers 80 percent of what you need straight out of the box.

Also in the Wharf Group's boardroom is Nancy Tse, the Hong Kong Hospital Authority's number two who was at the previous day's CEO roundtable. She's still carrying scar tissue from the last big software implementation she was involved with—the introduction of a large-scale client/server system. It was two years in the planning, three years in execution, and cost twice the agreed-upon budget. In short, a pretty standard big IT project. She wants to know when she should introduce new technology if she's going to have to go through the whole upgrade nightmare again. Ellison has two answers. The first is that the Internet model is the last model of computing. This is it, he says. What makes him so sure is that Internet-based computer networks work in a way similar to all the other networks that we depend on, from water, as invented by the Romans, to electricity and the telephone. The second is that migration from

---

*LE writes: Actually, I didn't invent the idea for a $20,000 version of the E-Business Suite on the fly during my meetings in China. The idea originated some time before, when a team of Derek Williams's engineers started a project to preconfigure the E-Business Suite for smaller Asian customers. This special edition of our business software is now in the market and sells for less than $20,000, including installation.

client/server to the Internet isn't trivial but shouldn't take too long. As long as Oracle can get the time with senior managers to work out how to change, standardize, and simplify every business process for the Internet, implementation can be very rapid—the model used so successfully with GE Power, he claims. Oracle was prepared to work on a guaranteed fixed-price, fixed-time basis. He promises, "We will make a very big difference." Tse doesn't look wholly reassured, and she's right not to be. Putting the E-Business Suite into a brand-new plant, such as GE Power's turbine factory in Hungary, should go fairly smoothly, but large-scale upgrades from "legacy" client/server systems tend to be a lot more painful than Ellison is admitting.*

• • •

As the cars race through the traffic back to the Grand Hyatt, Ellison casually suggests a change of plan for the weekend. "I thought that after Shanghai we might just fly down to Tahiti for a couple of days' R and R. The boat [the 192-foot *Ronin*] is down there and crewed, so we might as well use it." What really seems to tickle him is the idea of jetting straight from Tahiti on Sunday night to the next customer engagement—with HealthSouth in Birmingham, Alabama. "I bet that's a route that nobody's flown before: Tahiti to Birmingham."

Back at the hotel, Ellison is treated like visiting royalty and then some. Whenever his entourage arrives, flunkeys scurry ahead clearing a path, opening doors, and bobbing heads. That evening in the Grand Hyatt's fancy 1 Harbor Road restaurant, the chef is brought bowing and scraping to Ellison's table to explain the special banquet that has been prepared for the most honored guest. To his credit, Ellison appears to be neither embarrassed nor blasé but goes out of his way to be charmed and express his gratitude.

• • •

As the GV drops down toward the runway at Shanghai's slightly down-at-heel Hongqiao Airport, people on bicycles stop to take in the plane's unfamiliar silhouette. It's actually something of a miracle that the aircraft is landing at all. Just a few hours earlier, unknown to Ellison, the Chinese

---

*LE writes: When we implemented our E-Business Suite at JDS Uniphase, it was up and running globally in less than a year. We put the system in for a guaranteed fixed price. JDS's IT budget is now 50 percent lower than what it was before.

authorities had told the GV's pilots, Geoff and Pete, that permission to land had been withdrawn. But after haggling, negotiation, and string pulling by Oracle's advance party in China's biggest city, everything is back on again. The usual black Mercs (albeit of a slightly earlier vintage than those in Hong Kong) are on the tarmac to meet the plane, but in Shanghai there is also a police car with a flashing light to clear the motorcade's way through the city's gridlocked traffic. First stop is the towering Portman–Ritz Carlton Hotel, showpiece of the modern Shanghai Centre, where rooms have been booked and another CEO roundtable is due to start in forty-five minutes.

Although superficially grand, the hotel manages to be slightly tacky. The rooms, both public and private, suffer from that peculiarly Communist interpretation of luxury that requires acres of phony wood veneer and lashings of green (preferably cigarette-burned) velour. Everything is grubby, and nothing works quite as it's meant to. As it's about 8:30 in the morning, several of the elevators are emptying themselves of pretty young women wearing long raincoats in a vain attempt to conceal the evening finery they arrived in the night before. The atmosphere of pre-revolutionary loucheness is further heightened by the hotel's own female staff, who are kitted out in shiny red cheongsams, slit daringly high on the thigh. Touchingly, most are wearing shabby black sneakers or what look like boots from a People's Liberation Army surplus store. Two of these girls are standing at attention outside the room in which the roundtable will take place. Before Ellison shows up, one of the Oracle flaks orders them to find some more appropriate footwear.

The twelve guests, an impressive selection of local entrepreneurial talent, are all male, and most are in their early thirties. They lack the sleekness of their Hong Kong counterparts, and only two or three of them are sufficiently confident of their English to dispense with the simultaneous translation. But Derek Williams's warning that this audience would be even harder to get going than the one in Hong Kong turns out to be wide of the mark. After Ellison's opening remarks, carefully tailored to flatter Shanghai's massive building boom—"it seems like half the cranes in the world are right here in this city"—and the prediction that China would soon have more people hooked up to the World Wide Web than America thanks to the coming of the wireless Internet, the questions come thick and fast.

Although Ellison has talked enthusiastically about how lucky they are to be able to install Oracle's Internet-based software without worrying about legacy computing systems getting in the way—"client/server never happened here" he says, seeming to extol Chinese wisdom rather than hinting at any technological backwardness—they most want to hear his views on what's going on in the world. They want to know what he thinks will happen to the Nasdaq—four of the firms represented are stockbrokers with a lot of very perplexed clients—and whether the U.S. economy is going into recession. They also seem fascinated by the power cuts in California. Although Ellison would clearly rather be selling software, he's happy to oblige with his opinions and is stumped only when a banker asks him what impact the World Trade Organization (WTO) will have on the Chinese banking system and what steps Ellison would take to reform it.

After about an hour, the conversation meanders around to what Oracle actually does and might be able to do for them. They want to know whether this e-business thing is real (it is, says Ellison); how they should deal with rapid growth (it's risky, he says, but it's riskier not to grow fast; our software will help you scale your business); and how Oracle is doing against its rivals, especially Microsoft. At last Ellison gets the chance to pitch the E-Business Suite. To their surprise, Ellison explains that Microsoft isn't really a direct rival. Oracle's main competitors are the sprawling computer behemoth IBM and the leading business application firms, such as SAP and Siebel Systems, whose products IBM and other system integrators expensively try to knit together. The contrast is their complexity versus Oracle's simplicity. Yesterday, in Hong Kong, the idea of the E-Business Suite being installed for $20,000 and in less than an hour was an ambitious goal, but in Shanghai, Ellison turns it into something very like a product that will soon be ready to ship.*

Next stop is the Shanghai studios of CCTV, the state-owned television service. Ellison is to appear on a live lunchtime chat show that has an *Oprah*-style format and a claimed viewership of around 50 million people. While Ellison is wired for sound, the program's host, Wei Zhang, a smartly groomed young woman with an American university education, assures him that despite the presence of an invited audience of several hundred, who will be given a chance to question him later, the show is actually a good deal more intellectually serious than *Oprah*. Ellison is understandably relieved. He's been on the real *Oprah* and says that he felt like a rabbit caught in the headlights of an onrushing car.

---

*LE writes: The $20,000 special edition of the E-Business Suite came to the China market in 2002.

In fact, the show turns out to be pretty bad. The Chinese Oprah's idea of intellectual seriousness is to keep asking variations of the same question over and over again: Does he mind Oracle's being number two to Microsoft? How does he plan to become number one? How does he feel about being only the second richest man in the world, and how does he intend to overtake Bill Gates in wealth? Ellison becomes increasingly desperate to find ways of not repeating himself. Even when the audience gets its chance, it's the same questions all over again. Clearly, the Chinese think being number two is a pretty awful fate—watch out, America.

It gets worse when Ellison is asked about something different: How important is China to Oracle as a source of engineering talent? It's getting more important all the time, he says. In that case, says another member of the audience, how about moving R and D out here from California? Ellison blinks into the lights and suddenly realizes that the guy asking the question is Oracle's managing director in China, Andrew Hu. The Oracle events managers, who have organized Ellison's itinerary, are horrified: "What the fuck's he doing there?" As other equally self-serving questions from the audience come in, the thought comes to Ellison that maybe there are other Oracle plants among the guests. "Er . . . just how many people are there here from Oracle?" he asks nervously. A forest of hands goes up. "At least half" appears to be the answer. "Christ, I didn't know we even had so many people in China," groans one of the flaks. If this happened in America, says another, we'd never live it down. Luckily, the show has been seen by only about 50 million people.

The last meeting before returning to the plane is with the mayor of Shanghai, Xu Kuang Di. The room in the city hall is a vast, ornately decorated chamber with rows of large armchairs on three sides. Xu and Ellison sit on a slightly raised dais, their respective interpreters perched, absurdly, just behind them, like hiding puppeteers. Xu looks every inch the tough boss of a tough city. The mayorship of Shanghai is not only one of the biggest political jobs in China, it can lead to the very top—both President Jiang Zemin and the country's prime minister, Zhu Rongji, are former mayors of the city.

Ellison is at his diplomatic smoothest: Shanghai is one of the most exciting cities in the world, with the fastest growth and the most cranes (this is a line he clearly likes), and it's one that he always looks forward to returning to (though it's not fascinating enough to keep him in town for more than a few hours on this trip). Xu is equally flattering about Ellison's accomplishments and the contribution Oracle is making to the new China. He then gives a little soliloquy about the importance of the Internet to Shanghai, the need to keep constantly upgrading technology and the city's already quite impressive communications infrastructure. The growth of wireless was an example of how the new Shanghai was embracing technology, with more than 3 million mobile phones among a population of 13 million. He then asks Ellison the question that it seems everyone in China is desperate to have answered: What's likely to happen to technology and Internet stocks? He's very worried, he says, now speaking in quite passable English, that the experience of losses in the last few months could dent the appetite of inexperienced Chinese investors to hold stocks. You have to pinch yourself to remember that this is a Communist speaking, not the chairman of the New York Stock Exchange. The mayor suddenly asks what Oracle can do to put the city's customs operations online. Ellison and Derek Williams can hardly contain their excitement. They assure Xu that they have the software ready to go and the efficiencies will naturally be astounding. Arrangements are made to meet with customs officials and begin "scoping" the project. A meeting that was conceived as little more than an opportunity to show the flag and drum up some local media coverage has turned out to be a lot more interesting.

In fact, aside from the weirdness of the lunchtime TV show, everything has gone amazingly smoothly. But now we're not going to Tahiti after all: Geoff Glass, the senior of Ellison's two full-time pilots, has looked at a map. Ellison's idea that Tahiti is "on the way back" to the United States turns out to be wide of the mark—it's a seventeen-hour flight, including a refueling stopover in Guam. The Pacific is very big. The pioneering flight from Tahiti to Birmingham is left for someone else to do. Eleven hours later, but earlier the same Thursday thanks to the sixteen-hour time difference, the GV touches down at the San Jose Jet Center, where Carl Olsen, Ellison's driver, is waiting by the hangar with his boss's new Bentley Arnage Red Label.

• • •

It's a long Thursday. Ellison is back in the office by early afternoon to take a review meeting with the applications group. The meeting, in the eleventh-floor boardroom, is already under way by the time Ellison swings in. It's as if he had just stepped out to get a Coke from the fridge rather than flown in from China. Although the atmosphere is typically Silicon Valley informal—whispered side conversations, tinkering with PDAs and cell phones, frequent excursions to pick up juices and sodas from the fridge across the way—and no one is obviously chairing the proceedings, the focus subtly shifts toward Ellison.

It's all fairly routine stuff. There's an update on how a few big E-Business Suite installations are going. The most important are a major CRM installation at Silicon Valley neighbor Hewlett-Packard that's about to be rolled out to nearly four thousand marketing people and the vital "go live" at GE Power in Hungary. The good news is that there are "no software issues," but one small cloud on the horizon concerns the way GE is handling the next EBS implementation at its Houston plant.

Ron Wohl, Oracle's joint head of applications development, says that GE is warning that Houston is likely to be more complex than Hungary, because local managers are resisting the approach used in Hungary, where processes were adapted to work with the software rather than the other way around. At Oracle, this has become tantamount to heresy; a big part of the EBS campaign is to convince customers to take the software in "plain vanilla" form and install it rapidly without modifications. Wohl says that it may be possible to sort things out at a meeting of the GE-Oracle steering committee in a fortnight. But if that fails, either he or Ellison may have to go back to GE Power Systems' boss and current Oracle poster boy, John Rice, and persuade him to tell the Houston people to see sense. Ellison has a better idea. Tell Houston, he says, they must write down on paper exactly why they have to be different from Hungary. Don't let them argue about it at the steering committee, they'll come up with some wonderful reasons and put up a great argument. "Make them write it down," he says.*

The next day—Ellison usually doesn't arrive in the office until about 1:30 in the afternoon—is taken up with meetings, first with the application server group and second with marketing, to approve some press ads. Oracle's application server has been a problem for a couple of years. App servers are a vital layer in the software "stack" of Internet computing—

---

*LE writes: It has been my experience that people reflexively resist change. Change requires people to rethink the way they work and the way they are organized. When people write down their current processes and the reasons why those processes cannot be simplified, it forces them to carefully and methodically rethink their business. This usually results in business processes being changed, as opposed to our software. Simplified, modernized business processes are at least as important as good business software in delivering efficiencies to the enterprise. When we do turn up a serious shortcoming in our software, we add the required feature in a future version of the product at no charge.

the two main players in the market, BEA Systems and IBM with its Web-Sphere product range, market them as e-business platforms or even as the operating systems of the Internet.

But Oracle's offering has suffered from poor performance in running applications written in the popular Java programming language because Oracle's Java "container" has been taken from its database instead of being designed from scratch for the app server. As Oracle is a pioneer of e-business, it's strategically damaging and frankly embarrassing for it not to have a competitive product. The options on the table are to resell a direct rival's product, such as BEA Systems', persevere with developing an in-house solution, or do a licensing deal with a tiny firm in Sweden called Orion ("basically just two guys"), which seems to have come up with a container that provides one of the world's fastest Java environments. This last option is recommended by the application server group's Thomas Kurian, a young Indian who's a rising star at Oracle.

Interestingly, there is almost no "not invented here" vanity. It's a simple question of what will deliver in a cost-effective and timely way. Ellison is asked to approve the $5 million deal that has been negotiated with Orion, which will preclude selling a similar license to any of Oracle's competitors. The boys from Orion have also reluctantly accepted that they can't give the program to the open-source movement for three years—it's apparently the only requirement they balked at. Ellison is not only happy to cut the deal, he wants it done fast so he can avoid incurring any further parallel development costs. He even asks if there's a danger of lowballing Orion with the $5 million. It's not altruism. He wants to make sure that Orion has enough money not to stint on development that will benefit Oracle. The final question is whether the application server has been underpriced. Ellison is adamant about keeping a performance/price advantage over rivals. "It gets people downloading the software and generates buzz on all the tech bulletin boards. Keep the price low." This is a recurring theme: even if people steal your software, you get the money back in the end because they're forced to buy your other products and support.

At the last meeting of the week, marketing executive Stacey Torman has some new ads to show Ellison and Safra Catz, his formidable chief of staff. With an annual marketing budget of more than $300 million and a preference for displays in the business press, the company will soon be blanketing *The Wall Street Journal,* the *Financial Times,* and *The Economist,* among others, with ads. But Ellison doesn't like the pie chart that's in the ad, sourced from IDC, a computer industry market research firm, that's meant to show Oracle's dominant share of the database market, so he redraws the chart on the room's whiteboard. He says that some research organizations apply different metrics to IBM's share figures, but that anyway Big Blue fakes the number. Then he grumbles that he doesn't know why Oracle bothers to use an ad agency. For production and placement, volunteers Torman.

Another research company, Forrester, that's normally favorably disposed toward Oracle, has written a briefing note saying that when the E-Business Suite doesn't work, Oracle blames its customers. Ellison wants to come up with an ad that confronts the Forrester claim. He suggests something along the lines of "Don't try to finish our software for us. Let us finish it for you. Hiring a systems integrator to modify our software costs millions and rarely works as advertised. We have thousands of the world's most talented software engineers, but even they fuck it up on a regular basis before getting it right. Don't try this at home." Torman says she'll get someone to work on it.

After that, it's back to rewriting the current crop of ads. There's one that Ellison wants to run in Monday's *FT* that is aimed at countering some of the negative news that flowed from missing the quarter earnings number a couple of weeks earlier—the first sign that despite earlier boasting, Oracle was not immune to the problems of the slowing economy after all. The ad will say that despite everything. Oracle's profits and margins both went up, thanks to the E-Business Suite's effectiveness as a "cost reduction engine." The only problem is that the *FT*'s advertising sales office says that it needs two weeks to take a new ad. Ellison can't believe it and says maybe he should call Marjorie Scardino, the Texan chief executive of Pearson, the *FT*'s owner, over the weekend. Already, he's practicing his Texan drawl for Scardino's benefit.

• • •

It's a three-hour ride by GV from San Jose to Birmingham, Alabama—a place that Ellison proudly boasts he's never been to in his life—plenty of time for Ellison to mount a favorite hobbyhorse. The reason for this voyage of discovery is to announce a partnership with Birmingham-based HealthSouth, one of the country's biggest health care providers, to build a so-called digital hospital. It's an important deal for Oracle, even though it will be putting in more resources than it's likely to get back in the short term. But that's not the reason Ellison is so excited. He's been thinking for some time about how Oracle and the Internet could transform the efficiency of the health care industry, which is not only the world's biggest—he thinks he's read somewhere that its annual value is about $3 trillion—but one in which software-driven process automation has yet to make any major impact.

Once he starts describing the idea, the words come tumbling out. Almost all medical records, in America and elsewhere, are kept on paper. From prescriptions to insurance claims, medical practice is a never-ending trail of expensively generated and poorly filed paper. The computer systems that do exist are largely based on incompatible proprietary technologies that stop them from being able to communicate with one another—little pockets of automation. And although medicine in advanced industrial countries is seen as glamorously high tech with its array of diagnostic scanners, laser surgery, and sophisticated drugs that increasingly draw on biotechnology, there has been almost no attempt to integrate these new techniques synergistically. Add to that the problem of spiraling health care costs, standards of service that often fall below even the most basic consumer expectations, and the rise of expensively litigated malpractice suits.

Looking uncharacteristically pious, Ellison says that this may be one instance where it's possible to make money and do some good at the same time. He genuinely believes that the E-Business Suite, by combining customer/patient relationship management with resource planning applications into a single integrated system and leveraging the connectivity of the Internet and wireless communications, can bring huge benefits to the health care system. By eliminating unnecessary paperwork and duplication of effort, time and money can, in theory, be redirected toward patient care. Even more dramatically, Ellison is convinced that by keeping everyone's records on a single database and linking that wirelessly and in real time to what is going on in the hospital, it should be possible to eliminate many of the medical errors—misprescription alone is thought to be responsible for the deaths of more than fifty thousand patients a year just in the United States—that frequently kill or damage patients.

The importance of the deal with HealthSouth is threefold. First, as the world's first fully integrated, all-new, start-from-scratch digital hospital, the HealthSouth Medical Center will be a showcase for Oracle's technology—if only the 20 percent savings on administrative costs that Health-South is conservatively budgeting for are delivered, Ellison hopes that health care providers from all over the world will be beating a path to Birmingham. Second, Oracle is the first to admit that while it is the biggest provider of clinical trials software, it has gaps in its industry knowledge that need to be filled, and it will also have to adapt its software to the particular needs of health care. To achieve that, it's crucial to have a committed "anchor customer," such as HealthSouth, that shares its vision and will work with Oracle to get the software right; that's why it makes sense for Oracle to do the work for free. Finally, there are nearly a dozen other providers of technology to the project, from Carl Zeiss (optics) to GE Medical Systems (diagnostic imaging). Ellison admits that getting all of them to work together will be like herding cats but says it's a great opportunity to get all of them onto the E-Business Suite.

When the GV touches down in Birmingham, Jay Nussbaum, the avuncular head of Oracle's service industries division, based near Washington, D.C. in Reston, Virginia, is there to greet and brief Ellison. Although there are a couple of limos waiting to take us to HealthSouth's ninety-two-acre campus on the outskirts of the city, the firm's CEO, Richard Scrushy, has thoughtfully sent a HealthSouth-liveried Sikorsky S-92 helicopter as an alternative. As Ellison gets into the plush cabin, followed by two unsmiling minders, Nussbaum suggests that perhaps he should get a chopper like this for flying into and out of the Japanese imperial village that he is controversially building among the redwoods in snobby Woodside. "This the neighbors would really hate," says Ellison. "That would be it, they'd try and take me out with missiles if I got one of these. It's worth thinking about." But not for very long. Ellison hates helicopters—they're ugly, noisy, and unstable—and he usually avoids them whenever possible.

Ten minutes later we're inside Scrushy's office. It's as big as a tennis court, with an abundance of highly varnished wood and vermilion leather; curving plate-glass windows provide a panoramic view over the campus. Bizarrely, on the walls are pictures of Muhammad Ali's great fights, while the main ornaments are model airplanes—dozens of them, with pride of place given to a GV just like Ellison's.

Scrushy is an intense, wiry man, some ten years younger than Ellison but with suspiciously black, thinning hair. He and Ellison are scheduled to do a conference call with a reporter from *USA Today* before the main presentation. He talks at speed with a pronounced southern drawl ("We're gonna build somth'n' here you-all that's never been built before . . .") in an uninterruptible stream of unstructured hyperbole. For once, Ellison seems happy to play second fiddle, coming in only when Scrushy finally runs out of steam. The truth is that he doesn't have to say much. Scrushy has bought into the idea of the E-Business Suite completely and is a passionate preacher/salesman. Later, when Scrushy is making his big speech of the day and extolling the benefits of fully integrated software that works straight out of the box and automates every process, Nussbaum whispers, "It's like we slotted the tape right into his head."

When the *USA Today* interview is over, Scrushy steers Ellison toward the sumptuous HealthSouth boardroom, where executives from the other firms contributing to the digital hospital and the governor of Alabama, Don Siegelman, there to cast his official blessing on the project, are waiting to be briefed on what to say at the press conference. Young women wearing big hair, high heels, and revealingly tailored red suits are on hand to fetch and carry. For some reason, they present both Ellison and Siegelman with a golf putter. In appearance and attentive manner, they resemble fantasy airline stewardesses. Would Scrushy, who is a keen flyer, rather be running an airline than a health care business?

The press conference itself, in front of what looks like an audience of well over a thousand, is a fairly dull affair. Scrushy speaks too quickly, Ellison looks uncomfortable having to share the big platform with so many others, and everyone else is determined to plug their companies in the few minutes they have been allotted. The audience in the vast hall, made up largely of HealthSouth employees, is attentive and respectful, but the warmest applause is reserved for the governor when, after running through a long list of modern Alabama's achievements, he speaks of his happiness and pride that the state is home to the world's first hunting and shooting trail for the disabled. Welcome to the New South. The local media's questions are pretty desultory, but Ellison is happy to field one about the threat to patient privacy from storing everybody's medical details on one vast database. Just the opposite, he says. Right now, there's no security. Medical records are stored on paper folders in metal filing cabinets in doctors' offices. Anybody might get to see them; about the only privacy is that a lot of records get lost. In the future, patients will be able to authorize who gains access and to what. If Oracle databases are secure enough for the CIA and the FBI, they should be sufficiently secure to reassure most patients. And that's it. After a couple of interviews with the TV business channels, it's back to the Sikorsky and the airport.

But before boarding the GV for Washington, D.C., there's a customer meeting of a rather different kind. BellSouth, the local Baby Bell, has been having a torrid time with the Oracle software it's using to run its call center serving new broadband customers. The two BellSouth executives who feel most exposed have taken advantage of Ellison's presence in the region to fly a company jet down to Birmingham to tell him of their problems. The meeting is to take place in HealthSouth's hangar. The hangar itself is another testament to Scrushy's high-rolling ways. Within is a veritable air force of some eight planes, including a couple of Citations and the GV that sat in miniature on Scrushy's office sideboard. Ellison is taken aback and makes a joke about the kind of "shareholder abuse" that went out of style with RJR Nabisco a decade ago. To some, he is surprisingly puritanical about such things. He is always quick to point out that his own indulgences, such as the GV, are paid for from his, rather than the company's, pocket. It's also a reminder that Scrushy is a somewhat controversial character. Despite his achievement in turning Health-South into a $5 billion company in the seventeen years since he founded it with an investment of just $50,000, his brashness and towering ego have made him a target for gossip on Internet message boards—to such an extent that he has hired detectives to seek out his invariably anonymous persecutors. In 1997, he also made headlines when his pay for the year reached $106.8 million, including bonus and stock gains. He's received a number of death threats in recent years, and a very tough-looking security force constantly patrols the firm's headquarters.

The BellSouth team—Ralph de la Vega and Lowri Groves, respectively the heads of broadband access services and customer technologies—is waiting for Ellison and Nussbaum in a little conference room at the side of the hangar. De la Vega seems fretful, an impression amplified by his gloomy little moustache. Groves, who once worked at Xerox with Nussbaum, has the exasperated air of someone who has already heard too many excuses and is expecting to hear some more. The CRM software they have licensed from Oracle, which is supposed to provide a self-provisioning service to customers buying ADSL high-speed Internet connections, isn't delivering. In particular, de la Vega claims that the product is missing features that were promised some time ago. Smaller, nimbler broadband operators, he says, are meanwhile stealing market share from the Baby Bell. What's more, de la Vega reckons that he's in danger of going $20 million over budget, and he's looking for Oracle to find a way of helping him out. To make matters still worse, a factory supplying some of Bell-South's ADSL modems happens to be in Chechnya and has been bombed. De la Vega grudgingly accepts that this particular misfortune may be down to the Russians rather than Oracle, but he needs some convincing. Groves says simply, "You must get Ralph back on track and whole."

Ellison privately acknowledges that there may be some additional features that the engineering team needs to come up with. But he suspects that many of BellSouth's difficulties are self-inflicted—not least the overspend—and are the result of using systems integrators to modify Oracle's software: the big no-no. Rather than start an argument about what's gone, however, he declares himself "thrilled that you want us to change the software rather than change it yourself; it's the best way to add the features you need." He adds that he shares de la Vega's sense of urgency in getting in the new features: "It makes us more competitive as well as you. We want to be successful in the telecom industry, and that means we need to make you successful as well." He then asks de la Vega if he's ready to talk about changes to business processes to get the best out of the software. As long as BellSouth can be treated as a partner and involved in the process reengineering, de la Vega is ready to do anything that will get him to market more quickly. He says, "We agree, no customization, we've been through too much pain already." The quid pro quo is that he must have Ellison—"the guy at the top"—prepared to stay involved. There's been some friction with Oracle members of the project steering committee. Ellison confirms Oracle's desire to make "a substantial investment in telco CRM" and promises that he will lead the development teams.*

There is still the little matter of horse trading over where the $20 million is going to be found that de la Vega needs to stay in budget. It's kind of a challenge, says Nussbaum. De la Vega throws in an offer to be a customer reference. He suggests something along the lines of "We grew fastest, had the best customer satisfaction scores, and we did it with Oracle. I don't mind telling the world that you guys fixed it." Groves hints that the rest of BellSouth's consumer business might also move to Oracle if the steering committee can come up with a really telcocentric version of the E-Business Suite. Finally, Ellison suggests that they are going to need more storage disks to mine all the data they will be collecting on customers and that he might be willing to "see if I can let you guys purchase disks off our special deal with EMC [the leading computer storage firm]." Whether it will all add up to $20 million is far from clear. But for the time being, everybody is happy and optimistic. Ellison ingratiatingly concludes, "It's important that our developers work closely with our biggest clients, like you guys; that's the only way we can prove our software can solve your biggest problems." With that, the meeting ends and after a last incredulous look at the HealthSouth air force, both teams board their own waiting jets.

---

*LE writes: Oracle's e-business application software helped BellSouth become number one nationally in high-speed ADSL networking. Unfortunately, our software was heavily modified and extended to meet BellSouth's requirements. Making major changes to our standard e-business software—or anyone else's for that matter—is an expensive and time-consuming process.

• • •

After Birmingham, the next trip is to Washington, D.C. The visit has a double purpose: over lunch at the Four Seasons hotel, Ellison will host a roundtable of college heads to spread the word about what the E-Business Suite can do for higher education; later in the day he is to deliver the keynote speech at the Ronald Reagan International Trade Center to four hundred of Alcoa's top managers. Alcoa, the world's biggest aluminum producer, is just beginning its roll-out of the E-Business Suite and is potentially a vital reference customer. Jay Nussbaum has also sneaked into the timetable a secret meeting with Kevin Fitzgerald, a senior sales guy from Siebel Systems, the leader in CRM software and one of Oracle's bitterest rivals. With his Siebel options several fathoms under water, Fitzgerald is prepared to jump ship to Oracle. Poaching between the two firms is nothing new—Tom Siebel is himself a former Oracle salesman—but any opportunity to hire key Siebel people is too good to pass up, and face time with Ellison is deemed critical to closing the deal.

The dozen university presidents produce a different atmosphere from the CEOs who normally come to Ellison's roundtable events. They are administrator/politicians rather than businessmen, with some of the self-importance of the latter and the stiffness of the former. Ellison, with his youthful history of not hanging around long enough to complete university courses, seems slightly uneasy and goes into contortions to affect a respect that he almost certainly doesn't feel. But higher education is potentially a huge market if enough universities can be persuaded to work with Oracle both to standardize their processes and to help Oracle's developers adapt the E-Business Suite to their needs. Ellison is hoping that these men—and with only one exception, they are all men—have been sufficiently chastened by trying to integrate a spaghetti of specialized applications from the small software firms that focus on the academic market that they will be receptive to his message.

Almost as soon as Ellison draws breath from his preamble, one of the academics asks what kind of deal they might get from Oracle. He argues that Oracle's pricing should reflect the possibility that students introduced to the software at their university could become valuable customers in later life. Ellison says that Nussbaum has the authority to discount deeply but that what tends to cost most money in a software implementation is the labor to put it in, which can't be discounted. "Our goal," he says, "is to develop software that works out of the box, so you don't have to spend a lot of money to change it. But to achieve that, we need a much closer relationship with our customers so that we fully understand their business processes. Then we can help you modernize those processes before we help you automate them. Don't pay us or anyone else to adapt our software to the way you've been doing business for the last twenty years—if you do that, you'll spend too much money and get too little benefit."

Ellison goes on to say that what he wants is to open up a debate about finding standard ways—best practices—of doing things across a number of institutions. That way automation of things like student record keeping becomes cheap and easy. "Okay," says one of the presidents with the satisfied air of somebody who's about to say something extremely smart, "but we're going to want our own bells and whistles." It's as if he hasn't heard a word that Ellison has been saying for the last forty-five minutes. Adroitly, Ellison turns the remark on its head. The question, he says, is whether those bells and whistles are innovations that will work for other universities and become best practice. If they are, they should be added to the plain vanilla product.

Next comes the inevitable question about what Oracle is doing to "bridge the digital divide" and the equally predictable answers about all the virtuous things that Oracle is doing. "We are always looking for new programs that help narrow the digital divide," mouths Ellison piously. Suddenly, however, he has an idea. From what he heard today, he says, there's a need to link an individual's records from different academic institutions to create a single lifetime learning record to support accountability and validate credentials. Oracle could create such a database as a public service. "Up till now we've been focused on building software for individual universities. But we could build a national student record database and put it on the Internet. Every university could use the system for free. But don't mistake this for altruism. If we create a free student record 'hub' database, it's more likely that universities will purchase Oracle's 'spoke' software. In fact, most of you might find it more economical for Oracle to provide a national online student record service than each of you having your own student record system."

He goes on, "We're trying to think through the higher education market systematically. We want to make the same commitment to education as we've made to health care and manufacturing. Do we need more domain expertise? Absolutely, but we'll never know as much about your business as you do. We cannot finish the E-Business Suite for education without your help. And we can be successful only if you're interested in modernizing and standardizing your business processes. Look at our current software as a starting point and then help us better understand what we have to add to meet your needs. Is there the collective will to make this work? This is not just a pitch to sell software." It does the trick. As the lunch breaks up, there is a sudden rush for reassurance. "My most urgent need is the student services module. If we sign on, is there going to be a commitment of resource to match the urgency?" "If I partner with you, will you be there for me?" Ellison smiles. The exercise in humility is over. "We are the largest enterprise software company in the world. There is nobody better equipped to do this right than us." As Nussbaum works the table, fixing follow-up appointments, Ellison needs to say something funny: "The good news is that our E-Business Suite is brand new. The bad news is that our E-Business Suite is brand new." Luckily, he says it in a nearly inaudible voice and nobody is listening.

It takes fifteen minutes in a back room for the laying on of hands with the Siebel deserter, and then it's into the limos for the short ride across town to the Ronald Reagan Center for the Alcoa keynote. Steve McLaughlin, Oracle's VP for product industries, is waiting in the car to brief Ellison on the status of the Alcoa account, but first he's got some news about how relations are going with GE Power's John Rice. Rice may be Oracle's favorite customer when it comes to promoting the concept of the E-Business Suite, but McLaughlin complains he's proving a "take-no-prisoners" negotiator over financial issues. "He's a great guy," says McLaughlin, "but he seems to think he shouldn't have to pay. It's kind of a macho thing with him about paying."

McLaughlin's tactic has been to offer Rice a large discount as an incentive for paying up front. Ellison tells him not to worry and not to offer any more discount. He says, "GE already gets a huge discount." McLaughlin is concerned about not being able to book the revenue for the quarter, but Ellison just keeps saying that GE should buy the software when it needs it—not before.*

Before Ellison makes his speech, some time has been set aside for a

---

*LE writes: One of the oldest and worst habits of the Oracle sales organization was the use of aggressive discounting to get existing customers to buy software before they actually needed it. A customer might be planning a $2 million software purchase in 2004, but the sales force would offer the same software for $1 million if the customer bought in May 2003—the last month of our fourth quarter. Customers quickly figured out that the best time to negotiate for discounts was the last day of our quarters. It has taken years and a lot of management changes before we were able to break this habit.

meeting with Alcoa's CEO, Alan Belda, who's eager to give Ellison a progress report on Alcoa's E-Business Suite implementation. Alcoa, with revenues of more than $20 billion a year, has operations in 381 plants in thirty-seven countries. Belda is using Oracle software to create something called the Alcoa Business System (ABS), an integrated, enterprise-wide e-business system that has been designed to bind the sprawling company together in such close collaboration that it will operate as if it were a single entity with the same business rules, shared services, a common industrial language, and unencumbered knowledge transfer across divisions and geographies. Belda has committed to spending $800 million over the next five years, all on Oracle. He's taking the whole suite of manufacturing applications—order management, supply chain, human resources, financials, and manufacturing. At the same time, he's set a target of taking $1.75 billion of annual cost out of the company and is expecting information technology (IT) spending to fall to 40 percent of its level in 1998.*

The meeting with Belda is low key but verging on the mutually congratulatory. Ellison describes what Alcoa is attempting as "daunting" but promises that if Oracle's own experiences are anything to go by, the benefits will be "remarkable." It seems that Alcoa is doing everything the recommended Oracle way. Belda says that for sixty days the majority of his time was spent with Oracle, working out how key processes should be reengineered. "I'm basically betting the whole of my business on you guys," he says. What convinced him to go with Oracle was the promised speed at which the integrated suite could be deployed. There was a big internal debate, he says, between Oracle and SAP, "but it was kinda rigged." KPMG's (the consultants hired by Alcoa) idea of a fast SAP rollout was to do one location a month. "At that rate," Belda says, "I would have been retired before they were through."

Belda suggests that Ellison should concentrate his speech on the lessons learned from Oracle's e-business transformation and what he has seen at other companies going through the same upheaval. Belda says that the biggest challenge he faces is with people—"half want to change, the other half don't"—and he's already noticed that he is encountering more resistance in the United States to the idea of mapping processes to

---

*LE writes: The largest component of that $800 million was internal Alcoa labor cost. Oracle consulting and software were less than 10 percent of the cost of the project.

the software rather than doing it the other way round. It's just like with GE, says Ellison. If they got the processes right in Hungary, their Houston plant shouldn't need any modifications. "But that doesn't take into account the human factor," he says, "People are willing to automate their current processes but not change them. They think they're already doing it the right way. Big companies have to standardize their processes across all their different locations if they want to automate efficiently. That requires a lot of change, and a lot of resistance to that change is inevitable."

Now the speech has a higher purpose. It doesn't have to be a sales pitch. Instead it has to get the four hundred Alcoa managers, on whom the success of Oracle's software ultimately depends, to become true believers. It's an opportunity for Ellison to do what he does best—inspire, flatter, amuse, and, finally, steamroller skepticism with his own massive certainty.

It's the end of my first week on the road with Ellison. When you are around him, you cannot escape being evangelized. He can't help it. The ideas come bubbling out, and he's so excited about them that he has to share them. I have begun to think that selling software is a secondary objective for Ellison; what's far more important to him is to recruit believers.

3

THE WAR ON COMPLEXITY

Larry Ellison says he's happy only when everyone else thinks he's wrong, when he's "walking way out to the end of the limb and then jumping up and down." I don't think that's bravado. The core of his business philosophy is that you can't get rich by doing the same thing as everyone else. "In 1977, everyone said I was nuts when I said we were going to build the first commercial relational database. In 1995, everybody said I was nuts when I said that the PC was a ridiculous device—continuously increasing in complexity when it needs to become easier to use and less expensive. By then it was clear to me that PC-centric client/server computing was a mistake, a misguided model that just distributed complexity. And now they say I'm nuts because I said we could build a complete and integrated suite of application software. I always feel good when everyone says I'm nuts because it's a sign that we're trying to do something innovative— something truly new and different."

Ellison pauses and emits his strange, wheezy, high-pitched sigh of a giggle. "On the other hand, when people say you're nuts, you just might be nuts. You've got to constantly guard against that possibility. You don't want people saying you're nuts too often—once every three or four years is good. Any more than that, and you should be worried, because no one's smart enough to have a good idea more than once every three or four years."

The E-Business Suite was released at the beginning of June 2000. The suite was controversial right from the outset, and Ellison wouldn't have been true to himself if he hadn't gone out of his way to make it even more so by using it to challenge most of the belief system that the software business was founded on. In fact, the E-Business Suite was intended as an assault on the entire ecosystem of enterprise computing. It was an attack on every rival application company because of Ellison's claim that it was so complete customers could get everything they needed from one vendor; it was an attack on the huge and powerful systems integration industry because Ellison was arguing that gluing together programs from different software firms was an expensive waste of time; it was also an attack on the analysts in the consulting firms whose raison d'être was to identify the "best-of-breed" supplier in each category of application.

Ellison's advocacy of the E-Business Suite was not based on the belief that it had more features than rival products—in fact, he was ready to admit that in a straight features contest between Oracle's suite and most best-of-breed assemblies, the E-Business Suite would come off second best. He said, "It may not have one hundred percent of what you want, but it has a hundred percent of what you need. The advantages of out-of-the-box integration more than make up for a few missing nice but not necessary to have features."

What did he mean? The overwhelming reason, Ellison believed, for the failure of information technology to deliver on its overblown promises was the fragmentation of information that resulted from the computing industry's addiction to complexity. Expensively assembled best-of-breed enterprise computing systems, in which the cost of implementation might be ten times as much as the original software licenses, were Ellison's latest target but the origins of his "war on complexity" went back more than a decade.

Ellison started his career as a contract mainframe programmer, and although Oracle had been happy to join the stampede to client/server in the late 1980s, Ellison quickly became disillusioned with it. He says, "We installed lots of client/server systems. But it was a very ugly model. Our applications were installed on thousands of PCs, so if you needed to fix a bug you'd have to change the software on all those thousands of PCs. It was an incredibly labor-intensive, expensive, error-prone nightmare of a process. Worse yet, client/server worked fine on high-speed Ethernet LANs [local-area networks], but it performed terribly on [slower] wide-area networks [like the Internet]. We'd taken a huge step backwards because of this wide-area network problem. Mainframe systems had dumb terminals with a dumb user interface, but dumb terminals worked beautifully on wide-area networks, so you could build an airline reservation system on a single computer with a single database that could be accessed by terminals all over the world. But client/server systems didn't work on wide-area networks, so you had to use a separate local-area network in every location you did business. Attached to those local-area networks were database and file servers—lots of little servers everywhere, lots of little databases everywhere. Your information got hopelessly fragmented in the process."

Ellison isn't short of stories that exemplify the "insanity" of client/server: "I'll never forget when this reporter from *The Wall Street Journal* phones me to get my comments on a story he was writing on Grand Met's [the international hotels and catering group] information strategy a few years ago. They decided that they were going to put a 'low-cost' database server computer into every Burger King. 'What do you think of that, Larry?' I was stunned. All I could say was 'They're putting databases in hamburger stores? What? Are they crazy? They shouldn't put a database in every store.' But they were kind of stuck. The only way for them to deal with client/servers' dependence on fast networks was to put a server computer into every location where they did business, that is, in every location where they had client PCs. And if you think it's hard to manage lots of desktop PCs, just wait until you try to manage a database server in every location where you do business. Good luck. It's nearly impossible to manage all that distributed complexity; plus, you so fragment your data you can't keep track of what's going on in your business. But all these client/server problems weren't obvious until you got to the point of trying to run a large network of lots of little database servers in different locations. In contrast, the advantages offered by PC client/server computing were immediately obvious to everyone and quite seductive: better user interfaces; cheaper hardware; easier programming—all that made client/server seem irresistible. But the inherent problems of the client/server model were enormous. It was a ticking time bomb."

In fact, the bomb was ticking inside Ellison himself. The day it exploded was September 4, 1995, at the annual conference in Paris called the European Information Technology Forum. It was exactly eleven days since the launch of Windows 95 accompanied by the biggest marketing blitz in history. Bill Gates's face was everywhere. He was feted not only for being the inspiration behind the most exciting company in the world but for the powerful vision of the near future that he had articulated (with the help of Microsoft's chief seer, Nathan Mhyrvold) in *The Road Ahead*—a book all about the coming information superhighway that somehow managed to avoid almost any mention of the Internet. Gates was to be the keynote speaker at the conference, with Ellison scheduled to be the warm-up. Ellison's speeches are rarely scripted, predictable affairs. On this occasion the slide projector didn't work, so he just started talking. Did he know what he was going to say beforehand? "Sort of, but not exactly," he says.

What he thought was important to talk about that day was the "paradigm shift" to the Internet that was coming—similar to the shift from mainframes to client/server—and to express some dissent about the apotheosis of the Microsoft Windows PC, which had clearly taken its toll on Ellison. He says now, "It was really getting on my nerves. It was just such a surreal experience. There was peace in the Middle East and war in Bosnia the same week that Windows 95 was announced, and all the major networks seemed to cover was people in parking lots waiting up all night to get their first copy of Windows 95. It was very strange. Everyone was saying that Microsoft's PC-centric client/server computing would take over the world and then go on forever. Everything else would disappear. UNIX was going away. Mainframes were going away. There'd be little Windows computers everywhere; little database servers everywhere. Well, we were in the middle of installing all these client/server systems and trying to make them work. And they didn't work very well. Your information was chopped into tiny pieces, stored in lots of tiny databases, running on lots of tiny PC server computers. This data fragmentation was accompanied by distributed complexity. The PC was already a ridiculously complex device. And Microsoft had plans to make it still more complex. They were developing a new, more powerful operating system designed to run all the increasingly complex applications that were destined for your desktop PC. It was madness. You can't keep putting applications on the desktop PCs. You have to get as many applications off the desktop and onto servers as possible. And while you're at it, most data should be moved off PCs and onto servers as well. The PC needs to be much simpler and more appliance-like."

The big idea in the Paris speech was that even at the moment that the PC's dominance seemed beyond question, the rise of the Internet was already demonstrating a superior model of computing. Ellison had said, "When you have a networkcentric computing model, you don't need a device anywhere near as complicated as a personal computer. You can build a multimedia Internet terminal for $400 or $500 [compared to the $2,500 you needed to spend at the time to get a capable PC]. You just plug it into the wall to get power—electrons—and into the network to get to applications and information—bits. And you're done." The one mistake that Ellison made was in calling the new "thin" client (as opposed to the "fat" PC client) he had dreamed up a "network computer."

Looking back, he says, "If I'd been really smart I'd have called it an Internet computer. I called it a network computer partly because I liked Sun's slogan—'The network is the computer'—and partly because the word 'Internet' was not all that well known in 1995."

More than two and a half years later, when Oracle shipped an Internet version of its previously client/server-based Release 10.7 applications suite, Ellison still hadn't learned that particular lesson. The reengineered software was christened 10.7 NCA, the initials standing for network computing architecture, and no one was listening. Ellison recalls, "We had to change the name. Network computing architecture got absolutely no traction in the marketplace. So we announced a successor called Internet computing architecture, and sales took off. The big difference between the two? The name." *

The consequences of the Paris speech were profound. Although Gates, who had followed Ellison onstage, didn't stoop to reply to the attack on his beloved PC, the media had the bit between their teeth. Ellison was suddenly front-page news. He was actually not predicting the death of the PC (the PC, like the mainframe, wouldn't disappear, but it would no longer be at the heart of the computing universe); however, that was how it looked as the story gathered momentum. In an interview after the speech, Ellison, enjoying the attention, characteristically added a little fuel to the flames, boldly forecasting that within ten years, network computers would have overtaken PCs in sales. The ensuing publicity for Oracle and Ellison was beyond anything he had dared hope for. Suddenly he was much more famous than he would ever have been as the boss of a company that sold arcane technology to businesses. Now he was locked in a theological struggle for the future of computing with one of the richest and most recognizable people in the world. Oracle, instead of being bracketed with other database firms, such as Informix and Sybase, was suddenly being talked about in the same breath as mighty Microsoft.

It quickly became apparent that the world wanted to know what the newfangled network computer would look like and that Oracle, a software rather than a hardware company, would have to find a way of building one. Mark Jarvis, who now runs marketing at Oracle, recalls, "Microsoft was saying no, this will never happen, it's a stupid idea, so we were actually confronted with this problem of having something to show

---

*LE writes: It never ceases to amaze me how the product name can be the difference between success and failure in the technology industry.

people. Larry was a bit responsible for this, everyone thinking of the network computer as a physical device. Later on, as history now shows, the PC sort of became a network computer and so did the cell phone. But back then we had to make something that people could look at."

The official unveiling of the network computer was at Oracle Open World in Japan, one of the biggest computer shows in the world. Jarvis says, "We had them under cloth at OpenWorld. Larry unveiled them in front of all these people and they looked great, flash, flash, flash, there was a media frenzy. But you know what, they were made out of wood. I remember they cost a shitload to design—hundreds of thousands of dollars just for a piece of wood. But everyone thought they were real." In time, a specially set up subsidiary of Oracle called NCI (Network Computer, Inc.) managed to build about thirty thousand of the devices with the help of some hardware partners. One version, now called the NIC (New Internet Computer) struggles on today, mainly as a machine that Oracle donates to schools.*

Having gone so extremely public with his revolt from the whole client/server model, Ellison could hardly allow his engineers just to go on developing software as if nothing had happened. Ellison had spelled out his view that client/server was an evolutionary dead end and that a form of servercentric computing based on the open standards and protocols of the Internet was the future for Oracle. However, getting Oracle to change direction was not just a question of articulating a new strategy and expecting people to get on with it. The efforts of the entire company, from the developers building the applications to the sales and consulting teams who were selling and installing the software, were dedicated to making client/server a success. It was what customers expected and demanded. Whatever Ellison might be saying about the network computer and a new form of computing based on the Internet, client/server was, quite simply, the environment.

---

*LE writes: Digital Equipment Corporation (now part of Hewlett-Packard) had designed and built a beautiful ARM-based network computer they code-named "shark." They were in the process of marketing them in China, among other places, when they suddenly stopped. Bob Palmer, Digital's CEO, told me that Microsoft had threatened to retaliate against Digital's PC business if Digital continued to build NCs. So I had an early glimpse of the type of tactics Microsoft would later employ to destroy Netscape. Its attack on the NC was just practice before the main event—the browser war.

As for Ellison, it was as if he had needed the speech and the reaction to it to create a new set of circumstances, a new reality that would force him to lead the charge toward Internet computing, whatever that would turn out to be, despite the skepticism of many of his followers. Much later he said to me, "Once I'm finally certain of the right direction, I pick a fight, as I did with Gates. It helps me make my point, and it makes it impossible to do an about-face and go back. Once a course has been plotted, I sail a long way off and burn my boats. It's win or die."

How quick was Ellison to understand the significance of the Internet compared with others in the computing industry? There were undoubtedly others who saw the light even earlier, but he got there pretty fast. Farzad "Zod" Nazem, who worked at Oracle for ten years before leaving in early 1996 to become Yahoo!'s chief technology officer, remembers going out for meals with Ellison and "giving him kind of free tutorials on what you could do with this stuff." Mark Jarvis recalls a meeting at Oracle in February 1995 to tell Ellison about some software that a development team had come up with to allow access to the database through a Web browser that had been christened the World Wide Web Interface Kit. "My first slide was 'Here is the Internet, Larry.' Larry was, like, 'Next slide.' Next thing, I pulled up the World Wide Web and Larry was, like, 'Next slide.' So Larry was already into this. He knew it all. I thought I was educating him, but . . . Larry is always three months ahead of everyone."

What distinguished Ellison's take on the Internet from that of many other enthusiasts was that he saw it not just as a great new way to get information and go shopping—lots of people quickly understood that once they saw the first Mosaic Web browser—but as a platform for a completely different and infinitely superior kind of computing. Right from the outset, he believed that the Internet really did change everything. Six years later he says, "Internet computing is the last architecture. There will be no new architecture for computing—not in a thousand years—not ever. I know it sounds a bit crazy. But with the Internet, computing has adopted the same architecture as all the other major networks—the hundred-year-old telephone and electric power networks and the two-thousand-year-old aqueduct network. Internet computing centralizes data storage in huge databases and processing on large servers, while distributing information on demand across a global network. Internet computing hides complexity, provides economies of scale, and delivers information faster."

Ellison argues that while Internet computing architecture will not change, its technology components will continuously get better and better. Networks will get faster, high-speed wireless networks will be ubiquitous, processing power will multiply according to Moore's Law for years to come, displays will become more beautiful and user interfaces more intuitive. But the way the pieces are assembled architecturally, the fundamental structure of the Internet model—massive global databases, applications running on megaservers, applications and information accessed through a simple browser—that model won't ever change. He says, "The old PC-centric client/server architecture was the equivalent of everyone having their own well for water, Honda generator for electric power, and VHF two-way radio for communication. The client/server model distributed complexity, required huge amounts of labor, and precluded economies of scale. For these reasons, PC-centric client/server computing became an evolutionary dead end."

In this vision, the PC becomes just one of any number of network access devices—an appliance that connects to the Internet just as a television connects to broadcast signals, a telephone to the telephone network, or a light to the electricity grid. As with those networks, the user does not have to know anything about what it takes to get a television program, a phone call, or a sophisticated financial application to him. As with those networks, the technological complexity is hidden from view and managed by professionals. Nobody who points a mouse at a hypertext link has to know anything about the incredibly sophisticated computing and communications technologies—the programming languages, the transport protocols, the power routers, the massive servers and almost infinitely scalable databases—that have come together to deliver the application that's just been chosen.

The story of Ellison's struggle to make Oracle the first big software company to get to the Internet is for another chapter. But the philosophy of computing that triggered Ellison's outburst against the PC and the subsequent long and, at times, bloody campaign to end the dominion of client/server is precisely the same as the one that has led him to his current battles with best-of-breed software vendors and powerful system integrators—namely, that the cardinal sin of the computing industry is the creation of complexity: a complexity that invariably results in information systems that don't deliver timely and useful information because they use software architectures that result in chronic fragmentation of data.

Although Oracle first became active in the business applications market in the late 1980s, Ellison's own involvement in their development was, at best, sporadic until well after his Internet epiphany. But when, in early 1998, he was pushed into taking a more active role, a number of things soon struck him as odd. The first was that there was no consistent view of Oracle's applications among its customers. Whereas by this time just about all Oracle's database customers were getting a product that either met or exceeded their expectations, the same was not true of the people who were buying its applications.

Ellison says, "Some customers loved our applications, some didn't. That seemed very odd to me. How could customers react so differently to the 'same' product? My question revealed my fundamental misunderstanding of our applications business. Every applications customer didn't use the 'same' product. The applications business was not like our database business. We finish our database software, and then you use it. But with our applications software, the customer, usually assisted by a team of consultants, makes major changes to our software before it's used. Sometimes the changes work, sometimes not. No wonder customer satisfaction varied so widely. The business model of the customer 'finishing' our software for us seemed flawed to me. But that's the way Oracle's applications business worked, that's the way SAP's applications business worked, in fact, that's how the entire enterprise applications software industry worked."

What Ellison meant by the software not being finished was Oracle did not sell a complete range of applications. The chances were that anyone buying, say, Oracle's financial and manufacturing software would need to add the products of perhaps three or four other companies to get the computer system they needed, and the job of knitting these different programs together that had never been designed to work with each other was the job of either their own IT people or highly paid consultants. Ellison says, "The applications software industry sold components, not complete business systems. The customer bought the components and assembled them into systems as best they could—no instructions included. No other technology industry in the world works this way. I mean, every Boeing 747 has the same basic components: fuselage, wings, and tail. You don't buy a 747 and decide to speed it up by sweeping the wings back a little more. That would be expensive and dangerous. Who in their right mind travels in a heavily customized, one-of-a-kind 747? Why do people use heavily customized, one-of-a-kind business systems? Because they had no other choice. We wanted to give customers a choice of a complete and integrated suite of business applications."

If the lack of completeness was one reason why customers modified application software from Oracle and other application vendors, another was that it had become traditional to do so. As Mark Barrenechea, the Oracle executive responsible for the CRM half of the E-Business Suite, puts it, "When most of us buy a car, we select a standard design and then choose from a standard set of options. Think for a moment about what that has meant for the evolution of the automobile: every brand has been able to incorporate every major advance in design because the factories have not been busy reworking every unit to the customer's preconceptions about how, say, the transmission should work. But the convention with software has been for companies to buy standard products and then pay somebody to change those products so that they conform to the company's peculiar business processes. And who is that somebody? Either an employee, who's probably familiar with those processes but not with the software, or a consultant, who's probably familiar with the software product but not with the company's business processes."

It was the usual problem with the computer business: a deeply ingrained preference for creating the maximum complexity for customers whenever possible and customers who were often their own worst enemies. Ellison became convinced that the peculiar characteristics of the enterprise application industry—the need to glue together a kit of parts purchased from multiple vendors and the urge to customize still further in an effort to make the software fit the way customer companies did business—were responsible not just for the frequently expressed dissatisfaction with Oracle's own application software but for a general and widespread conviction that long and costly ERP and CRM implementations often failed to deliver the expected return on very large investments.

For Ellison, as always, the most pernicious consequence of unnecessary complexity was the resulting fragmentation of data. In the era of client/server computing, companies with global operations could not escape the problems caused by having to maintain multiple databases. But as Mark Barrenechea points out, it was, at best, a necessary evil: "Multiple databases mean duplication of data, conflicting data, inconsistent data formats, and multiplication of effort whenever data needed updating. Multiple databases also mean multiple data centers and multiple IT staffs." However, the advent of Internet computing meant, at least in theory, that it was now possible for any company, however big and complicated, to move toward having just one central database with reconciled and integrated business data that could be accessed from anywhere in the world. But that wasn't happening.

Ellison says, "The World Wide Web is a single unified network—all users who are connected can communicate with each other. We would never connect our users to separate networks that couldn't communicate with each other. That would be nuts. However, we think nothing of having a marketing system from E.piphany with a separate marketing database, a sales systems from Siebel with a separate sales database, a customer service system from Clarify with a separate customer service database, a Web store from BroadVision with a separate store database, an accounting system from SAP with a separate accounting database, and so on. It's incredibly difficult and expensive to make these systems communicate at all—and it's impossible to make them communicate well."

In Ellison's mind, this was the inevitable result of buying "best-of-breed" software, or, as he preferred to put it, buying pieces of kit. Even though the Internet was making it possible to consolidate data all in one place, best of breed, in which every application from every vendor ran on its own little database, was conspiring to undermine it. Supposedly there to fix the problem were the systems integrators from the likes of IBM and Accenture, who would write the custom programs that were needed to move, say, customer information from one database to another. Skillful consultants may be able to overcome some of the problems. But there are others that can never be fully resolved. Software from different vendors will have different semantics—even something as simple as defining what a "customer" is may differ—different underlying data schemas, which have to be coordinated but will scarcely ever be fully reconciled, and different user interfaces with conflicting design conventions and display elements. Even if the consultants have a proven integration method to link two pieces of software, APIs (application program interfaces) still have to be specially constructed to pass messages among distinct database schemas, limiting the amount of information that can be extracted as well as duplicating storage requirements.

The Internet should have made it possible for multinational corporations around the globe to exchange large amounts of information quickly and easily, but in practice, because every system was different and each one used multiple databases to store and manage information, that remained impossible. Most multinational companies found themselves with systems that couldn't talk to one another. The Internet might make access global, but without global systems, that was of limited value.

Making all this complexity even worse was the fact that different and often competing software firms had no interest in coordinating their releases. When one of the software vendors whose products a company was using announced an improved version of the application, putting it in would involve upgrading the entire integration backbone and rewriting all those custom interfaces, not just for one system in one country but for different systems all over the world. The expense and trouble often meant that customers elected to reject new features that could be of real, albeit marginal, benefit to their business. The fact that every computer system was more or less unique meant that it was either frozen in time or required almost constant attention from teams of ever-helpful consultants to keep it up to date. No wonder Ellison described systems integration as "the gift that keeps on giving" or that in May 2000, IBM's then CEO, Lou Gerstner, was able to boast at analysts' day that for every dollar spent on software licenses up to seven were spent on services.

Ellison's analysis was informed by what he'd encountered at Oracle. Although Oracle was using only its own applications, before the advent of the E-Business Suite, they were scarcely more integrated than many best-of-breed systems. Whenever Ellison meets customers, he describes what it was like: "Here I was, running the company that provides most of the world's information management software, and our internal applications systems couldn't provide answers to the most basic business questions. Like: How many people work at Oracle today? I didn't know. Why? Well, the French had their own HR [human resources] system and database, the Germans had their own HR system and database, so did the Japanese and the Americans, and the Canadians, etc. In total, we had seventy separate HR systems. To find out how many people worked at Oracle worldwide, I'd have to inquire into all seventy HR systems. All our business data was fragmented into so many separate databases, it was difficult to get answers to many seemingly simple questions. How much did we sell yesterday? Sorry. Our sales order data was fragmented across a hundred and thirty separate accounting databases—one per country in which we did business. How many new customers did we get last month? Simply impossible to answer. Our customer data was fragmented into four hundred separate customer databases. Worse still, it was just about impossible to combine the customer data into a data warehouse because the customer data was not consistent across all those separate operational databases. For example, the same customer, Michelin, would have one customer ID number in the French database and a different customer ID number in the German database. In the data warehouse one customer, Michelin, thus looked like several separate customers.

"No wonder people have a hard time getting information out of their business systems. The current state of the art is inconsistent information fragmented across lots of little databases. And integrating and maintaining all these separate little systems costs much more than a single unified set of applications running on a single global database. So businesses are paying extra not to be able to get answers to their questions. But it's worse than that. If your systems can't easily share information, then the people within your company can't communicate effectively. If they can't communicate, they can't cooperate. This results in a lot of friction between groups. Marketing doesn't cooperate very well with sales. France doesn't cooperate very well with Germany. Sound familiar? What was unbelievably frustrating was the fact that we were paying top dollar to maintain this mess—all these separate systems with their fragmented, inconsistent data. We had a huge IT staff running hundreds of loosely connected systems. We wanted one unified system with one global database. With all our information in one place, we could easily access and share information. We'd make better decisions, groups would cooperate, and IT costs would go down. All that would happen, but first we'd have to build a global applications system. That's why we built the E-Business Suite."

The high cost of implementing and running these systems, the fragmentation of data that resulted in very little useful information being available in real time—Ellison described them as billion-dollar clerical automation systems—and the near impossibility of being able to take advantage of upgrades gracefully were not the only things that customers were unhappy about. One obvious one was the vendors' refusal to take responsibility for the failure of their software to deliver once it was integrated with the third-party applications that it had never been designed to work with. Consultants would blame the software firms for bugs in their products, and the software firms would blame the consultants for changing the code of their products to meet the requirements of individual customers. The customer was left standing miserably in the middle, paying huge bills and saddled with "shelfware" that had proved too difficult to install.*

---

*LE writes: Even today, most customers split their applications software purchases between the software provider and the system integrator. While the software provider sells the software for a set price, the system integrator will provide only a cost "estimate." If there is a shortcoming in the software, the systems integrator will charge extra to fix it. These extra charges are typically many times higher than the original estimate. The best way to solve this problem is to make

A new and emerging problem was that the "e-business transformation" that the Internet was supposed to have made possible and that all the technology companies were hyping for all they were worth was far more demanding than the ERP era in which automation tended to take place inside a company within tightly defined functional silos. E-business not only demanded extending the enterprise to its business partners and customers, it also required highly choreographed interactions among all parts of the business. A significant point of e-business was to save time and money by exponentially accelerating the velocity of transactions. Ellison believed that best-of-breed software solutions, in which every application had to sit on its own database and information had to be moved laboriously and usually in incomplete form from one database to another through a custom-designed integration layer, would always struggle to achieve the seamlessness and speed implicit in the e-business promise.

The answer to the problems that enterprise application customers were facing, Ellison concluded, lay in doing two things, which he calculated that Oracle alone was capable of. The first was for all of Oracle's applications to be tightly integrated both with one another and with the database through an architecture based on a single shared-data model. The second was to produce the first-ever complete suite of applications that would be capable of automating every aspect of a company's business, from the traditional ERP or back-office tasks, such as financials, manufacturing and HR, to the fancy new stuff that included customer relationship management (sales, marketing, and customer support), the supply chain, procurement, and Web stores. Ellison calculated that Oracle's advantage lay both in its genes as a database company and in the sheer size of its development teams.

The starting point was to see the database as the hub and the applications as the spokes. Ellison says, "We had been thinking about the problem upside down, and as a result we were building the wrong software. We had been building process automation systems. We needed to build information systems—with the process automation layered on top. Traditional

---

the applications software vendor or the systems integrator unconditionally guarantee the price of the software product and the cost of the project to put it in. And while you're at it, you might try to pin down the cost of running and maintaining the systems once they're installed. It never ceases to amaze me that companies continue to enter into large software projects without knowing the cost of installation, integration, operation, and maintenance.

applications design focused on automating one particular process—like taking an order. Modern application design must focus on one piece of information—customer orders—and then layer on *all* processes that touch the order information: taking the order, billing the customer, initiating customer service, marketing additional services to that customer, and so on. It's not the process at the center, it's the data. It's the 'information age.' If you're building a marketing system, the marketing application should use the same exact customer information as your sales system, as your accounting system, as your customer service system. That way, every time you interact with a customer, it changes the same central customer database. All your customer information is in one place. All your product information's in one place. All your applications share the same data. If you draw a picture of Oracle's application architecture, the database is at the center and the applications are attached around the periphery. This is a radically different view of the world. If you draw a picture of Siebel's CRM 'suite'—they have a bunch of separate applications each with its own separate database—it looks like a charm bracelet. But there's no charm in lots of separate databases. A single global database connected to a single global network—the Internet—is the ideal architecture."

What followed was that Oracle's developers had to rewrite every ERP and CRM application so that they could all use a common data model. That meant overcoming the resistance of development teams who were convinced of the design superiority of their particular models. It also meant fixing on a data model that would be consistent across an entire range of interactions. For example, what is a customer? Is it someone that just buys stuff from us? Is it someone that buys our stuff through other channels? Is it someone we ship stuff to or who pays us for stuff we ship? Or is it someone who asks questions before buying stuff or after buying stuff, and does that someone expect to get service? A further problem was the inclusion into the data model of what are known as "multis"—languages, places, currencies, contact addresses. And so it goes on. If Ellison's concept of a unified data model for all of Oracle's applications was vital to waging war against complexity, achieving it would be a far from simple undertaking.

Almost as important as the datacentric approach that Ellison evangelized was the notion of completeness. "It can't be simple if it's not complete" had become Ellison's latest mantra. Although rivals immediately derided the idea that any one company, even one as big and financially strong as Oracle, could do it all, Ellison did have software history on his side. He was only too happy to point out that he was only copying the successful strategy of Microsoft with Office, its market-dominant suite of personal productivity applications—"There used to be a best-of-breed PC software industry, but there isn't anymore"—and SAP with its R/3 suite of ERP applications, which had swept nearly all before it, including less comprehensive offerings from Oracle, in the 1990s.

For Ellison, the central argument in favor of the suite approach was that it would give customers all the functionality they needed to transform their efficiency and even become e-businesses without the need to integrate other pieces of software from a multiplicity of vendors. Ellison was convinced that the suite would deliver all the things that best of breed had failed to: fast, fixed-price implementation; rapid information flows across and beyond the enterprise; seamlessly integrated operations between functions and territories thanks to the "single global instance" made possible by the Internet; real-time business intelligence for senior executives accessed through browser-based "dashboards"; a consistent user interface common to every application, reducing training requirements; speedy and graceful incorporation of anything from patches for fixing bugs to full-scale feature upgrades and new releases; lower ownership costs thanks to data consolidation and Internet-based support.

But to arrive at this IT Nirvana, customers, Ellison made it clear, would need to do more than just buy Oracle's software: they had to sign up for the vision behind it—Ellison's vision. And being Ellison, the way he expressed the vision was deliberately expressed to stir up the maximum amount of controversy. The messages were, "Just say no to systems integration," and, "Don't finish our software for us." Some nine months after the E-Business Suite was released, Ellison used a speech at Oracle's AppsWorld convention in New Orleans to explain the perils of customizing Oracle's applications. To Oracle's critics and competitors, it sounded very much as if Ellison was arrogantly (and if true, very foolishly) blaming his own customers for the problems many of them were having installing early versions of the E-Business Suite. The influential technology consultancy Forrester Research put out a vicious report accusing Ellison of attacking customers when Oracle shipped a piece of software that was allegedly so buggy that it had needed five thousand patches to stabilize it. *

---

*LE writes: "Patch" is an unfortunate choice of words. A "patch" includes both bug fixes and enhancements to the E-Business Suite. So many of the five thousand patches were not bug fixes at all, they were new features we were putting into the suite in our never-ending quest to be functionally complete.

In fact, Ellison wasn't criticizing his customers at all. What he was actually doing was outlining a different sort of relationship between a software supplier and clients. In New Orleans he said, "We used to deliver incomplete software, and you would finish it. Now we're delivering nearly complete software—software that will meet eighty to ninety percent of your needs without any changes. So we're asking customers not to try to put in the last ten, fifteen, or twenty percent. If you do, you'll fall into an old trap. If you heavily modify our software, it will be difficult and expensive for you to take a new version of that software a year from now. If you heavily modify our software and you call us with a question, we'll have a hard time answering the question because you wrote a lot of the system, not us. You are better off, I submit to you, with an eighty percent solution installed and working in six months than fantasizing about a hundred percent solution that you might finish in two years after you write lots of custom code."

The second part of his plea not to modify the E-Business Suite was based upon another aspect of what he saw as a changed relationship with the customer. The systems integration industry has successfully taught enterprise software customers how to buy software so that costly customization is an inevitable outcome. Typically, prospective users put together a team to draw up a Request for Proposal (RFP) of desired features and functionality. As a rule, partly these RFPs reflect the way the firm has traditionally done business, and partly they are a wish list of features that often quite low-level people suppose will improve the operation of their small bit of the organization. The result is software that is expensively adapted to lock in outdated and ill-considered business practices—a major reason why ERP installations have only rarely given an adequate return on investment.

With the E-Business Suite, Ellison wanted to turn that practice on its head. Instead, Ellison wanted customers to change their processes to take maximum advantage of the Internet-based best practice captured by the software. Ellison said, "Don't tell us how you've been running your business for the last twenty years. Instead, let's try to figure out how you want to run your business for the next twenty years. It's a classic business mistake to say, 'This is how we do business; change your software so we can automate it.' A new approach is needed. First, you must simplify and modernize all your business processes, then move those newly standardized processes to the Internet. Only then can you expect the system to improve your business. Only then can you expect the system to be delivered on time."

There was something reckless in all of this. Ellison was challenging customers to share his vision and, in doing so, change the way they operated their businesses. He was daring them not to touch the software he wanted them to buy from Oracle: "We don't think our customers should try to finish our software. It's too hard. We're the world's biggest employer of engineers from MIT and CalTech, and mathematicians from Harvard and Stanford, and even we have a hell of a hard time finishing our software. Customers shouldn't try do it for us." He was challenging the enterprise computing industry's basic assumptions: "IBM says that what you need to do when you buy that Siebel system is modify it so it fits your business. So you modify it, and you modify SAP and you modify i2 and you modify PeopleSoft. You modify and enhance all this incredibly complex software. When you finish, your company is the only company in the world that is running this unique software configuration. I don't care if this is the way everyone does it; we're going to try a completely different approach."

4

BEGINNINGS

When Larry Ellison says that he honestly thinks Oracle has it within its grasp to become the most important company in the world, he believes it. His eyes shine with sincerity, his smile is almost apologetic. It's as if he knows that he shouldn't say such things, but keeping something so exciting and so wonderful to himself would be unbearable. There are, of course, other reasons for saying it. It's that business of burning his boats again. Just being successful isn't enough. There has to be something more to play for, a reason to keep challenging oneself and others. When you have more money than you could spend in a thousand years, the stakes have to be big enough to get you into the office each day (or at least most days). Yet when Ellison makes these statements, it confirms the opinion of many people in their belief that he is slightly crazy, someone who has become so addicted to hyperbole that he inhabits an alternative reality.

That Oracle today is one of the world's most successful companies is beyond argument. From its birth as a public company in 1986, its revenues have gone from a little over $20 million a year to a peak of more than $11 billion by 2001. It has operating margins of at least 35 percent even in a down economy and a cash pile that fluctuates between $6 billion and $8 billion. In the middle of 2000, its market value was more than $200 billion. Even after the "tech crash" it is still worth nearly $70 billion, twice as much as the combined values of Ford and General Motors. Many of Oracle's 43,000 employees, particularly key developers and those who have been with the company since the mid-1980s, have become multimillionaires thanks to their stock options.

Most people are far less aware of Oracle's software than they are of

Microsoft's, but it is just as ubiquitous and may have even more impact on their daily lives. Ninety-eight percent of the Fortune 100 companies depend on Oracle software to manage their information. Every time we use a credit card, buy a plane ticket, reserve a hotel bedroom, order from a catalogue, search Yahoo!, get a video from Amazon, settle a phone bill, or withdraw cash from an ATM, the chances are that we are interacting with an Oracle database. From its six shining blue-green towers overlooking San Francisco Bay, Oracle's operations span more than 145 countries. Oracle's OpenWorld convention in Tokyo attracts more than a quarter of a million visitors and outstrips even Comdex as the largest computer show in the world. In contrast to Microsoft, few would dispute that Oracle has been a ceaseless innovator, rarely working far from the technological bleeding edge.

Yet . . . it's equally remarkable how many observers of the technology scene see Oracle as a company that never quite manages to realize its potential, never mind scale the vertiginous peaks of Ellison's overactive imagination. Among the defects routinely identified are the failure, despite well over a decade of trying, of Oracle's applications to match the success of its database; a habitual willingness to use customers to debug unstable application software; a cowboy sales force that's good at driving through deals but couldn't care less about what happens to customers afterward; hyperaggressive marketing that not only overclaims but insultingly belittles rivals; a consulting organization that complicates and sours relationships with channel partners by competing directly with them; a shallow management bench caused by an inability to hang on to executive talent; and (take your pick) Ellison's excessively dominant role in the business or Ellison's semidetachment from the business.

Who should we believe, Ellison or his critics? Does Oracle have the capacity for real greatness, as Ellison contends? Or is there something deep in its DNA and, by extension, Ellison's, that will deny it the kind of respect, almost love, that people once had for Thomas Watson's IBM?

A large part of this story is about Ellison and Oracle as they are today. But without an understanding of where Oracle has come from and how it has been forged by both triumphs and disasters in its twenty-five years of existence, the present is without meaning. Oracle's founding and turbulent early years, leading up to what became known as its "near-death experience" in 1990, have been well documented. But relatively little is known of the struggles and rivalries that have made the modern Oracle: how, in the aftermath of that crash in 1990, the company regrouped, stabilized, and was forced to reinvent itself not once but twice; and in the process, how it increased its revenues more than tenfold in the course of a decade.

• • •

When, in the summer of 1977, the thirty-four-year-old Larry Ellison founded a little firm that he and his two partners, fellow programmers Bob Miner and Ed Oates, rather grandly named Software Development Laboratories, his ambition was pretty much in line with his thus far fairly modest achievements: namely to avoid having to do, as he saw it, unrewarding work for people he didn't respect. He remembers, "My original goal was to build a company doing about ten million dollars of revenue and employing about fifty people. What motivated me was the desire to control my environment so I wouldn't have to do things I didn't want to do or spend time with people I didn't enjoy working with."

Ellison had left his hometown of Chicago eleven years earlier, having failed to graduate from either of the universities he had sporadically attended. Looking back, Ellison says, "I went to the University of Illinois for a couple of years, but during finals week my mother passed away, so I just packed up and left without taking exams. I didn't like exams or the university or the town it was in, for that matter. I recall one exam where I just sat there for an hour, unable to begin because I was so angry that I had to spend the next three hours writing answers to questions I cared nothing about. I never had the discipline to do things I didn't like. The classes at the University of Chicago were better, but I had such a short attention span that it was simply impossible for me to finish anything. However, I was intrigued by physics because it seemed to answer the most basic questions about our world. Like a lot of young people, I was looking for answers." *

The one good thing that came out of studying physics was that Ellison ended up working at the Argonne National Laboratory as a contract programmer. As part of a physics course, he had to learn basic programming. "I just read the book. It was similar to doing math proofs. It was logical, and I was good at logic." He quickly learned how to program the latest IBM mainframe computer. "I started doing contract programming. My short attention span didn't work against me because I could get programs written very quickly. I ended up making quite a lot of money, and I only

---

*LE writes: No longer young, I am still looking for answers. Today the science I find offering the most insight into our world is molecular biology.

had to work a few days a week. It was fun and it was easy. And nobody cared if you were a Ph.D. from MIT or had never finished high school. Either you could do the job or you couldn't. I loved that."

For Ellison, discovering he was good at programming was both a validation of his intelligence and liberation from what he regarded as "absurd conventions." He says, "People—teachers, coaches, bosses—want you to conform to some standard of behavior they deem correct. They measure and reward you on how well you conform—arrive on time, dress appropriately, exhibit a properly deferential attitude—as opposed to how well you do your job. Programming liberated me from all that. I could work in the middle of the night. I could wear blue jeans and a T-shirt. I could ride my motorcycle to work. And I'd make more money if I could solve the problem faster and better than anyone else."

With the money Ellison was now earning and skills that he knew would be in demand, he bought a secondhand Ford Thunderbird and headed for Berkeley, California. It was the summer of 1966, and "it seemed like the place to be." Was he looking for a career? Not exactly. "Basically, programming gave me the freedom to screw around through my twenties. All I knew I was capable of was short bursts of energy. So I found jobs working on weekends as an IBM systems programmer. I would help run these huge data centers and fix the operating system on big IBM mainframes. Most people didn't want to work weekends, so I had no trouble getting these jobs. Monday through Friday, I'd be hiking or rock climbing in Yosemite, kayaking down the Stanislaus or American River, or on a long bike trip down the California coast. I was in my twenties and having fun."

Soon after moving to Berkeley, he met and married Adda Quinn. But the marriage didn't last: "She was very bright and very pretty. But although we were the same age, she was mature and I was not." The breakup triggered all sorts of feelings of self-doubt in Ellison. "My father had told me that I would never amount to anything, and now it seemed he might be right. I knew I could earn a living as a programmer, but where was my life going? I wondered if I could ever be disciplined enough to be anything more than a technology pieceworker."

Despite the soul-searching, Ellison continued to live pretty much as before, doing less contract work but flitting from one Silicon Valley firm to another. Amdahl, a would-be competitor to IBM in mainframe computers, laid him off in 1973. He then went to work for Ampex. The company that had invented the magnetic tape recorder was working on a way of dramatically increasing the amount of information that could be stored in computer databases. The Ampex terabit memory system was, according to Ellison, a "very cool" project that the CIA had funded and code-named Oracle. At Ampex, Ellison also met his future partners, Bob Miner and Ed Oates.

But as usual, Ellison didn't stick around for long. By 1976, he had moved to a firm called Precision Instruments (soon to change its name to Omex), that, like Ampex, was also working on a mass storage system. The difference was that for the first time Ellison had a title—vice president of R and D—and some seniority. "I had always believed that at the top of these companies there must be some exceptionally capable people who make the entire technology industry work. Now here I was, working near the top of a tech company, and those capable people were nowhere to be found. The senior managers I saw were conformist, bureaucratic, and very reluctant to make decisions. Much to my surprise, I gradually became convinced that I was better at solving problems and making decisions than they were. Or at the very least I was willing to make a decision to do something, while they seemed paralyzed by endless analysis and fear of making the wrong decision."

Ellison suddenly began to think that maybe he could run a company. But he wasn't motivated by either great ambition or the vision to do anything in particular. Having his own company would simply allow him to go on with his life but with more control over it and with better rewards. "I thought that if I ran a small consulting company, I could work on a lot of interesting projects and make more money. The key was finding enough projects that were 'hard' enough. The ideal 'hard' job is one that is generally perceived as being difficult but can quickly succumb to a bit of cleverness. All we needed were a few really smart people who could do these so-called hard jobs quickly, and we would make a lot of money while not working all that hard. That had been my favorite approach to work from the beginning."

The job at Omex gave him his opportunity. Omex was preparing to put the contract for writing the software for its mass storage system out for bidding. "I said I knew some super programmers who could save the company a lot of time and money. Do you want to me to ask them to put together a bid on the contract? My boss, the CEO, said, 'Sure.' " The team that Ellison had in mind included two of his former colleagues from Ampex, Oates and Miner. The three of them formed a company—Software Development Laboratories—and they won the contract from Omex with a bid of $400,000, a third the price of the next lowest bidder. Ellison would stay at Omex to design and oversee the project while

Miner and Oates wrote the software with the help of a hotshot young programmer named Bruce Scott.

When it came to negotiating the ownership of SDL, Ellison says, "Initially, I proposed splitting the company evenly between Bob, Ed, and me. Then I went home and thought about it. The company had been my idea, and so far I had done all the work. So I changed my proposal. I wanted sixty percent, while Bob and Ed would get twenty percent each. We agreed that this division of ownership was just a starting point and that both Bob and Ed could earn additional stock so long as they performed well. Bob did a great job, and his ownership percentage was increased to thirty percent. Ed went through a very messy divorce, which affected his performance, and he ended up leaving the company. Eventually Ed returned, but his ownership was reduced." Over the years, as Oracle grew, went public, and became a blue-chip stock held by many institutions, Ellison's share has inevitably been diluted, but he has always been acutely aware of the value of his stock both in financial terms and because of the power it gave him within the company.

Alongside doing the work they were doing for Omex, the SDL partners, with Ellison at last installed as president, began thinking about what sort of company they wanted it to be. For Ellison it seemed obvious. He says, "I wanted to get out of the consulting business. Consulting proved to be much more work than I ever imagined. My 'hard problems, cleverly solved' business model did not scale up beyond a few people, proving I was not nearly as clever as I thought. I was working eighty hours a week—at least. We were making a lot of money, but we were working insanely long hours. The closest I got to Yosemite was the Ansel Adams poster on my office wall. So we decided to abandon the consulting business and go into the software product business. A software product offered the ultimate leverage: build it once and sell it over and over again." The problem was deciding what it was they would make. Ellison says, "When I was working for Bob Miner at Ampex, I built a database management system for the PDP-11 minicomputer. It was a CODASYL database, basically a ripoff, excuse me, 'modeled after' Cullinet's successful IDMS mainframe database. Cullinet had been quite successful competing against IBM in the mainframe database business. Surely there was a market for minicomputer databases as well."

The SDL guys scoured the technical literature about databases for new ideas. Ellison says, "The first time I heard about a relational database was some years back at a meeting with the CIA. Since then I had read a series of technical papers by [Edgar "Ted"] Codd, an IBM fellow, about relational database theory. But Codd's papers were much too theoretical to be used as the basis for a product. Then IBM Research starts publishing this series of papers by Don Chamberlain about a prototype relational database they were building called System R, including a complete specification for System R's Structured Query Language, or SQL. After a lot of careful reading and rereading of the System R papers, I decided we should throw out the work I had done on the CODASYL database and use the IBM papers as an architectural blueprint for our new database product. The opportunity was huge. We had a chance to build the world's first commercial relational database. Why? Because nobody else was even trying.

"The other relational database projects were pure research efforts. They were spending little to no time on overall system performance and reliability, both of which were essential for a successful commercial database product. If we could build a fast and reliable relational database, we would have it made. At the same time I thought it would be smart to avoid the very competitive and highly conservative IBM mainframe market. So we decided to build our database for the minicomputer market. Bob thought that the relational database strategy was risky, but he left the final decision up to me. I thought that relational was clearly the way to go. It was very cool technology. And I liked the fact it was risky. The bigger the apparent risk, the fewer people will try to go there. We would surely lose if we had to face serious competition. But if we were all alone in pursuit of our goal of building the first commercial relational database system, we had a chance to win. But we had to be first to market with the new technology. This was the first in a pattern of apparently high-risk decisions I made throughout my life at Oracle. But I only ever picked the high-risk approach when I thought that it would increase our chance of winning and our share of reward." *

In the relational model, information in the database is viewed as a number of linked two-dimensional tables consisting of rows and columns. Each table has a specified set of named columns, while each column name is distinct within a particular table, although not necessarily between tables. Within a particular column, each entry must be of the

---

*LE writes: Virtually all of these so called high-risk decisions, from building the first commercial relational database to building the first complete and integrated E-Business Suite, involved innovation. Whenever you travel an untraveled path there's risk.

same type. Unlike the hierarchical approach, no predetermined relationship exists between distinct tables. By combining the data items in related columns, it is possible to find information that would either be hidden in a hierarchical database or would take far longer to find. Relational users don't need to understand how stored data is represented in order to retrieve it. What was so exciting about SQL was that it was the only language needed for working with relational databases. It could be used not only for queries but also for data manipulation, data definition, and the setting of access or privileges for groups of users. No wonder Ellison thought it was "cool technology."

Given that IBM was doing most of the important work in the relational area, apart from the CIA-funded Ingres project at Berkeley under Mike Stonebraker, what made Ellison think that he and his tiny team could come up with a commercially viable product before anyone else? "First, conventional wisdom had it that relational databases couldn't be made to run fast enough to be commercially viable, so people didn't enter the race. Second, IBM feared that introducing a relational database would destabilize its large existing IMS [Information Management Systems] database business. Third, even if IBM did deliver a relational product, it would probably be for mainframes. Since we were targeting the minicomputer market, we didn't need to worry about IBM—at least not in the beginning, when we were most vulnerable."

The money that was coming in from Omex basically paid for SDL to create a first version of what would become the Oracle database. This prototype didn't really work, but SDL was creating intellectual property for itself, changing from being a consulting firm into a software company at a time when there were still very few pure software companies around, as opposed to hardware companies that wrote the code to run their boxes. When Ellison looked around, Boston-based Cullinet, with its market value of around $100 million, seemed like the company to emulate. "Cullinet was our role model. We never thought we could get as big as they were because they had an expensive mainframe product and we were focused on these cheap little minicomputers."

After completing the work for Omex, doing just enough to get paid for its software despite the fact that the firm's thin-film laser storage hardware still didn't really work, SDL changed its name to Relational Software, Inc., or RSI, and moved into some smart new offices at 3000 Sand Hill Road near Palo Alto, the address of the top venture capital firms in the Valley. RSI's first customer turned out to be the CIA. The CIA had been interested in the relational model ever since Codd had first expounded his theories and had avidly followed the work IBM's System R research group had done to make SQL into a key to unlock information from a database that could be used by any half-competent user. Unfortunately, IBM wasn't yet interested in making anything that might undermine IMS, so the CIA had to find somebody who might be interested in coming up with a commercial project. Dave Roberts, the man whose job it was to find a potential vendor, soon tracked down RSI. Two things that encouraged him to bet the agency's money on the tiny firm were the discovery that Bob Miner, who had worked with him on the Ampex terabit memory project, was involved and that RSI was committed to SQL and therefore had IBM's stamp of credibility. The other thing that appealed to the CIA was that RSI was building its database to run on the PDP-11 minicomputer. Ellison says: "Digital's PDP-11 minicomputers were heavily used in government, especially within the intelligence community, because the computers are small enough to fit into airplanes and submarines."

The money that came from the CIA enabled RSI to finish work on the first commercial release of the Oracle database. Ellison recalls that the moment it actually worked brought the kind of thrill the Wright brothers must have had when their plane took to the air. "The first version of our database was called Oracle Version 2. I didn't think anyone, not even the government, would buy Version 1 of a database from five guys in California. Unfortunately, the Version 2 label didn't change the fact that we were experiencing those very serious performance problems predicted by conventional wisdom. We just couldn't make our database go fast enough. We tried one thing after another. Finally we got a breakthrough that delivered the tenfold performance improvement we needed for commercial viability. In our final test we ran faster than the CODASYL system, which was then considered the fastest PDP-11 database.

"I was stunned by the final test results. I had never thought about the consequences of failing, but I had never thought about the consequences of succeeding either. On my way out that evening I ran into Tony Spoor, our auditor, in the elevator lobby. I was a bit light-headed and euphoric, still trying to fully grasp the import of our performance test results. I spontaneously decided to explain what it all meant. After laboriously rattling off the details of our performance test results, I said 'Tony, do you know what this means? Do you? Do you know what this means?' He said, 'Ugh . . . no.' I said that it means Oracle's worth at least $100 million. Tony's lips parted slowly and his jaw lowered. He did not respond, but his look said it all. He thought that after all the late nights and weekends my mind had finally snapped like a dry twig. This hundred-million-dollar valuation I just proclaimed seemed so far from reality that he thought I should be sedated and put into a padded cell so I wouldn't hurt myself."

Ellison adds, "It gradually dawned on me that this thing was going to take on a life of its own. Not because we were going to grow to be a big company. I think we all had the fantasy that however successful our database product, there would never be more than fifty of us, and customers would be sending us checks and we'd be sending them software. Even with just fifty people on board, I thought that my management ability would be stretched to the limit. I remember when we hired our first salesman, Bob Preger, who came from a mainframe database company called Software AG, Bob Miner came in and asked me, 'What do we need a sales guy for?' I smugly replied, 'To sell more of our software, perhaps.' That's an inside glimpse of our top management team at work discussing the expansion of our distribution capacity. I knew we needed to build a sales organization, although I certainly had no idea how one worked. Bob, however, remained unconvinced as to the need for salespeople. He just said, 'Okay, we'll try one.' "

The only way to convince people that RSI had a product that worked—albeit, according to Ellison, "not all that well"—was to demo the new database system to anyone who could imagine a use for it. Ellison had to hit the road and sell. "The news about our hot little database traveled around the intelligence community pretty quickly. I'd make a presentation at one agency on Monday, which would result in a phone call on Tuesday to visit another agency on Wednesday. One week I flew to and from Washington, D.C. three times. In a little over six months' time we had won several deals—the CIA, Navy Intelligence, Air Force Intelligence, and the NSA [the highly secretive National Security Agency]."

But as so often happens with young companies, just at the moment that things appeared to be taking off, RSI came perilously close to running out of cash. "Once we started making database sales, we decided to stop doing consulting work. We needed everyone working on finishing the bloody product.* So the consulting money stopped coming in. All we

---

*LE writes: It turns out you never really "finish" a software product. Programmers never run out of good ideas. Customers never stop asking for more features. We've been working on the Oracle database for twenty-five years, and we're still not "finished."

had was $235,000 in the bank, and that didn't go very far even in those days. But the real killer was that I didn't have the slightest idea about how much time could elapse from the moment the government says they're going to buy and the moment you get the cash. I thought we'd have our money in sixty days, max. Not even close. When the government wants to buy anything, they have to adhere to a congressionally mandated process, which includes the publication of the pending purchase in the *Commerce Business Daily* so other firms can offer a competitive bid or protest the purchase. So, after you're told you've 'won' the deal it can still take six to nine months before you actually get paid. No consulting money was coming in, so we were going to run out of cash. The solution was simple: we had to stop paying some people, starting with me."

• • •

Far from finding running his own company liberating, Ellison was working harder than he'd ever imagined, to the extent that it probably contributed to the breakdown of his second marriage, to Nancy Wheeler, a grad student at Stanford, after only eighteen months. "Self-absorption will crush a young marriage, and I was completely absorbed by my own ambition. I was totally immersed in making the business succeed. I neglected everything else. I was writing computer programs, writing documentation, answering customer support calls, giving training classes, and sending out marketing literature. The very last thing I would do every evening was stamp a stack of manila envelopes stuffed with this spiral-bound Oracle introductory manual I'd written. Everyone and anyone I spoke with on the phone that day would get one. I'd arrive home around midnight most evenings. Nancy eventually tired of this routine and left. She was the second wife I managed to drive away. The first left because I refused to work enough. The second left because I worked too much. Both cases were caused by my self-indulgent, without-compromise mode of living. My personal life had fallen apart, and work was the only thing left that mattered. So I worked even more—until the hours of the day ran out."

The long hours being put in at RSI were noticed by another occupant of the building, Don Lucas, a doyen of the Valley venture capital community. Lucas recalls, "I was one of the developers of 3000 Sand Hill Road, and I had a nice corner office on the second floor. I was keeping some pretty odd hours myself, but I noticed that whenever I left for home the lights in this particular spot in the complex were always on. So I finally went by and asked them what they were doing and I met Larry and Bob

Miner and Barbara [later to be the third Mrs. Ellison], the receptionist. And we just got talking. They clearly didn't have a lot of money, and they weren't very sophisticated in the ways of corporate America. The first thing they asked me was if I'd go on the board. So I said, 'Sure,' and I became chairman of the board."

Although it was part of Lucas's job to make equity investments in promising young companies, Ellison and Miner were insistent that they didn't need money. When they urgently needed to get inside Digital's new VAX, a sort of PDP-11 on steroids, to ensure that their software could run on the minicomputer that over the next ten years would sweep all before it, rather than push for a stake, Lucas arranged and guaranteed a loan. "They were very energetic, very positive, driven. These guys worked not round the clock but pretty close to it. There was a very interesting relationship between Larry and Bob. Larry was the visionary, the top salesman, the top cheerleader, the driver, and Bob was clearly a very good software architect."

Making sure that the Oracle database worked on the VAX (Virtual Address Extension) was a no-brainer for Ellison and Miner. The VAX (which made its debut in 1977) was the most impressive minicomputer to come onto the market, and all RSI's intelligence agency clients were buying them as quickly as Digital could make them, while corporate customers saw them as being capable enough to take over at a departmental level many of the tasks previously reserved for mainframes. By 1984, more than 70 percent of the firm's software license income was coming from Digital's machines—the vast proportion from VAX seats. What was less obvious, but what rapidly became a key part of Ellison's pitch to customers, was Oracle's ability to run on just about every conceivable computer its potential customers might own.

Portability, as it's known, is the ability to "port" software to a given hardware platform. It not only meant that Oracle could sell to the widest possible market, it was also crucial for customers, the majority of which operated a heterogeneous mix of computers but wanted to have only one database. The architecturally elegant solution, and one that allowed Oracle to run on the dozen or so proprietary operating systems that were current, was to maintain a single code base and take the gamble of writing Version 3 of the software in a new programming language called C. Inexpensive C compilers (the software that translates a program into a form the computer can understand) were also becoming available for most of the machines that Ellison needed Oracle to run on. Ken Jacobs, who arrived at RSI in 1981 as employee number eighteen, says, "It was done at a time when the rest of the industry couldn't even spell C." Even today, Oracle is the only database that can run on all the main operating systems likely to be found under corporate databases, from Microsoft's Windows through all the various flavors of UNIX to open-source Linux and MVS (Multiple Virtual Storage) on mainframes.

By the time Version 3 made it out of the door in 1983, RSI had sensibly changed its name to Oracle Systems (later, Oracle Corporation) and was getting ready to move to an 84,000-square feet site in nearby Belmont. Much of Ellison's time was spent talking up the relational model. Don Lucas says, "People just didn't believe that the relational model would work. There was a great need to do a very high level sell and say, 'Hey, this is going to be the thing and these are the things you could use it for.' I'll never forget being with some guy, an analyst, and he just said that relational will never work. It's a toy, you know, fun and games. We had to fight that for maybe ten years. Larry was very good at this. He was like a spiritual leader, an evangelist for the relational database model."

While that kind of "high-level sell," which included doing a lot of public speaking at conferences, suited Ellison's talents, RSI/Oracle quickly needed more than just Bob Preger and Ellison to sell its product. Don Lucas had brought onto the board his friend John Clark, who had a background in sales. Ellison says, "He patiently explained the basics of sales to me. If you have a good product, the more salespeople you have, the more you'll sell. If you want to sell twice as much, get twice as many salespeople. I said, 'Really? It's that simple? Okay, we'll hire some more salespeople.' And then we started getting these sales guys in and they just started to replicate, kind of like a virus inside of your company." A virus? It's an odd choice of word and one that indicates the ambivalence that Ellison has even today about the people he employs to sell Oracle's products.*

For the first few years of its life, Oracle grew rather slowly, by the standards of today. Jenny Overstreet, Ellison's assistant and confidante for thirteen years, remembers that when she joined the company in 1983, there were only fifty employees in California. "Larry still thought that

---

*LE writes: I have no ambivalence about good salespeople—the ones that understand our technology and how to apply it to solve customer problems. Those salespeople are among our most precious assets. I admire those salespeople. I try to be one of them myself. The other type of salesman—the hired gun, the too-creative deal maker—not only do I not admire them, I think they're dangerous.

was probably about all Oracle was ever going to need." In fact, by this time Ellison had already realized that Oracle had the potential to become something much bigger. The combination of Version 3's (at least theoretical) portability and those replicating sales guys meant that sales were suddenly beginning to explode. Ken Jacobs says of Version 3, "It was a vision of what could be done. One of the most gratifying things was the tremendous faith of our early customers who stayed with us through difficult times. For many of them it was like going through one of those shared experiences when a couple faces death but they survive together."

One of the smartest and most driven of those first salespeople was a young Mormon named Gary Kennedy, who had started up a midwestern sales operation in 1982. Among his first hires was Sohaib Abbasi, a quiet-spoken Pakistani who has run Oracle's tools business for the last decade, and Tom Siebel, who went on to found Siebel Systems. Abbasi recalls, "The technical press was saying at the time that the relational database would never be useful, and even IBM had raised doubts as to whether it would ever be suitable for transaction processing. Our job was to call up prospects and tell them that if they would give us a day we would come and show them what the technology was capable of. We'd show up in the morning, they would explain what their system was—obviously everything was custom applications back then—and what they wanted. I had to build it in front of them."

It was a formidable team. Abbasi and Siebel were both highly qualified computer scientists who had even written theses on the relational model, while Kennedy, despite his intense religious convictions, was about to become perhaps the most aggressive sales manager in software history. In 1984, Ellison was sufficiently impressed by Kennedy's efforts to put him in charge of the entire eastern half of the United States, and a year later he made him national sales manager. On the eve of Oracle's initial public offering in 1986, when Kennedy was thirty-two and a Mormon bishop, Ellison made him vice president of U.S. sales and service.

While a U.S. sales organization was being created, Ellison realized that Oracle could expand overseas without significant investment by doing deals with distributors. Two teams were signed up, one for continental Europe—Tom Peddersen Associates—and one in England, the U.K. arm of CACI, a famously tough systems integrator and consultancy. Over time Oracle bought out its distributors, but with a minimal initial outlay it began to build an international presence that also brought in funds when the product was immature and the money was desperately needed. Peddersen's friends Bo Ryden and Brian Cassidy became the founders of

Oracle Europe, while CACI's Geoff Squire, a highly accomplished computer industry executive, left to run Oracle UK. For several years, Oracle's sales grew faster overseas than in the United States. Ellison says, "The salespeople we hired in Europe were very professional and service-oriented. The European management team's strategy was to build long-term relationships with our customers and do business with them on a regular basis. This European 'farming' strategy was in stark contrast to the U.S. sales organization's 'hunting' strategy. U.S. salespeople tried to sell the largest possible transaction to a given customer and then move on to the next customer and the next deal. It took me until 1991 to figure out that the U.S. hunting strategy was both shortsighted and unsustainable. It took another decade to change the culture of the U.S. sales force from hunters to farmers."

The responsibility for building up the U.S. sales organization fell first to Mike Seashols, a confident and highly competitive salesman who, like Kennedy, was religiously devout. A member of the intensely evangelical Covenant Church who read the Bible every morning before going out to do battle, it was Seashols who recruited Kennedy, while Kennedy hired other super salesmen, such as Siebel; Greg Brady, who went on to found i2, the supply chain specialist; and Craig Conway, who became CEO of the ERP vendor PeopleSoft. Seashols was fired by Ellison and replaced by Kennedy in 1986 for reasons that remain obscure. Seashols claims that he had expressed discomfort with some of the statements in the company prospectus that was circulated to investors before the public offering. Others suggest that he wasn't making his numbers, which is difficult to believe given that Oracle's U.S. sales were pretty much doubling every year while Seashols was responsible.*

One possibility is that Ellison had concluded that he wasn't hungry enough. Seashols recalls a dinner with Ellison: "It was right before we went public. Larry asked, 'What are you going to do with all your money?' I had no idea. My house was paid for. I was driving a new car. I didn't have any needs I could think of. I said something about just wanting to be content. I think that really took him aback." That said, Ellison

---

*LE writes: I replaced Mike Seashols with Gary Kennedy for the very simple reason that Gary's numbers were better than Mike's. Mike's sales results were good. Gary's were astounding. I have never met a more driven person than Gary Kennedy. Gary would rather die than lose. For years that extreme drive worked to Oracle's benefit. But in the end it proved to be a two-edged sword.

was still not giving much of his attention to what was or wasn't happening in sales. As far as Ellison was concerned, overwhelmingly the most important contribution he could make to Oracle's success was to concentrate on making the product better. He simply didn't regard himself as competent to concern himself with all the other things that a CEO is supposed to be responsible for. To some at Oracle, Ellison's approach was one of enlightened delegation. "You could say that," he says. "But it was closer to abdication than delegation."

In fact, Ellison had every reason to concentrate on the product. Mike Stonebraker had taken the Ingres relational database project he had overseen at the University of California at Berkeley and formed a company around it called Relational Technology, Inc. Although a commercial version of Ingres had come to market a little later than Oracle, Stonebraker's outfit was growing faster than Ellison's. In 1984, Oracle's sales had doubled to $12.7 million, while Ingres, as RTI was increasingly known, had tripled its sales to $9 million. Ellison says, "They were really kicking our butts. They were catching up fast because we had just rewritten our database product and we were having software quality problems. Sound familiar?"

The Berkeley team at Ingres had had much more time to refine their user language, QUEL, than Oracle had to develop SQL, and many relational experts thought it was intrinsically a superior language. Ellison says: "Maybe QUEL is better than SQL. Maybe French is better than English? It didn't matter: English and SQL were going to win." What Ellison was most worried about was the sheer engineering talent at Ingres. "It had become painfully clear to me that our development organization wasn't good enough to keep up with the team at Ingres. So we had to rebuild it. If Stonebraker was hiring the best kids from UC Berkeley, we would hire the best kids from CalTech, MIT, and Stanford. We would also recruit the very best experienced programming talent in the Valley. In a real coup we hired a superb team from Xerox PARC. One of those guys, Derry Kabcenell, was among the most important people ever to work at Oracle. Thanks to Derry and the new engineering team he led, we overcame the software quality problems in Oracle Version 3. He delivered a superior database product—a product we could be proud of—a product that would kill Ingres. We called it Oracle Version 4."

Kabcenell now works at Oracle only part-time, but he still contributes his ideas and experience to major software architecture projects. He's a slightly built man who talks softly with an almost professorial air. The thing that he remembers most vividly about his hiring was the speed at which the little company was recruiting—a friend had joined in January 1983, when there were about thirty people on board, but by the time Kabcenell arrived in September the number had grown to seventy—and the intensity of his interview with Ellison. "I was really impressed at his grasp of the technology and also his respect for the professional practice of programming. I was doing a pretty extensive set of interviews with different companies and had a chance to meet a bunch of people, including CTOs. Nobody I'd met was as addicted to technology as Larry was. In my interview he described a feature that was just being developed in the database that's still important today called 'read consistency'—he described that to me and asked what I thought about it. I was just amazed that I was having that kind of conversation with the CEO the first time I'd met him."

It was a technique that Ellison used with all the recruits to the development team; it made them want to work for Oracle, and it ensured that he was hiring only people who were smart enough to debate technical issues with him at the highest level. Andy Mendelsohn, like Kabcenell a graduate of MIT, who joined in the same year, remembers, "In the interview with Larry I was very surprised by the technical level of the questions. He discussed different ways to use indexes to resolve results from a SQL query. It was a real detailed kind of thing, but it showed me that he actually understood the technology."

Hiring people such as Kabcenell, Mendelsohn, and another recruit from the same year, Roger Bamford, was the only way that Ellison believed Oracle could have a future. Eighteen years later, nearly all the people that Ellison brought into the engineering team at that time are still at Oracle and are still, despite middle age and huge wealth, involved in cutting-edge work on the latest versions of the Oracle database. For all the company's reputation for revolving doors in the executive suites and a hire-and-fire culture in sales, the people responsible for creating and developing the core product, known within Oracle as the "kernel group," have been an extraordinarily loyal and stable team. While many parts of the business actually need staff turnover to stay fresh and vigorous, Ellison believes that keeping the elite kernel group together has been vital. The process of building a software product teaches a programmer what to do and what to avoid. The accumulated knowledge and experience within the forty- or fifty-strong kernel group comes from continuous work on improving the core code rather than from some extension of the product that will make a flashy new release.

Derry Kabcenell's impact at Oracle was immediate. Ellison says, "The first version of our database, Version 2, was a good working prototype written in PDP-11 assembly language—the same language that I wrote the earlier CODASYL database in. Version 3 was totally rewritten in C. It was much bigger and more complex than Version 2 and, as a result, plagued by quality problems. Derry made Version 3 work by going around rewriting other programmers' code and fixing their bugs. One of our programmers had been working on a problem for six months, and Derry, bless his heart, just came in one weekend and rewrote the whole thing. Of course it worked perfectly. Derry combined brilliance with discipline and endurance. It's a rare combination. Of course he had perfect grades at MIT. Derry's not a perfectionist—he's an obsessive perfectionist. Sometimes his thoroughness went over the top. I remember when he was buying a condominium, he told me that he had carefully read all twenty pages of the sales and owners' association contracts. He read a law book to make certain he fully understood what he was signing. Several years later Derry confided in me that he was worried that his brain might have filled up because his memory was not as good as it used to be. I told him it was his own fault for cluttering up that wonderful brain with all those stupid condominium agreements."

As well as ensuring that Oracle had the talent to compete with Ingres, Ellison made sure that the development team was building the right things. "If we built the right products the right way, we would win. That was my view of the world then, and that's my view of the world now." Ellison bridles at the suggestion of some former colleagues that Bob Miner was running the development team while he was out selling. "I loved Bob. Everyone did. He was an uncommonly humane, generous, and caring person. But his egalitarian nature prevented him from ever crossing over from labor to management. He loved being one of the guys too much. He wouldn't give that up for anything—certainly not for money or fame, neither of which interested him much. So Bob became the head of the 'Oracle programmers union': shop steward, and father confessor. He was the moral and spiritual leader of the engineering team—of the entire company, really. He was the guy you went to if you had a personal problem. When the person I considered our worst programmer lost half his Oracle stock in a divorce, Bob thought the company should make it up to him. I had wanted to fire the guy for years. Bob wouldn't allow it. He protected his people like a mother bear. While I couldn't fire any of his people, Bob was perfectly happy to let me recruit the new members of the programming team, which I did, and manage the development process." The kernel group veterans I've spoken to bear out Ellison's claim.

Very often, Ellison would say that something was in the database that hadn't yet been done. After Version 2 had come out, he wrote a little spiral bound book describing Oracle and the SQL language. He says, "Someone jokingly said, 'It took us eight years to make the database product look like your book.' Not exactly true, but what is important is that we were making steady progress and we were ahead of the competition—most of the time. The database just kept getting better and better." If Version 3 was all about portability, the most significant feature of Version 4, which came out a year later, in 1984, apart from the all-important reliability that Derry Kabcenell had given it, was "read consistency," or the assurance that a query against the database will read a set of data that remains consistent during the time it takes to execute the query. For example, money being switched between bank accounts during a query could not be miscomputed, and employees being added to an HR database not be counted twice.

With the solidity of Version 4 and Oracle's increasingly aggressive sales force, Ingres was hard pressed to maintain its momentum, but the real threat was the decision of the American National Standards Institute (ANSI), supported by IBM, to declare SQL the standard relational database language. Mike Stonebraker of Ingres didn't even bother to show up at the committee meeting to make the (quite strong) case for adopting QUEL because he was ideologically opposed to setting technology standards. It was the behavior of an intellectually arrogant academic rather than a prudent businessman protecting the interests of his company. Ellison says, "Stonebraker invented QUEL and stuck with it like a proud father, while IBM and Oracle supported the SQL standard. Lack of SQL support hurt Ingres badly. But so did lack of portability and read consistency. And Ingres had fallen far behind in performance. All this together conspired to kill off Ingres as a competitor in the database market."

No sooner had that threat of Ingres been diluted than others appeared. In 1985, IBM released a relational database for big mainframes called DB2, but it was part of the process by which SQL became a standard, and Oracle did only a small amount of business on mainframes anyway. Two newer rivals, however, were determined to grab a large part of Oracle's fast-growing business. The lesser of the threats came from Informix because of its concentration on the nascent UNIX market. Although UNIX would become the enterprise server operating system of choice in the 1990s, at that time it was more popular in the universities than in corporate computing environments. Sybase, on the other hand, came from nowhere to become a dangerous competitor.

A spin-off from a hardware firm named Britton-Lee, Sybase had come up with the first database specifically designed for the new paradigm of client/server computing. With Sybase's architecture the database lived in one computer, the server, while the application would live in the client machine. Although Oracle's Version 5 supported client/server and 5.1 contained a feature that enabled so-called distributed queries, allowing a single query to access data stored in multiple locations, Oracle's database had not been designed from the beginning for the separation of client/server. Ellison says, "The key thing that Sybase had that we didn't was a programmable server, the ability to write programs called stored procedures that ran inside the database. This allowed Sybase to build and advertise two features—referential integrity and two-phase commit—that they had and we lacked. These key differentiators gave Sybase immediate traction in the market."

Two-phase commit made it possible to execute a transaction spanning a number of databases on different computers. If you have two databases and you make a savings withdrawal out of one computer and a checking deposit into the other with a separate database, that whole thing would have transactional integrity—either both updates would occur or neither would. Referential integrity provides for an automatic existence check to make sure that if, say, you enter "department 57," there is in fact such a thing in the department tables as 57. One of the things that customers liked about Sybase was that with its programmability and stored procedures it was a database that could be used to enforce business rules across an organization.

Although Sybase was a lot smaller than Oracle, its advertising was getting plenty of attention from both Oracle's customers and, to an even greater extent, Oracle's sales force, who were demanding something to hit back at Sybase with. A few months before Oracle's IPO in early 1986, Ellison had declared that the company would double its revenues every year. Indefinitely. A year later, with revenues of $131 million, Oracle claimed to be the world's biggest database software company, having overtaken a rapidly failing Cullinet on the way down. However, Ellison, sensing that the original code base would not allow the product to evolve as it would need to, had ordered a complete rewrite of the kernel, effectively the entire "bottom half" of the database's software, for the next major release. "Version 6 included a complete rewrite of the most complex part of the database. It took so long and had so many bugs, it almost killed the company. But its advanced architecture laid the foundation for much of what differentiates our database today—including clustering.

Version 6 was something we had to do to move ahead of the competition.* But while we were trying to finish Version 6, Version 5.1 fell further and further behind Sybase."

With Oracle's ambitious revenue targets, its sales force (now under the relentless Gary Kennedy) screaming for a new product, and Ellison's fear that Sybase was gaining real traction, the development team found itself subjected to appalling pressure to declare Version 6 ready to ship. Ellison says, "There was an overwhelming sense of frustration. We had delayed Version 6, and then delayed it again and again and again. Delaying it one more time seemed unbearable. We had done a lot of testing, and I thought that it was good enough to go. I was wrong. When we did release Version 6 in 1988, it had more bugs than any of us believed was possible."

The decision to ship Oracle 6 unfinished was the beginning of a sea of troubles that came close to overwhelming Ellison and destroying the company.

---

*LE writes: Rewriting the database software for Version 6 was a much bigger effort than the Version 3 rewrite. But in both cases the rewrite led to software quality problems, and it took some time before the software stabilized. The only other project of similar scope and complexity to the Version 6 database rewrite was the Release 11i applications rewrite, which gave birth to the E-Business Suite. These rewrites are periodically necessary if you want to make major advances in your technology. Invariably there is a lot of pain before the payoff, but the payoff—for both Oracle and our customers—has been huge.

5

TO THE LIMIT

To what extent was Ellison responsible for releasing an unfinished product because of a treadmill of his own creation? In 1985, with sales running at $24 million, Ellison had declared that from that point on Oracle would double its revenues each year. Amazingly, for the next five years, Oracle did precisely that, hitting sales of $916 million in 1990. But Ellison argues that the sales projections were not his overriding concern. "We were small, and we had to grow fast or die. But the most effective way to grow sales is to make the product better. That's why I spend most of my time with our engineering teams." *

Maybe. But the notion that Ellison was measuring success purely in terms of Oracle's technological prowess is far-fetched. The original idea of Oracle's being a vehicle to provide him with a nice life, a reasonable amount of money, and plenty of time to goof off whenever he felt like had quickly evaporated. In his early forties, Ellison was willing to say and do whatever was necessary to defeat Oracle's rivals. Apart from engineering genius, brashness and aggression were the most prized qualities at Oracle in the late 1980s. The only thing that seemed to matter was market share,

---

*LE writes: I admit to pushing our sales force to grow faster than the competition. Without increased sales we would have been unable to increase the investment in our engineering team. We had to increase sales to maintain our technical leadership.

and increasingly Ellison didn't seem to care how reckless Oracle became to get it.*

However, the strain of achieving such phenomenal growth and the increasingly dangerous business practices needed to underpin it nearly killed the company. When Oracle went public with a market value of $270 million on March 12, 1986 (by an extraordinary coincidence, just twenty-four hours before Microsoft's IPO), Ellison, with 39 percent of the stock, was suddenly wealthy beyond his wildest expectations. But if anything, the fact that he now had something to lose intensified the demands he was prepared to make on himself and his company. Shipping Oracle 6 before it was ready was a risk, Ellison calculated, that had to be run.

Despite its bugginess and lack of the key features that Sybase boasted about, Oracle 6 introduced many new features, including row-level locking, which meant that a transaction performing writes would lock only the affected rows and not the entire table, thus greatly improving the throughput of the system with a large number of users. That helped to make Version 6 the first scalable database that could grow as a customer's business grew. Row-level locking, combined with another Version 6 feature, multitasking, enabled Oracle to perform extremely well on the symmetrical multiprocessor (SMP) computers, which were just starting to become important and are now the norm in enterprise computing, some high-end boxes today having as many as sixty-four CPUs. Unfortunately, the market was not yet crying out for that kind of scalability, and the instability of Version 6 disqualified it as the enterprise-strength system it aspired to be. The launch was itself a bad omen. In grand style, Oracle chartered Concorde to fly the press and analysts to Bermuda for a formal briefing on the wonderful new database, but because of a technical fault the plane had to turn back.

At about the same time, Oracle was getting serious about the emerging market for the packaged applications to automate businesses that became collectively known as enterprise resource planning (ERP) software. Late in 1985, Ellison had persuaded Jeff Walker to come to Oracle and set up an applications division—even then some people were predicting the imminent saturation of the database market, and Ellison was deter-

---

*LE writes: The only thing that mattered at Oracle was results—not brashness or aggression. The European sales force was neither brash nor aggressive, yet their results were just as good as the U.S. sales team's. The personality of our different sales forces reflected the personality of their sales leaders.

mined that Oracle's growth shouldn't depend on one product. Walker was about the same age as Ellison and had founded and run his own software business, Walker Interactive. But unlike Ellison he had taken money from venture capitalists, and when his firm had badly missed its numbers during a brief technology spending slowdown his investors had concluded that Walker, although technically brilliant, was not enough of a businessman to manage the company. He says, "I left because my venture people would have driven me out." Pretty soon after, he had a conversation with Ellison. "Larry said that his strategy for getting into the applications business would have been to have hired somebody from Walker Interactive because it was the emerging technology leader. He had never thought he could get me [at the time Walker Interactive was slightly bigger than Oracle]. I told him that I thought I was unmanageable and I didn't really want to work for anybody. He assured me that I would not really be working for him, that we would be merely collaborators."

When Walker arrived, there was just one other person in the "applications division." True to his word, Ellison gave Walker a free hand to work out a strategy, hire people, and design the initial applications. Walker, who now runs another troubled applications company called TenFold, has a very high opinion of his own abilities. He claims that in the six years to his departure from the company in 1991, "Oracle came from being a nonplayer to being the industry leader in applications. SAP hadn't really entered the market at that point with their R/3 client/server product. They were selling R/2, their hosted product, but they weren't really as successful as Oracle." It's an interesting point of view. However, just running Oracle's applications operation was not a big enough job for the multitalented Walker. After a spell, when he both had his development responsibilities and had become head of marketing, in late 1986 Ellison asked him to take on the job of CFO while staying as head of apps. Walker says, "Larry quickly realized that I had management strength and experience that he needed on his team. It was not something that I had done before, but I think that I did a credible job as CFO."

Don Lucas remembers, "Larry just announced to me that Jeff was going to be CFO. Jeff's a nice person. I like Jeff. But I spent hours, probably an average of an hour a day, on the telephone trying to talk through finance with him . . . But he's an engineer,* and, to be honest, it was a

---

*LE writes: I am most comfortable working with engineers, so I wanted a company where most of the managers were engineers. But making Jeff Walker

personality issue, he never got it. Larry's approach was to delegate massively, completely, almost totally. That's the good news—as long as he gets good people, it really works. But when he gets a person like Jeff, who is a very smart guy but not a brilliant CFO . . ."

Walker's appointment wasn't the strangest thing that happened at Oracle during that time. Gary Kennedy was under appalling pressure to meet the Herculean targets that were implied by Ellison's commitment to continually double revenues. Kennedy had become convinced that the corporate legal department was actively preventing deals by taking too long to vet sales contracts. The answer, he argued, was to give U.S. sales its own contracts and finance organization. Ellison acquiesced. "Gary told me he couldn't get the job done because the legal department didn't report to sales and they were slow in processing deals. I said, okay, you can have the legal department. What kind of CEO lets the salespeople write their own contracts? I just didn't know any better." *

The buzzword at Oracle became "decentralization"—another manifestation of the extreme form of delegation that Ellison appeared to favor. Noosheen Hashemi, an intense young Iranian who was running the financial administration for U.S. sales, was asked to write something called "The Decentralization White Paper" that was meant to define the checks and balances that would be needed in Kennedy's brave new world. She says, "Decentralization occurred, and none of the things mentioned in the white paper were executed. Not one. All the regions implemented their own processes and started doing their own thing. Decentralization happened because U.S. sales didn't want corporate to be watching over their shoulder. They didn't want to have to justify what they were doing. It was like, here's the deal, book it, let's move on."

Hashemi insists that Gary Kennedy never asked her personally to do anything unethical, but all hell was breaking loose. Essentially, U.S. sales was now responsible for oversight of its own deals, reviewing contracts and booking revenue without any interference from the corporate center. The consequences were myriad. Huge discounts were offered to induce customers to buy software they wouldn't need for years; risks were taken

---

the CFO while he was still in charge of applications development was a big mistake. Accounting is a control function and should always be separate from sales and development. Unfortunately, I didn't understand that at the time.

*LE writes: Legal, like accounting, is a control function and has to operate independently of the sales department.

in selling to companies that didn't have the money to pay their bills; exotic barter deals were entered into. In one, Oracle was given a couple of jets by Israeli Aircraft Industries in exchange for software.*

To make matters worse, Kennedy wanted a huge expansion of the sales force and told Hashemi to organize the recruitment of 1,500 additional salespeople within nine months. Not surprisingly, few of those taken on had time to be properly trained or inducted before they were sent out into the field. Unless the new recruits started selling quickly and bringing in revenue, the cost of such breakneck hiring would be crippling.

It's hard to say how much more Jeff Walker could have done, other than to threaten to resign as CFO. But he made things worse by supporting the extreme form of delegation that Ellison had carelessly encouraged. Amazingly, even today he defends it: "Larry had found a management team of very strong individual guys that could work together and yet autonomously run their areas. It was almost a feudal environment, in terms of feudal lords over whom Larry as king only had very weak controls. He chose to make them weak. I think it was a wonderful decision on his part because it allowed Oracle to come out of nowhere and become this huge market force."

Walker made things still harder for himself by believing so passionately in the efficacy of his own financial applications that he thought he could operate with only a fraction of the people he really needed. Eventually, in response to Walker's concerns and Hashemi's whistle-blowing to Ellison, in 1989 Ellison asked her to go and work for Walker in an attempt to clean things up. Hashemi says of Walker, "There he was, building products to use internally and sell to the outside world. He wanted to shove whatever he made in applications down my throat. To prove how fabulous his applications were, he wants to fire two thirds of the hundred and fifty I have working for me in finance." Walker was also to some extent conflicted in reining back the increasingly desperate sales antics of Kennedy's people. His bonus was tied to the sales of applications. If Walker came down too hard on sales, the applications he was so proud of would appear less successful.

A good test of how well a sales organization and its financial department are working together is the efficiency with which money is collected

---

*LE writes: Not true. The deal was proposed and passed to me for approval. I did not approve the deal, and it never happened.

from customers. By the end of fiscal 1989, although revenue had doubled to $584 million, trade receivables were running at $262 million. A year later, the corresponding figures were $971 million and $468 million. Hashemi says that Walker wasn't prepared to face up to the problem: "Instead of acknowledging it, addressing it, going through every statement, Walker was still lying to himself."

Kennedy had developed what he liked to call a "commitment" culture at Oracle. He was committed to achieving the revenue targets set by Ellison, and in turn his own team were committed to realizing the quotas set for them. Commitment meant that you did what you had undertaken to do. Period. It sounded good, but the consequences of Kennedy's terrifying insistence on commitment were appalling.

If ever a company was heading for a crash, it was Oracle. And it duly came, almost exactly four years after the company's IPO. Steve Imbler, Walker's number two in finance and, unusually for Oracle, a qualified accountant, had become so anxious about the ballooning receivables that he had started to trawl through as many of the dubious-looking contracts as he could. By the time the third quarter of fiscal 1990 was due to close on February 28, he had found $15 million worth of deals in which the likelihood of payment was minimal. What followed was more than a devastating year of purgatory for both Oracle and Ellison.

Imbler managed to persuade Walker and Ellison to write down the missing $15 million when the results for the quarter were reported on March 27. Although revenue, at $236 million, was still up by 54 percent over the year before, net income was more or less unchanged, while earnings per share, at 18 cents, were little better than half the upper end of analysts' forecasts. The following day, Oracle's stock lost more than 30 percent of its value, falling to $17.50 at a time when such precipitous single-day drops were much less common than they are now. It should have been the warning that Ellison needed to put Oracle's house in order. But far from being chastened and repentant, Ellison told investors that he fully expected to make up the lost ground in the final quarter and that Oracle would be back on what he called its "annual plan." Eighteen months earlier, at the company's annual strategy meeting, with just five slides, Ellison had made a presentation that he titled the "Five in Five" plan: "I was simply extrapolating the annual doubling of revenues. We would reach $5 billion in five years. I had absolutely no idea how absurd and naive the plan was."

He didn't have any better idea how his March 27 promise was going to be achieved either. But a commitment was a commitment, and it was Gary Kennedy's job to deliver the number. Astonishingly, given a slowing economy and Oracle's continuing product problems, he just about made it. Revenue was up 63 percent, to $334 million, and earnings per share came in at a respectable 39 cents. A great deal has been made of Kennedy's idea of incentivizing the sales force by giving them the option in that crucial quarter of having their commissions paid in gold coins. Kennedy's "Go for Gold" campaign is a nice metaphor for the hysteria that accompanied selling Oracle software during that period, but it was relatively harmless compared with the other things that were going on.

The real damage was being done by the way future sales were being mortgaged against the present. Customers were being encouraged by outrageous discounts to buy software licenses they might not actually need for years. By the time the next quarter arrived, instead of the "planned" 50 percent increase in sales, the figure was closer to 30 percent. With expenses still geared to doubling revenues, Oracle was heading towards its first-ever loss. Geoff Squire, who was by this time running European sales from London, says, "Every customer had been squeezed as much as possible to help the May quarter, with the result that the cupboard was really bare. I got a call from Larry in late August, and he said, the quarter's gone and Gary's going. He said he was going to focus personally on fixing America and he wanted me to take over International." Squire argued successfully that International could look after itself and that he would come over to America to help Ellison restructure the company. He started by giving Ellison a list of all the things that needed doing. Ellison interrupted: "Okay, what time does your plane land?" *

When Squire arrived, he found Walker telling Ellison that with the company about to miss its numbers by a mile, he had to make a statement. A warning issued two and a half weeks before the scheduled earnings call suggested a loss of 20 cents a share. Within days Walker was saying that he had gotten his sums wrong. Squire says, "By this time Larry was getting a little upset about this—that was two hits. He didn't scream and shout, but you could tell he was angry. I was in the room when he took the decision that Walker should go. He didn't say anything. It was just a realization—he simply wrote a note to himself and carried on with the executive committee meeting."

When Walker announced the real losses during International Oracle User Week in Anaheim, California, on September 24, 1991, they were 27

---

*LE writes: Geoff Squire was nothing less than heroic during this crisis. Without his efforts, the company probably would not have survived.

cents a share and $36 million. Ellison, having fired Kennedy a couple of weeks earlier (Kennedy claims he resigned because he had been offered the chance to lead a Mormon mission and wasn't prepared to commit another two years of his life to Oracle), was eager to put as much of the blame for the "fiasco" on a botched reorganization of U.S. sales. He was also able to point to the fact that he was at last pruning costs, having laid off four hundred people a week earlier. Squire says, "We basically had to find a revenue number we couldn't miss and then build a cost plan underneath, which meant getting rid of an awful lot of people." By way of painful irony, the day the layoffs were announced was also the day that the magnificent pool and gym complex opened at Oracle's spectacular new campus at Redwood Shores.

Whatever Ellison had said, it wouldn't have cut much ice. On November 1, less than eight months after Oracle's stock had reached an all-time high of $28.38, the shares were trading for $4.88. To make matters worse, Oracle also had a serious cash crisis. It was this, as so often happens with ultra-fast-growing companies that suddenly hit a wall, that turned a painful reverse into something almost terminal. Jeff Walker stills likes to play down the seriousness of what had happened to Oracle: "It was one lost quarter coupled with some accounting irregularities as a consequence of rapid growth, lack of central control, and a far-flung empire of somewhat autonomous organizations. If the company had held adequate cash at the time, it would have been nothing more than a little blip. What made it a near-death experience was the lack of cash. As the CFO of Oracle, I and the board worked hard to encourage Larry to raise cash in a variety of ways throughout the late 1980s. I wanted to do additional equity rounds. We came within days of doing convertible debentures to raise large amounts of cash. Larry at the last minute decided not to do it. The board could have done something about it had it chosen to do so." *

Ellison was determined to avoid the dilution of raising new equity and by his own account was too uninterested to read the new numbers. A prudent insurance policy against a downturn in the economy or Oracle's fortunes was simply too boring, and the board did not press him on it. It was a recklessness that came very close to losing him the company.

---

*LE writes: Actually, I wanted to raise cash and was working with Safra Catz, who was then at DJL [an investment bank], to do just that. We just could not come to an agreement on structure. I wanted a bond deal. Others wanted a convert. Without an agreement on structure we did nothing.

In August, Oracle had entered into a three-year revolving loan agreement of up to $250 million from a thirteen-bank syndicate, but by December the banks were so shocked by the deterioration in both Oracle's business and its stock that it forced a renegotiation of the terms. The size of the credit line was scaled back to $170 million, the maturity date was brought forward to November 1992, and additional covenants relating to Oracle's future financial performance were imposed. Unfortunately, most of the $170 million had already been borrowed. Squire, who by now was in charge of worldwide operations and effectively number two at Oracle, was doggedly trying to bring in cash by running the receivables down: "I'd ring the customer up and ask them why they hadn't paid. It was always the same thing: the product didn't work; I never ordered the product; the salesman said I didn't have to pay until whenever . . ." Squire, an accountant by training, remembers that the cash position was so bad that at one point Oracle was within $3 million of its overdraft limit.

The danger of a hostile takeover was small because without its key people to develop the product, Oracle had little value to a rival. A much bigger danger was that those people would walk because their options were so far under water that a deep-sea diving bell would be needed to find them and because many thought that the company was finished. Squire says, "Every time the phone rang, you feared it might be a headhunter. They were all over the place like leeches, trying to take all our top people away." One of the brightest talents to leave was Tom Siebel. Siebel was not only one of Oracle's most successful sales managers, he had designed and built from scratch a highly effective telephone sales operation running on an early version of the customer relationship management software that he was later to pioneer. He said later, "Oracle looked to me to be an organizational disaster at that point. Larry offered me the position as president of Oracle USA to stay, an offer which I declined. I was tired. I was vested. I was looking for a higher-quality work environment in an organization committed to higher ethical standards and committed to fulfill customer obligations. I left."*

For Ellison, a personal as well as professional disaster was unfolding.

LE writes: Tom's crisis of conscience was coincident with the drop in our stock price, which made his huge option grants worthless. Tom, like many other U.S. salespeople, left Oracle because he thought the big-money days were over. And I certainly never offered Tom the Oracle USA president's job. In fact, I had already given that responsibility to Geoff Squire.

He had borrowed heavily against shares that had slumped to a point where he faced the equivalent of a margin call from his creditors. And a great many people were only too happy to see him getting his come-uppance. His marriage to Barbara had broken up, and Bob Miner, who should have been his closest friend at Oracle, wanted out. Ellison says, "Even after our stock dropped, Oracle was worth much more than Bob ever imagined. He thought the prudent thing to do was to sell the company." It was personal in another way for Ellison. His adoptive father, Lou Ellison, had always told him that he would never amount to anything. "My father said I would never succeed. It seemed he might be right after all."

Although he was clearly shaken and depressed, it didn't occur to him to give up. Geoff Squire says that he never thought that Ellison would walk away. "He had some low points. I remember, the day my father died, finding my mother clinging to the bedpost not knowing what to do because the rock on which her life was built was no longer there. I saw Larry almost like that a couple of times. There was desperation. But what he clung to was his belief in the company." Jeff Walker says, "My observation is that he dealt with it in a forthright and manly way. No one was happy about it, but there were things that he had to do and decisions that he had to take. I never saw petulant or childish behavior. I never saw withdrawal or a fear to face facts. Pressure can make us react in perverse ways, but I never saw any of that. He dealt with it." Ellison says, "I couldn't run away. I had to save Oracle to save myself. I had no choice."

In one sense Ellison was very lucky indeed—he could easily have lost his job before he had a chance to fix the mess he had helped create. Don Lucas says, "I can say this now, and Larry knows this, that not all the board was in favor of keeping Larry on. I was chairman, and I was one hundred percent convinced that this was not a good time to make a change. Larry was inspirational to the company, he understood the technology, and despite the problems with Oracle 6 the technology was great. The problem was in not having proper accounting and the need to clean up and push that out to the field, to sales, and say, 'Thou wilt not do this, and this is the way you will do things.' This was a simple problem. What we really needed to do was get a good financial officer." Ellison says, "I'll always be grateful to Don for trusting me and giving me another chance, even though I probably didn't deserve it."

How much of the blame for what happened should stick to Ellison and how much to Kennedy and Walker? As CEO, Ellison clearly has to take overall responsibility. The extreme form of delegation he pursued—what he describes as his abdication model of management—was a form of self-indulgence rather than a brilliant insight into how to get the best from talented managers. "I was interested in the technology. I wasn't interested in sales or accounting or legal. If I wasn't interested in something, I simply ignored it. The managers who wanted to run their part of the business with minimum interference were quite happy that nobody was looking over their shoulder. Unfortunately, if people ran amok, the problems they created would not become visible until they had grown so large that they were difficult to fix. All I had to do was keep legal and accounting organized as separate control functions, and a lot of the problems we had in '90–'91 could have been avoided. You cannot run a company without strong checks and balances."

Ellison's defense today is still pretty much what it was at the time—that he was naive and inexperienced. But he knows that it's not enough to absolve him. He adds, "I just wasn't paying proper attention to my job. I was doing only the things that interested me. It was the same problem I had in school. But this happened in my forties. I wasn't a kid anymore." Exactly. The truth is that Ellison found almost everything about running a company, other than creating a vision of what Oracle's technology could do and driving the product development strategy to achieve it, boring and, in some sense, beneath him. But later, after he realized he had a duty to know about the supposedly tedious details of how a sales force should be compensated and revenue recognized, he discovered it wasn't so dull and trivial after all.*

Ellison also had a genuine respect for Walker's intellect, which blinded him to his other faults. "I like very smart people, and Walker's very smart. In those days, whenever I was defending somebody, my defense would be to point out how smart they were. Geoff Squire wasn't impressed by this argument. He said, 'Yes, Larry, he's very smart, but can he do his fucking job?' I just stared at Geoff and said nothing, but I was thinking, 'Oh, God. He's right. Brilliance is not enough.' "

As far as Kennedy was concerned, Ellison seemed to think that his religious fervor would prevent him from doing anything morally dubious.

---

*LE writes: These days I believe that every process within an organization—marketing, sales, service, everything—should be carefully engineered. This can be done only if a company implements systems that automate and monitor its business processes. I'm still an engineer at heart, but now I apply engineering discipline to our entire business, not just product development.

"I never thought Gary was capable of being unethical. But I also knew he hated losing more than anything." Ellison used to play basketball with Kennedy. On one occasion, the Oracle team was down by twenty points in the fourth quarter to a team from Stanford. "Late in the game I passed the ball to Gary and jokingly said, 'Hey, we can still beat these guys.' Gary gave me a look of total disgust. How could I give up before the game was over? He hated losing. The feeling was so strong, it could only have come from his childhood. Gary came from a very modest background [his father worked as a miner in Wyoming, forty miles from the family home in Randolph, Utah]. In his family, you were taught never to give up. Gary would fight to the limit not to lose."

But surely that refusal to accept defeat was precisely the quality that convinced Ellison to put Kennedy in charge of U.S. sales? When Ellison committed Oracle to doubling its revenues each year, when he presented the "Five in Five" plan, didn't he realize he was creating the conditions in which somebody as driven as Kennedy would be unable to stop himself from going too far?

I think Ellison is disingenuous in arguing he was not responsible for a good deal of the pressure that turned the Oracle sales force into an out-of-control monster. If a demand from the CEO to keep doubling revenues each year, even with a shaky product and weakening economy, is not pressure, it's hard to know what is. The frequently declared determination to wipe out database rivals, such as Ingres and Ashton-Tate, and the testosterone-charged advertising that Oracle indulged in to convey its message of dominance—one series of ads depicted Oracle as a sleek F-15 shooting down Ashton-Tate's World War I biplane—bred a win-at-all-costs culture that came at least as much from Ellison as from Kennedy. Given Ellison's abdication model of management, it was also surely his responsibility to have a qualified, tough CFO to establish and police business rules. Making Walker CFO just because he was "smart" and was designing financial applications was a decision of extraordinary frivolity, while integrating the legal department with U.S. sales was equally irresponsible.

In partial mitigation, however, it has to be remembered that the software business more than a decade ago was extremely immature. Until the early 1980s, nearly all software had been sold with hardware according to the vertically integrated model established by the likes of IBM and Hewlett-Packard. Enterprise software, because of the peculiar nature of the product and the time it usually takes to install, lends itself, more than anything else, to companies that are likely to spend large sums of money on exotic and innovative deal making.

Don Lucas says, "Software by its very nature is an intangible. The same tape can be worth $100,000 or $200,000 and so is susceptible to a vast number and variety of business relationships. And of course at that time we didn't have standardized contracts, and the accounting profession was just coming up to speed and, you know, we were called cowboys, but there were many different ways to enter into a contract, with the provisions and the details and so on. Some salesmen gave customers the right to return the software. Of course that's lunacy, that's not competent. But in between that, which is zero, and a clean booking, cash down, there's a vast array of considerations." Ironically, given Tom Siebel's strictures about the ethical standards at Oracle when he was there, Ellison always cites Siebel as a salesman whose "creativity got him and the company into trouble." "Tom was and is a super salesman. He is the king of the deal. But not every deal was good for the company."

Ellison hasn't seen Kennedy since he left Oracle. (To almost everyone's consternation, when Jeff Walker founded Tenfold in 1993, he asked Gary Kennedy to be its CEO, even if it meant basing the business in Salt Lake City.) "Gary and I didn't have a lot in common other than work and the occasional basketball game. We never spent time together." Although he won't quite say it, it's clear that he still blames Kennedy in large part for Oracle's crash and for the humiliation of having to restate earnings for three quarters and submit to a brutal SEC investigation that resulted in a $100,000 fine. It has left Ellison with a profound distrust, not to say distaste, for the things that salespeople will do to get a deal.

In one particular, however, Ellison does recognize something of himself in Gary Kennedy. "Like Gary, I've always been more motivated by fear of failure than by greed. And I hate losing. But bending the rules is a bad strategy. It's more likely to bring on defeat than victory."*

There is something slightly disturbing in Ellison's treatment of Kennedy. Ellison gives the impression of having been almost Kennedy's victim. Yet Kennedy recruited the most talented and feared (by both competitors and customers, it has to be admitted) sales force the technology business has ever seen. Some of them may have gone off the rails and

---

*LE writes: I know that Microsoft seems to be getting away with breaking the antitrust rules, but it will probably catch up with them in the end. Or they may stay lucky and get away with more slaps on the wrist. Who knows? Still, by breaking the rules Microsoft took a huge and unnecessary risk. If not for a few careless comments by Judge Jackson, it would have paid dearly for that.

gotten Ellison into trouble, but without them it's doubtful that Oracle would be the powerhouse it is today. Ellison likes to believe that, by and large, great products sell themselves. But Oracle's were not always unambiguously better than those of its rivals, whereas its sales force was invariably smarter, tougher, and more relentless.

The question of how much blame attaches to Ellison remains difficult to gauge. One thing he accepts without equivocation is that he practiced management by abdication. He does not deny negligence. There is even some justification for his abdication model. It wasn't just that he enjoyed driving product development more than the other stuff, he was convinced that it was in that area that he could make the greatest contribution to Oracle's success. While Bob Miner was supposed to be running development, he was never prepared to lead his programmers in the kind of "death marches" that winning software companies have to be ready for when products are late or failing.

Ellison says with fond exasperation: "Bob loved and took care of the people that worked for him. He would never ask them to work weekends because he thought they should spend time with their families." The fact that Oracle was having such a terrible time getting Version 6 of the database to work properly and the advances that were being made by Sybase made that focus on the product all the more urgent. Ellison says, "To beat Sybase, we had to deliver Oracle Version 7. That's what I spent my time on. I ignored everything else."

Nor is it obvious that making Oracle as big as possible as quickly as possible and relentlessly pursuing market share was the wrong strategy. Ellison says, "Among our early competitors, Ingres and Informix are gone and Sybase is on life support. Silicon Valley is a killing field. Very few technology companies survive. We did." It was this rather than the pursuit of a particular revenue number that fueled Ellison's competitive drive. Ellison understood that once a customer committed to a database vendor, he was pretty well locked in for the next ten years or so. Releasing Oracle 6 when it wasn't ready was extremely risky, but delaying it still further would only have allowed Sybase to become more entrenched in the market. It might have been a lousy way to treat customers and it might have done damage to Oracle's reputation, but to Ellison, the alternative of losing those customers for good would have been worse.*

---

*LE writes: I did not release Version 6 of our database, or any other software product for that matter, knowing there were serious bugs in the product. When

Perhaps Ellison's gravest fault was being instrumental in allowing the firm's cash position to become so nearly terminal. He might not have been sufficiently aware of his duties to note the fragility of his own company's balance sheet, but remarkably he felt qualified to ignore the warnings of others. That single sin of omission may well have had the most serious consequences of all. If, as Jeff Walker and Don Lucas had advised, Oracle had raised money when it hadn't needed it, the consequences of the lost quarter and the revenue restatements would have been little more than an embarrassing stumble.

Ellison's claim that he was "incompetent" is only half true. He combined arrogance and recklessness to a degree that was very nearly lethal for Oracle. But against that he built something so inherently resilient and valuable that both he and Oracle would have the chance to reinvent themselves. As Jeff Walker puts it, "If you take a brilliant, compulsive personality and you subject them to a learning experience, they learn brilliantly and compulsively."

---

you rewrite a large portion of a complex product, as we did with Oracle Version 6, it is virtually impossible to test thoroughly enough to find all the bugs. Unfortunately, you do not discover some of the bugs until the product is in use by customers.

6

GROWING UP

By the beginning of 1991, Ellison had recovered enough from his very public humiliations to be fully engaged in digging Oracle out of its hole. Jenny Overstreet says, "There were a lot of people saying, 'Told you you'd get your comeuppance, you sonofabitch.' He was badly frightened, but the Larry I knew responded to great fears by regrouping quickly. He'd decided, 'I'd better go back to the only thing I know, which is to work really hard and focus all my best energies and all my best talents on fixing this because I'm not really ready to quit.'"

Marc Benniof, who had taken over the telephone sales operation on the recommendation of Tom Siebel, sees it slightly differently: "I don't see Larry as conventionally resilient. I see him as a driving force. Larry gets what he wants, and when he focuses on something he gets it." Benniof, who became one of the few people working at Oracle in the 1990s to become a close friend of Ellison, is even reluctant to buy the idea that Ellison was all that surprised by what had happened: "Larry had his foot to the floor at a hundred fifty miles per hour, trying to leave all his competitors behind. He knew that eventually he would shoot the car over the cliff. But it was like in a James Bond movie—the car makes it across to the cliff on the other side even though it's broken into ten thousand little pieces. It's like he had to go back and say, 'Sorry, Q, look what I did to the car!' But he'd accomplished his goal."

Ellison had to do three things if he was to put Oracle back together. The first was to deal with the cash crisis. The second was to bring in seasoned managers who would bring some solidity to what was now a billion-dollar company and give confidence to investors that the mistakes of the past would not be repeated. Finally, he had to overcome the reliability problems of Version 6 and make sure that the next release would more than hold its own in the features race with Sybase.

Of all these, the most urgent was Oracle's dangerous cash crunch. Ellison knew that a conventional financing solution would not be available on anything less than the most punitive terms, terms that would undermine his position as Oracle's dominant shareholder by destroying the value of the equity held by the company's most important employees: the key developers. Ron Wohl was a young product manager who for several years had been a notably loyal staff officer. He remembers, "Not only did we not have cash, we had not made good banking or other arrangement for financing. We were in danger of violating our covenants [which could have resulted in the bank syndicate calling in the $170 million already borrowed], so we needed to raise some money. At that point, the Japanese economy was extremely strong and Japanese companies were very interested in participating in high tech. Larry had a very strong personal interest in Japan. So he began some initial discussions with Japanese companies which rapidly centered on Nippon Steel, a very, very capable company. Larry asked me to take a lead in the negotiations because our CFO at the time, Jeff Walker, had lost credibility and Larry was in the process of looking for a new CFO."

Ellison made it Wohl's mission to get $200 million while giving as little Oracle equity away as possible. Although initially the Japanese were bewildered to be dealing with a rather junior thirty-year-old, Wohl turned out to be an inspired choice. Wohl has an almost oriental inscrutability that makes him an extremely cagey negotiator and, at times, an infuriating colleague. Even in normal conversation his wariness and reluctance to commit himself can be unsettling. Ellison says, "Ron is extremely smart and very cautious. He hates errors of commission, which means he can be slow to make decisions. That's very Japanese." Not surprisingly, the negotiations proceeded at a glacial pace. Wohl says, "Given the complexity, it was a long-drawn-out negotiation involving a lot of money, a lot of complicated financial arrangements, some partial ownership of Oracle, and some board arrangements in Japan. During that time, Oracle's financial position was getting better by the day and we needed much less money." So much better, in fact, that it dawned on Wohl that his boss didn't really want him to do the deal at all.*

---

*LE writes: I wanted a deal; I just didn't want to give up any Oracle equity, so I slowed down the negotiating process. Time was on our side. Every day our cash position got stronger, so our negotiating position got stronger.

With an agreement imminent with the cash-rich Japanese, Ellison was able to hold off Oracle's bankers and buy time to renegotiate a different and much more advantageous deal with Nippon Steel than originally conceived. By the end of 1991, with expenses under reasonable control and the beginnings of recovery in the economy, Oracle had returned to robust, if unspectacular, profitability and the stock was climbing. Instead of surrendering equity in Oracle to pay off the banks, Ellison had secured a deal that gave Oracle an $80 million loan on highly favorable terms, in exchange for which Nippon Steel had warrants to buy up to 25 percent of Oracle Japan at an exercise price that gave a value to the subsidiary of $400 million. It wasn't quite a case of "and with one bound, Jack was free," but it was getting close.

Another reason for the restored order of Oracle's finances was the arrival in early 1991 of a new CFO. Ellison accepted that Oracle needed a high-class, conventional, professional CFO rather than someone else who, in Geoff Squire's words, was smart but couldn't do the job. About the only thing that Jeff Henley had in common with his predecessor was the same first name. According to Don Lucas, Henley was "a straight arrow," a perfect choice. "We were extremely fortunate in finding Jeff. He was very highly considered by his peers. He'd been there, done that. He'd worked for Memorex and one of the semiconductor companies. You don't have to understand software per se, you just have to know how to do things right."

At the time Lucas approached him, Henley was CFO at the real estate firm Pacific Holdings Company, controlled by the controversial entrepreneur David Murdock. Henley had worked for Murdock for four and a half years and "couldn't stand the guy." He feared that on the basis of what he'd read, Ellison sounded very similar to Murdock. "Murdock was a self-made guy, much like Larry, very opinionated, very volatile temper, and wouldn't listen to anybody. And here's this Ellison, that they say is an egomaniac and all this other stuff, so why would I go and work there?"

Henley was won over in December 1990 at a dinner with Ellison at the Sofitel hotel across the road from Oracle's new "Emerald Towers" headquarters. Henley says, "He had clearly been in deep shock, but now he had gotten over that and was trying to get things going. He was very concerned and, as I would later discover, worried for his own job. I found him very resolute and committed to turning the company around and that he had taken a very active role after a number of people in the leadership had been fired. He was even signing all the checks in the United States as a way of really trying to get his arms around what was going on, but he clearly acknowledged that he needed more experienced management."

Far from Ellison's personality being an obstacle to him, Henley wanted a guarantee that Ellison would not be forced out. "I didn't want to join the company and see Larry leave. I found him very different from Murdock—Murdock thought he knew everything and was in a thousand different businesses, but Larry was very focused on the business of technology. Murdock had street savvy, but nothing like the intellect of Larry. Murdock had no sense of humor, while Larry had a great sense of humor, so I saw a guy who I could also have a lot of fun working with. I'd been ten years in the tech industry, and I came to believe that most tech companies lose their way because they don't have leaders who really understand the technology, but Larry did."

Ellison also liked Henley a lot more than he expected to, finding in him much more than the kind of super bean counter he feared being saddled with. What impressed him was Henley's calm rationality. Although he was only a year or so older than Ellison, in his late forties, with gray hair, craggy features, and the quiet confidence that only the truly well grounded have, he had a somewhat senatorial air that was far removed from the Oracle of the 1980s. Henley also appreciated Ellison's willingness to learn from his mistakes. "He acknowledged that he had created too much competition inside the company. He hadn't pushed teamwork enough, so he had a group of people on his executive team who just hated each other. He also realized that hiring really smart people, very smart young engineers or whatever, had to be balanced by bringing in people who had some business experience. The blowup made him modify some views he'd held for a long time, it was like 'I had a couple of blind spots, and now I need to go work on them.' " *

Henley's arrival made an immediate difference. Noosheen Hashemi had been banging her head against a wall trying to get Jeff Walker to agree to bring in fifty accountants from Peat Marwick to go through the

---

*LE writes: From the first day, I found Jeff very easy to work with. He says exactly what he thinks. He has no personal agenda at all. He's fiercely loyal to the company. He looks out for the interests of our shareholders, employees, and customers. And he's a leader. As they say in the military, it's been an honor to serve with him.

boxfuls of weird contracts and deals that had to be reconciled to get the numbers into shape. "Walker said I could spend just twenty thousand dollars after letting go two thirds of the people who worked for me. I said, 'We can't. We have to restate. This is serious.' He had his head in the sand. The day Henley walked in, he just said, 'Go clean it up, go do it.' He signed up just like that."

Other things also began to change with Henley's arrival. He began to modify Ellison's policy of hiring only exceptionally clever young people. Hashemi says, "We had honor students delivering the mail. That was superb for the company when it was growing so fast because people could take on jobs that evolved in value very quickly. When Henley came in, he said, 'I don't see growth like that. I'm going to hire a payroll clerk for fifteen thousand dollars that has twenty years of experience and no college degree, not some twenty-four-year-old prima donna who doesn't expect to be doing the job for more than six months.' From that moment on, I felt the company lost the incredible culture it had."

Henley also started chipping away at expenses such as lavish parties and massive bonuses. Hashemi, a zealot who thought nothing of working eighteen or twenty hours a day for her beloved Oracle, says that in the past it would have been unusual to find an empty conference room at nine in the evening. "Oracle became a job, when it had been a mission." Most shockingly of all: "People started having children." In other words, Oracle was doing what it had to: evolving into a more stable, grown-up company. Something may have been lost in the process of dialing down the manic intensity that had helped get Oracle into trouble, but not much of it was worth keeping.

With Henley in place bringing reassurance to Oracle's investors and order to the company's finances, Ellison's next task was to find someone to run U.S. sales and consulting. After the departure of Gary Kennedy, Ellison had appointed his polar opposite to run U.S. sales, a genial, almost cuddly man named Mike Fields. Hashemi says, "He was sort of like a teddy bear, he was what we needed for a short period of time. The worst thing that could have happened was to have put in someone arrogant like Tom Siebel. What was needed for a year was for Mike Fields to go around shaking hands with customers, saying, 'Sorry, we're a different, kinder, gentler company now.' "

Although Ellison eventually fired Fields, he is still quite fond in his recollection: "Mike was an exceptionally nice man—he was the Bob Miner of sales. He was a father figure. He was effective at sales because people trusted him. But Mike had never managed a sales organization as large as Oracle's. I wanted someone experienced managing a large organization. And I wanted someone who was servicecentric—not salescentric."

Ellison knew what kind of manager he was looking for to change the cowboy culture of the U.S. sales organization. "I had never heard a customer say, 'Gee, what I need are a few more salespeople calling on me.' Customers always want better products and better service. With Oracle Version 7 we were about to introduce a greatly improved product. Now we had to improve our service. The era of the cowboy was over. We needed someone who could build and run a railroad."

For practically the first time, Ellison used the services of a headhunter, Heidrick & Struggles, to identify candidates for Mike Fields's job as head of Oracle USA. The two men who were shortlisted were a world away from the old Oracle. One was George Conrades, who was running IBM's sales in America and later went on to be the CEO of Akamai, the successful pioneer of Web-caching technology. The other was Ray Lane, a senior partner of the big consultancy firm Booz Allen Hamilton. Lane had been at Booz Allen for about twelve years and had built its IT practice—the Information Systems Group—into one of the four major lines of business within the firm. With the handsome features and firm voice of a film director's idea of a cliché presidential candidate, and a good opinion of himself to match, Ray Lane certainly looked the part.

However, Lane had to be talked into seeing Ellison by Heidrick & Struggles' John Thomson. Oddly, Lane had never heard of Ellison and knew next to nothing about Oracle. Thomson suggested that even if nothing came of meeting Ellison, Lane might be able to sell himself some consulting work down the road. When Lane agreed to fly to California from his base in Dallas, he decided to do some research on Oracle. "It was all really bad. I remember one article in *Upside* magazine which had Larry portrayed as Don Quixote [tilting at windmills], and there were others about the demise of Oracle and its near bankruptcy. Frankly, I didn't know why I was going to meet him. But I did, and I spent three hours with him, talking more at each other than having a conversation. About eighty percent of the discussion was my views of how companies don't understand how to use computer technology and what they needed to be doing. He kept on talking about the technology. So at the end we were really firing each other up in different dimensions—talking about the same things, but looking at both sides of the elephant. He wanted somebody who understood what the technology did for customers and who could sell solutions. Finally, it got to the point after two hours when he says, 'You're the guy. You're exactly what we're looking for. Will you do this?' " *

Although Lane was excited by Ellison's pitch that the combination of the forthcoming Oracle 7 and a reformed, professional sales force represented a great opportunity, he played hard to get, claiming that he stood a good chance of eventually becoming CEO of Booz Allen, which, compared with Oracle, was a global and highly respected firm. But if Lane was cautious, Ellison was convinced. "Larry tripled the number of options on the spot and said I could run things from Dallas—it's Oracle USA, not Oracle California—and just turn up at Redwood for management meetings."

Lane returned to Dallas without having given Ellison his answer and continued looking into the kind of company he might be joining and what working for Ellison would be like. "I started talking to people I could trust about Oracle, about ten people in all. All but one said that the company was gone and the earth would be better if it was gone, and everyone said Larry couldn't be trusted, was the scourge of the earth and was legitimately hated. They were saying 'You'd be going from a classy, professional environment to a bunch of wolves. If you go, don't call me—I'll never buy an Oracle product, even from you.' I was hearing that there was a true love/hate relationship with every employee who works at Oracle. It's an exciting place to work because you're in the middle of everything. You make good money, the sales force makes incredible money. Yet every day, you're dying to go home and you're saying 'I hate this place, I hate this company.' "

The one dissenting voice was a friend of Lane's named Robert Shaw, a burly, dynamic ex-marine who ran the Booz office in San Francisco. Shaw, who was willing to back his judgment by going with Lane to Oracle, said that he thought Oracle had more potential than any other company in the Valley. Lane says, "I trusted him. He knew something about Oracle and had worked with them in the past. He thought they had just been mismanaged. Larry was a lunatic, but a lunatic with vision. They

---

*LE writes: I thought then and still believe that a good consulting manager is ideally suited to sell complex software products. Ray could sell the business benefits of our technology. That's what we needed to do more of in our field organization. And of course Ray could improve our consulting service delivery. He was the right guy for the job.

had kicked ass in the 1980s, and they could kick ass again. Robert was very influential with me, saying, 'Gee, if you go, I'm going with you.' " *

Lane had also more or less convinced himself that he could work with Ellison because they were so complementary and that Ellison's propensity for delegation would result in "a degree of separation." He felt, too, an urge to move to California: "If you're in the oil business, Texas is the place to be. If you're in the computer business, you've got to be in California. Also, at the time, I was not close to my wife and we had already talked about splitting up." If there were attractions in making a new life, Lane is candid enough to admit that it was the prospect of getting rich that made up his mind for him. Speaking of himself and Jeff Henley, he says, "I think Larry bought both of us. I think it's an MO—Larry will first charm you and then he'll buy you. With three hundred thousand stock options, he knew I could do the math, and if Oracle stock moved five points it would be more than I would ever make at Booz Allen."

The funny thing is that Ellison was so desperate to hire Lane. As Geoff Squire says, "If you had done a criteria matrix, you wouldn't have picked Ray. He'd never really seen software, and he'd never run an organization doing more than $50 million. Conrades had more ticks on the scoreboard. But he was intelligent, a good consultant, very quick to understand things. I think it was actually quite an inspired decision." As for Lane, whatever his initial doubts about joining Oracle, his relationship with the "lunatic" Ellison would be pivotal in creating the company that Oracle became in the 1990s.

Lane's timing couldn't have been better. His first day at Oracle on June 14, 1992, coincided with the launch of Oracle 7 in New York. "Larry stuck some makeup on me and threw me up on stage. After he had introduced Oracle 7, I ran a little analyst panel that was to talk about why they thought it had the right features and how if we delivered on time, the prospects looked pretty positive." In fact, Oracle 7 was a little late to ship and didn't get out of the door that day. But it quickly became apparent that it was the product that Oracle's long-suffering customers had been waiting four years to get their hands on.

Ellison says simply, "Oracle 7 was a working version of Oracle 6 plus a few very important new features." Specifically, it had all the features

---

*LE writes: Robert Shaw was a great addition to Oracle. He deserves most of the credit for building our consulting organization in the United States. He's also a pretty good sailor.

that Sybase had differentiated itself with and more. Oracle 7 had an advanced architecture and, like Sybase, was fully programmable via its elegant new PL/SQL programming language. And Oracle 7 one-upped Sybase on both referential integrity and two-phase commit. Ellison says, "With Sybase you had to write hundreds of lines of code in their server programming language to get two-phased commit or referential integrity to work. In contrast, Oracle 7 implemented both of those features using standard SQL. What took hundreds of lines of code in Sybase, we could do with a few keywords. The two features Sybase had marketed most heavily suddenly became technical advantages for us, not them." Whereas Sybase supported neither standard SQL queries nor update transactions that accessed data on more than one server, Oracle 7 could automatically retrieve and modify data on multiple computers using standard SQL, even when some of that data was stored in the databases of rival vendors, making it much easier to build client/server applications that worked with the database than before.

In addition, Oracle 7 was much faster than any other database on the market, thanks to Ellison's passion for the clustering and multiprocessing technology that had made its first appearance in Oracle 6. Although it would be nearly a decade before the full fruits of Oracle's commitment to clusters based on the pioneering Oracle 6 shared-disk architecture would become evident in Oracle 9i, there was already one important marketing benefit. Ellison says, "We were the first to use clusters in performance benchmarks. We won the TPC benchmarks by such huge margins that everyone else just gave up." Running on a pair of UNIX servers, Oracle 7 supported more than ten thousand users and smashed through the thousand transactions a second barrier. Clustering may not yet have been of much practical benefit to customers wanting to run real-world applications, but combined with Oracle 7's other strengths, it was to prove a knockout blow to the likes of Sybase and Informix. Jay Nussbaum, who had joined Oracle from Xerox in early 1992, summed up what Oracle 7's product superiority meant to the sales force: "A dog with a note in its mouth could sell it technically."

Apart from having a great product to sell, Ray Lane was also pleasantly surprised by the quality of the people he discovered at Oracle. He was expecting to "find people who were kind of average—not thinkers, but doers." But "everywhere, there were a lot of very creative people." Even so, Lane resolved that if Ellison didn't pass two "tests" in the first few months, he would return to Booz. The first of these was whether Ellison would back him in choosing his executive team. Lane says, "I had to figure out who the good apples and bad apples were. I fired about seven people, and one was a particularly bad apple, Craig Conway, who's the CEO of a big company [PeopleSoft] today. Craig was a smart guy, and he was also a friend of Larry's." *

Although Lane at first wanted Conway on his team, he soon changed his mind. He came to the conclusion that Conway had undermined the still popular Mike Fields by constantly feeding Ellison with poison about him. Lane says, "Poor Mike was trying to sell a bad product [Oracle 6] against Sybase and he was doing a great job trying to correct the years of bad behavior with the customer, always out on the road. And back at the ranch, there's Craig saying to Larry, 'Why don't you give it all to me, I'll make it work.' He was very smart, very Machiavellian, always trying to figure out an angle, and so he got Mike Fields." What convinced Lane to get rid of Conway was not only the belief that he was also plotting against him but the ill feeling against Conway that he found during the annual company jamboree in Hawaii for salespeople who had met their quota (the "Hundred Percent Club"). "It was like hell. Everybody was calling my room . . . all the fingers were pointing at Conway. It was such an easy decision."

Whether it would be so easy for Ellison was another matter. When Lane told Ellison what he was going to do, Ellison asked him whether he was sure, because he might need some help getting through the next couple of quarters. Lane said, "I'm very sure and . . . I want your commitment that when he comes to you, you will either not talk to him or you'll tell him that it's Ray's decision." Ellison told him he had it, and when Conway duly went to Ellison and demanded to be put in charge of something else, Ellison was as good as his word, saying "It's Ray's business to run. Ray has to make the call." †

The second test was whether Ellison was willing to listen and respond to criticism and unpalatable facts. On his arrival Lane had tried to find out why Oracle had been losing market share to Sybase and Informix. "I

---

*LE writes: I don't think Craig was or is, as Ray put it, a "bad apple." The fact that Craig managed a turnaround at PeopleSoft proves he's a very capable software executive. But Craig was not Ray's guy. Ray wanted people that were totally loyal to him.

†LE writes: I didn't agree with Ray's decision, but I didn't overrule it. Ray had to build a management team he was comfortable with. It was clear that he and Craig didn't like each other.

was just getting stupid answers, like, 'We never see Sybase,' so I hired McKinsey to do a study and collect data on our customers and business practices. How did deals get approved? How did the field actually work? How do the customers actually feel? Why do they feel so bad about us? I was hearing stories like customers would call because the product didn't work and they would get answers like 'Bummer, dude'! When I presented the McKinsey study, it was the first time anyone had presented real data. Now here it is, we've talked to hundreds of customers, and now tell me we don't lose to Sybase. Tell me Sybase is not viewed as a better company than Oracle."

If Ellison was convinced that Version 7 on its own would enable Oracle to triumph, Lane was more skeptical: "He believed that, I didn't. I think it certainly brought parity with Sybase. But Larry . . . thinks that ninety percent of the company's success is made on the product. I think the product is really important, but Oracle's problems were not going to be solved just because Oracle 7 came out. The McKinsey survey showed that Sybase was a beloved company. All I got was Larry telling me stuff that, you know, Oracle 7 gets introduced and your life is wonderful and it's plain sailing and all that. I would talk to the sales force and say, 'Why did we lose?' They said, 'We never lose.' They had no respect for Sybase. What came back from McKinsey was that customers hated us, and Sybase was revered as a trusted partner."

However confident Ellison might have been about the prospects for Oracle 7, he passed Lane's second test by allowing him a completely free hand in reorganizing the sales and support operation. With Lane and Henley on board, supposedly providing the "adult supervision" that Oracle had previously lacked, Ellison felt free to revert to his preferred role, directing engineering. He was no more interested in those parts of the company than he had been in the past and was just grateful that they now appeared to be in safe and steady hands. Lane says, "He was very helpful, very supportive of what I was doing—and I was changing everything, bringing in a whole new management team [many of them from Booz Allen]."

At the same time as Lane was shaking up sales, his former Booz colleague Robert Shaw, who now reported to him, was determined to yank Oracle's tiny consulting operation out of its torpor and turn it into something much bigger and more powerful on the back of the applications that Jeff Walker had begun to develop a few years earlier. Whereas databases were sold to the techies running corporate data centers, selling applications required understanding every aspect of a customer's business.

Shaw says: "I walked into a two-hundred-person consulting business and probably a hundred ninety-five of them were the wrong people. The mandate was: how do you grow this, how do we get it better integrated with the sales force? I took the job because there was a real opportunity to really drive the customer proposition from a services perspective. It went from an ugly duckling losing a lot of money doing little three-day projects, and customers complaining about consultants just out of training class who think they know more than their own people, into, by the time I left in 1998, a very profitable organization with seventeen thousand people and pushing three billion dollars in revenues."

Building a vast consulting organization was as strategically daring as it was risky. It would have enormous consequences, both good and bad, for Oracle. The danger was that if it became a direct competitor to the Big Five IT consulting companies it would risk having its immature applications business cold-shouldered by the firms who made software choices on behalf of their clients in favor of the much-better-established SAP and the promising new kid on the block, the client/server-focused PeopleSoft. On the other hand Oracle had come to recognize that developing and selling apps was very different from the database business, and having its own consulting operation was a way to gain the skills it needed to succeed.

Shaw says that in his first year the decision was revisited many times: "Larry came to me when we reached the first milestone for us, which was when we did a hundred million dollars. We were probably celebrating and we thought we'd just really pulled a coup, and Larry's reaction was 'Do you think you could ever make this larger than Andersen Consulting?' I said, I doubt it, but in the back of my mind I was thinking, the next plateau is becoming a billion-dollar business and then a multibillion-dollar business. Larry was always insightful. He said, 'Look at the evolutionary state of a set of our products. Arrogantly, you can think that we don't really need to listen to the customers on the database because we know more about database technology than they do, so you can really drive the requirements internally towards the external market.' But when it came to applications, the users knew a lot more about the functionality they needed to run their business.

"And at the stage we were at, of trying to integrate the core database technology with the development tools and then adding applications on top of that, Larry said, 'This is going to be a mess to manage if I also have to integrate with a bunch of systems integrators and have them bothering my development organization. They'll slow down the implementation of projects because they're not serving a single master; they're serving whatever they can generate services around.' So I think Larry and I and Ray basically made the decision, we're going to go for it. We'll be channel friendly as long as the channels bring the business, but if the channel is just looking for us to hand off all systems integration business without helping us influence it, we're probably not interested. Would a third party really invest the time to learn our products, or would it slow us down in terms of penetrating accounts with our applications? We had so many people questioning either their functionality or the integration of the technology that we decided to cover ourselves and build the business ourselves. So the decision was, let's go build a very successful consulting business around that."

Nine months after Ray Lane's arrival, Oracle managed to beat analysts' expectations for the traditionally tough third quarter of its fiscal year, bringing in revenues of $371 million and nearly doubling net income over the previous year to $29.2 million. Lane says, "The message was starting to get out that we were serious about serving customers. We'd shipped the product [Oracle 7], not empty boxes. International, run by Geoff Squire, was doing well—average growth numbers but with great profitability. People were saying that it looked like a turnaround was in progress, and that's all you need to move the stock. The day we announced the Q3, the stock bounced eight points, from fifteen dollars to twenty-three." The message was that Oracle had turned the corner. Lane's gamble had already paid off financially: "I was in the game, and after the first year, I thought, I can do this. It's going to be a good ride."

Lane's focus continued to be on bringing order, discipline, and a service ethic to the sales force. By the end of the 1993 fiscal year, he felt confident enough to change all the compensation plans. The two biggest changes he made were to insist that the sales organization should not be paid extra for service and to change the quotas for individual salespeople in relation to the size of their accounts. "They were saying to me, 'If you want service, Ray, if you want us to be good guys, then pay us for being good guys.' I said, 'No. That's something that comes with your DNA.' " *

"When I came in," says Lane, "I also found that all the quotas were

---

LE writes: Interestingly enough, the sales force eventually wore Ray down and he started paying them for selling consulting services. It was fascinating watching Ray interact with our sales force over the years. Sometimes he changed them. Sometimes they changed him.

the same—everyone had a two-million-dollar quota. Even the guy at General Motors. The list price of all the Oracle products he could sell to GM would probably come to two hundred million or more. He could say, 'If you buy the whole book, I'll discount at ninety percent.' With a twenty-million-dollar deal and a two-million-dollar quota, he makes a lot of money and the CIO that buys the stuff is a hero. So the salesman leaves Oracle because he can't sell anything more, having sold the whole book. Meanwhile, the customer is saying 'What can I do with all this crap?' We had thousands of customers in that situation. So I customized the quotas for potential and a lot of the cowboys left. I knew I would drive them out. Now if you've got GM, you're going to get a ten-million-dollar quota, you're going to sign up to stay, and you're not going to be allowed to sell everything in the price book in one deal."

Ellison couldn't have been happier with Lane's impact on the company. He had brought in other senior managers from Booz Allen, as well as a number from EDS and IBM, who were a different species from Kennedy's pack dogs and who had precisely the effect on the field that Ellison had hoped. Jenny Overstreet says, "Larry was just totally jazzed to have Ray and Jeff Henley around to teach him about what happened in grown-up companies." In fact, Ellison was so thrilled by Lane's performance and the impression of gravitas he lent the company that when Lane began to suggest taking on more responsibility, he didn't hesitate to give it to him.

Ellison says, "Ray had done a great job in the U.S., so when he asked for more responsibility I gave it to him. The problem was I gave him too much, too fast. Ray went from running U.S. sales to running global sales in October 1993. That was mistake number one. I removed Geoff Squire from running Oracle Europe. That was mistake number two. Then I gave Ray customer support. That was mistake number three." The rapidly expanding consulting organization run by Robert Shaw also reported to Lane. When Lane had arrived at Oracle, his position, if anything, had been slightly beneath those of Jeff Henley and Geoff Squire.

Lane, however, bears no responsibility for the firing of Squire, which Ellison now so bitterly regrets. The two men got on well from the outset despite Ellison's having (typically) failed to explain clearly to either who was the other's boss. Squire, who had moved back to London after the company had stabilized, says that he would have been happy to work for Lane, knowing that management of global sales would at some time revert to the United States. But Ellison had other ideas. Meeting Ellison for what he expected to be a routine session over breakfast in a London hotel, Squire kicked off his "to do" list with some senior appointments he had been waiting for Ellison's approval on. Ellison said, "Ah yes, that's what I wanted to discuss with you, we won't be needing them. Ray is taking over International." Squire says: "I then asked him what he wanted me to do. He didn't say anything, and it was about five to ten and I had another meeting to go to. He looked uncomfortable, so I said, 'You're surely not . . . you don't want me in the company?' He nodded and I said, 'That's ridiculous,' and I left him there. After that, it got silly with lawyers."

Looking back on it now, Ellison says, "Removing Geoff Squire from Oracle Europe was the mother of all the management mistakes I made that year. Geoff was probably the most talented field executive we've ever had at Oracle. He proved just how good he was by building Veritas out of an acquired amalgam of tech company flotsam and jetsam. Geoff is an extraordinarily gifted guy—and I fired him. Ugh."

Within two years, Ray Lane was not only very clearly Ellison's number two but was in practice running far more of the business than his boss. From Ellison's point of view, it meant that he was able to spend most of his time doing what he liked best: leading the developers in the database and the tools groups. It was also good timing because Ellison's cofounder Bob Miner had quit his development role at the end of 1992. He was unsuited to managing the big teams of engineers that Oracle by now employed and was fed up with the unrelenting pressure to meet product deadlines. Things had come to a head at one of the Monday management committee meetings over the release date of Oracle 7.1, and Ray Lane had banged the table in frustration.

Ellison recalls, "In the meeting, I asked Bob to commit to a date for Oracle 7.1. He wouldn't provide a date. I kept asking. Finally Bob got angry and threw a crumpled-up piece of paper in the middle of the table and said, 'Okay, there's your fucking schedule.' The room went silent. After a long pause Bob said, 'Everyone is working their ass off. It's done when it's done.' That evening Bob called me at home and said, 'Look, I'm going to make it easy for you. I'm going to let Derry run database development.' Bob knew I would never take him out of his job—so Bob did it himself."

A year later, Miner was diagnosed with lung cancer, and a year after that, he was dead. Ellison says of him, "Oracle changed a lot of people, but not Bob Miner. He never bought a new house. He never bought a fancy car or boat. He never ever changed. He never got swept away by ambition."

The departure and death of Miner affected Ellison personally, but without him, the little group Miner had taken off to San Francisco disbanded and returned to Oracle, mainly to the database group. One of them was Ed Screven, who had previously worked with Jeff Walker. "Bob was an incredibly smart guy with great technical intuition. We were trying to build a kind of next-generation application execution environment. We had a lot of good ideas and it was fun, but we didn't make much progress. It was just way too ambitious."

As for Ellison, despite a fair amount of turmoil in his personal life (see Chapter 20) and having survived a couple of near-death experiences of his own (between the end of 1991 and the middle of 1992, he had managed to break his neck while body surfing in Hawaii and smash one of his elbows when his front bicycle wheel stuck in a disused railway track while he was careering downhill near Napa), he was fully focused on propelling Oracle clear of the pack of other database vendors. His strategy rested on three legs. The first, and most important, was achieving real product superiority over Sybase and Informix, Oracle's main rivals in the early 1990s. With the release of Oracle 7 and, in particular, Version 7.1 in 1993, Oracle had, for the first time in several years, unambiguously the best database on the market. The second was in some ways a repeat of what had worked for Oracle in the 1980s when Ingres had been the target. Ellison was determined to exploit the strength of Oracle 7 by building market share no matter what the cost.

Ray Lane believes that Ellison's obsession with growth may have been one of the factors behind his sacking Geoff Squire. Although Europe was extremely profitable, it was not growing fast enough for Ellison. The country managers appointed by Squire to run subsidiaries, such as Michel Rocher in France, had considerable autonomy, and some of them preferred slow growth and big profits. Lane says, "Larry was constantly saying he wanted better numbers out of France, out of Europe. He was saying that we were losing market share to Sybase every day in France and he didn't care how profitable France was. I told him, 'Larry, if we do this, ramp up growth, we'll need to hire more salesmen, really saturate the market, but we're going to have a profitability problem.' He said, 'I don't give a shit about profits. I want to beat Sybase.' So that's what we did." *

---

*LE writes: It's true. I wanted to knock out Sybase while they were technically behind and vulnerable, even if it meant sacrificing profits in the near term. If we were successful, the profits would be greater in the long run.

It didn't take long to work. Lane remembers, during a trip to London in early 1994, Ellison getting him out of bed at three in the morning to deliver the news that Sybase had badly missed its quarter. "He just said, 'It's over.' He was the happiest I'd ever known him. They never, never recovered. Then it was Informix. I remember we broke Informix in about a year and half. We had more salespeople, we went for their key accounts, and we made sure that we never lost on price." Tellingly, the bonus scheme that Ellison, Lane, and Henley shared in was based on one thing: market share. If Oracle was growing at twice the rate of Sybase, the bonus would be doubled. Lane recalls, "The year Informix hit the wall the bonus got multiplied times thirty-three, but of course, the board couldn't let that happen. Larry has to have an enemy. Larry's the most focused individual I've ever seen when he has something to beat."

The third leg of the strategy was for Oracle to be increasingly seen as more than just a maker of databases. Ellison's interest in massively parallel processing (MPP), or clustering technology as it was also known, was as strong as ever. It had helped deliver the crushing benchmark performance figures that Oracle's marketing machine had blitzed the opposition with, but Ellison believed that it might have another application that could take Oracle into a very different world from the corporate computing engine rooms that had been its sole habitat up to that point.

In the early 1990s, there was growing excitement about the perceived convergence among the telecommunications, media, and computing industries. The idea was that the telephone and cable companies would build incredibly high capacity fiber-optic networks, replacing old twisted copper wire and primitive one-way broadcast cable systems; the computer firms would come up with ways to move data from one end of the network to another at high speed and convert bits of information into high-quality streamed sound and pictures; the television companies and the film studios would digitize their huge programming libraries and develop interactive and transactive content with retail and financial services partners; the killer applications, many believed, would be video-on-demand (VOD) and home shopping. The whole caboodle went by the name of the "information superhighway," and everyone, it seemed, wanted to be a part of it. Including Larry Ellison.

Ellison reckoned that he had at his disposal a number of the pieces that were needed to make the information superhighway, and VOD in particular, possible. The two assets Ellison controlled were the leading relational database management system and a majority stake in a Silicon Valley–based computer hardware company called nCUBE, which he had acquired in 1988 for around $11 million of his own money (Bob Miner had put in about $5 million). Ellison maintained that Oracle should never go into hardware itself because it must always be seen to be platform-agnostic. nCUBE had been started five years earlier by some engineers from Intel, and it was an early leader in building massively parallel computers—relatively compact machines with multiple processors and the ability to calculate far faster than conventional mainframes.

Ellison hoped that one day an ultrareliable version of the Oracle database would run on the nCUBE boxes. It was partly his belief in MPP as the way of the future that had resulted in the rewriting of Oracle 6 with all the consequent problems of lateness and chronic unreliability. Unfortunately the nCUBE machines were very tricky and time-consuming to program, which made them unsuitable for the rough-and-tumble of corporate computing. But Ellison realized that it might be possible to use them for the much more specialized task of serving up streamed video.

What attracted Ellison to video-on-demand was not just the possibility of being able to sell more software and finally make some money from nCUBE but the opportunity to link Oracle with something that everybody was talking about and that was more glamorous and consumer-oriented than Oracle's usual business. Ellison says: "VOD had become very fashionable.* The technical problem presented by VOD was moving very large amounts of data, all those bits that make up the movie images, off disks and onto the Net fast enough. The performance bottleneck was the video server computer's memory system. But if you have multiple memories, as you have with a massively parallel machine, then you have all the bandwidth you need for VOD. Problem solved. So we set off to build the software for a massively parallel video server."

In 1993, Ellison co-opted a team of some of his brightest young engineers to solve the technical problems of building a media server that could handle video, audio, and text on the nCUBE platform. Within a

---

*LE writes: If you work in Silicon Valley long enough, you can't help noticing how much the technology industry resembles the women's clothing business. Both are fashion-driven. Fashionable ideas are hot, while the others are not. In the early '90s, VOD was fashionable and everyone—Oracle, Microsoft, Sun—was doing VOD. These days "Web services" are hot, so everyone is doing and talking about Web services. If you are out of step with the latest fashion in the tech industry, the tech analysts say nasty things about you and you don't get your picture on the cover of magazines.

few months, they succeeded. How much the software had to do with Oracle's database technology is debatable, but at least the shared-disk approach to architecture that had made Oracle 6 so hard to finish finally came into its own. By January 1994, the technology was sufficiently stable to be rolled out at an event hosted by Walter Cronkite at the CBS studios in Hollywood.

Ellison was already experiencing a degree of limelight that didn't normally come with selling databases. He met entertainment moguls such as Michael Eisner of Disney, Rupert Murdoch, and Barry Diller, and also made his first appearance on the cover of *Fortune* magazine. The accompanying article by Alan Deutschman, gratifyingly entitled "Software's Other Billionaire," was in marked contrast to the kind of press that Ellison had been getting only a couple of years earlier. Best of all were the pictures showing Ellison in the Japanese garden of his home in Atherton surrounded by lots of little television sets. The message couldn't have been clearer or better for Oracle: here was the man who was making the dream of video-on-demand into reality.

Was it all a dazzling digression from Oracle's real business, a bit like the network computer that was still to come? Marc Benniof strongly disagrees: "With both the network computer and the video server, you can see a very important part of the way Larry thinks about things. He will create a strategy that elevates Oracle and also destabilizes a competitor in one movement. It's like the martial arts of business. He's very good at this. The video server strengthened Oracle because it made people much more aware of Oracle, the Oracle brand, and Larry the visionary. After the *Fortune* article there were a bunch of other pieces all saying the same kind of thing. It not only drove people to Oracle, all the competitors were going crazy saying, 'Gee, what should we do?' Microsoft had to respond and so did Silicon Graphics, which was very hot in those days, and the other database companies. They don't even know what's happening to their own psychology when Larry is out there doing his stuff."

The glitzy presentation of Oracle's all-singing, all-dancing VOD technology at CBS didn't go quite as planned, but not because of the gremlins that traditionally conspire to undermine carefully rehearsed tech demos. At 4:30 on the morning of the rollout a powerful earthquake measuring 6.7 on the Richter scale struck the Northridge area of greater Los Angeles, destroying buildings and collapsing freeways. Ellison was in his hotel. "People were pounding on my door telling me to get out of the hotel because of the earthquake. I told them to go the hell away so I could go back to sleep. I had already been awakened by a huge crash in my room followed by what sounded like a series of gunshots coming from the bathroom. I didn't care. I wanted to be well rested for the presentation the next morning. I went back to sleep. The next morning I discovered what caused the noises in my room. The 'gunshots' were ceramic tiles exploding off the bathroom wall as the building swayed back and forth. The big crash was the armoire with the big-screen TV falling face first onto the floor."

Maybe it was also an omen. The demo had to be postponed because Cronkite was pulled out to work on the earthquake. Unlike the television in Ellison's room, VOD went out with a whimper rather than a bang. It wasn't, however, because the technology didn't work. Time Warner ran a big pilot for a couple of years down in Orlando, Florida, while Oracle partnered big telephone companies in similar pilot services on both sides of the Atlantic. One was with British Telecom, involving two thousand paying customers in Ipswich, which ran for a year, until the end of 1995. Oracle provided the software, nCUBE the servers, Apple had been persuaded by Ellison to build a set-top box based on the Macintosh computer, BT ran the high-speed network, and a group of media companies from the BBC to some of the Hollywood studios contributed content.

The findings of the experiment were pretty uniform. The technology scaled perfectly, as Oracle had promised it would, although the nCUBE boxes were expensive because of their proprietary processors. People also liked the service a lot and were prepared to buy some of their television on a program-by-program basis (in Ipswich, the most popular feature was the chance to watch favorite soaps a day before they were broadcast, thus enabling subscribers to be one up on their friends). Unfortunately, they weren't spending enough, either on entertainment or on the primitive online shopping that was also provided, to give the telcos any confidence that they would get a return if they spent billions building out the new networks and running fiber to the doors of their customers.

Ellison says, "It's really embarrassing looking back on it. We all believed this was going to happen. Bill Gates even wrote a book about it. I thought I was so smart figuring out how to use a massively parallel computer to solve the VOD technical problem. Unfortunately, the barrier turned out to be economic, not technical. Consumers were unwilling to pay very much for VOD movies, and the market for training videos and shopping services was too small to make up for it. It didn't matter how good our video server was, it just didn't make economic sense to spend billions building a broadband network to everyone's home."

Three other developments also explained the telcos' failure to push ahead. One was an emerging technology called digital subscriber line (DSL), which offered the promise of turning standard paired copper wire into a much fatter pipe. While the bandwidth would still be much less than that of fiber, advances being made in digital compression offered the possibility of soon being able to deliver broadcast-quality video through the existing network. BT said it might mean the difference between spending $3 billion and well over $20 billion. The second was the imminent arrival of digital television with the capacity to deliver more than five hundred video streams, a good many of which could be used to offer movies with staggered start times on a pay-per-view basis. Near-video-on-demand was nothing like the real thing, but the telco bosses were worried that a lot of people would think it good enough.

Finally, there was the arrival of the Internet as a mass-market platform, thanks to the creation of the World Wide Web by Tim Berners-Lee and Marc Andreessen's point-and-click browser. While the Web still needed big bandwidth to provide video of acceptable quality, it was a fundamentally different approach to the proprietary networks that the telcos had had in mind. And while the Internet might not yet be a good way of distributing movies, it was likely to be much better at delivering most of the other online services that the telcos had hoped to earn commissions from. By the end of 1996, almost nobody was talking about the information superhighway anymore. Video-on-demand might have been only resting, but nobody could say when it would be revived.

But for Larry Ellison, the whole interactive TV thing had been a wonderful ride that had cost very little money and had fundamentally changed the public perception of Oracle. At the beginning of the 1990s, hardly anyone had heard of Oracle except for IT managers. By the middle of the decade, if it wasn't exactly a household name, it was widely recognized by technology investors and readers of the business press. Ellison had set out to stop people talking about Oracle and other database companies and get them talking about Oracle and Microsoft. "Oracle was now perceived as a software heavyweight, ranked just behind Microsoft and IBM. Customers who bought our products could trust that we were going to be around for a long time. We were a survivor. The same could not be said for Sybase and Informix. And if customers don't believe you're going to survive—you won't."

Oracle, by 1994, barely three years after so nearly self-destructing, had conclusively triumphed in the vicious database wars, in large measure thanks to Ellison's incredible competitiveness and strategic brilliance. But the same could not be said of the applications business that was supposed to become the main driver of the company's growth as the database market matured. Applications would become Oracle's and Ellison's crucible.

7

BEST-OF-BREED

When Ray Lane arrived at Oracle in the middle of 1992, the still relatively young applications business that Jeff Walker had founded six years earlier was growing fast. Its first products might have been thin on features and bug-infested, but by the early 1990s Oracle had nearly 1,500 customers, made up of mainly fairly small or midtier American companies, running their financial, human resources, and manufacturing packages without too many complaints.

Lane says, "Walker was brilliant. He created some very innovative things in those applications and he used Oracle's technology better than either SAP or PeopleSoft. The customers were happy, they liked the innovations, and they bought them because they were open systems, whereas every other application company's at the time were all closed and proprietary running on mainframes or minicomputers." What Lane meant by "open" was that Oracle's apps were built on the UNIX operating system and on the relational database—two major differentiators from the competition that, moreover, a sales force used to selling databases understood and felt comfortable talking about.

Lane believed that these qualities, combined with the rapidly expanding consulting organization that Robert Shaw now had a mandate from Ellison to build, would ensure growing success for Oracle's applications. There was a lot riding on it, given that nearly everyone at Redwood Shores, even Ellison, to some extent, believed that the database market was fast maturing. Oracle might never get back to doubling its revenues each year, and it was too big for that anyway with sales running at $1.2 billion for the 1992 fiscal year, but the combination of applications and consulting would ensure that Oracle recovered and held on to its status (and its stock rating) as a growth company.

However, for anyone who wanted to look problems were already beginning to build up in applications. Unlike Ellison on the database side of development, Walker had not stuck to a policy of hiring only the best and brightest. Ellison says, "Jeff wanted people who were totally loyal to him and his ideas. That made it hard for him to hold on to the best people." Ed Screven, who worked with Walker, says that he was a bully who had favorites while picking others out for vilification: "I mean, the guy literally made them cry." The consequence was that when Walker was fired, he failed to leave much talent behind him. Screven says, "We had a series of very poor managers who were no good at building a competent engineering organization."

Part of Walker's legacy that stored up trouble for the future was that he implemented his own tools. Oracle's own tools operation under Sohaib Abbasi was concentrated on going after the market for building customized applications for the database. In other words, Abbasi was creating tools to leverage the database as it evolved from host-based computing to client/server, while the tools in applications were stuck without a migration path to the new platform. The consequence was that Oracle's applications were not rewritten to run in client/server mode until 1993, and even then Oracle's tools proved extremely difficult to adapt to the kind of graphical user interface (GUI) that PeopleSoft was making popular and that customers expected to find on their Windows desktop PCs.

To make matters worse, in 1992 Ellison and Abbasi had taken a fateful decision to extend Oracle's portability proposition to supporting as development platforms a wide variety of emerging graphical user interfaces. The list included Windows, Apple's Macintosh, IBM's OS/2 Presentation Manager, OSF's Motif, and Sun's Ultimate. The decision was based partly on what had worked for Oracle in the past and partly on not wanting to give too much of a helping hand to Microsoft by betting more strongly on Windows. However, as Abbasi says, "The pressure was on me to deliver technologies that would enable portable user interfaces, but it was much more difficult than we expected and original estimates were off by two or three years, but by then the market had already determined that Windows would be the dominant GUI. It ended up being a very expensive decision." *

---

*LE writes: It was a big mistake, and it was my mistake. I didn't think that Microsoft Windows would crush IBM OS/2 and all the other desktop systems— but it did.

What both of these costly mistakes showed was that Oracle's technology development was being driven almost entirely by the requirements of the database rather than the applications business. Not surprisingly, as by his own admission Ellison was barely thinking about what was needed to help applications. He admits, "I paid no attention to the goings-on in applications. I was a disinterested bystander." The truth is that Ellison found applications and the mainly clerical functions that the software of the time was designed to automate unspeakably dull compared with the intellectual purity of the mathematics and physics that were at the heart of database development, never mind the glitz of Hollywood and interactive television.

Ellison's neglect meant that Oracle's applications were in no shape to respond effectively to what was about to hit them. It was called R/3. In 1992, the German software powerhouse, SAP, which had been founded by five former IBM systems engineers in 1972 (it stands for Systemanalyse und Programmentwicklung—Systems Analysis and Program Development), had at last announced a client/server version of its R/2 applications suite. Launched in 1979 after several years of painstaking development, R/2, which ran on mainframes, was widely recognized as the most complete and thoroughly engineered of the new breed of packaged applications. Typically, SAP hadn't skipped to the new client/server paradigm with great speed or nimbleness. But it had done so with precision and meticulous planning. At the same time as R/3 was being developed, SAP was also preparing a serious assault on the largely untapped U.S. market, with SAP America establishing a development center just a few miles from Redwood Shores in Foster City.

For Oracle's applications, R/3's arrival in 1993 was a disaster. Ray Lane says, "R/3 changed the game. Although we'd had some success in that area, we weren't really an application company. Our sales force and our consultants didn't really understand how to compete in the applications business.* They had been able to sell saying 'open' and 'relational,'

---

*LE writes: Ray and I both agreed that our database sales force was not very good at selling applications. But we disagreed as to why and what to do about it. Ray thought the problem was they didn't understand how to sell applications due to lack of training and relevant industry experience. I agreed with those points but thought the problem was compounded by the fact that our salespeople would be foolish to spend their time competing for applications deals when they could make much more money by concentrating on selling the data-just like when they sold databases. But when R/3 came along, it took that advantage away. We now had to fight on a different battleground, and that was business functionality. No contest. We didn't even come close. Against SAP, we were a fraction. So we went on what turned into a four-year binge to try and catch up with SAP. From 1993 through to 1997, our entire application effort was devoted to trying to build the features to compete."

Lane realized from the outset that competing against SAP would be very difficult. SAP had slowly spread from its base in Germany to one European country after another, adding localization and translation as it went. By adding the features that American companies needed, it was able, at a stroke, to double its potential market. For Oracle, it was the other way around. Lane says, "We didn't have Italian accounting, say, or German manufacturing. To double our market size, we had to go to twenty-seven different countries in Europe." Nor was it just a case of not being able to attack local markets in which SAP was entrenched; for any global business with operations across many borders, Oracle in 1993 wasn't even an option. While SAP could aim for the biggest and most profitable accounts, Oracle faced being left scrabbling for smaller customers, which were now in SAP's sights because unlike R/2, which could run only on mainframes, R/3 would work on just about any computer.

Nor did Oracle really understand just how different the applications business was from selling databases. The Oracle sales force wasn't used to dealing with senior management, nor did it have the expertise about the requirements of different industry "verticals," such as energy or financial services, how customers ran their organizations, and therefore what functionality was likely to be most important to them. Lane says, "SAP called very high. They called at the boardroom and the CEO, and our guys are used to calling at the CIO and down—talking about technology with database administrators." Jeff Henley says, "Even today, it's hard to get some of our sales force to move beyond the CIO, because

---

base. No amount of training and experience could ever solve that problem, so I thought we should create a separate, dedicated applications sales force. But I could never convince Ray. He wanted Oracle to have one sales force because he insisted that customers wanted to deal with one and only one Oracle sales force. This grew to become a huge point of contention between Ray and me, and it wasn't until after Ray left that we began splitting and specializing our sales force.

that's where they get their meat and potatoes—learning how to sell to a financial guy or an HR or a sales guy or whatever is a big challenge." Over the years, Oracle has struggled with this issue, with some, including Ellison, arguing that there ought to be separate sales forces for the technology and applications products.

Nor was it clear whether Robert Shaw's aggressively expanding consulting empire was helping applications or not. It helped to the extent that Oracle was, as Shaw had promised, gaining a great deal of knowledge about integrating Oracle's products. Ellison believed strongly then, as he does now, that for plenty of customers the direct model, in which a single vendor takes responsibility for building a solution, is attractive. However, even by 1994 it was becoming apparent that there were significant costs to the way Oracle was going about building its consulting business.

SAP had carefully nurtured relationships within the Big Five consulting firms, especially with Andersen Consulting, the largest systems integrator in the world. When companies were deciding whether and how they were going to implement an ERP system, they rarely started off by talking directly to the software vendors. Instead, they would ask one of the consultancies, usually one with which they had an existing relationship, to evaluate their business processes and then recommend the software that would best fit their requirements.

Although SAP's suite was far from perfect—it was notoriously inflexible and hard to put in (not that that worried consultants too much, who were paid according to the length of the job)—most of the required functionality was in place and, critically, the consultants would not be pitching the software of a company that appeared intent on stealing their lunch. What's more, a recommendation in favor of Oracle's applications would run the risk of the customer then inviting Oracle Consulting to pitch for the work. It made choosing SAP a no-brainer. Jeff Henley says, "We totally screwed up partnering by building this big consulting group. We totally pissed off our partners."

Ellison, as he does so often, claims naïveté: "I wasn't aware of how important the consulting companies were in recommending applications, because they weren't very important making recommendations in the database market. I didn't understand that building a big consulting business was making it much harder for us to sell our applications, so I supported building up our consulting business while SAP was off building alliances. We made very little effort to work with consulting partners."

Robert Shaw, unsurprisingly, sees it differently: "SAP obviously made the decision to go the other way from us with consulting. But you've got to remember, they were starting from a company that's twenty years old in the business of applications. I think we lost some market share and penetration to SAP because the partners didn't recommend our product but, at the same time, our product wasn't ready for the Fortune 100 world that they inhabited. It didn't have the globalization and a lot of the functionality it took, so we were probably better off losing that work. At the same time, as SAP grew and we grew, I think they came to be so dependent on the systems integrators that they were unable to compete with us when we moved to rapid implementation and single point of accountability." [*]

Ellison's response to the threat from SAP was to appoint thirty-three-year-old Ron Wohl to clean up the mess inside applications and produce a package that would stand comparison with R/3 and PeopleSoft's successful HR and financial packages. He knew that it would not be easy, but he had no idea what a bed of nails he was consigning his protégé to. Ellison, however, had huge faith in Wohl's ability. He had handled the complicated negotiations with Nippon Steel with calmness and intelligence. Since then he had operated as Ellison's chief of staff, and, despite often having to play the difficult role of go-between, he was recognized as technically very smart, straight to deal with, and utterly loyal to Ellison. Ellison believed that Wohl could build the kind of applications development team Oracle needed if it were to compete effectively with SAP—one that was both disciplined and talented. [†]

The only problem was that Wohl knew very little about the applications business. When Ellison told the rest of the company that he was putting Wohl in charge, there was consternation and then anger. Ray

---

[*]*LE writes: Robert's analysis is right on. Building our own consulting organization was a two-edged sword. There were as many pluses as minuses.*

[†]*LE writes: The biggest problem in applications development was the mediocrity of the management team—people who were promoted because of their unquestioning loyalty to Jeff Walker. Ron's job was to analyze the organization and figure out who was good and who was smart, and put them in charge. Ron has no tolerance for muddy thinking, so I knew he would quickly find and weed out the mediocre managers. Ron also had to prioritize what features we were going to put into the applications to become more competitive. We needed someone extremely detail-oriented and very, very analytical. Ron is one of the best thinkers in the company so I gave him the job.*

Lane says, "When Larry put Ron in charge of applications, all of us were just shocked. He'd never run a large organization, never done any development of any consequence. He was a smart guy, but he knew nothing about applications, didn't know our products because he'd lived with Larry. He was kind of a thinking guy. Very seldom do software companies succeed when they try and build a second front, a second product, and second market. This was going to be our big play—by the year 2000 this was going to be billions of dollars of revenue. So I said, 'Ron Wohl, I don't think so.' I was probably negative from the very beginning on Ron Wohl."

From the outset, Lane seemed unwilling to understand the extent of the difficulties that Wohl was grappling with. The organization Wohl had been asked to take over was a shambles. Oracle had been late to client/server in both technology and applications, it had embarked on a disastrously flawed strategy in tools with devastating effects for applications, and much of the business functionality that had taken SAP's much larger development team many years to complete was simply absent. Yet within a year, Lane was denouncing Wohl as a failure.

It's possible that if Wohl had been a different type of personality, the relationship between himself and Lane would not have deteriorated so rapidly. Jay Nussbaum, who was running Oracle's federal government operation, says, "At school, Ron would have been the smartest guy, but he doesn't have street sense. He can outthink you and outpause you, but nothing comes back." For Ron Wohl, read Ron Wall.

Ellison says of Wohl, "The things that make him good—his analytical ability, his detail orientation, and most of all his caution before he makes a commitment—make Ron so different from Ray that it was a constant struggle for them to work together. Ray is the type of guy who believes when something needs to be done you do whatever is necessary and make it happen. Ron believes when something needs to be done you analyze it thoroughly so you understand exactly how it can be done—if it can be done at all. Ray manages by force of personality. He wills things to get done. Robert Shaw, an ex-marine, strongly shared Ray's 'can do' attitude. Ron frustrated the hell out of both Ray and Robert. They'd come to him and say, 'Okay, to get this deal done we have to promise this,' and Ron would say, 'Well, that's nice, but we can't deliver it.' They hated hearing that. Ron was killing their deals. It drove them crazy. So Ron got nicknamed 'Doctor No.' Ray never saw Ron as someone he could do business with."

The frustration of Lane and Shaw over running a features race with

SAP that Oracle could never win, and their inability to relate to Wohl, was understandable but not exactly helpful. They were in the front line, dealing with protests from the field, and were only reacting to the difficulties of delivering on the commitments made to customers. Tensions between the development and distribution organizations in software firms are almost inevitable. Sales and consulting think that developers sit in ivory towers, insulated from the real world of deals, implementations, and dissatisfied customers. They are the ones who suffer, above all in their wallets, when development is late in delivering anticipated functionality or when the products that do ship are buggy and unstable. For its part, development tends to believe that sales will say anything that customers want to hear to snag their fat commissions and then expect engineers to perform miracles to rescue them from the consequences of their overpromising. But at Oracle in the mid-1990s, the divisions and the factional warfare were beginning to get out of hand.

Robert Shaw says, "The consulting business was there first and foremost to drive product adoption and to have experts on site who knew the products and could get the stuff to work better, quicker than outside consulting firms. But what was not there from the beginning was a good interface between consulting and development to get product issues and future requirements from the field back into the development organization. The number of bugs, the number of deficiencies in the applications being uncovered by the field, was just overwhelming. It was almost catastrophic. We were always the ones that found the problems that would embarrass development. We were always on their case because we wanted relief in our budget * because we were spending so much time building around the product to make it work in a customer site."

It didn't take long for Ray Lane to lose patience with Wohl completely. "I went to Ron one day, and I said that I had finally had it and that I was

---

*LE writes: If consulting claimed that a product bug had cost them extra unbillable time at a customer, Ray would give the consulting team "budget relief" and the team's bonuses would not be affected. It sounds reasonable, but it created a perverse incentive to blame everything on product bugs. If consultants admitted they had made a mistake, their bonuses would go down. If consultants blamed it on development, their bonuses would be safe. Not surprisingly, just about every delayed and failed consulting project was blamed on the product. This perverse process of paying for the placement of blame poisoned the relationship between applications development and consulting.

going to go to Larry and recommend he take him out of the job. I said to him that I'd never stab him in the back, but I would stab in the chest. Ron didn't say anything except, 'Okay, fine.' It was like, 'I think you're kind of crazy for doing it because I know Larry loves me.' " If that's what Wohl was thinking, he was right. It wouldn't be the last time that Lane would try to get Wohl fired. It was the beginning of a war of attrition between the two men that would last for years.

However, it wasn't in Lane's nature to accept what he felt was an intolerable situation. If development under Wohl couldn't or wouldn't produce the weapons to make the fight with SAP more equal, Lane's side of the company would come up with an answer of its own. The idea came from Shaw's hard-charging consulting operation. Shaw says, "We'd made the first step of training the sales force on how to sell solutions. Then, at the next level, when we started competing for the major accounts with SAP, it became obvious that if, say, you're going to a major oil company you'd better have somebody who knows how an oil company works and can talk about the issues—the same with a pharmaceutical company or any of the retail process industries. So Larry and Ray gave me the task of building a sales force that could compete more successfully and aggressively by vertical markets with SAP."

Apart from manufacturing industries, where Oracle was relatively strong, the verticalization of the sales force* only rammed home the absence of business functionality in the markets that Oracle was now trying to target. Shaw says, "When we looked at the development plan and how long it would be before we would have a competing product with rich functionality on a global basis, it was measured in years, not months. So that's why we came up with the strategy of, 'Can we go out and build partnerships with other applications companies?' where we'd preintegrate suites made up of Oracle and third-party software for verticals like the CPG [consumer packaged goods] market and the energy business."

Ron Wohl acknowledges that he could not give Lane and Shaw what they wanted: "When Ray and his team demanded a CPG solution, development didn't have any good answer because we couldn't build it in anything like the time frame that sales wanted. Sometimes, the engineering

---

*LE writes: Verticalizing an applications sales force by industry made sense. Verticalizing our database sales force did not. We needed to segment into separate sales forces. But Ray refused. He verticalized everything. It was a costly mistake.

answer may not be acceptable to sales. They tried to convince Larry that Oracle's strength was its sales force rather than its products—if we need to license the product from somebody else, let's go ahead and do it. Robert and Ray really wanted those markets so badly."

Faced with apparently insuperable time-to-market problems, Oracle embraced a best-of-breed approach by identifying the vendors that had products that could fill the gaps in its own package and by coming up with a methodology for gluing them together into complete suites that would be a match for SAP. Lane says, "The idea was that we would design these templates that would convince the customer we had the right foundation. We had financials and we had HR, but it had taken us four years to build global financials. To compete against SAP, who had everything, we would work with these other companies to fill the gaps. I endorsed the strategy, and Larry endorsed it." He also maintains that Ellison was as enthusiastic as he was to go down the best-of-breed road: "Larry bought it hook, line, and sinker." Ellison, however, claims that he was always "a little uncomfortable about using the Oracle sales force to sell third-party products." But he was won over both by the arguments that Shaw presented and by the need to take some of the heat off Wohl.*

In early 1995, board member Joe Costello of Cadence Design had come out in support of Lane's campaign to oust Wohl. Costello had complained to the board that a presentation that Wohl had given to the board of Oracle's applications strategy was "uninspiring, uninsightful, with no clear picture of how he was going to beat the competition." At the subsequent board meeting, he rounded on Ellison, who he believed was protecting Wohl and failed to understand how disastrous things in applications were. Ellison was shaken by the intensity of Costello's attack: "Joe jumped up and started screaming at me, 'Larry, you're fucking up, you're fucking up the company again, just like last time, you're fucking it up!' all because I wouldn't fire Ron Wohl."[†] After such an outburst, Costello

---

*LE writes: Frankly, I was getting tired of hearing Ray tell me over and over again how he could do a better job than Ron by having consulting build vertical industry application suites by integrating best-of-breed third-party products. I decided to let him try. If he succeeded, great; if he failed, he would better understand the complexities of application development. Expensive mistake. I never should have let Ray build and sell best-of-breed suites.

†LE writes: Joe had joined Ray in demanding that I fire Ron. But I don't think that Joe wanted to stop there. I believe he wanted me fired as well.

could not remain on the board. His parting shot was to pick SAP for his firm rather than Oracle.

Ellison had already agreed to the idea of selling some third-party content if it meant Oracle could win deals it would otherwise lose. "Selling ten million dollars' worth of Oracle applications along with two million dollars' worth of i2 [a supply-chain specialist] and a custom integration project was just fine. I had no objection to selling third-party applications so long as seventy-five percent of the deal was Oracle product. This phase one of selling third-party products and custom integration worked pretty well, and we won some deals we otherwise would have lost. Phase two was much more ambitious. We'd become the king of best-of-breed by preintegrating our applications with a number of third-party products. We'd develop a best-of-breed suite for a number of different industries. Rather than selling third-party products on an exception basis to win the occasional deal, we'd transform our entire applications business into a best-of-breed suite business. And Ray's consulting organization would run the new applications engineering and marketing teams.

"Why did I agree to this? Well, we weren't doing well in applications and there was tremendous tension in the company as a result. I didn't think that this was the time to fight Ray over applications because I wasn't sure I'd win the battle at the board level. And I didn't have any good answers on how to solve our applications problems quickly. Ray would tell me over and over again how he could do a better job at applications development than Ron. He just wore me down. So I said, 'Okay, go ahead and build your best-of-breed suites. Maybe you're right. I don't think so, but give it your best shot.' * So Oracle started buying and partnering with lots of applications software companies. We built a consumer packaged goods [CPG] suite, an energy upstream and downstream suite, a retail suite, etc. Very quickly we were in several new applications markets. Unfortunately, prepackaged reusable integrations proved very difficult to do, so every time we sold a best-of-breed suite we had to do lots of custom integration for the customer. We lost money—lots of it— on every one we sold."

Jeff Henley says, "Larry sort of said, 'This is a horse's ass thing to do, but okay.' It was a moment of weakness. He felt that we were getting screwed and that the field was mad at him." It seemed sensible to

---

*LE writes: One of the most expensive mistakes I have ever made at Oracle. I never should have let Ray do software product development of any kind.

Ellison to adopt a twin-track strategy. Lane and Shaw would be given their head to work on best-of-breed, while Wohl would continue to slog away, trying to make Oracle's own apps more competitive.

Whatever Ellison's misgivings about allowing the establishment of engineering teams within consulting, once he had given it his blessing he had no choice other than to back it to the hilt. He says, "I wasn't going to try to undermine Ray's strategy—that would have been madness. While I didn't think it would work, I didn't know for certain it wouldn't work, and I certainly didn't think it was unreasonable for us to try. And maybe we'd win more deals if the sales force got behind a strategy they believed in." *

To demonstrate his commitment, Ellison pledged that development would help engineer the vital interfaces between Oracle's own products and those of its partners. Wohl was opposed to the strategy, believing it would divert resources away from making Oracle applications better and because he wasn't sure it could be done. Consequently, Ellison moved a young engineer called Nimish Mehta into applications to work with Shaw's industry groups and provide them with what they needed. Mehta had previously worked on getting Oracle's core technology to work with Windows, but despite his lack of applications experience and Wohl's profound skepticism, he was confident that he could pull it off. For Lane, Mehta was a breath of fresh air compared with the nitpicking Wohl.

If there were uncertainties about the "experiment," the 1995 annual report gave no hint of them. "With more than 4,000 consultants in 43 countries, Oracle Services can assemble a global team with the skills necessary to deliver the solutions customers require. . . . Oracle Vertical Markets offers comprehensive industry solutions for selected market segments. Under the Certified Application Partners (CAP) program, Oracle integrates data products from its partner companies to deliver 'best-of-breed,' turnkey solutions to customers in important targeted industries." Reading it, anyone might have thought that this was something that Oracle was already successfully delivering. They would have been wrong.

Nevertheless, the best-of-breed strategy got off to a flying start. Just as Lane and Shaw had hoped, they suddenly had a story that was capable of convincing multinational companies to buy an Oracle solution rather than turn to SAP. Many companies, especially in America, disliked the inflexibility of SAP's software and were happy to back a U.S. competitor

---

LE writes: In fact, we did win more deals. But they weren't profitable.

that promised to deliver an alternative based on gluing together the best software around. Nothing summed it up better than a landmark deal Lane negotiated with the breakfast cereal company Kellogg. In late February 1996 Oracle was committed to providing a viable "Consumer Package Goods Industry Supply Chain Management Solution" to Kellogg within three years that would "maintain a best-of-breed level of functionality, which, at minimum, meets or exceeds the functionality of its foremost competitor's product(s)."

From the suite, Oracle would provide only one component, the financials. The rest would come from other software firms: order management would come from IMI, logistics from Manugistics, maintenance management from TSW, manufacturing from Datalogix (later acquired by Oracle to prevent it from going bust), and warehouse management from McHugh Freeman. Oracle would serve as the system integrator and would market "the resulting solution." All of this would be achieved through "an Oracle CPGI defined interface technique that is based on open application transaction and database standards. The complexity of this interface technique will provide for external bolt-on interfacing, which is significantly easier than interfacing to competitors' solutions."

Naturally, Kellogg would also be expecting and getting massive discounts on both license and consulting fees. However, Oracle would be gaining valuable experience in CPG by working with Kellogg and would be able to use it as a reference account in selling to other companies in the same business. Similar deals were put together with other flagship customers to announce Oracle's arrival as a serious player in a particular sector. Typical was a deal with British Petroleum to provide a complete refinery inventory management system.

Suddenly Oracle's revenues from applications went into overdrive. In the last three months of fiscal 1995, Oracle's sales topped a billion dollars in a quarter for the first time, helped by a 115 percent surge in applications sales. The following year, applications sales showed a 73 percent gain in the final quarter, capping a tenfold rise in profits and share price over the previous four years. Ellison, now chairman of Oracle as well as chief executive officer, singled out Ray Lane for having contributed more to this "unprecedented success" than anyone. Such was Ellison's confidence in Lane that he also announced his promotion to president and chief operating officer. It was probably the high-water mark in their relationship.

In early 1997, Ellison was able to boast that Oracle was not only the number two applications company in the world but was rapidly "gaining on number one, because our applications install more quickly, adapt to change more easily, and operate more economically." It was a nice story, but it wasn't really true.

The theory of Oracle's best-of-breed strategy to take on SAP was elegant and convincing, but the execution turned out to be almost the exact opposite, partly through the absurd commitments that Oracle was prepared to make to win business, partly because what it was trying to do was extremely difficult, if not actually impossible. Systems integration is difficult enough at the best of times, and SAP implementations became a byword for the time, money, and agony that companies would have to go through to come out with a functioning ERP system at the other end. Many of those that bought into the hype over ERP in the 1990s are still trying to figure out the return on their investment, while a good number would rather not even ask the question.

Although Oracle's applications were designed to be more flexible than SAP's, much of the flexibility was lost by trying to integrate with the applications of other vendors. But the real problem was Oracle's ambition. In most cases, best of breed can be made to work with lots of customization. But even though the same group of vendors' applications may be used in combination on many different occasions, each customer ends up with a computer system that is essentially unique to itself.

What Lane, Shaw, and another ex-Booz consultant named Charlie Schneider set out to do through their integration methodology was to make the whole process repeatable. While Oracle might not make much money on a contract like the one with Kellogg, out of it would come a preintegrated suite that could be sold profitably to other CPG companies at a competitive price. In other words, repeatability equaled leverage. That way Oracle could convince itself—and, more important, Lane could convince Ellison—that it was still a software firm and not just a distributor/integrator.

Ellison remembers, "They had all these wonderful names for the new integration technologies that they were developing: the message backbone, integration glue, and all this other stuff. I tried to get a detailed technical explanation as to how it all worked, but nobody was able to explain it to me. I just couldn't understand what they were saying. One of two possibilities here: I'm too stupid to understand, or they don't understand it either. Even though they couldn't describe how this stuff worked, they just knew it would solve all their product integration problems. Charlie Schneider is a capable guy, but he had never developed software before. I don't think he ever understood the unbelievable difficulty of building this magical integration technology. Just because they wanted it and needed it, they believed they could build it. It was like, wouldn't it be nice to have flying cars? All we have to do is interface the wings to this Oldsmobile and it will be phenomenal. We just need really good glue. Brilliant."

One of the things that made it so difficult was having to use the proprietary tools of each application partner. Another was getting all the pieces to run on the Oracle database platform. Sohaib Abbasi says, "There were components that had never been built for our database and had to be adapted for it. From a technology point of view, we could never get those applications to fit in with any of our products." But the killer was the upgrade cycles of the third-party vendors.

Ellison says, "IMI would finish a product in June, but Manugistics wouldn't have their new version done until November. The customers were allowed to say which products they wanted, which versions of which product and in what order they wanted them implemented. The customers had so much flexibility that there was no repeatability in the systems integration at all. Each implementation turned out to be unique. The Kellogg contract was a key deal Ray was able to snatch away from SAP at the last minute by making some astoundingly open-ended commitments. The Kellogg contract basically said, 'Oracle will make its applications software do whatever Kellogg needs to run its business, and make the IMI software and all our other partners' software do whatever Kellogg needs too.' Needless to say, Kellogg's software enhancement list was long and our losses were large on that one."

Interestingly, even Robert Shaw, the main evangelist of best-of-breed, doesn't fundamentally disagree with Ellison about the practical difficulties: "At the application layer . . . it rapidly became an engineering nightmare." Ray Lane, however, is unrepentant. He accepts that repeatability was a goal that was never reached and that Oracle went through a lot of pain, especially in CPG, but he doesn't see it as the failure that Ellison does today. "It was the right decision. The only alternative was to let it all go to SAP. Take CPG: we generated a lot of CPG clients, not without a lot of pain, but there are maybe thirty-five to fifty clients in CPG alone, who are still Oracle today, including Kellogg. It generated hundreds of millions of dollars of business."

Lane argues that one of the reasons for Ellison's jaundiced view of best of breed is that he still doesn't understand the applications business. "It's not true what Larry says about Kellogg. No, it wasn't the greatest contract ever, but I think we went into it with our eyes open. Larry's not an applications guy. With the database, Larry's used to building a product where he can ignore customers. We were building a suite of products, connecting them together and trying to figure out what Kellogg wants it to be at the same time. SAP had hundreds of these projects. Look at the stories of SAP trying to install their suite at Compaq or P&G—a billion dollars, two billion dollars. They lost incredible amounts of money doing this. They had the same problems as we had except that our job was a little tougher because of integrating third-party apps.* But this is something Larry is measuring relative to the database business, which we totally owned and in which you just sell the software and don't change it.

"In many ways," says Lane, "the whole CPG thing was wildly successful. Larry would probably say the problem was it was wildly successful—it sold to too many clients, and we didn't know how to do it. Well the truth is, if Ron Wohl wasn't in charge of applications we could have done it. It can be done. IBM does it today, others do it today.† Larry started off very enthusiastic about this stuff, and then halfway along he started turning on it because Ron would go to him and say, 'IMI needs us to design this thing and that's not in my budget, I need more money.' So these partners became irritants. Larry has always hated channel partners, and Ron was the only one who had his ear. Best of breed was very difficult, hard to do, but we were doing it because our own applications sucked. He doesn't acknowledge that."

Even with the benefit of hindsight, it is difficult to know exactly where the truth lies. The only question that really matters is whether, despite all its problems, Oracle was better off doing best-of-breed. Lane believes that Oracle still has customers that it would have lost forever without his strategy, while Ellison believes that the business was so unprofitable that it was a disaster. Ellison says, "We'd sell all this stuff from Manugistics and i2 and the others and package it up with services. I'd say, 'Ray, this

---

*LE writes: A little *tougher*? Nobody has found a rapid, low-cost way to integrate a lot of applications from different vendors. Not yet, anyway. But I have to give Ray credit. He didn't give up on the idea after he left Oracle. He immediately helped start up a couple of companies to solve the application integration problem, this time using Web services. So far these companies have been unsuccessful. It's a hard problem.

†LE writes: Nonsense. IBM does software product integration with a lot of labor for a lot of money. Low-cost software integration is still beyond the state of the art.

doesn't make any sense to me, we're not making any money.' And he'd say, 'Well, Larry, it's what customers want to buy.' But Ray, the fact that customers want to buy it is not very interesting if every time we sell it we lose money."

From a sales perspective, Jay Nussbaum says, "The real danger in doing these smart things was that they were forgetting their mission. Their mission was to sell the damned database and sell applications, sell software, not create solutions that were one of a kind. Compensation became ludicrous because you'd be paying two or three people—salespeople, applications people, solutions people—for doing the same thing. There was too much energy being spent without enough margin."

Not surprisingly, Robert Shaw doesn't think it was all bad. He says, "I see both Ray and Larry's point of view, and I was in the middle of having to make it work. There was failure at Kellogg, but there was success in other places. I think Larry was being crowded by Jeff Henley to make money from applications. He kept saying this was a black hole; how much was it going to cost us to maintain these applications based on the contracts we were signing? We were making a ton of money on the consulting side, were also dragging database, so overall it was probably a pretty profitable business. But I think what Larry figured out was that when he started handing out the assignments to the development managers to take responsibility for integrating the suites, he kept seeing failures."

Jeff Henley had initially accepted that some margin erosion was the price to be paid for "playing the game and keeping some momentum." However, "What turned out to be horrifying to all of us was that we underestimated what we were getting into. When everybody started wanting slightly different permutations of this or that best-of-breed combination, it became clear that supporting this stuff and migrating it was just horrific. We knew we weren't going to make a lot of money reselling software—that was okay—but when we discovered the real implications, how much it was really costing us, we were horrified."

An example of how it was possible to see the same thing very differently at Oracle was something set up by Lane called the Max Account to deal with the cost overruns of implementing buggy applications or creating interfaces with partner software that hadn't been delivered in time by development. Shaw says of his consultants, "We wanted relief in our budget because we were spending so much time building around the product to make it work in a customer site."

Shaw's argument was that it was unfair for either the consulting team or the customer to eat the additional cost. Consulting managers were paid on the profit margin of the engagement they were working on. The idea was to steer cost they felt was not their fault into the Max Account. Lane expected development to cooperate, putting its hands up if it had failed to produce something that had been promised. According to Ellison, a consequence of the Max Account was that the consulting group dramatically improved its profitability: "The company's profitability was deteriorating, but according to our accounting reports each of Ray's groups was controlling expenses fabulously well. I didn't understand how this could be possible. But I found out. Ray had a system where his managers could spend money and not be charged for it. For example, when Ray wanted to encourage training he told his managers they didn't have to pay for the cost of training their people. Suddenly every sales meeting became a 'training' meeting. There were lots of ways to get expense relief. It was like the goddamn tax code. It created financial incentives for people to do what you wanted them to do. Unfortunately, like the tax code it was loaded with perverse incentives and people learned how to game the system and increase their profit bonuses." *

Another side effect of the Max Account was that it increased the already dangerous amount of finger-pointing. Ellison says, "The idea of people not having to pay for things that aren't their fault sounds fine. But it meant we had to set an adjudication process to determine fault. 'Oh yes, I've spent the money, but it wasn't my fault.' How much was your fault? Are you just pretending it's not your fault? Was about seventy-three percent not your fault? The whole notion of finding, quantifying, and assigning fault within the company was perverse and poisonous."

Jeff Henley says, "Larry always felt like the Max Account was a dark hole. It's a difficult issue. Ray was right that if it was a product problem,

---

*LE writes: Ray's managers constantly lobbied him for expense relief, and over time he gave in to it. Once that happened, managers who wanted to increase their profit bonuses could do it one of two ways: cut real expenses or lobby Ray for more expense relief. Thus the company's profits went down while managers' profit bonuses went up. Oracle now has a very simple way to hold managers accountable for expenses: If a manager makes the decision to spend the money, then that manager pays for it out of his budget. If somebody else decides to buy something and you use it—like our global network, for example—you don't get charged back for it. I believe managers can be measured and held accountable only for expenses they control.

why should the poor consultants have to fix it for free? Ray wanted to expose the product problems to development. But Larry was right that if you give them an account to charge they'll go crazy charging everything they can get away with."

If the best-of-breed strategy had started coming apart at the seams, Wohl's other track, to deliver homegrown products with the features needed to catch up with SAP, wasn't doing much better. Early in 1997, Wohl finally managed to push Oracle's first full-fledged client/server suite out of the door; it was called Oracle 10.7 Smart Client (it sounded better than Fat Client) because all the program logic was located within the application on the client. It turned out to be something of a misnomer. Smart Client was both buggy and unstable.

The problem, according to Byron Miller, an analyst at Giga Information Group, was that the software absorbed too many resources of the desktop client, with the result that performance deteriorated and the ability to run the applications in a distributed, multisite environment suffered badly. In other words, 10.7 didn't scale and was likely to crash your PC. Oracle was not only late to client/server, it didn't seem to be very good at it.

Part of the reason for the inadequacies of 10.7 lay with the need to divert developers into the unending catalogue of problems thrown up by the effort to integrate the best-of-breed suites. But the larger reason was Ellison's growing conviction, following his September 1995 speech in Paris launching the idea of the network computer, that client/server was not the way to go. It was, as he put it, "an evolutionary dead end." Instead of defending 10.7 Smart Client's shortcomings to irate customers, Ellison agreed with them, condemning client/server as "an awkward, expensive, and slow technology." By bringing together the distributed complexity that was inherent to client/server with the attempt to achieve repeatability with a number of industry-specific, pre-engineered best-of-breed suites, Oracle, always with the best of intentions, had created a quagmire for itself. By 1997, the applications business was continuing its strong revenue growth and Oracle was a clear, albeit distant, second in the applications market. But nobody at Oracle thought that it had anything other than a continuing embarrassment on its hands.

Worse still, the rows over applications strategy were having an increasingly corrosive effect within the company. Even after the release of 10.7, which was by far Oracle's most complete suite to date, the sales and consulting organizations would frequently recommend that clients buy third-party software rather than the homegrown stuff. Ellison claims that the sales force was equally compensated whether it sold Oracle applications or a partner's products. Lane vehemently disputes this, saying that it got paid only on the royalty that the third-party vendor handed on to Oracle for making the sale—typically 30 to 50 percent.

However, despite the weakness of Oracle's applications—perhaps partly because of it—the consulting business was continuing to grow at a tremendous clip. By 1997, Oracle Services, which wrapped up consulting with support and education, accounted for half of all Oracle's revenues. It was a success of a sort, but many within the company were becoming increasingly concerned at its side effects. Jay Nussbaum says, "We were content to grow the revenue number even if the margin was playing between sixteen and eighteen percent. As long as revenue was growing, we fed the monster. But the reality was that nearly all the margin was coming from technology licensing. We may actually have been losing money while consulting was growing at forty percent. We were taking on projects we should never have done because of their sheer size. It was alienating all the other distribution partners, but Robert was a take-no-prisoners type of guy."

Lane's dissatisfaction with Ron Wohl was also becoming an obsession. He could not restrain his criticisms even when speaking to journalists and analysts. What made him even wilder was his frustration with Ellison. Although Ellison had given Lane control over nearly all of the company, development was still a no-go area. When Lane had proposed that Nimish Mehta take over from Wohl, Ellison ignored the idea. But he still seemed to have little interest in the nitty-gritty of applications, and from Lane's point of view he seemed perfectly willing to let the drift continue. While Lane and Shaw were dealing with constant complaints from the field and from their relationships with major customers—which were far closer than Ellison's—and learning how serious the shortcomings were, Ellison seemed fired up only when he was talking about Microsoft or how the network computer was going to take over the world.

By the late summer of 1997, database license growth had slumped to little better than flat while applications had hit a wall. Growth in the previous quarters, artificially pumped up by sales of third-party products, had been respectively 60 and 95 percent. But with the wheels starting to come off the best-of-breed implementations, applications managed only a feeble 7 percent, while SAP had turned in an impressive 62 percent. If Oracle lost its second-place spot in apps to either the Dutch company Baan or PeopleSoft, which were both breathing hard down its neck, the long-term damage would be immense.

The perception within Oracle, particularly among Lane's people, was that customers had heard about all the problems with 10.7 and were sitting on their hands. To make matters worse, Ellison, who had bought his first megayacht the previous winter, the 192-foot *October Rose*, from fellow billionaire Kirk Kerkorian, had decided to spend most of the summer cruising the Mediterranean. The idea of Ellison sunning himself on his $10 million new toy for months on end (he says that he was actually away for no more than five weeks) while the company once more seemed to be imploding did nothing for employees' morale.

Gary Bloom, a fast-rising young executive vice president who had been running both the platform group and the partner programs and was about to take on management of the database team, says, "Larry had simply carved out a subset of the CEO job that he wanted to do and really disengaged, so Ray was pretty much running the company. . . . He wasn't paying any attention to the engineering teams, the applications were getting further and further behind the competition. It was driving Ray wild."

Although Lane was quite happy to allow respectful journalists to take away the impression that he was now the guy in charge at Oracle, few within the company believed that he could solve its problems. Jeff Henley says, "I'll always remember calling Larry and telling him that the company was blowing up and he had to get off his frigging boat." When Ellison returned at the end of September, Bloom confronted Larry. "I said, you've got to decide whether you're going to re-engage and run the company as CEO or not. If not, I said, he'd have to go and hire one. Oh, and by the way, Ray's not it. Ray couldn't manage the technology groups by any means, and he was frankly creating a scenario that was not effective for the company. A bit earlier I had also talked to Ray about it and said, 'Your job is not to make Ron Wohl fail. You're the president, you're the guy everybody listens to right now because Larry's not here.' The real kind of negative turning point for me was when he went public, saying in front of huge audiences and Oracle staff that our applications are a disaster. That's when it became crystal clear that Ray couldn't be CEO because you can't have a leader that's out there trying to make other leaders fail. It just doesn't work."

Bloom had an offer to become CEO of another software company. If Ellison wasn't prepared to take the reins, he had decided to leave. "The job offer meant that I had a catalyst to get him interested in the topic. I told him that I wasn't looking to leave but that I couldn't work at a place where we were going to fail. I told him that Ray couldn't run the company and that in fact many of the areas that he was running were out of control. He's busy drawing attention to other people's problems when he's got a million of his own. I think he took it pretty seriously. He asked me to come back the next day to his house. When I arrived, Don Lucas was there as well, and Larry said, 'I want you to have a private discussion with Don and to tell him your views without me there.' "

At about this same time, Oracle was forced to issue its first earnings warning since the dark days of 1990. The moment markets opened on December 9, there was a rush to unload Oracle stock. Within hours, 30 percent of the company's market value had been wiped out.

Ellison soon faced what amounted to another ultimatum, this time from Lane himself. It was about the same issue as usual. Lane says, "The subject was about how Ron had to come out of his job. The thing that provoked us into having this specific meeting was that Barry Ariko, who was in charge of all American sales, and Robert Shaw had both threatened to resign. That's actually not how they put it to me. They came to me and said, 'Ray, sign up with us. The three of us will go to Larry and tell him that if he won't replace Ron we're all leaving.' I said that I understood why they were asking me to do that but that as president of the company I couldn't do that, I couldn't give an ultimatum to the CEO like that. But I would carry their message to Larry. . . .

"They were really suffering. They were saying that they were having to sell stuff that was subpar and that if we did sell it, it was the worst of all worlds because then we had to fix it and we had to try and deal with Ron, who would just ignore us. Randy Baker, who was running support, was living in sheer hell. . . . The bug counts on 10.7 were so high that it was an environment that was impossible to manage. This is the worst incrimination of Ron I can think of. At one time we had to stop development completely and put all of Ron's staff on crunching bugs."

The meeting between Lane and Ellison took place in January 1998. Lane said that the situation with Wohl had to come to an end or Shaw and Ariko would quit. "I said, 'There needs to be a Mr. Applications, somebody who can really go head to head with SAP.' I wanted Larry to throw Ron out and hire a professional. I said, 'You brought in me, you brought in Jeff Henley, why in hell can't you bring in somebody to run applications development?' " When, as usual, Ellison raised the objection that actually finding such a person might not be very easy, Lane said he even had a suggestion: Robert Shaw should become Mr. Applications. It wasn't clear who Shaw would report to. Lane said he could report to Ellison. Ellison had no doubt that Shaw would have continued to have

Lane as his boss. Shaw says, "I knew about the proposal, and I was willing to do the job. It made a tremendous amount of sense. I also knew that Larry would never agree to it . . . never, never."

Lane insists that he was interested only in finding a way out of the impasse over applications. This was not, however, the way Ellison saw it. He believed that Lane was using the threatened departure of Shaw and Ariko to grab still more power. What's more, in doing so, he had stepped over a critical line. Ellison had been willing to let Lane run just about everything else at Oracle, but development would always be his domain. Ellison says, "Ray asked me whether I thought he should run development. I said no, not really. I think he genuinely believed that he was better equipped to run development than I was. He felt the most serious problems in the company were in development. He had decided he couldn't solve them without me out of the way and without him running development." Jay Nussbaum puts it succinctly: "Ray had stepped into the sacred burial ground."

Ellison knew he could no longer placate or ignore Lane as he had in the past on the subject of Ron Wohl and applications. Jeff Henley says, "Things had changed with that last quarter. We'd set a record on Wall Street for the most amount of value lost in a single day, and the stock had gone on being pummeled into January. The board was pissed and Larry was embarrassed as hell by the way we'd fallen on our rear end. There were lots of things going wrong, like Ray's disastrous sales reorganization. But the real recurring issue was the product." However, Ellison was damned if he was either going to hand apps over to Shaw, whom he didn't consider to be technically qualified, or get rid of the loyal Wohl.

Ellison says, "Ray's solution was to put Robert Shaw in charge of everything. But Robert had never developed a software product in his life. Finally, out of extreme frustration and great fear of putting Robert in charge of development, I said, 'Okay, I'll be Mr. Applications. I'll do it. I can do it. I don't want to do it. I really don't want to do it.' Order management, tax tables, accounting—are you kidding me? I'm working on parallel server, man. I didn't want to go from computer science to accounting. I thought that understanding and automating all these business processes would be dull and duller. It just wasn't a book I wanted to read." *

As for Lane, he says, "I had no choice . . . I sent an e-mail out to the en-

---

*LE writes: After I got started, I found engineering our business processes (it wasn't reengineering because they had never been engineered in the first place) was just as interesting as engineering the database.

tire field saying Larry is taking over applications as head of development. I showed it to Larry before it went out. He did a few edits to protect Ron. But it was very direct." What Lane didn't realize was the speed at which he was losing Ellison's confidence and support. It wasn't long before Ellison was able to convince himself that after the thwarting of his power play to replace Wohl with Robert Shaw, Lane was now hoping that, having taken responsibility for applications, Ellison himself would fail.

Jeff Henley thinks that Ellison may well have felt threatened, but he has no time for the idea that Lane was trying to take Larry's job. George Roberts, who succeeded Barry Ariko as head of U.S. sales, is convinced that Lane never wanted Oracle to be anything other than successful and, while he might have sounded off against Ellison at times of great frustration, never thought he could replace him. Jay Nussbaum, no ally of Lane, says, "Let me make something perfectly clear. At this point, Ray had such a huge financial upside that if Larry failed, Ray also failed. There was no rooting for Larry's failure. None whatsoever." Gary Bloom, who was shocked by what he saw as Lane's undermining of Wohl in public, agrees: "I don't think Ray wanted Larry to fail. I would not put that burden on him. I think they had different views on how to fix applications and how to make it better."

The truth, I think, is that Lane was determined to make Ellison take his responsibilities for fixing applications seriously and that the best way of achieving that was to put his boss under as much public pressure to deliver as possible. When I put the question to Lane, he looked shocked and sad. "I'm going to give you a very strange response to this. Had Larry read the situation right and had he worked on the real problem, . . . then maybe we'd still have a relationship and there's no question Oracle was much better off with both Larry and me there as a team. He totally misread it. I was tired of not being competitive. I was tired of Ron producing sucky applications that we couldn't sell, and I desperately needed somebody to replace him. When Larry said, 'How about me?' I totally supported that. I went out and sold that strategy to everybody. I said, 'Larry's going to do it,' and three months later he comes up with a strategy. At first I doubted he would spend the time, but he did. I didn't want to run applications. It wasn't a power play at all."

In which case, why did Ellison, who so recently had seemed to think that Lane was close to being the perfectly complementary number two, someone he was prepared to give virtually equal billing in what was now the world's second biggest software company, turn so dramatically against his deputy?

8

FALLING OUT

On June 30, 2000, Ray Lane was enjoying the last day of a family vacation when a call came through from Larry Ellison. Lane remembers, "Larry says that he didn't know I was on vacation and that he's sorry about calling me and telling me this, but he wants to take the president's title back. I said, 'Really? Why?' He said, 'What we're doing here at Oracle, the reengineering of the company, is so important that authority has to be driven from my office. The whole company needs to understand that there is one single centralized point of authority, and it will be with the CEO.' I said, 'Well, Larry, I have never really opposed that. I'm on your team.' He said, 'It's kind of like kids playing off Mom against Dad. If they get a no from Mom, they go to Dad.' He was very uncomfortable because I was asking direct questions. I said, 'Larry, let's just step back. What went wrong? Everybody in the industry would look at this team and say that this is the reason I want to do business with Oracle. You on the technology and the vision; me on the business. What went wrong?' He said, 'I don't know. It's like a marriage that went bad. I don't know.' "

Characteristically, Ellison did what he could to avoid an embarrassing confrontation. The main reason he gave to Lane for wanting him to leave was his concern about how divided the company had become with two leaders. Ellison says, "I explained that . . . there was too much ambiguity of authority at a time when we were trying to reinvent ourselves and restructure the company to make it more centralized, more automated, more of an e-business. It's very difficult to make changes when a lot of the existing managers didn't believe in the changes I wanted to make. Most of our senior people liked being autonomous general managers. They wanted to be given a budget and left alone to run the business as they saw fit."

Lane insists that Ellison didn't have the stomach to sack him. "Larry was incapable of firing me. I said, 'I guess I have got to leave if you've taken back the president's title.' He said, 'Well, that's your choice.' I now wish I'd said, 'Okay, you've got the title. What do I call myself now?' He couldn't fire me. He doesn't know how to do it." * The two men then briefly discussed a press release, and Lane suggested that they should talk about the terms of his departure. He had $70 million worth of options due to vest in three weeks, and he proposed a termination agreement "so that I say good things about Oracle and we both have the same story about why I left—Larry said, of course, 'Let me look into it and I'll call you back.' He never called back."

The terse press release that Oracle released that evening offered no explanation for Lane's sudden departure. Attempts had been made by the PR department to dress it up with a tribute from Ellison to Lane's years of service. But Ellison admits that in the end, he couldn't bring himself to say what he didn't feel; Lane had already been more than adequately rewarded for his time at Oracle. Lane says, "The press release was in the papers the next day. My mother, my sister, my friends were all with me in Oregon, and they got the paper the next day. What's this? So I had to explain it to the family. It was totally below the belt."

Nor was there any termination agreement. Lane claims that the board tried to put together something that was "fair"; a payoff of $13 million was suggested. Ellison rejected it, offering instead $1 million in cash. Ellison says, "I can't understand why a receptionist who gets laid off gets two weeks' salary and has to worry about paying the rent, when some rich senior manager who made millions gets additional millions when they get laid off."

Lane refused to sign the deal. He really didn't need the money anyway. In subsequent interviews, his version of events was that he had resigned over changes within the company that Ellison was proposing to make and with which he disagreed. For his part, Ellison insisted that Lane was leaving because, as a result of the way Oracle had recently centralized its

---

*LE writes: Very interesting but not true. During our conversation Ray asked me if I wanted him to leave the company, and I said yes. Later on he sent me an e-mail stating, "Now I know why you started behaving the way you did and ended up firing your most loyal employee."

operations around the Internet, he no longer had a big enough job to do. Only later, when he could no longer control the urge to trash his former business partner, did he admit that he had fired Lane.*

What happened was that the man who many people outside Oracle believed to have been responsible for the firm's reinvention and much of its success in the 1990s had been slowly frozen out and systematically stripped of authority. When Ellison said that he had no need to replace Lane, it was because there really wasn't much left of Lane's job by the time he left.

Within three years of his arrival at Oracle, Lane's reputation in the industry was so high that he was soon receiving a stream of job offers. With most, he never went further than the first step. However, there were a few that Lane was willing to explore further. One came from John Doerr, a senior partner at Silicon Valley's most exclusive venture capital firm, Kleiner, Perkins, Caufield & Byers, and Jim Clark, the former boss of Silicon Graphics and the founder of Netscape, the software firm that triggered the mania for investing in Internet with its pioneering Web browser. Doerr and Clark wanted Lane to come and run their latest big idea, a company called Healthscape (later Healtheon and later still WebMD) that was going to bring the Internet to medical practice. After taking a close look at what was involved, Lane said no. "I didn't see myself as a start-up guy."

Much later, Lane would be on the short list of candidates to become CEO of Hewlett-Packard, the stately computer hardware company that launched the Silicon Valley phenomenon in the 1930s. But the job he came closest to taking was with the once high flying networking firm Novell. At first he wasn't interested. Novell, once the leader in network operating system software, was being badly beaten up by the onward march of Microsoft's Windows NT, while its GroupWise collaboration software was being squeezed on both sides by Lotus Notes and Microsoft Exchange. Novell still had plenty of cash, but what it lacked was any kind of strategy to get it out of its hole.

---

*LE writes: It had nothing to do with an uncontrollable urge to trash Ray. I avoided talking about this subject for as long as I could. But everyone was so interested. There were numerous "Why Ray left Oracle" articles in the press. I was asked about it repeatedly. On a few occasions and only privately did I tell people that I had asked Ray to leave. I had to get permission from the board before I could ask Ray to leave. I did that. And then I asked him to leave.

What changed his mind was an unannounced visit by David Burn, one of the toughest and most persuasive headhunters in the business, and John Young, who was not only a Novell board member but a highly respected former chairman of Hewlett-Packard. "They came into my living room and put this offer in front of me that included $15 million of cash that would be put straight into my bank account and $4.5 million in options at the current price, which was an all-time low for Novell. And I'm just going 'holy mackerel' and said, 'Give me an hour and I'll just write down some thoughts about a strategy for a turnaround, because that will help tell me whether it's possible.' So I wrote four pages that I shared with them and said, 'Here's what I'd do,' and they said, 'That's why we want you—you've just written a strategy on the back of an envelope. . . .'

"I was nervous. I was an Oracle devotee, there for life, and I was very, very nervous about this. But I was saying, CEO, turnaround, lots of money, and I agreed that I'd go and see Larry and tell him I was resigning. So I went to see Larry that afternoon in his house and I said, 'I've got an offer from Novell.' He said, 'Novell!'—just like that. Novell, that brain-dead company. I said, 'Larry, look at it my way, it's a turnaround opportunity and they're going to pay me all this money.' He said, 'You're not going. Their server isn't programmable. You have no APIs to build applications. It's dead meat, and Microsoft will take them out.'

"So he basically had scared me out of taking the job anyway, but then he said, 'How about two million options, would you stay for two million options?' I said, 'Yes, it's more than adequate—I'm not doing this because I think Novell's great, it's for the money.' I went to Young and Burn, and said, 'Sorry guys, I'm staying at Oracle.' That night I went to the fiftieth birthday party of Robert Shaw's wife and Larry called me on my cell phone. He said he'd talked to the board and he thought $2.5 million in options was the right number. You deserve it. I thought he'd gone way overboard, so of course I stayed. I didn't find out until I left Oracle that the board was pissed off about this. No one ever told me, and I certainly wasn't holding Oracle up for money." *

Ellison's recollection of what happened is a little different. He says that the figure of 2 million was Lane's price for staying at Oracle and that the main reason he increased the number to 2.5 million was that, per-

---

*LE writes: Not a holdup? He said he was going to Novell because of the money. I offered him more money to stay. It was a classic holdup. He stayed.

versely, by volunteering additional options he felt a little more in control of the situation, a little less responding to blackmail. He also wanted to ensure that Lane really would give Novell the brush-off. That said, the most convincing explanation for Ellison's excessive generosity to Lane is that he panicked.

His first reaction was sheer amazement that Lane actually thought that he might be able to fix Novell. "I said, Ray, Novell doesn't have a service problem, and it doesn't have a sales problem—they distribute through third parties. Those are the things you're best at. What Novell has is a very serious product problem. I don't know what I'd do if I went to Novell. I think it's too late." However, his second reaction was fear that despite his demolition job on Novell's prospects (correct, as it turned out: even Eric Schmidt, a first-class technologist, proved unable to save Novell) Lane might still go through with his resignation. "At this point in Ray's career, he thought he could do just about anything—even turn around Novell, which I thought was impossible. But I couldn't afford for him to take the Novell job. I felt terribly vulnerable because he was running such a large portion of the company. With the problems we were having in applications development, which was where I thought I should focus my time, I didn't have the bandwidth to take on anything more. Besides, I really didn't know how marketing ran or how sales ran. I just didn't feel I had the time or competence to take over those things if he left . . . so I paid him off."

Ellison was right. Oracle would have been in a jam if Lane had suddenly quit in early 1997. But there was a substantial price to be paid by both men for Ellison's bribery. If Lane was getting inflated ideas of his talents thanks to the flattering press coverage that Ellison was happy for him to receive, learning that Ellison thought him so important to Oracle that he was willing to make him fabulously wealthy was bound to puff his ego up still further.

Don Lucas says he warned Larry about the possible effects. "I'll never forget it. I very, very seldom have disagreed with Larry. . . . This was a huge stock option, like a bribe as opposed to an incentive. That's going to twist people's minds. It has all these bad effects. Ray says to himself, 'I'm worth all this money, I'm irreplaceable, I've got a lot of power, I'm like Superman.' So it reinforces all the bad things. If we'd given him regular incentives and if Ray would have stayed, I think that would have been better for everybody. If he wanted to be loyal to the company and get compensation, reasonable compensation, he stays. If he wants to go be a big shot, be a CEO, have all that power, that's fine, leave. It would have been better for everybody. So I think that was a critical juncture. I'm not saying I was right and Larry was wrong,* but I think you have to stand by your principles and I think to overcompensate can have deleterious effects."

From his perspective as a senior member of Lane's team, Jay Nussbaum was convinced that something had changed. "The Novell thing pissed off everybody at Oracle. Ray would always argue about loyalty, trust, and integrity. But everyone saw what he did. He put on a mask and took a gun to Larry's head. . . . It gave a signal to the world that Ray didn't respect Larry and he thought he should be CEO, he had this blind ambition. It became obvious that there was no love affair. So much so that Larry starts to wonder what life would be like without Ray."

Even though Ellison used the threat of Lane's departure to get another 1.5 million options for himself and 1 million for Jeff Henley, he felt increasingly sick about what he'd done. I don't think he really blames Lane for what had happened, but he thought that he had in some sense been manipulated, and the feeling festered. Carolyn Balkenhol, who took over from Jenny Overstreet as Ellison's close assistant in 1995, has an interesting perspective: "I think the things that always upset him most are his own issues. I think that when he seems really angry it's because he's done something that he perceived to be a mistake, particularly when he's made a decision that he thinks has set in motion a series of events which didn't have the desired result. I think most often if he's really angry it's because . . . he did something that took a wrong turn."

Ellison began to realize that not for the first time, in his eagerness to carve out just the portion of the CEO's job that he enjoyed, he had delegated too much power and responsibility. It's a characteristic of Ellison that when he thinks he has found someone who is competent and who can help him, he invests an excessive amount of faith in his or her ability. Just as when Gary Kennedy said he needed more authority to get the job done, Ellison would give it to him without much thought, the same applied to Lane, albeit on a much grander scale. Ellison says, "I've been to this movie. I'm not going to let this happen again." At some point, in Ellison's eyes, Ray Lane stopped being the solution and started to become part of the problem.

---

*LE writes: I'll say it. Don was right and I was wrong. I should have let Ray go to Novell.

Within a year of Lane's receiving his option grant of January 20, 1997, Ellison had begun the process of peeling away his direct reports. Strongly influenced by Gary Bloom's critique of Lane's management and his plea that Ellison should assume more of the responsibilities that normally go with being a CEO, Ellison began to shift whole departments from Lane to Bloom. Among the first were marketing and education, but inevitably, the first battleground was applications. Ellison's realization that the commitments that Oracle was entering into with customers such as Kellogg and the never-ending litany of lengthy and money-losing implementations, especially those involving the CPG best-of-breed suite, had convinced him that development must regain control of product engineering.

By this time even Lane was prepared to admit that best-of-breed had proved a great deal harder and more costly to execute than he had initially realized, but tensions increased between him and Ellison over the broad strategic direction that the applications business should take. Although Ellison had put a stake in the ground in Paris two years earlier, to mark his profound disillusionment about the unmanageable complexity that was inherent to client/server, Oracle was only now near the point of releasing software designed for the Internet. Once Oracle became committed to engineering client/server software, it was inescapably locked into that architecture for years, even if theoretically a better alternative might have existed. Ellison's public statements about the coming of Internet computing were not just about attracting media coverage and tantalizing customers, they were also a deliberate tactic to open up the debate within Oracle.

Ellison says, "You can't tell engineers, 'Just do it.' You have to persuade them that the Internet is a better architecture than client/server. You have to persuade them the Internet is going to win in the marketplace—even though Microsoft is backing client/server all the way. They have to believe in what they are doing. If you simply bark out orders, you get malicious obedience—they'll build exactly what you want and make sure it doesn't work. I had to proselytize in every meeting. It took years before we killed off our last client/server product. It wasn't fun. I'd say, 'You know that thing you've been working on for the last year and a half? Throw it all away. We don't want it.' It pissed people off. They'd say, 'I've been working hard for a year and a half, and now you want me to throw it all away?' 'Yeah, I do.' 'Are you crazy? I quit.' It was very difficult to get all the developers inside Oracle to change direction. Everything they were reading said that Microsoft and client/server would go on forever. I got the same looks that Galileo got when he told people the earth revolved around the sun. 'Sure. Whatever you say, boss.' "

For the first year, most of Ellison's Internet evangelizing was confined to technology—the database and tools, the things that he knew and cared most about. But it began to dawn on him that the impact on Oracle's struggling applications might be even more profound. Ron Wohl took only a little convincing. He says, "In the applications business, you can never catch and pass someone who has dominant market share unless something else changes. If you do the same thing as a competitor who's ahead of you, you'll never catch up. That's the position we were in with SAP."

Ellison believed that Oracle was so far behind in client/server that the only way to win in applications was to change the game. There were two reasons why Oracle might be able to pull it off. The first was the increasing number of customers that were discovering the difficulty in making client/server systems work effectively over a wide-area network. Client/server might be all right for departmental use, but for any company that wanted to unify its operations over a number of different sites, it was a nightmare. After a decade of client/server as the dominant computing architecture, at least some disillusioned customers were ready to hear about alternatives. The second was that, quite simply, Oracle had much less to lose by betting everything on the Internet. If SAP had done the same and had failed to make the technology transition gracefully, it would have destroyed a wonderful business for no good reason; it's the dilemma of all incumbents and the reason why the short history of the software business is littered with the bones of once successful firms that failed to adapt to new paradigms in time.

It therefore made sense to Ellison to devote an increasing amount of development time to working out how to make a Web-based, servercentric version of 10.7, even if one of the consequences was to deny 10.7 Smart Client the resources needed to debug it properly before its release. Ron Wohl says, "From 1996 we started moving a small number of key technical people onto the underlying architecture, then a larger number of people, then gradually the whole division. We ran the risk that by pouring energy into the Internet version, we were not making the improvements we needed in the client/server version." For Ray Lane, it was just another example of Ellison and Wohl's failure to understand the applications business. As far as he was concerned, customers weren't interested in esoteric architectural issues: what they wanted was reasonably stable software that had all the functionality they needed to run their operations. The fact that 10.7 Smart Client was a couple of years late to market was bad enough; the fact that it still wasn't much good was intolerable.

What's striking is that there was so little consensus between the two men running Oracle as to what the applications strategy should be. If Ellison had worked hard to convince the development organization that Internet computing offered a better way than client/server, either he failed to let Lane in on the secret or Lane wasn't listening. The idea that there was a trade-off between getting 10.7 Smart Client right and Oracle being first to the Internet is not one that Lane has much time for. He claims that when the Internet version of 10.7, known as 10.7 NCA (network computing architecture), came out in early 1998, it wasn't any better than the client/server release that had been rolled out five months earlier. He says, "NCA wasn't what it was sold as. We said it was browser-based, but you had to have Java code running on the client or it wouldn't work." The only reasonably reliable variant of 10.7, Lane maintains, was the unglamorous character mode version that ran on green-screen dumb terminals and that few customers wanted. While Ellison was busy talking up the brave new world of Internet computing that Oracle was ushering in, one that would solve all the problems with applications, Lane says that customers were still having to live with a very different reality.

In fact, although flawed, 10.7 NCA was a considerable technical achievement, given the compromises that had to be made because of Java's immaturity. Lane's suggestion that running client-side Java code meant that it wasn't really Web-based is technologically naive. Even today, the E-Business Suite runs Java on the client for things such as expense reports. NCA was essentially a three-tiered architecture for delivering Web-based applications made up of an Oracle database engine running on a powerful UNIX server, a lightweight Java application on the client, and a midtier "forms server" to provide the gateway between the two. Among other things, users discovered that since the forms technology now ran on the server, patches to fix bugs could be delivered without having to relink and regenerate customizations. Most important of all, according to Mark Jarvis, who took over as head of marketing a month after the launch, the existence of 10.7 NCA meant that "everywhere Oracle's sale's force went, it was pushing the idea of the Internet as being about business, not just a consumery thing—we were educating customers long before the competition."

Where Lane has a point is that for any customers who had started with 10.7 SC, upgrading to NCA was a nightmare, whereas those with the character mode release found it relatively easy. Unfortunately, communication between development and the field was so poor that customers received little worthwhile advice about which version they should buy. As Ron Wohl admits, "Development must always move ahead of the sales and consulting organizations. It means that half the time they are implementing one product while we are already building the next one."

If shifting the emphasis away from client/server to the Internet was controversial within Oracle, the issue reached boiling point with Ellison's decision to halt all further work on client/server in early 1998. Having reluctantly become "Mr. Applications," Ellison threw himself into the task. One of the problems was that Oracle was now trying to support three different versions of its application suite. Ellison says, "We were the only vendor supporting three different modes of operation: terminal, client/server, and Internet. Life isn't hard enough—we had to have three fucking versions? The client/server version worked poorly on a wide-area network and was nearly impossible to maintain because the applications code was on hundreds or thousands of desktop PCs. Our so-called Smart Client version was not smart. It was unnecessarily complex, and I wanted to dump it."

Ellison was desperate to move ahead—"I decided to get out of the client/server applications business just as fast as possible." He wanted Release 11 to ship as soon as possible to expunge the memories of 10.7, and this time he wanted only one version. If Ellison had his way, 11.0 would be engineered for the Internet only. Ellison was certain that Oracle could not succeed if it had both an offensive and a defensive strategy. The analogy he used was taken from the Six-Day War, when the Israelis had been willing to bet everything on taking out the Egyptian and Syrian air forces on the ground even if it meant leaving their own airspace unprotected. Lane strongly disagreed. It wasn't that he was against Oracle's trying to get ahead of the field by embracing the Internet, but he was opposed to leaving in the lurch customers who had signed contracts for client/server software. His fear was that if Oracle was seen as dictating to the market a lot of customers would simply walk.

Ron Wohl comments, "The idea of moving to the Internet was a no-brainer. The hard decision was cutting off client/server and committing ourselves totally. That's why 10.7 NCA was so important. It would give us references. People had to believe that the Internet version of our applications worked. That allowed us then to go to the next stage and say, 'Guess what, this Internet technology not only works, but it's so superior to client/server that we're not even going to offer client/server.' We were saying that when Release 11 comes out five months after 10.7 NCA, it's one thing and one thing only: Internet."

Ellison is convinced that Lane mounted a serious challenge to his Internet-or-bust strategy. He says, "Ray didn't want to bet the farm on Internet applications. He thought it was risky to the point of being crazy. He thought that we should do client/server too. But I'd already decided that the Internet applications were our best shot at being successful, and we didn't have the resources to do both." In early 1998, soon after Ellison had taken charge of applications, he was briefing some consultants when he received a phone call from Ray Lane. Lane had called a meeting of his top 150 sales managers. He wanted Ellison to come down and answer some of their questions. Ellison remembers, "I got a call from Ray at about midday. He wanted me to come and listen to what the field had to say about giving up on client/server. And they wanted to tell me what customers were saying. When I got there I was treated to what seemed to me to be a carefully choreographed show. The message was clear: our customers wouldn't tolerate being forced away from client/server and pushed to the Internet. 'Can you guys just tell Larry that what he's doing is crazy and he's putting the entire company in danger.' I had heard it all before. Relational database will never be commercially viable. The customers want client/server. Blah blah blah. They were mistaking the present for the future. It's the worst mistake a tech company can make. Client/server was dead, and the people in the room would figure that out at the funeral. By then it would be too late for Oracle to change course. We had to change to Internet applications now—before SAP and the rest figured it out. But Ray was having none of it. I couldn't convince him or his people.

"This meeting came at a time when I was feeling a bit insecure in my position at Oracle, and if push came to shove, I wasn't sure whether the board would support Ray or me. Maybe it was paranoia on my part, but the meeting seemed like the beginning of a revolution with me playing the part of Louis XVI. At the very least, Ray was trying to split the company down the middle—his field guys versus my development guys. When that dawned on me, I realized I had to do everything I could to keep a split from happening. So I changed tacks. I carefully and patiently listened to all the field people's comments and said, 'You know, you guys are right. I promise we'll go on doing client/server if we need to.' But I knew we'd never, ever *need* to do a client/server version, and I never planned to build one. But I left the meeting letting them believe they had convinced me. They hadn't. I knew I was right and they were wrong."

Ellison concluded that Lane had attempted to set him up. "I think Ray was trying to do two things: He was trying to make sure that he got a client/server version of the applications. And he was making a power play for more control within Oracle. I was astonished that Ray wouldn't support my decision to kill client/server and put all our resources on Internet applications. He was fighting a technology decision that was the key to the company's future. This wasn't simply about our applications. This was about predicting the future of computing. We needed to move everything—our tools and our database as well as our applications—to the Internet as soon as possible. What was Ray thinking? First he wants to build industry-specific best-of-breed application suites; then he wants to run application development; now he wants to set the overall technical direction of the company. What the hell is going on? That's my job."

Lane's version of the episode is at odds with Ellison's. He says that the issue of moving away from client/server had not been that important. "It was the same old story that the applications didn't work and they weren't competitive and how Ron Wohl was a joke.* I had about three hours of trying to respond to this and telling them that Larry was in applications now. He is trying to fix these things, guys, give him some time. Finally, I said, 'You know, guys, you're talking to the wrong person. You need to talk to the head of engineering, and that's Larry.' So I called Larry and said, 'Come down here.' It wasn't a setup at all—how can you set up the CEO? I just wanted him to answer some questions and tell them he was working on it. That's all. I actually thought he did a great job of handling them."

"So this stuff about Internet was not even a debate. I have a feeling that Larry is trying to position himself as this Renaissance man who saw the light and saved everything. He doesn't have to. He did. That doesn't take away from the fact that our application business was a disaster. But by then Larry had come up with a strategy and everyone knew that it would take time before we had applications that did it. . . . A great strategy, Larry. We love it, we'll do it, but when we stick this stuff in our quotas, it

---

*LE writes: Ray calling Ron Wohl a "joke" is as unprofessional and unfair as it is factually inaccurate. The applications that Ron Wohl built run nearly fifteen thousand companies around the world, second in success only to SAP.

has to be something real. We have to ship a real product that works. Otherwise we don't get paid." *

As usual, the truth seems to lie somewhere in the middle. Ellison exaggerates the degree to which Lane was orchestrating a campaign against the strategy of getting to the Internet ahead of the competition. As a salesman, Lane was as keen as anyone to have a new story to tell. As Ellison himself frequently says, technology is a fashion business, and by 1998, the Internet was nothing if not fashionable. Lane's overriding concern was that the transition to Internet computing would not happen as quickly as Ellison hoped, leaving his sales force and consultants to carry on the struggle with a suite of client/server applications that had been effectively orphaned by the development organization. He was worried that without any prospect of Oracle's client/server software getting better, customers would desert in droves, unwilling to be guinea pigs for Oracle's first Web-based applications.

That said, Ellison was almost certainly right in thinking that Oracle couldn't afford the luxury or manage the complexity of developing radically different versions of all its application software. It's a measure of Lane's understanding of the technology that he either couldn't or wouldn't see that continuing with client/server would make it far less likely that the Internet strategy would succeed. Ellison's determination to cut off client/server entirely might have looked reckless, but in fact, it was the only option open to Oracle that gave it any chance of shaping a future in applications that would be better than its troubled past. By not only questioning that decision but making it clear to the field that he disagreed with it, Lane was straying perilously close to challenging Ellison's judgment on a major technology issue, something that even he would agree he was ill equipped to do.

He was also ensuring that Oracle would become an even more divided and factionalized company. His long crusade against Ron Wohl, whether justified or not, had become morally corrosive and commercially destructive. Furthermore, while Lane constantly demanded personal loyalty of a high order from the people who worked for him, increasingly he did not appear to think it necessary for them to extend that loyalty to Ellison or the people who built Oracle's products. There is little doubt that Lane believed that he was acting with the best of intentions, but his years of frustration over applications, the flattering media coverage that he had

---

*LE writes: That's why I wanted to put all our resources on one version—the Internet version. He still doesn't understand.

encouraged, and the boost to his already sizable ego from the Novell episode had eroded his judgment, certainly regarding his relationship with Ellison.

As had happened with Gary Kennedy and Jeff Walker, somebody who had once been bathed in the beneficent glow of Ellison's approval and admiration was about to experience the chill of his displeasure. Ellison says that the thing that disturbed him most was not so much the feeling that Lane was invading his territory but that he had lost touch with any realistic idea of his own capacity. "When Ray first came to Oracle, he spent most of his time with customers. He built the kind of personal relationships that he could rely on when it came time to close a big deal. That made him a fantastic salesman. But now, all of a sudden, he thinks he can come up with a technology strategy that would enable Novell to compete with Microsoft in PC server operating systems. Oh my God, fight with Microsoft in the PC operating system market! Not my first choice if I'm looking for a fight. So Ray's a technology strategist now. That's why he thought he could turn around Novell. That's why he fought with me over client/server versus the Internet. Ray decided that he's good at things I didn't think he was good at. Scary. Thinking you know things you don't know leads to a lot of mistakes. But I was also vulnerable to him leaving because I wasn't yet competent to take over from him all the things he did. First I had to move his departments to other managers. And that would take time."

I put it to Ellison that there was something ruthlessly calculating about leaving Lane in post while submitting him to a kind of corporate death by a thousand cuts. Ellison replied, "I had to start repairing things piece by piece and transferring responsibility from Ray's team to the 'shadow management team' without overwhelming it. I'm not confrontational, but I am pretty calculating. This was carefully calculated."

Ironically, by pushing Ellison into deciding that he had no choice other than to take over applications, Lane had triggered the process by which his own authority would unravel. Having removed all application development from Lane's part of the company and put Ron Wohl in charge of sorting out the mess that had been created by best-of-breed and the industry vertical suites, Ellison stripped two other functions from Lane: first marketing and then education. Marketing was run by a bright, attractive, but somewhat controversial woman named Karen White who was something of a Lane protégée. Ellison says, "I had hired Karen into the company a while back. I always felt that she was exceptionally bright and one of the most determined people I had ever met. But I also felt that she was miscast in marketing, and I suspect that she felt the same." White was pushed sideways, and Mark Jarvis, a personable Englishman with a background in engineering, was put in charge and reported not to Lane but to Gary Bloom.*

The next to go, in May 1999, was education. For most big software companies, educational programs fulfill two important functions. The first is to spread expertise to IT professionals about the use of a company's products. The second is to make money: companies and individuals are prepared to pay substantial amounts to gain useful and highly marketable skills. However, as Ellison discovered during budget review in March 1999—the first he had been fully involved in for years—Oracle's education business was becoming less and less profitable.

The executive responsible for running education was Randy Baker. Lane hired Baker from Tandem Computers to run Oracle's product support organization. Later Baker was given the additional responsibility of running education. Ellison says, "Randy proposed an education budget for the following year where margins were planned to drop from seventeen percent to thirteen percent. I thought margins should go up—not down. In fact, I thought margin should be much higher—at least thirty and as much as fifty percent. Nobody could give me a satisfactory explanation why our education margins were so low, so I moved the education business away from Ray and Randy and to Gary Bloom and John Hall." †
Within a year, Baker had left and support was also reporting to Bloom.

Lane professes that he wasn't worried about losing either marketing or education: "I really didn't care. I wasn't interested in keeping marketing; marketing was the most hated function at Oracle. With education, I

---

*LE writes: When Ray was running marketing, they produced our one and only Super Bowl ad. The ad was a series of scenes from a Vietnam-like war. The fighting stopped when the camera focused on a red wooden chair called "the seat of knowledge." The red wooden chair was supposed to become our new corporate symbol. I didn't like the chair, but the war scenes were amazing—bombs, flames, even a running elephant. But I'm not sure it was worth a million dollars.

†LE writes: It turns out our education business taught several hundred different courses, but ten of them brought in 90 percent of the revenue. It was an easy business to fix. After we got rid of the unprofitable courses, education margins increased continuously until they reached 50 percent a couple of years ago. They have recently fallen back to between 30 percent and 40 percent because of the ongoing tech slowdown.

guess it probably was the first signal that Larry was either doing something for Gary or taking something from me. But I didn't mind all that much; it was a small business that wasn't important to me."

Even now, Lane seems to have only a relatively hazy idea about what was actually going on. Ellison's immersion in the applications business and his determination to reduce his dependence on Lane had a number of consequences. Most obviously, Ellison was carefully and deliberately building up Gary Bloom at Lane's expense. Ellison wanted people both inside and outside Oracle to see Bloom as a manager who had been given "tremendous stature." Bloom says, "I became the guy who got all the broken stuff and went and fixed it. But I was also building up a following based simply on respect for delivery." What Lane didn't realize was that Bloom, whom he had generously praised and encouraged during his rise up the hierarchy, was an enemy, contemptuous of his competence and eager to bring back to Ellison any information that would cast Lane in a bad light.

Wherever Ellison looked, he seemed to find glaring examples of inefficiency, wastefulness, and intellectual sloppiness. A prime example was something called the Energy Center of Excellence. This was intended as a place to showcase Oracle's best-of-breed suite for the energy industry. In the course of the 1999 budget sessions, Ellison says that he uncovered plans to spend millions of dollars to run the center. "I asked how much energy upstream and downstream software we were planning to sell next year. The answer was about $10 million. So I said, 'Does it bother anybody here that we are forecasting sales of $10 million and we're spending $5 million to run an Energy Center of Excellence? Does that strike anyone as strange?' What struck me as strange was the fact that Ray had approved all of this.* I asked Ray to explain why we were spending so much money on the Energy Center of Excellence. He says, 'Larry, that's not what you're paying me for [managing the Energy Center of Excellence]. You pay me to bring in big deals.' I guess that's true. But while he was out selling, somebody needed to look at our sales costs and say no to things like a multimillion-dollar Energy Center of Excellence. But nobody was."

In part because of the work he had been doing in applications, Ellison was beginning to realize how chaotic many of Oracle's own processes

---

*LE writes: I am not certain that Ray personally approved Energy Center of Excellence expenditure. Ray had a policy of delegating even very large expenditures to his staff.

were. At the same time, he was discovering that in many of the areas that Lane was responsible for, getting hold of the basic information required for the budgeting process was disturbingly difficult. "The most basic budget-planning module we have in applications asks a few basic questions: How much did you sell last year? How much are you going to sell this year? How much did you spend last year? and How much are you going to spend this year? Simple, right? Wrong. It took many hours and multiple meetings to pry answers to these four basic questions from some of Ray's senior managers. One of Ray's people, George Kadifa [now CEO of the leading application service provider (ASP), Corio], came in with two hundred slides. I'd said, 'George, I've got four questions. Once you've answered these four questions, I'll look at however many slides you want me to.' He was quite offended. He thought it was very important for me to look at his slides *first* because they explained and justified why he would sell less [than last year] while spending more [than last year]. After a while I realized these weren't really planning sessions at all. They were compensation negotiations disguised as budgeting and planning. Everyone wanted me to approve as low a profit target for their group as possible so they could easily exceed it and get a big bonus. I learned that a key to making money in sales at Oracle was negotiating a low profit target or quota. I decided to fix that problem."

Ellison was determined to get involved in another area that had been entirely Lane's responsibility: the design of sales force compensation. Patronage is power, and, after hire and fire, there is no greater power within a company than setting the remuneration of the sales staff. By deciding that he, rather than Lane, would in future determine how the sales force was paid, Ellison was signaling in the clearest possible way that Lane's power was in terminal decline.

In any sales-driven organization, the way in which the "comp plan" is structured is a vital ingredient in determining success or failure. The objective of a good comp plan is simply stated: it should be transparent and fair and encourage the achievement of carefully worked out "stretch" targets; the salespeople who do most for the bottom line should be able to get rich themselves, while those who are hoping for a free ride should be penalized and cleared out. In other words, the best comp plans are simple to understand and work with the grain of human nature. When comp plans start delivering the opposite of what's intended, it's usually because they have become too clever by half. That was precisely what Ellison thought had happened at Oracle.

Jay Nussbaum recalls, "The 1999 budgeting sessions were a real watershed. I was telling Larry about how there was so much fucking abuse and waste in the system. And Larry's saying, 'Tell me more, tell me more, tell me more.' So I called Ray and told him that Larry was asking me a lot about compensation and do you want me to brief you about it. So I started to tell him, and he said, 'You have no fucking right to talk to him about that.' I said, 'What am I to do? He's the CEO. If he calls me and says, "Talk me through this compensation," am I supposed to tell him I'm under instruction from you not to talk to him? Let me help you and then you can tell him.' And from that moment, it was like we were on different sides of the world."

Ellison says, "Ray would experiment with different compensation ideas and sales force organizations every year. One of the worst ideas I can remember was when Ray decided we didn't do enough selling through partners. The sales force convinced him that the way to fix this was to pay more money to the sales force if the deal went through a partner than if the deal came directly to Oracle. For example, if you sold a million-dollar deal directly, Oracle would get a million dollars and you would get a $100,000 commission. But if you sold a million-dollar deal through a partner, Oracle would get $600,000 and you would get a $120,000 commission. Needless to say, our sales force pushed as many deals as they could through partners that year, so the partners were happy. The sales force got higher commission payments for going through partners, so they were happy. The only loser was Oracle Corporation. We ended up paying huge partner bonuses and larger sales commissions, so our sales margins went down. The only possible justification for this extra pay for partner deals was if the partners started bringing in large numbers of deals on their own. But they didn't.

"Our sales managers converted Ray to the fundamental belief that the best way to change the behavior of our sales force was to pay for it. So when Ray wanted to encourage better cooperation among our different sales groups, he decided to pay multiple groups on the same deal. We had industry sales teams, product sales teams, geographic sales teams, global sales managers, etc. All could get paid on the same deal. They wouldn't split a commission—no, no, no—instead we'd pay double commissions, triple commissions, and so on. But Ray told me not to worry because we could afford to pay everybody on the same deal so long as we raised everybody's quota. I said, 'Ray, paying people for things they don't sell is not a good idea. Raising quotas is not a good idea.' So one of the very first things I did when I took over the sales comp plans was eliminate most double compensation on deals. It allowed us to bring quotas down dramatically. And it smoked out the people who were making a living getting paid on other people's deals. But something else happened when I took control of the comp plans. When Ray lost the power to pay the sales-people, he lost most of his influence in the organizations that still reported to him."

The final nail in Lane's coffin was the unheralded arrival in April 1999 of Safra Catz, a former investment banker from Donaldson, Lufkin and Jenrette (acquired in 2000 by Credit Suisse First Boston) who had covered the software industry since 1986, the year Oracle had gone public, and who had become a close friend and admirer of Ellison. Catz, a petite, black-haired Israeli American, had come to take Ron Wohl's old job as Ellison's chief of staff. Ellison had been keen to hire her for some time but had initially thought she might run one of the companies he had recently bought in Israel. But Catz made it clear that if she was going to work for Ellison in any capacity, it would be at Oracle itself. Disillusioned by the investment hysteria over dot-com firms that had little or no proprietary technology, she was ready to quit banking. She suggested to Ellison that she could come and do corporate development—a role that was vacant following the departure of the able David Roux to run the interactive television company Liberate Technologies.

Catz had been an Oracle partisan for years: "I was already on the Or-acle bandwagon. I said that if Pets.com or Ariba trade at those kinds of numbers, then Oracle's worth a hundred or a thousand times that. This is kind of the center of the universe, right, not Wall Street. You want to be in the sun, this is the sun. I thought, you know, shame on me if I don't try this. And of course I thought Larry was great, awesome, with this ability to think without walls."

Catz didn't have any operational experience, but Ellison quickly realized that she had precisely the combination of qualities that he needed to help him run Oracle. As a lawyer, she had an almost forensic approach to digging out information, while her thirteen years as an investment banker had left her with finely honed analytical skills. She says, "I came in with absolutely no agenda other than to help Larry. That actually made my job incredibly easy. If Larry wants something done, now it happens because I'm going to check that it has. That was the thing that was really missing. Larry would make a decision, and nobody would check that it had been carried out. People would hope that because he had so many things to do, he would forget."

The first thing she did on her arrival was analyze previous years' budgets in the light of those submitted for the next financial year. She says, "It was clear we were spending a lot of money for no good reason, that there was an enormous amount of duplicative effort and overlapping objectives." Much of the inefficiency that Catz found, she laid at Lane's door. "We had any number of initiatives in place that when I got up the actual numbers it was obvious that they would lose us money. Ray would say, 'This is what the customer wants to buy. He wants lunch. You want to sell him lunch?' I was looking at this stuff and saying to Larry, 'Did you know this. As far as I can tell so far, I can find at least $100 million we've lost.' "

Ellison says, "Safra is a slave to facts. She is unwilling or at the very least extremely uncomfortable about making decisions without the facts. Not all managers are like that. Some managers rely on their 'gut' to help them with difficult decisions—especially if the facts are hard to find. The fundamental clash between Ray and Safra was that Safra dug out the correct facts while Ray relied on what people told him. In an argument when nobody has any facts—and I've seen a lot of those—the person with the strongest personality wins. But when one person has the facts and the other doesn't, the one with the facts always wins. When both people have the facts, there's no argument. Safra never tried to embarrass Ray in a meeting. He just kept saying 'This is true' or 'That is true,' and she would say, 'No, I don't think that's true and here's why.' It was painful to watch."

That, of course, is not how Lane sees it. "Safra just arrived. . . . I had no idea who she was, there was no introduction. . . . Safra and Gary started working together and appearing in every meeting. Larry would ask the questions: How much does it cost to do this or that? And she would go out and write in the headline first and then fill in the rest from Larry's perspective." All the while, Catz was going to Lane's people and pumping them for information about old contracts and sales practices that found its way quickly back to Ellison. Lane's first response was to try to ignore what was happening to his authority. "I just kind of said, 'Maybe if I just continue to do my job, this thing will pass.' "

However, that illusion didn't last very long. In February 2000, Lane received an e-mail from Catz informing him that Ellison wanted the European operation (under Pier Carlo Falotti) to report directly to the CEO.

Remarkably, for the first time, Lane decided to raise the issue of what was happening to their relationship: "I just confronted him direct. I said, 'I don't feel good about it. You have moved organizations to Gary. What's wrong?' He said, 'Nothing, nothing—you and I just have to spend more time together and get on the same page. The company is in a state of change now, we're reengineering business processes and all that. The CEO has to drive that. You and I are public figures, seen by a lot of employees, and we just have to be on the same page and spend time together.' I said, 'Okay, great.' I totally fell into the trap that everybody falls into when you have a meeting with Larry; no matter how depressed you are, you come out happy. It happens over and over again."

The next time they actually managed a one-to-one meeting was in Lane's office three months later, in May. The atmosphere could hardly have been much worse. Ellison had recently moved support from Randy Baker to Gary Bloom, and Lane had had "this awful meeting with Safra."

In her hunt for facts, Catz was occasionally finding Lane's people less than cooperative. Lane claims that when she thought she was being thwarted, she would threaten to have the individual responsible fired.* "After three or four people had come to me to complain about being threatened, I went to her and said, 'Safra, this has got to stop. This is no way to behave; I don't want you in my organization.' When I got done, she became totally woman. Tears. Emotional, she just blew up. She said, 'Why are you always criticizing me? Why can't you and I work together?' I said, 'I just came in here to tell you please don't threaten my people anymore.' She just came unglued, and I said, 'What is this based on? I don't know that we've actually spent two minutes together.' She said, 'I know what you are telling people around this organization about me.' I said, 'Guilty to a point. I have criticized you and the way you've worked here, but it's not something that can't be rectified.' We ended the whole thing by hugging each other and I said, 'If Larry would agree, why don't you work for both of us. Don't do the witch-hunts, but work for both of us.' I probably appeared to be the most naive person in the world to her. She was thinking, 'He doesn't understand what's going on.' I think she was clearly promoting the thought to Larry: you need to get rid of Ray, he's not good for you."

As for the subsequent meeting with Ellison, it took much the same course as the one in February. Lane says, "He gave me the same thing. We hadn't spent the time together, I was always traveling." Lane felt strongly that his absences from Redwood Shores were more than justified by the results they were producing. In November 1999, Oracle had announced

---

*LW writes: Absurd. I don't believe it.

a partnership with Ford to build an Internet-based business-to-business exchange that would link the carmaker to the many thousands of companies in its supply chain. Over the following months, a rival exchange planned by GM and the software firm Commerce One had been folded into the Ford/Oracle scheme and other car manufacturers, such as DaimlerChrysler, were also preparing to come on board.

Under the terms of the deal that Lane had negotiated, rather than simply selling software licenses, Oracle would be a minority partner and provide some of the operational management. Lane estimated that within a few years, Covisint, as it was later named, would handle transactions worth tens of billions of dollars a year, raking off a small commission for each one. The plan was to float Covisint as an independent entity. At a time when the name-your-price airline ticket exchange Priceline.com had a market value greater than the combined worth of the airlines whose seats it sold, the idea that Oracle would be a stakeholder in B2B (as they became known) exchanges across a range of industries had an electrifying effect on its stock price.

Lane says, "All that stuff was going on in the background at the same time that the Gary/Safra show was undermining me. I personally take credit for the run-up of Oracle stock that happened then.* As soon as the market realized that we were a real B2B player, our stock took the run-up that we'd always been waiting for—it went from forty dollars to eighty dollars overnight." Two months later Lane received the call from Ellison that would bring his relationship with Oracle to an end. Soon after that, Safra Catz renegotiated Oracle's position within the Covisint consortium to that of pure software supplier. She and Ellison had decided that as a risk-sharing partner within an increasingly unwieldy alliance of competitor companies and at a time when the initial euphoria about the prospects of B2B exchanges was fast deflating, there was a very good chance that Oracle would never see a penny from the deal that Lane had been so proud of.

What should be the final verdict on Ray Lane's eight years at Oracle? His outstanding achievements made Oracle a company that learned to

---

*LE writes: He takes personal credit for our stock price run-up? Amazing. Oracle rode the Internet wave because our database powered virtually every major Web site on the Net. If you plot the stock price of Cisco, Oracle, and Sun, you will see that all three companies rose and fell together in perfect synchronization as sentiment about the Internet rose and fell.

care about its customers and to preside over the creation of a large, powerful consulting organization. However, even in these areas the record is not unambiguous. While he did a good job cleaning up (though by no means clearing out) the cowboy U.S. sales force, his attempts to overhaul the culturally very different European operation added considerable cost without any obvious gains in effectiveness.

Perhaps the biggest myth about Lane, which he was happy to propagate, is that he was the disciplined, process-oriented manager who made the trains at Oracle run on time, in contrast to Ellison, the impulsive visionary. The truth is that until Ellison became interested in mastering the nuts and bolts of process, as a precondition to understanding how such things could be automated, neither of them was paying much attention to the things they should have been. Both were essentially doing what they liked best: Ellison kept Oracle at the leading/bleeding edge technologically; Lane worked corporate America and brought home "the big deals."

Many of the people I spoke to about Lane were highly critical of the negative way he has spoken about Oracle since leaving, including giving aid and succor to the enemy by appearing as a guest speaker at SAP's annual Sapphire Convention. It's undignified, they say, particularly when you consider the billion or so dollars Lane made during his time at Oracle. They have a point, but given the way Ellison treated him during his last two unhappy years and his subsequent trashing of a man whom he had once been prepared to entrust with running the greater part of the company, it's not really surprising.

What is more surprising is how little Lane seems to understand the reasons for the deterioration of his relationship with Ellison (a relationship which both men in conversation compared to a marriage, despite the fact that they were never close friends and had few shared interests). When I told Lane how Ellison had reacted to his threat to jump ship to Novell and then how he had interpreted as a kind of putsch the suggestion that Robert Shaw should take over application development and report to him, Lane seemed genuinely shocked. After one of our interviews he e-mailed Ellison thus:

Larry,
I think it's unfortunate you feel the need to continue to trash me with the press. It's irrelevant to me since your opinion of me is not relevant to my self esteem, but I assume you don't think I'm credible to criticize your abilities in leading development, the same way I don't think

you're qualified to criticize my abilities in sales. I guess we can both continue the war of words; the press loves it.

I almost picked up a telephone Saturday to have a conversation with you based on insight Matthew Symonds gave me about 1997. Now I know why you started behaving the way you did and ended up firing your most loyal employee. It's a shame you read it so wrong, but all that's irrelevant based on what you want to continue to tell the public, which causes me to do the same.

Seems a more typical divorce every day. . . . unfortunate.

Ray

Lane even asked me whether I would broker a meeting between him and Ellison. He suggested that I should act as a marriage guidance counselor, helping the two of them to understand what had gone wrong between them. I'm not sure that Lane was looking for a reconciliation with Ellison, but rather some kind of closure. Despite all the signals he got that he no longer had Ellison's professional respect and the fact that a full twelve months had passed since Ellison had fired him, his ego was unable to come to terms with what had happened. He also quite clearly wished he had handled Ellison differently. Lane told me, "I regret that I didn't work on a one-to-one relationship with Larry." *

I asked Ellison what he thought of the idea of meeting Lane with me. His response was that he might be more receptive if Lane weren't supporting an age discrimination lawsuit against Oracle that had been brought by Randy Baker. But even without that obstacle, I don't think it's something that Ellison would have wanted to do. Combined with his dislike of emotional confrontations, he really didn't see much point in seeing Lane again.

The last word on what passed between Lane and Ellison should go to the scrupulously fair Jeff Henley: "Larry got very excited about the idea of automating all of Oracle—this is big stuff, man, something I can get my teeth into, which was great. But it's a shame that Ray became the fall guy because I never saw Ray really try to make Larry look bad or work against him. Ray was critical of Larry at times, as I have been, perhaps more critical than me because he had to deal with all those damn cus-

---

*LE writes: In the beginning we actually did try to build a social relationship, but it didn't take hold. Ray's a serious duck hunter. I raise mallards every spring. We couldn't be more different in personality and pastimes.

tomers who were mad at us . . . but he was just trying to make sure the product got better—that was his whole goal. Ray's a good guy, and he did a lot for Oracle. But Larry was also absolutely right in getting involved and exposing a lot of nutty things. There were some areas like support and education that, to be honest, Ray didn't spend any time on. Ray was a little thin-skinned about that because the fact of the matter was that some of that stuff was really screwed up and I think Ray was embarrassed.

"And once Larry got so deep into Ray's pants, it was clear to everyone that this was not going to last, but it could and should have ended a little better than it did. Ray was actually willing to leave, but he just wanted to do it in his own way. . . . He was a trouper, a team player . . . for many years he and Larry were a real strong team. And then it turned. I believe it was Gary Bloom and some other people who undermined Ray to a large degree. But when Ray says he was surprised by what happened, that's just bullshit. He said to me that Larry never told him. I said, 'Ray, you've been here a long time, you know how Larry works, you're a smart guy.' He said, 'Yeah, but I just can't believe he'd do it to me.' "

9

THE LABORATORY

A couple of days after the announcement of Ray Lane's departure, I spoke to Larry Ellison for a piece I was writing about Oracle in *The Economist*. When explaining why Lane's job had diminished to the point of insignificance, Ellison said, "We're going to be an e-business. We're going to use computers to run everything. Okay. I understand computers. I should be good at this. So suddenly I'm competent to be CEO." How many successful CEOs, I reflected, who had built their company from scratch over more than two decades and at the age of fifty-six would declare themselves in an on-the-record interview to be "suddenly competent"?

Although Lane may not see it like this, the pressure he put on Ellison to do something about applications may have been his greatest service to the company; from that, a great deal else would follow. Just as Ellison, by his own admission, had "never really wanted to be a CEO, never really wanted to run a company," for similar reasons he had never had any real interest in applications. As he said, "I thought understanding business processes was dull and automating them even duller."

However, with his reputation on the line as the new Mr. Applications, there was nothing halfhearted about the way he threw himself into learning about the business. When Ellison talks about the experience, he does so with something approaching religious fervor: "It really was a crisis situation. I felt my job was at stake. The company would survive, but I might not. Anyway, it was about six months before Release 11.0 was due to come out and everyone was very concerned about fixing bugs and improving product quality, so I started having regular applications quality meetings. The meetings started about two o'clock in the afternoon and ran until to eight or nine o'clock in the evening. We quickly made progress fixing bugs, so I moved on to asking a lot of questions about what our applications actually did. I had no idea. I never used them. Wait a second, I'm the CEO. How come I've never used our applications? Can someone explain that to me, please? I never got a good answer, but I finally figured it out. Oracle, SAP, and the rest of the ERP vendors don't make applications for CEOs. CEOs just aren't important enough. ERP applications are built for clerks.*

"I'll never forget my early days in applications. This large aerospace company was doing an evaluation to decide whose applications they were going to buy. They had a huge amphitheater filled with clerks—mainly low-level purchasing people. And they were comparing our applications to PeopleSoft's applications based on keystrokes. Whoever needed fewer keystrokes to enter a purchase request had the best application. It was like a time-and-motion study from the 1930s. If we required twenty-six keystrokes and they required twenty-four keystrokes, they had the better application. I thought they were joking. The most important thing in purchasing is buying things for less. You've got to identify your low-quality suppliers so you can throw their ass out and move their volume to the good suppliers. Of course, before you give the good guys the additional volume you beat the crap out of them so you get a better price. Nobody in their right mind is going to spend a fortune putting in a brand-new purchasing system just so they can get rid of a few clerks. That's fucking nuts.

"Our purchasing system has to provide the purchasing people with the information they need to weed out low-quality suppliers—guys who deliver late, that kind of stuff—and negotiate the best possible price from the good suppliers. We do that, right? Oh, no. Nobody does that. We automate the process of entering purchasing requests, approving the purchase request, sending the purchase order to the supplier—the entire

---

*LE writes: The term "clerks" was an intentional exaggeration in a number of internal speeches at Oracle. I was trying to make the point that ERP systems delivered very little value to senior managers because they were process automation systems, not information systems. ERP systems were pretty good at automating a business process like issuing purchase orders, but they were terrible at providing information, such as telling you if this purchase order put you over your capital budget.

purchase-to-pay flow. The people who decide what software they want to use to automate the process are the people who will be using the systems. The clerks decide? What does the CEO think about this? I mean, how much you spend buying stuff is a big deal, you'd think the CEO or the CFO would be deep into this. I just can't believe they're going to spend all this money on a new purchasing process automation system without making sure that they were getting a great information system to go along with it. But they did. Because ERP vendors don't make information systems.

"So I had this radical idea: we type stuff into our applications; we should be able to get stuff out. I said it just like that. When we type stuff into our applications, it goes into our database. I know the data's in there. We should be able to get it out—in a useful form. I wanted all our process automation systems to come with tightly integrated information systems. It's so simple. What's wrong with you guys? It took a while to dawn on me just how hard the problem was. Companies have so many systems, they can't see the forest for the trees. Companies have lots of separate process automation systems, each with their own separate database. Simple example: Oracle had seventy separate HR systems, each with its own database. To find out how many people worked at Oracle, you had to look into seventy separate databases. If we had one HR database, we'd know. But we had seventy. Now, seventy HR systems cost a lot more than one HR system, so we were paying *extra* not to know. Why are we doing that? I felt like an idiot.

"But it was worse than that. Our HR systems kept track of all our employees. Our sales systems kept track of all our sales employees. Because the systems were separate, every salesperson had to be entered into both systems. When a salesperson moved from one group to another, both databases had to be updated. The duplicate data entry was expensive, but worse yet, it often wasn't done. The sales database might be kept up to date while the HR database wasn't. So we had conflicting and inconsistent data. If we had one database that kept track of our people, we would eliminate the duplicate data entry and the inconsistent data. With all these separate databases, we were paying extra for inconsistent data—paying extra not to know.

"We had hundreds of separate databases. You couldn't ask any questions because your information was so badly fragmented. Your purchasing information was over here. Your quality database was over there. So it wasn't easy to find out who your low-quality suppliers were. And all the problems seemed to have the same source: too many separate systems, too many separate databases. It really was a stunning discovery. All these separate process automation systems have to be integrated and sit on top of one database. Then and only then can we have a true information system. And we'll save a fortune by getting rid of all these separate systems."

Mark Barrenechea, a chubby, confident young programming manager who had come to Oracle in 1997 to build a CRM development team, remembers the moment when the truth about the applications business first hit Ellison. "He asked a very good business question. He said, 'How many employees at Oracle do we have?' Because, logically, as in all complex networks, everything is centralized. He just assumed HR data was centralized. So he asked how many employees there were at Oracle. Ron replied, 'Well, we'd have to put a data warehouse together. We'd have to go out and put a team together. We'd have to consolidate formats. Larry, in ninety days I'd give you an answer' and the guy went off the wall. He said, 'Why isn't all this data in one place? We have the Internet now, right. We can consolidate this into one global schema.' That was the spark."

Ellison continues, "Taking over applications at the same time we were moving our database and tools to an Internet architecture was serendipity. In a fairly short time the right application strategy became obvious. It was a horrifyingly big job; it wasn't going to be a short ride. But then neither was building real application clusters—game, set, and match in the database business. Building all our applications around a single database—building a single integrated global information system—that's game, set, and match in the applications business."

This was Ellison's epiphany. It was not just a question of suddenly understanding how Oracle needed to go about developing its applications to make them both better than and different from the competition's; it was also about how Oracle itself could become a different kind of organization and how Ellison could reinvent himself as a CEO. Ellison's other realization, as he became increasingly involved in applications development, was that in trying to consolidate systems and get business intelligence out of them, just as much effort would have to go into better processes. Ellison says it was like a yin-yang diagram that shows how one opposite produces another: "Better information allows you to improve your processes. The more complete your process, the better your information. It's a virtuous cycle." All of a sudden, the things that he had always assumed were intellectually beneath him became very interesting indeed.

Ellison shared his revelation with senior colleagues during a strategy meeting in March 1998 at the Hotel Nikko, a stone's throw from San Francisco's Union Square. Mark Jarvis, who became head of marketing a month later, remembers the occasion well. "We had the heads of sales for all the regions, the heads of consulting, Ray, Larry, the heads of development, and a few other people, including myself. The sales force started off by saying that in the database business we can beat anyone because we can differentiate ourselves, but in the apps business, whatever SAP says, we say. They didn't have features to sell that you couldn't get in SAP.

"So Larry stands up and says, 'You're all wrong. We lose because clerical administrators don't like our product. All these wonderful features you want are irrelevant because all they care about is the user interface and the number of keystrokes.' Larry's insight was to change the game by saying that instead of just talking about transactions we had to start talking about extracting business intelligence from our applications. Instead of talking about keystrokes to executives who never used the applications, we should start asking, Do you know this and do you know that about your business. The idea in marketing terms is to move up a ladder. If everybody else is on one rung of the ladder, you move to the rung above them with a different message. The next rung of the applications ladder for us was business intelligence, and we built a campaign around 'Do you know . . . ? ' Then, after six months, when SAP started talking about business intelligence too, we moved up the next rung and started hammering on the Internet. It was a very big turning point. Even before we had the products, it began to change our ability to compete with SAP."

Ellison's excitement was almost unbounded. In his own mind, he'd not only worked out how to make Oracle's perennially underperforming applications business into a winner, but simultaneously it had been revealed to him how Oracle could become a dramatically more efficient company and how the CEO's job, which he had spurned, would now be worth doing. Better still, what would make it all possible would be leveraging the Internet and the thing that Oracle understood better than any other software firm in the world, the relational database. Nor was there any question of having to put reengineering the company onto a back burner because of the need to sort out applications. One would lead directly to the other. Oracle would become a giant test bed for its own software developers.

And what better way to demonstrate the coming revolution than to make the much-maligned Ron Wohl responsible for putting Ellison's idea into action? Ellison says, "I decided to make Ron our CIO. I said, 'Ron, we're going to test our new applications inside Oracle. I'm going to turn our entire company into a laboratory. If the applications are any good, they should save us a lot of money, and for the first time I'll actually know and be able to control what's going on inside the company."

Although Ellison had been touting the benefits of centralizing data for a couple of years and had been canceling client/server development right and left since 1996 in favor of Internet-related projects, the operational reality at Oracle was very different from the marketing message. While a few high-tech companies were seen as e-business pioneers—Dell and Cisco Systems, for example, had already gone quite a long way toward using the Internet to put key business processes online, including their customer service, sales, and supply chains—Oracle was a pretty good example of the pernicious effects of client/server computing, especially as practiced by a fast-growing global company with plenty of money to spend. Although some of the applications that Oracle was using were by now Web-based and everybody who worked at Oracle was connected to the Internet and used e-mail, on its own that wasn't making a lot of difference. Information was scattered across more than a thousand databases in different parts of the world, and every functional organization within Oracle had its own computer system, replicated, naturally enough, in every major territory.

Ellison says, "We had hundreds of large server computers managing hundreds of separate databases. For example, every major country had six customer databases—one each for marketing, Web store, telesales, field sales, accounting, and services. So we had hundreds of customer databases. We had seventy human resources databases. We had ninety-seven e-mail databases. Data, data everywhere, and not a drop of information." Oracle had no fewer than forty-three full-fledged data centers around the world, each one stuffed with computer hardware and each with its own IT staff maintaining the multiple systems.

Gary Roberts, the executive Ellison would put in charge of sorting out its IT mess, recalls, "We were actually running in excess of 140 customized applications; in some cases, we'd bought third-party products to do some things that Oracle applications couldn't do. When I told Larry about the number of servers we had around the world—two thousand in Europe alone—he almost choked. And that was just counting servers that were four CPUs or more. Part of the reason was all those customized apps. You have to have test environments and staging environments and of course the production environment itself. Larry had one question that set us all back on our heels: 'We're the second largest applications company in the world. How come we have so many custom applications? And if I need these applications to run the business, why aren't they part of the product suite?' We looked at each other: Yeah, that's a damn good question."

One of the consequences of each bit of Oracle having its own computer system was that each one of them could make up its own mind about how it wanted to do business. Ellison says, "Every country invented its own business processes for marketing, sales, service, everything, and operated the way they deemed best. Everything was nonstandard." Both Ellison and Lane had supported the principle of having strong, highly autonomous general managers in each country. But the combination of a high degree of decentralization, global scale, and the functional silos formed by client/server resulted in a structure that was very nearly unmanageable and that encouraged "appalling" duplication of effort. Ellison says, "We, like most other large corporations, had a feudal structure. We were organized like medieval Europe. I was a weak king surrounded by a bunch of strong and fiercely independent dukes. I would sit in my capital in California and make policy decisions—which the dukes promptly ignored."

Ellison's favorite example of the way this system operated was the work of the supposedly powerful pricing committee. Chairing the committee, which sets prices for all of Oracle's software, used to be a pretty thankless task. "The pricing committee was 'responsible' for deciding how much we would charge for our products—our new application server for example. So we'd do some competitive analysis—what's IBM charging, what's BEA charging, what's Microsoft charging? How does our product compare? What are the market dynamics? After that we'd make a decision, say, $10,000 per processor.

"We'd then produce an updated price list and send it across the hall to our global sales headquarters. Unfortunately, our global sales team had their own pricing people who felt they weren't doing their jobs unless they did their own analysis and—for the good of the company, of course—corrected any pricing mistakes we might have made. They'd say, 'Larry's an engineer, what does he know about setting prices? We're salespeople, we know about pricing.' So they'd reset the price to $20,000 per processor and send out a pricing memo to our European headquarters in Geneva. Of course we had another pricing team in Geneva that redid the analysis and reset the price once more. They'd say, 'What do Americans know about selling software in Europe? We're Europeans, we live in Europe.' So a team in Geneva decides that the right price for Europe is \$15,000 per processor. They then send that price out to Paris, Munich, London. The same thing happens all over again. The guys in Germany ask, 'What do French people in Geneva know about selling software in Germany? The right price in Germany is \$25,000 per processor.' Every country had a different price. It was crazy.

"We had about two hundred people around the world involved in analyzing and reanalyzing, setting and resetting prices. It cost us a fortune in duplication of effort. It delayed the process and confused most of our customers—but not all of them. One day I get a call from one of our largest customers, located in the northeastern United States. He tells me, 'Larry, we've decided to buy all of our Oracle software from Oracle Brazil.' I said, 'But you're headquartered in Connecticut, Connecticut's not part of Brazil. Why are you doing that?' He said, 'They gave us the best price.' Shit. Everything is so duplicative and decentralized, the right hand doesn't know what the left hand is doing. We're competing against ourselves. This is embarrassing.

"I realized that there were two very important things we had to do, neither of them easy. First we had to move as quickly as possible toward the ideal of 'one company, one database.' Then we had to complete and integrate our applications suite. That meant building application modules we didn't have, like contract management and pricing quoting. If you have gaps in functionality, it's impossible to completely automate the flow of data through a business process. If there are manual processes left lurking around your process automation systems, it means you have big gaps in your information systems. Incomplete process automation causes cost problems, quality problems, and delays. Incomplete automation is almost as big a problem as data fragmentation.

"Take the flow of data between sales automation and order management. When the customer says he wants to buy one of our products, we send out a price quote and a contract. Creating a contract, quoting a price, sending out a contract, negotiating changes, and actually entering an order into the system were all labor-intensive manual processes. Process automation is just like a manufacturing assembly line. If you want to get the efficiencies of automated production, you have to keep the car on the assembly line and not keep pulling it off to do things to it manually. But nobody had built applications that completely automated business processes end to end, like lead-to-quote and order-to-cash. This incomplete automation problem meant that companies consistently failed to get the cost benefits they expected from the process automation they invested in.

"To remedy all this, we had to automate every fundamental business process end to end. That artificial separation between applications products—CRM and ERP—had to be bridged, because the data process flow from lead-to-quote to order-to-cash spanned marketing, sales, order management, and accounting application modules. We had to rebuild all our separate application modules into a complete and integrated E-Business Suite. And we had to rebuild them on top of a single global database."

Critically, Ron Wohl and Mark Barrenechea quickly saw that working independently of each other, one concentrating on back-office functions and the other working on the new customer relationship software with which Oracle was going to take on Siebel, made no sense. Barrenechea says, "We'd use the same data schema, the same application program interfaces, and the same standards. That's what became known as the E-Business Suite."

Not only did Ellison insist that development break out of its silos of specialization, he also demanded that development and Gary Roberts's IT organization become, in effect, a single entity. The development group became intimately involved in defining and understanding the business processes that were to be implemented at Oracle and taking the final responsibility for deploying the software and validating its operational use. Roberts says, "We took all the application support people who used to be part of internal IT and moved them into the development groups. Today, we have what we call the three-legged stool for development. There's me, Ron, and Mark. When those two develop a product, they hand it to me to implement. I also do final quality control against our entire employee base. What better way is there to see whether a product is reliable, can scale and perform to expectations?" The ratio of support staff to employee at Oracle has fallen from about 1 to 25 to as little as 1 to 75.*

Roberts admits that at first there was a certain amount of suspicion on both sides: "It wasn't exactly confrontational, but it was strained. The attitude was 'You guys just run data centers, what do you know about developing products?' But we were able to sit down with some of Oracle's

---

*LE writes: I thought that a major test of our new applications should be the lowering of IT expenses within months and consistently thereafter. I never bought into the notion of "investing" in Internet systems or any other kind of computer system. Internet systems should save you money very quickly, or you shouldn't put them in.

technical gurus, and they said they would have made exactly the same recommendations as us. So that legitimized our position, and from that time on it's been transformed into a collaborative effort."

As well as forcing IT and development to work together as one, Ellison began the process of globalizing Oracle with IT. He decided to move all the IT people from their country and regional headquarters to a new global organization headed by Roberts. Not surprisingly, Ellison encountered fierce resistance from the feudal barons. The idea of relying on the corporate center for their mission-critical systems was anathema to them.

Rather than just mandating the change (and then waiting for the shifting of blame every time a country manager missed a quota), the way around their resistance was a crafty mix of financial incentives and proof points that the new systems would actually work. First, the decision was made to provide the new global IT systems for "free" rather than as an allocated cost. Ellison wanted to establish the principle that managers should have to absorb only costs that they were directly responsible for incurring. Country managers who wanted to keep their IT in-house could do so, but it would be at the expense of both their operating margins and their bonuses.

Second, Ellison identified an easy-to-implement project that would provide "cheap thrills" and immediate proof that the new Internet systems actually worked: global e-mail. Instead of those ninety-seven separate e-mail systems, Oracle would run on a single Internet e-mail system running exclusively on two computers at its main data center in California (plus standby servers in the Colorado-based backup data center). Ellison says, "It was a stunning success. We used our global intranet and our database e-mail system, now called Collaboration Suite, to link everyone in the company together. The new global e-mail system cost one tenth as much as the ninety-seven local e-mail systems it replaced. And it was faster, more reliable, and more secure. Our users were happy because they could keep using the user interface they were familiar with: Microsoft Outlook." One senior executive in Tokyo, betraying a limited faith in the Internet technologies that Oracle was selling, couldn't see how an e-mail system in California could be faster than one in Japan. "Something to do with the speed of light," muttered Ellison to him. "Please don't act so surprised in front of customers."

Next up for globalization were marketing and sales. And in the case of marketing, it was not just its computer systems but the organization itself that was unified. Unlike with IT, marketing people were left in their countries, but from now on they all reported to Mark Jarvis rather than to their country managers. But it was the same deal as for IT: if you wanted to keep your own marketing organization, you paid for it. Ellison was trying to instill a new culture in which the status of senior managers was based not on the amount of money they spent but solely on how much profit they earned. But as Ellison had anticipated, there were other benefits from globalizing marketing: "The Internet made all our marketing programs visible in every country in which we did business. The programs that worked became global. The programs that didn't were killed. Duplication of effort was minimized. Prices set by our pricing committee were published on our global Web site, where our customers could see them. That made it impossible for every country to set its own prices.* We now have less than ten people working on product pricing. That's down from two hundred. So duplication of effort ended, delays eliminated, and our costs greatly reduced. The pricing bureaucracy was gone. I could always make policy, but now, for the first time, I could enforce it."

By April 1999, Ellison felt sufficiently confident of the progress he was making to start talking about Oracle's "e-business transformation," claiming to the board that he believed it was possible to take out a billion dollars of annual recurring costs in just the next year. Two months later, at a headquarters press conference, he went public with the target. He was desperately hoping that before the end of the year, Release 11i, the E-Business Suite, the most ambitious software package in the history of enterprise computing, would be ready to ship, and he wanted the world to believe that it was thanks to using its own software that Oracle was saving unimaginable amounts of money. However, to reach the billion-dollar target and get beyond it, Ellison, Gary Bloom, Gary Roberts, and the other executives leading the e-business charge were now going to have to do something much more difficult than globalizing HR or accounting.

Despite the degree of professionalism that Ray Lane had, at least initially, brought to U.S. sales after the near catastrophe of 1991, Ellison's distrust of Oracle's own sales force and the potential for trouble that stemmed from its wheeler-dealer ways was largely undiminished. Just as

---

*LE writes: At least a country could not set its own prices without justifying the difference to the global pricing committee. We approved different prices in India and China. Everywhere else in the world our product prices are the same.

the Internet could help restore centralized control over Oracle's Tower of Babel–like marketing operation, Ellison believed that an Internet-based sales system could not only make sales more efficient, but just as crucially, it could standardize much of it. What Ellison wanted was a uniform process that would minutely choreograph every single step of the sales process.

Ideally, an increasing number of sales would be made through the Oracle Web store without any human intervention. When sales prospects visited Oracle's Web site, the information collected would automatically steer them toward information about products or services that might interest them. Follow-up e-mails would be automatically generated to keep up interest and to discover whether a telephone call or a face-to-face visit from a salesperson was needed to close the sale. Where appropriate, some leads could be instantly shared with approved consulting and hardware distribution partners. At least in theory, the prices posted on the Web would be the standard prices that all but the very biggest customers would pay, thus avoiding the hugely time-consuming (for all concerned) ritual of protracted negotiation on every deal. A by-product of this transparent sales process would be far more accurate sales forecasting.

But Ellison wanted to go much further than that; he wanted to use the technology both to help change the entire sales culture at Oracle and to make each salesperson vastly more effective. He says, "I wanted to get the 'creativity' out of the sales process. If you want to be creative, go write a novel. I want to 'engineer' the sales process. I don't want the field people spending all their time wheeling and dealing on price. The primary function of our salespeople is to communicate and quantify the business benefits of our products. There should be a carefully engineered step-by-step process for most common sales situations—like selling our database against IBM's. First, identify the decision maker and enter their e-mail address into our sales automation system. Second, send them a set of key customer references—case studies showing how much customers saved by converting from IBM DB2 to Oracle—showing how they got better performance and ran on lower-cost hardware. Third, send them a proposal quantifying their cost saving in hardware, software, and labor if they pick Oracle rather than DB2. Finally, send them a standard contract and a price quote. If we have an engineered, proven sales process, we will sell more software. The purpose of new sales automation systems is to allow standard sales processes to be defined and implemented across the sales force. That's real sales automation. Most so-called sales automation systems simply automate opportunity management and sales forecasting.

If you are going to spend a lot of money on sales automation, make certain you are automating selling—not just forecasting." *

Ellison adds, "An engineered sales process can also be effortlessly updated. If the sales pitch we want to use against IBM changes, as it does from time to time because of some cool new feature we put into Oracle or because we have a great new reference, I want every salesman to change the way they sell against IBM. Press a button, and everyone's PowerPoint presentation becomes the latest version of the pitch. Press a button, and great new references are automatically sent to our sales prospects. Press a button, and the new demo is online."

Ellison recognizes that applications can't be sold the same way as database technology. But instead of sending four or five people to, say, Slovakia to demonstrate those applications they know something about and think the customer might be interested in, why not use cobrowsing on the Internet to run the demos and presentations? That way, the best people are always conducting the demos, the customer is seeing the latest version of the software, and money is saved on travel expenses. It also happens to be a pretty good way of showing customers the difference between client/server applications and apps that run over the Internet and can be accessed with a browser regardless of where the computer they're sitting on happens to be.

Ellison is unrepentant about the charge by rivals, such as Tom Siebel and some of the analysts, that what was once the most feared sales force in the industry is being "dumbed down" and emasculated. Many of Oracle's top sales guys, they say, have left to join other software firms because Ellison no longer allows them the flexibility they need to do their jobs. It's typical Larry, they say; because he's an engineer, he thinks that everything in the business can be engineered. He laughs. "Yeah, the Oracle sales force certainly was feared—mainly by me! Seriously, I think some of our competitors have been hiring our old cowboys—the kind of guys who will only be happy as long as they have horses, lariats, and guns. But I've never thought that our very best salespeople were these crazy deal makers. Our best salespeople are very knowledgeable and

---

*LE writes: For the same reason we're trying to persuade our customers not to customize our software, because the lowest-cost way to get quality is with a standard product—a customized sales process is expensive and generally of low quality. Very few people can sell well. An engineered process is almost always— not always but almost always—better than an ad hoc process.

service-oriented. I love and respect those guys, and I want more of them. I want a sales force made up of the kind of people you'd want your son or daughter to marry."

It's understandable that Ellison should think the way he does, but I wondered whether George Roberts, the head of U.S. sales and a former protégé of Ray Lane, would feel the same way. Did he feel that Ellison was engineering the testosterone out of selling? "Oh God, I think that's a ridiculous assumption. I think that what Larry is trying to do is find a way to make every sales rep behave like an 'A'-grade sales rep. I have had this discussion with Larry many times, and what I tell him is that we will know we've arrived as an e-business when we release the product and the next day forty thousand Oracle employees can deliver the same-value proposition around the globe. Because that's when size becomes an advantage. Historically, as companies get bigger they become more inefficient, and this whole e-business effort is all designed to leverage Oracle's size and make it more effective all around the world. I have seventeen thousand people. Closing that $2 million deal isn't going to solve my problem for me, but if I can make seventeen thousand people more effective in their job every day, that has a real impact top line and bottom line. That's a huge win."

Doesn't Roberts lament the passing of the "crazy deal makers"? "Absolutely not," he says. "We want to make sure that people understand our key differentiators against the competition, what our value proposition is, and how we then match it against customer needs. That's it. A salesman shouldn't want to cut deals. Okay, at the high end, the top hundred accounts, there may be some relationships and arrangements. But as you move further downstream, the more standard the business should be. A large part of our e-business effort is aimed at optimizing our distribution model in a way that leverages all the different channels a customer can buy through. That's tremendously important in helping us get market share. As for our competitors saying that we're dumbing down, they're nuts. And you know what? They all want to do what we're doing. I've had a dozen companies through here in the last few months—one of them was BMC, a software company—and there isn't one that doesn't come away saying you guys are so far ahead of anything they've seen even if they've been doing telesales for years and years."

Chuck Phillips of Morgan Stanley Dean Witter, who is not only the doyen of Wall Street enterprise software analysts but, unusually, is held in high regard by Ellison, takes a balanced view of Oracle's attempt to change the way software is sold. He believes that some "dumbing down" was necessary just to make things simpler for the customer. "Buying from Oracle was like trying to buy a building rather than a piece of software. I think Larry's simplifying it is something customers like . . . but I don't think he ever gets rid of those high-testosterone sales guys either. Those guys are still very important for the big deals. It's not like people wake up and decide to spend thirty million on the Web site. You need hungry guys that can sell and sell high, and I think he knows that. . . . You still want those top five hundred guys who know how to move mountains and who won't take 'no' for an answer. There is still a human element to selling software." *

Not everyone at Oracle was as enthusiastic as George Roberts about the changes, many of which were being driven through by Ellison's "shadow management team" of Gary Bloom and Safra Catz. According to Ellison, one group that felt particularly threatened—perhaps not surprisingly, given the amount of independence they had enjoyed under Lane—were the country managers in Europe. That may have been true of some who equated their power and influence within Oracle with the size of their budgets and the autonomy of their systems. But the major obstacle to changing the way things were done in Europe was the man whom Ellison had himself chosen to run EMEA (Europe, Middle East, and Africa), a polished ex-Digital and ex-AT&T executive with a background in services named Pier Carlo Falotti.

After joining Oracle in 1996, Falotti had built a substantial European headquarters in Geneva. Unfortunately, the infrastructure that Falotti had built around himself was extremely expensive to run, while contributing little to revenues. As Ellison demanded increasing cost savings, Falotti forced his managers to absorb the costs of the "services" that were being provided from Geneva. Philip Crawford, a tough salesman who ran the very profitable British business until being fired by Lane in 2000 for overaggressive customer license audits, says, "The problem with Falotti was that he said one thing and did another. I sat in meetings where blatant lies were told about costs. Blatant untruths about European and about EMEA cost structures. When Larry started to ask for lower costs, quite understandably the answer in EMEA was that the

---

*LE writes: Chuck, as usual, is right. The big deals will always be driven by our best and most senior people. I believe that means our best managers, best salespeople, best consultants, and best engineers. In a great company everybody sells—not just the salespeople.

countries have to eat more of the cost of services. In the United Kingdom I got almost zero in the way of services that I actually wanted."

Safra Catz recalls, "It was not pleasant dealing with the senior European management team. I think some were well intentioned but didn't know what to do. The guys had to push Ray's line that they couldn't change because they'd always done it in this way." Ellison eventually fired Falotti on the last day of May 2000 by calling him on his mobile phone. The date of his dismissal meant that Falotti lost $10 million worth of options that were soon to vest. To avoid that fate, Falotti secured a note from his doctor stating that he was "ill and unable to work as of May 30 for an indefinite amount of time." According to Swiss law, an individual can't be sacked if he is too ill to work. Suspecting a scam, Oracle promptly slapped in a lawsuit against Falotti arguing that the doctor's note "plainly misrepresented the facts." So far, the legal decisions have gone against Falotti. His consolation is that he had already made nearly $30 million from the earlier sale of shares from an option grant.

Another senior manager who left as a consequence of Ellison's e-business crusade was Ray Lane's old chum Randy Baker. Having already had education stripped from him in early 1999 because of the "dismal" 13 percent profit margin he was targeting, later in the year his leadership of Oracle's six-thousand-customer support organization was passed to Gary Bloom. Two months later, in February 2000, the fifty-five-year-old Baker was fired. Like Falotti, Baker believes the timing of his sacking was linked to the date when options were due to vest. He sued Oracle for $18.5 million on grounds of wrongful dismissal and age discrimination. He had indicated that after seven years' service he wanted to leave the company in August, by which time his options would have vested, but Ellison had other ideas.

Ellison says, "Randy and Pier Carlo both felt they needed more people to do a good job. I didn't agree. I wanted Randy to leave because his margins were dropping like a rock and he still wanted to hire more people. What's more important to me, profitability or someone's age? I'm actually slightly older than Randy. I wanted to automate, cut expenses, and improve profitability. That's what I insisted on. It proved to be a very difficult time for many of our most senior managers, who were long accustomed to operating independently." Ray Lane regards both men as "among the finest executives" he has ever worked with.

By moving all of Oracle's service information to the Web and everyone within customer support to a single Internet-based global system, Ellison maintains, customer service and satisfaction have increased without the need to hire any additional people. He's especially proud of the fact that much of the support work is done out of Bangalore by Indian engineers, who earn a fraction of the wages expected in California or Europe. Problems can now be tracked around the clock, exploiting different time zones, and the best-qualified people can work on problems wherever in the world the customer may be based.

Remarkably, within not much more than a year of Ellison's beginning his campaign to cut costs by turning Oracle into an exemplary e-business, the targeted first billion dollars of savings—a number pretty much plucked from the air to help dramatize the project—had been secured and Oracle's profit margin had moved from a little under 20 percent to more than 30 percent. Ellison had been helped by the rapid growth in all parts of the business coming from the dot-com and telco-generated boom in technology spending, but Ellison was already talking about getting a second billion dollars in annual expense savings.

The savings gave Ellison the marketing message he needed to sell Release 11i, which had finally been released in May 2000. Selling brand-new software is always difficult until a reference base of satisfied early customers exists. Ellison decided that Oracle's own Internet-derived efficiencies would be the first reference. Soon, Oracle's $300 million marketing budget was pumping out the insistent message: "By using our own E-Business Suite, Oracle saved $1 billion in one year." The grammar might not have been precise, but the meaning could not have been clearer: Oracle's new applications suite was a cost-cutting engine that could do the same for any business with the vision to use it. It was the kind of boast that was bound to attract both attention and skepticism in equal measure. Partly because of Ellison's reputation for stretching the truth when it suited him, critics were keen to find explanations for the cost savings that didn't depend on the performance of Oracle's software.

An article in the magazine *InternetWeek* by Mitch Wagner published in March 2001 and entitled "Oracle's Savings Don't Add Up" was fairly representative. It began, "Don't buy into Oracle's claims that it's saving billions of dollars by implementing its own e-business software. Much of the savings actually have come from cost-cutting measures that could have been achieved without the Internet, according to experts and an analysis of Oracle's financial statements." One such expert, John Puricelli, an analyst with A. G. Edwards & Sons, opined that most of the savings had come from old-fashioned belt-tightening: "A lot of the cost savings that came were changes in employee behavior, and software doesn't do that," he said. Chris Shilakes, an analyst with Merrill Lynch, said that "revenue momentum" as much as cost saving had been responsible for the margin improvement. Spurred on by such pieces, a group of shareholders, disgruntled by the fall in Oracle's stock price since the beginning of the recession, even filed suit in early 2001 alleging that the company's savings were due to head count reductions (from forty-four thousand to forty-one thousand since 1998), as opposed to Internet-driven efficiencies. Stung by these criticisms, Oracle invited the Harvard Business School to carry out one of its famous case studies and an independent management consultancy to carry out a meticulous department-by-department investigation.

A review of both investigations by the Economist Intelligence Unit concluded, "These studies provide impressive evidence of a company in the midst of dramatic changes inspired by the Internet—although as Oracle's senior executives freely concede, many of the efforts at transformation derive as much from old-fashioned sound business practices as they do from Internet-driven innovation." Pointing out the huge gains in Oracle's own IT operation—spending nearly halved since 1999 and average help desk response times down from three minutes to less than ten seconds with 44 percent fewer IT staff—the EIU summed up, "The company undertook simultaneously to transform every aspect of its operations in accordance with three key principles: standardisation, centralisation and web-enabled automation. Driven with near-fanatical zeal by the CEO, Larry Ellison, this trinity has shaken up virtually every job function within the company. There is little doubt that an Internet-based business transformation has taken place."

What the EIU and most others fail to note, however, is that while standardization and centralization may sound like "old-fashioned sound business practices," it was the Internet that made it possible to achieve the Ellisonian ideal of "one network, one database" so rapidly and so completely. The suggestion that most of the savings were simply the result of cutting head count is absurd; it was only successful automation that meant Oracle could do more with fewer people. As for the accusation that much of the margin improvement came from the revenue momentum fueled by the dot-com boom, that too appears simplistic.

The second quarter of fiscal 2002 was hard pounding for Oracle—its earnings per share of 10 cents were a cent lower than the previous year, while new software license sales were down 27 percent and services revenue was flat. Announcing the numbers, Jeff Henley said, "For Oracle, this quarter included the September eleventh tragedy and its impact on an already weak economy. In a difficult economy, we are gratified that our business automation has allowed us to continuously take cost out of our business while expanding our engineering capacity." Ellison put it differently: "It was our toughest quarter in a decade, but we still made over $800 million in operating profit and a thirty-five percent operating margin. When the economy improves, we will earn a lot more." Ellison was pointing out two things. The first was that in extremely difficult selling conditions its margin gains had not deteriorated despite the fact that, almost alone among technology firms, Oracle had not been forced into large-scale layoffs in 2001. The second was that when business picked up there was likely to be a nearly one-for-one relationship between increasing revenue dollars and profit—Ellison believed that Oracle had effectively uncoupled expenses from revenue growth and that in an "up" economy, Oracle was capable of getting near a 50 percent margin that would beat even Microsoft's phenomenal profitability into a cocked hat.

Software was as much a catalyst as a cause of the revolution in Oracle's business practices. Ellison frequently tells prospective customers that unless they are prepared to review all their business processes in the light of the Internet and unless their top management is willing to make available the best people in the company to work out what should be done, they shouldn't buy Oracle's software because they will only be disappointed by the return on their investment. His constant message is: Don't change the software to fit the way you have always done business; use it to figure out how you want to do business for the next twenty years. Gary Bloom, who left Oracle to run the software firm VERITAS in November 2000, agrees. "I was the driving force behind the idea that the way we were spending money and making business decisions at Oracle was lunacy. But the software forces you to think about exactly how you want to do business, and that makes you go do it. It gets your attention, and it's very powerful."

Ellison believes that one of the greatest benefits of Oracle's e-business transformation has been to the way people within the company now behave: "Oracle had been a company made up of many independent business groups, managed by these self-reliant generalists who valued their autonomy. Now it's a company of interdependent business groups managed by specialists who value their knowledge and excel at teamwork. As a result, it's more fun to work at Oracle these days and there's less management conflict because decisions are based on up-to-date, shared information."

As Oracle's own information systems improved, Ellison was increasingly struck by how executives who had accurate data at their fingertips were able to overwhelm managers who were nominally senior to them who didn't. He had seen Safra Catz relentlessly drive home arguments with Ray Lane by virtue of better information. "She always had the facts. I was watching how people manage, how they make decisions and how they debate during meetings. When you have someone who has facts versus someone who has none, facts, not personality, rule the day. The more we know, the more rational our decisions and the less we argue. Because once you knew that certain facts were true, the argument is over. It's really quite extraordinary how different an organization becomes when decisions are based on facts rather than force of personality, rank, and opinion."

Despite his enjoyment of controversy, Ellison doesn't have a great appetite for argument, at least not in a professional context. While he's always prepared to listen to the views of developers when they differ from his and is willing to be persuaded if he's wrong, he doesn't enjoy debates about business issues that depend on hunch and feel. Ellison is a self-confessed "hyperquant" who feels fully in control only when he's processing data. Even when he's flying a plane or racing *Sayonara,* he prefers to be guided by the numbers coming out of the computer systems rather than to put all his trust in what he's feeling through the seat of his pants.

Another of the cultural changes that Ellison feels proud of is the attitude toward budgeting and expenses that he insists has now spread through the company—an approach, he says, he learned from close observation of one of Oracle's biggest customers, GE. He says, "A few years ago when we had a budgeting session, it used to go something like this: A bunch of people walked into the room. There was a big pot of gold sitting on the table. The team that came in felt it was their job to use all their rhetorical ability and cleverness to leave the room with as much of that gold as possible in their budget. My job, on the other hand, was to hold on to as much of the gold as possible. The fight—excuse me, budgeting sessions—would go on for days and days. It took a long time for them to explain why every department needed to spend more money than it had spent the previous year.

"I said, 'Wait a second. We all work for the same company; we're all shareholders here. Why am I the only person in the room trying to hold on to as much of the gold as possible? If we spend less gold, we'll make more money. That's a good thing.' Something I learned from working with and watching GE over the years was that GE expected its managers to come into planning sessions with budgets showing profit margins going up. Good idea. Now every manager in Oracle is required to come to planning sessions with a first slide that says 'How we're going to do more while spending less.' The rest of the presentation goes into detail as to what you're going to do this year that you didn't do last year and how you're able to spend less while doing it. During hard times, like the last few years, this approach to planning is essential if you want to have any hope of preserving profitability. If people are looking for an outlet for their creativity, this is the place for it. We learn from each other. We no longer have a culture in which people think that the more money they spend, the more important they are. We have a culture that finally understands: expenses are bad."

The changes that Ellison has driven through at Oracle since 1999 are extraordinary—all the more so because almost nobody who knew him before would have dreamed that he could ever get so fascinated by every mundane detail concerning how Oracle operated or that he would have the determination to drive such profound cultural changes through a large and far-flung organization once the first quick wins had been realized. Nor is there any doubt that he has done it by turning Oracle into an e-business laboratory, creating a virtuous circle that greatly benefits the development of Oracle's application software. It's a measure of his success that during the last technology industry downturn at the beginning of the 1990s Oracle was nearly sunk by poor cost control and the ensuing cash crisis, whereas in the tougher business conditions of 2001, an admittedly much bigger Oracle remained formidably profitable. Nonetheless, there are some important qualifications.

The first is that Oracle was unusually ripe for an e-business transformation. By any normal standards, it had grown extremely rapidly over a twenty-year period and, as in many high-growth companies, controlling expenses was not a priority. It had also adopted a highly decentralized model, partly to enable it to establish a global presence quickly. Because it was a technology company, spending large amounts of money on the latest IT systems was lodged deep in its DNA. However, in the era of client/server, as Ellison is fond of saying today, the more you spent, the worse it got. Thus when Ellison began his campaign to standardize, centralize, and automate everything that moved at Oracle, he quickly realized that the returns had the potential to be spectacular.

The second reservation is the risk that having created systems that have turned Oracle into a disciplined machine capable of responding very quickly to inputs from the top, Ellison may be in danger of isolating himself from the influence of colleagues and depriving the company of some of their creativity. It's one thing to curb the "creativity" of deal-crazy salesmen; it's quite another for a company full of very smart people to become obsessively rule-based. Ellison is clearly fascinated to see how far he can go in bringing the principles of engineering to the running of a complex business. There is a danger, however, that he may go too far.

Jeff Henley articulates some of those anxieties: "Larry has played a very healthy role in coming back in and cleaning everything up. But my worry would be that he has become very powerful and is not delegating very much at all. There's a danger that he's trying to control everything so tightly himself that he'll stifle the growth of the company. It's nothing immediate, because he's done much more good than harm. I'm just saying that in the longer term, he'll have to figure out a way to be a little bit more inclusive. He'll disagree with me that we can't grow and flourish, but the fact of the matter is that there will be limits because of the approach he's taking right now.

"I think a lot of it goes back to our software. To create the E-Business Suite, he's been figuring out the entire enterprise and how it can be programmed. He's obsessed with this idea of programming every aspect of the way we all work. The idea that everything can be engineered is as intellectually exciting as hell to him, so he wants to get right down to the lowest levels of detail and work through the processes. So we've been making our product much better because he's been getting so deep into it, and I'm all for that. It's just that there's a risk [that] Larry, who's a very able guy, will choke off free thought and expression in the company because he's trying to make too many of the decisions."

Jeff Henley may be overstating the dangers. Although dominating, Ellison is usually open to ideas from people who are not so overawed that they forget to express them. But as Ellison candidly puts it, he now uses Oracle as a laboratory for product development. And in any laboratory some experiments are bound to fail. He needs colleagues who are not afraid to tell him when that happens.

The final qualification about Oracle's story of transforming its efficiency by using its own E-Business Suite is that the claim is only partly true, because the first billion dollars of savings was pretty much in the bag before 11i was finished. The software that Oracle used to turn itself into an e-business was, in fact, a combination of modules from Release 11.0, which shipped in late 1998, and a number of customized prototype applications that were global, Internet-based systems. A key element of the E-Business Suite, however, was missing: the underlying information architecture, including the vital shared data schema that were the basis for Oracle's claims about the tight integration of all the applications. Ellison says, "That's absolutely right. The software that saved Oracle a billion dollars in the first year was a combination of our standard applications products plus prototype applications that had not yet been integrated into the E-Business Suite. But all the applications, products, and prototypes were global Internet applications systems. It was these systems that became the driving force in Oracle's transformation. Once the prototype applications proved their worth, they were rewritten and integrated into what would become the E-Business Suite. As we automated every part of Oracle, just about everything went into the E-Business Suite."

So was it a stretch for Oracle to brag in its ads that it had saved a billion dollars by using its own E-Business Suite? Not from Ellison's point of view. For him, the process by which the suite had evolved and Oracle had been transformed into an e-business was utterly symbiotic. But in one sense, the marketing claims were misleading. The reassuring message to prospective customers was that Oracle had been successfully running the same E-Business Suite that they would buy for at least a year. That was very far from the case. Not for the first time in Oracle's history, early guinea-pig customers would pay a price for taking too much on trust. Not, however, as great as Oracle and Ellison would pay.

10

READY OR NOT . . .

For Larry Ellison and Oracle, it probably didn't get any better than this. The May 8, 2000, issue of *Business Week* magazine carried a portrait of Ellison on its cover wearing shades and what had become his trademark black crewneck pullover. He looked good—a little too much like a Mafia heavy, but pretty good all the same. Even more satisfactory was the unequivocal headline "Oracle Is Cool Again." The story inside by Steve Hamm wasn't bad either. After noting the quadrupling of Oracle's stock price in less than a year that had taken it past IBM in market cap and the widely reported fact that three weeks earlier the value of Ellison's stake had surpassed Bill Gates's holding in Microsoft ($52.1 billion to $51.5 billion), Hamm argued that with the shipping of the E-Business Suite, Oracle was set to be perhaps as dominant a force in the new era of Internet computing as Microsoft had been in the heyday of the PC. The piece was balanced by the attacks of rivals and the skepticism of some analysts who questioned whether Oracle could pull off its grand designs, but the implication was clear: the future was Ellison's to lose. Over the next twelve months, he came pretty close to doing exactly that.

In 1999, it had become accepted as fact that Oracle was one of four companies whose products were the foundation stones of the Internet and e-business—the others being the powerful servers made by Sun Microsystems, the massive information storage systems that came from EMC, and Cisco Systems' ubiquitous routers. No serious dot-com company would look further than these four for the essential IT infrastructure it needed to do business. Amazon, eBay, E*TRADE, and Yahoo! were all Oracle customers. And the dot-coms weren't alone: the deregulating impact of the 1996 Telecommunications Act meant a massive surge in spending by spectacularly well funded "bandwidth barons" and new "challenger" telcos, such as Qwest, and an equally determined response from incumbents determined to match their technology and conquer new territories to offset the effects of the intensifying competition in their traditional markets. Fueled by the prevailing Internet fever, never before in history had there been such an appetite by businesses to buy the latest in computing technology, and Oracle was one of the leading beneficiaries. Instead of the evangelical "The Internet Changes Everything," the company's ubiquitously displayed promotional message was now the much more assertive "Oracle Software Powers the Internet."

Not only did Oracle appear to have the right products for the times, Ellison's unrelenting focus on the Internet and the e-business revolution had also turned out to be spectacularly right. The latest version of the flagship database, Oracle 8i ("i" as in "Internet," of course), had shipped in March 1999, and Oracle's first true Web-based ERP applications suite, 11.0, was actually winning market share against SAP's product because, with "Y2K" fast approaching, it was proving much quicker and easier to install. According to Dataquest, Oracle was the only leading ERP player to show significant growth in the first half of 1999. While PeopleSoft suffered a 53 percent revenue decline and SAP managed only a measly 3.8 percent year-on-year growth, Oracle's applications revenue grew by nearly 30 percent. As Ellison said, 11.0 was "really smoking" the competition. As for Oracle 8i, when announcing its forthcoming release at a New York press conference in September 1998, Ellison had declared that 8i was not just a database but a platform for Internet computing. With its built-in development tools, it was all that companies needed to deploy business applications that could be accessed using a standard Web browser.

The "first Internet database," as Ellison described it, was packed with hip-sounding new features: a built-in Java virtual machine that could execute applications written in the new Java programming language, which was taking the development community by storm; the latest messaging technology and directory services; additional Common Object Request Broker Architecture (CORBA) interfaces and better support for clusters. Most customers would initially buy it for the traditional reasons— increased speed and performance—but others raved about 8i's Java capabilities from the outset. One was Jeff Grant, the IT manager for the recording company Nettwerk Productions, which represents Barenaked Ladies, Gob, and Sarah McLachlan. With sixty thousand subscribers to its mailing lists, he described the Java Mail package as a "lifesaver": "No more using another mail server, no more screwing with building database cartridges for the server. Now you have the ability to call the Java routine straight from the database and no longer have to use a go-between." Similarly, Grant found that if he wanted to make a change to any of the applications he was running, instead of having to upgrade the software on five thousand PCs, he could now make the changes in one place. "Developing apps like this makes all the sense in the world," he said.

Jeremy Burton, then responsible for server marketing at Oracle, said, "The features that are important now are scalability and reliability. But over time customers will figure out what this Internet model can do for them." Merv Adrian, an analyst at Giga Information Group, observed, "You can't just sell a database by saying it works better. It has to have the latest thing, like new, improved XML support with JavaBeans. 8i represented a dramatic shift in focus to Internet-driven changes. People are buying it because it meets today's *and* tomorrow's needs."

One of the most significant 8i innovations wasn't ready until more than a year after the database came out. Called Internet File System, it allowed any Windows application file, such as Word or Excel, or any Web page or e-mail, to be dragged and dropped into a directory and integrated into the database. Among other benefits, developers would be able to build Web applications that linked both relational data and Windows files. When Ellison said that 8i was not just a database, he meant that users would no longer have to rely on Windows. The database was agnostic about which operating system it ran on! They would be "insulated" from the operating system; in other words, the OS would be merely a utility.

It was an important propaganda message to get out at the same time Microsoft was launching the supposedly much improved Version 7 of its SQL Server database. Unfortunately it lacked a reliable operating system to run on, and Microsoft was still laboring mightily to finish the long-overdue new version of Windows that it believed would finally win SQL Server 7 a ticket into the corporate data center and thus into Oracle's heartland. Ellison was saying, in effect, that for all Microsoft's efforts to become an enterprise computing player—it claimed that Windows 2000 was one of the biggest and most difficult engineering projects of all time, with armies of developers struggling to find the bugs in the 45 million lines of code—it was already out of date. To amplify the message that operating systems were not very important anymore, 8i would also run on Linux, the free operating system developed by the open-source movement. Furthermore, Oracle, in partnership with hardware companies such as Sun and Hewlett-Packard, would market something Ellison called a "database appliance." Known as Raw Iron, it would run straight out of the box using a stripped-down operating system. Raw Iron didn't take off commercially, but it reinforced the idea of simplicity versus complexity.

If Ellison was happy to describe Oracle 8i as the Internet database, he had no difficulty officially christening the forthcoming application Release 11i the E-Business Suite. For Ellison, 11i would be the summation of everything he had learned about the applications business since his forced introduction to it in early 1998. Above all, it would deal conclusively with the curse of fragmented data that had begun with client/server and that best-of-breed had exacerbated regardless of whether applications were Web-enabled or not. Apart from its new Internet computing architecture, which superseded that of 10.7 NCA and 11.0, the new suite would have three unique characteristics to ensure that Ellison achieved his holy grail of "all of your information, all of the time in just one place."

For the first time, 11i would offer tight integration between traditional enterprise resource applications that managed back-office functions such as financials, HR, and manufacturing automation, with the newer customer relationship software that ran marketing, sales, and service. In addition, 11i included an advanced planning suite, enterprise asset management, and online procurement. It is axiomatic that information about any customer transactions, supplier transactions, or internal business processes can affect every part of the organization. The best example of this is the apparently simple one of orders. From sales to marketing to customer service to supply chain to production, just about everybody needs to be able to access order information to do his or her job properly. Without integration between front- and back-office software, the ideal of "order information everywhere" is unachievable.

The second claimed point of difference for 11i was its completeness. Ellison had realized that data fragmentation was not the only reason for the difficulty users of enterprise applications had in getting worthwhile information about their businesses out of their multimillion-dollar systems. Another was the problem of gaps in automation. If a business flow was interrupted by manual processes at any stage, it almost always meant that the information stored was, at best, partial. By attempting to provide all the core functionality to run most businesses from end to end, Oracle was promising seamlessness and with it the speed, efficiency, and responsiveness that were supposed to be inherent in the idea of e-business.

The key to everything was the seemingly esoteric concept of a common data model uniting every piece of the suite. Every module—and there were about 140 of them—would be written to the same shared data schema, allowing semantic consistency (for example, the definition of a customer remained the same no matter from which application the information was coming and could thus be shared by all the other applications in the suite) as well as a complete view into every transaction. The underlying simplicity of the architecture was designed not only to make the gathering of useful business intelligence much easier than with multiple component systems but also to make implementation radically easier and therefore cheaper and quicker.

The scale of Ellison's ambition with 11i was breathtaking. While Microsoft boasted about the size of the project to build Windows 2000, it was, at the end of the day, only an operating system. The E-Business Suite, by comparison, had modules designed to run nearly every aspect of even the biggest and most complex multinational company's operations. From its inception, more than four thousand developers had been working on it nonstop (and still are refining the software and adding features demanded by customers or required to match competitors). When it shipped at the end of May 2000, as well as a new architecture, at least 40 percent of the modules themselves were entirely new. When Ellison described it as the largest and richest software product ever created, for once nobody accused him of exaggerating. The question was: Could Oracle pull it off?

Although Oracle first started talking about 11i in April 1999 at the Oracle Applications Users Group's (OAUG) conference in San Diego, the official announcement of a shipping date and what customers could expect from the new suite had to wait another five months. When ten thousand Oracle users showed up at the fall OAUG conference in Orlando to see Ellison make his keynote speech in the flesh, all they got was his image beamed from Redwood Shores on four giant screens. Many of them were also disappointed by what he said.

After an almost perfunctory fifteen-minute ramble, throughout which he appeared to be wrestling with an uncomfortable earpiece, he declared that the anticipated November launch date had been put back until February 2000. The suite would be complete only when the CRM component became available sometime in the second quarter. Ellison explained that technology glitches were causing the delays: he had also decided to include a brand-new order management module that had been scheduled for a later release, rather than bolt on the old one as originally planned.

One man in the audience, apparently speaking for a good few others, groused that the constantly shifting release dates left him losing credibility with customers, who were forced to put updating their applications on permanent hold.*

Both Ellison's apparently casual remark about the decision to go with the new order management module and the pressure from customers eager to get their hands on 11i would have profound consequences. But the immediate aftermath from Orlando, where Oracle executives had been energetically briefing analysts about the wonders of the new suite, was pretty positive. Gartner Dataquest wrote bullishly that 11i, by making Oracle the first big applications vendor to "use ERP/CRM integration as a loud, primary marketing message," would only add to the superior momentum of Oracle's license revenue growth over its rivals. It noted that apart from being easier to manage and deploy, the suite approach, as defined by Oracle, would provide "richer business intelligence and decision support." It summed up: "Dataquest awards Oracle a thumbs-up for pouncing on an opportunity to present a clear message. . . . Oracle would benefit wildly if ERP/CRM integration becomes the key driver for vendor choice in the enterprise applications space."

There was, however, a word of warning—"Of course, Oracle must now deliver"—which the author had some doubts about, given "its somewhat less-than-sterling past performances" in applications. The META Group made a similarly qualified prognostication: "Oracle, somewhat hampered in the past by offerings that lacked coherence and differentiation, has recently demonstrated a consistent vision. Although it remains to be seen how smoothly its plans are carried out, Oracle is positioning itself to aggressively increase its share of the overall enterprise application market." The analysts were saying that for pretty much the first time Oracle had a potentially appealing story for customers who were sick of bearing the risks and costs of integration. Their caveat was that Ellison's "change the game" strategy required near-flawless execution. Oracle was on a roll, but if it became apparent that it had bitten off more than it could chew, the company could expect little mercy.

Many of the industry analysts regarded Oracle as an arrogant company that had never shown much interest in engaging them in dialogue.

---

*LE writes: We were getting a lot of pressure from our customers to deliver the 11i applications. I made a lot of them mad by delaying the release for several months. I should have delayed it even longer.

But it was more complicated than that. Oracle had spotted what it thought was a serious conflict of interest for the tech consultancies when it came to accepting the single-data-model concept behind the suite. Mark Jarvis, Oracle's head of marketing, says that he never expected an easy ride: "I thought that the Gartners and the Forresters of this world would find it hard to accept the idea of buying everything from one vendor. If they no longer have to advise clients that you need to buy this software for marketing and this software for sales, ending up with buying software from fourteen different vendors, they will be out of business. Their advice and their expertise are no longer important. You also have to bear in mind that some of those firms are in the systems integration business too, so we were threatening their revenues on two fronts. The financial analysts were likely to be more open-minded. But many of them were advising people to buy the likes of Ariba and Commerce One [which were threatened by Oracle's suite strategy], so they had some vested interest too."

However, the initially largely favorable analyst coverage, which Oracle suspected wouldn't last, added to the pressure on Ellison to ship 11i. There was pressure of a different kind from Wall Street. Because customers sit on their wallets when they know a radical new release is imminent that is more than just an upgrade from existing software, earnings can stall. With Y2K out of the way and company IT spending on e-business-enabling software expected to boom, for Ellison the cost in revenue postponed or even lost because of further delays in 11i was unacceptable. If that meant putting heat on development, especially Ron Wohl and Mark Barrenechea, to declare the software customer-ready, then so be it.

As Ellison frequently says about himself, he doesn't have any difficulty in making decisions, even if they sometimes turn out to have been wrong. In this situation, he concluded that the risk was asymmetric. As well as the hit to Oracle's enviable earnings momentum, with its inevitable impact on the company's heady stock price, if Oracle were seen to be struggling, critics would be only too happy to declare Ellison a victim of his own vaunting ambition. At the same time, more delays would give rivals time to undermine, perhaps critically, the credibility of the suite concept before customers had even had a chance to try it. On the other hand, pushing 11i out of the door before it was finished ran the risk of generating a raft of unhappy customer stories for the analysts to feed on.

But maybe that wouldn't happen. The certainty of a launch date would undoubtedly concentrate minds. Maybe 11i would work perfectly out of the box. In the software industry, it was not unknown for miracles to happen. Even if a miracle didn't happen on this occasion, Ellison was cynical enough about the development process to believe that however much work is done in-house to iron out problems, it's not until the product is in the hands of real customers that you really start to find out what's right and what's wrong. Ellison was also prepared to take the apparently sensible path of having a controlled customer release and staggering the launch, rolling out first the more mature ERP part of the suite in February and then adding the CRM modules and the brand-new order management application in May.

It sounded prudent enough, but the reality was very different. In the first place, Oracle was breaking one of the cardinal rules of the applications business: don't release software to customers until you've tried running on it yourself. While much of 11i was based on the custom-built applications that Oracle had used to turn itself into an e-business and save $1 billion, Oracle would not have time to move its own operations onto 11i before it began selling it to customers. They, rather than Oracle, would be playing the guinea pig.*

To make matters worse, the idea of a controlled release to early-adopter customers who were ready to trade some pain for the gain of getting their hands on the software before competitors wasn't strictly adhered to. Part of the problem, according to Ellison, was that customers in Europe were getting their systems ready for the introduction of the euro and had been planning on implementing 11i as part of that process. If 11i came out later, they would not only lose vital time but would incur heavy costs from extending their contracts with systems integrations firms. Ellison says, "I had already delayed the 11i release date, and that forced our customers to revise their implementation plans. There was tremendous pressure not to delay again. Our customers had their resources all lined up and were ready to install our software as soon as we released it. It was a bit like the beginning of World War I: once the troop mobilizations began, there was no turning back."

Under the circumstances, a prudent general might have done everything possible to eliminate any unnecessary risk. Instead, Ellison decided

---

LE writes: The biggest lesson I learned from the release of 11i was to make sure we used the applications internally before we gave them to customers. That's how we operate today, and it's made all the difference. Once we're using an application successfully at Oracle, it's much less likely that a customer will run into problems.

on the software equivalent of a blind cavalry charge. It had never been the intention to put the new order management module into the early releases of 11i. The idea had been to start off with the old one and upgrade customers later. But because the launch of the whole suite had been delayed, somebody suggested that it might be possible to sneak the new and much more capable system in at the last moment.

Ellison says, "We had just finished a complete rewrite of our order management system. It was a huge job. The new order management system was dramatically better than the old one, but it hadn't been tested yet, so we thought it was much too risky to put it into the suite. Then someone—not me this time—had this very innovative idea: let's put both the old one and the new one into the suite. That way, conservative customers could stick with the old reliable order management system while our most avant-garde customers could get the benefits of the new one. Cool idea. Unfortunately, it turned out to be technically impossible, but it was a hell of an idea, and Ron and I took our time before we gave up on it. There were five stages to the order management decision. Stage one: We have time to put the new order system into the suite; let's do it. Stage two: No, too risky; we have to go with the old order system. Stage three: Let's put them both in; absolutely fantastic idea. Stage four: Fantastic idea, but we can't make it work. Stage five: Well, then, let's put in the new one. It was my decision. It's in my nature to go for the highest-risk/highest-reward option. That's my cross to bear. We went from having an average order management product to having the premier order management product on the planet. The only problem was that it was brand new and we hadn't done enough testing."

Ellison had no illusions about how critical the order management system was: "The order management system is the heart of the sell side of our e-business suite. Order management is the funnel that captures the information about the sale. The better your order management system, the more information it captures. Our new system captures all the details about the products sold, contractual obligations, payment terms, everything. It manages marketing promotions, vendor rebates, and tracks what salespeople should be compensated on the deal. The flexible pricing engine handles complex and arbitrary rules—like buy two and get the third one free. And the automatic configurator keeps people from buying the wrong combination of products—like computer components that won't work together. It's a great system. But when it first came out, it had a lot of bugs."

Ellison was not acting on his own, however. Ron Wohl fully supported his view that putting in the new order management system was a risk worth taking. Wohl says, "Technically, we really had to include it to fulfill the objective of the E-Business Suite. If it had the flexibility to meet modern e-business practices, you're in great shape, if it doesn't, you don't really have an E-Business Suite." What's less clear is whether Wohl was giving Ellison an accurate picture of the state the work on the order entry system was in. Mark Barrenechea complains that although Ellison had instructed both his and Wohl's teams to standardize all their outward-facing applications on a completely rewritten customer master called Trading Community Architecture (TCA), "the ERP organization had kind of missed it along the way." Critically, the new order management system wasn't using the TCA. A close colleague of Wohl told me, "With most people, Ron comes over as cautious to a fault. But not with Larry. He always wants to look good in front of Larry, and he often ends up telling him what he wants hear." When Wohl told Ellison that he believed that everything was ready for prime time, Ellison wasn't going to argue.*

Another mistake in the testing process was that a handful of chosen customers were trying a beta version of 11i under artificial conditions. Instead of the software running in their own data centers, it was running on Oracle's own computers. Consequently, the severe upgrade problems that some customers would experience after the official launch were masked. Mark Jarvis says, "We were completely in control. We were solving their problems for them. We were doing seventy to eighty percent of what the customer should have been doing himself. It was a mistake." Some good did come out of this botched testing program: it encouraged thinking about delivering software as a Web-based service, allowing the evolution of the earlier Business Online initiative, aimed at small businesses, into the current E-Business Suite Outsourcing.†

Even with Oracle's vaunted rapid implementation procedures for installing 11i, it would be at least three or four months before any signifi-

---

*LE writes: Not true. Ron explained the risks, and I understood the uncertainty surrounding release of the new order management system. And I made the decision to release it.

†LE writes: This accidental discovery that our customers were uniformly more successful and happier with our applications products when we were managing the software for them—upgrading to new versions, fixing bugs, tuning performance—caused us to rethink our approach to applications delivery. E-Business Suite Outsourcing is now the fastest-growing business inside Oracle.

cant "go-lives"—the moment when a business switches its operations to new software. Oracle itself would be moving onto 11i only in stages, between the fall and the end of the year. When I met Ellison for lunch in mid-October at his home in Atherton, he appeared not to have a care in the world. It was the calm before the storm. Clad only in a *Sayonara* T-shirt and shorts and enjoying the sunshine, he oozed confidence about every aspect of the business. The new version of the database that was nine months away was "unbelievable," while 11i was building unstoppable momentum. Even with the clouds gathering over Silicon Valley as the dot coms imploded one by one and the hype about Internet-driven B2B faded, Ellison was sanguine. Just as in 1990, he seemed to think that any economic slowdown might pass Oracle by. His argument was that the E-Business Suite was such an extraordinary "cost-cutting engine" that customers were likely to need it all the more to preserve their profits in difficult selling conditions.

After lunch, Ellison showed me a draft of the chairman's letter to shareholders that he was writing for the annual report. "Tell me what you think when you've had a chance to read it," he said. It was a five-thousand-word account of Oracle's e-business transformation and a marvelously clear exposition of the philosophy of computing that had driven it. One passage went to the heart of what he was trying to do: "To eliminate inefficiency, we had to make information easier to find and easier to share. But how? The solution was quite simple. If we put all our information in one place—a global database on the Internet—then everyone would know where to look to find the information they needed. While conceptually simple, this single unified database approach required fundamental changes to our application software. It turned out to be a massive engineering effort involving thousands of computer programmers. But when we finished the Oracle E-Business Suite, it was the first and only set of applications to work with a single global database. We also developed several new applications, so that the E-Business Suite would be complete. Today, the suite includes every application you need to run your business—marketing, sales, supply chain, manufacturing, customer service, accounting, human resources—everything. It works in every country and in every language. The E-Business Suite is the first and only complete set of applications ever to have been built." Ellison signed off with this: "The more we know, the more rational our decisions. Oracle's getting smarter. Oh, the possibilities. . . ."

If Ellison had known what was coming, he might have restrained himself a little more. In October, the first reports from the field described early 11i implementations afflicted with more than usual bugginess. At the Oracle Applications Users Group conference in Honolulu at the end of October, the complaints were legion. Attendees griped about a lack of reliable information concerning the status of applications, malfunctioning modules—especially CRM and order management—a constant stream of bug-fix patches, and poor support from the customer service organization, which, according to some, hadn't been properly trained on the workings of 11i. In particular, customers that were upgrading from previous versions of Oracle applications were finding that theirs was not a favorable position to be in. During the conference, word got around that Oracle had released around five thousand patches for 11i. That was an oversimplification—many of the patches were to improve functionality rather than to fix bugs and many fixed multiple bugs, but the five thousand figure stuck in the memories of journalists and analysts, who would gleefully include it in almost every piece on Oracle for the best part of a year. Mark Jarvis says, "The five thousand bugs haunted us at least until midsummer of 2001."

Over the next couple of months, customer complaints poured in. Instead of working on the planned features and functions to flesh out the suite's capabilities as planned, development was increasingly engaged in a feverish attempt to produce patches that would fix the bugs that seemed to be flying at them from all sides. It was all made much worse by the sheer number of implementations that were under way. Yet, there was little air of crisis at Redwood Shores. Ellison says, "11i was a huge new product, so I knew there would be a lot of bugs, but there was no way to know how many there were or how long it would take us to fix them. I thought we could fix most of the bugs pretty quickly, during the controlled release phase. I was way too optimistic. It just kind of got away from us, and that became a very big problem."

The software business likes to play the blame game when products don't work as billed. At about the same time that users started beating up Oracle, i2, a specialist in supply-chain planning, was involved in a fierce "debate" with one of its most high profile customers, the sports goods firm Nike. According to Nike, the malfunctioning of the i2 order entry software it had bought to power its demand and inventory management system had been the cause of an earnings shortfall. Not so, said i2; Nike had overcustomized. It was not unusual for Oracle's senior executives to assume at first that customers' problems might be the result of shoddy work by integration partners. They also had plenty of anecdotal evidence that Ellison's well-publicized arguments against excessive customization and his pleas to put in Oracle's software as "plain vanilla" were being ignored by some customers and their integrators.

Out in the field, however, George Roberts had a rather different take on where problems lay: "Larry is very fact-based, very logical with decisions and processes. Customers saying they are having issues is one thing, but being able to track down and point directly at the issue is another thing. It's a new product. Does the customer understand it? Is there a third party implementing it who's been trained on it? The problem was that Larry really thought that his development leaders had it done. He listens to them closely, and that's what they had been telling him. You know, the baby's never ugly. We should have done two things: installed it in-house first and engaged with the early implementations at an executive development level. I think if either of those things had happened, we would have rapidly found out that it wasn't done. As it was, it took us until November to realize we had issues here and to start to mobilize."

By this time, people from Ron Wohl's and Mark Barrennechea's organizations were being parachuted into troubled implementations—"customer escalations"—and were learning about "issues" firsthand. But what rammed the message home was that Oracle itself was, at last, beginning to go live on one part of the suite after another. By December, Oracle was running financials, some HR, field sales automation, and telesales on 11i. Barrenechea says, "The next really big push was to get in contracting and order management over New Year's. What happened was one of the most dramatic moments I'd seen during my five years at Oracle. Everyone except Ron knew that we could not place an order with the new system.* And Larry, knowing we can't place an order, not knowing when we would be able to place an order, and knowing that once we turned off the old bespoke system that there was no going back, said, 'We're going live anyway. I need a forcing function, so off we go.' So we upgraded, and Oracle went down. We were down for fourteen days. For fourteen days that January, Oracle could not place a single order. It was frightening. But we got it to work. Larry was right. It was a great forcing function. At that point I became acutely aware of the customer dissatisfaction and immediately started drilling down into the implementations we were doing."

Ellison's view is less dramatic: "We knew that we were going to go

---

*LE writes: Nonsense. Of course Ron knew about the problems with our internal order management implementation. He was personally running the project to put it in and make it work. We planned to be down for a while, and we were.

down for some time, so we scheduled the installation over the Christmas/New Year's holiday. I had decided on a massive big-bang implementation: we were going to upgrade all our software at once. I never, ever recommend that to our customers. But I wanted to get all our latest application software installed, up, and running at Oracle, and I wanted to do it fast. We should have done it before we released 11i to customers, but we didn't. Okay, that was my mistake. Now I wanted to remedy that mistake as fast as possible. That meant installing 11i at Oracle the first opportunity we had. The fact that we got everything up and running in a couple of weeks was a major accomplishment. We uncovered a number of problems in our software, and we fixed a number of problems in our software. By the time we had finished the Oracle implementation, we had fixed most of the order management problems."

A revised release (11.5.3), which incorporated everything Oracle's developers had painfully learned, was rushed out to customers in early February. It was the third revision since May and by far the most reliable. Barrenechea boasted that 11i was now at least as solid as any rival enterprise software products, most of which had been around much longer. Cap Gemini Ernst & Young, one of the biggest consulting and integration houses, declared in March that "Oracle had made significant improvements and fixes." As a result, the suite was now sufficiently stable for Oracle to begin using the CRM modules in its own practice.

However, just as it took time for the problems with the E-Business Suite to surface, the fact that Oracle had now overcome many of the defects did little to stanch the flow of bad news. The technology press and the analysts were on the hunt for stories about 11i implementations that had run into trouble. Fairly typical was this story of woe in the March 12, 2001, issue of *Information Week*, a magazine aimed at information managers and integrators: "International courier DHL Worldwide Network NV in Brussels, Belgium, for example, was unable to complete transactions based on the euro currency using Oracle's 11i financial applications. Problems included defective currency-to-currency payment functions and slow performance. The glitches put the courier three months behind on its plans to deploy the suite in 12 European locations. DHL came within two days of a drop-dead January 31 deadline before Oracle engineers delivered software patches that fixed the flaws, says Jeremy Young, DHL's finance business-process manager. 'No software is perfect in its early release, but it took seven months to resolve these problems,' Young says."

Young also happened to be the president of the Oracle Applications

Users Group, which been locked in a bitter feud with Oracle about who had the right to stage conferences—the users or the company. In 1995, Oracle had taken over the conferences, which had previously been run by the database user group, launching Oracle OpenWorld later that year. OpenWorld had been a huge marketing success. The number of attendees had gone from 2,500 or so to events that regularly pulled in 40,000 people, blowing the doors off some of the biggest venues in the world. Mark Jarvis reckoned that with the E-Business Suite soon to debut, Oracle needed to do something similar with applications.

The issue was that Oracle was putting a lot of executive time and money into the OAUG's conferences but not getting enough of what it wanted out of them. Jarvis says, "The OAUG ran two events a year in the U.S., and we were highly restricted in what we could do at them. The OAUG insisted that it was very independent. For example, they didn't want Oracle logos and signage around—a bit odd. There were other peculiarities, but their primary goal was to have users talk to other users, while our goal was to get out there, market our products, and educate people on all of the new stuff. The third factor was that a lot of the guys in the user group are not always on the leading edge. They are more interested in running a version of our software from three years ago and they want to talk about that, whereas, of course, we wanted to always talk about the latest thing so that we can get people upgraded and sell them more stuff. We were at cross-purposes. In early 2000, we told the user group of our desire to run a conference and we asked them if they wanted to be part of it. They took it as a declaration of war."

The result was a stalemate. Oracle went ahead with its plans to hold its first AppsWorld conference early in the first quarter of 2001 in Paris and New Orleans. The OAUG continued to hold its conferences, albeit without the official presence of Oracle executives and no keynote speeches from Ellison. Jarvis says, "They also started a very active PR campaign against us, continually emphasizing their 'independence.'" It proved very successful. Whenever industry analysts or press wanted to find out how Oracle customers were getting on with 11i, they started going to the user group for references rather than Oracle. "OAUG board members were suddenly being quoted in the press saying negative things, knocking whatever we were claiming, and attacking the company's whole approach. They wanted to point out to everybody that they weren't on 11i yet. We'd be saying in all our messages that people are starting to use 11i, and they'd be saying, 'But we don't know anybody who's on it.' They provided a counterpoint to everything we said."

If Oracle hadn't been vulnerable to criticism because of the early 11i quality issues, the damage caused by OAUG's revolt would have been easy to limit. But with plenty of people happy to take a swipe at "arrogant" Oracle for claiming more than it had been able to deliver, the user group was the perfect stick to beat it with. Even quite early on, Oracle could have pointed analysts in the direction of many pretty successful 11i implementations if they'd been interested, but it was much more fun to get the horror stories from the OAUG. Ellison maintains that the fight was never with the users as such but with the user group management: "Some of the officers in the users' group were not customers or users of our applications at all—they were independent consultants who made their living running the Oracle Applications Users Group meetings. We were threatening their livelihood by running our own meetings. It was unfortunate that at the same time we were having the quality problems with 11i, we were also having the spat with the user group. They bashed us every chance they got."

If Oracle had gone on making its numbers, the bad blood with the user group would have been no more than a minor irritant. Even the fallout from the buggy early versions of 11i would in all probability have been containable. But on the eve of the first AppsWorld show in Paris, the moment when Oracle had planned to deliver to the world a confident message about its winning applications strategy, a series of almost uniformly gloomy reports from Wall Street analysts thudded on the mat, including one by Morgan Stanley's Chuck Phillips. He argued that Oracle's forecast in December of 15 to 20 percent year-over-year revenue growth in its core database business, along with 75 percent for applications, would be extremely hard to achieve given the fact that no fewer than thirty of Oracle's dot-com customers had gone bust and that around 12 percent of the firm's total database license revenue had come from dot coms in the previous year. A prescient report by Bank of America analysts noted, "Though management seems confident in the progress Oracle has made thus far in the quarter, we remind investors that a good amount of the quarter's business remains to be done. The next three weeks will tell the tale." As shareholders chewed over the possibility that Ellison might have exaggerated the extent of Oracle's immunity to the forces that were blighting other tech companies, Oracle's stock price plunged by 13 percent, to $23.56. In response, Oracle reiterated that it was standing by its bullish forecast.

A few days later in Paris, Ellison seemed unusually nervous and flustered. The main theme of his speech was on the folly of customizing Oracle's software and why it was better to buy a complete suite from

Oracle—in Ellison's analogy, a finished car that you knew would work—rather than a bundle of kit glued together by mechanics from IBM. He said, "We've worked hard to be the first car company. We don't want to sell you parts and labor. If you customize our software, when we bring out a new version you can't use it. You trap yourself in an old version." Ultimately, customizing the E-Business Suite was futile because Oracle itself would soon add the functionality customers were looking for. "We will bring out a new version of the software before you can finish customizing our old version." *

There was nothing wrong with the familiar argument. But without a prepared text, Ellison sometimes puts things in starker terms than he—and certainly Oracle's marketing department—intends. A significant part of the speech was a rant against system integrators—evil folk who persuaded customers to part with huge sums of money to let them mess up perfectly good software. As usual, IBM was singled out as the worst villain: "IBM has thousands of consultants who are eager to help. IBM has alliances with five hundred software partners. IBM has thousands of guys with glue guns who come and stick it all together. At least that's what I think happens. What is systems integration, anyway? What do those thousands of people do all day?" Unfortunately, most of the AppsWorld sponsors just happened to be systems integrators. Mark Jarvis says, "I was just thinking how proud we were of ourselves that we had done a great first AppsWorld, when we suddenly picked a battle with every systems integrator in town." Oracle had lined up a series of anti–systems integration ads. One said, "Just Say No to Systems Integration," while another asked, "Do You Have the Big Systems Integration Blues?" Naturally, "Blues" was written in the style of IBM's logo. After Paris, they never saw the light of day.

The other big "take-out" from the Paris speech was Ellison's frank recognition that the E-Business Suite didn't yet do everything its cus-

---

*LE writes: Worse than being overzealous in this presentation, I was ambiguous, imprecise, and easily misunderstood. The problem was that I failed to be clear as to what I meant by "customize." Of course customers can tailor our applications to their business processes, but they should never modify our software. Customers can add to our applications and connect our applications to non-Oracle applications, but they should never go in and change the application program itself. If they do that, they will create quality and support problems and find it difficult to upgrade to new versions of our applications products.

tomers wanted and maybe never would but that an "80 to 85 percent so-lution" that could be implemented in five months was better than the 100 percent promised by some vendors that would take three years to put in and still wouldn't work. Immediately, the chorus went up that Ellison had claimed that the suite was complete and now he was saying that it wasn't. The following week, when AppsWorld moved to New Orleans, Jarvis per-suaded Ellison to ease up on the systems integrators. However, although the speech went down much better than the one in Paris, once again there were unintended consequences. Jarvis says, "A whole new thing came out, which was that he gave everyone the impression that you had to have the entire suite or nothing. I've looked at the videos many times. He didn't actually say that, but that was the impression he created."

Ten days later, on the first of March, after the markets had closed, Or-acle issued a profit warning for its third quarter. It now expected to miss its earnings-per-share number by 2 cents. Although applications had con-tinued to grow strongly thanks to the buzz that had been generated around 11i, database revenue growth was flat to negative. Ellison ex-plained, "It's very disappointing. A bunch of deals were approved at the senior vice president level, but once they got to the CFO and CEO level, they were pushed off. We have a lot of nervous executives looking at this economy and being very cautious. They want to wait thirty to sixty days so they can get a better read on this economy." In after-hours trading, Oracle's stock fell 21 percent, to $16.88, about half the price it had been as recently as early January.

When Oracle got around to making its official earnings announce-ment in mid-March, the mix was different but the overall result was the same. But while database did a little better than predicted, applications revenue was slowing at a worrying speed. From the 75 percent growth projected by management on February 14 to the 50 percent expected on March 1 at the time of the profit warnings, the real figure had turned out to be only 25 percent. It didn't take a genius to see that not everything that was going on could be explained by the weakening economy and edgy CEOs waiting for "visibility" to return. For anyone who wanted to see, there was mounting evidence that it wasn't only the economy that prospective Oracle applications customers wanted to see stabilize.

To complete a miserable few weeks for Ellison, from the moment of the earnings warning legal vultures had been stirring up their clients to file class action suits against Oracle for misleading investors about its numbers and the true state of the E-Business Suite. One law firm, Milberg Weiss, alleged that Ellison was involved in the "largest case of insider dealing in U.S. financial history." It claimed that he had dumped nearly $900 million worth of shares during the third quarter, knowing that the stock price was likely to fall soon. The suit, on behalf of a small pension fund, accused Ellison of concealing information about the cost of the "massive technical problems" of 11i. In fact, the shares that Ellison had sold, his first disposal for five years, were stock options that were due to expire in August. Oracle said that the suit was "entirely without merit and would be defended vigorously."

Adding insult to injury, the fashionable technology consultancy Forrester Research leapt on the speeding anti-Oracle bandwagon with a particularly vicious briefing note, charging Ellison with "stooping to a new low—blaming its 11i unhappy customers for doing too much customization." The note, by an analyst named Laurie Orlov, attacked the whole proposition of the integrated suite, blithely advising Oracle: "By unhinging apps like CRM from tight links to order management, the individual apps can be coupled with apps from other vendors and can then be revised or released in chunks." Only three months earlier, Forrester had enthused that its "all-integrated approach will make Oracle outperform any best-of-breed technology vendor in the long run."

As usual, Chuck Phillips brought some level-headed perspective. His view of the numbers was philosophical: "Is this the beginning of the end? We don't think so. Every time Oracle misses a quarter—which is about every five to seven quarters—there are a rash of proclamations about market saturation [database] and fatal strategy missteps [usually applications] that point to eternal doom. Even in the best of times, Oracle has not produced smooth license or product line growth from quarter to quarter. The numbers generally fall where they may without, much to our chagrin, a ton of backlog management. Billions of license revenue gets booked in the last five days of the quarter and it's difficult to smooth out that business model. Usually, investors throw in the towel on Oracle for three quarters and don't want to hear the name mentioned for a while. But then, comparisons get easier, customers eat through their licenses and need more capacity, the product footprint expands into higher growth areas, the buying cycle improves with the economy and recently released products get seasoned and get some traction in the installed base. The only cure is time."

The mood at Oracle was bloody but unbowed. There was an embarrassed realization that it had fallen down badly on execution in sending a hugely important new product out to customers in an unfit state. But at the same time, there was complete conviction both that the suite message was right and that Oracle was well on the way to dealing with the outstanding quality issues. Talking to me nine months later, Ron Wohl said, "Fundamentally, we tried to do something that I think was much larger in scope than even we realized and was much larger than the scope of any software we had released beforehand. In retrospect, we didn't do a good enough job up front—our QA [quality assurance] procedures didn't work because they had outgrown our scale.

"I would have liked to have done two things differently: we should have changed a number of processes within development to deal with the scale of the release, which we have now done; and two . . . we would have been wiser to withhold the release a little bit. We would have been better off as a company if we had deferred the release by three or four months. The stability actually improved at a very rapid pace. You could see it in the bug numbers, you could see it in customer satisfaction by anecdote. Customers who had started on a later version [11.5.3 and above], they were extremely happy. Customers who started on one of the early versions weren't happy, and they had a right to be upset with us."

Mark Barrenechea thanks God for the recession: "We actually got a little lucky that the economy turned down. It gave us more time to deal with the problems. Of course we'd like the satisfaction of stabbing our competitors before they hang themselves. But the downstep in the economy meant that a lot of them were just dying. It couldn't have happened at a better time for us. It meant that there were fewer choices among the best-of-breed vendors and customers were more nervous about making those choices. Secondly, in a boom economy, there's a lot more IT dollars. If something isn't working the customers can say, 'Fuck you' and go to another vendor, spend some more money. So companies weren't willing to double down on their mistakes and bet the farm, they couldn't abandon us. So they forced Oracle, and we were forcing ourselves to walk through the issues and fix the problems. To quote John Milton, I was not displeased that there was a downturn in the economy."

Ellison is rueful but philosophical. There's little in the software business left to surprise him. "A little over ten years ago we undertook a massive rework of our database software. It strained our company to the limit, but it resulted in a database product that was so much better than anything offered by the competition that we became the number one database company in the world. We have to make big leaps forward in technology or sink slowly into obsolescence. The pain is worth the gain. It's very much like childbirth. It's a lot of pain followed by great joy. The joy helps you forget the pain. When Version 7 of the database came out, customers loved it. The pain of Version 6 was largely forgotten. The applications release 11i birthing process was not nearly as painful as Version 6 of our database, and I think the 11i gain will be even greater. We'll see. People haven't forgotten the pain yet. In fact, during the worst of our bad publicity and our sinking stock price, somebody said to me, 'Oh my God, this is as bad as 1991.' Jeff Henley and I both laughed. In 1991, we were on the brink of bankruptcy. At the worst point in this recent downturn, we had $6 billion in cash and profit margins of thirty-five percent."

Ellison had previously said that the only thing that would make any difference was a quarter that beat expectations. "Most analysts try to foretell the future by understanding and explaining the recent past. If you have a bad quarter, if your sales are going down, they will attribute part of that sales decline to product problems that are creating competitive pressures. If you suddenly have a good quarter, better than the competition, they explain that it's because your product is getting better. It's as simple as that—they just look at the numbers. So the best way to improve perception of the E-Business Suite is to sell more of it. Then the analysts will say, 'Good job, Oracle, it's a great product you got there.' "

Despite everything, at least the idea of the integrated suite was beginning to win acceptance, not just from customers but even from rivals, like SAP and PeopleSoft. George Roberts soon began to notice that he no longer had to bang the table with suite-versus-kit arguments. "If you have a strong strategy, it forces your competition to respond. Whether the release was premature or not, every major competitor has been forced to respond to the Oracle message and the value proposition that we brought out with 11i." The initial execution might have left much to be desired, but Oracle is a company that learns from its mistakes. Oracle, and Ellison in particular, have a reputation for arrogance. But during the difficult first six months of 2001, I discovered an impressive determination to face facts and put things right combined with an iron conviction that the E-Business Suite was still destined for greatness. Establishing it would not be the early-round knockout that Ellison had predicted, but as the going got tough, his certainty of ultimate victory, if anything, seemed to increase.

11

TAKING STOCK

April 2001

In the weeks immediately after the "lost" third quarter and the trip to China, Ellison has been trying to get a handle on how bad the financial situation really is. But immediately after what could have been a rather tricky board meeting, he shows no sign of stress. The previous day, he flew in from a two-week spring break with his children in Tahiti on the recently renamed *Ronin* (its previous name—*Izanami*—spelled "I'm a Nazi" backward, which Ellison didn't think quite right for its Jewish owner).* His only grumble is that he strained his neck and sprained his toe while trying to crash tackle eighteen-year-olds during a game of beach football.

Ellison's next appointment is a press conference to announce a shift in the marketing strategy behind 11i. To some extent, the change is being driven by the worsening economy. However, he also wants to try to correct some impressions about the E-Business Suite that may be damaging its prospects in the market and for which he feels largely responsible. Ellison has already acknowledged that he made a mistake in sounding too hostile to systems integration—some integration with legacy software is

---

*LE writes: Izanami and Izanagi are the names of the two Shinto deities that gave birth to the Japanese islands, or so legend has it. When the local newspapers started pointing out that Izanami was "I'm a Nazi" spelled backward, I had the choice of explaining Shintoism to the reporters at the San Francisco Chronicle or changing the name of the boat.

inevitable in all but the newest businesses. It's modifying code that's the real crime. But there's another misapprehension that he thinks could be holding back sales: by spending so much time and money extolling the benefits and uniqueness of 11i as both integrated and *complete*, Oracle may have frightened off potential customers by making them think that they have to buy and install the whole suite at once—a massive undertaking that implies getting rid of any existing software no matter how recently acquired and fit for the job.

The new line is that the E-Business Suite can be broken down into bite-size chunks that automate discrete "business flows." The idea is that you can decide which "flow" of business processes you want to automate first, get that done quickly and relatively cheaply, and then move on to automate others when the first has proven its worth. To dramatize the idea and to differentiate Oracle's offering from that of its deadly rival, Siebel, Ellison has come up with the idea of installing "global CRM" within ninety days of purchase for a fixed price—any time or cost overruns "will be on our nickel," he says.*

The press briefing is held in the ground floor executive dining room at 500 Oracle Parkway, the headquarters building. There's a good turnout of about twenty journalists, including reporters from *The Wall Street Journal*, the *Financial Times, BusinessWeek, Fortune,* and *Forbes.* Ellison starts off by saying that the software industry's preoccupation with offering separate applications for what are really continuous processes has made "the graceful flow of information" hard to achieve. For example, says Ellison, although Siebel provides sales automation, it doesn't have contract automation. By contrast, the Oracle E-Business Suite automates complete business flows that reflect the way businesses operate in the real world; the alternative is to automate functional departments in separate modules. But unless data is to stay fragmented among different applications, you need to write separate programs that attempt to move the data between each application. It's an approach that, as Ellison never tires of saying, frequently fails, meaning one group can't work with another. Even when it doesn't fail, it's still very expensive.

---

*LE writes: Our new sales force automation software was an Internet system that ran on top of a single global database. We were able to get it up and running very quickly and inexpensively. Guaranteeing a firm fixed price for the software and the labor to put it in seemed the best way to differentiate us from Siebel.

Louis and Lillian Ellison in the 1950s

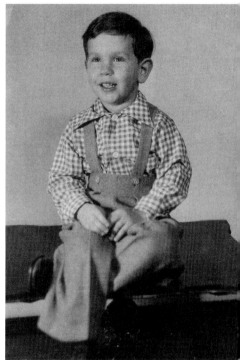

Larry Ellison in 1948

Larry Ellison and Jimmy Linn in 1950

Larry Ellison rock climbing in Yosemite in the late 1970s

Larry Ellison playing folk guitar in the early 1970s

David, Larry, and Megan Ellison in 1989

Annual report picture in 1988

Kathleen O'Rourke in 1990

Larry Ellison, President
Clinton, and Melanie Craft
in 1996

Sayonara in a hurricane in the 1998 Sydney-to-Hobart race

Melanie Craft and Larry Ellison at the finish of the 1998 Sydney-to-Hobart race

Katana in Capri in 2001

Carl Djerassi and Josh Lederberg on *Katana* in Sardinia in 2001

Prince Alwaleed's son, Prince Alwaleed Bin Talal, Melanie Craft, Larry Ellison, and Matthew Symonds in Cannes in 2001

Judge James Linn, Larry Ellison, and Melanie Craft in *Katana* in 2001

Melanie Craft and Larry Ellison kayaking in Alaska in 2002

Ronin in Alaska in 2002

Larry Ellison and his Marchetti S211 jet fighter

Melanie Craft in 2003

Cameron Hirigoyen

Woodside Project, 2003

Woodside Project, 2003

Matthew Symonds, Melanie Craft, and Larry Ellison at Woodside in 2002

Melanie Craft, Larry Ellison, Joe Montana, and Mayor Willie Brown at Woodside in 2003

Larry Ellison in China in 2001

The example he gives of Oracle's alternative is a flow called "campaign-to-cash"—one of ten other "fast-forward flows" that are being announced with names such as "plan-to-campaign," "procure-to-pay," "click-to-order," "opportunity-to-forecast," and "call-to-resolution." Once a decision is made to initiate a sales promotion, the software filters prospects and leads from the customer database and sends thousands of targeted e-mails—all within minutes. When a prospect turns up at the Web store, his or her identity is known. If a sale isn't made, the details will go to telesales, which will follow leads that didn't transact. Once a sale is booked, every other part of the process is automated, right through to the moment when the order is fulfilled and the vendor gets the money—hence campaign-to-cash. Ellison boasts that while a Siebel implementation can take nine months to complete in just one country of operation, Oracle guarantees to "go live" globally within ninety days.* While the cost of the software license fee to the consulting charges for big CRM implementations is typically in the ratio of 1 to 7; Oracle is betting on getting nearly 1 to 1.

Ellison goes on to predict that previously high-flying Internet software firms, such as Ariba and Commerce One, which are already suffering from the sudden downturn in demand for e-business applications, will not survive. "These aren't one-product companies," he asserts. "They're one-feature companies. Ariba has a little piece of the procure-to-pay flow—Internet purchasing requests. It's just a tiny component part of a procure-to-pay system." Oracle has already drawn attention to Ariba's difficulties with a nasty piece of copy on its Web site entitled "Ariba Derci." Siebel, by comparison, has a full CRM suite, but Ellison claims that it's the product of acquiring other software companies and putting a Siebel label on their products. "It's complete, but it's not integrated. It's a lot easier writing checks than writing software."

The reporters are politely interested in the "CRM in ninety days" message; the next day there is widespread, albeit fairly muted, coverage. But it's clear that they see it more as smart marketing than as anything fundamental—although Carleen Hawn of *Forbes* asks an interesting question about the impact on Oracle's business model of switching to a high-volume, low-price approach. (Ellison's answer is that the cost has never

---

*LE writes: We can't do all the business flows in ninety days. Campaign-to-cash takes longer. But we can do opportunity-to-forecast—global forecast—in ninety days, even in a fairly large company.

been in the software but in the labor needed to put it in—Microsoft got it right, the enterprise guys got it wrong.) They're also pretty used to hearing Ellison banging on about Oracle's "war on complexity" and the dreadful consequences of fragmenting data, even though he's always funny and they can't help laughing at his jokes.

What they most want is to get Ellison talking about the economy and its effects on the competitive landscape. Marc Boslet of *The Industry Standard* (a tech magazine in Silicon Valley that at the height of the dot-com boom was running to more than two hundred glossy, ad-packed pages but is now in what turn out to be terminal financial difficulties) asks in what way the B2B market has changed. It's time for Ellison to start enjoying himself. "A lot of wild things were going on," he says. "People were watching the stock market more closely than they were watching their businesses. Commerce One was giving big customers stock in their company if they bought its B2B exchange software. Companies were buying Commerce One products because they expected to make a lot of money on Commerce One stock. It seemed a brilliant plan because every time one of these big deals was announced the Commerce One stock would go up. On top of that, some of these companies would then spin off their purchasing departments and call them B2B exchanges. They thought they'd get rich taking their purchasing department public. It was crazy." *

Another question, from the *San Francisco Chronicle*'s Kelly Zito, is about whether Oracle is finding itself squeezed in the database market by IBM (the following day, IBM announces that it's buying an old but much-weakened survivor from the brutal database wars of a decade ago, Informix). No problem, says Ellison. Oracle 9i with real application clusters runs SAP or Siebel five times faster than IBM's DB2 or Microsoft's SQL Server, with ten times the scalability and one hundred times the reliability. "RAC [Real Application Clusters] is the most important new technology from Oracle in the last ten years. It's game, set, and match in the database business," he crows. The briefing is already running half an hour overtime, and the Oracle PR people are trying to pull Ellison out. Appropriately, one of the last questions is about the battle between Siebel and Oracle. The previous week, Tom Siebel claimed that he

---

LE writes: At the height of this madness, we lost a very big sale to Commerce One because I refused to give the prospective customer any Oracle stock as a part of the deal.

didn't often see Oracle win big new accounts when the fight was on. Ellison is both outraged and amused. He says, "Very interesting. Possibly Tom needs an optometrist."

The meeting that Ellison is late for is the regular Monday afternoon PDMC (product development management committee) meeting attended by the heads of the key engineering teams. It starts off with fairly routine pricing and licensing issues. Among them is a proposal that Oracle's e-mail server (which, Ellison says, is faster and more reliable than Microsoft Exchange because it runs on top of a database) should cease to be sold as several separate products. Oddly, there's a feeling that telcos that license Oracle Internet Directory "product" in the millions at $5 a seat might not like the change. "It makes no sense to price every feature as a separate product," says Ellison. "But that's the way the enterprise software business has been for a very, very long time." Another mystery to Ellison is the poor reception of a proposal from Ron Wohl to stop talking about exchange software and to refer instead to "hub-and-spoke" software. Wohl convinced Ellison to make the change, and Ellison has been using the new terminology for several weeks. Unfortunately, nobody else agrees. Ellison says jokingly: "Okay, okay, I give up. I promise never to say 'hub' or 'spoke' again. I just want to get out of here before midnight. What's next?"

The next item on the agenda is rather more serious. It turns out that one of the "fast-forward flows" that Oracle is formally to launch the next day and that Ellison has just previewed with the press doesn't work as it should. It's a package called "incentives to performance" that is designed to allow members of a sales team to calculate their compensation precisely. The software has to deal with a fiendishly complicated set of variables, determining rules for who should get what as a lead is turned into an order and eventually becomes a sale. In the approved manner, Oracle has been using its own business and processes as a laboratory for developing its applications.

Ellison starts off by asking detailed questions about how the software maps and automates the set of interactions that begins with sales forecasts and ends with accounts receivable. He doesn't like what he hears. Always suspicious about the ability of sales organizations to extract more than they should by counting the same sale more than once or by spreading the commission around to too many people, he concludes that the detail isn't there. Suddenly he asks crossly, "Just what is it that we're announcing tomorrow?" The tension in the room is mounting. Is Ellison going to pull tomorrow's announcement? One of the team involved in the

"CRM in ninety days" initiative is licking his lips nervously and starting to sweat despite the air-conditioning. He agrees that the product isn't ready. Ellison says with rising incredulity, "You want to announce this, but not deliver until May . . . can anyone tell me why we're doing this? Why should we announce it now? Why shouldn't we wait until it works?"* It's a nasty moment, but Ellison is assured that the other flows are ready. The decision is made to pull the sales force compensation package until the problems are resolved and go ahead with launching the other flows on Tuesday.

• • •

When the day is over, Ellison and I drive the half mile to a canalside house he owns in Redwood Shores, where we can sit on the deck and watch the pelicans. Ellison's earlier belief (sincerely held) that Oracle alone might miraculously escape the recession sweeping through the rest of the technology industry now seems ludicrously optimistic. What really happened during those last few days in February at the end of the quarter? Was it a question of two or three big deals falling through at the last moment, as Ellison had earlier appeared to suggest, or was something more fundamental going on?

"No. It was a lot of deals—dozens, I'd say. Sometimes a deal was delayed. Sometimes the size of the deal dropped from $6 million to $2 million. All of a sudden people stopped buying in anticipation of their needs for the next couple of years. Instead they bought exactly what they needed for the next three months. There were even cases where companies that were already using our software were trying to find ways not to pay for it. I'm not going to mention names, but a very large wireless company that was supposed to give us $15 million or $20 million this quarter, based on their own published subscriber numbers, decided to dispute the amount. It was just a negotiating tactic. If we lowered their bill, they'd pay us this quarter. We didn't. Lots of tech companies and telcos are under financial stress, so they're being much more careful with their cash these days. The dot-com die-out is getting worse. Suddenly, moving all your business processes to the Internet doesn't seem so important anymore. It seems like e-business and the Internet are going out of fashion."

LE writes: It made no sense to release the compensation flow until it was working successfully at Oracle. I had made this mistake too many times in the past. Never again.

I suggested that perhaps companies were no longer worried about Web-based "stealth competitors" coming from nowhere to eat their lunch. "That's exactly right," said Ellison. "Wal-Mart is no longer worried about Amazon.com—if Wal-Mart ever was worried about Amazon. A lot of companies have realized they don't have to move quite so quickly. They can be more deliberate and automate at a more rational rate. Flying the Internet flag isn't so cool anymore." Perhaps another factor was that simply making an announcement about what you were doing on the Internet was no longer likely to have a major impact on their stock price? "Absolutely," replied Ellison. "All these B2B exchanges . . . there were lots of companies that issued a press release about a B2B exchange and saw their stock price shoot up. Commerce One dished out about three of these B2B press releases for every one that we sent out. They killed us in the press release war. But that exchange business is gone now. And it's not just the exchange business that's dried up. Companies are much more cautious about buying any kind of new technology."

It is almost as if Ellison were talking about some semi-mythical period remembered only through the mists of time. I can't help reminding him that in mid-February, only ten weeks ago, he still thought Oracle would make its number. "Absolutely," he says. "We went into that quarter extremely confident. We got off to a great start. If you look at our quarter month by month, we had great growth in December, we were still way ahead in January, and then we hit the wall in February." When did he first know that something big had changed, and why didn't Oracle's own much-vaunted e-business systems provide any warning? "Our sales-forecasting system tells us how many deals are in the pipeline and multiplies their value by a historic close rate. If there's a change in close rate we detect that, but in our case we don't detect it until the last day or two of the quarter, because that's when we close so much of our business. I hate that. Consulting firms actually go out and train software buyers to negotiate right up until the last hour of the last day of our quarter before signing a multimillion-dollar deal. Most software companies will increase the discount on the last day just to get the deal into the quarter. It's a monster the industry has created by mapping its sales compensation plans to its fiscal reporting. I think that's a bad practice, and we've tried to put a stop to it at Oracle. But that hasn't stopped our big customers from asking— and taking us right up to the end of quarter before they sign."

I asked Ellison what he had expected the reaction to be when he issued the earnings warning. He said, "Well, the reaction had already occurred. The stock had already gone down dramatically. It was one very loud 'I told you so.' It turns out that the analysts were looking at the macroeconomic forecast and that proved to be more accurate than our internal systems sales forecast." So how bad did he think things were going to get, and how did he plan to adjust to the new circumstances? "Well, first off, I thank God that we spent the last two years reengineering our company into an efficient global e-business. If we had just started the process of moving to the Internet now, we would really be in trouble. Yeah, we were disappointed in the quarter, but it wasn't a disaster: our sales went up, our margins went up, and our profits went up. I'm not happy, but I'm not going to go out and kill myself. We're really in pretty good shape. We're making a lot of money, and our products have never been stronger. We have release 9i of the database coming out soon. We have a cool new version of the application server that's going to drive BEA nuts. Our products are competitive, and our organization is efficient. Those two things allow me to sleep at night. The last time the economy slowed down [in 1991], Oracle lost money."

Even if the product cycle was in good shape, it was clear from the "CRM in ninety days" initiative that the marketing message was changing with the times. "That's true. Without the same sense of urgency about moving to the Internet, we have to sell differently. What we're selling now are very rapid, low-cost, low-risk implementations of automated business flows. The E-Business Suite contains several separate business flows. We can automate one flow at a time—like "procure-to-pay" or "opportunity-to-global-sales-forecast" and so on. We provide the software and the labor to get it up and running for a guaranteed fixed price, so customers get a guaranteed return on their investment with a minimum of risk. That's what's selling these days—return on investment. People have lost their appetite for risk.

"Selling separate flows solved another key problem for us. By talking about the E-Business Suite as complete, people thought that you have to buy and install the entire suite all at once. It's an all-or-nothing kind of deal. No, no, no. Not true. But our competitors used it against us quite effectively. So we thought that we had better start talking about the separate E-Business Suite flows inside the suite. That also lets us sell better against the best-of-breed specialists. We'll sign a contract guaranteeing to do a CRM flow in ninety days for X number of dollars. We tell our prospects to go ask IBM and Siebel how long it will take and how much it will cost for them to do the same thing. It was the best way we could think of to drive home the point that Oracle applications install faster and are much less expensive to run than the competition. Even today many companies make the incredibly expensive mistake of failing to ask for a guaranteed implementation cost and guaranteed annual operating cost of the applications systems they are about to buy. We'll guarantee everything. The competition won't."

Would Oracle have gone down this route if the economy hadn't gone bad? "Well, marketing the flows separately is a good idea with or without the downturn. We marketed the complete integrated E-Business Suite as a cost-cutting, productivity-enhancing engine. Now we emphasize the fact that you can install the suite a flow at a time. So we have two applications marketing messages. The first message is, we have a complete integrated E-Business Suite—we saved $1 billion at Oracle using it. The second message is that you can install one business flow at a time, quickly and at a guaranteed price."

A big part of Ellison's 11i campaign has been centered on the idea that systems integration was to be avoided at all cost. Yet the assumption behind being able to install the software to manage a particular flow was that it was being integrated at some point with legacy systems. Didn't that mean that he was backtracking on something pretty fundamental? "Yeah, the 'Just say no to systems integration' slogan was poorly thought out on my part. It wasn't systems integration that had to be avoided; it was code modifying that had to be avoided. Of course, some systems integration may be necessary. So wake up! Try a little harder!"

Perhaps another reason for the flip-flop on systems integration could be the damage that was being done to Oracle's relations with the big consulting firms, which frequently recommend what software their clients should buy. Ellison said, "I don't think so. We still think it's important to *minimize* systems integration. It's just not always possible to eliminate it completely. 'Say no to systems integration' was right some of the time, but it wasn't right often enough for it to be our primary message. 'No code modification' is the correct message. If you've integrated our accounting application to your custom telephone-billing systems, you can easily move to the next version of our accounting system so long as you haven't modified our code. If you've modified our code, you're stuck." And the integrators, the consultants? "Now that we've cleaned up our message, the integrators that compete on price love us because we install faster and cost less to operate than the competition. The integrators that do the giant time-and-materials projects still don't like our message."

How was Oracle doing in efforts to win a massive deal with AT&T that Ellison had recently been pitching in New York? "They'll make a choice in very, very short order. I think we're ahead. We're the only one that can do the business flows. By the way, we did a very similar business flow for their ADSL division. The business we're trying to get now is fixed-line. They're trying to decide whether they're going to do the flow with us or take a more traditional, functional piece of sales automation from Siebel. We'll know in a week or so." As is often the case with Ellison, he was being overoptimistic about the time frame. The negotiations with AT&T dragged on interminably as key executives on both sides left and the decision-making process at the troubled telecom giant stalled. Apart from the sheer size of the deal, winning it would create a vital reference point in Oracle's struggle to catch Siebel.

How was the fight against Siebel, the market leader in sales automation and CRM software, going on other fronts? What about Tom Siebel's remark, quoted earlier in the day, that he hardly ever saw Oracle competing with CRM on major accounts? It's the kind of dismissive claim that incumbents always like to make about the pretensions of challengers, but it had seemed to needle Ellison. Obviously Mark Barrenechea lived and breathed the idea of one day destroying Siebel as a serious rival, but what about Ellison? Did he get up in the morning thinking about how to take the fight to Siebel? Ellison replied, "At one point I ranked Siebel as our most important applications competitor, because they're the largest best-of-breed software company and they have a close partnership with the largest best-of-breed integrator, IBM. I thought we had to beat Siebel for the suite approach to triumph over best of breed. But even now the outcome of that war is now fairly certain. We'll end up with a couple of suite companies, and SAP will be our only major competitor."

It's true that the tech downturn isn't all bad news for Oracle. The likes of the once fashionable Ariba and Commerce One, which had been carried to extraordinary market caps by the Internet tsunami, were now in danger of being left high and dry. But Siebel Systems was a much tougher proposition. Founded and run with iron discipline by the former Oracle salesman Tom Siebel, the company was still outselling Oracle in CRM by a factor of four to one. Revenues in 2001 broke the $2 billion mark accompanied by net earnings of $255 million. Siebel also had a war chest of well over $1 billion—useful rainy-day money to ride out a prolonged tech slump. I first met Siebel in the summer of 1999 at his office, which cheekily stands just three miles north of Oracle's on the opposite side of Highway 101. A small, intense man with a harsh, gravelly voice, he lost little time in launching a bitter attack on Ellison and what he called his "pathological lying." When he heard I was having lunch with Ellison later that day, he immediately scrawled on a piece of paper "The six lies of Larry Ellison" and said, "Give him that." Which, to Ellison's vast amusement, I did. Siebel's main point about Oracle was that however much it was prepared to throw at building a competitive CRM package, he would believe it when he saw it: "This isn't simply something you can throw a thousand software programmers at. It's something that somebody in the organization has to know something about."

In much the same way that Ellison uses Microsoft and IBM as the points to Oracle's counterpoint, Siebel uses Ellison and Oracle to define what Siebel isn't. He says, "It is critically important to me that Siebel Systems never develops yet another pathological [a favorite Siebel word] Silicon Valley corporate culture. Too many companies here have an arrogant self-image. Their attitude is 'We are geniuses and visionaries who make insanely great technology.' And there's the cult of the software CEO, where it's all about 'me, me, me' and my transitory fulfillments— my parking lot filled with Ferraris, my crushing the competitors, my money, articles with pictures of me in my fighter jet or being escorted around by PR assistants." * Who could he be talking about?

Although Ellison patronizingly refers to him as "Tommy," he has a grudging admiration for what Siebel has achieved in defining and dominating a market (much as Oracle did in its early days), but he doesn't have much respect for Siebel's technology. "Siebel Systems is all about sales automation. They defined the category and made the market. They were the first mover. They built a ruthless, big-deal-focused sales force. But they have a couple of problems. Despite what Tom says, their software's still client/server and their Internet version isn't due out until the fall. Two years ago the Siebel Web site claimed their software was architected for the Internet—but it wasn't. Now they say that their Internet version is on its way. So I guess they moved to the Internet two years ago and it was so much fun, they're going to do it again. So, who's lying? Tom and Craig Conway were both key lieutenants in Gary Kennedy's sales team. Were they hard chargers? Jesus, were they ever. They're both killer salesmen and hard-driving sales managers. That's what made them successful. But they're not choirboys. And now that they're both CEOs they'll live and die as their quarterly results rise and fall. Tommy talked a

---

*LE writes: Gee, I guess I should have named the company "Ellison Systems" and put a huge ELLISON sign on the side of our buildings so everyone could see it as they drive by. And can someone please tell me what "transitory fulfillments" means?

lot about the 'pathology' of Oracle. And when Tommy talked people listened, because he was delivering the goods quarter after quarter. But that's all about to end. He really struggled to make his last quarter. He pumped it up with software swaps and a big deal with IBM. He can't do that two quarters in a row. Tommy's going to crash." * Siebel was indeed finding the going harder, but Ellison's predictions about Siebel hitting a wall had been wrong before. Two years earlier he had forecast that by the middle of 2000 Oracle would have knocked Siebel off its perch.

Part of Oracle's problem was that it had taken the company so long to build a product with enough features to match Siebel's even remotely. And whereas Siebel had gone out and bought companies to fill feature gaps, Ellison had insisted on making everything at home to ensure the architectural integrity of the integrated suite. As usual, Ellison put a higher priority on the benefits that derive from engineering elegance than the crude business functionality that Siebel's hotshot sales force expertly leveraged with customers. However, a new report from the Gartner Group had found that while Siebel remained well ahead in terms of customer wins, in the last year Oracle had emerged as its only significant challenger, putting distance between itself and the rest of the chasing pack.

Ellison says, "We don't have every feature that Siebel has with all their different CRM products. But our CRM front-office systems are tightly integrated with our ERP back-office systems. Our CRM systems and ERP system share a common database, so it's easy to find the information you're looking for. All our applications are architected for the Internet, so it's quick and easy to roll them out globally. We have enough advantages to win our fair share of CRM deals. Siebel built their feature-rich portfolio of CRM products by acquiring lots of different CRM companies: Scopus and about a dozen others. Then they rebranded all these separate products as the 'Siebel CRM Suite.' But it's not a true suite. The products are barely integrated, and they don't share a common database. Writing checks is easy. Writing software is hard.

"Could we have caught up with Siebel any faster? Sure. All we had to do was buy a bunch of companies like they did. But we wanted to stick to our product strategy of an integrated suite built on top of a common database. The only way to get one of those is to build it from scratch. You can't go out and buy it because it doesn't exist. We're building software

---

LE writes: And crash he did.

about as fast as we can. We have nearly four thousand applications developers working on the suite, about nine hundred of them in CRM. [According to Mark Barrenechea, the true CRM figure is nearer to fifteen hundred, up from ten when he arrived at Oracle four years ago—Ellison still doesn't know how many people work for him!] They may have built the Empire State Building in nine months, but the E-Business Suite has already taken us several years, and we're still not done. Complex business software takes a long, long time to build. Sometimes you have to build it two or three times before you get it right. Mark Barrenechea still has a lot of work left to do. Mark worked for Scopus when Siebel bought them but came to work at Oracle rather than going to Siebel—something to do with having to wear a tie while programming." [Tom Siebel insists on suits and ties as a mark of 'respect' to customers and as another way to differentiate the company from the Silicon Valley norm.] As Barrenechea tells it, "I remember going over to Larry's house in Atherton. This was my first experience of Larry—he shows up in shorts and a pink tank top, holding a glass of carrot juice. And I'm thinking, this is my kind of guy." *

I ask Ellison if he sees Siebel in the same category as niche players like the Internet procurement specialists Ariba and Commerce One. "Yes, Siebel is a best-of-breed specialty player," he says, "I'd put Siebel and i2 into the same category. Why? Their stuff is too expensive to install, integrate, and operate. I'd guess that more than half the software these guys sell sits on the shelf and never gets used—shelfware. Companies still buy from Siebel because they're the CRM leader and people think it's safe to go with the leader. But i2 was the supply-chain leader, and look what's happened to them. Oracle and SAP are rapidly getting i2 out of our EPR accounts. We'll get Siebel out too. Every year Siebel and i2 will come under more and more pressure. I don't see how they can survive."

The idea of speeding up that market consolidation through acquisition doesn't much appeal to Ellison, even though the battered and reeling niche players would now go for peanuts. One possible exception was Clarify, the call center specialist acquired by telecom equipment maker Nortel a couple of years ago. He says, "We're cheap, too cheap, probably. We've never paid more than $125 million for an acquisition. Clarify's in that range these days now that SAP stopped reselling it. Selling Clarify

---

*LE writes: I met Mark out on my deck just as I arrived back home from the gym. I was wearing a black cotton tank top with a Sayonara logo on it. I have never owned, nor would I ever wear, a pink tank top. This is very important.

and Commerce One was SAP's brief experiment with best-of-breed integration. They weren't any better at it than we were. At a recent conference in Florence, I was on the same speakers' panel as Hasso Plattner [SAP's co-CEO]. Hasso was explaining about how hard it is to integrate with the third-party products they're reselling. Tell me about it! SAP's in the process of declaring their integration experiment a failure and going back to building and selling their own suite of applications. So will we buy Clarify? We'll look at it. We'll analyze it. We'll talk about it. But we won't buy it, because we can't integrate it."

One deal that Ellison wishes he had done was to buy PeopleSoft in 2000, when its stock was on the floor and Oracle's was riding very high. "PeopleSoft was amazingly cheap. We could have bought them for two or three percent of our [outstanding common] stock. I wanted to do it at first, but I gradually became convinced the timing wasn't right. Most of our executives thought doing our first big acquisition at that time was just too risky. We were in the midst of a massive reengineering of our own company that consumed a hundred and ten percent of our management capacity. No available management, no experience in big acquisitions— sounds pretty risky to me. But something else bothered me even more: PeopleSoft pretends to be a suite company, but they're not. Sixty-five percent of their business is HR systems. They're really a best-of-breed HR specialist, and you know the fate of best-of-breed specialists. I think their HR product will gradually get replaced by Oracle HR and SAP HR. Still, PeopleSoft was so damn cheap we probably should have bought them anyway. It was close, but we probably made the wrong call." They certainly did. Although, in a predictable echo of Tom Siebel's remark about Oracle, Ellison says that he never "sees" PeopleSoft competing for big accounts, there's evidence in both the numbers and the analysts' reports that the firm from Pleasanton is making something of a comeback with its version of the E-Business Suite, PeopleSoft 8. Although still in recovery, PeopleSoft is a much-loved company.

Ellison accepts that one rival that is definitely not fading away yet is SAP. "SAP made a couple of exceptionally good decisions that resulted in them becoming the number one applications company in the world. First and foremost, they invented the applications suite business when they built the first integrated ERP system. Being first got them lots of big customers all over the world. Even when the going gets tough—it's been difficult for them to get new customers in the U.S. over the last couple of years—they can always sell into their installed base and into the hyperloyal German market. Nobody can compete with SAP in the German market—they own it. Second, SAP has executed its strategy pretty well because it's an engineering company at its core. In that respect Oracle and SAP have a lot in common: we're both engineering-centric companies, and we both have software engineers as CEOs. Most other application software companies are run by salesmen. The Oracle and SAP engineering teams have great respect for each other and get along together quite well. Their engineers love our database. In fact, when we launch Oracle 9i in June, they'll be there up on the platform with us* [they weren't, as it turned out], which is really pretty incredible considering the rivalry in applications. But their customers desperately need the speed and reliability of Oracle 9i Real Application Clusters [RAC]. For all the things SAP has done right, they still face one overwhelming challenge: their system is very, very inflexible, and that makes it extremely expensive to install and operate. The big consulting firms charge a fortune installing, integrating, and customizing the SAP system. The cost overruns on big SAP implementations are legendary. In this new climate of constrained IT budgets, it's going to get harder and harder for them to sell to new customers. If people start asking for a price guarantee before buying or expanding an SAP system, then they're in big trouble. SAP's best hope is that people don't ask."

• • •

Hardly a month goes by without Ellison's hosting at least one or two CEO roundtables. While he has frequent meetings with Oracle's biggest customers and increasingly makes the vital calls that help to close deals, the roundtable format allows both efficient use of Ellison's time and the opportunity to talk more widely about the issues that concern Oracle's customers. Today's roundtable is being held at his house in San Francisco. The Pacific Heights house couldn't be more different from the restrained simplicity of his Japanese-style villa at Atherton. Four stories high, the house is famous for its extraordinary panorama of the bay, sweeping from the Golden Gate Bridge to Alcatraz. It's also well known for being fitted out like a James Bond villain's hideaway with touch screens directing the industrial-strength computers that control every

---

*LE writes: SAP wasn't on the stage with us, but they did officially certify and start reselling Oracle 9i Real Application Clusters under their applications. Interestingly, SAP did not certify either IBM's or Microsoft's database-clustering technology. So our biggest applications competitor is now our best database reference. SAP loves RAC.

function inside the house. It's gorgeous but so minimalist that it's not a cozy place to live in. It is, however, a spectacular venue for corporate entertaining. A few of the twelve expected guests are relatively local, such as Dick Kovacevich, CEO of Wells Fargo (and one of Oracle's bankers), and David Lawrence, the chairman of Oakland-based Kaiser Foundation Health Plan, one of America's biggest medical insurers. But others, such as Jim Courter of IDT, a telco in Newark, New Jersey, and Ron Orr, who runs the air force's logistics operation from Washington, D.C., have flown across the country to attend. And while an invitation to lunch from Ellison is on its own probably enough to get the attention of most CEOs, the fact that the lunch is being held in a house that you will want to tell your friends about is an added lure.

After the guests have had an opportunity to admire the view from the first-floor drawing room before the fog closes in, they are led down to the dining room and seated around the huge, rectangular white table. Oddly, there seems to be no seating plan. Other top Oracle executives, including Safra Catz, Sandy Sanderson (the head of Oracle Consulting), and Mark Jarvis, just spread themselves around, while a handful of the guests politely jockey for a seat near Ellison. The meal, served by a team of several black-uniformed waiters, is elegant but simple. Despite the opulently over-the-top surroundings, the atmosphere is serious and professional.

At least until Ellison starts talking. With this group, he's confident and ready to entertain. It's a variation on the usual theme: what he's learned from his own efforts to turn Oracle into an e-business and why it's a process in which CEOs must become directly involved; the profound impact of the Internet; the failure of IT to deliver on past promises because it is an industry founded on a model that both celebrates and distributes complexity; and, finally, the extraordinary benefits to be had, in terms of efficiency and knowing what's going on in your business, by adopting Oracle's approach of implementing a fully integrated suite of applications on top of a single consolidated database. But the anecdotes of the chaos at Oracle before he saw the light are well honed and funny. What's more, they strike an immediate chord with his guests, as he knows they will. The confessional tone is calculated to get others to tell blood-curdling horror stories of their own. And then for Ellison to point them in the direction of salvation.

There is, however, a potential danger in being funny about the night-mares that the IT industry has visited on its wretched customers. In his own imagination, Ellison had long since moved on to a simpler and more rational kind of computing that banished armies of expensive consultants and the associated problems of tying together software packages from a multitude of vendors. Oracle, Ellison boasted, could now, uniquely, offer computing solutions that, for the first time in IT history were guaranteed—that's right, guaranteed—to provide a spectacular and speedy return on the customer's investment. However, even at Oracle, with its much-trumpeted $1 billion of savings and the boast of being able to extract as much again this year (recently slightly moderated because of "the economy"), Ellison was, according to his own CFO, Jeff Henley, running slightly ahead of reality. But for customers, including some of the ones around the table on Broadway, what might be galling was the fact that until very recently, Oracle had enthusiastically been selling the very approach, namely customized best-of-breed solutions, that Ellison was now describing as madness.

By the time Ellison stops speaking (after a good forty-five minutes), one of the guests, George Buckley, an English expat who runs the Brunswick Corporation, a medium-sized conglomerate that operates boating and leisure-focused businesses such as Mercury Marine, is seething to say something. He has written a number of points down on his pad. Looking intense and white-faced, he begins, "Larry, we've spent $250 million on systems in the last few years, and we've got jack shit. I feel like we were led down the primrose path by the IT guys. It was always jam tomorrow. We have all the best stuff in the candy store—PeopleSoft, i2, Oracle—it's a real hodgepodge of systems." Ellison has a "There you are!" kind of smirk on his face. He says, "That's the absolute archetype of what not to do." Buckley looks furiously across the table at him: "Well, I've got to tell you that it was Oracle consultants who, when pressed by my IT people on a perceived deficiency in your software, would say that maybe PeopleSoft or i2 might be better. Well, I'm not going to throw in another $200 million to fix it now." IDT's Jim Courter chips in, saying, "We were fed all kinds of promises that it will all work, and it doesn't." Buckley adds, "We're in so deep now that spending money is not the way. We're spending $100 million a year now. So how do we get out of this mess?" *

LE writes: CEOs as a group are incredibly pissed off about how much they spent for their computer systems and how little they got in return. They have a right to be. As for our own consulting organization recommending best-of-breed, well, that happened regularly in those days. All consulting organizations, including our own, made a lot of money pushing very large, very expensive best-of-breed integration projects.

It will be interesting to see how Ellison gets out of the hole he's dug for himself. What he'd like to do is disown the advice that Oracle's own consultants were peddling only a couple of years previously, when Oracle had some major gaps in its applications suite and couldn't afford to be so dismissive about best of breed if it was to compete with the more complete product from SAP. But with Sandy Sanderson, who has run consulting since the departure of Robert Shaw in 1998, a few feet away from him, doing so might be embarrassing. Instead he tells Buckley that he should actually be cutting his IT budget. He suggests that Buckley stop the work on some of his existing systems integration projects and swap a portion of the budget out to install 11i in one part of the business. Once it has proved itself, Buckley can start rolling it out across the rest of his company. By firing some of the consultants wrestling with his existing software and starting again, Buckley will be able to save some of the money he's currently spending. Says Ellison slightly smugly, "SI is the gift that keeps on giving." *

Buckley doesn't look any happier. The expression on his face suggests that Ellison is the worst kind of snake-oil salesman. It turns out, however, that one of his firm's divisions is in the process of doing a 100 percent 11i implementation. Ellison suggests that they audit how it goes and the time it takes to get a return from the software. Sandy Sanderson will follow up and report back. If that works, maybe Buckley will be more inclined to take up Ellison's suggestion of diverting funds from other projects.†

The message that Ellison wants to emphasize is that his guests should spend less on their IT rather than more. By stalling some spending and taking his recommended path of putting in 11i without modification, he genuinely believes that they will save money. The key, he says, is speed. Most SAP failures happened because the projects never got finished. The

---

*LE writes: I wasn't feeling smug. I was feeling frustrated. Over and over again I hear about consultants' recommending overly complex systems that end up costing far more than the customer planned to spend. If customers would demand a price guarantee for the total cost of the system before they signed a contract, it would go a long way toward solving this problem. (Total system cost includes: hardware, software, installation, and annual operating costs.)

†LE writes: We did a complete E-Business Suite implementation at one of Brunswick's divisions. The project was delivered on time and under budget. They're a very happy customer. The integrated suite approach works.

money spent went to IBM and Andersen. Don't take a three-year flyer like that. The longer a project runs, the less likely it will be to finish. Freeze your budget, and we'll get you a return in very short order. It's the 80/20 rule: a project aiming for 100 percent of the benefits will never finish. But if you go for 80 percent, you can get it done in six to nine months. David Lawrence of Kaiser, who has the manner of a kindly M.D., asks whether there is any evidence that going for the last 20 percent of functionality ever paid back. Never, Ellison says. That last 20 percent can cost you tenfold.*

It's just the opening Ellison needs to describe the approach he used at Oracle—what he calls spending less to know more. The pitch has now been carefully honed to the new reality of shrinking IT budgets, disenchantment with the Internet, and the absolute requirement for rapid payback. "When we first started planning the replacement of all our local country systems—there were hundreds of them—with a single global e-business system, the planning team told me I needed to increase our IT budget by $250 million and not to expect to see any payback for at least three years. Sound familiar? Of course, our IT budget was already way too high; it needed to go down, not up. We had to find a way to fund our global e-business transformation out of our existing IT budget. So I reviewed every one of our internal IT projects; if a project wasn't going to pay for itself in twelve months, we killed it. That didn't mean we canceled every big project. It just meant we had to break up our big projects into multiple steps and make sure we were getting deliverables with benefits and cost savings at every stage along the way. If we couldn't break a big

---

*LE writes: Even if the software could be made to do 100 percent of the things customers say they need, there are still a couple of serious problems that remain. First, the customer may not fully understand each and every one of its own needs, and second, even if it does, those needs are likely to change over time. A far better approach is to buy a system that delivers 80 percent of the benefits of a "perfect" system at 20 percent of the cost. After the 80 percent solution is installed and delivering substantial benefits, you then have the option of incrementally enhancing your system's automation and information capabilities a little at a time. Going for a 100 percent solution requires a perfect understanding of your business before the project starts and a lot of customization to make the software fit. That is a very expensive and risky approach; you might end up with nothing.

project into steps, then we killed it.* Every time we killed something of questionable value, we freed up people and budget to work on the global e-business project and a couple of other cool new things I had in mind.

"Now we targeted two operational systems that were burning money like it was going out of style. We had so many e-mail systems and Windows file servers that we couldn't figure out how much we were actually spending on them—but we knew it was a lot. Replacing our ninety-seven local country e-mail systems with one global e-mail system saved a fortune. Replacing our two thousand Windows file servers with one global file-sharing system saved even more than global e-mail.† These two projects were the closest you get in my business to 'cheap thrills.' Both projects were quick and easy to do and had huge near-term payoffs. Everyone should do them. It only takes about ninety days to lower your e-mail and file-sharing costs by 50 to 75 percent. We actually ended up saving *more* than the $250 million we needed to build our global e-business system. By the time we finished putting in our global e-mail and file-sharing systems and consolidating our data centers, our IT budget had dropped by half.

"As predicted, our global e-business system did take about three years to put in, but we saved money every step of the way. Every time we folded another local country's system into our global system, our IT costs went down and the quality of our business processes and information went up. The first local systems we turned off were in Latin America. Separate off a small part of your business—a country or a division—and move that small organization to the E-Business Suite first. The 'start small' approach minimizes both risk and cost; you'll find out very quickly if the suite delivers value to your business. If it does, then you can start adding other countries or divisions into your working E-Business Suite system.

"We started in Latin America because they were the least automated part of our business and they were the most willing to move to our new standardized Internet business processes. After we got Latin America running smoothly, we started moving other countries into the global system. In our big countries—like the U.S. and Japan—there was a lot of re-

---

*LE writes: The longer a project runs without delivering value, the greater the likelihood it will never deliver value. Go to zero-balance budgeting for IT projects, and beware of throwing good money after bad on long-overdue projects.

†LE writes: Both our global e-mail system and our global file-sharing systems are based on what has become the Oracle Collaboration Suite.

sistance to the change, but it had very little to do with our e-business software. People didn't want to adopt our new global business processes because it meant they'd have to change the way they worked. The resistance was fierce, but we finally broke through by making the people *write down* exactly why they couldn't or wouldn't change to our new business processes. Making them write it down forced people to carefully study and think through the new process. Most of the time that resulted in them realizing that the new process was okay—98 percent of the cases—but sometimes they found real deficiencies in the software and they wrote down exactly what the engineers needed to do to fix it, which they did. Once our users and systems people were communicating in writing, we started making real progress. We added country after country to the global system in rapid succession. Every time we added another country to the global system, our information got better and our IT budget went down. The less we spent, the more we knew. It was amazing."

After Buckley, the two other voices of skepticism are from Wells Fargo's Kovacevich and from Justin Jaschke, the CEO and founder of Verio, a big Colorado-based Web-hosting specialist that was bought by Japan's NTT Communications a few months before the dot-com crash for an eye-watering $5 billion. The point that Kovacevich wants to make is that surely there's a danger of companies' losing competitive advantage and whatever is unique to them if they slavishly adopt business practices that suit the software they're putting in. It's a common misperception that has to be dealt with politely. Oracle's Steve Perkins, who handles much of Oracle's federal government business says that compared with SAP, Oracle's apps are very flexible and you have plenty of choices about the way you want to work.

Jaschke, not surprisingly, is more of a geek than the other guests. He wants to know what's wrong with the currently fashionable approach to systems integration in which applications from different vendors are made to work together using specially designed software, known as middleware, that acts as glue, and central data schema created to form a common language. It's the kind of question Ellison loves. "It just can't be done very well," he replies. "If you glue, say, E.piphany and Clarify [two popular CRM applications] together, the customer databases don't map to each other, so the systems can't pass data back and forth very easily. It's like one guy speaks French and the other guy speaks Japanese. You can get them on the phone together and they can hear each other talking, but they can't communicate. The only thing that really works is a common database schema like we have in the suite. Engineers have tried the data-

passing and messaging approach for twenty years without much luck."
IDT's Jim Courter helpfully adds that he's trying to do something like
that now and "it's a complete nightmare." "Absolutely," says Ellison. "It
might work a little bit some of the time, just enough to tempt you to keep
trying. You can put wings on a car, drive very fast, and it will take off . . .
landing safely is another matter."

The next question turns out to be trickier. The air force's Ron Orr
wants to know, reasonably enough, where Oracle has an example of 11i
up and running that has stood the test of time. Ellison points out that the
suite has been out for only a year but that a few customers had adopted
the "no-modifications" model early on out of poverty. One such is
Techtronics in Oregon—five years ago its business "fell off a cliff," so it
put in global systems because that was the cheapest way to go. It's an odd
example to give. Sensing it, Oracle's Mark Jarvis adds that Cisco is a
well-known example using Oracle financials to achieve a daily "virtual
close." Somebody points out that it didn't help Cisco from making a hash
of its forecasting.*

Afterward, when the guests have gone, the Oracle execs strike a res-
olutely upbeat note, confident they will get solid orders out of the
re-evangelized customers. But with the prospects for the economy as
foggy as San Francisco Bay, the question is: For all Ellison's eloquence,
how much software will they actually buy?

---

*LE writes: As I've said before, our forecasting system is not clairvoyant. Our
forecasting does statistical extrapolations based on historic trends. If something that's outside our mathematical model of the business changes, like a war
in the Middle East, our forecasting becomes inaccurate.

12

HUNGARIAN LESSONS

Hungary
May 2001

The customer Larry Ellison refers to more than any other when selling the E-Business Suite is GE. It's a good choice: there are few more admired companies.* But the bit of GE he's improbably declared a model 11i customer is in a far-flung outpost of Jack Welch's sprawling imperium.

The road east from central Budapest toward the tiny market town of Veresegyház some forty-five minutes away is not a bad metaphor for modern Hungary. The capital itself is a job half done. There are plenty of new buildings—mainly banks and office blocks—and a concerted effort is under way to refurbish the grand government buildings, such as the absurdly Ruritanian Parliament that sits on the Buda side of the Danube and is covered in scaffolding. The road to Veresegyház, narrow, rutted, and bordered with ads for the latest in mobile phone technology, carries a mixture of modern European cars, a few wheezing Trabants, and, as the tatty suburbs give way to open countryside, increasing numbers of horse-drawn carts. On a warm afternoon in early May, the rolling landscape of neat fields is unspoiled and beautiful, until the view is interrupted by a shining new steel-and-glass factory that stretches across more

---

*LE writes: Working up close and personal with GE was like going to a real-world business school. What separates GE from most companies is its willingness to force change after change into its business in a relentless, never-ending pursuit of efficiency.

than 500,000 square feet and has changed forever the view of the valley. There's nothing to indicate what goes on inside—a reasonable guess might be some kind of agribusiness plant producing fertilizer or turning out farm machinery. Except that every few days a noise that blasts out of one of the huge metal containers lined up outside one end of the plant sounds oddly like a Boeing 747 taking off.

This building is a $100 million investment by the Power Systems division of America's mighty GE, put up in record time to make replacement parts for industrial gas turbines—highly sophisticated nozzles, shrouds, and combustors—and to manufacture what are known as "aederivative" power packages. These are $15-million-a-pop transportable gas turbines that harness the thrust of GE jet engines to produce up to 50 megawatts of electricity—enough to run a large factory or keep a small town humming. Before each of the turbines is disassembled and packed into twenty or so containers for shipping, it is given full load testing to verify its power output and heat rate. Within a year of the groundbreaking for the factory construction—even before the offices for site managers and engineers were completed—the first turbine package rolled out of the gates, on its way to a customer in Paris.

The man who makes it happen is Craig Kipp, a tall, athletic-looking forty-five-year-old who was yanked out of his job at GE's nuclear fuel business in Wilmington, North Carolina. When he arrived in April 2000, Kipp knew that he was facing the challenge of his life to get the plant up and running in the time demanded by his unrelenting bosses in Atlanta. What he didn't know was that Oracle's Larry Ellison would turn out to be staking even more on his success or failure than either GE's legendary Jack Welch or even John Rice, the hard-charging new head of the Power Systems division.

GE has been in Hungary for several years and has several major businesses in the country. The first, Tungsram Lighting, was acquired in 1990 in the first major phase of post-Communist Western investment. Since then, GE Capital has bought Budapest Bank, and GE's Medical Systems and Engine Services divisions have established outposts. Welch early on decided that Hungary would be one of the leaders in the Eastern European pack and the decision to build the turbine plant wasn't a difficult one, with the country expected to accede to European Union membership by 2005. As Kipp puts it, he can plug into an existing GE infrastructure for support services, and he has access to low-cost, well-educated local engineering talent. What's more, for American expats, Budapest is a "livable city."

However, within GE, the significance of Veresegyház would be more than just a new facility to help meet the booming demand for the firm's power generation products. Under Welch's project to digitize every aspect of GE's extraordinary spread of businesses, Veresegyház was to be given the status of a laboratory to test how far, using Internet technologies, the power systems operation could be transformed into a full-fledged e-business. There was also another consideration. The speed with which Welch and Rice's predecessor, Bob Nardelli, now boss of Home Depot, were insisting that the plant come on stream meant that a traditional approach to systems integration wouldn't work, particularly as the other outfits in GE that Veresegyház would be dealing with, such as oil and gas, based in Italy, and energy products, based in France, had a mishmash of ERP systems from different vendors.

At a strategic level, GE was already convinced that going down the integrated suite route made more sense than best of breed, and anyway, time wouldn't allow for anything else. Nor was there much doubt that Oracle would get the nod—Release 11 had already been installed elsewhere in GE, for example, in medical systems, and was doing all right. In July, a month after the bulldozers started clearing earth at Veresegyház, the big discussion was whether to take the chance of going with 11i only weeks after its release. Kipp asks, "Did we really want to take the risk? Putting up a new plant in Central Europe and having to hire a workforce from scratch is risky enough. In the end, what swung it was the superior upgrade path. Because it was all Internet, Oracle convinced us that we could seamlessly get new versions and new features as they became available. The attitude here is that everything's going to the Internet, so we just decided on making a leap of faith. The whole thing had to be installed in just a few months, and we kind of figured that Oracle couldn't afford to let us down." It was a shrewd calculation.

The contract was signed in late October with a clear understanding that if Oracle delivered at Veresegyház, GE would start rolling out 11i across its thirty or so other turbine plants. Within a month, the project was in trouble. Kipp was using a local IT consulting firm named Ejiva, which had done work for GE in Hungary before but was now struggling. Worried, Kipp told Nardelli that at this rate he would never hit his milestones. Nardelli and Rice decided to call Larry Ellison. Kipp says, "Within a week we had thirty to forty Oracle consultants. It was like a MASH unit arriving." Kipp was working from hastily converted offices on a run-down industrial estate that he christened "the bunker." "There were lots of things going on: hiring people, riding the builders, working with local government. Until December, I thought things were under control. On the other side of town we had all these people from GE and Oracle—there were about eighty of them in an office designed for forty. They were working through the night, mapping processes and figuring out what they wanted the software to do."

When the consultants invited Kipp over for what is known in the business as a "conference room pilot" (CRP), the first of a series of trials that the software has to be put through before it is deemed to be ready, he realized that things were far from "under control." Basically, a CRP involves running the business in a simulation mode—putting the systems that will run the manufacturing and financial operations through their paces. Within the first couple of hours, as he moved from room to room, Kipp felt increasingly uncomfortable. "It just dawned on me that a twenty-six-year-old recent graduate from Budapest Technical University and three guys from Oracle in San Jose were designing how to run my business. I realized I'd been focusing on the wrong thing. Pouring concrete may be important, but what was going to determine on a daily basis sixty to eighty percent of what my people would be doing was being written into the software. And I thought, shit, have we got the right people making the right decisions?"*

What convinced Kipp that he was in trouble was a simulation that involved picking up hypothetical parts from the stockroom to assemble on one of the turbine units. By the time they had taken all the parts out on the shop floor, they realized they were working on the wrong job. Kipp says, "The software was designed that way because people from my finance team were putting in very strict requirements for tracking costs. As I learned more about it, I said this is crazy, if this were to go live we'll just crash the whole business. So we had a meeting in the hallway that night at eleven P.M. There were people hanging off the doors. I'll never forget it. I said, 'What are you trying to do? We don't need this level of sophistication and complexity to run this business.' Because to have this very structured financial cost system means that everything has to be done differently on the manufacturing side."†

---

*LE writes: This was the turning point of the project. Once senior management got involved—deeply involved—we started making real progress.

†LE writes: Only senior management looks at and makes decisions for the business as a whole. Individual department managers optimize their internal departmental functions without much sympathy for or understanding of the

Kipp knew that if they continued down this track there was no way they'd meet the promised "go-live" date of March 7. His message was to make it simpler. The problem was that GE's finance and manufacturing specialists from America had believed they were expected to add value by getting Oracle to customize the software to deliver all the features Kipp might possibly want. Unfortunately, they hadn't thought to ask him, and the Oracle consultants were trained never to say no to a customer.*

Kipp says that what had happened was the key to understanding why the installation of business software systems so often goes wrong. "You decide on buying a piece of software that pretty much has what you need to run your business. But then the consultants ask, 'What would you really like it to do, because we want to optimize your business processes.' So the guy says, 'Well, what I'd really like is for it to do the following . . . ' and they have the same conversation with the finance team and the manufacturing team and the sales guys. And of course, the consultant doing his job writes down all the little other things that would be great to have. So Oracle has this great product that will do eighty percent of what you want just by throwing the right switches in the software—no special code or anything—and it all falls down because someone asks that innocent little question: 'What else would you like it to do?' "

Kipp says that if they hadn't been sucked down the path of customization, they might have gotten the software installed in three rather than five months. The key was the commitment of his own time—as much as half of each working day for at least a couple months—and that of his dozen best managers. He says that it's no good expecting junior people to make the right decisions about how the business should be run, and it's crazy to ask them to do it. He admits that the strain of it nearly killed them, but that you have to use the people "who've really got that mental expertise to configure the system right from a process standpoint."

It's exactly what Ellison's been saying all along. Just after Veresegyház

---

burdens they may be placing on other departments. That's why it's treacherous to automate one department at a time. You're better off taking a self-contained segment of the business, like the Hungary plant, and automating the end-to-end business flows that cross departmental boundaries.

*LE writes: Today, Oracle's consultants are trained to say "no" when it comes to customizing the code. The less a customer changes our software, the more of it they're likely to buy. We make more money selling software than consulting. When consulting is your moneymaker, it's a lot harder to say "no."

went live, John Rice called Kipp over to Orlando to share his experiences with some of GE's other senior managers. Kipp says, "I told them: don't let it happen to you. Just take the software, install it. If you simplify and standardize your business processes along the lines of the way the software's configured, you're going to get eighty percent of what you want. If you want to go back after the next year or three to get some special feature you need, you can still do that." By way of example, he told Oracle that if he needed improved data on quality, the chances were that most of their other customers would too. Oracle's response was that if he could wait six months they'd write it and give it to him in the next upgrade. Instead of saying that was too long and demanding a customized solution, Kipp said, "OK . . . the world's not going to fall apart in six months. Plus, I've got supported software that's in all their upgrades—not some special code that I have to take responsibility for."* It's another example of what Ellison calls his "80 percent rule": take 80 percent functionality now rather than risk never finishing by holding out for a 100 percent perfect solution that exists only in the imagination.

If the lessons for GE are clear, they should also be for Oracle. When the project nearly came off the rails because the consultants were obliging requests by junior managers that were at odds with the approach laid down by John Rice, there was, in Kipp's words, "no one on the Oracle side who was going to tell the customer, 'No, you can't have that.' " Kipp says that GE's managers, culturally used to demanding "everything and now" needed to be told more clearly what's in their best interests. "If they're offered this feature, they're not going to say, 'Well, I don't need that.' But somebody with authority has to be able to say no."

---

*LE writes: Our five thousand applications developers put lots of new features into the E-Business Suite based on customer priorities. This close collaboration was what made it possible for most of our customers to avoid the complexity and cost of custom code.

13

HILL BY HILL

May 2001

A year after the E-Business Suite was launched with such high hopes, the world has become a very different and, for Oracle, more hostile place. It would be tempting to describe Ellison as "beleaguered," but that over-worked word doesn't really fit. He is still cracking jokes and generally en-joying life. At Oracle there's no hint of crisis. There's a good deal of grumbling about the evaporating value of stock options and the disap-pearance of bonuses, but at least Oracle isn't laying off swaths of work-ers like many companies in Silicon Valley. There's an atmosphere of sober determination. There are enough veterans around at Redwood Shores—guys who have been through far worse times than this—to steady the ship and calm the anxieties of young engineers who really did think, as Oracle's advertising insisted, that the Internet had changed everything, including the abolition of the business cycle.

We're on the road again—or, more accurately, flying at 45,000 feet in Ellison's Gulfstream—heading for more customer meetings and CEO roundtables. This time we're going to Chicago and then on to Fisher Is-land, an exclusive resort near Miami. It's a strange moment in the E-Business Suite campaign. Ellison is convinced that the bugginess and instability are a thing of the past. But the media and the analysts have gotten their teeth into that story and won't let go. The only way to turn it around will be increasing numbers of references from happy customers. But the bad publicity and the economy have persuaded many to delay planned installations. For Ellison, it's a waiting game.

Nonetheless, he says, "We've had some very significant E-Business Suite 'go-lives' lately. Alcoa went live at a major location in less than five months, start to finish, without any modifications. Liberty Mutual went live. More and more customers are going live on 11i. That's really important. People love the idea—the concept—of a complete and integrated E-Business Suite. But the question is 'Does it really work?' And if it does, 'How do I get there from where I am today?' "

I'm curious to know how many of these customers, if any, are actually using the whole suite. In Hungary, GE Power Systems was deploying the ERP part of the package—the manufacturing and financial apps plus the hot new order management system—but they had no need yet for the fancy CRM piece of the action. What about Alcoa? "Well, when I say that some company is using the E-Business Suite I mean they're using several E-Business Suite applications, not all of them. Nobody, not even Oracle, uses all of the E-Business Suite. We don't use manufacturing because we don't manufacture anything. However, I still describe Oracle as an E-Business Suite user. If a company is using a number of the release 11i applications, I call it an E-Business Suite user. GE Power is running a lot of our applications but not all of them. The same is true of Alcoa. Both GE and Alcoa are industrial giants in the process of modernizing their businesses. They're using E-Business Suite applications to modernize their supply-chain processes, their procurement processes, their manufacturing processes, and their accounting processes. Step by step, one location at a time, they're modernizing their companies using the E-Business Suite."

Alcoa will be an enormous Oracle installation, involving all 362 of its plants worldwide. "I started participating in regular conference calls at GE Power after we ran into some problems a couple of months into the project. We quickly solved those problems and stayed on top of new ones as they arose. During every call we go through major product and implementation issues in excruciating detail. I've learned a lot in the process. I'm going to try to spend more time with Alcoa because it's a huge project that automates all the different Alcoa businesses, from making and selling boxcars of aluminum ingots to consumer-packaged aluminum foil. Another big project I'm watching closely is at POSCO, the world's largest and most profitable steel company. They're doing a big-bang go-live in July. They're switching over the entire company all at once. Not many companies take that approach because of the risks involved. But if you pull it off, it's the by far the fastest way to go.* It takes iron balls to go

---

*LE writes: The POSCO go-live went nearly flawlessly. It did a lot of planning and testing before moving the entire operation to the E-Business Suite.

that route, but hey, they're a steel company so. . . . Anyway, I always recommend a safe, step-by-step implementation process: define a set of standard processes, bring up one location or one division using those processes, then start adding more locations or more divisions. That's what we're doing at GE, that's what we're doing at Alcoa, that's what we did at Oracle. But you must automate one business at a time, not one department at a time. One-department-at-a-time automation, best-of-breed systems that don't work across departmental boundaries, that's how companies got in the mess they're in today. Companies need a road map to move from their detached departmental systems with their disconnected processes and fragmented data to a modern integrated system built on a single global database."

While the campaign for 11i continues, Ellison's main focus is about to switch back to his first love, the database, and the launch of 9i, the latest and most significant new version of Oracle's flagship product for many years. "I'm back to spending about half my time on the database. 9i is a very big deal because for the first time our database clustering works with real applications—Oracle applications, SAP applications, Siebel applications, custom applications, everything. We've been trying to do this for more than a decade. It's not an easy problem. Microsoft's and IBM's clustering technology works fine for performance benchmarks, but it's useless for real applications. They run clustering tests and then run an ad bragging about their database performance. That's good marketing, but marketing can only carry you so far. Their database clusters can't run real-world applications, so their clustering performance tests are meaningless. Eventually people will notice.

"But our clustering isn't just a marketing scam. Our clustering works with real-world applications, and *that* fundamentally changes the database business forever. But it doesn't stop there: clustering changes the entire computer industry. The computer industry is based on the principle of scale: a big application runs on a big, expensive computer. But if you can make a bunch of cheap little computers 'look' like a big computer, then you've altered the economics of the industry. And that's exactly what we've done with 9i clusters. We've been able to take a group of cheap Windows or UNIX computers, cluster them together, and run SAP applications, PeopleSoft applications, Siebel applications, and everything else. We can do it. Nobody else can. Nobody.

"Before, if you wanted to run faster, you bought a faster machine. Once you bought the fastest machine there is, you're done, you can't run any faster. With Oracle 9i clustering, those limits no longer apply. You can have multiple database computers running your SAP application. To add performance, you add another computer; to add reliability, you add another computer. Rather than having one expensive computer, you have four inexpensive computers, you run faster, you run more reliably, and you run much more cheaply using an array of small machines. We broke the code. We made it work. That's not good news for people who build huge expensive machines. IBM says, 'Gee, our database software costs less per processor than yours.' We say, true enough, but you have to buy software for twice as many processors and then spend five times more for hardware to run IBM's database. IBM would have to pay you to run their database for it to make economic sense. Even if they gave you all the software and hardware for free, it still wouldn't be nearly as fast or reliable as an Oracle 9i cluster. So Oracle9i is the 'last database.' This is game, set, and match in the database business. Oracle 9i clusters make it very difficult for IBM and Microsoft to compete on performance, reliability, or cost. We've got to do a good job getting the clustering message out there, but I think within three to six months it will become obvious that Oracle 9i really is the last database" *

The trouble is that people think of databases as mature technology and not as sexy as applications. How will Ellison communicate his excitement? "Well, it's pretty interesting if you can show eight Compaq PC servers running faster and more reliably than the largest IBM mainframe. And those PC servers could be running Linux. People say Linux isn't reliable enough for enterprise computing. Now, it doesn't have to be reliable. Not if you use lots of them. If one fails, who cares? Not fast enough? Use more of them. 9i is great computer science, not just another software product. It's, I hate the expression, a 'breakthrough.' Bill's been talking a lot about Microsoft's horizontal scalability [using a cluster of little machines to get performance rather than one big machine] strategy. But they can't make it work. We've got horizontal scalability for every application ever written; they have horizontal scalability for one and only one application—their custom version of the TPC-C benchmark [an industry standard database performance test]! It's amazing. And, it will take IBM and Microsoft a long, long time to catch up. Maybe ten years, but probably never."

---

*LE writes: SAP has certified and started reselling Oracle Real Application Clusters, but SAP has not certified either IBM or Microsoft clusters. That says it all.

If Ellison's claims for 9i are borne out, it's not only bad news for Microsoft's and IBM's database products; it will also have some pretty serious implications for the hardware makers. It's a point that hasn't escaped him. "It will fundamentally change the high end of the computing business. Today, our big customers, like eBay [the Internet auction site], are running big Sun 10000 servers. When one of them goes down, part of their service is down. Now they can run a cluster of four 6500s, or run six 4500s rather than one big 10000. The cluster is cheaper, faster, and a lot more reliable. Why wouldn't you run a cluster?" Ellison had just met with Scott McNealy, the combative boss of Sun Microsystems and an important Oracle ally. Does he realize that Oracle 9i is a big threat to his business? "I don't think he does right now. For the first few years people will cluster two big machines together to double their performance and get fault tolerance. But as they gradually see how well clustering works, they'll start replacing their big machines with clusters of small machines. That's not good news for anyone who builds big, fast computers. The Sun 10000, the HP Superdome, the IBM S80, all these expensive sixteen- to sixty-four-processor computers, why buy them? You want sixty-four processors of power, buy sixteen four-processor PC servers. You don't need to buy these really big machines anymore. They're expensive and they're unreliable, because a single machine is a single point of failure. If it breaks, you're down. Why would anybody spend more for something that's slower and less reliable? Big boxes are going to be replaced by arrays of small boxes. And we're the ones with the software that makes it all work."

Ellison needs 9i to be the success he's so convinced it will be. Although Oracle has maintained its overall share of the relational database business, a report from Gartner that's due out in a few days suggests that IBM is growing its share of the UNIX market a good deal more quickly than Oracle, thanks to aggressive pricing and the naturally much cozier relationships it enjoys with the other ERP and CRM vendors thanks to the fact it doesn't compete with them. Meanwhile, through its willingness to bundle SQL Server with its other BackOffice products, Microsoft has overtaken Oracle for the first time in the Windows NT/2000 segment. Clearly, 9i has the potential for Oracle to open up more blue water between itself and its database competitors, while also providing an economic case based on total ownership costs to justify its much fancier price tag. But can the strength of 9i be leveraged to the advantage of the applications business?

"Well, I do think 9i will be a huge success. This is a little bit like when Oracle 7 showed up and it just creamed everybody. I think 9i will sweep away the competition. 9i is also very important for our applications business. Clustering is so fast and so reliable, now even our largest applications customer can move to a single global database. In fact, we're thinking about repositioning our applications and focusing on the single database message. At the heart of the E-Business Suite is the one database idea: one customer database, one supplier database, all your information is in one place. We have this wonderful unified 'information architecture.' With SAP and Siebel, you have dozens of customer databases, dozens of data warehouses; it's really hard to find the information you need to do your job. Positioning our unified information architecture sitting on top of our clustered database will help us explain the benefits of the E-Business Suite. We're looking at the same picture, but we're looking at it through a different lens.

"Focusing on the database as the center of our applications strategy has another advantage: it allows us to tackle some new application areas where we're not going to write all the applications ourselves. Instead we're going to provide and publish a database schema with the necessary APIs to allow other apps vendors to write on top of our data model. We're going to start with health care. I think we need a national health records database where doctors input information, hospitals input information, laboratories input information. All your health care records are in one database. It's highly reliable, it's highly secure, it's auditable, privacy is guaranteed. And rapid access is assured in case of emergencies. We have a variety of partners like GE Medical who we're trying to get to build applications on top of our national health records database."

If Oracle were to succeed in persuading lots of independent software vendors to develop their applications using the same data model as Oracle's own applications, it would be big stuff. It would make the E-Business Suite limitlessly extensible by offering a different approach to integration that still kept all the information in one place. Paradoxically, it would even be a way of making best-of-breed work. Unfortunately for Oracle (and maybe its customers), Ellison will probably have to wait a long time for rival enterprise application vendors to allow Oracle the kind of leverage over them through its database that Microsoft exercises over the battered and submissive PC software industry through Windows. Working with niche players that target particular industries, such as health or education, with highly specialized software is a smart way for Oracle to fill out the functionality of the suite.

To try to draw a line under its early instability, Mark Jarvis, the senior VP for marketing, had told me that the E-Business Suite might soon be given a symbolic 2.0 release. Ellison was skeptical: "Yes, I thought about that, but it's a bad idea. Instead, we're just going to try to do a better job of explaining how we approach applications from a databasecentric point of view. We don't need a relaunch. We just need to tell the market about how much specific customers have saved and how fast the software went in because they didn't modify the code. The other thing we need to do is talk more about the notion of databasecentric applications—all your applications built around a single central database. People already believe Oracle's good at database stuff, so they might also believe we're good at databasecentric applications. And you know what, it's not only believable, it's true—we are good at that."

Despite Ellison's confidence about overall strategy and the quality of Oracle's products, the impact of the slowdown in technology investments and the deteriorating economy were plenty to worry about. With one of the trickiest final quarters for years ready to close, had the "visibility" that has been so clouded a month ago improved? "It's very odd, our business in Japan is doing extremely well, and they've been in a recession for around ten years. It's hard to understand exactly what's going on now that the bubble has burst. Those who enjoyed the ride up are now having an unpleasant ride down. Those who missed some of the ride up, like IBM and Microsoft, don't have as far to fall. But it is what it is. We can't control the market. I don't think it makes much difference whether our stock is flat or down a bit; in the long run what really determines our success and our stock price is how good our products are. And our products are really, really good right now. All we need are more references. References are the key to selling software. That's what gives people the courage to buy a complex, almost incomprehensible piece of technology. Selling the architecture only works with a few early adopters. In most cases, even when they agree that our applications architecture is much better, they'll still go with the market leader. People buy Siebel because 'everyone buys Siebel.' People have an innate belief that there is safety in numbers. It's deep inside everyone's biology. So until we have a significant number of references, including people who threw Siebel out, it will be slow going. So for now we're just going to take it hill by hill, deal by deal, until we have a strong enough foothold for our sales force do what it does best, reference selling."

Something I'd been wondering about is the effect on Oracle's business of Ellison's bad-mouthing of systems integrators. Ellison had sort of apologized and recognized his error, but was he doing anything positive to rebuild bridges with the consulting and SI partners whom he has managed to insult and annoy? Ellison says, "I've had meetings with all the heads of the big five consulting firms, so the answer is yes. More importantly, we've made a couple of important changes in our business that they seem to like. First, we changed our motto from 'Just say no to systems integration,' which was stupid, to 'Just say no to custom code.' That helped. Second, we've been gradually downsizing our consulting business because of our focus on rapid, low-cost implementations, so we don't compete with the big integrators very much anymore. We specialize on getting in and out very quickly."

That made sense, but there's been no letup in deriding Accenture and IBM Global Services. Were they more resistant than the others to what Oracle is trying to do? "Oracle and IBM are point, counterpoint. They say 'best of breed,' we say 'integrated suite,' they sign ten-year integration and outsourcing contracts, we want to implement in six months or less. It's unlikely that IBM will ever do much applications integration business with Oracle,* even though they do a lot of work with our database. The IBM hardware and service guys *love* our database. Accenture has been even more difficult to deal with than IBM. I really don't understand why, but they seem to think meeting with us is a waste of their time. Maybe the hard feelings date back to the Robert Shaw days, or maybe it was something I said. I really don't know. I've had a couple of conversations with George [Shaheen] before he went to Webvan [a struggling Internet grocery firm that would soon fold], but they led nowhere. We'd love to work with Accenture, but so far we've been unable to get them interested." Accenture, it's also worth pointing out, is an investor in Siebel.

Ellison and I then turned to discussing the future of the spin-off from Oracle that makes network computer devices—now known as New Internet Computers—the same ones that were meant to replace the PC. He's thinking of merging the company with a little firm called Be that's focused on developing software, particularly operating systems, for Internet appliances. Ellison relaxes, and his tone changes to that of someone talking more about a hobby than a business. "Be is a public

---

*LE writes: When IBM bought PWC [in July 2002], they inherited a large Oracle applications implementation business. That gave us an opportunity to try to work more cooperatively with IBM in both application implementations and outsourcing. Early on the signs are very promising. I don't agree with their best-of-breed strategy, but there is no denying the quality and professionalism of their people.

company, and they're having business problems, not good. But they've got great user interface technology and an important relationship with Sony. NIC is doing OK, $2 million last quarter, $4 million this quarter; they're tiny but growing. All NIC really is is a $200 desktop computer running Linux and a Netscape browser. If we put the Be user interface on top of Linux, the NIC would be easier to use. Maybe we should glue these two companies together." *

A potentially much more important initiative is Ellison's plan for Oracle to buy NetLedger, a start-up run by a former Oracle programmer named Evan Goldberg that has produced an award-winning suite of Web-based applications aimed at small businesses. It's a little awkward for Ellison because he has backed NetLedger with nearly $40 million of his own money and consequently owns most of the company. But now that the bursting of the Internet bubble has killed any hope of an IPO, Ellison wants to bring NetLedger and its five thousand subscribers into the Oracle fold and rebrand the software as Oracle Small Business Suite. He hopes that Intuit, the firm that makes the PC-based QuickBooks accounting application for professionals and small businesses, will make an offer for NetLedger and thus establish fair market value for an Oracle purchase. He says, "My conflict of interest prevents me from getting involved with an Oracle purchase of NetLedger. That said, if NetLedger proves to be successful, they could play an important role in Oracle's applications strategy. We're talking to a large auto company that's interested in providing an online service to all their dealers. The NetLedger system is designed as an online service for small businesses, like car dealerships. It's an ideal fit. It's also an interesting new business model. By connecting the NetLedger service to our E-Suite software we can link a bunch of small companies that are doing business with a large company. In other words, we can automate networks of companies, rather than one company at a time."

---

*LE writes: To Be or not to be, that may have been the question (sorry), but it didn't matter one way or the other. Microsoft killed both companies like a rogue rhinoceros trampling a couple of disoriented field mice. But the Linux-on-the-desktop idea lives on. If anything breaks Microsoft's monopoly, it will be a desktop version of Linux. The ingredient still missing is a replacement for Microsoft Office. Once the open-source version of StarOffice matures a bit, Microsoft might actually have to compete for business. Watch what is going on in India and China for early signs of cracks in Microsoft's desktop monopoly.

NetLedger/Oracle Small Business Suite could turn out to be important for other reasons. Microsoft has been dipping a toe in the small-business applications market with its bCentral Web site. In December 2000 it also spent more than $1 billion to buy Great Plains, an applications firm with a decent franchise in the small and medium-sized business sector. It's clear that Microsoft wants .NET to offer a range of services and applications to what it sees as a largely untapped market. Ellison agrees. Market research predicts that the small-business software market will be worth $47 billion by 2006, and Ellison thinks that he can use NetLedger both to get a big slice of the action and to head off Microsoft's efforts to extend its applications franchise beyond the desktop. He says, "Intuit is one of the few surviving PC software companies. They've done a terrific job. But NetLedger is an online service company, not a software company. It's a totally new business model. An online service has a much lower cost of ownership and offers a lot more features than Intuit's QuickBooks or any other small-business software, including Microsoft/Great Plains. Nobody is going to beat Intuit or Microsoft in the small-business software market. But if it's a war between service and software, then I think the service model will win." I wondered what would happen if Microsoft decided to offer $200 million for NetLedger. "I'd tell them to get fucked. I suppose Evan might take a swing at me, but I own 55 per cent of the company, and there's no way in hell Microsoft's going to get it."

• • •

When we land at Chicago's Midway Airport, there's a limo waiting to take us to an Italian steak house downtown where we're going to meet Jimmy Linn, or "the Judge," as Ellison usually refers to his nephew. Linn is the son of Doris, the much older sister he grew up with and the daughter of his adoptive father, Lou Ellison. Although there's no blood relationship, the Linns are Ellison's family and they're a very important part of his life. By the time we get to the Erie Café, a former meatpacking plant near River North, the dinner's already in full swing. There are about twelve people at the Judge's table, nearly all of them are lawyers, and most of them seem to have met Ellison before. It's a very traditional place with dark-paneled walls and bare brick, every plate groaning with bleeding slabs of meat (the twenty-four-ounce T-bone is a specialty) or mountains of steaming pasta. And the lawyers don't really look or sound like lawyers. From their appearance (loud sports jackets, open-neck shirts, and plenty of gold hanging from wrists and necks) and conversation (mostly about criminal mayhem of one kind or another), you'd think it was a scene from *The Sopranos*. The Judge, who's only a few years younger than Ellison, has a dark tan, long black hair, and a Zapata moustache. It's the first time I've met him, and although he's outgoing and friendly, he's also guarded. He doesn't like the treatment Ellison has received from journalists, and he's protective of his famous uncle.

Although Ellison is, inevitably, the center of attention, he's not accorded any special treatment. There's a lot of joking and telling of mostly horrifying anecdotes about Chicago lowlifes. There's also quite a bit of grousing about the fall in Oracle's stock price. Ellison has made Jimmy wealthy by giving him shares in the company (it's the reason he could afford to follow his father onto the bench), and several of the others at the table have personally invested in Oracle. Ellison assures them that the business is in pretty good shape, but he's not prepared to say when he thinks the stock will start to recover. The only thing that fazes him is when a massive plate of lamb chops arrives for him. Ellison loves his food, but the sheer size of the portions seems to rob him of his appetite. He's been in California too long. When the dinner breaks up, Jimmy, who's picked up the tab, puts a braceleted arm around me and says that unless I'm nice about his uncle, he'll personally kill me. I *think* he's joking.

• • •

The next day's roundtable event turns out to be for chief information officers rather than CEOs. There's some embarrassment about this on the part of the Oracle people who've made the arrangements. According to protocol, Ellison really shouldn't be wheeled out in front of this lower-level audience. Maybe Sandy Sanderson, who heads Oracle's consulting organization, should take the meeting instead. Ellison decides that he will show up, but not until after lunch is out of the way. He's decided that from now on, even with a room full of CEOs, they should eat before he makes his grand entrance. It's difficult to make the pitch, he says, if you have already used up all your best lines on the people sitting next to you. In fact, perhaps because the audience is made of CIOs, who are more technically savvy than their bosses, it turns out to be a rather good occasion.

Most of those present are in service industries such as health, education, and the Chicago Police Department. When Ellison finishes his standard confessional riff on why information fragmentation is the reason that expensive computer systems promised much but delivered little, he's drawn into an interesting dialogue with the CIOs about what they need to do if they're to get their own organizations to follow Oracle down the path to e-business. There's near unanimity that, in the words of one,

"From an IT perspective we have islands of automation—little fiefdoms that like spending money on their own bespoke systems." The CIO of Western Digital, a maker of hard disks and storage for computers, says that he figures his firm is running on a total of thirty-eight different applications when it could be using just six—five of which are within Oracle 11i. But when he tried to change things, eight functional directors "slapped me down—the message was, you're in my penalty box." *

Without having the CEO "in their camp," Ellison admits, they'll find it tough. "New software is a great catalyst for change, but unless people are willing to change the way they work, the benefits will be elusive. New business processes are at least as important as new software. At Oracle we began with a project to put in new software. The software made us change the way we worked. Those new business processes led to a more efficient global organizational structure. The sum of all these changes was a new Oracle culture in constant pursuit of higher quality and lower costs. It was a surprise ending to what began as a software project." However, the message that Ellison most wants to leave this technical audience with is the idea that the database comes first. "Count your customer databases. Every year you should have fewer. You're not done until you get to one. Once you have a single customer database, your company has entered the information age. Technology is important. Applications are important. But chief information officers should focus on delivering better information to the business. That's what Oracle applications and Oracle technology are good at, managing and delivering information."

• • •

Next stop is Fisher Island, Miami. The private resort is reachable only by boat. The island was owned by the Vanderbilts, and the centerpiece is still William's former mansion, now converted into a hotel and surrounded by rather tacky guest bungalows that are reached by golf carts, the only

---

*LE writes: Functional directors, aka department managers, do a good job of optimizing business processes inside their own functional areas: marketing, sales, service, manufacturing, accounting, HR, and the rest. Functional directors have no authority to optimize processes between and across functional areas. That's why things break down between marketing and sales, manufacturing and service, manufacturing and sales, etc. Only the CEO is responsible for the business as a whole. If the CEO doesn't connect the dots, the company will never operate efficiently.

form of transport allowed on the island. The following day's roundtable is for the CEOs of eighteen of Oracle's Latin American customers. It's a sybaritic place but a boring meeting. There are language issues, and the guests are much more diffident about engaging Ellison in debate than their Yankee counterparts.

Perhaps it's just as well. As we're leaving, one of them, Paolo Bassetti, the president of Exiros, a big Internet exchange spun out of the Techint Group, an Italian-Argentine industrial conglomerate, starts telling me about the problems his company is having with Oracle's procurement software. Bassetti's company had opted for Oracle's Exchange Marketplace Platform because it promised a high level of scalability and the ability to integrate with most known ERP systems. But Bassetti felt let down: his clients were finding it difficult to close transactions; California power outages were undermining Oracle's hosting service; and the critical functionality that had been promised in subsequent releases was several months late in arriving.* When I say that he should have mentioned some of this to Ellison during the roundtable, he says that his fellow guests would have thought him ill mannered.

On the way back to California with Ellison, I tell him about Bassetti's complaints. It doesn't come as a total surprise to him and he says he'll look into it, but he looks a bit tired and fed up. I ask him if he doesn't sometimes think it's a little odd that at his time of life and with his kind of money, he's still flying all over the country trying to sell software. He smiles wryly. "It's not something I really enjoy. But right now, I have to do it."

---

*LE writes: At the height of Internet mania, our B2B exchange business spread around the world faster than Asian flu. I've never seen anything like it. Unfortunately, every customer wanted its Exchange Web site to operate slightly differently. As the bubble began to deflate, all our commercial Exchange customers began to alter their business plans. It was simply impossible for us to keep up with their constantly changing requirements. Then, to make matters worse, the lights in our California data center started going out on a regular basis. We moved our B2B exchange customers to our Texas data center as fast as we could because California was running out of electricity. California is a strange place. A few years back we almost ran out of water.

14

THE LAST DATABASE

June 2001

I'm meeting Ellison by his hangar at tiny San Carlos airport, five minutes' drive from Oracle's headquarters. Ellison keeps four aircraft there: a couple of high-performance prop-driven stunt planes, one of which belongs to his son, David; an Italian Marchetti jet fighter that he acquired after the authorities told him what he could do with his plans to import a supersonic MiG-29 from Russia; and a Cessna Citation business jet, which is unquestionably the biggest and most sophisticated airplane that flies in and out of San Carlos. The Citation is more convenient than the San Jose–based Gulfstream V for trips of less than five hundred miles, and it's the Citation that we're flying to Las Vegas, a one-and-a-half-hour hop over the Sierra Nevada, for an Oracle sales conference.

Right on time at 4 P.M., we drop out of a cloudless sky over the famous strip that is home to the most incongruous set of buildings on the planet, including replicas of the Eiffel Tower and one of the Giza pyramids. As we emerge from the little white plane, a blast of heat hits us. On the taxiway are the inevitable black Lincoln limos and Ellison's bodyguards, George and Rich. On the short ride to Caesar's Palace, I ask Ellison whether he feels at all nervous. It's not only a big audience but one that's expecting to be inspired. Sales for the last two quarters of the year have been flat, and few, if any, of the 3,300 Oracle salespeople in the room will be taking home the bonuses that can bump their salaries up to more than a million dollars. Ellison says, "No, I'm not nervous. I just wish I didn't have to do this. All these guys are going to want to talk about is comp."

The Las Vegas bash is an annual event that takes place just after the close of the final quarter and costs Oracle the thick end of $10 million. It's a perpetual mystery to Ellison why the field needs this kind of thing or the ridiculous awards they love handing out to one another. He says that when he holds a modest party each year for the developers before Christmas, half of them don't turn up and those who do don't stay for long. The team that built 9i might go out for a few drinks when the software ships, but they're back at their desks the next morning, working on what will turn into the next release. When Ellison talks about the sales force, it's as if it's a strange, childlike tribe with odd customs and rituals that are impenetrable to anyone else (i.e., who's grown up). Ellison is willing to concede that Oracle's sales force is full of smart, intensely hardworking people—but the subtext is that most of them are emotionally immature and motivated only by money. It's not contempt, more a kind of fastidiousness combined with intellectual snobbery. The idea that Ellison might spend the night in town striving to be "one of the boys," as, say, Microsoft's Steve Ballmer would, is ridiculous. "If I stayed, they'd hate me for it," he says, "If I was around, they couldn't enjoy themselves."

We arrive at the rear entrance of Caesar's Palace, where Judy Sim is ready to brief Ellison. She says the audience has had a long day and has been "PowerPointed out" with one presentation after another from other Oracle executives. The message is that they're waiting impatiently for a bit of Ellison knockabout and he'd better not disappoint. As we pass one of the swimming pools on the way in, Sim points to what the hotel describes as its policy of allowing "European-style"—topless—sunbathing. The implication is clear: there are competing attractions.

The ballroom is jam-packed. It's standing room only, and people seated in the wings of the giant hall are dependent on the huge screens that fill both sides of the room. As news of Ellison's arrival ripples around the overwhelmingly male audience, all eyes swivel in our direction. On the stage, Jay Nussbaum, Oracle's vice president for service industries, has been presenting BellSouth's Lowri Groves with an award for completing a large CRM implementation at the firm's consumer broadband division. This is the same Lowri Groves whom we met three months earlier in the HealthSouth hangar, who had pleaded with Ellison to do what it took to make Ralph de la Vega, the division's nervy boss, "whole again." BellSouth appears so happy with de la Vega's restored wholeness that it's well on the way to a commitment to extend the Oracle system to its huge fixed-line residential business. Oh, and she's got a prize for Ellison. As Ellison gets up to mount the stage, I whisper to him that she's changed her tune. He whispers back, "Software implementations are like childbirth. You go through terrible pain, but once you get through it, you have a beautiful new baby."

Nussbaum introduces Ellison—"We welcome our great leader"—who receives a hug from Groves and a piece of fragile-looking modernistic glass sculpture that stands as much chance of making it into Ellison's office as a bust of Bill Gates. The applause subsides; Ellison grabs a microphone and begins to prowl up and down the stage. It's curiously effective, giving the impression of pent-up energy, like a big cat restlessly pacing a cage that's too small to hold it.

Ellison wants to get across the message that despite a tough second half of the year, Oracle has never been in better shape to take the battle to its competitors. "Let's start with our products," he says. "The 11i suite is a revolutionary idea. All the information in one place. All the pieces fitting together. There's never been this breadth of functionality in an applications package before. After just one year we have more than four hundred customers running their businesses on it." He then starts to reel off some names. High up the list, which as usual includes the likes of Ford and Alcoa, comes the story of GE Power Systems and how GE Power in Hungary was able to complete something that might have taken two years in little more than three months by mapping its processes to the software rather than the doing it the other way round—a method of implementation that was now being rolled out in Houston and thirty-seven other sites around the world. For a little light relief and to show that not only huge companies are turning to 11i, Ellison brings up Papa John's Pizza and Pizza Hut: "We're dominating the business of configured pizzas—pineapple and anchovies, whatever you want, our software can configure the pizza. The telecoms business is also pretty important, but it's less familiar to me." The line, which is unrehearsed, gets a big laugh.

But Ellison isn't prepared to lighten up too much. He wants them to know how much more capable 11i is than the products of rival vendors: ERP and CRM combined . . . you can't do business without it . . . SAP and Siebel don't have it . . . Ariba can't automate procurement . . . we're the only ones who can automate whole business flows . . . don't take the whole E-Business Suite all at once . . . take it one integrated flow at a time. And then something close to an admission, an acceptance that the birth of 11i has been far from easy for both Oracle and its customers: "11i has been the most complex product transition in application software history—building a complete suite of applications with Java and HTML front ends. PeopleSoft says we're not as 'pure Internet' as they are because they have no Java, just HTML, in their user interface—but ninety-nine percent of their apps are written in PeopleTools! Is People-Tools an Internet standard? It's the same with Siebel, their apps are written in SiebelTools—Tom won't sell any software that doesn't have his name on it! Siebel got into the CRM market early, and they didn't have any competitors for a long time. That time is over. The first year of selling the suite was the hardest year. It's difficult to sell without customer references. Maybe we began to doubt whether we could pull it off. They said we couldn't. But we did. We have four hundred references now, and next year there will be thousands. No one else is even trying to build what we've built."

He's brought with him the slides that will be used in two days' time at 9i's official launch. The idea is to see how the presentation goes down in Las Vegas and tweak it as necessary. At first, Ellison promises "no more PowerPoint," remembering Sim's warning on the way in. But just as suddenly he decides to use slides anyway because they'll help him show just how "amazing" a database 9i really is. "Oh, put the slides up. And then afterwards we'll talk about comp."

One of the slides compares the transaction speed of Oracle running on IBM's fastest UNIX computer compared with DB2; it's based on an ad that Oracle is about to run. It shows a tall red column for Oracle and for IBM a blue stump that doesn't extend much beyond the bottom of the chart. Ellison explains, "When IBM wanted to show how fast their fastest computer ran, they used Oracle. IBM won't even say how fast DB2 runs on the same computer. There are two possibilities. The first is that DB2 is so fast that IBM doesn't want to embarrass us. That's one possibility. The second possibility is that they run like a snail. I think we're dealing with escargot, folks." In the testosterone-charged atmosphere that Ellison has carefully stoked, it brings the roof down.

An important part of Ellison's argument is that IBM's DB2 is actually two entirely different products: an excellent database that runs on mainframes and that is capable of running real-world applications across clusters, albeit slowly and expensively, and a vastly inferior product that has a completely different architecture and can run only (briefly) the TPC-C benchmark across different computers. Ellison jeers, "It's like painting the word 'Boeing' on the side of a roller skate and calling it a 747. DB2 on mainframes is a fine product with real clustering capability. DB2 on Unix and Windows is a totally different product with clustering capability that's only good for marketing. It's totally useless for running real applications. You expect this kind of thing from the boys in Seattle [Microsoft]. They're new to the database business. They might not even know their clustering is useless. But IBM should know better." Ellison then explains the different architectures: "shared disk" for DB2 on main-frames and Oracle 9i on Unix, Windows, and Linux versus "shared noth-ing" for the other DB2, which he describes as a piece of garbage. "Who's right?" he asks. "The mainframe DB2 guys at IBM or the UNIX DB2 guys? The products are totally different. They can't both be right. It's a difficult question for IBM to answer. So we're going to keep asking it. DB2 on UNIX is an imposter. Its shared-nothing architecture is good for nothing. It doesn't deserve the IBM logo. Oracle 9i is the last database."

With that Ellison turns to sing the praises of the newly released 9iAS application server as being now the "fastest and cheapest middleware in the world." A week earlier, Ellison made a rambunctious appearance at the Java One conference for Java developers at the Moscone Center in San Francisco. Despite the near hysterics of Sun's PR people, who had wanted Java One to be an anodyne celebration of the Java community, Ellison used his time on stage to proclaim the superior performance of 9iAS over the rival product from cosponsor BEA Systems that currently dominates the Web application server market. Ellison had set out to demonstrate that while BEA was much better than IBM's WebSphere—according to Oracle's tests, twice as fast rather than half as fast, as IBM claimed ("It's so easy to get those metrics confused," joked Ellison), 9iAS was three times faster than the market leader. BEA's boss, Bill Coleman, as Ellison now gleefully related to his troops in Las Vegas, had not been amused. "Bill liked the first slide showing how much faster BEA was than WebSphere, but he didn't like the second slide. Major bummer. In fact, he said afterwards that 'Larry had just made the numbers up onstage.' He said I lied. Shocking. He really hurt my feelings. A bit later, when he found out that all my numbers were based on certified performance test results, do you know what he said then? Bill Coleman said, 'Performance doesn't matter.' Performance doesn't matter? Is that right? We're going to feed those words right back to Bill in our next BEA comparison ad. Yes, folks, we *are* a kinder, gentler Oracle these days." The audience roars its approval.

It's time for questions from the floor. The first one's easy. What's Ellison's take on Microsoft? Ellison replies: "The X-Box looks fabulous. They've finally found something they're really good at. We don't compete with Microsoft. SQL Server is a joke. We don't make spreadsheets or word processors, so we don't see much of Microsoft in the market. The only time I think about them is when my Windows machine blows up."

Having spent much of the second half of the 1990s appearing to fight a holy war with Microsoft over the direction of computing, Ellison's approach now is to portray it as irrelevant to Oracle's future. While Oracle is the leader in the serious world of supplying complete business information systems to companies, Microsoft is derided as a company that is increasingly focused on consumer markets, where its main rival is AOL Time Warner.

The next question is a little trickier, although it's one that Ellison has been expecting. An intense-faced, clearly nervous young man, sitting near the back of the hall, asks Ellison about "comp." He says that they've recently been told via a conference call that there will be no money for raises in the second half of the fiscal year just ended. Is this really true? The hall is suddenly completely silent. But by the time he's through, the young man sounds more angry than frightened. And when he sits down he gets a big cheer for being bold enough to say what's on everybody's mind. Even though he's been expecting the question, Ellison still looks slightly uncomfortable. "You obviously drew the short straw," he jokes. "But the truth is that we've had a really crappy year, especially the last two quarters. We share the success, and we share the pain. When things are going well, we pay out huge raises and bonuses. When things aren't going so well, we don't give out raises and bonuses because there's no money for them. The stock's down to fifteen dollars. I'm sorry about that. But it's a fact of life. We're all suffering together. But because we're watching every penny we spend, we've been able to avoid layoffs—Cisco laid off thousands. We're watching every penny we spend so we can preserve our team intact—so you're all here to fight again this year. We have a long tradition of paying people well at Oracle. You can make it all back and more this year, it just depends on how much you sell." I wonder how the stuff about shared pain will go down. Most of the people in the ballroom know that Ellison cashed in $900 million worth of stock at the beginning of the year. Either they're too polite/scared to mention it, or the juxtaposition doesn't trouble them.

One of the more senior salesmen gets up to say that the current situation reminds him of 1990, when Ellison sent all employees an e-mail describing the crisis and the steps that he was taking to resolve it. What was he doing to help Oracle through its present crisis? Ellison is a little shocked at the comparison and starts to talk about some of the things that he's doing to lower costs, such as using the Internet to move customer support from high-price markets such as Britain and the United States to India. But, he says, this has nothing to do with the economy, it's what Oracle would be doing anyway, "automating away jobs, saving head count, and improving service." The whole point of the E-Business Suite is to do more with less: "That's what we sell it for." Then he starts to waffle about adding people in development and maybe in sales too but says that Oracle is a tough place to be if you're a mediocre sales performer. Realizing he's losing his audience, Ellison stops himself and says what he ought to have earlier: "This is nothing like 1990. We were on the verge of going out of business then. Our performance this Q3 may have been disappointing for us, but it would have been glorious success for almost anyone else."

A couple of questions later Ellison is asked what Oracle's greatest challenge is. His answer is interesting: "The biggest challenge was this year's applications technology transition. It put huge stress on the entire organization. It was like the move from Oracle 6 to Oracle 7. It was Oracle 7 that saved Oracle. The E-Business Suite has been a difficult transition, but we've crossed the chasm. 11i wasn't perfect when it came out, how could it have been? It's five times more complex than the product it replaced. But we were right to be ambitious. There's nothing else like it. First we have to persuade ourselves; only then can we convince the rest of the world."

With that Ellison is done. He leaves the ballroom with the audience still standing and clapping. The effect is clearly calculated. While other Oracle senior executives are accessible and will stay overnight to get drunk and party, the charismatic leader maintains some distance between himself and his troops.

• • •

A couple of days later, it's time for the official launch of Oracle 9i. After the troubled infancy of the E-Business Suite, Oracle could do with some good publicity, and Ellison is convinced that the advanced technology of 9i, especially Real Application Clusters, will blow the minds of the journalists and analysts who have been invited to Redwood Shores. The main theater in the Oracle conference center is decked out with huge red banners, boldly proclaiming the extraordinary qualities of the new database. A spotlight sweeps over the banners, rock music pulsates, and a giant video screen projects swirling images of speed and power. The audience has been carefully segregated: the press occupies tables to the left and near the front; the analysts are behind them; and to the right are the Oracle employees: some from marketing, but mainly the middle-aged, rather academic-looking guys from the database development group, who are on hand to do one-to-one briefings when the main show is over.

When Ellison sweeps in, he moves quickly into the pitch for 9i that went down well in Las Vegas. He's trying to get across an idea that he fears cynical journalists and analysts will be naturally resistant to—that 9i is not just an incremental improvement over its predecessor but a breakthrough product with the potential both to transform the economics of corporate computing and to render the rival databases from IBM and Microsoft terminally obsolete. To Ellison, this is not just marketing bombast. He is convinced it's true. He can hardly contain his excitement. Oracle 9i is the superweapon that will not only win the war but convince the enemy that further resistance is futile. That's why Ellison calls the database team "the boys from Los Alamos" and why he talks of 9i as "the last database."

Although 9i has, according to Ellison, at least four hundred "incredibly cool new features," the one he wants even people who know nothing about databases to understand is RAC. Oracle's top computer scientists, led by a prickly genius named Roger Bamford, have been working on the technology for more than a decade. Although clustering, in which several computers are linked together to work as one, has been around for some time, there has always been a trade-off between scalability and reliability. As corporate IT departments have tried to add computing power to their applications, they have had to spend months reconfiguring data if their applications were to run at all. Even then, the applications were limited to highly specialized activities such as data warehousing, in which groups of machines laboriously look for patterns in their stock of information. The packaged applications made by the likes of SAP, Oracle, and Siebel do not run on clusters because they are unable to cope with the speed at which data changes with applications of this kind.

The only exception to this rule is clusters of IBM's ponderous and costly mainframe computers. Customers who needed both speed and scale to run their applications had no choice other than to buy very-high-end sixty-four-processor UNIX computers such as those made by Sun Microsystems, Hewlett-Packard, and IBM. However, not only do these complicated pieces of hardware typically cost upward of $2.5 million, but to get the reliability required for mission-critical applications or to support an e-business platform able to withstand the onslaught of millions of users, you have to buy twice as many machines as you really want—the one you actually need and one to act as a "hot standby" in case the other crashed. And once you fork out for the biggest, fastest, most powerful computer that money could buy, if you want even more performance, tough. You just have to wait for Sun or HP to get around to building something even bigger and more expensive.

Oracle's RAC is designed to get customers out of this bind by allowing groups of machines to share the same short-term memory or "cache," allowing them effectively to operate as one computer. With RAC, IT departments can start with just one low-cost computer, if that's all they need, and then add more boxes without making any configuration changes or rewriting the code in any of their applications, as demand increases. Not only can they scale their operations remarkably cheaply—thirty-two Compaq four-processor boxes cost less than a fifth of a couple of giant Sun E10000s—but with every server added, they increase redundancy and therefore reliability. Oracle's claim for RAC is that it delivers virtually limitless scalability, absolute fault tolerance, and dramatically lower hardware and operating costs. No wonder Ellison has convinced himself that it is the firm's most important step forward in database technology since it came up with the world's first commercial SQL relational database management system a quarter century ago.

Ellison begins the show with a slide outlining Oracle's original design target for 9i: to improve performance by a factor of five while halving the cost. A further goal was to achieve ten times the reliability. There are, he says, just two ways to get better database performance: use either faster software or faster hardware. Making Oracle 9i the fastest database on a single computer wasn't the problem. On the TPC-C standard benchmarks it could comfortably handle four times the number of transactions a minute as Microsoft's SQL Server, while IBM was not prepared to publish any benchmarks for the UNIX/NT version of DB2. Interestingly, Ellison says, when IBM wanted to show how fast its most powerful UNIX computer was, the benchmark was run using Oracle rather than DB2. Ellison jeers, "IBM couldn't even persuade its own hardware guys across the hall to use DB2, even though it was free!" But hitting the ten-times-improved cost/performance target simply wasn't possible on a single computer. "Really fast computers are not only very expensive," says Ellison, "but one high-end computer is also a single point of failure." So the aim of getting ten times better reliability was also not possible. Why had nobody used clusters? Because the only database that would run real applications was DB2 on mainframes. Pretty much the only application that would run on clusters in a UNIX/NT environment was the benchmarking software used to measure TPC-C performance. So unless you happened to run your business on a benchmarking application, clustering wasn't likely to be a whole lot of use to you.

The problem, Ellison explains, was one of architecture. The architecture of the DB2 clusters on mainframes is called "shared disk," which means that any computer in the cluster can get at 100 percent of the data. But the clustering architecture used by "the other" DB2 and SQL Server is known as "shared nothing." Apart from the benchmarking software, the problem with "shared nothing" is that the only applications it will run are customized "one-offs." It won't run the packaged apps that are used in the real world. And, Ellison says, it gets worse. First of all, shared-nothing clusters are very hard to manage. If you need to add computers, all your data has to be repartitioned, a job that might take months. Worst of all, as you add computers, the whole system becomes increasingly unstable. With four computers, each holding 25 percent of your data, the failure of just one will bring down the others. In other words, from a reliability point of view there is not just one single point of failure that might bring down one application but multiple single points of failure.*

Oracle's achievement, according to Ellison, is to have taken the same shared-disk architecture that works within the tightly controlled, hermetically sealed environment of an IBM mainframe and make it work using clusters of the cheap computing boxes churned out by Compaq or Dell in their millions. It is, he says, true fault tolerance with commodity hardware—one of the holy grails of computing. The result, says Ellison, is not just ten times greater reliability than before but one thousand times, with no need for redundant "hot-standby" computers and no need for expensive twenty-four-hour-a-day human monitoring of the data center. If one computer, or "node," goes down, it doesn't matter. The system may slow down a little, but otherwise it carries on as normal.

What comes next is that staple of software presentations: the live demo. Onto the stage comes Mark Jarvis. His job is to run the demo while Ellison plays the role, rather unconvincingly, of the guy who asks the dumb questions. The aim of the demo is to show what happens to two clustered four-node computer systems when one node is brought down. One, represented by a thick blue bar that fluctuates in size according to the number of transactions being processed, is running DB2 with the "shared-nothing" partitioning architecture, while the other, in red, is on Oracle 9i with its "shared-disk" approach. Jarvis claims that the demo is live and hooked up via the Internet to an Oracle data center. At first, both systems chug along at pretty much the same rate. Then Jarvis

---

*LE writes: Simply stated, shared-nothing clusters get less reliable as you add computers to the cluster. An eight-machine shared-nothing cluster is one fourth as reliable as a two-machine shared-nothing cluster. Hard to believe, but true.

takes out one of the nodes of the Oracle system. The speed of transaction processing falls by about 20 percent, the red bar reducing slightly in size, but otherwise the system remains stable. He then applies the same treatment to the IBM cluster, which predictably, but nonetheless quite dramatically, can't take it. Within a minute, because only part of the data is now available to the application, thus rendering both the offline and the online data worthless, the blue bar collapses, indicating that the entire cluster has failed. The press and analysts are trained not to react to this kind of thing, but it's impressive. They know that the software business has an inglorious history of rigging demonstrations when products are late or can't do what they're meant to.

After the demo, Ellison turns to the issue of how Oracle 9i will be priced. Over the last year, Oracle has been pricing its database licenses according to a formula known as "power units," which measure the overall power of a customer's computer system and price it accordingly. It's been unpopular because some customers, upgrading their hardware, have resented paying Oracle more money for the same software and because both DB2 and SQL Server licenses are sold according to the number of processors the database will be running on. By using a different metric from its rivals, Oracle has left itself vulnerable to accusations that it is overcharging. It's a stick that several of the market research analysts, principally Gartner's Betsy Burton, have been using to beat Oracle with while claiming, somewhat against the evidence of their own surveys, that it's been costing Oracle market share. Ellison has decided to return to the processor-licensing model used by IBM and Microsoft. He's incensed by the suggestion that DB2 works out cheaper than Oracle.

Under the new formula, the price of the enterprise edition of 9i is to be $40,000 per processor against the $20,000 charged by IBM. But whereas Oracle includes "essential" features such as queuing, work flow, and files in the basic price, DB2 customers must pay extra for them. Quoting IBM's own price list, Ellison says that DB2 turns out to cost 65 percent more than Oracle 9i before you even start to add in the advantages of running on cheaper hardware and lower running costs. And if you want data mining, Ellison claims, IBM will charge you $60,000 per processor compared with Oracle's $20,000. Although this seems like another well-aimed shot at IBM, it has the unfortunate consequence of turning the main story of the day away from 9i's fancy technology and into one about pricing policy, one with a pretty negative spin. The headlines next day are predictable: "Oracle Backs Down on Pricing" and "Oracle Cuts Prices to Stem Market Share Slide." It's a mystery how a company that spends as much time and money on marketing could have made such an elementary mistake.*

But it gets worse. When Ellison finishes speaking, a local newspaper reporter named Tom McEwen wants a quote from Ellison—or "Captain Midnight," as he calls him—about a court ruling a few days earlier on whether he could fly his Gulfstream into San Jose Airport late at night. Ellison had claimed that the airport authority was unfairly discriminating against him on account of the weight of his plane rather than its noisiness, and the ruling, by federal judge Jeremy Fogel, was a big win. Still, he's shocked to be asked about it now. "Oh my God," he groans, raising his hand to his forehead in a gesture of exasperation.[†]

Most of the questions that follow are about pricing. Is this a disguised price cut because of the pressure from IBM, and if so, what impact will it have on revenues? The answers are "no" and "none"—it's just a question of using a comparable metric, and anyway, Oracle is always making its software cheaper and selling more of it as a consequence. An analyst says that in interviews he's conducted with DBAs (database administrators) about half of them are saying that Microsoft and DB2 are "good enough" and what's the point of paying extra for Oracle? Ellison responds almost wearily, "With Oracle, you use less hardware and less labor. The economics of the database industry actually have very little to do with the price of the software."

Only a few questions are about the radical clustering technology, but a couple of them raise interesting issues. Ellison has been keen to get endorsements from rival application vendors for 9i and has succeeded in getting a glowing reference from even SAP. So has Oracle been working with application partners? Ellison seizes on the opportunity to amplify a key point: "Our clusters don't require us to work with them. They don't

---

*LE writes: Right. We should have held the pricing change until the following week. It was really dumb to mix it with the RAC announcement.

†LE writes: San Jose Airport had a bizarre noise abatement program based on the weight of an airplane rather than the noise it made. My quiet plane was banned from landing after 11 P.M. because it was too "heavy." Noisier planes were allowed to land anytime because they were "lighter" than my airplane. Call me crazy, but I thought that noise ordinances had to do with restricting noisy airplanes, not heavy airplanes. The judge agreed. But in the meantime the press wrote lots of nasty articles about my not obeying the rules. It was quite the little local controversy.

have to change a single line of code. It just works—it's transparent to the app. The app doesn't even know it's running on multiple machines." One perceptive questioner wants to know what RAC means for Oracle's close relationship with Sun in terms of the latter's do-or-die battle with Intel.

The answer is up there on the stage in the form of a rack of Compaq four-processor boxes and in some of the slides that Ellison has shown indicating the price difference between getting sixty-four processors with sixteen Compaq boxes and a sixty-four-processor Sun E10000. Ellison equivocates, "We have a good relationship with both Sun and Intel. But we've always hesitated to recommend Intel for mission-critical applications because their server hardware is relatively small and the Microsoft operating system is so fragile. But with RAC none of that matters anymore. You get the performance you need from clustering lots of small servers together, and if a few should fail, no problem, the system keeps running. So RAC makes low-cost Intel servers viable in the data center.* But Sun has very competitively priced small servers, and they have a great operating system. It's really about small machines versus big, high-end machines, not Sun versus Intel." The truth is that Sun is pretty competitive at the low end because it has to be—but it's not where it makes its money. If big, fast computers can be replaced with groups of little ones, it's seriously bad news for Oracle's old hardware partner, and Ellison knows it.

What Ellison isn't letting on is that he has decided to throw Oracle's weight behind Intel's sixty-four-bit McKinley processor when (and if) it finally debuts next year. Ellison isn't about to say anything disparaging about Sun in public, but what he's planning, not to mention what Oracle has already done with RAC, could turn out to be far more damaging to his feisty Valley neighbor than anything so far achieved by their mutual enemy Microsoft.

• • •

A week later, at Oracle's OpenWorld event in Berlin's huge and hideous ICC conference center, Ellison does a repeat of his 9i launch presentation.

---

*LE writes: The Linux operating system running on Intel servers is rapidly on its way to becoming the most popular hardware/software combination in large data centers. This presents a great opportunity for Oracle because our unique clustering technology lets us deliver our high-performance, fault-tolerant database on low-cost Intel servers running Linux. We can't continue to let Microsoft be the only software company to exploit low-cost Intel hardware.

This time, however, the seven-thousand-strong audience is largely made up of enthusiastic Oracle partners and database administrators. The professionally skeptical analysts and reporters have their chance to question Ellison in a side room, but it's a fairly tame affair despite the presence of one or two known Oracle scourges, including Gartner's Betsy Burton.

Burton has suggested in recent interviews that Oracle's database is losing ground because of intense pricing pressure from IBM and Microsoft, even though the evidence, and even the market research data—itself of questionable quality—is ambiguous. While it's taking flak over the early bugginess of 11i, the last thing Oracle needs is for the biggest technology research and consulting house to be suggesting that there are chinks in the armor of its core database product. In fact, in the course of Oracle's fourth-quarter earnings call earlier that week, Ellison had to admit to a 5 percent falloff in database revenues. While the financial analysts took comfort from the fact that Oracle's earnings had held firm, industry watchers such as Burton took it as further evidence that Oracle's database business was coming under pressure.*

The next day we're in London at his favorite hotel, the Lanesborough. After yet another CEO roundtable, Ellison is going to meet with a group of industry analysts from different firms, among them the dreaded Betsy Burton and two or three of her colleagues from Gartner. Although Mark Jarvis has been trying to mend fences with Burton, Ellison is more inclined to be confrontational. "Like a lot of these analysts," he says, "all she does is predict the past."†

About fifteen analysts from firms such as IDC, Forrester, AMR, and, of course, Gartner, are seated around a long table. Their demeanor is

---

*LE writes: Every survey that asked customers what database they were using or planning on using showed Oracle gaining share against IBM. A Morgan Stanley survey had Oracle six times more popular than IBM's DB2 under enterprise applications like SAP and Siebel.

†LE writes: The most respected analyst in our industry is Chuck Phillips. When Chuck publishes his survey results, he includes all of his supporting data and his methodology. Anyone can independently verify the data and double-check his calculations and conclusions. Chuck is completely devoted to the scientific method, invented by Sir Francis Bacon more than four hundred years ago. Betsy Burton uses a more modern approach: she publishes her results without any supporting data or details about her methodology. You can't check a damn thing. You just have to take her word for it.

mostly earnest and respectful, although one, Paul Mason, a senior analyst from IDC, soon starts to rub Ellison the wrong way with a fatal mix of overfamiliarity and sarcasm. Ellison starts off by ramming home his message about data fragmentation: "It's *the* issue. It's that simple." What's unique about Oracle, he argues, is its combination of a datacentric information architecture and the ease with which the E-Business Suite can be extended because Oracle uses Java rather than the proprietary tools of its rival applications vendors. The key difference between Oracle and the others—its counterpoint—is information management. Ellison says that he doesn't believe in separating data warehouses from transaction processing because too much time is lost. The combination of RAC and another feature on 9i that automatically maintains both old and new versions of the same data would make warehousing irrelevant. Burton volunteers that one of the benefits of this is that it "reduces conflicts between two separate instances." "Absolutely," purrs Ellison.

Ellison feels strongly that the analysts haven't yet given Oracle enough credit for RAC because they are hostile to real innovation. "It's like Galileo and the pope. Every time he had a new idea, the pope threatened to kill him." Instead of talking up IBM's DB2, why not point out that with its shared-nothing architecture all it can do is share nothing really fast? "Drill down into this," he demands. "Write this down. Ask IBM why its UNIX database takes a different architectural approach from its mainframe versions. Please write this down. Why won't IBM demonstrate the speed of their hardware with their own database? You guys always say we're more expensive than IBM. But it's the cost of ownership that matters—the networking, the hardware, the labor. The software is always a tiny proportion of that. I'm almost done. This is a scam, and you guys have all fallen for it."

Having let off steam, Ellison answers questions on everything from peer-to-peer computing (which he dismisses as a "cute little technology that's good for exchanging music" but not something for the enterprise) and software as a service. Ellison says that in a very few years, the bulk of Oracle's business "will be on servers we manage." But the conventional ASPs (application service providers) were all wrong. Where the computers were located was irrelevant; what mattered was who provided the skilled labor. "It doesn't matter where the computer is. As long as it's running in a standard certified configuration, you can put hardware wherever you want and we'll run it for you. And another thing: everyone focuses on our new license revenue, but the real value in our business is recurring revenues from license updates and support." IDC's Mason suggests that this is typical Ellisonian arrogance. Everyone's wrong except him. Ellison responds, "Sure. If you're the first to say something or do something that conflicts with popular conventional wisdom, then what you're saying is, in effect, 'I'm right and everyone else is wrong.' That's what innovation means—being first. People never forgive you for being right too early.*

Ellison had been forceful, funny, and brilliantly controversial, but I didn't think he had necessarily won them over. He was more than capable of charming them; but it was as if he was too fastidious to try. Eight weeks later, Betsy Burton produced a report for Gartner entitled "Oracle Under Fire," which began with this broadside: "During the past 12 months, Oracle has been under increasing scrutiny from many of its customers, the business and technology press, investment firms, and Gartner. Some of the press attention is because of Oracle's sheer size, its impact on U.S. financial market indicators, and its 60 percent and larger stock price slippage in the past twelve months. Some is because of Oracle's flamboyant and contrarian CEO, Larry Ellison. Much of the attention, however, is because of real product, marketing and business issues."

The report itself was a mixture of the obvious and the out of date. Oracle, Burton said, would have to: provide "proof points" for 9i's "clustering scalability" and ability to "support very large databases"; regain "customer trust" after a U-turn on power unit pricing; "continue a sustained level of commitment to its application server"; resolve the quality issues with some of its ERP components, such as order management; deliver CRM product parity with Siebel; make sure that Oracle consulting

---

*LE writes: If you speak out in support of small, unimportant innovations that fly in the face of widely held beliefs—I do it all the time—you are likely to be dismissed as stupid or arrogant, and that's pretty much the end of it. However, if you defend a really big idea that challenges widely held beliefs, you're likely to generate a mass of hatred, and you just might pay for it with your life. When Galileo defended Copernicus, he was ridiculed, imprisoned, and then threatened with death unless he recanted. Charles Darwin cautiously postponed publishing On the Origin of Species and The Descent of Man for more than twenty years, but that judicious delay did not save him from vicious personal attacks coming from all ranks of contemporary society, from the dons at Oxford to the man in the street. In pleasant contrast, big discoveries that don't come into conflict with popularly held beliefs are quickly embraced and the discoverers are rewarded with love and fame. Such was the good fortune of Jonas Salk.

and Oracle.com (its ASP offering) complemented its other channel relationships. Burton pointed out that she was far from suggesting that "Oracle, as a company was failing—quite the opposite," but the overall impression the report gave was highly negative, thanks in part to its last line: "We believe that recent actions and events will leave an indelible scar on customers' views of Oracle."*

Around the time that Burton's report came out, Oracle hired one of her Gartner colleagues, Peggy O'Neill, to take charge of analyst relations. I asked O'Neill what Oracle needed to do to get on better with such an influential constituency. She was in no doubt: "We fundamentally need to change the relationship with the analysts. We must talk to them more. . . . Don't broadcast to them. Listen to their advice and, if at all possible, incorporate it in your planning, marketing, and development. Historically, Oracle has never had that kind of interaction." I told her that I found it hard to imagine Ellison, whom she had yet to meet, taking that advice to heart. "The analysts are prepared to give Larry a bit more room because he's Larry," she said. "But the folks underneath Larry who copy that style won't get away with it. I've seen them with customers: they know how to be charming. They should try treating analysts like customers."

O'Neill was almost certainly right. But I found it hard to imagine Oracle schmoozing analysts and journalists with the polish and attention of, say, an IBM or a Cisco Systems. Technology companies that are run by engineers, such as Sun Microsystems, Microsoft, SAP, and Oracle are characterized by a particular kind of intellectual competitiveness that is highly unreceptive to the opinions of outsiders, who they think (usually correctly) are not as smart as they are. As long as they execute flawlessly, it's not a problem. But when something goes wrong, they can't expect any slack. O'Neill made another point: analysts, she said, "are a jaded lot." She might as well have said that analysts and technology journalists are professional cynics and that someone like Larry Ellison, who is relentlessly optimistic, calculatedly contrarian, and shamelessly devoted to hyperbole, brings out the absolute worst in them.

---

*LE writes: What most analysts say about your company has more to do with the financial results of your last couple of quarters than anything else. If you're growing revenue and earnings, they usually say nice things about your products and management. As Tevye says in Fiddler on the Roof, "When you got the money, they think you know." But our previous two quarters had not been good, so we got hammered.

15

ENEMIES

A subject that's close to Ellison's heart is Oracle's enemies. He strongly believes that Oracle is always at its best when it has an identifiable enemy to go after: "We pick our enemies very carefully. It helps us focus. We can't explain what we do unless we compare it to someone else who does it differently. We don't know if we're gaining or losing unless we constantly compare ourselves to the competition." When Oracle was fighting its relational database rivals for market supremacy in the late 1980s and early 1990s, it was famous for the in-your-face aggression of its "attack" advertising.

The aggression hasn't altered, but the size and power of the firms with which Ellison wants Oracle to be compared have. These days, none other than IBM finds itself the regular target of Oracle's ads and Ellison's combative speeches, while not a little of Ellison's own fame has come directly from his highly public assaults on Microsoft and his obsession with one day overtaking the colossus of Redmond to make Oracle the number one software company in the world. When people think of Ellison, it's all too often as a kind of alter ego to Bill Gates, software's other billionaire.*

An odd effect of this was to diminish Oracle's own extraordinary suc-

---

*LE writes: If you're a fighter, the only way up is through the top fighters in your division. So we picked fights with IBM and Microsoft because they're the ones we had to beat to reach the top. By constantly measuring ourselves against the two top heavyweights, we constantly improve the competitiveness of our products and services.

cess. Surely it was better to be known as the world's biggest enterprise software firm than to be seen as Microsoft's perennial challenger. As for Ellison's attacks on Gates, they could make him seem "chippy" and resentful, both of which were far from the truth. What made it even stranger was the fact that Microsoft and Oracle compete only at the margins. To be sure, Microsoft has a database product, originally licensed from Oracle's old rival, Sybase, more than a decade ago. But despite attempts by Microsoft to present the latest versions of its SQL Server as being sufficiently capable for data center duty, its deployment is still mostly departmental. Although Microsoft would like nothing better than to destroy Oracle's profitability by commoditizing the database business, the demands of Internet computing have so far thwarted that ambition. SQL Server remains essentially a "good enough" database that's bundled into Microsoft's BackOffice server suite to put some price pressure on Oracle at the low end of the market. As for applications, Microsoft has remained content to dominate the desktop with Office, preferring to partner with Oracle's competitors, such as SAP, than to compete with Oracle head-on.

However, from Ellison's perspective, the assault on Microsoft and all its works, which he initiated in September 1995 when deriding the PC as "a ridiculous device," had not only evolved into the much broader war on complexity, but created an awareness both of Oracle and of its vision of computing that nothing else could have achieved. Since then, although Microsoft's wealth had grown almost exponentially thanks to its near-monopoly profits from Windows and Office, it no longer had quite the aura of invincibility it had previously enjoyed. Thanks to the Internet, computing had moved decisively toward a model that played much more to Oracle's strengths than to Microsoft's. As for the antitrust case against Microsoft that had arisen from its brutal suppression of Netscape, it had not only hugely distracted its senior management but done great damage to the company's reputation. A few days after, I discussed these issues with Ellison. The Washington, D.C., Court of Appeals found Microsoft guilty of serially abusing its monopoly power while rejecting the controversial remedy of District Court Judge Thomas Penfield Jackson that it should be broken into two companies.

Ellison's antipathy toward Microsoft seemed to go much further than simply seeing it as a dangerous business adversary. He once said to me that what he really didn't like about Microsoft was that it didn't have any taste. What did he mean? "Well, actually I was quoting Steve Jobs. He said that the thing that really bothers him most about Microsoft is not how successful they are or how much money they have; it's the tasteless mediocrity of their software.*

"I totally agree with Steve, Microsoft's software is rarely first rate. They never, ever innovate, but they're pretty good copiers. All those bright people up in Redmond remind me of the guys you see sitting in museums making beautiful copies of great art. Their pictures are beautiful, but they're copies—forgeries. Ever since the guilty verdict in the antitrust case, Bill began chanting Microsoft's new mantra: 'Please, please don't take away our right to innovate.' Microsoft innovate! Give me a fucking break. The innovation for the Internet came from Netscape. All Microsoft did was copy Netscape's browser and bundle a 'free' copy of the browser with Windows. But it wasn't really 'free' at all. Microsoft got paid for its 'free' browser by raising the price of Windows. But Netscape couldn't charge for its browser because Microsoft included a 'free' browser as a part of Windows. It was a brilliant business strategy. It killed Netscape. But it's illegal. Now Microsoft is trying to do the exact same thing to RealNetworks [the innovators of Internet streamed video and audio] by bundling a 'free' media player with Windows. They'll just keep doing it over and over again until somebody penalizes them for doing it. You're got to give them credit for balls, but not for innovation. Even Bill's business strategy is just a copy of Standard Oil's strategy back in the 1870s. But when Rockefeller used his monopoly to crush his competitors, it wasn't illegal. There were no antitrust laws back then.

"So what's Microsoft's single greatest innovation? Take your time. It's a trick question. There aren't any. All that money Microsoft spends on research; what have they got to show for it? Nothing! Compare that to IBM's research results. IBM invented the disk drive, they invented core memory, they invented the scanning tunneling microscope, they invented fractal geometry. The list of IBM inventions goes on and on. IBM researchers have won Nobel Prizes. IBM, at the height of their greatness, was a national treasure, an institution that anyone would be proud to be a part of. They don't do software very well anymore, but their old mainframe stuff was great. I make fun of a lot of other databases—all other

---

*LE writes: What bothers me most about Microsoft is the fact that they've been found guilty of repeatedly violating our antitrust laws but they've escaped all punishment—so far, anyway. Those guys are lucky as well as smart. I hate that.

databases, in fact, except the mainframe version of DB2. It's a first-rate piece of technology. Microsoft may have more money than IBM ever did, but they don't have more ideas. It's the difference between a great fashion designer in Paris and someone who just does knockoffs in Brooklyn. Except that Microsoft would bundle the dresses with Windows and give them away for 'free.' "*

There are few things that Ellison loathes more than hypocrisy. It's one of the reasons that people often find him objectionable—he almost never says the politically correct thing, whether the subject is dating Oracle employees or how he spends his money. If he thinks he's in danger of sounding sanctimonious, he'll suddenly shut up in the middle of a conversation. More than anything, it was Gates's hypocrisy about the "right to innovate" that infuriated Ellison: "I didn't despise Bill for destroying Netscape, which wasn't very nice—or legal, for that matter. Bill just calculated he could smash his competitors by breaking the law and get away it. Who knows? Maybe he can. But when Bill defended Microsoft's murderous behavior by saying, 'All I ask is the right to innovate,' that kind of pushed me over the edge. *Netscape* did the innovation, Bill—that's why you killed them! All you did was copy the innovation and destroy the innovator. To kill the innovator in the name of innovation was such an incredible lie, such a cynical piece of deception, such hyperhypocrisy, I just couldn't stand it. If Bill had said, 'We killed Netscape because they were in our way; they weren't tough enough to survive, so fuck 'em. Hey, Andreessen [Marc Andreessen founded Netscape when he was twenty-one], welcome to the software industry, punk. I've got a little present for you; it's a pine box and a bullet with your name on it. That'll teach little kids

---

*LE writes: Recently, in a Wall Street Journal *article, I predicted "the end of Silicon Valley as we know it." I believe that a thousand Silicon Valley companies are in the process of going out of business and that the computer industry will consolidate around a few giant technology survivors. These large companies will dominate the industry and be the source of innovation in the years to come. Marc Andreessen, Netscape's founder, responded in both horror and disbelief. He said that large companies are incapable of innovation; that innovation is done in small companies by nineteen-year-olds. Of course that's what Marc believes. Marc is in his thirties. All he's seen is the complete absence of innovation at Microsoft. He never witnessed the cornucopia of inventions that poured forth from IBM in the 1960s and '70s.*

to stay the fuck out of my neighborhood. Mess with Microsoft, you die.'
Okay, cool. That's still not very nice, but at least it's honest."*

For a couple of years—between 1990, when Microsoft did its deal
with Sybase, and 1992, when Oracle 7 arrived to save his bacon—Ellison
regarded Gates as a direct competitor. But for most of the time, at least
until Ellison launched his attack on the PC in the wake of the release of
Windows 95, these were profound differences between Oracle and Microsoft—one was a desktop company, the other was server-based; one
was Windows, the other largely UNIX; one believed in the proprietary
software route, the other was committed to standards—actually made it
easier for the two men to get along. Ellison says, "Bill and I used to be
friends, insofar as Bill has friends. Back in the eighties and early nineties,
all the people in the PC software industry hated Bill because they feared
Bill.† But Oracle didn't compete with Microsoft very much back then, so
we got on pretty well. As I got to know Bill, I developed a great respect
for the thoroughness of his thinking and his relentless, remorseless pursuit of industry domination. I found spending time with Bill intellectually
interesting but emotionally exhausting; he has absolutely no sense of
humor. I think he finds humor an utter waste of time—an unnecessary
distraction from the business at hand. Scary stuff. I don't have anything
like that kind of focus or single-mindedness."

One telephone conversation with Gates in 1993 sticks in Ellison's
mind. "It was the most interesting conversation I've ever had with Bill,
and the most revealing. It was around eleven o'clock in the morning, and
we were on the phone discussing some technical issue, I don't remember
what it was. Anyway, I didn't agree with him on some point, and I explained my reasoning. Bill says, 'I'll have to think about that, I'll call you
back.' Then I get this call at four in the afternoon and it's Bill continuing

---

*LE writes: During Netscape's heyday, John Doerr, Silicon Valley's top venture
capitalist and a big investor in Netscape, told me that Marc Andreessen liked to
say, "Microsoft just didn't get it." That's a saying in Silicon Valley. It means
you're technically behind the times, you can't feel the change of seasons, you're
a dinosaur just waiting to die. But in Microsoft's case, they were a dinosaur
waiting to eat. Netscape was just getting fat before they were served up for
lunch.

†LE writes: They had reason to be afraid. They're all dead now. There is no PC
software industry anymore. There's just Microsoft.

the conversation with 'Yeah, I think you're right about that, but what about A and B and C?' I said, 'Bill, have you been thinking about this for the last five hours?' He said, yes, he had, it was an important issue and he wanted to get it right. Now Bill wanted to continue the discussion and analyze the implications of it all. I was just stunned. He had taken the time and effort to think it all through and had decided I was right and he was wrong. Now, most people hate to admit they're wrong, but it didn't bother Bill one bit. All he cared about was *what* was right, not *who* was right. That's what makes Bill very, very dangerous.

"Most people are so in love with their own ideas that it confines their thinking—creates boundaries and limits their ability to solve problems. Bill, however, has this Asian-like ability to manage his intellectual vanity and take ideas, regardless of where they come from, and put them to work for Microsoft.* The terrifying thing about Bill is that he's smart enough to understand what ideas are good—what's worth replicating— and he has the discipline and resources to get on with it and make it just a little bit better. That's very Japanese. That's very scary. Add that to Bill's ruthless perseverance and the fact that Microsoft has more money than God, and you get a most formidable foe—the ultimate foe, the perfect enemy. We pick our enemies very carefully. We decided to pick a fight with the biggest, most dangerous bully in the schoolyard. There's no way to avoid this fight, so let's start it."

Ellison's decision to start attacking Microsoft in 1995 was based on the same reasoning as today's attacks by Oracle on IBM: "If I want to make a point, I have to compare it to a counterpoint. I can't explain hot without comparing it to cold. In fact, there's no such thing as hot without

---

*LE writes: Bill Gates, like most of the other very smart programmers I know, loves to prove his brilliance during arguments with other smart programmers. But if Bill has to choose, he'd rather win the war than win the argument. He doesn't really care where the ideas come from as long as he's the one who gets paid for them. The very last time I ever spoke with Bill was in 1999, when he called and invited me to visit Microsoft and debate the future directions of technology with their top technical people. When I declined, he asked me to reconsider, arguing that I would find it interesting "because there are a lot of very smart people at Microsoft." I told him that was exactly why I didn't want to go. He had expected me to show up and show off by explaining how clever Oracle's ideas and plans were. Many of Microsoft's competitors fell into that intellectual vanity trap. Not us. We want to get paid for our ideas.

cold. Everything's relative. So I attacked Microsoft: this is what they think, this is what we think. Constant comparison between our Internet-centric server technology and their Windows-centric desktop technology provided increasing clarity. The battle lines were now clearly drawn. It was Microsoft versus the Internet—the common heritage of all mankind. We were part of Team Mankind, the last, best hope to prevent total world domination by the evil empire in Redmond. Very colorful stuff. Anyway, it made it interesting for journalists, analysts, and customers. We got a lot of press. It was supposed to be a battle between two rival computing architectures. It wasn't supposed to degenerate into a me-versus-Bill thing, but people are more interested in personalities than technologies, so that's what it became: Billionaire A versus Billionaire B. I got onto the cover of *Fortune* magazine as 'software's other billionaire.' Oracle's technical ideas and products went along for the ride. The 'battle of the billionaires' was good brand building for Oracle. At that time the company we wanted to be compared to was Microsoft."

To what extent had Ellison really believed that his network computer was going to take over the world, or had it always been more of a stick to beat Microsoft with and a way to dramatize philosophical differences about computing architecture? "When I introduced our new Internet computing architecture, I emphasized what was new about it; how it was different from the client/server architecture that came before. What was different was that we stored the application software on the server, not the desktop client PC. One implication of running the application on a server is that you no longer need a desktop PC to access the application; all you need is a simple device running a standard Internet browser. Now, we make our money selling server software, so I wanted to talk about the server aspects of our new architecture. But the press wasn't interested in our architecture or any other difficult-to-photograph concept. They wanted to see the new, simple device—the Network Computer. The NC story just exploded beyond anything I imagined. It took on a life of its own. Some hardware companies even started manufacturing network computers. Then people started asking me how we were going to make money with the network computer. We're not, I told them. We make money selling server software. As long as the application is on the server, I don't care what's on the desktop.*

---

*LE writes: Actually, I do care a little. It sure would be nice if desktop Linux took off. I'd love to see Microsoft's desktop monopoly broken and their revenue stream reduced.

Almost everyone now sees this Network Computer episode as an example of Ellison's shooting his mouth off and getting it embarrassingly wrong. When I asked him whether he'd put much real thought into it, he just laughed and made a zero sign. I pointed out that I'd never seen him using a network computer (or, for that matter, a Mac). "Well, my desktop PC has this big, beautiful screen. That plus the speed of my network connection is about all I care about. Ninety percent of the time I'm either in e-mail or on the Internet. In other words, I use my PC as if it were a network computer about ninety percent of the time. And when this book is done, that will go to ninety-nine percent of the time. Right now I'm spending more time in Word than I'd like, plus I still read the occasional PowerPoint file or Excel spreadsheet. That's a complete list of what I do on my PC. As for the network computer, I don't care about it at all. Why should I? It makes no difference to me what computer people have on their desk: a network computer, a Mac, or a PC, just so long as their shared applications are on Oracle's application server and all their data is in Oracle's database. The only applications that belong on your PC are personal productivity tools [e.g., Office], an e-mail and calendar interface [e.g., Outlook], an Internet browser [e.g., Explorer], and games, if you play games. All shared applications and all your data, all of it, belongs on a database server. You should never have any data stored on your desktop PC that isn't also stored in a database, unless you don't mind losing it.* Everyone's adopting the Internet server architecture or at least says they are. Look at PeopleSoft's new Version 8—one hundred percent of the user interface is via an Internet browser, and all the applications are on a server. Siebel's not there yet, but they say they are, which means that they know they should be, they just haven't gotten the programming done yet. But Tom knows what's hot, so that's what he sells. Anyway, the debate's over. The Internet computing architecture has won; the client/server architecture is dead."

I put it to Ellison that although the war had unquestionably been largely on the architectural front, he had been wrong about two things: the ability of the PC industry, through its extraordinary volume efficiencies, to turn out full-featured boxes for little more than the price of a

---

*LE writes: We created our Collaboration Suite [about which more later] to make it easy for users to replace Microsoft's Exchange e-mail servers and Microsoft's file servers with an Oracle database. Data, all data, belong in a database.

stripped-down network computer and the reluctance of people to give up having their personal productivity software running on their local hard drive. Ellison's response was that he hadn't been alone in underestimating how the price of PCs would fall. He recalled a conversation with Intel's Andy Grove in 1996.*

"My idea for a $500 Network Computer had been heavily ridiculed in Intel's internal magazine. They ran a mock ad showing 'Larry Ellison's magic $500 box.' It was an orange crate containing two tin cans connected by a string. Andy Grove, Intel's CEO, carefully explained to me that people wanted more powerful PCs and they were willing to pay for them. He said that PCs would keep getting more powerful and their selling price would stay about the same, around $2,500 for the foreseeable future; PCs would keep getting better but not cheaper. He compared my cheap NC to an inexpensive but unpopular car called the Yugo. I can still see Andy disdainfully spitting the word 'Yugo' at me as I responded back with my most adolescent smirk. Fine, I thought. A $500 NC will compete quite well with a $2,500 PC."

Unfortunately for both Grove and Ellison, the foreseeable future didn't last very long. A variety of competitive pressures forced PC prices to drop to around $700. Ellison says, "That $700 PC surprised the hell out of Intel, killed the NC, and made me look stupid. But it didn't cost me any money. Oracle's server software business was unaffected. However, for the PC hardware companies it was an extinction-level event. Most of them saw their margins drop, their profits disappear, and their life expectancy shorten to that of a fruit fly."

The implication was that if even Andy Grove, one of the founders of the PC industry, hadn't foreseen $700 machines with ten times the performance of high-end PCs of only a few years ago, why should Ellison, an enterprise software guy, have read it any better? As for Microsoft's Office, Ellison concedes, "Microsoft's real stranglehold monopoly has turned out to be Office, not Windows. Like everyone else, I could easily move to desktop Linux if Microsoft Office ran on Linux. But it doesn't. Microsoft maintains their desktop monopoly with Office; Windows isn't nearly as important."

---

*LE writes: Andy's the only guy whom both Steve Jobs and I agree we'd be willing to work for. Andy's absolutely brilliant and brutally honest. I've always loved him, but I fear my love has gone unrequited. I'm afraid Andy thinks I'm a bit of a flake. That's what he told me, anyway.

One of the things that made Bill Gates so livid about the government's antitrust case was the active support it received from powerful commercial rivals, such as Oracle and Sun, which he considered to be no less ruthless in the way they competed than Microsoft. In June 2000, it emerged in the press that Oracle was employing private detectives to root through Microsoft's garbage for evidence that apparently independent, but pro-Microsoft, institutes with names such as Americans for Technology Leadership and Association for Competitive Technology were just front organizations, set up and entirely funded by Microsoft. Ellison's so-called Dumpster diving hit the headlines when Oracle passed the information it had gathered to the newspapers. Later the same week, Ray Lane's departure from Oracle was tersely announced. According to the rumor mill, Lane had left after fighting with Ellison over his "inappropriate" behavior. Far from being embarrassed or chastened, a grinning Ellison had appeared before the cameras dressed in a blue suit, red tie, and white shirt (intentionally invoking the flag) and had spoken proudly of having done nothing more than his patriotic duty in helping to expose Microsoft's wrongdoing.

He still feels pretty good about it: "I'm an American. I think it's important that America's technology is competitive. Absolutely. But I don't think we stay competitive by killing off innovative companies like Netscape and RealNetworks, which was Microsoft's modus operandi. So why were they warning all patriotic citizens that anything that hurt Microsoft would hurt America? It was all part of Bill's Big Lie. Whatever's good for Microsoft is good for America? Microsoft's freedom to innovate must be protected? What? I think Bill must be some kind of reincarnation of Milo Minderbinder from *Catch-22*.* Microsoft was bankrolling all these bogus operations, such as the Independent Institute,

---

LE writes: Joseph Heller's novel Catch-22 is set in Europe during World War II. One of Heller's characters is Milo Minderbinder, a budding entrepreneur serving in the U.S. Army Air Corps. To supplement his army pay, Milo forms M & M Enterprises with the grandiose marketing tag line "Whatever is good for M & M Enterprises is good for the world." Milo gets into a bit of trouble when M & M Enterprises signs a contract with the Germans to bomb American forces. But Milo strongly defends his actions by explaining that the war was being fought to "preserve the free enterprise system." Any restrictions on the behavior of M & M Enterprises would conflict with the goals of the war and be bad for the world.

which was neither 'independent' nor an 'institute.' But we had to find proof that Microsoft was paying them off to parrot the Microsoft party line. So we found a bunch of invoices and canceled checks in the garbage proving Microsoft was paying all these phony front organizations. Why should I be embarrassed about that? We didn't break the law. They did."

Back in late 1997, when Netscape, the target of Microsoft's aggression, was already on the ropes and the Department of Justice had begun to take action against Microsoft, I had asked Ellison whether Oracle might buy Netscape. If Netscape was so important, surely it was in Oracle's or Sun's interest to offer it protection. Ellison's answer then had been that Netscape didn't have any technology that Oracle wanted, his "cat could write a browser," that it was terribly overvalued, and that, anyway, Microsoft was going to kill it. I came away with the impression that perhaps Netscape was more valuable to Oracle as a very public victim than as a going concern. Even now, it's hard to gauge Ellison's real feelings about Netscape. "Netscape was the most innovative Silicon Valley start-up during the nineties. Netscape's Navigator browser ushered in the Internet age. They single-handedly changed the Valley. eBay, Yahoo!, and all the other Internet companies exist because of Netscape. But Netscape had a big problem. It's just not very hard to write a browser. Andreessen wrote Mosaic [the Mosaic browser was the precursor of Navigator] in his spare time when he was in college. So there was no technical barrier preventing Microsoft from writing a competing browser. To emphasize that point, I said that my cat, the one that recently died, could write a browser. For some reason that made Jim Barksdale [Netscape's CEO] and Marc very angry at me. I don't know why. She was a very smart cat. The two cats I have left, incidentally, can't program worth a damn.

"Okay, I accept that most people don't believe that a cat, even a smart one, can write a browser—all by herself, anyway. Reasonable people can disagree. But there's no question that a team of competent programmers can build a pretty darned good browser in about a year. And that's exactly what Microsoft did. When they bundled it with Windows for 'free,' Netscape's days were numbered. They were just this little itty-bitty company—just a few kids and Jim Barksdale—in a fight to the death with Microsoft, for God's sake. They had no chance at all. Bill liked to say, and I quote, 'If Microsoft gives away all of its Internet software and Netscape gives away all of its Internet software, I like Microsoft's chances of survival better than Netscape's.' Yeah, no kidding. The most powerful company on Earth had decided to kill off a little newborn company called

Netscape. No holds barred. It was Godzilla versus Bambi—and Godzilla didn't bother to play by the rules."

On the question of whether Oracle should have bought Netscape, Ellison repeated that under the circumstances, the company had been horribly overvalued. "There was this big Netscape acquisition meeting at Oracle shortly before they sold out to AOL. John Doerr, Jim Barksdale, and Marc Andreessen represented Netscape. The gap between what they thought Netscape was worth and what I thought Netscape was worth was gigantic. They thought they were the heartbeat of Silicon Valley; I thought they were a corpse on the dark side of the moon. They wanted five to ten billion for the company. I thought that Netscape was near worthless. They were a money-losing proposition, and I couldn't figure out what we could have done to save them. If we had immediately open-sourced the Navigator browser, then browser revenue would have instantly gone to zero. What's the point of that? We would have paid billions for nothing. Some people at Oracle didn't agree. They thought that we should buy Netscape just to make certain that Microsoft wouldn't have the only browser in the market. But I really didn't feel like paying a $5 billion entry fee into a one-sided browser war. It's a colossal mistake for us to battle with Microsoft over desktop software for one very simple reason: desktop software will not determine the ultimate winner of the software wars. It's not a desktop browser war, it's a server software war. I don't think that we can beat Microsoft on the desktop, and I don't care. We're a server software company. The Internet is all about network server software. Oracle is CBS, and Microsoft is Sony. We run the network, they make television sets. We make much better server software than Microsoft. Server software is a battlefield where we can fight them and beat them. We do it every day. Let them have the desktop. They can build all the television sets they want."*

Ellison thinks that the sheer distraction of destroying Netscape and dealing with legal consequences damaged Microsoft more than is generally realized. He's fond of saying that Microsoft "robbed the wrong bank." He says, "Microsoft wasted a tremendous amount of moral capital, credibility, and time destroying Netscape. At Oracle we used to call Netscape the 'heat shield.' Microsoft was so busy burning Netscape to a crisp that they fell further and further behind in database technology. We

---

*LE writes: I suppose they could build televisions that receive only MSNBC and give them away for free. I'm sure they're thinking about it.

have a big lead in server software, and I don't think that they can catch us. Unlike Netscape, we're protected by a huge, almost insurmountable technology barrier."

I couldn't help feeling that there was at least a whiff of the hypocrisy that Ellison detests in the tear-jerking way that he talked about the crushing of poor little Netscape, while he seemed quite happy to try to snuff the life out of smaller competitors such as Ariba and Commerce One, which he derided as "features rather than software companies." It's a charge that nettles Ellison: "We've never seen anyone compete like Microsoft. Nobody. Microsoft very effectively and illegally threatened and bullied PC companies that dared to distribute Netscape's browser. All the PC companies stopped distributing Netscape because they were afraid of Microsoft's reprisals. Microsoft will go on breaking the law until someone stops them. They're going after Real, using the same exact bundling techniques they used against Netscape. They're bundling instant messaging to go after AOL. That's how they compete: bundle, bundle, bundle. Why not? From their point of view, they're getting away with it. I've never seen anything like this degree of abuse of monopoly power. IBM used to have a monopoly. But they never engaged in the kind of behavior that's business as usual at Microsoft."

Okay, but if Oracle bundles its application server with its database, which is pretty much the case, and goes to war with BEA, which a lot of people see as an innovative company that has created a new market, what's the difference between what Oracle's doing and Microsoft? "First, we don't bundle our application server with our database; we charge separately for our application server. Second, even if we did bundle our application server with the database we wouldn't be breaking the law because we don't have a monopoly in database. Under the provisions of the Sherman Anti-Trust Act, standards of behavior are different if you have a monopoly versus not having a monopoly. The law says you can't use one monopoly to obtain another monopoly. Microsoft has a monopoly in desktop operating systems. Microsoft bundled its browser in their desktop operating system, and they succeeded in getting a monopoly in browsers. That's express violation of our antitrust laws. Now Microsoft is bundling a media player in its desktop operating systems to get a monopoly in those. Microsoft is bundling instant messaging. See any pattern here? We have no monopolies; we don't bundle; we don't break the law."

I wondered whether Oracle, if it ever did get monopoly power, would behave more like Intel than Microsoft. When Andy Grove first realized

Intel was on its way to having a dominant market share in PC processors, he made certain that everybody at Intel who dealt with the world outside understood exactly what the limits on their behavior should be. It didn't stop Intel acting, at times, in a fairly brutal way toward competitors, but it had always accepted that the law was there and that it applied to Intel. Ellison laughs. "I think that obeying the law's a really good idea. IBM and Intel managed their monopolies and competed aggressively without ever operating outside the law. But Microsoft is different. They understood the law. They had lawyers advising them. They're smart guys. They're not naive. But Bill's an ideologue. I think he believes that the antitrust laws are wrong, so he doesn't need to obey them." *

I had often thought that one of the reasons for Gates's apparent willingness to flout the antitrust laws time and again was simply the arrogance and sense of inviolability that comes from unimaginable wealth. If anyone had a take on that, it should be Ellison. His answer was complicated. "Bill's hyperrational side is in a losing battle with his emotionally fragile side. Bill goes out and methodically searches for good ideas to steal. That's perfectly rational behavior. That's made him very successful. But then, one by one, Bill starts to claim credit for the stolen ideas. He actually starts believing that they really were his ideas in the first place. He's pretending to be someone else. He wants to be someone else. He can't bear to see himself as Rockefeller; he sees himself as Edison. And he can get very childish and upset when other people don't see him as the great inventor." He tells a story of a dinner party at Andy Grove's house during which Grove was asked whom he admired most in the PC industry. Grove replied that it had to be Steve Jobs: he had either invented or popularized everything to do with the PC industry. News of this eventually reached Gates, who called Grove and asked him to dinner. When the meal was nearly over, Gates finally let it all out: His feelings have been terribly hurt. Doesn't Andy admire Bill?

Ellison says: "Here's this guy who built the most successful company

---

*LE writes: More likely Bill simply calculated the risk-reward ratio in breaking the law to break Netscape and acted accordingly. Getting rid of Netscape benefited Microsoft approximately $25 billion to $50 billion in market cap. The punishment for breaking Netscape and the law seems to have been a few harshly worded editorials in The New York Times and The Economist. So far Bill's calculations seem to be correct; for Microsoft the benefits of breaking the law have been great and the financial cost near zero.

on earth, but he's still very unhappy with himself. He's unhappy with how he's perceived, not just by the public but by the people who are close to him: his primary partner, the guy who ran Intel. His behavior during the antitrust trial wasn't so much recklessness coming from extreme wealth as self-destructiveness because he felt persecuted and unappreciated. Bill just wants to be loved. Who doesn't? But historically America has never offered great love to people who accumulate vast fortunes. Just the opposite. If you're rich, the best you can hope for is to make the transition from robber baron to philanthropist with a great deal of humility and a lot of check writing. Fair enough. That's a perfectly reasonable and time-honored bargain. What else can you do with all that money, anyway? You can't spend it, so you have to give it away."

America hasn't yet "offered great love" to Bill Gates, at least inasmuch as he is now seen by most people as a latter-day Rockefeller, a ruthless bully, rather than the benignly grinning and blinking supergeek who built America's most admired company. The government had been successful beyond all expectation in making its case against Microsoft, thanks to the courage of many witnesses, the courtroom skills of David Boies, and Microsoft's own almost cavalier self-incrimination through both the testimony of its executives and the damning trail of e-mails.

One consequence of the trial, I reckoned, was that the hardware makers had become braver about not being used as Microsoft's pawns, and there were greater opportunities for Oracle to forge strategic partnerships with the likes of Compaq (before it was absorbed by HP) and Intel, as it was now doing. Ellison agreed up to a point. "Do you remember when Microsoft invited all those people to New York to get up onstage with Bill and say how much they liked him and how much they like working with Microsoft? It reminded me of Al Capone doing a similar thing in Chicago back in the thirties. It's the 'Be nice to the alligator and maybe he'll eat you last' theory of survival. Well, I've got a better idea. Let's kill the fucking alligator before he kills us! If we fight back, maybe we'll survive. Maybe we won't kill the alligator, it's a huge fucking alligator, but trying to kill it will improve our chances for survival. Being nice to this alligator will never work. If you think Microsoft's competitors dislike them, you should talk to their 'partners.' Microsoft has bullied Intel and Compaq so many times they've lost count. Everyone in the industry is looking for an alternative supplier of software for Intel's mass-market computers. Everyone's thrilled about Linux. And I believe they're looking to Oracle to provide some balance against Microsoft. IBM's really not a big player in the software business except on mainframes, so it's up to us. We're the last, best hope for mankind in the battle against Microsoft and its plans for world domination."

To that end, Ellison was devising a strategy for Oracle to go into the operating system business. He believed that despite the hype over Linux and IBM's enthusiasm for the open-source operating system, it would still be years before it was sufficiently hardened to do service in the corporate data center. For that reason, he was in discussions with Compaq's boss, Michael Capellas, an ex–Oracle hand, to rework, and eventually take over, the immensely fast and robust Tru64 operating system, which had been developed over more than two decades by the best engineers at Digital, so that it would run on Intel's new 64-bit processors.

Ellison eventually wanted to see all the Intel-based computer makers selling certified servers preinstalled with Tru64 and Oracle's database software. It would mean that Oracle would have preintegrated every part of the software "stack" from the applications at the top of the stack through the applications server to the database and, finally, the operating system at the bottom. "We're going to build our next generation of database clusters out of a bunch of low-cost Intel computers. Our Intel clusters will be highly secure, totally fault-tolerant, and much faster and cheaper than anything else on the block. As for the operating system—don't ask, don't tell. You don't ask what operating system a Cisco router is running. Why should anyone care what operating system our database cluster is running?" *

It seemed that regardless of the final outcome of the Microsoft case,

---

*LE writes: Perhaps people shouldn't care, but they do. So we had to adapt our operating system strategy from "Don't ask, don't tell' to the very latest, hippest fashion—namely, Linux. The Linux movement was gaining tremendous momentum, so we decided that we'd better jump on the train, not in front of it. But we had to add a number of critical features to Linux to enable it to run our fault-tolerant database clusters. We had to assign a number of our engineers to work with Red Hat [a Linux distributor] and the open-source community to build the features we needed into the Linux operating system. We even took our distributed file system and donated it to the open-source community so that it could become a standard part of Linux. After a lot of time and effort, Linux has now developed into the prime-time, mission-critical operating system that we need to compete head-to-head with Microsoft Windows. Today, Linux on Intel beats Windows on Intel in every important area: performance, reliability, security, and cost.

Oracle had already benefited from it. Even if Microsoft emerged constrained by only mild conduct remedies, Ellison seemed to think that Oracle could withstand any vengeance that Gates might want to exact. Rather than Oracle being on the firing line, Ellison believed that the companies that had most to fear were in the consumer and entertainment businesses. In particular, he thought that AOL Time Warner and Sony were about to feel the full effects of competing with Microsoft.

Ellison frowned. "I think AOL is in deep trouble, but what do I know? I really don't understand AOL's business at all. To me it seems like a simple online service for people who don't like computers. Whenever I prowl around their system, all I can find are a bunch of twelve- to fourteen-year-olds in chat rooms. Chat rooms are closely related to instant messaging. Both have been critical to AOL holding on to their customers. AOL chat and instant messaging is a closed network; they only allow you to communicate with other AOL members. That strategy works fine for a while, but it will fall apart over time. Imagine an e-mail system that only lets you e-mail other AOL members. No one would use it. As instant messaging matures into a standard service, AOL must open their system up or be isolated from all the other instant messaging users in the world. AOL has no good choices here. Either way they lose. Microsoft is bundling instant messaging with the next version of Windows. Instant messaging will soon become a standard service in business. There will be more instant messaging users outside AOL than inside AOL. It's not a pretty picture. To make matters worse, Microsoft can underprice AOL whenever they feel the government heat is off. What if Microsoft priced MSN at half the cost of AOL for the next ten years or so? Then there's the small issue of the upcoming competition from the broadband carriers—the phone and cable companies. Maybe they'll squeeze out both AOL and MSN. Who knows? All you really need is a fast line from a carrier and Yahoo! Why should the broadband carriers share any money with Microsoft or AOL? AOL has a very uncertain future. Steve Case pulled off the deal of the century by buying Time Warner. AOL shareholders should give him a medal. On the other hand, Time Warner shareholders have a right to be very, very upset. And I think they'll get more upset over time. What was Gerry Levin thinking?

"X-Box [Microsoft's game console] is likely to get killed by Sony's Playstation 2 for the next couple of Christmases. However, Microsoft has great patience and endurance. They'll be around year after year. Microsoft's monopolies generate so much cash that they can blow billions in the game business and keep coming at you. That's what Sony faces. Perhaps Microsoft won't kill Sony's game machine business, but they'll be Sony's number one competitor. And as games go online with broadband, Microsoft is likely to start building games that work with both PCs and the X-Box. The online game business is brand new, and that presents opportunities to a newcomer like Microsoft. Sony's a great company, but Microsoft has unlimited financial resources. It's no fun competing with a company that has an infinite amount of monopoly money—real monopoly, real money. So I think AOL and Sony are both vulnerable to competition from Microsoft. The barriers to entry into their businesses are primarily financial, not technical. Fortunately, the opposite is true for us. The reason we're able to compete with Microsoft is because our technology is so hard to replicate. It took us more than twenty years to build our database. And our guys are every bit as smart as theirs. Sometimes I think that we'll be their last competitor. The last one standing."

Hating and baiting Microsoft, software's evil empire, is one thing, but I wondered whether Ellison could really get himself so worked up about IBM, a company he had admired all his life and was even now ready to call a "national treasure." "Well there are two different IBMs—the IBM of Christmas past and the IBM of Christmas present. The old IBM, the real IBM, was created by Thomas Watson, Jr. That IBM was the greatest company in the history of the earth. When I grew up in this industry, IBM wasn't someone against whom you competed; IBM was the environment in which you competed. But that was then and this is now. IBM never really recovered from the loss of Tom Watson. He was followed by a string of anonymous sales executives who just kept doing what IBM had always done: develop and sell mainframe hardware and software. As the center of gravity of the computer industry moved away from mainframes, IBM failed to adapt. The world changed, the industry changed, but IBM didn't. Eventually IBM was forced to hire an outsider, Lou Gerstner, to come in and change the company. He abandoned IBM's technology-centric past for a service-centric future.

"IBM hasn't developed any interesting software since the mainframe version of DB2 nearly twenty years ago. That's a long dry spell. All of their great software is their old mainframe stuff: OS/390, VM, the mainframe version of DB2—all first-rate pieces of technology. The new IBM no longer develops much software; instead they go out and buy it. They bought Lotus, Tivoli, Informix, Rational, and so on. IBM's products on UNIX and Windows are not close to being competitive. Their database on UNIX and Windows used to be called UDB [Universal Database] but they changed the name to DB2 to try to fool people into thinking it was the same database product that they had on mainframes. Now, DB2 on mainframes is a great product. DB2 on UNIX and Windows is a totally different product with a totally different architecture, and it's a very distant third in the modern database business behind Oracle and Microsoft's SQL Server.

"Lou Gerstner turned IBM into a giant service organization. You have money; we have people. Want to trade? There is very little leverage in that. It's really just a bigger version of EDS [a big systems integrator and hosting firm founded by Ross Perot]. But I don't think building lots of oil and lube places to service your car is a very good idea. What if someone builds a car that only requires the oil to be changed every 100,000 miles? IBM's service business model depends on computer technology remaining very complex and labor-intensive. IBM ran this series of ads showing a roomful of business executives saying: 'Good grief, if this merger goes through we'll have seven different platforms, fifteen different databases, fourteen different operating systems, a wireless project, and so on.' Then you hear this woman's voice speaking to the roomful of desperate execs, and the voice says, 'And that's when you know it's time for IBM.' In other words, computing is so enormously complicated that a normal business can't hope to understand or cope with it, so you should call in IBM. I have a different idea. Use better technology that's easier to understand.

"Our strategy is to simplify our software so you need *less* labor to install and run it. You don't need a big systems integrator if you don't do much systems integration. IBM recommends that you buy lots of different applications from lots of different vendors. In fact IBM resells applications from SAP, Siebel, i2, Ariba, pretty much everyone I can think of except Oracle. Then IBM makes a bundle by selling you guys with glue guns to stick it all together. The old IBM's strategy was creating value by creating intellectual property. The new IBM's strategy is based on servicing complex systems; the more complex the system, the better it is for IBM. But if I'm right and the industry turns away from these labor-intensive, highly customized best-of-breed software systems, then IBM's service business will slowly melt away, like a glacier."

The essence of Ellison's hostility toward IBM is a form of intellectual snobbery. A company that was made great by its technology and applied engineering skills had lost its way and sold out. It was now run by sales and marketing guys who were cynically selling out the greatest name in American business. For the pragmatic Gerstner, remaking IBM as "the solutions provider with the deepest bench," as his successor, Sam Palmisano, once described it to me, has been a triumphant success. But it's easy to understand why Ellison sees the shift not only as an exploitable point of difference with Oracle's main competitor in the database market and the aggressive reseller of its rivals' applications, but also as a kind of betrayal. What most riles him, however, is the cavalier approach to facts that Big Blue routinely adopts in its marketing: "IBM went on the attack about six months ago. They sent out a bunch of letters to CIOs claiming that they were number one in database market share and number one in database performance. Well, they are number one in mainframe database market share, but on UNIX, Linux, and Windows we have five times the market share they have. Tons of surveys—Morgan Stanley, Goldman Sachs—support that. As for being number one in performance, well, I'm stunned that IBM would make such a completely indefensible and easily disprovable claim. The old IBM would never, ever have done that."

Although Oracle's big philosophical battle with IBM is about complexity—the integrated Oracle suite versus the best-of-breed applications recommended by IBM and expensively glued together by Big Blue's army of integrators—Ellison has decided that the first stage of the campaign against IBM will be "to go after their software technology products because their software technology isn't what it used to be." And it's not just IBM's database that's in the firing line, but also its application server: "IBM's got this thing called WebSphere. WebSphere is not a product; it's many products: around a hundred separate products, I believe. It's a bit confusing. IBM has gotten into this odd habit of using the same name for totally different things. DB2 is one name, but IBM applies it to two totally different products. The confusion is intentional. The WebSphere name takes the confusion to a new level. WebSphere includes a hundred different products. It's the same naming scheme that George Foreman uses to name his kids: they're all named George. Anyway, one of the products that falls under the umbrella name of WebSphere is IBM's Java system. In a fit of creative license IBM put a statement on their Web site claiming that IBM's applications server—WebSphere—runs Java twice as fast as BEA's applications server. They didn't publish their benchmark results, but they did put a copy of the benchmark program on their Web site. Now, we were ready to take IBM at their word because, after all, they're IBM. They wouldn't just make this stuff up. We had already tested BEA's applications server and found that our Java was twice as fast as BEA's Java, so we figured that we must be around the same speed as IBM's Java. That was a little disappointing, but those seemed to be the facts.

"But the night before we were scheduled to make our big Java announcement, I asked Richard Sarwal, the guy in charge of our server performance group, to download the performance test on IBM's Web site and test IBM's Java. Richard looked extremely depressed: it took him twelve hours to download everything he needed. But he finally got the test running. When I came in the following day, I found out that IBM was not twice as fast as BEA; BEA was twice as fast as IBM. IBM just confused the subject with the predicate. That's a pretty serious typo. After we completed all our testing, our Java ended up running twice as fast as BEA and four times as fast as IBM. I don't know how IBM gets away with making claims that are so easily disprovable. I guess because they're IBM." *

The ads that Oracle had started running against IBM were as aggressive as anything it had done during the 1980s, when it was just a scrappy upstart. I wondered whether a self-confident, mature company should feel it necessary to define itself by trashing its competitors. Wasn't there something undignified about it? Ellison grins. "I know it's bad manners to publicly point to your competitors and say, 'Nyah, nyah, nyah, we're better than you.' I know this style makes people think I'm a rude jerk. So be it. But I don't know any other way to prove the superiority of our technology without directly comparing it to our competitors' technology. We urgently need to make our points. There's no polite way to point out that what IBM's saying is not true. We present verifiable facts as clearly as we can, and then we ask the market to decide. Here's us; here's them; here's the proof. You decide."

Another part of the logic in going for IBM, as Ellison sees it, is that many of Oracle's other rivals march under Big Blue's banner, companies Ellison describes as IBM's vassals. He says, "A lot of Siebel's success is due to the fact that IBM recommends Siebel. It costs you $2 million for Siebel and another $20 million for IBM to put it in for you. IBM says, 'We've looked at Oracle, we've looked at Siebel, and we really think you

---

*LE writes: IBM continues to make numerous incredible claims about its software. Perhaps the strangest was the claim that DB2 was the only database that ran on UNIX, Linux, and Windows. After we called them up and pointed out that we ran on UNIX, Linux, and Windows, they quickly took the claim off their Web site. I don't think IBM is lying when it makes these claims; I just don't think it knows the facts. This is not the IBM I so admired when I first started working in the computer industry. This is not your father's IBM.

should buy Siebel.' IBM is the supermarket for all of our competitors. They do two things. First they provide the skilled labor to install the stuff. Fair enough. The problem comes with IBM's pretense of objectivity when they recommend application software: 'We're IBM. We're an independent agent. We've done a careful and detailed analysis, and we honestly think SAP or Siebel or PeopleSoft or i2 or anyone is always a much better choice than Oracle.' Of course they're going to recommend SAP or Siebel because it costs five or ten times more to install and run that stuff. That's how IBM makes their money: installing and running the software. IBM brings Siebel, i2, Ariba, Commerce One, and other economically fragile software companies brand credibility. Without IBM they'd all die. Even with IBM they'll all die, just more slowly.

"We compete with IBM directly in the database and application server business and indirectly in the applications business. We're beating IBM in the database business and the application server business. The only place they do well is on mainframes, and mainframes matter less and less every year. Time is on our side. In the applications business, it's not IBM's to win or lose. That battle is between best of breed and the integrated suite. If the integrated suite wins, then IBM loses. We'll win the database and applications server war. I'm confident of that. And the integrated suite will kill best of breed. I'm confident of that too. But we need to beat SAP in the integrated applications suite war. That's the hard one, but it's doable. If we win all three battles—and that's a big if—then we'll replace Microsoft as the most important company on earth. But I don't dream of an Oracle that's like Bill's Microsoft or Lou Gerstner's IBM version 2. Our role model is Tom Watson's magnificent creation, the technically brilliant and innovative IBM of old. That's who we want to be like when we grow up."

16

CHAINED TO THE JOB

Early on I had wondered just how committed Ellison really was to making Oracle as great as IBM in its heyday. I thought that given his age, the range of his interests, his unimaginable wealth, and his own self-confessed dislike of much of the routine drudgery that's involved in running any business, it was almost inconceivable that he would have the necessary stamina and the hunger. Two things made me realize that I had underestimated him. The first was Ellison's evident willingness to put in fourteen-hour days while on the road. The second was sitting in on the meetings in Oracle's eleventh-floor boardroom, from which he drives and directs the company. This was not a "big-picture" chief executive who passively absorbed sanitized briefings at ten thousand feet from nominal subordinates who were actually running the business.

Whether he was suggesting a solution to some obscure engineering issue concerning the database, deconstructing some back-office process at Oracle to understand what was needed from applications to automate a business flow seamlessly, tweaking a sales compensation plan to eliminate perverse incentives, designing a "portlet" for Oracle's executive dashboard, penning the latest ad, or sharpening an online sales presentation, Ellison was everywhere. Nor did it strike me that he was interfering with the work of others for the sake of it. Although most of the people who work at Oracle are formidably intelligent, Ellison's constant probing and refining seemed both to put them on their mettle and genuinely to add value. Ellison also constantly monitored every shift in his competitors' business tactics or product strategies, ensuring that Oracle could rapidly exploit any emerging weakness or block off any new threat.

Ellison had told me that he was unable to strike a balance between an extreme form of laissez-faire delegation and an equally extreme obsession with influencing every aspect of the business. He could either be semidetached from the day-to-day management of Oracle, as he had been during the mid-1990s, or furiously involved, as he was now. Although Ellison's energy and commitment were hugely impressive and there was hardly anyone at Oracle who preferred the hands-off Ellison to the hands-on version, I could not help remembering Jeff Henley's anxiety that perhaps Ellison was now being too controlling and that the creativity of some very smart people might fail to flower as a consequence.

Overdependence on Ellison carried other risks: according to some people who knew him, there had been a cycle in the past in which Ellison's appetite for running Oracle would wax and wane depending on the challenges facing the business. Henley actually believed that in some ways the pounding that Oracle was taking in 2001 was a stroke of luck because it meant that Ellison had no option but to tie himself to the job. If success with 11i came too quickly, there was a danger that Ellison might relax. Henley and other Oracle executives were also worried about the commitment Ellison was making to winning the America's Cup. When I inadvertently mentioned to Henley, in July 2001, that a successful America's Cup campaign might mean Oracle's losing its CEO for the best part of five months, he had been horrified. At the very least, he said, it would mean that some important deals, which only Ellison could close, would be lost, maybe forever. He was so upset that he called Ellison, who was cruising the Mediterranean on board *Katana*, and threatened to resign if it was true. Ed Screven, Oracle's chief software architect and the man whose job it is to make sure that the various development groups are working synergistically, had an additional concern: "Larry casts a pretty long shadow, so he can be gone for an extended period of time and his shadow is still there. But what will happen is that some disputes that only Larry can settle will remain unresolved." I asked Ellison how seriously he took their misgivings. No matter how much he wanted to win the cup, he said, if Oracle needed him, Oracle would come first.

• • •

A typical day for Ellison starts when he gets up at about seven o'clock and checks his overnight e-mails. Unlike many CEOs, Ellison has only one e-mail address. He gets more than a hundred e-mails a day, most of which he answers himself or forwards to the appropriate person. He prefers short e-mails that deal with one specific issue rather than essays because it makes collaborative working easier. After dealing with e-mails he heads for the spacious deck that overlooks the exquisite Japanese garden. There he usually breakfasts on scrambled eggs and bacon (Ellison's Judaism is of the lapsed variety) or fish, rice, and miso soup while reading the newspapers (the *Financial Times* and *The Wall Street Journal; The Economist* on weekends). Even if it's raining and cool, he likes to sit out of doors as much as possible.

At about nine, he heads back inside to continue work on e-mails, writing memos, checking through ads, and working on larger "think pieces" both to clear his mind and to outline strategic issues and forthcoming challenges for colleagues. Some of the papers that Ellison writes will go straight onto Oracle's intranet, especially those aimed at sharpening the message of the sales force. Also part of the routine is a visit to Oracle Sales Online, which might prompt him to leave a message questioning the status of a particular sales opportunity. During the morning, he also takes telephone calls, patched through to him by either Carolyn Balkenhol at Redwood Shores or by Joyce Higashi, the highly efficient Japanese American who works from his home and meshes together the personal and professional sides of Ellison's life. Some of these are regular conference calls with major customers in the middle of implementations. Every fortnight for a year, for example, Ellison talked to the senior management at GE Power during its rollout of the E-Business Suite.* Another part of the routine is to check out the Web sites of rivals: software companies tend to tell the world about what they are intending to do long before they actually have the products ready to ship. Thanks to the Internet, there's no excuse for ever being taken by surprise.

At about eleven o'clock, Ellison usually jumps into one of his cars—his current favorite for everyday use is a Mercedes SL55—and drives a couple of miles to his gym for a workout until lunchtime. Although he has a well-equipped gym in his house, he prefers to exercise with other people rather than at home with a personal trainer. He says, "I can't work unless I work out. I can't push myself mentally unless I push myself physically."

Sometimes, usually on a Friday, Ellison will host a business lunch at home in Atherton. For instance, in July 2001, Ellison's entertaining the top management team at The Gap to celebrate a deal to install the

---

*LE writes: For a time I had regularly scheduled conference calls with POSCO (the world's largest steel company) during the final phases of its implementation of the E-Business Suite. The calls started at 4 A.M. Pacific time.

E-Business Suite to run the retailer's financial and purchasing systems and various other modules to cut costs in its core business functions, including a nifty piece of Internet software called Oracle Product Development Exchange. On hand to greet the khaki-clad Gap executives as they roll up in their black Lincoln limos are Jeff Henley and Sandy Sanderson, the head of consulting. As usual, Ellison waits to make his appearance until all the guests have arrived (he can be heard playing classical guitar in an adjacent room) and are being seated at the immaculately laid table outside on the deck—he is conscious of his celebrity CEO status and knows how to nurture it. With its new clothing lines failing to find favor with its traditional customers, The Gap is having, if anything, an even more bruising time in the market than Oracle. So, while much of Ellison's conversation is aimed at encouraging his guests to buy into Oracle's philosophy of redesigning processes to get the best out of the software, he and The Gap's CEO, Mickey Drexler, also want to compare notes about the economy. It's an interesting contrast: Drexler, who along with Ellison serves on the Apple board, sees everything through a consumer lens, whereas Ellison is more concerned about the confidence of business customers to invest in an uncertain climate. Naturally, both are far too polite to suggest that any internal factors could be contributing to their current problems. When the guests eventually tear themselves away from their beautiful surroundings, Ellison expresses his frustration that despite the Oracle sales pitch, The Gap seems determined to go down a partial best-of-breed route, mixing custom software with the E-Business Suite. "They're going to have a hard time with Retek [a retail software package]. It's not an easy package to implement or integrate. They need to understand that," he tells Sanderson.

When he doesn't have lunch at home, Ellison usually heads to the office at around 1 P.M., driving himself the ten miles along the congested Highway 101 to Oracle's headquarters at Redwood Shores. When she knows he's on his way, Balkenhol will phone around, telling everyone who's scheduled to attend Ellison's meeting to gather. She then uses his travel time to update him on anything he needs to know, run through the afternoon's schedule, get approvals on spending and hiring decisions, and find out whether he wants his lunch of chicken nuggets and ice cream.

Until Ellison's arrival, Safra Catz will push things along in the eleventh-floor boardroom. But it's slightly awkward for her, a fact reflected by her unwillingness to sit center stage. An important part of the way she sells herself within Oracle is that she doesn't give the impression of running the show in his absence, in the way that Ray Lane and, to some extent, Gary Bloom might have done. When Ellison does stride in, the atmosphere becomes highly charged. It's not that Ellison's presence exactly makes anyone nervous (although a relatively junior executive waiting to make some careful PowerPoint presentation might disagree), nor do people become overtly respectful. There's still plenty of tinkering with PalmPilots and frequent visits to the fridge in the hall to get drinks. If Ed Screven is there, he'll be sprawled in his chair, his feet in decaying running shoes planted on the expensive table top. It's more that there's an air of expectation. Ellison is always in performance mode, cracking jokes, telling stories, and generally dominating every part of the discussion. It's almost as if he feels the need to relegitimize his leadership each day by demonstrating the completeness of his grasp.

What's noticeable in these meetings, which typically continue until six or seven in the evening, is how differently Ellison relates to the programmers compared with other workers at Oracle. They know that they are the elite, and a good few of the old hands are confident enough of their standing with Ellison to argue with him if they think he's wrong and they have the facts on their side.* From that point of view, the concern that an excessively controlling Ellison may be squeezing the creativity out of colleagues seems overdone. Although I have been present in a few meetings when there's been an air of tension, usually when it turns out that somebody has fallen down on the job, Ellison no longer goes in for public executions. By his own admission, it's quite a change from the way he used to operate, and, as always with Ellison, it's the reputation he earned in a different era that stays with him now.

---

*LE writes: Our senior engineers don't hesitate to argue with me when they think I'm wrong. And if I'm way wrong, they'll cut me off midsentence. Ed Screven will blurt out, "No, that's not right," and rapid-fire the reasons why. Ron Wohl will let me finish my sentence and say in a considered tone, "Larry, I don't agree with you." Then he'll carefully, point by point, explain where I've gone wrong. Andy Mendelsohn will let me finish what I'm saying, and then he'll just stare at me for a while. Gradually, this pained look takes over his face and he'll say, "I really just don't understand what you're saying." That's a bad one. I must have been totally wrong or completely incoherent. (Fortunately it's not possible to be both.) But the worst is when Roger Bamford catches me saying something stupid. He just giggles. It makes him so happy.

• • •

When Ellison was fourteen, he had an argument with his sister Doris, then in her early thirties: "She asked me the question 'What's more important to you? To be loved or admired?' I said I'd like to be admired. She just said, 'No,' gave me her 'You're just a stupid adolescent' look, and left the room. It took me a long time to understand that we *all* want to be loved. Even me. Imagine that. Anyway, I used to have a management style that earned neither love nor admiration. Rather than using conventional MBO [management-by-objectives] techniques, I invented my own style of management called MBR. MBR stands for 'management by ridicule.' MBR is perfectly suited to a young smart-ass programmer who just started his own company. A popular book at the time, *The One Minute Manager,* recommended that managers spend a minute a day praising their employees. MBR takes more time. You need to spend hours every day in meetings with your key senior people where you point out at length exactly why this person or that person's ideas are utterly ridiculous. Not everyone can do it. You've got to be good at intellectual intimidation and rhetorical bullying. According to MBR theory, your brilliant arguments establish a clear intellectual dominance that gives people the confidence to accept you and follow you—their leader. Interesting theory, isn't it? I was pretty brutal in attacking ideas and embarrassing people. I'd excuse my behavior by telling myself I was just having 'an open and honest debate.' The fact is, I just didn't know any better. All my experience in business had been as a programmer. Programmers routinely play a game called 'Who's the smartest person in the room?' It's still a popular game at Oracle. I see it played all the time. When playing WTSPINR— pronounced 'wet spinner'—you get points by showing how irrational or suboptimal other people's ideas are. It happens in all disciplines to some extent, but programming is similar to mathematics in that there are clear right and wrong answers, so there are clear winners and losers. It's classic primate behavior, figuring out where you are in the monkey troupe."

I thought that maybe Ellison's use of "MBR" was fairly typical of an insecure CEO trying to establish his leadership; he disagrees: "No.* In fact, CEO is a title that's looked down upon by most programmers. Remember, the name of the game is who's the smartest in the room, not who's got the most stars on their shoulder. There's very little respect for

---

*LE writes: Actually, in retrospect, I do agree. I was an inexperienced and insecure CEO trying to establish my leadership. Very embarrassing.

rank among programmers. Programmers have tremendous intellectual integrity, and you have to be able to clearly explain why something is right or wrong if you expect to win an argument. What is unnecessary and unacceptable is to humiliate people in public while you're explaining something. People didn't sign up for that. You know: 'Oh great, between ten and twelve I get to go to a meeting and be publicly humiliated. I can't wait.' "

What was it that convinced Ellison that beating people up was not always the way of getting the best out of them? "I was in a big meeting between Oracle and another company. The other company's CEO, an absolutely brilliant guy, started attacking ideas and people in a frighteningly brutal and destructive way. I was an MBR amateur compared to this guy. The overall dynamic in the room instantly changed. Everybody became afraid to talk because they didn't want to be intellectually embarrassed. But it was worse than that. People started to line up against this guy, not because he was wrong—he wasn't—but because he was inhumane. They grudgingly accepted that he was smart, but that didn't keep them from wanting him to fail. From then on I was very careful about using MBR. Maybe it's okay for programmers, but it's certainly not okay for CEOs. It's hard enough to run a company; you don't want everyone rooting against you. Ninety-nine percent of the time MBR is degrading to the practitioner and damaging to the business."

Although Ellison has learned from past mistakes, there are still aspects of the way he runs the company through these quite large meetings that can have some negative consequences. Ellison feels he has to perform to demonstrate his leadership and his prowess. Is it possible to be in both performance mode and listening mode? It makes picking up the nuances of a meeting more difficult and makes him all the more dependent on a few trusted people, Safra Catz above all, to tell him what he may be missing. And some very bright people, who might have important contributions to make, simply freeze in that kind of environment. And although Ellison no longer practices "MBR" and now tries hard to encourage debate, there probably still isn't enough of it at Oracle.

Gary Bloom says, "The way Larry uses these meetings, they're a fine environment for communicating strategy and decisions he's already made, but it's not a fine environment for debating those decisions once he's made them. It's an issue I raised with Larry, and I think he's been working on trying to get people to be more open if they disagree with him. I once said to him, not long after I became a member of the PDMC (Product Development Management Committee), that I didn't get what the meetings were for. Is it for you to articulate what you want or is it for people to tell you what you need to hear? He said, 'It's for people to discuss and tell me what I need to hear.' I told him, 'That's not what happens.' I said, 'Larry, we have separate discussions from you, and we might sometimes all be in agreement that you're wrong about something. . . . But as soon as you violently disagree or get emotional, everybody folds their cards. . . . The debate's over—they're unwilling to take you on.' The very next day in the meeting, he took up a deliberately controversial position on an issue against me. I kept debating him, and eventually he turned to everybody and said, 'You must all agree with my position because none of you are jumping in on Gary's side.' And they all went, 'Oh, actually, we do agree with Gary.' But even if he's got better about this, a group meeting is still not a substitute for a one-to-one interaction between a CEO and key leader within the company." *

This is an issue about which Bloom feels especially strongly. From the end of 1997, for at least two years, during the period when Ellison was slowly wresting power back from Ray Lane, Bloom was Ellison's right hand. Whenever Bloom wanted to speak to Ellison in private, his boss made the time, especially if Bloom had uncovered yet more evidence of what they both at the time regarded as Lane's incompetence.† When the Oracle board insisted in 1999 that there should be a formal plan of suc-

---

*LE writes: Gary's right, I should do more one-on-ones. That said, I feel my time is more efficiently spent in larger meetings, where I can do a better job of gathering facts, debating, and communicating decisions. Harold Genin (the man who built ITT) defined management as "gathering facts and making decision." He also said that the hardest thing for a manager to do is to "distinguish facts from true facts." I can get at the true facts much more easily when a couple of layers of management are present at a meeting. The senior guys sometimes don't know the facts, and occasionally they don't want you to know the facts. Oracle's current management team has a much better grasp of the facts than any previously, and they never try to hide things. That makes my job much easier these days.

†LE writes: I don't think it's fair to describe Ray as an incompetent manager. It just seemed to me that Ray wasn't very interested in the daily details of management, especially on the expense side of the business, so he delegated that responsibility to others. Ray thought that his time was better spent doing deals, so that's what he did. Unfortunately, some of the people whom Ray relied on to manage expenses let them get way out of control.

cession in place, the only internal candidate whom Ellison was ready to endorse was Bloom (the top choice outside Oracle was Sun Microsystems' Scott McNealy).

However, within twelve months Bloom was finding it difficult to get the kind of access to Ellison that he had come to expect. In part, it was because Ellison was beginning to think he might have promoted Bloom a little too fast and as a consequence, like Lane before him, his ego was starting to outstrip his ability (although Ellison denies it, I think he was riled by Bloom's claim in *Fortune* magazine's "Why Oracle's Cool Again" cover story that he was perfectly capable of running Oracle). But it was also because of Ellison's growing reliance on and trust in Safra Catz. Although Bloom and Catz got on well, respected each other, and were united in their contempt for Lane, it became increasingly clear to Bloom that he was losing out to Catz in terms of influence with Ellison. Bloom says, "This isn't a slam on Safra. I like her. She's very smart, and she really does understand what needs to be done. But what happened is that Larry, out of convenience, started using her as a path of communication. He felt it was easier to tell something to Safra and then have her go and communicate it to everyone else, including me. She became the filter and the funnel through which everything from Larry came. If I had to communicate something to my organization, which was about sixteen thousand people, I needed to get that little bit of background or color directly from Larry to provide the context for a decision. I never wanted to be in the position of a leader saying, 'We're doing this because Larry says so.' It was so damaging to our culture. All I would need was thirty seconds of discussion direct with Larry. But when things started coming through Safra and I couldn't get that, I couldn't effectively do my job. I'm not criticizing Safra. I told Larry this and he said, 'Okay, I see your point; I'll try to change.' But there was never any change. It got to a point where I was responsible for the vast majority of the company, yet I had no contact with the guy who actually ran the company."

Carolyn Balkenhol confirms that Ellison became increasingly reluctant to see Bloom. As well as being frustrated and personally wounded, Bloom also calculated that Ellison's new appetite for running the company meant that his own role, let alone his chances of one day becoming CEO of Oracle, would diminish. When, in November 2000, Veritas, then the fifth biggest software company in the world (thanks in no small measure to the efforts of Geoff Squire, the man Ellison most regrets firing), offered forty-year-old Bloom the top job, it wasn't a difficult decision.

Although Ellison was annoyed about Bloom's departure, partly because of the bad impression it gave to investors, coming so soon after Ray Lane's "resignation," that he couldn't keep his senior executives happy, he has some sympathy with him. "I understand Gary's frustration. Safra and I share a high-bandwidth communications link. We finish each other's sentences. We come to the same conclusion in the same amount of time. We rarely disagree, but when we do, she's not shy about expressing her opinions. If she thinks I'm wrong, she freezes me with one of her piercing stares and tells me I'm wrong. She's not afraid of me or any other human. Anyway, I can count on her telling me the truth as she sees it. I respect her and rely on her as my chief confidante and counselor. In that respect she did replace Gary. That was very hard for Gary to take. Actually, come to think of it, he didn't take it. He left."

Although Ellison accepts that his key "directs" should have a right to one-on-one time with him, it's still something that he feels ambivalent about. "It's true. I don't like doing a lot of it. If it's something personal, then you have to do it one-on-one, but if you're trying to decide a business policy issue like pricing, then I'd much rather have the whole team there so that everyone can weigh in. That way everyone will understand how we arrived at a particular decision rather than having to guess. Meeting with the senior management team as a group forces us to focus on the goals of the company as a whole rather than one department at a time. Looking at the gestalt of the business has resulted in less infighting between departments and a more open and collegial work environment."

• • •

What's very clear is how much these days Ellison leans on the slight, black-haired, black-clad figure of Safra Catz. He says, "She makes up for one of my biggest areas of weakness. She's disciplined and thorough. I'm not. I'm pretty good at separating the good ideas from the bad ideas, and I'm pretty good at drilling into detail and solving problems. But once a problem is understood, once a plan is in place, I usually move on to the next thing rather than following up and making sure that the agreed-upon plan is actually implemented. It's called execution, and Safra is brilliant at it. Safra is so exceptionally bright that she keeps all the whys and wherefores of all our policies and plans in her head. That enables her to make interpretations, modifications, and improvements during the execution phase of the plans without any intervention from me. Now when we decide on something, it actually gets done."

Catz has always downplayed the extent of her power and influence, insisting that she has no agenda of her own (unlike, by implication, Ray

Lane) and is there only to make sure that the things that Ellison wants to happen get done. She says, "I'm not interested in building power and I don't have any individual power here. People will send me things for my approval and my response will always be okay, if it's within the scope of a decision I already know Larry has approved. I say that as a reminder that I don't have any power of my own."

It's an impressive (and genuine) demonstration of loyalty as well as being clever—it puts her out of the firing line when she's doing something that ruffles feathers or bruises the egos of senior executives, especially on the sales side, who resent the degree of oversight and supervision she represents. But one of the criticisms that I sometimes hear about Catz both within Oracle and outside is that, unlike other managers, she is not really accountable—an impression that's strengthened by her reluctance to become a public face in the way that Ray Lane and, to a lesser extent, Gary Bloom did. Ellison says, "She's accountable to me—and to the board. Together with Jeff Henley, we're collectively accountable for the performance of the company. If we're not doing a good job, it will show up in the numbers. I understand her desire to stay in the background, but that's going to be very hard to do over the long term. She's gradually becoming more visible. Joining the board of directors was a big step in that direction." Given that Ellison had sometimes referred to Catz as a possible successor, how did he want her role to evolve over the next few years? "I'm not sure it needs to evolve much. We work extremely well together. Sometimes we're too aggressive about pushing new systems and procedures into the company, but we keep on improving our margins, so it must be working. We're trying to define how a modern business operates. We're continuously improving Oracle and our applications software suite at the same time."

From Ellison's point of view, Safra Catz is the answer to his prayers. She makes him much more effective within Oracle than he could be without her, he can trust her completely, and he can communicate what he wants through her almost intuitively. But I think there are potential dangers in the relationship for both of them. Ellison must be careful not to do what he did in the past with favorite subordinates, which is to load more and more responsibility on them until something snaps. In Catz's case, there's little chance that it will go to her head, as happened with Ray Lane; she is a remarkably grounded person. I once asked how she felt when Ellison said in interviews that she could run Oracle. She said, "I don't want it, and why would I? My parents used to say to me that I could do anything I wanted to and that gave me confidence in life. But equally, I never felt I *had* to do something, I didn't feel that I had to prove anything. I don't have an individual agenda, so don't make me one."

She's also smart enough to know when she doesn't know something. But there is a risk of Ellison's trying to turn her into something that she's not. Some people feel more comfortable and are more effective working behind the scenes. If Catz doesn't want the limelight, Ellison shouldn't push her into it. He must also guard against making her the main channel through which he deals with other senior executives. Amazingly, Catz hasn't yet become an object of envy and mistrust in spite of her unique degree of access to Ellison, because people don't see her manipulating the situation to her own advantage. But she's nonetheless highly vulnerable to the backbiting and jealousy that exist in all organizations. She says, "People have been really nice to me. A number of folks appreciate that decisions can be made faster because I've done my homework. But you never really know what they think."

• • •

One of the most frequent criticisms of Ellison is that even in an industry that lives on hype, he takes boasting and overpromising to new levels. It's not only Tom Siebel who talks about "the lies of Larry Ellison," it's an article of faith for half the journalists who cover the software business that Ellison is an incorrigible liar who deliberately distorts the truth about both his professional and personal life. I frequently observed him stretching the truth to create a better impression, while his ebullient optimism routinely put him in the embarrassing situation of having to explain why something he had seemed certain of hadn't happened.

Ellison says, "I piss people off because I'm quite willing to say what I think and I'm reckless enough to make public my predictions about the future—about Oracle and about the industry. As an old Chinese proverb says, 'Predictions are very dangerous, especially when they pertain to the future.' Sometimes I'm right, sometimes I'm wrong. I was right about relational database technology. I was wrong about the network computer. I was right about Internet architecture replacing client/server architecture. You don't have to be right all the time to make a good living. When I was wrong, I was not lying, I was just wrong. When I say Oracle clusters can run real applications and DB2 clusters can't, some people think I'm lying. I'm not. It's a fact. When I say Oracle Java is faster than BEA Java, some people think I am lying. I'm not. It's a fact. When I predict one of our products is going to come out on a certain date and it doesn't, some people think I lied. I didn't. I was just wrong. Give me a specific example of a lie I've told in business. There's only one. In my early twenties, when I first came to California, I lied about having a college degree so I could get a job. Big fucking deal. That's it.

"Being optimistic and exaggerating is another matter altogether. The entire history of the IT industry has been one of overpromising and underdelivering. Software executives routinely say that a product is going to be ready on a certain date, and then it turns out to be literally years late. It's happened at Microsoft. It's happened at Oracle. Software development is notoriously unpredictable. Maybe the only honest schedule is the one Michelangelo gave the pope when he was painting the Sistine Chapel: 'It will be done when it's done.' Anything else is a guess, and sometimes we guess wrong. Most senior software executives don't tell out-and-out lies about their products or their businesses.* But optimism and exaggeration, those are the standard rules of engagement for combat in this industry."

I suggest that maybe Ellison had done as much as anybody in the software industry to establish those rules of engagement and had both lived and thrived by them. He grins as if to say that's all in the past. "Since I've got this notorious reputation for exaggeration, the press denies Oracle any leeway to exaggerate at all. I know that, so we make sure that all our advertising is one hundred percent fact-based and provable. Our current campaign is called 'Just the Facts.' We're absolutely rigorous about making claims about our products. Any claim we make must be independently verifiable and provable. I believe in ads that list the cold, hard facts about your products and your competitors' products—a side-by-side comparison of irrefutable facts.

"Unfortunately, just sticking to the facts doesn't necessarily mean you'll avoid criticism. When I said that GE Power runs the Oracle E-Business Suite, a front-page article in *The Wall Street Journal* took me to task for being intentionally misleading. They thought that I should have listed the names of the specific GE Power locations that were currently running the suite and identify exactly which parts of the suite each location was running. Give me a break. I never said that GE Power runs the E-Business Suite everywhere for everything. I never said that GE Power

---

*LE writes: Every once in a while there's even a kernel of truth in some of the things Tommy Siebel says. I don't like Tommy very much. He says nasty things about me all the time. I hope he will have run his company out of business by the time this book is published. He appears to be working hard at it.

has no other software except Oracle software. I said that GE Power runs the E-Business Suite. Period. I suppose I could say that GE Power runs lots of parts of the E-Business Suite at lots of locations. That's true too, and it's a bit more specific, but it sounds strange. So I'll just keep saying that GE Power runs the E-business Suite and leave it at that. That may not be precise for some, but it's the truth."

What about Ellison's claim when the E-Business Suite came out that it was complete, wasn't that an example of deliberate overclaiming that came close to lying? Ellison laughs. "Well, words like 'complete' and 'unbreakable' are relative, not absolute. Our E-Business Suite is much more complete than any other suite of applications. In the high-tech manufacturing industry the E-Business Suite is close enough to being complete to be called complete. In the insurance industry it's less complete. Our database is so much more reliable and secure than any other database system that it's okay for us to call it unbreakable. Tandem [the fault-tolerant computer company] called their computers 'nonstop' because they stopped much less frequently than other computers, not because Tandem computers never, ever stopped. I read that some analysts say that our claim that the 9i database is unbreakable is outrageous because everyone knows that nothing is truly unbreakable. Fine. If the earth falls into the sun, our database will break—that's true, so I'm a liar. Whatever." Ellison does, however, accept that he can sometimes push an argument or an idea just that little bit further than it can stand. "Once I believe in a new, important idea I get very enthusiastic and push it hard. Once I started believing in Internet architecture, I couldn't say anything nice about client/server. Once I started believing in integrated applications suites, I had a hard time admitting that there was any value at all in any best-of-breed product. Once I've thought something through, there's no intellectual uncertainty remaining. Once I enter a crusade, I cease being objective and I become a zealot."

Another aspect of Ellison's bravura style is equally calculated: leadership. "You cannot lead if you're filled with uncertainty. Imagine two officers each leading a company of marines up a hill. The first one says, 'Men, we're going up this hill and we're going to kill every fucking enemy solder on our way to the top. I'm going first, and you're all going to make it to the top with me. I haven't lost one of you yet. Follow me, men.' Cool, competent, and confident. I'm ready to follow that guy. The second guy says, 'Men, we're going to try to take this hill. I have to admit that I don't know how many enemy solders are on this hill. And I've never really done anything like this before. But I'm willing to go first if you're willing to follow me. We might make it; we might not. There's no way to know for certain. Even if we make it to the top, it's highly likely that some of us will be killed. Follow me, men.' Well, the second guy is impressively honest about his fears and uncertainties. Maybe he should become a psychotherapist. But there's no way anyone is following that guy anywhere."

• • •

Like a lot of people, I still find it hard to understand how someone with as many choices as Ellison, who for most of the last fifteen years has had more money than he could spend and who clearly has a low boredom threshold, can bring himself to keep on doing the same thing. He says, "My sister told me that whenever I got too close to a goal I'd raise the bar for fear of actually clearing it. We're endlessly curious about our own limits. The process of self-discovery is one of testing and retesting yourself. I won the Sydney-to-Hobart. Can I win the America's Cup? I'll find out. The software business is a more difficult test; it's a much higher stakes game; there are more people playing this game; it's a lot more interesting game; and it's a lot more exciting. If I wasn't doing this, I'm not sure what else I would be doing with my life." * It seemed like a far cry from Ellison's original motivation of founding Oracle—to have enough control over his own life not to have to spend time with people he didn't like or doing things he didn't like. "We change as our circumstances change. Financial independence means you no longer need to trade time for money. But once you've been liberated, the freedom that comes afterwards can be difficult to manage. The good news is that suddenly you have all these choices; the bad news is that suddenly you have all these choices. So you've got to figure out what it is you really love to do, because there's no other justification for doing it. And if you can't find anything you love, you have to settle for doing something that's merely important."

Did Ellison still love his job when Oracle came close to self-destruction in 1991? He says simply, "It's not like I had a choice then. I had to save Oracle to save myself." What if he had been forced out? What if Don Lucas had denied him that chance? "I'd have done what Steve [Jobs] did [after being booted out of Apple]: I'd have started another company to

---

*LE writes: I'm chairman of the board of Quark Biotech, a molecular biology research and drug company. If for any reason I left Oracle, I'd probably go to work for Quark full time. That prospect should scare the hell out of the guys at Quark.

try and prove it all over again, first and foremost to myself." So he would have put at risk his entire fortune, at that stage around $150 million? "Without question. Oh, yes! It was my life that was at risk, not my money. It has nothing to do with courage; I just can't accept defeat until I've been carried dead from the field. I'm one of those chess players who will stare at the board for as long as it takes to find a winning line of play. I have a lot of endurance: intellectual, emotional, physical. The clock in the software game is measured in years, not minutes. It took twelve years to make our bloody database-clustering technology work. But we knew if we could make it work we'd win. If we can make the E-Business Suite work, and I think we can, we'll win again. I'm optimistic, but not irrationally so. We're pretty good at coming up with winning strategies; the problem is, our strategies are technically very, very hard to implement. But difficult strategies, well executed, can lead to great victories. Hannibal crossed the Alps with elephants to beat the Romans at Canae. Napoleon crossed the Alps without elephants to beat the Austrians at Marengo. Database clustering was really hard—it required elephants. The E-Business Suite is just a march over the mountains. It's a long way to the top, but we'll make it."

If the prospect of beating IBM or Microsoft is one of the things that gets Ellison up in the morning, there are other satisfactions. One is the straightforward pleasure that comes from solving a problem or making a piece of technology work. "Watching a cluster of eight Compaq PCs running faster and more reliably than a big-ass IBM mainframe is just so incredibly cool. It's the same kind of thrill as when the Wright boys took off on *Kitty Hawk*. It's off the ground! Oh my God, it actually flies! This changes everything. Database clustering is cold fusion that works—it works." *

What Ellison hasn't said is that he gets satisfaction from making the businesses of Oracle's customers run better. It's the kind of thing that politically correct CEOs are supposed to say. "GE is a wonderful company, but it's not my company, it's not the team I play on. I'm happy if General Electric is happy with our software because that means our software's good and we'll probably sell a lot of it. We work very hard to make our customers successful, because that's how we make Oracle successful. When the Lakers win a basketball championship, they may say they did

---

*LE writes: Okay. Maybe database clustering is not as cool as flight. But it's close.

it for the fans, but I don't really believe them. I think they did it for themselves. As a fan that doesn't bother me at all. I'm just glad they won.

"I get a lot of satisfaction from my job. There's the intellectual satisfaction that comes from solving a really hard problem. There's the satisfaction of seeing our software help our customers, especially in health care and government, where good information can actually save lives. But it's not altruism, and it's certainly not the money. Maybe it's just vanity that motivates me. You can never really be certain of anyone's motives, including your own. You are better off measuring people on what they do rather than the unknowable 'why?' I don't know why the Lakers played well, I'm just glad they did. I don't know, can't know, and don't care what motivated Jonas Salk to try to make a polio vaccine, I'm just glad he did. If you want to understand why people do things, then take a course in evolutionary psychology. What we want to do with our lives is the most important question we all have to answer. So if I could do anything at all with my life, what would I do? I'd cure cancer.* I'd much rather cure cancer than become the richest guy in the world. Why? Because I'd be a much happier person if I cured cancer. Why? Because I'd be loved. Why? Because people don't want to suffer painful death. Why? You know why."

Although Ellison talks about a life after Oracle in which, among other things, he would spend time working on his new passion, molecular biology, the level of success that he says that Oracle must achieve before he can leave is so daunting that he may never be able to escape. "I'm stuck here for the duration; there's no way I can stop until I know how this story ends. I think even if I found out I was dying and I had a year to live, I wouldn't change my life very much."

---

*LE writes: Yes, I know that cancer is a collection of diseases and it is very unlikely that there will ever be a single cure. Still, my mother died of cancer and I want to cure cancer. That's where most of my money and all of my time after Oracle are likely to go.

17

ALTERNATIVE STRESS

May 2001

Approaching Ventura Harbor by road from the little airport where Ellison has just landed his Citation, we can see the strange gunmetal gray sails from a mile or two away. The flat, featureless countryside and the low-rise buildings that straddle the slightly run-down little port offer no visual competition to the two tightly sculpted, towering airfoils that move balletically together as if directed by some hidden choreographer. The sails belong to the two boats that Ellison's Oracle Racing team is using to train for the 2003 America's Cup. Previously, they belonged to AmericaOne, the top-placing U.S. challenger in the 1999 series, and were purchased in August 2000 as part of a deal in which Oracle Racing beat rival Craig McCaw's Seattle team to acquire AmericaOne's physical assets and many of its key people—an invaluable foundation for a team that had not collectively competed for yachting's most prestigious trophy before.

Since April, most of Oracle Racing's nearly 100-strong team and their families have been quartered in and around Ventura, California. The spring and summer breezes at Ventura are a good match for the conditions the team can expect to meet in New Zealand in twenty months. Oracle Racing contributed $75,000 to have the harbor dredged to a depth of sixteen feet to accommodate the team's giant eighty-foot yachts after Ventura Mayor Sandy Smith convinced Oracle that its closely guarded design secrets would be safer from prying eyes there than at the more populous Long Beach harbor. It's a boost for the port because the team will spend several million dollars, and their presence will encourage visits from other sailing enthusiasts.

We've been met at the airport by Bill Erkelens, who has managed
Team Sayonara, Ellison's world championship–winning maxi-yacht
team, for the last six years and is now chief operating officer of Oracle
Racing. Every evening, all the information on the day's sailing is down-
loaded onto an Oracle database (which is running on a Digital super-
computer donated by Compaq). From there, it's e-mailed to Bruce Farr
and Mickey Ickert in Annapolis, Maryland, the designer of the new boats
that will contest the cup and the team's sail designer, respectively. There
has been no word from the trophy holder, Team New Zealand, about a
meeting with the challengers to agree on the ground rules for the 2003
competition, and Erkelens wants to know the dates for the qualification
races, called the Louis Vuitton Trophy, and where exactly off New
Zealand the races will be run. One of the reasons why holders of the trophy are traditionally so difficult to unseat is that they keep challengers in
a permanent state of uncertainty. While Team New Zealand will want to
avoid being accused of deliberately unsportsmanlike behavior, it's not
about to surrender any of the incumbent's advantage if it can help it.

After inspecting the team's headquarters—a series of portable offices
and a dry dock big enough for both boats when they are hauled out of the
water each night to have their hulls scrubbed and be reconfigured with
the latest ideas from Annapolis—we board one of the chase boats, a high-
powered thirty-six-foot whaler. Once clear of the harbor, the chase boat
closes in on the two racers out in the bay. Even though the team owner is
about to come on board, there's no question of interrupting the racing.
The whaler expertly comes up alongside USA 61, and Ellison, Erkelens,
and I jump aboard, allowing the chase boat to career smoothly away
without hampering USA 61's chances of overtaking USA 49, slightly
ahead. At first, Ellison seems content to crouch out of harm's way near
the stern of the boat. But not for long. As USA 61 goes about, Ellison signals that he wants to drive. Without any fuss, John Cutler, the team's
number three driver, hands over to Ellison. The trimmers and grinders go
about their work with the same intensity, the numbers are called from instruments that provide telemetric data on the other boat's speed and position, and the race tactician continues to feed his thoughts to the driver.

And how does Ellison do? It takes him a few minutes to adjust his balance to the boat's progress through the water, but after that, he's sailing
pretty well, taking in the mass of data being hurled at him and losing no
ground to the other boat, which is being driven by Peter Holmberg.
Thanks to a lucky guess about where the wind might be blowing more
strongly, we actually overhaul and beat USA 49. Did the other boat let

Ellison win? It's not very likely. Ellison is treated by the crew with respect but no hint of deference.*

No sooner has that race ended than we're maneuvering to begin another. Erkelens, who says this is about the first time he's been out on the water since the team arrived at Ventura, describes the crews' time out in the bay as being like "groundhog days"—a continuous loop in which one race follows relentlessly and repetitiously after another. Thoroughly pleased at his earlier success, Ellison decides he will drive at the start of the next race. Despite the fact that these are essentially sparring sessions, any advantage at the start, which, as in Formula One racing, is frequently decisive, must be fought for. It's not uncommon for the boats to make contact and even sustain quite significant damage. Before the start, which is closely overseen by the two chase boats and an umpire's boat, *USA 49* and *61* circle each other aggressively. The boats are making nearly ten knots—fast enough to have a fairly big accident.

Suddenly the race is on, and immediately Ellison is muscled out of position. *USA 49* makes it past the starting buoy a few meters ahead and with the right of way on the starboard tack. This time Ellison doesn't get any breaks, and the distance between the boats becomes unbridgeable. The concentration required to maneuver these highly strung machines under the critical gaze of some of the world's best sailors is draining, and he has been at the wheel for the best part of two hours. The boats are now running downwind, something that Ellison finds less entertaining than sailing close-hauled, and he seems happy to hand over the helm.

• • •

Bill Erkelens met Ellison late in 1994 through an Atherton neighbor of Ellison, a New Zealander named David Thompson. Erkelens has sailed all his life. During summer vacations from university, he would earn money delivering boats for wealthy owners to and from Hawaii and

---

*LE writes: Passing another boat in America's Cup match racing is both difficult and rare. But I was able to maneuver USA 61 into a nice position and capitalize on a favorable wind shift. I was very pleased when we tacked and found ourselves clear in front by a boat length. There is no way Peter would willingly let me pass him. He was trying to become the number one driver on our team, and you don't get that job by losing races to anyone, especially me. He was pissed when he got passed. He was looking to get even in the next race, and he did.

prepare boats for sailors in the annual Trans-Pac (San Francisco to Honolulu) race. One of these was Thompson, whose boat won his division and came in second overall. About the same time, Thompson had begun encouraging Ellison to take up sailing. Ellison recalls the day that he was working out on the StairMaster at the public gym. "The guy next to me was David Thompson. David just casually asks me if I sail. I said, 'Yeah, I used to sail. I used to sail a lot.' Then he asked if I've ever raced, and again I said yes. So he goes on to ask me if I'd be interested in racing a maxi—the biggest, fastest class of racing sailboats. I'd always loved sailing, but I had to give it up in my late twenties because it was too expensive. I couldn't afford it then—but I could afford it now. So we started doing some research, and we signed up the best designer, Bruce Farr in Annapolis, and the best builder, Mick Cookson in New Zealand, the best spar maker, Steve Wilson in New Zealand, the best sail maker, the best this, the best that. We found the right people to design and build the fastest maxi in the world. Shortly after David put the idea into my head, *Sayonara* was being designed as an all-out race boat whose only purpose was winning."

Thompson had promised Ellison to find someone who would help to oversee the project and run the boat. Since one of the first races that Ellison wanted to enter was the Trans-Pac, Thompson had no hesitation in recommending Erkelens. He went out to Atherton to meet Ellison and go through the first set of drawings of *Sayonara*. Erkelens was hired on the understanding that he would go and live in New Zealand for the six months that it would take to build *Sayonara*. He says, "I was keen to do it, so we signed on. But it was a big decision for us. My wife, Melinda, was an attorney, and leaving her career a couple of years from making partner and going to work on boats meant that I was not very popular with her family."

For the first year of the "campaign," Erkelens took his orders from Thompson. But when Thompson's businesses began to suffer due to the time he was spending on *Sayonara,* he withdrew and Erkelens was left in charge of running the program. Ellison was clear that his objective was to win races. But Erkelens says that it soon became something more than that. "Initially, it was a results-oriented thing. But then we sailed a nine-day race to Hawaii, and he just absorbed it all. He was up all night staring at the stars, sailing along in the middle of the night with the dolphins and the whales—he just loved it. It was a beautiful place to be, and he was proud of the boat. . . . One thing that struck me was how important the people were to him. He got a group of people he was comfortable with and enjoyed their company. That became a really important part of the whole campaign.

"The one thing that strikes everyone about Larry is that he has confidence in the crew. He does not second-guess them or question them or want to show that he can do a better job. He is quite happy to be part of the team, working with the team and doing his part. I don't want to demean other owners, but he does not seem to stick his finger into the pie just for the sake of doing it. He knows what he wants done, but he does not tell people how to do their job. I guess he gets people who can do their job well, and he respects them for that. I think that is why the people are so comfortable about it." What about when Ellison is driving the boat? Is he willing to be influenced in terms of tactics and other inputs from the rest of the team about what he does? Erkelens says, "Yes, he works really well with our trimmers, who really have a direct line to the feel of the boat through the sail. Then there are the numbers from the onboard computers—it's a very technical game. Quite a few people on the boat stay on the numbers, and there is also the feel of the rudder. He has the force on the rudder, which he needs to react to, so it's a very dynamic job. He has to work with those people; otherwise he will not be able to do it."

Although I'd now seen Ellison sailing for myself, I found it hard to believe that, never having sailed at this level, Ellison could so quickly contribute something other than money to the team. Erkelens insists, "The first two races *Sayonara* did were down the coast of California. He did a lot of driving in the Cavalier race, which we won, and he did a phenomenal job. A lot of it is about numbers and concentration. He has a mind for numbers, it seems, and he concentrates, so he did really well at it. But I must admit these were ocean races, so he was not right next to another boat. It's harder to judge. . . . After that we took the boat to New Zealand and did a little refit to adjust to the new handicap. We got it prepared because for the first time we were going to race alongside other boats in Hawaii. But when we got there, he did an excellent job and we won the regatta. We did not win every race—I think we might have got a few seconds—but we won most of our races. Then we thought, 'Well, this is all good for us,' because what was shaping up was that the Owners Association decided they were going to enforce the owner-driver rule. The owner has to drive at the start and the first lead and then two thirds of the race after that. What happened in San Francisco, in 1996, was that there was a bit of a standoff where the other boats were going to withdraw from the regatta before it started if Larry did not commit to their rules of driving the boat. I think he was a little reluctant at first, but he agreed to do it. He started the boat and did the first upwind leg, and we won every race by a long shot. All of a sudden we overcame this confidence hurdle. He was better than all those other owners."

Nevertheless, Ellison had been frank (or modest) enough to admit to me that with the best boat and the best crew, he could be 10 percent less good than the next guy driving and still stand every chance of winning. Erkelens says, "We always had, in my opinion, a little bit better crew, a little bit better sails. But I still think Larry was better than the other maxi yacht owner-drivers."

Chris Dickson, *Sayonara*'s skipper for most of the last four years, is now on a retainer of nearly $1 million a year, fulfilling the same role for Oracle Racing. Dickson is notorious for his willingness to scream criticism at some of the world's best sailors, and the yachting press has been running stories about a bust-up in the Oracle Racing compound a few days before in which fists flew. He says of the approach he brought to Team Sayonara, "We have an uncompromising commitment to winning. We don't accept excuses for anything. We have an absolutely ruthless approach to doing the best we can." What is also not in doubt is his genius. Few who have sailed with him, including those who have endured his volcanic temper, dispute that there is anybody better at skippering a racing yacht.

Ellison recalls the arrival of the Kiwis: "We made some key crew changes, and we immediately started sailing better. Chris Dickson and Brad Butterworth were both great to get on board. If there are better sailors in the world than those guys, I haven't met them. The Kiwis are the world's best sailors, no question about that. But what I really enjoyed was the greatly improved chemistry on the team. The Kiwis we had on board were older than their American counterparts, and they came from more diverse backgrounds. A lot of the American sailors are privileged yacht club kids. Not all of them. Mike Howard, one of our American grinders, is as regular as a guy can be. Anyway, the Kiwis are more blue-collar types. You know, 'My dad is an auto mechanic, and he taught me how to sail.' 'My dad is a postman, and he taught me how to sail.' 'My dad is a farmer.' 'We raise red-tail deer—and sail.' Everyone in New Zealand sails, young and old, boys and girls. Everyone. So New Zealand's best sailors are a true cross section of the community.

"The America's Cup really should be renamed the New Zealand Big Boat Championship. New Zealanders are the key sailors on Alinghi [Switzerland], Oracle [USA], and Prada [Italy]. And of course Team Zealand is made up of mainly Kiwi sailors. That's not to say that there aren't some pretty good American sailors; there are. But the Kiwis are better—much better."

Ellison says that Dickson reminds him of his friend Steve Jobs, the founder and once-again boss of Apple Computer. "Dickson wants everyone to do everything perfectly all the time. He's so brilliant at what he does and so unforgiving of himself that he becomes unforgiving of others." Erkelens adds, "The parts of Chris's personality that rub some people up the wrong way don't really seem to get to Larry. He's getting all the benefits without the negative impacts of Chris's methods, which isn't to say that Chris doesn't qualify his behavior around Larry a little bit . . . even though I'm pretty sure that Chris has had a little shout at Larry here and there under extreme stress." * But while Dickson may be willing to yell at Ellison just like any other member of the crew, he doesn't forget that it's Ellison who's paying the bills. When Ellison made it clear that he wanted to sail the start of the 1998 Hobart, despite the risk of an accident because of the hundreds of yachts jockeying for position in Sydney Harbor, Dickson had no objections. On the eve of the race, he told the other *Sayonara* helmsmen, "He'll have the helm for the start, and he'll keep it until he gets sick of it. I'll be there to give him guidance. He's the boss, and that's it."

The 1998 Sydney-to-Hobart, which *Sayonara* won, has gone down in yachting history as one of the most lethal ocean races ever: only 43 of the 115 boats that started made it to Hobart. When the fleet hit hurricane-force winds in the Bass Strait, which separates Australia from Tasmania, seven boats were abandoned at sea, five sank, and six sailors lost their lives despite the heroism of the air-sea rescue services. Ellison has said he was traumatized by the experience, and he has sworn never to enter the race again.†

Erkelens had a close-up view of how Ellison responded to the stress and the physical danger: "Well, I think he and the rest of the crew were in

---

*LE writes: Once, right after the start of a race, Chris wanted me to sail the boat between 10.4 and 10.5 knots. He had good tactical reasons for having me do that. If the boat ever dropped to 10.3 knots or got up to 10.6 knots, I heard about it. I like that about Chris. His job is to win races, and he expects everyone to perform, me included.

†LE writes: I wasn't "traumatized" by the race, but I sure didn't enjoy it. I'd have to be an idiot to spend any more of my Christmas holidays throwing up on a sailboat. (The Sydney-to-Hobart race starts on December 26.)

awe of the size of the seas, the conditions of the ocean, not just the wind. There was wind, sixty-eight knots or whatever, but the sea state was much bigger than that wind would normally kick up. Even people on our boat that had done three or four Whitbreads (the around-the-world yacht race) were amazed at the size of the waves. It was difficult for everyone, it was physically stressful . . . you could not sleep, you were being bruised by the waves smashing you. Larry told me that he was comfortable in the situation as long as we—the rest of the crew—were comfortable. The point is, I think, that he had confidence in us, confidence that we would get through it. He could have been in a safer place, that's for sure. But if you were going to do it, you could not have been with a better group of people. I think that helped him deal with the situation." *

For Erkelens, Ellison's finest hour as owner-driver of *Sayonara* was not the 1998 Hobart but a long-distance race to Bermuda that was part of the 1997 Maxi World Championships. The race was worth 1.5 times the normal number of points to the winner, but it didn't go well for *Sayonara*. Erkelens says, "It was a real light-air race, and on the evening before we finished, we saw boats several miles ahead of us on the horizon jibing to make Bermuda on starboard. We were losing the regatta at that stage." The leading boat was *Alexia*. If *Alexia* won the race and *Sayonara* failed to finish higher than fourth, *Alexia* would win the World Championship by half a point. The race tacticians thought they had come up with a way to use the wind angles to bring *Sayonara* back into contention. But if they guessed wrong and the winds became lighter again, *Sayonara* would not be able to take advantage of her superior size. In fact, the wind did begin to lighten. Erkelens says, "I remember Larry saying, 'You guys . . . I think we need to jibe.' So we jibed back and he made a strong call, some people were rumbling a little bit, we jibed back into the cloud and got another six knots' breeze or so and sailed for another hour and a half. It turned out we had sailed around them all except *Alexia*. At that stage *Alexia* was fifty miles ahead, but by the finish we had shaved that down to about six. It took another ten hours for the rest of the boats to even finish. That really impressed me. It was the biggest single gain we ever made in a race."

LE writes: The crew was simply amazing. The boat was leaping off these huge waves, but somehow they managed to put up the storm sails. Think about a rodeo cowboy trying to change shirts while riding a bull. I've never seen anything like it.

• • •

Ellison first learned to sail when he came to California in the mid-1960s. He took a sailing course at the University of California and got started on "a little plastic boat called a Lido 14." He says, "I should tell people I attended the University of California and majored in sailing." He enjoyed it so much that a year or so later, when he was twenty-five, he bought first a twenty-four-foot boat and then something quite substantial: a thirty-four-foot racing sloop. "I was passionate about sailing and the idea of sailing . . . the idyllic independence . . . traveling with the wind . . . that kind of stuff. I guess a lot of people have dreams of sailing around the world. I was one of them. I remember reading Robin Lee Graham's story of sailing his twenty-four-foot sloop, the *Dove,* around the world. It was published in *National Geographic.* I'm pretty sure it was the most popular story they ever ran." But if Ellison, like most other leisure sailors, fantasized about circumnavigation, the reality was more prosaic: "I was just racing around the bay, sailing out to the Farallons [islands 27 miles west of San Francisco] and back. I was having a good time. The trouble was, I really couldn't afford it." The point was driven home to him when racing *Galilee Hitchhiker,* the thirty-four-footer he had bought by borrowing $25,000. During a slight storm at the start of a light-ship race, the jib halyard broke and Ellison's first wife, Adda, nearly fell overboard trying to bring the expensive sail back on board. Soon afterward he sold the boat. "I finally had to accept that eating came before sailing in Maslow's hierarchy of needs." Adda had become so worried about how much money the boat was eating that she was driven to seek counseling.

It was years before he got back on the water. He was a wealthy man from the day that Oracle went public in 1985. Surely, when he looked at other people's boats, he must have thought, "Why don't I go and get one like that?" "It just never really occurred to me. When I wanted to go on holiday, I'd always go to warm places near the water, like Kona Village in Hawaii, but I never went on boats. I read, rode my bike, surfed a bit, but no boats. As my son, David, got older, he rekindled my interest in a lot of things. He got me back into flying. He got me back into playing guitar. Another David [Thompson] got me back into sailing. Then my ex-girlfriend Kristine convinced me to buy my first motor yacht. It was the summer of 1996, and we were in Sardinia for the maxi sailing world championships. Kristine was standing at the dock and staring at this huge, white 200-foot luxury motor yacht. Suddenly she pointed at *Sayonara* and said, 'That's not a yacht.' She then pointed at the 200-footer and said, 'That's a yacht.' To my credit, I immediately recognized that she was right, so I went right out and bought *October Rose* [renamed *Sakura* by Ellison and subsequently the center of a legal dispute with the yacht broker], a 192-footer, from Kirk Kerkorian for around $10 million. I'd never even been on a big motor yacht until I bought one."

What Ellison seemed to be saying was that it had taken him a while to realize he was rich enough to indulge whatever desire he might have. "It's true," he says. "My life had been focused on work, work, and more work. Oracle had crashed in 1991, and I couldn't rest until it was healthy again. I didn't have any time to spend money or think about spending money. I bought a house [in Atherton] in 1992, but that was my only house, and I only had one car. The car was a Mazda RX7. Don Lucas told me I had to get rid of the RX7 and buy a more appropriate car for business. I loved my old rotary-engine RX7, but Don was right, so I sold the RX7 and bought a big silver Mercedes. A few years back Mike Seashols [Oracle's then head of sales] had looked at my cheap Seiko watch and said, 'Come on, Larry, you shouldn't wear a watch like that. You should have a Rolex.' He then handed me his solid gold Rolex President so I could feel how heavy it was. I went out a bought a Rolex, but in stainless. I just couldn't deal with the gold. Anyway, it took a while and a lot of help from my friends, but I'm now world class at buying things. I moved from Rolex to Patek Philippe. I still have a Mercedes, a couple of them actually, plus the new BMW Z8, a McLaren F1, and a Bentley. It took me a while to learn how to spend money, but once I got started"—Ellison laughs—"I discovered that I have a real talent for it." *

So when David Thompson put the idea into Ellison's head that he might like to get himself a maxi yacht, he was pushing on an open door. But why did he want a pure racing machine instead of just a really nice, big sailing boat? "I talked with Rupert Murdoch about the big luxury sailing yacht that he and his family enjoy spending time on. But I never thought of sailing as a form of relaxation. To me, sailing is about adventure and competition. Sailing is completely unpredictable. If Mother Nature decides to make things difficult for you, it can get pretty intense, pretty fast. You always have to be prepared for that. If I want to relax, I'll read a book." I'd mentioned to Ellison a few days earlier a theory I had that people who had very intense work lives often found relaxing diffi-

---

LE writes: While I enjoy spending my own money, I still hate spending Oracle's money. I'm very cheap at the office. We have no company planes, no company cars, no company art, etc.

cult and that the best they could do was to find some alternative stress that so fully engaged their attention that it drove everything else out of their mind. Ellison said, "That's certainly true for me. I'd never heard the expression 'alternative stress' until you said it, but it immediately struck me as a perfect explanation for all my hobbies. Sailing and flying are definitely alternative stress activities. Driving the boat or the plane demands total concentration. Playing classical guitar is not stressful, exactly, unless I do it in public, but it requires one hundred percent of my attention."

So the idea of racing at the very highest level just seemed like an obvious thing to do if you were going to do it at all? "Why not? I could afford a big maxi boat—they're slightly larger than the America's Cup boats and maybe slightly faster—and the idea of racing one seemed very exciting to me. My nephew, Judge Jimmy, wanted me to buy a basketball team. But if I bought an NBA team, league rules would prevent me from playing point guard—that plus a strong aversion to public humiliation. Anyway, the point is, I don't want to watch; I want to play. I want to be a part of the team. I want to be taught by, coached by, and sail with the best people in the business. I like feeling a part of the team at Oracle. I enjoy the people I work with very, very much; otherwise I couldn't spend so much of my time with them. Sailing is similar in one way, because I love working with the *Sayonara* crew, but it's totally different in another, because I'm not the star. I'm just a pretty good amateur driver. The rest of the *Sayonara* crew are the best professional sailors on the planet. Chris Dickson, Brad Butterworth—these guys are unbelievably good at what they do. They're the best. When we won our four maxi world championships, I usually raced against other amateur drivers, but some of the time I got a chance to drive against the best professional drivers in the world. I've even been at the wheel of *Sayonara* when Russell Coutts was driving *Morning Glory*. Imagine going head-to-head with Russell Coutts! How cool is that?" *

From 1996, *Sayonara* competed in all the maxi-yacht series and nearly all the major ocean races. Ellison says that he missed only one, when his daughter, Megan, was graduating from grammar school. Sailing for several weeks every year, he also thinks his driving skills became better than

---

*LE writes: I drove our America's Cup boat quite a bit during the Louis Vuitton Cup leading up to the 2003 America's Cup, but I never got a chance to drive against Russell. I sure would have liked to have driven my America's Cup boat against Russell, just to be able to say I did.

respectable: "I'm very focused. I put the time in, and my driving got better and better. I did most of the driving during all four of our maxi world championships. *Sayonara* won every buoy regatta she ever entered. The second-best maxi team, *Morning Glory* [owned by SAP CEO Hasso Plattner and skippered by Russell Coutts], never beat us, not even in one race. We came second in a couple of ocean races, like Bermuda, but we won every buoy regatta. I'm very proud of that. One of the reasons I did the 1998 Hobart was to find out how much I had improved as a driver since 1995, the first time I did the Hobart. I thought I had improved a lot. I wanted to test myself." The time Ellison spent sailing—the alternative stress—coincided with accusations from within the company that his new interest and his new toys were taking him away from Oracle.

Naturally, he doesn't agree. "Winning is a habit. So is losing. Competing and winning at sailing has made me more confident, intense, and determined to win at Oracle. Winning breeds winning. The more you win, the more you want to win. The more you win, the more you think you can win. Three of our four world championships were very close. I won a key start against *Morning Glory;* I drove past *Boomerang* during the first windward beat after she got out ahead of us at the start; and I made the critical tactical call on the Bermuda race. Had I screwed those three things up, we would have won only one world championship. But I didn't screw up, and we won four. I did my job, and so did everyone else on the crew. So we ended up winning them all—even one that seemed utterly hopeless.

"One year, the final race of the maxi world championships was the ocean race to Bermuda. We were comfortably in first place after the buoy racing finished, but we still had to finish at least fourth in the Bermuda race to take the championship. Now, ocean races are rarely included in world championship regattas because they are much more subject to chance than racing around the buoys. You can have the fastest boat and the best crew and still lose an ocean race. In an ocean race the boats are often tens of miles apart, some in much more favorable wind than others. Well, the wind gods really had it in for Brad [Butterworth] on this race. The first two nights, the moment Brad came on watch the wind just died. [During ocean races *Sayonara* races with twenty-four people, who are divided into three groups of eight. Two of the groups are on watch up on deck while the third group sleeps below.] We were becalmed for two nights in a row. We just went nowhere for hours and hours. After the second day's position report, we knew we were in tenth place, behind some boats we had never even heard of. Desperate times call for desperate measures. I looked at the latest weather charts on the computer and decided our best chance would be to head as far to the left side of the race-course as possible, where we might pick up more breeze and a better wind angle. This was a very risky bet. Conventional wisdom says that on a long race you stay near the middle of the racecourse and keep your tactical options open. Anyway, I overruled the tactical team and sent the boat to the far left-hand side of the racecourse. We were so far behind I thought that the only chance we had was sailing in a part of the ocean where there were no other race boats. If we got lucky, we'd get a favorable breeze all to ourselves. That's exactly what happened. The further left we sailed, the more breeze we got. Then we got a favorable shift in the wind direction. Everything came good. We rocketed on by all the boats that were in front of us except *Alexia*. It was a high-risk call, and I got lucky, okay, I know that. It was a lucky call. But it was my call at a critical time, and it gave us the championship. I'll never forget it.

"Another thing I'll never forget is the start of one of the buoy races during the world championships in Newport, Rhode Island. It was just before the gun, and *Morning Glory* was well set up near the starboard end of the starting line. I had *Sayonara* to the right of *Morning Glory*, and it looked like there was no room between them and the buoy. We were both on starboard tack, and *Morning Glory* had right-of-way because she was the leeward boat. If I couldn't squeeze between *Morning Glory* and that right-hand buoy, I was going to have a very bad start. So we eased the sails a bit and headed directly for *Morning Glory* at about twelve knots. As we closed to about half a boat length of *Morning Glory*, the guys on *Sayonara* started screaming, 'No room, no room, turn the boat.' Anyway, at the last second I turned up hard. I was going to get a penalty if I touched either *Morning Glory* or the buoy. But I made it. We started two feet to the right of *Morning Glory* and two feet to the left of the buoy. It was very close to a massive high-speed collison. We had lots of speed at the start, so we quickly got over the top of *Morning Glory*, and Chris had me tack onto port and head out to protect the favored right-hand side of the course. I said, 'Chris, Chris, did you hear those guys screaming, "Turn the boat, no room, turn the boat"?' He stares intensely right at me with those blue laser eyes and asks, 'Did you hear me screaming?' I said, 'No.' Then Chris smiles slightly and says, 'Nice start.' I think, 'Wow; Chris never smiles.' It was my best start ever."

• • •

Ellison knew that the 1998 Sydney-to-Hobart race was likely to be tough. The wave conditions in the Bass Strait usually guarantee that.

"The Southern Ocean, the ocean that circles Antarctica, is unique because there's no landmass interrupting a wave's journey around the world. The waves just continuously travel around and around, getting bigger and bigger. The world's biggest waves, sometimes more than a hundred feet high, form in the Southern Ocean. The shallowest part of the Southern Ocean is a ninety-five-mile stretch of water between southeastern Australia and the island of Tasmania. It's called Bass Strait. When big waves pass over a shallow sea floor, they become very steep. The friction of the sea floor slows the bottom of the wave and causes the face of the wave to become a vertical wall of water [he makes a gesture with his hands]. Under severe conditions the waves can break. The shallows trip the wave and topple it over forward, just like a wave approaching a beach. In Bass Strait the waves always have steep vertical faces, and they come very close together. They hit your boat in rapid succession—bang, bang, bang—very unpleasant. But they almost never break. In an ocean storm it's not the speed of the winds or the height of the waves that threatens your survival, it's the steepness and the frequency of the waves. The constant battering of steep, high-frequency waves can break critical gear and cause crew injuries. A single breaking wave can cause severe structural damage and send a boat to the bottom in a couple of minutes."

Ellison had wanted to do the race again because he thought he was now good enough to be the primary driver and it was a way of proving himself both as a sailor and as a man. Compared to the big-wave body surfing in Hawaii a couple of years earlier, where he had broken his neck and nearly been left a paraplegic, sailing the Hobart seemed perfectly sensible—macho, but not potentially deadly. It made you more impressive in the eyes of others and gave you a collection of exhilarating memories. He says, "The Sydney-to-Hobart is one of those events that everyone thinks of as cool because it's dangerous. But it's not really a dangerous race, I mean, it's not life-threatening, it's just a hard, demanding race. You have to be reasonably fit to cope with the pounding in Bass Strait, but it's pretty unlikely that you'll get hurt. In 1995, we hit winds of about forty-five knots, got banged around a bit, and won the race. It was just your typical Sydney-to-Hobart. The 1998 Sydney-to-Hobart was not typical. I don't know how, but somehow I managed to pick the one year out of a hundred when the risk wasn't an illusion. We sailed into a hurricane.

"During the morning weather briefing, we were warned that there was going to be a storm—forty-plus knots—in the Bass Strait. What a surprise. Predicting a storm in the Sydney-to-Hobart is like predicting a cool summer night in San Francisco. Summer nights are always cool in San

Francisco. So wear a sweater. No one was concerned about the storm forecast. No boats pulled out of the race. The weather in Sydney was absolutely perfect. It was warm and sunny, and nearly a hundred and fifty boats were tacking and jibing around the most beautiful harbor in the world, trying to get into a good position for the start of the race. During our prerace maneuvering we managed to break a carbon fiber gear in one of our brand-new winches. Dickson got really pissed off: 'How the hell can we break one of our main winches in light air before the goddamned race has even started?' It was a good question. We only had about ten knots of breeze, and you're not supposed to break stuff in light air. I was driving the boat, and I was glad he didn't blame me for the damage. Anyway, we didn't have time to fix the winch before the start of the race, so I had to tack the boat very slowly and very carefully. That made starting more difficult.

"Chris was standing right behind me, barking out tactical instructions. I was at the wheel, doing what I was told. Chris had me stay away from *Nokia,* the biggest boat in the fleet, because they had a nasty habit of banging into nearby boats. We were looking for a safe start. We got *Sayonara* into a good position for the beginning of the race, the gun went off, and we got up to speed. We did our tacks slowly and precisely. It was a good start. We rounded the first mark ahead of the rest of the fleet. *Sayonara* was the first boat to sail out of the harbor, through Sydney Heads, and turn to the south. Hobart is due south of Sydney; you set a course of exactly 180 degrees. As we made our right turn to the south, we dropped the jib and set the spinnaker. The breeze was out of the northeast and increasing. We were going through the water at about fifteen or sixteen knots. It was just about as perfect as sailing conditions could get. We had no idea what was going to happen to us over the next three days. If we had, we would have turned left and gone up north to the Great Barrier Reef. That's where all the sensible people having sensible Christmas holidays go. Instead we turned right and raced down the Australian coast toward the island of Tasmania.

"The wind was very puffy and heavy with moisture. These big puffs would hit the chute [spinnaker], and the boat would suddenly lift up and accelerate through the water. We were absolutely flying down the coast. It was very exciting. Then this really big puff hits the chute, and it just explodes—gone—ripped to pieces. We had a nice lead on *Brindabella,* the number two boat, but they caught up to us before we were able to set another spinnaker, a smaller one this time. I blamed myself for blowing the chute. If at the beginning of the puff I had come down fast enough—

turned the boat five or ten degrees to the right—maybe I could have saved the chute. I had been driving the boat for a couple of hours, and maybe I was getting tired. I thought I must have been sailing the boat at too high an angle. That's what put too much pressure on the spinnaker. Maybe I should get off the wheel. So I asked Brad [Butterworth] if he wants to drive. The wind is getting stronger, and it's very puffy, very heavy. It feels different from anything I'd ever experienced. We're now doing eighteen or nineteen knots, and I'm looking back, checking our lead on *Brindabella*. Then bang, we blew a second chute. The wind was twenty-five, gusting thirty. And the wind was continuing to build. After blowing two chutes we decided to be safe and set the mini—our smallest, strongest spinnaker. The mini is an unbreakable sail. The mast will rip off the boat before the mini blows up. Brad and I were taking turns driving, and the wind just kept on building. *Sayonara* was surfing through the water at amazing speeds: twenty-two knots, twenty-four knots, twenty-six knots. It was amazing. Maxi racing sailboats don't go twenty-six knots. But we were going twenty-six knots. Twelve hours into the race, *Sayonara* had gone twice as far—twice as fast—as the Sydney-to-Hobart race record holder. Wow, that's incredible. But what the hell is happening here? Why the fuck are we going twenty-six knots?

"Then this monster puff hits the boat. And the minispinnaker is gone. That's impossible. The mini can't break. Then I realize the mini didn't break, the spinnaker pole lost its fitting. The spinnaker pole is no longer attached to the mast, it's just swinging wildly through the air. That metal alloy fitting is threaded into the spinnaker pole for about a meter. A meter's worth of three-quarter-inch metal alloy thread had just been extruded through our carbon-fiber spinnaker pole. What kind of force would that take? A hundred thousand pounds, something like that. That can't happen, can it? But I had seen it. We're talking about bringing up our other spinnaker pole, but the wind is rapidly clocking right—from the northeast to the east—so we set a jib instead. Soon the wind will be coming from the southeast. We're almost to Bass Strait.

"At the beginning of the race, just after you leave Sydney Harbor, you get prevailing winds out of the northeast. As you make your way south, the wind starts to shift around to the right. This clockwise shift is called the 'southerly buster,' and it rapidly takes the wind around from the northeast to southeast to the southwest. We were now well into the southerly buster, and the new wind was coming from the southeast. We had been carrying a jib for some time, and now we were hard on the wind, pointing the bow of the boat as close as possible to the direction the wind is coming from. The sun was setting, the sky was covered with black clouds, and it had started to rain. The wind was blowing over forty knots and still building. As we entered Bass Strait, the sea state got dramatically worse. The steep waves started pounding against the bow of the boat, making it difficult for me to hold my course. We ease the sheets a bit to reduce the stress on the boat, the driver, and the rest of the crew. The winds pick up to over fifty knots, and it starts raining harder. Rain and salt spray at fifty knots feels like someone is repeatedly stabbing you in the face with an ice pick. Everyone except the driver and the trimmers are facing away from the wind. The sea state is getting worse and worse. The twenty- to twenty-five-foot waves are straight up and down—they look like row after row of three-story bubbling glass office buildings. I think to myself, 'It's a lot worse than last time, but I can do it.'

"The winds hit sixty knots, and the seas continued to build. The sky is black. The ocean is black. There's no horizon. The waves I could see were huge, but I couldn't see most of them behind the rain and spray. As we rode up a wave, the wind would increase and I'd have to compensate for the change in apparent wind angle by turning the bow toward the wind. Then the boat would fall and slide into the trough. The wind speed in the troughs was half the wind speed on the crests. I had to constantly adjust the angle of the boat. But I couldn't see a thing, and the instruments were reacting too slowly to be of any help. I had to drive by feel. The roar of the wind and the waves made it impossible to be heard unless you screamed. Brad was trying to help me through it. He screamed, 'Larry, head up, head up now, now!' I screamed back, 'I'm trying, I'm trying!' But then, 'I can't do it, Brad. Take it, take it, you take it.' I let go, and Brad Butterworth grabbed the wheel. I couldn't drive in those conditions; I just couldn't do it. But Brad could. Brad Butterworth is a sailing god.

"The 1998 Sydney-to-Hobart wasn't even a day old, and I had already been overwhelmed and beaten by the Southern Ocean. I wanted to find my limits, and I found them in Bass Strait. I couldn't imagine conditions getting any worse, and for a while, they seemed to be getting better. I was on deck when the wind suddenly started dropping. Brad was driving, and the winds had come down to around ten knots. It was eerie. The waves were still big, but the sky was clear and you could see the stars and the horizon. I thought, 'If I can see, I can drive.' It seemed as if we had passed through this enormous weather front and we were now safe on the other side. We had our small storm sails up, and we weren't making much progress in the light breeze. We were just wallowing up and down in the big waves. After about ten minutes or so of this I thought that we should set our heavy number one jib. Brad thought that we should wait a while longer, but I was impatient so I said, 'Brad, let's set the heavy and get going.' Brad was still hesitant, he thought that we should leave the storm sails set, but he agreed to put up the larger jib while I headed down below to the nav station to check the satellite weather charts that were due to come in shortly.

"*Sayonara*'s navigation station is located belowdecks in the aft portion of the boat right below the boat's two steering wheels. It consists of a forward-facing bench with enough room for two, three if you really squeeze. In front of the bench are some radios and two laptop computers. I sat down next to Mark Rudiger [the boat's navigator] as the satellite images were being slowly painted on the computer screens. This image starts to appear on the top of the screen, we can see the Australian coast, and it works its way down to where we are in Bass Strait. I just can't believe my eyes. I keep staring at the screen. It's displaying a circular weather formation with our boat positioned right in the middle of it. Still staring at the screen, I ask Rudiger, 'Mark, have you ever seen anything like this before?' He doesn't say anything, so I turn and see him staring at the screen and slowly shaking his head. I say, 'Well, I have. It was on the Weather Channel. It was called fucking Hurricane Helen. We're in the eye of a fucking hurricane.' Then all of a sudden I hear Brad up on deck; he's screaming, 'The wind's coming, the wind's coming fast, get that fucking jib down, get it down on deck now.' The wind went from ten to over fifty [knots] in less than a minute. Unbelievable. We had sailed into the eye of a hurricane. I thought we had sailed through a front."

Along with everyone else, he was shocked by the ferocity of the weather conditions and physically drained by the battering and the sickness, but he was still able to come up with a steady supply of quips that Ellison himself admits sound rather smart-alecky in retrospect. But how had he coped with what must have been real terror?*

"Fear is interesting. Everyone on the crew was loaded up on adrenaline, the fight-or-flight thing. But we were all stuck in fight mode for one simple reason: there was no place to run. When you're busy in fight mode, you don't have time to think about being scared. The worst time for me was when I was in my bunk trying to get a little sleep. I hadn't

---

*LE writes: I remember very few quips and a lot of throwing up. I threw up so many times I lost count. I was very surprised because I never get motion sickness, not flying aerobatics, not sailing in heavy seas. But this was different. The entire crew was sick, even the guys who never get sick.

slept or eaten for a couple of days. I had thrown up so often that I was dehydrated. Throwing up over and over again with nothing in your stomach feels like your guts are being ripped out. I was totally exhausted. So I wedged myself into my bunk and tried to sleep. It was hopeless. After two days of seventy- to eighty-knot hurricane-force winds the seas were massive. The waves I saw were forty or fifty feet high, but some guys on the crew saw waves higher than the top of our mast [the top of *Sayonara's* mast is 105 feet above the deck].

"The waves were so steep that we didn't get the normal ride up the front of the wave and down and back. Instead, *Sayonara* would bury her bow deep into the wall of water coming at us, then the buoyancy of the boat would lift us up to the crest of the wave. It was like going up in an elevator. Then *Sayonara* would exit the wave and free-fall into the trough. It felt like she was being pushed off a five-story office building and landing on asphalt every twenty seconds. If guys didn't hang on when we started falling, they would float up off the foredeck. I saw one guy up at the first spreader [more than forty feet above the deck]. Several guys on deck broke bones, one severely enough that he had to be put in an inflatable leg cast, pumped full of morphine, and strapped to his bunk.

"Riding out the storm in your bunk was no picnic, either. Every time Sayonara would go airborne—start falling off these huge, steep waves— you'd go weightless in your bunk, then the boat would crash down into the water, crunching you back into your bunk. The impact of the boat hitting the trough sounded like an explosion. The noise below was amazing. The hull acts like a huge bass amplifier. It sounded and felt like we were being hit by explosive shells fired from the *Bismarck*. The bow hits the wave, we take the elevator up, we go weightless, then BOOM. Over and over, again and again. BOOM—BOOM—BOOM. Then I see Tugboat [Mark Turner], our chief engineer, with a red Magic Marker, and he's drawing these red circles on the inside of the hull where the bow section meets the forward bulkhead. I say, 'Tugsy, what are you doing?' He says, 'I'm marking the spots where the bow is delaminating.' I say, 'What? The bow is delaminating? You mean the bow is coming apart? This is fucking ridiculous!'

"I push myself out of my bunk and head back to the navigation station, and I ask Mark Rudiger to pull out a chart and show me where we are. We're about seventy nautical miles off the northeast coast of Tasmania. The winds are out of the southwest, and we're banging our way south on starboard tack. I want to tack the boat onto port and head west toward Tasmania. I figure if we can get close enough to the lee of the island we should get some relief from these big waves that are trying to kill us. I tell Rudiger to tack the boat. He tells me that he thinks that tacking the boat will hurt our chances of winning the race. I say, 'We won't win the race if we sink. Tack the fucking boat.' Mark says, 'Okay, I'll go up and talk it over with Chris.' As soon as we tack over onto port, we get immediate relief. The new angle the boat is hitting the waves is less punishing. After a few hours we start to get close to the lee shore of Tasmania, and the wind and the waves begin to diminish. We had made it through the storm. The worst was over. Then we pick up this favorable wind shift. Tacking the boat turned out to be the right thing to do for the race, too. God was smiling on us. We won the race by quite a bit. But no one really cared. We were all just glad to be alive."

When *Sayonara* arrived first across the line in Hobart, after the inevitable "What was it like?" questions, Ellison was asked if he would be coming back to defend his title. "I remember saying, 'No, not if I live to be a thousand.' Then I thought about it for a moment and said, 'Hold it, wait a second, if I live to be a thousand, I'll come back. Chris, do you want to come back with me? Mark this down, a thousand years from now, we'll be back.' "

But for now, Ellison is going America's Cup sailing. He says, "The best thing about the America's Cup is that they don't sail it in Bass Strait during a hurricane. In the America's Cup you never race in more than twenty-five knots of breeze. You just go out for a few hours, race around the buoys, and come back in for a nice seafood-and-pasta dinner. Everyone dresses up, very civilized, perfect for my old age."

18

SAYONARA SWAN SONG

July 2001

Although Ellison will spend most of his seven-week summer vacation aboard *Katana* in the Mediterranean, he's starting his holiday by flying the Citation to his hometown for the annual "Chicago Mac" sailing race. With a fuel stop at Grand Junction, Colorado, it's a six-hour flight into Midway Airport. Despite the rigors of the weekend ahead, Ellison insists on flying the plane with Jeff as copilot. It's a gorgeous, clear night, and the burning lights of Chicago are clearly visible an hour before we begin our descent. Although tired, Ellison exults in the view of his hometown. One of his more endearing qualities is that he never loses his capacity for excitement. Although the technical demands of flying a plane appeal to him, like many pilots he is in love with the sheer beauty of what he sees from the cockpit.

The next morning, some fifteen Ellison family and friends have gathered in the dining room at the Ritz-Carlton, where he has stayed overnight. His sister, Doris, is there with her son Judge Jimmy Linn. Jimmy is coming on the race, and he's already in the Team Sayonara gear: logoed caps, T-shirts, and shorts. Jimmy is an unlikely sailor, but it's his third Chicago Mac. It's a race that Ellison enjoys, partly for the opportunity it gives him to turn it into a family event and also because it allows him to cut a dash in front of people who knew him as a kid.

The running joke over brunch is how appalling the food is on *Sayonara*, and Ellison claims to be furious with himself for having failed to take personal charge of provisioning, leaving it to the boat's engineer/

cook, Tugboat.* On the previous year's Chicago Mac, the food was so dreadful that it almost caused a fight. Ellison says, "It wasn't just disgusting, it was actually dangerous. I don't know how Tugsy managed it, but the chicken was burnt on the outside and still raw and frozen on the inside. I really thought Robbie Naismith was going to kill him, and Robbie's a pretty easygoing guy. But first Robbie burned his mouth, then almost broke a tooth biting into the frozen part. He was convinced that Tugsy was trying to murder us. Robbie said we were going to lose the race because the whole crew was going to die of salmonella." Ellison thinks it can't be so bad again. But just to be on the safe side, he decides to stop off at a deli on the way to the boat and stock up on cans of sardines. It turns out to be a smart move.

By the time we arrive at the marina, *Sayonara* and most of the other three hundred or so boats that will contest the 333-mile race—the world's longest on fresh water, up Lake Michigan to tiny Mackinac Island—are a mile or two offshore, jockeying for position and making last-minute inspections before the 2 P.M. start. Even amid such an armada, *Sayonara* is easily identifiable. Not only is her mast taller than anyone else's, it is made out of jet black carbon fiber. Whereas for the others, this is perhaps their most important race of the season, *Sayonara* is more used to competing and winning in the world maxi-yacht championships against the fastest and most expensive sailing boats ever built. In fact, after winning four out of four world championships, *Sayonara* has more or less killed off the class—the owners of the other boats, such as Hasso Plattner, chairman of Oracle rival SAP, are fed up spending their millions and routinely losing.

And despite the warm sunshine, the gentle breeze, and the sheer beauty of Chicago's skyscrapers shimmering on the shoreline, there is a quiet intensity about Ellison's crew—it's as if you had put down the McLaren Formula One team amid some weekend club racers. The most striking thing about the crew, almost all of whom have sailed together on *Sayonara* for all six of the years it has campaigned and are now part of

---

*LE writes: I was more apprehensive than "furious." Years of experience had taught me to fear the food on Sayonara. Tugsy wasn't solely responsible for our history of bad food. Jeff Stag would bring only freeze-dried stuff because he wanted to save weight. T. A. McCann was a vegetarian who thought the crew could live on PowerBars and nuts. I think we sailed faster than other boats because the crew wanted to finish, get off, and get a good meal.

Ellison's Oracle Racing America's Cup team, is that they are not young guys but grizzled veterans with lined faces and graying hair. *Sayonara* has won this race for the last two years, and the Chicago Yacht Club has handicapped her harshly. To win outright, she must cross the line seventy-five minutes ahead of the next most potent yacht in the race, a big turbosled named *Decision* that beat *Sayonara* once before in the Trans-Pac from Los Angeles to Hawaii.* If we get a following wind for any length of time during the race, the sleds, with their flat sterns, are quite likely to outrun us, whereas *Sayonara* is unbeatable upwind. Ellison claims that she is still the fastest upwind boat ever built. The forecast is for the wind to turn all the way around the clock in the next thirty-six hours.

I'm already hoping that it's not going to be a long race. As Ellison promised, *Sayonara* is an uncompromising racing machine with almost nothing in the way of creature comforts. When Bill Erkelens takes the guests below, he warns us to try to avoid using the solitary toilet—the message is to piss over the side and shit only if you really have to. To comply with local environmental regulations, *Sayonara* has been fitted with a holding tank, but to keep weight down it's relatively tiny—certainly too small to deal with the digestions of twenty-four men if it's a slow race. The second shock is the realization that there are only eight berths to share among us. The idea is that there will be alternating watches of three hours off, six hours on. To call them berths is an exaggeration; they are more like narrow hammocks placed one on top of the other. As for the cooking, there's a solitary gimbaled burner.

Ellison informs me that other maxi yachts have owner's staterooms that provide their skippers with a bit of comfort and privacy. "Nobody told me about owner's staterooms when we were building *Sayonara*. Then I found out that Hasso had one on *Morning Glory*, and I said, 'I'd like to have one of those.' But it was too late." He's actually quite proud of the fact that he doesn't get any special treatment on *Sayonara*, and maybe it's one of the things he enjoys about the whole experience. Although he owns the boat, he says he regards himself as a junior crew member in terms of status and ability. And while that's not quite the way

---

*LE writes: Decision beat us back in 1995. Back then she was called Cheval, and she beat us to Hawaii by forty minutes. It was a long race—nine days—and we came in second. It was Sayonara's first and only loss in our first few years of racing.

the others treat him, it's also true that there's no standing on ceremony. Being one of the guys at Oracle ceased to be an option nearly twenty years ago, but it's not something that worries him greatly. He does seem more relaxed in this environment, perhaps because the burden of performance is much more shared with others.

After the excitement of the start, there's the fun of overtaking all the slower boats that began the race in front of us. What's impressive is the constant searching for tiny improvements in performance by changing sails whenever there is the slightest shift in wind speed or direction to justify it. It helps having Robbie Naismith and Joey Allen aboard, both Kiwis and respectively the best sail trimmer and bowman in the world. As night falls, *Sayonara* appears to be in the lead and putting ever more distance between it and its nearest rival—as predicted, *Decision*. The mood onboard is relaxed, and nobody questions skipper Chris Dickson's strategy of heading as close to the mark as possible and not to go searching for better wind. We're making about ten knots with a gentle breeze on our port beam. Ellison drives for a while, but with Dickson trying to get some rest, he hands over to Mike "Moose" Sanderson, another New Zealander, content just to chat and enjoy the night.

The conversation is exclusively about sailing. With the collapse of the world maxi series, the richest and most competitive owners are building ever-bigger and more extreme boats. It seems that the years of *Sayonara*'s domination are coming to an end. Ranged against *Sayonara* in open-class racing now are likely to be monsters such as Gianni Agnelli's ninety-foot *Stealth* and Hasso Plattner's new 140-foot *Morning Glory*. But although they are very fast, especially downwind thanks to their huge sail areas, Moose reckons they have a flaw. Their vastness means that the tried-and-tested America's Cup–class equipment that could be used for the old maxi class is simply not up to the job, but the custom-built winches and the towering masts are inherently less robust. Ellison thinks that the answer may be to build a 150-foot two-masted ketch that could fly the same amount of sail without having to size everything up by more than 50 percent. The idea grows on him as we sail through the night. Racing in something a little more comfortable and less stripped down than *Sayonara* has a lot going for it. But only if a new boat can be as successful. The idea of racing and not regularly winning has no appeal to Ellison.

Meanwhile, it has become clear that *Sayonara* is going to have to fight to win this race. Through the night, a light on a boat sailing on the other side of the lake has been steadily making ground on us. At first nobody is concerned. It may not even be another racer, and if it is, it is sailing well away from the more or less direct route to Mackinac that Dickson has opted for. But as the light draws level and then overtakes us, the complacency evaporates. In the light airs in the middle of the lake, *Sayonara*'s speed has dropped to about eight knots, while the other boat seems to be making at least twelve knots. It's Dickson's turn to drive, and he asks Erkelens to give us accurate readings of how much ground we're losing each fifteen minutes or so. After half an hour, Dickson decides to bear off toward the rival boat in search of the extra wind that's pushed him past us. Suddenly, the idea that we might actually lose has entered everybody's head. Ellison is below, trying to get some sleep. Although nobody says anything, they don't want him to emerge at dawn to find us a distant second.

With hindsight, we should have moved to cover the other boat much sooner. As we move across the lake, the wind kicks up from little more than ten knots to nearly twenty, and *Sayonara* slowly starts to close the gap. By 4 A.M. we're close enough to see that *Sayonara*'s old nemesis *Decision* has managed to get the jump on us. Dickson has decided to close right in on *Decision* and then take her wind. It's a brilliant and ruthless piece of sailing. As we come within what seems like touching distance, *Decision* suddenly heads up to try cut us off. Immediately Dickson shouts, "No luffing, no luffing!" warning that what they're doing is illegal and that if they persist we'll flag them—issue a protest that will certainly lead to penalties. For a moment *Decision* seems anything but decisive. But by then *Sayonara* is level, and it's as if *Decision* has stopped dead in the water. Within twenty minutes *Sayonara* has opened up a gap of nearly a mile. By the time Ellison surfaces, unaware of the drama, *Decision* is a couple of miles distant but managing to match *Sayonara*'s pace.

For the rest of the morning, as we crawl northward to the Manitou Islands, the two boats cover each other, neither making ground on the other. If it carries on like this, *Decision* will finish ahead of *Sayonara* on corrected time because we carry a handicap of about an hour and a quarter. But as soon as we draw near the Manitous, the wind veers round to the north and picks up speed. By 2 P.M. it's raining hard, the breeze is blowing at a steady twenty-five knots down the channel, and *Sayonara* is doing what she does best—sailing close-hauled at fifteen knots into a mounting sea, the water creaming over her decks. It's also the kind of sailing that Ellison loves, and it's not long before he grabs the helm. If the conditions are now perfect for *Sayonara*, they're miserable for *Decision*, whose lack of stability means she is constantly being blown sideways. As

Decision falls ever farther behind until she becomes little more than a distant speck, Ellison exults, "Boy, we're really smoking 'em. They're not having any fun back there. They can kiss that corrected-time trophy good-bye."

But before dusk, the speck of *Decision*'s sail becomes just visible on the horizon some ten miles away. Despite Ellison's braggadocio, with only another two or three hours to Mackinac it's still touch and go whether *Sayonara* will have enough of a lead to overcome her handicap. I ask Ellison what matters more to him, winning on corrected time or being first to cross the finishing line. "That's easy," he says. "Being first to finish is what it's all about. This corrected-time stuff is totally arbitrary. A fully tricked-out turbosled like *Decision* should beat us in the Mac—actually finish in front of us—under some conditions. If the sailing is mainly upwind, we'll win. If the sailing is mainly downwind, they'll win. Some years the Mac's an upwind race. Some years the Mac's a downwind race. So how do they figure we owe her seventy-five minutes? Why not fifty minutes? Why not a hundred fifty minutes? The handicap is just a wild-ass guess." The other thing that would make Ellison happy would be to beat the record for the race, something he might have achieved when *Sayonara* sailed her first Chicago Mac if a piece of equipment had not failed a couple of miles from home. That's not going to happen now.*

Just then an appalling smell of burning comes drifting up from below. After a succession of cold meals, Tugboat has decided that what the crew needs to warm up is a steaming bowl of spaghetti bolognese. Unfortunately, the distinction between cooked and burned has once again eluded him. As the bowls of pasta are passed up on deck and the very brave or very hungry begin eating, the sheer nastiness of Tugboat's cooking becomes apparent. Some eat from necessity but immediately regret it. Others simply tip the muck into the water. Tugboat is furious and hurt by the ingratitude and is not even mollified when one of the grinders innocently asks him how he managed to introduce such an interesting "smokiness" to the flavor. Thank heaven for the sardines.

Ellison suddenly asks whether *Sayonara* should enter the Fastnet Race in a month's time. It's a notoriously tough course from the Isle of Wight to the Fastnet Rock off the southwest coast of Ireland and back again. The first thing to establish is whether it's possible even to get *Sayonara*

---

*LE writes: We broke the ram on our backstay a few minutes before finishing our first Mac. We missed the record by about a minute. Very disappointing.

there on such short notice. Unfazed, Bill Erkelens gets on the satellite phone to see if he can get a giant Russian Antonov transport plane to fly *Sayonara* to England. But Ellison's concern is whether *Sayonara* has a reasonable chance of winning against the new breed of supermaxis, *Stealth* and *Mari Cha*. Moose, who's sailed on both boats, is doubtful. The problem is that they won't be giving much away to *Sayonara* upwind, and downwind they're likely to give her a beating. Surely, Ellison persists, if much of the race is upwind, which it often can be, *Sayonara* has a chance. A chance, agrees Dickson, but a fairly slim one. Ellison decides to call Bruce Farr, *Sayonara*'s designer and the man responsible for coming up with the design that's meant to deliver Ellison the America's Cup, and get him to do some computer simulations. If *Sayonara*'s chances of winning are less than 50 percent, he doesn't want to do it. Besides, he has the excuse of not wanting to disrupt the training of the America's Cup team any more than it has been already. By the time Erkelens, looking very pleased with himself, announces that he has an Antonov on standby, Ellison's enthusiasm has significantly cooled.

It appears he also has other problems to deal with. Speaking low enough so that others can't hear, Chris Dickson tells Ellison that he's having problems in his relationship with Paul Cayard, the distinguished American sailor with whom he shares Oracle Racing's "afterguard." When Ellison bought the two boats from the AmericaOne syndicate that challenged for the cup in 1999, he bought with them a large part of the team and its infrastructure, including Cayard as the leader of the team and skipper. Although he and Ellison had never much liked each other after they had sailed together on *Sayonara* in her first year of competition, Cayard saw that Ellison's millions might bring him the cup after his own effort failed for want of funding. For his part, Ellison was prepared to go along with Cayard's involvement as long as he didn't try to take over Oracle Racing. But according to Dickson, that's exactly what's happening, and, even more dangerous, the AmericaOne veterans had become a team within a team, leaving some of the *Sayonara* boys isolated.

Suddenly, the rumors in the sailing press of a quayside fight a couple of months ago at Ventura Harbor, where the team is based, seem more solidly based. Ellison asks a couple of the guys closest to us how they feel about Cayard but gets back only cautiously noncommittal answers. The truth is that Cayard is not unpopular, while Dickson's edgy perfectionism and intensity can put a strain even on colleagues who are in awe of his abilities. While Cayard is happy to go drinking with the lads after work, Dickson unwinds only when he is back with his family. But for Ellison, a choice between Cayard and Dickson is a no-brainer. He had always expected that sooner or later he would have to sack Cayard from the team and even suggests that he might fly down to Ventura to see Cayard before leaving for Europe in three days' time. "Decisions like this are better made sooner than later," he says.*

When we eventually arrive first across the line at Mackinac and moor, the only welcoming committee is the wives and girlfriends of Team Sayonara. It's not entirely surprising. Not only is it 10:30 and a miserable, rainy night, but Ellison managed to offend the local yacht club after the near-record-breaking run a couple of years back. Asked by the beaming and beblazered commodore what the club can possibly do to make his stay on the island a happy one, a frustrated Ellison suggests a taxi to the airport. I'm worried about whether Ellison is in a fit state to fly the seven or eight hours back to San Carlos without sleep, but he's as keen to get away as before. We decide to go, leaving the crew, after midnight, downing drinks in the bar at the Lilac Tree and repelling the advances (or not) of local girls.

There are no cars allowed on the island, so we hail one of the horse-drawn taxis that ply for hire along Main Street, while Ellison rushes to the grocery (everything is open to greet the arriving fleet) to stock up with ice cream bars. We tell the young driver that we want to go to the airport (airstrip, more accurately) and load our bags onto the cart. It's only then that he delivers the bombshell that his horses have been working for six hours and local regulations demand that he change his team on the way to the airport. Dickson and the Judge, who has been seasick and looks shattered, implore the young man to take us to the airport directly. When he refuses, they get angry, telling him how important the passenger buying the ices is. Finally Dickson tries bribery, which is grudgingly accepted. When Ellison returns, the youth informs him that he's doing this only because he's been told that Ellison will "look after him."

And off we go at what seems like little more than walking speed. At the top of a hill, the driver suddenly halts his horses, to the consternation of Dickson and the judge. "The horses need a rest," he says stubbornly. "The horses shouldn't be doing this anyway. I look after my horses." Although as tired and desperate to get to the plane as the others, Ellison

---

*LE writes: Unfortunately, I didn't go to Ventura and I didn't make a sailing team leadership change at that time. My delay seriously hurt our chances of winning the America's Cup.

talks gently and approvingly to the young man, praising him for putting the welfare of his animals before the requirements of impatient passengers. From then until we get to the tiny airport fifteen minutes and several more stops later, Ellison and the driver chat about the horses and how they need to be cared for. When Ellison gives him a hundred-dollar bill at the end of the journey, a strange thing has happened. It no longer seems like a tip for bending the rules but a reward for standing up for his horses.*

*LE writes: When I was a kid, I used to like animals more than people.

19

FAMILY VALUES

Until his twelfth birthday, it had never occurred to Larry Ellison that he was adopted. "I can remember exactly where I was. I was standing in the doorway between the dining room and the kitchen, and my father tells me I'm adopted. That was it. They didn't give me any details. It was like 'Tonight we're having meat loaf, and, by the way, you're adopted.' It was many years down the road before I found out that my biological mother was my mother's niece."

Ellison's reaction to the news was in character: "I don't think I told anybody for a long time. I'm not sure I even thought about it that much. I just went straight into repression mode." Ellison once jokingly described himself as a "repressions-'R'-us kind of guy." He said, "If something's really unpleasant, I just don't think about it. I'm very good at doing the Scarlett O'Hara thing: 'I can't think about that today, I'll think about that tomorrow.' Repression has been a very useful tool for me to manage things that are painful or delay a confrontation until I'm better able to deal with it. Something made me put off dealing with the adoption until I was much older and more mature. So I just put it into cold storage and didn't deal with it at all. I'm sure that there are consequences to repression—knowing something like that and not dealing with it—but I have no idea what the consequences are. Anyway, repression makes the pain go away; I just freeze it and go live my life as best I can. When I'm a little bit stronger, a little bit smarter, I'll deal with it then."

In fact, it was thirty-four years before Ellison felt strong enough to deal with the emotional issues raised by his adoption. It was probably no coincidence that his resolve to confront his past was finally summoned up in 1992. In resolving the events that had come close to destroying the company, Ellison had come through eighteen months of fear, embarrassment, and public vilification. In doing so, he had learned something about his own resilience and ability to deal with intense pressure. He was also more confident than ever that Oracle had the strength to survive and prosper. Not only did he now have seasoned managers, such as Jeff Henley and Ray Lane, to keep the show on the road, but, with the release of Oracle 7, he knew that he now had a product that would sweep away the competition. In turning Oracle around, Ellison had been forced to ask questions about himself and to fight both inner demons and external threats. He decided that the moment had come to try to discover something about who he really was.

Ellison says, "I'd always been curious about my biological parents, but don't ask questions unless you want answers. After Oracle's crisis, looking into the abyss and surviving, I felt emotionally strong enough to take a more realistic look at myself. I was tired of striving to be the person I thought I should be. If I was to have any chance at happiness, I had to understand and accept who I really was. That required me to ask some questions about my past and live with the answers, regardless of what they turned out to be."

• • •

The facts of Ellison's early life are these. He was born on August 17, 1944, on the Lower East Side of Manhattan. His nineteen-year-old mother, Florence Spellman, had fallen in love with a handsome, broad-shouldered third-generation Italian who was a pilot in the air force. By the time Florence knew she was pregnant, her lover had been posted abroad. What happened to him, despite Ellison's efforts in later life to find out, remains a mystery. At the age of nine months, Florence's baby contracted pneumonia and nearly died. Reluctantly, she concluded that it was impossible for her to work to support the two of them while giving her son the care he needed. And in those days the only solution was to have the baby adopted. Fortunately, Florence had an aunt living in Chicago who was prepared to bring Larry up as her own son.

Lillian Ellison was the second wife of the considerably older Louis Ellison. A Russian Jew, Louis had come to the United States in 1905 aboard a Black Sea steamer. He is said to have escaped the Crimea's grinding poverty on the back of a hay cart, carrying his only possessions: a brass samovar and a gold locket. Louis was a model immigrant. He changed his unpronounceable Russian name to Ellison (after Ellis Island), worked hard, married, had two children, and, during the 1920s, prospered in the Chicago real estate business, buying up properties for rental with borrowed money. Intensely patriotic toward the country that had given him his chance in life, he even had political ambitions.

However, as happened to many others, when the Depression struck, the modest fortune he had made was largely wiped out—his tenants could no longer pay the rent, which meant that the highly leveraged Ellison defaulted on his interest payments. Under the strain, in 1929, his wife left both him and the two children, Jack and Doris. Lou Ellison managed to put his life back together, remarrying and finding respectable, if relatively poorly paid, work as an auditor for the Federal Housing Authority. His second wife, Lillian, who was childless herself, persuaded him to take Larry in.

It seems likely that Lou, old enough to be Larry's grandfather, was not exactly enthusiastic about the arrangement. For one thing, it would have been an additional financial burden. The family wasn't poor, but money was sufficiently tight that they needed the additional income Lillian made as a bookkeeper. In any event, he and Larry never became close, Lou finding it difficult to display much affection to his adopted son. Looking back, Ellison has some sympathy with Lou's predicament, but he is still resentful about being denied the paternal love and approval that he "promiscuously" showers on his own children.

Part of the problem was that Larry and Lou had very different attitudes toward authority. Ellison says, "His worldview went way beyond Nathan Hale's, 'My country right or wrong.' He believed that our country's officials, and authority figures in general, were always right and should be obeyed without question. The governor, the mayor, the police are in their jobs for a reason, he'd say; 'They know things you don't.' I thought, 'Sure, they're brilliant, just like my teachers.' I understood his gratitude toward the United States, but I couldn't accept his blind faith in authority figures. In fact, I had the opposite point of view. I questioned everything. It's like Mark Twain says, 'What is an expert anyway? Just some guy from out of town.' This lack of respect for authority made it just about impossible for me to get along with my father."

A consequence of Ellison's insistent questioning of authority was that his grades at school were usually poor. "I didn't respect or like most of my teachers. I didn't think they were very smart, and half the time they didn't seem to know what they were talking about. They constantly made mistakes, and I enjoyed pointing them out. They didn't like that at all, but I did." Although he was good at mathematics and enjoyed reading, he was never prepared to submit to the rigors of uncongenial course work or accept the fact that progress at school depends on jumping through the hoops that teachers specify. When somebody told him that he would look back on his school days as being the best years of his life, he replied, "If that's true, I'm going to kill myself right now." He says that he never felt as if he fitted in but denies believing that he was in any sense "special." "I was a quick-witted and aggressively glib teenager. As I got older, humor became as important an emotional defense mechanism as repression. Humor was also my primary social skill, equally useful for charming friends and attacking enemies. Because I was so quick and glib, I thought I must be reasonably smart. But underneath the bravado there was a lot of doubt and insecurity."

He still bitterly remembers a confrontation with his biology teacher at South Shore High School. She happened to be the mother of his best friend, Dennis Coleman, and the wife of Harold Coleman, a chemistry professor at the University of Chicago whom Ellison admired for his intellect and commitment to reason. "I was having dinner over at the Colemans', and she says to me, 'Ellison'—she never called me Larry—'I'm going to flunk you in biology because you don't attend the labs.' True, I was cutting lab to play basketball, but what's attendance got to do with anything? I was getting As and Bs on the exams. I knew more biology than most of the people in the class. So I said, 'What if I get the highest grade in the final, would you still flunk me?' She said, 'Yes.' I said, 'Let me get this straight: even if I clearly prove I know more about biology than anyone else in the class, I will be the only one in the class that flunks. Is that correct?' She said, 'Yes.' I said, 'Okay. I understand completely. That makes a lot of sense.'

"It was yet more proof to me that school was just a bad joke—not that I needed any additional evidence. Anyway, her husband, Dr. Coleman, noticed the absurdity of it all and suggested that if I did indeed get the highest grade on the final that I should get a C. She eventually agreed. I was sure that I could get everything right on the final. All I had to do was study for a change. The only thing left that could go wrong was a tie. So as I left, I told her to make sure that the exam was hard; I didn't want there to be a lot of people getting everything right. She was really pissed, and she gave us a very difficult final. I ended up earning my C by getting a 96 on the final while the second highest grade was around 60. I always thought it interesting how teachers, coaches, and other authority figures value obedience more than knowledge or skill, and effort more than results. They just love being the boss." *

The frustrations that Ellison experienced because of his inability to establish good relationships with people in authority would stay with him until he discovered the liberation of computer programming, a discipline in which you are judged only on your ability to solve a problem. "I was working at this Silicon Valley company as a computer programmer. The CEO called me into his office to complain about me coming to work late all the time. So I asked him, 'Are any of my programming projects late?' No. 'Are anyone else's projects on time?' No. 'Would you rather me come in on time and deliver late or come in late and deliver on time? Maybe you should ask the other programmers to get a little more sleep and come in later. They might be more productive.' I couldn't believe it. Why should the CEO care what time I come to work? He's measuring the wrong thing. The only thing that matters is results. Shortly thereafter the board fired him, and the new CEO promoted me to VP of development. Silicon Valley usually values function over form, results over effort. I finally found my place in the world."

Not surprisingly, Lou Ellison concluded early on that Larry's failure to comply with authority would be his undoing. Sadly, he could never resist any opportunity to remind his son that he would amount to nothing. Yet it would be wrong to say that as a boy Ellison was unloved. Lillian never gave him less than unconditional affection, and Doris, nineteen years older, was full of tough, wisecracking love for her wayward baby brother. Soon after Ellison learned of his adoption, his family moved to Clyde Avenue on Chicago's South Shore to set up home in a second-floor two-bedroom apartment next to the bungalow where Doris now lived with her lawyer husband, David Linn, their nine-year-old son, Jimmy, and

---

*LE writes: People regularly mistake obedience for intelligence. That's why we think that dogs are more intelligent than cats. We measure intelligence as the speed at which animals learn to do what we want them to do. A dog will fetch a stick every time you throw it. A cat will look at you and wonder, If you wanted the stick, why did you throw it in the first place? Get it yourself, idiot. In reality, cats and dogs have similar intelligence levels but different survival strategies. The dog is dependent and must please to get regular meals. The cat will mooch off his human roommates, but if the food runs out the cat can survive on its own. I love golden retrievers, but I don't want to be one. I'd much rather be a cat.

their daughter, Leslie. Jimmy Linn, now, like his father before him a judge in Chicago, says that he and Ellison were like brothers: "It appeared to me that he looked on my mother and father as quasi parents because of the limitations of the relationship with his own parents, especially his father. He saw my father as a role model, and he always felt very comfortable at our house. My father was very generous with his affection because Larry was there and he could see that he needed it. I think he felt a little sorry for him because he didn't have that much encouragement in his own home."

For all their support, the Linns didn't see anything in Ellison to mark him out as exceptional, just a little odd. Jimmy Linn says, "My father liked Larry but didn't perceive him as anything particularly special. Although it's not a word I would have used at the time, I remember feeling that he was eccentric, a little bit unbridled but very bright. He was very witty, constantly wisecracking, and he would always talk in superlative terms about everything, always exaggerating about the best of this and the best of that. I used to think that Larry was kind of blowing hot air, he was full of baloney—his sense of humor was built on gross exaggeration. Now, with hindsight, I see that he was visionary at a young age. But at the time that wasn't clear. Mainly we just played sports. He would never, ever let me win unless it was on merit. I will attribute this to him: he helped me become a better athlete, and he taught me all about competitiveness."

Ellison might have been competitive, but he was incapable of channeling it into anything useful. After graduating from South Shore High School, he enrolled at the University of Illinois in Urbana-Champaign as a premed student. He found the lectures tedious and had the same problems with authority that had contributed to his poor grades at South Shore. He says, "It was unbearable. In comparative anatomy we had to memorize the names of all the bones, muscles, nerves, etc., of a dogfish shark and a cat. Why? They weren't teaching us about the fundamental mechanisms of the evolutionary process. That would have been interesting. That's important. That's essential to understanding how the world works. But no. Instead, we spent all our time memorizing a bunch of Latin names of animal body parts. That's not learning. It's some form of medieval torture. I thought it was a total waste of time, and I couldn't do it."

Ellison never got around to taking his finals at the University of Illinois. Whether he would have even if Lillian Ellison hadn't fallen sick and died of pancreatic cancer is doubtful, but the death of his mother further destabilized him and he just upped and left. Oddly, however, he wasn't quite ready to give up on academic study, later enrolling as a physics and math major at the University of Chicago. Despite his evident unsuitability for university life, he maintained a fantasy that one day he might be a professor like Harold Coleman. The University of Chicago was a marginally more positive experience than Illinois, but he still lasted only a couple of quarters.

The one positive thing that came out of it was that he learned enough about computer programming to earn rather more money than in his previous job as a beach lifeguard. It gave him the confidence to quit university for a second time and, at the age of twenty, to make a break with his old life. He bought himself an almost new 1964 turquoise Ford Thunderbird and headed west. He says, "I just packed all my stuff into the car and headed for Berkeley. It seemed like a good idea." If it occurred to him that the Linns might feel abandoned, it didn't seem to bother him. It was as if the death of Lillian had finally jolted him into reacting to his adoption and he did so by getting as far away from his adopted family as possible. Part of the Linns' disappointment was that Larry seemed to be proving that Lou Ellison had been right all along. Jimmy says, "There was some anger. My father thought it was another example of Larry being immature and not focused. I felt a sense of being abandoned by my big brother. I felt a sense of loss because he didn't make any effort to stay in touch."

The separation from the Linns proved to be temporary. While at college, Jimmy ran into a personal jam: "I needed some help, and it was something I couldn't go to my parents with. I hadn't talked to Larry in a few years, but I wrote him a letter and he immediately responded, providing the help and support I needed without question. I was very relieved—both to get the help and to start up the relationship again." David and Doris were also relieved to have Larry back in their lives, although they were still worried about the lack of direction in both his personal and professional life: he seemed to be drifting, never staying long in a job, and his marriage to Adda Quinn was falling apart. When, on the verge of his second marriage, Ellison seemed to be in need of their help, they were determined to do what they could for him.

Jimmy says, "I've talked this over with Larry several times, and there's a big difference of perception about this. I was at home with my parents when we got a call from Larry. My father had a long talk with him over the phone, and when he hung up, he said: 'Larry's in trouble. He wants to start a company, and he needs money.' At that time, he'd just become a judge and his salary had dropped dramatically from what he'd been making as a lawyer, but he said, 'I'm not going to say no to the kid.' He went into my sister's savings account and sent him $6,000. The feeling was, he's calling us for help and we'll do all we can for him." Ellison's version is indeed a little different: "I told them that Oracle would go public in about a year or so and that anything they invested in the stock now would increase by a factor of ten. Of course, at the time they honestly believed that they would never see any of their money ever again. In spite of that, they gave me the money. It was an act of kindness. And it turned out to be a pretty good investment too." *

• • •

Ellison's relationship with the Linns grew in importance to him, and, gratifyingly, it was no longer a one-way street in which they did most of the giving and Ellison most of the taking. As Oracle established itself and Ellison grew rich and (moderately) famous, he made sure that the Linns benefited. Before Oracle went public, he gave Jimmy and Leslie stock that would make them financially secure for life. Among other things, he also provided David with a chauffeur-driven limo to take him to court each day. Crucially, the money that Jimmy made from his Oracle shares meant that he could afford to give up his lucrative work as a defense attorney to become a judge without making the kind of financial sacrifice his father had accepted as the price that you paid for entering public service. But there was still something missing. Jimmy says, "He was successful. He was a very wealthy man, but I think he was still trying to figure out who I am in this world, where do I come from? He would have long talks with my mother, telling her that he didn't understand his wealth and whether or not it was all a dream that he would one day wake up from. But above all, for the first time he had this curiosity about who he really was."

David Linn was able to help. By pulling some strings, he was able to track down the original adoption papers and other records that made it relatively easy for the ex-FBI agent they hired to find Florence Spellman. For the Linns, there was the anxiety that another family would replace them in Ellison's affections, but for Ellison it was a risk that he could no longer avoid. Forty years earlier, Lillian had taken Larry on a trip to New York to meet his "cousins"—Florence and her young family. "I did all the things you do when you're a kid visiting New York. I remember going to the top of the Empire State Building and going up the Statue of Liberty. I

---

*LE writes: I was wrong about Oracle stock's increasing in value by a factor of ten; it increased by a factor of ten thousand.

had a great time, but my mother didn't. She never took me back." Jimmy Linn confirms that Lillian feared she might lose Larry if it were repeated.

After Ellison had located Florence Spellman in New Haven, Connecticut, he decided one day just to call her out of the blue. Ellison says, "I felt a little apprehensive, but calling on the phone seemed like a better idea than just knocking on the door."

When he made the call, he had almost no idea what he was going to say, not even what he was going to call her. "I didn't call her anything. I said, 'Hi. My name is Larry Ellison, and, uh, this is a bit awkward but, uh, you and I are related.' Florence's reaction was predictable surprise: "Oh my God! The son I gave up for adoption!" Ellison says that he tried to describe himself very slowly, "like a telemarketer giving a detailed description of a product unfamiliar to the person on the other end of the line." When Florence asked her son what he did, Ellison just replied that he worked in the computer industry on the West Coast as a software executive. Suddenly the questions and answers started pouring out on both sides—"it was tense and exciting," Ellison admits. "She kept on saying 'Oh my God, oh my God.' " Ellison learned that she had married, had two children (both grown up), and was now divorced. He told her that he would soon be in New York and suggested that he fly up to nearby New Haven and just "drop by to meet and talk." Ellison recalls, "She was agitated, crying a bit, but happy. She told me that she had often wondered about me—how I was getting on. She was most interested to know if Lou and Lillian had treated me well. And she asked me to forgive her for giving me up for adoption."

He found her living in a house he describes as "modest but not poor." His half brother, Steve, was in his early forties and was a helicopter pilot who had recently left the army, while his half sister Anne, several years younger, was at loose ends after a spell in the air force. There was some slightly forced hugging and lots of looking at old photographs as Florence explained to Larry why she had had to give him up to her aunt for adoption. Ellison says, "She felt guilty and wanted my forgiveness, but I didn't think there was anything to forgive—she had tried her best and had done what she thought was the best thing for me. In fact, I'm quite certain it was the best thing for me."

But if Ellison had been expecting an emotionally cathartic experience on his side, he didn't find it. "It just didn't feel like she was my mother or even a part of my family. There was no emotional attachment, no bond, no connection. But in that meeting I did finally discover the identity of my real family; it was now clear to me that the family that had raised me, the family that I had known all along, that was my real family." For all that, he felt in some way responsible for these people he couldn't bring himself to accept as family. He found that all three were eager to move to California, and he bought a house for Florence and Anne in Redwood Shores, a stone's throw away from Oracle. He put Anne through college, where she earned a teaching degree. Steve, having been in one too many helicopter crashes in the army, wanted to work in the computing industry. Without ever revealing the identity of his brother, Steve Janicki went to work at Oracle, married, had children, and rose on his own merits to be second in command of Oracle's data center. Ellison says, "Steve's been very careful never to take advantage of our relationship. I've hardly helped him at all. He worked his way up the organization entirely on his own. He has done an extraordinarily good job for Oracle. I'm thrilled to be related to such a hardworking, wonderful guy."

Things have been more difficult for Anne. Ellison describes her as "bright and talented," but he thinks that she's not found it easy adjusting to the reality of her half-brother's extraordinary wealth. "Anne and Steve are quite different. I supported Anne through school and I've given her money when she's needed it. That's very easy for me to do because I have lots of money, but sometimes I've wondered whether it was the right thing for her. Happiness and self-reliance have a funny way of going together. She's just got her teaching credential, so she's chosen a very difficult, poorly paid but otherwise rewarding profession. I admire anyone who tries walking down that road."

As for Florence, she lived on for eight more years in her comfortable new waterside home with Anne before getting terminal cancer. If the relationship with Ellison deepened at all, it's not something he's willing to admit. He visited her two or three times a year and at least a couple of times when she was near the end in the hospital. He never wanted his two children to meet her. If he had trouble showing her much warmth, the same seems to have been true of her. Although, according to Ellison, she liked to boast about her son the multibillionaire, she never expressed much in the way of pride in his accomplishments to him. To that extent, it was like Lou Ellison all over again.

Ellison confesses to feeling some anger about what he rather harshly describes as her willingness to "trade" on his success: "I thought it was undignified for her to brag about 'her son's' money. I wasn't really her son—she had given that up a long time ago." Ellison saw Florence on the night she died, and again he felt that she was still asking forgiveness. "I told her she had been very, very young and in an impossible situation. She had no choice, really. She had to give me up. I said everything I could think of to try to help her cope with her emotional pain, but there was nothing I or anyone else could do about the cancer pain. It's a hideous, sadistic disease. In its late stages, the only effective painkiller is death."

Finding and coming to terms with his blood relations meant that, for the first time, Ellison had no doubt who his real family was. He says, "Anyone who's been adopted has an uncertain sense of belonging. There's this ambiguity about which family is your 'real' family. Meeting my birth mother resolved all that for me. The family that raised me is my family. They're stuck with me. I'm very attached to my sister and the Judge!" Jimmy Linn remembers the moment well: "He looked in my mother's eyes and said, 'As soon as I met her, I knew who my real family was. I know who I am now.' "

The relationship with the Linns continues to be of huge importance to Ellison, and he sees them as often as possible. Usually Doris and Jimmy with his wife, Elyse, and two daughters join Ellison for holidays on his boats several times a year. Whenever possible, Ellison sends his plane to Chicago to fly them to wherever *Katana* or *Ronin* is cruising. Whenever a car in Ellison's automobile fleet is up for renewal (a pretty regular event), it's more likely to be shipped to Jimmy's garage in Chicago than traded in. With the Linns he's probably more relaxed and happy than at any other time in his life. With Jimmy in particular, the affection seems almost physical, with much hugging and kissing. There may be an element of overcompensation in Ellison's emotional outpouring toward his adopted family; it's as if he's making up for the time when he was confused and uncertain about his identity. But there is something touching about his urgent need to both give and receive unconditional love; the kind of love he felt he didn't get from Lou. The scars of adoption never quite heal.

• • •

Ellison's need to demonstrate unconditional love is, naturally enough, at its strongest with his two children, David and Megan. It would have been easy—and not exactly unusual—if Ellison had lost contact with his children, given that they were both still very young (David was three, Megan still in diapers) when he and their mother, Barbara, were divorced. But, to the surprise of many, Ellison, from the outset, worked hard on his relationship with them. Part of that meant staying on reasonable terms with

Barbara. Ellison says, "I was determined to remain friends with Barbara and provide as much emotional and financial support as I could. It's impossible to raise healthy, happy children if their parents are at war."

It's often underestimated how much fatherhood changes even men who are not paragons of monogamy. Ellison says, "It was amazing. My personality fundamentally changed as a result of me becoming a father. I had expected a change when I got married, but I woke up the next morning feeling exactly as I did the day before. But being a father made me sensitive to the needs and feelings of my kids, and then that gradually seeped over into my other relationships. I became a more considerate friend and partner. I grew up." Barbara and the children continued to live in Woodside, while Ellison moved to nearby Atherton. Most weekends, they would go and stay with him. He even claims to have gotten pretty good at dealing with Megan's diaper changes and enjoying the experience: "A primal bond is formed between a primary caregiver and a small child. Biology takes over. Your brain is flooded with oxytocin, and this little person becomes a part of you." Imagining Ellison, the "new man," mystically in touch with his female side while taping up Megan's diapers in the lonely small hours is a stretch, but he insists it's true.*

The weekend routine was interrupted only by occasional crises at Oracle. Ellison admits, "When the company was in trouble, I was a less attentive father. Barbara knew that as long as I was seeing the kids regularly, everything at work was okay, even if the stock was down. But if I disappeared from the kids' lives for a while, like in 1991, something bad must be happening. During those times I became so focused on work and survival that I locked everything else out—even the kids." The children were also kept away from casual girlfriends, getting to know only the two women with whom Ellison has had serious long-term relationships, Kathleen O'Rourke and Melanie Craft. As always, Ellison is ultrasensitive to any taint of hypocrisy or political correctness. "I don't claim to be a dutiful father. I just get so much pleasure from my kids. I suspect I need them a lot more than they need me."

Ellison makes no attempt to pretend that his children will have to

---

*LE writes: Okay. I don't think I'm ever very likely to "get in touch with my female side." But I did get pretty good at wiping and powdering bottoms and then taping on Huggies without ever being fully awake. Changing your kids' diapers while you're still asleep is an essential survival skill for parents of young children.

make their own way in the world or to shield them from the potentially corrosive knowledge that they can have whatever material thing they want whenever they want it. David has a BMW M3 at college and a Honda NSX at home to drive, while Megan's first car was a Lexus 430SC convertible. With the best coaching and equipment, both excel at their (expensive) chosen sports—competitive aerobatics for David, equestrian events for Megan. Although two of David's best friends are relatively poor (Ellison has helped finance their education through both school and university), most of their circle is made up of rich kids who seem to think nothing of being transported by private jet for a week's holiday on "Camp Ronin" in Tahiti. Does Ellison not worry about the effects that exposure to enormous wealth and privilege might have on them?

One evening, sitting with Ellison aboard *Katana* at anchor outside the picture-perfect Italian resort of Portofino, I asked him what it is that he wants for his children. He says simply that he hopes they will be happy. And what does he think will constitute happiness for them? Twenty-four hours earlier, Megan had been racing speedboats across the bay of Saint-Tropez with the son of the Saudi billionaire investor Prince Alwaleed. She certainly seemed to be having a good time. Was that enough? Ellison says that he has come to believe that an essential precondition of happiness is self-esteem—maybe because it's something he's found only fairly late in life: "It takes a good deal of confidence and self-esteem before you're able to look at yourself and the world honestly. I do my best not to deceive myself, and I think I see the world pretty realistically. I wasn't able to do any of that until I became reasonably successful at the two things Freud says are important in life: love and work. When my family and friends and Oracle are doing well, I'm happy." Ellison is convinced that growing up with unlimited money shouldn't be an obstacle to success in either of those things—love or work—for his children. "I think it's wonderful that my kids don't have to worry about money. For them, earning money isn't necessary for survival, so they can move on to the other challenges in life."

He recognizes that it may be difficult for his children to emulate his business success, which, he says, "was largely responsible for initially building up my self-esteem." But he believes there are plenty of other things they can do and things they can achieve other than amassing money. It will be up to them to decide what it is that they want to be good at. The second component of self-respect, according to Ellison, is the simple matter of treating other people decently. Some would say that this is, for Ellison, a pretty recent discovery, but I know that he means it. He insists, "Being insensitive, rude, or mean to someone close to you, or to a perfect stranger for that matter, is self-destructive and self-degrading behavior. You'll think less of yourself for doing it. Being nice is an essential strategy for pursuing happiness. That plus excelling at your life's work are the only avenues leading to happiness that I've found so far. I don't think that masses of money increase or decrease your chances for finding happiness in this life." *

I think he's being a little glib. Both of his means of achieving happiness are more difficult to find if you have a lot of money: if your choices are unlimited, it's too easy to be a dilettante, and the rich are doomed to wonder whether they are loved for themselves or for their wealth. Ellison strongly disagrees. "It takes about five seconds for me to detect that someone is interested in me solely because I'm rich. It's really very easy to tell." As for work, he says, "If you have to work to eat, you have to choose a profession fairly early in life. Search too long, and you'll starve. You may get lucky and pick something you're good at and enjoy doing. That's what happened to me. But if you have money, you can keep searching forever. Seemingly there's no need to choose. But it just seems that way. You must find a meaningful life's work, or you'll starve emotionally. It's your work that defines you. Rich kids start a couple of rungs up on Maslow's hierarchy of needs, that's all. They don't have to earn money, so they have more options. They can go into politics, play in the orchestra, or run a charitable foundation. But unless they work and succeed at something, they'll never be happy and they'll never know who they are."

Ellison has always given his children access to a lot of money. "You can't create artificial poverty to teach your kids what it's like to be poor. It's like sending a kid to bed without dinner to teach them about hunger. It's phony, and kids see right through it. The sooner my kids get experience dealing with the pluses and minuses of having a lot of money, the better." He hopes they will get used to making the decisions that go with extreme wealth while they are still young enough to accept some parental guidance. He says it's like taking a drink. He'd prefer his children to learn to drink at home rather than discover alcohol for the first time when they pass some arbitrary age qualification.

---

*LE writes: I don't, however, believe in being nice to my enemies. My enemies are trying to deprive me of the success that led to my happiness. I want to beat my enemies, and it's hard to be nice to them at the same time.

I'm curious about why Ellison has encouraged David to take up the seriously dangerous sport of stunt flying. It seems it all comes back to self-esteem. Early on, Ellison realized how difficult David might find it growing up in the shadow of such a famous and successful father. He wouldn't have been the first child in such circumstances to damage himself, either through a vain attempt to compete or by retreating into a form of personal nihilism. Ellison says, "It's incredibly important for teenage boys to be cool. The danger lies in trying to be cool the wrong way—drinking and driving fast, taking drugs, and all that other self-destructive stuff. Even if they don't die in a traffic accident, they can still sustain a lot of emotional damage." So Ellison thought about what was the best way he could guarantee his son a really cool self-image and hit on flying. From the age of thirteen, David has had his own plane and has regularly flown both Ellison's Citation jet and his Marchetti jet fighter.

Did Ellison not worry at all when David was flying? His answer is no, because worrying doesn't make it any safer.* He argues, "The statistics are on our side. We have wonderful airplanes that are perfectly maintained, and David has the best aerobatics instructors on the planet." I point out that despite all that, just the other day David could have gotten into trouble when he lost his canopy. "He managed the emergency quite well and landed the airplane without incident. David has developed into a very calm and mature kid. Putting him into an airplane early had that effect on him. One serious mistake, and it's over. He became responsible for his own life the first time he went up in an airplane by himself."

Ellison is close to both his children, but it's clear that his relationship with David is currently a good deal easier than the one with Megan. While David gives every impression of being relaxed and at ease with himself, Megan is suffering from all the angst and rebelliousness of adolescence. But I suspect she is naturally wilder and more headstrong than

---

*LE writes: I seriously object to sports that are truly odds-on dangerous. David's skydiving and sky-surfing days are over. After more than a hundred jumps he had an equipment failure that caused part of his primary parachute to wrap itself around his neck. He was able to cut away the failed primary chute and his air board and then deploy his reserve chute just in time. It was a very close call. He was going fast when he hit the ground, and he was seriously banged up. If I had understood how dangerous sky surfing was, I never would have let him do it in the first place. After his accident I learned that the two top-ranked sky surfers in the world had both recently died in accidents.

David. In other words, she is more like her father. One question that Ellison hasn't discussed with his children is how they would feel if he were to start a new family with Melanie. They both seem very fond of her, but who knows?* My guess is that if the idea of it made either of them unhappy, Ellison would back off. From an unpromising start, he's worked hard and consistently to keep his children close to him. Many of his friends regard it as both his greatest and most unlikely achievement.

---

*LE writes: Melanie and the kids have spent a lot of time together. They're nice kids, and she's quite attached to them. They're also both quite fond of her. Anyway, my kids get to pick who they marry, not who I marry.

20

THREE STRIKES, YOU'RE OUT

Larry Ellison thinks he's pretty good at most things. He's forgotten more about programming than some of the kids working for Oracle will ever know. If he has a fast boat for the America's Cup, he'll drive it and still expect to win. He's even quietly pleased about how he's turned out as a father. But there's one important life skill that has so far eluded him: holding a marriage together. His third and most recent marriage, to Barbara Boothe, ended when she filed for divorce in April 1986, less than three months after the birth of his second child, Megan, and a month after Oracle's initial public offering. The marriage had lasted less than three years. He says, "After that, I decided I just wasn't any good at marriage. There's a criminal law in California called three strikes and you're out. . . . Maybe after three marriages, you shouldn't be allowed a fourth."

It's a reasonable, and in many ways convenient, conclusion. It's meant that ever since breaking up with Barbara, Ellison has had a wonderful excuse for not entering into the kind of commitment that many of the women he has dated were hoping for. It's also one of the main reasons for the playboy image that he has encouraged and resented in equal measure. By the time his third marriage ended, Ellison was already worth the best part of $200 million. Apart from the dog days of 1991, when he came close to losing nearly everything, since his early forties Larry Ellison has been in the enviable position of being one of the most eligible bachelors in California. It's a status that he's enjoyed, but it has also come close to destroying him.

Ellison was married for the first time in early 1967, about a year after arriving in Berkeley in his turquoise T-bird. He was twenty-two, and Adda Quinn was about five months younger. She was a graduate of San Jose State University, and they met when he rolled up at an employment agency where she was working. He felt comfortable with her because she came from a similar lower-middle-class background. While the marriage lasted seven years, most of that time they didn't live together. It was clear from the beginning that while Adda took the relationship very seriously, Ellison was a long way from being ready for the sort of commitment that he had entered in to.

Ellison says of her, "Adda was very bright and exceptionally pretty. Our problems stemmed from the fact that, unlike me, she took life seriously and worked hard at it. She'd get home from her full-time job, make a gourmet dinner, clean up, and then start to wallpaper one of the bedrooms in our house. She wanted me to help her. Perfectly reasonable request, but I didn't want to wallpaper the bedroom. I wanted to go for a bike ride. I didn't want a full-time job either, so I did just enough contract programming to pay my part of the monthly bills. Most of my time was spent backpacking in Yosemite and kayaking in the Sierras."

To bring in money, Ellison frequently worked nights and weekends doing routine software maintenance on IBM mainframes in data centers. While he thought the money he earned was best spent on having fun, Adda wanted to use it for home building. Whereas he never had the slightest idea how much money they had, she kept all their accounts in neat notebooks—"It was like the early days at Oracle. I never looked at the numbers!" He says, "We responded differently to not having any money while growing up. I was irresponsible and careless about money, while she was cautious and disciplined to the point of being obsessive." While Adda would save up for cheap pieces of furniture and would even change the oil in Ellison's car as an economy measure, Ellison was perfectly happy to go and make a down payment on a thirty-four-foot yacht even before selling his smaller boat. He confesses, "I was awful. She said that buying that boat put her into therapy. Here she was carefully managing our finances while I was spending money we didn't have on a sailboat."

Another strain on the marriage was that in an effort to establish some sort of "detente" with Lou Ellison, Larry and Adda asked his now-widowed father to come and live with them. Not surprisingly, most of the burden fell on Adda, and Larry started finding excuses not to come home. Although Ellison was unfaithful to Adda, the main reason she eventually decided to leave him was her conviction that unless she escaped, he would drive her mad. She had found him extraordinarily stimulating and never dull, but the combination of constantly worrying about money and their entirely separate agendas for the relationship was literally making her ill. Luckily, there were no children ("I certainly wasn't ready for that!') and precious few assets to complicate the divorce.

Ellison felt liberated from a relationship that he clearly wasn't ready for. But the fact that Adda, whom he remained very fond of, had taken the step of leaving him was hard to come to terms with. The rejection revived all the feelings of emotional insecurity stemming from his adoption that he normally repressed. It seemed to support Lou's contention that he would never amount to anything. He says, "I thought I was reasonably smart, but I was going nowhere. I was a very good programmer, but I didn't have the discipline to work on problems that couldn't be solved in a few days. I had no endurance. I doubted I ever would." Ellison was thirty, and his father's jaundiced prediction seemed to be coming true. He maintains now that it was a turning point in his life.

However, after Adda left, he carried on pretty much as he had been: hiking in Yosemite whenever possible, dating a succession of girls, and earning reasonable money as a quick and skilled programmer who could usually be relied upon to solve problems. But something had changed. Slowly Ellison began to have a growing conviction that he was at least as capable as most of the people who were running the businesses that employed him. He also eventually wearied of the sexual freedom that the return to bachelorhood had brought—a pattern that was to repeat itself over the years. He says, "I doubt that anybody really enjoys a steady diet of dating different people. Nobody in their right mind trades in a working long-term relationship for an endless series of fantasies and adventures." Whether it was the shock of Adda's departure or something else, Ellison was beginning to realize two things about himself: the first was that he was ready in his professional life to be more than the equivalent of a hired gun; the second was that he needed the support of a stable relationship more than he thought.

That said, Ellison met his second wife, Nancy Wheeler, when he was looking for a car, not a partner. "I'm writing a check for this classic Mercedes convertible, and out of the blue the woman who's selling the car says, 'I've got just the perfect girl for you.' Yeah, right. I just kind of ignored her and tried to change the subject." What got his attention was when she described Nancy as the best-looking girl she'd seen in her life and her husband agreed. "It was a brief but compelling description." Armed with her telephone number, it didn't take him long to find her.

More than a decade younger than Ellison and from a well-to-do Louisville, Kentucky, family, Nancy Wheeler had recently transferred to Stanford University.

Ellison doted on her, and they were married soon after meeting in late 1976. Nancy could not have been more different from the practical, responsible Adda. "Nancy was gorgeous. She had this sexy southern accent and a wicked sense of humor. She had a rare combination of athletic grace and feminine charm. My male friends simply adored her. My female friends thought she was a self-centered, superficial, materialistic vamp. What's wrong with that? She did have a couple of quirks, though." Ellison recalls that the first time they spent a night together he was disconcerted by her complete stillness while sleeping. "She slept on her back with her arms at her sides—kind of like a vampire in a coffin. She didn't move all night." Her explanation was that she had taught herself to do it since coming to Stanford: she hated getting up early, but this way she could put on all her makeup and fix her hair the night before and leap out of an undisturbed bed at the last moment and go straight in to class.*

While Adda had counted every penny, Ellison noticed that Nancy never bothered filling in the stubs in her checkbook. She couldn't see the point of it. "I said, 'Nancy, what if you write a check for more money than we have in the account?' She asked, 'Is that possible?' I answered, 'It is now.' " Ellison claims that Nancy had been inside a grocery store only once before they met, let alone learned to cook.

On another occasion, the couple had decided to go backpacking in Yosemite. Ellison recalls, "I was wearing normal hiking clothes: khaki shorts, tan army surplus shirt, old leather boots with wool socks. Nancy's dressed for a game of tennis at the country club: white hot pants, white tennis shoes, and a skintight red-orange tank top that's perfectly color-coordinated with her lip gloss. I'm carrying this huge fifty-pound pack with all our stuff in it. All she's carrying is extra lip gloss. Anyway, we begin hiking from the valley floor to our campsite, about eight thousand feet up. An hour and a half into the climb, I ask her if she wants to stop and rest. She says she's not tired and wants to keep going. I notice there is not a single bead of sweat on her. She's standing there looking like a cover girl from *Seventeen* magazine. Very annoying. I'm sweating so much I look like I've been hiking under a waterfall. It's a hot summer day and I

---

*LE writes: Nancy was always willing to go the extra mile to look good.

need a break, so I say, 'Hey, I'm the one carrying the pack. I want to stop for a minute, okay?' She just smirks at me for a moment, and then she offers to carry the pack for a while. I'm thinking, no way can she carry this pack up this mountain. But I'd dearly love to see her try. So I say, 'Fine, honey, you carry the fucking pack.' I adjust the pack's shoulder straps and belt and latch this huge thing onto her. The pack begins below her butt and ends a foot over her head. I figure she won't last a hundred yards before she falls on her face, but off we go. We'd taken no more than ten steps before we see these three guys descending the trail. Then they see us. And what they see is this cover girl in hot pants and a tank top carrying this huge backpack up a very steep trail. Not a bead of sweat on her. They see me soaked with sweat—carrying nothing all. They just stared at us mouths agape. They didn't say a word, but as they passed us they turned around and stumbled backward still staring. I thought they were going to fall over the trailside cliff. When they disappeared around the bend, I took the pack back and carried it the rest of the way."

When Nancy walked out on him after little more than eighteen months of marriage, returning to a former boyfriend just back from Harvard Business School whom she subsequently married, Ellison was devastated. This time, it wasn't Ellison's lack of seriousness or infidelities that ended the marriage. More likely, it was the stresses and financial problems associated with founding Software Development Laboratories (SDL). Without money coming in from late-paying customers, Ellison was not only failing to meet the bills of the contractor who was building the couple's new home in Orinda, he was also being threatened with foreclosure on the couple's house in Woodside. Ellison says, "Starting a company and a marriage at the same time is a very bad idea. I was working insanely long hours and getting home around ten o'clock every night. Nancy was going to graduate school at Stanford. We had different schedules, different friends, different priorities, and different lives."

The divorce was friendly. Ellison agreed to pay a small amount of maintenance and got to keep the houses. Nancy also gave him the truck they owned and agreed to sell him her stock in SDL for $500. Ellison remarks, "She didn't care about the stock at all, but she was pretty upset about losing the truck. Years later she called me to joke about the value of 'her half' of the stock—then worth about half a billion dollars."

Ellison used work as an escape from his feelings of emotional emptiness and failure after Nancy's departure. "I started working sixteen-hour days. That helped, but I remember some long nights and longer weekends fighting with feelings of despair." It wasn't very long, however, before he found someone new to take Nancy's place. Ellison says: "I know I have this reputation as a playboy. But the truth is, I find dating lots of women very confusing. My memories become blurred together. I'll be talking about a movie and suddenly I'll realize I saw it with somebody else. Life is a series of shared experiences and memories. If you can't remember something, it's like you never lived it. You've lost part of yourself. If you date too many people, your life gets broken into little tiny pieces— disconnected bits of experience and memory that are easily lost. It's like you're dividing yourself up into all the people you spend time with."

• • •

Barbara Boothe was a twenty-three-year-old Stanford graduate who came to work as a receptionist at Oracle in early 1981, when it was still called RSI: she was the company's tenth employee. Ellison had a policy of hiring bright, overqualified young women for administrative roles because he didn't want a two-tier company of highly educated male engineers and lesser females. As the company was growing fast, it wouldn't be long before they could be promoted to a job that would better suit their abilities. Besides, Ellison had a weakness for good-looking grads fresh out of Stanford.*

Barbara broke up with her boyfriend soon after joining RSI and needed to find a place where she and her two Irish setters could live. It didn't take Ellison long to offer her accommodation in the guest house at his new home in Woodside: It was a short step from there to suggesting that she move into the main house with him. Ellison was getting enthusiastic at the idea of having children. Having grown up with a father who was already old, Ellison didn't want to have a similarly distant relationship with his own children. "I was getting to the age [midthirties] where I wanted children. I didn't want to wait until I was too old to shoot baskets and go hiking with them." Although much younger, Barbara was ready to have children too, and a few months after moving in with Ellison she was pregnant. Engagement followed, but plans to get married were shelved after Barbara miscarried: an indication that becoming a father was more important to Ellison than the relationship itself.

Barbara became pregnant again and gave birth to David (named after

---

*LE writes: Bob Miner once said that as long as Stanford keeps turning out good-looking twenty-two-year-olds, I'll keep marrying them. I don't think this is true, but I do think it's funny.

Ellison's brother-in-law, David Linn) in January 1983, but it was another eleven months before the couple married, and from the beginning, the prospects for the marriage were dim. After David's birth, Barbara gave Ellison the ultimatum that if they were not wed by the end of the year, she would go home to Oregon, taking David with her. Ellison says, "We had a number of problems in our relationship. Barb thought the problems were caused by the fact that we weren't married. I didn't think so. But despite my doubts I decided to get married—again. I had one really good reason: a baby boy I didn't want to lose."

However, Ellison admits that he was far from certain that he wanted to go through with the marriage: "It was the most traumatic period in my life." Ellison thought that he had to get married in order to establish legal rights of access to David if things didn't work out with Barbara, but he was terrified that by getting married to someone with whom he had a failing relationship, he risked losing control of Oracle if it ended in divorce. With the company's growing success and the prospect of a lucrative initial public offering only a couple of years away, he calculated that he wouldn't get off as lightly this time as he had when Nancy had left him.

His answer to the dilemma pretty much destroyed whatever small chances of success the marriage might have had. A few hours before the wedding at Ellison's home in December 1983, he presented Barbara with a prenuptial agreement that she would have to sign if the wedding was to go ahead. It detailed Ellison's assets and included an optimistic (though as it turned, not unrealistic) valuation of his 2.2 million Oracle shares (about 40 percent of the company) in the event of either a trade sale or an IPO—up to $16.5 million if the former were to occur but as much as $44 million in the event of the latter. It then set out the terms of any divorce settlement: 25,000 Oracle shares would be used to establish a trust fund for David, while Barbara would get $100,000 for each year the couple had been married and a $250,000 home in Portland. Any additional support payments mandated by court order would be based on her needs rather than Ellison's ability to pay.

To Barbara, it was a bolt from the blue. Ellison may or may not have mentioned the possibility of a prenuptial some weeks earlier, but he certainly hadn't pursued it. "As the wedding date got closer, I panicked. I had visions of Barbara leaving and me losing my family and my company on the same day. So I had this prenuptial prepared—several weeks before the wedding, actually. But I chickened out of showing it to Barbara until the very last moment. What a disaster." As usual, Ellison's desire to avoid emotional confrontation was just a way of storing up future trouble.

Ellison knows that springing the prenuptial on Barbara (as the flowers and food for the wedding were being brought into the house) was not his finest hour, but he explains it as an act of desperation. Given the hurt and damage caused by the document, it's ironic that it was of almost no legal value to Ellison. The final drafting of the agreement was left to the two lawyers who happened to be staying at the Woodside house for the wedding: Barbara's father and David Linn. Ellison says, "It was my idea; my worst ever probably." Ellison now says that according to California law, you can't spring a prenuptial agreement on someone at such a late stage that they're almost forced to sign: "It was legally useless, and the emotional damage it caused was irreversible."

Even more ironic was Ellison's discovery later on that under California law his rights as a father were little altered by marriage. The only legal advice Ellison had sought on the prenuptial was from his corporate lawyers. He says, "They didn't have a clue about this area of the law. They never should have advised me. The prenuptial thing was completely unnecessary. If they hadn't been so ignorant—or I hadn't been so insecure—the whole terrible experience could have been avoided." Ellison also maintains that he didn't even need the prenuptial to hold on to his stock. He claims that because he had owned the stock before his marriage, Barbara could have no claim on it.

When the marriage inevitably ended in divorce a little over two years later and after the birth of a daughter, Megan, Barbara's lawyer took a different view, arguing that most of the value in the shares had been created during the period of the marriage and that Barbara was therefore due half of Ellison's estate. After months of wrangling, they settled out of court on terms far more generous than those laid out in the ill-fated prenuptial. Ellison says, "I offered more than what's required under California law for the simple reason that I wanted her and the kids to be able to afford to live in Woodside and have all the things they wanted. Barb was pretty happy with the settlement. She once described her divorce as better than most of her friends' marriages."

Once relieved of the burden of living with each other, Ellison and his former wife became good and dependable friends. Barbara has never re-married, preferring a life devoted to her children and horses. Ellison claims that he was determined to provide "unqualified" emotional and financial support for his family and that he worked hard to rebuild the relationship. Ellison's closest friend, Steve Jobs, gives him high marks for his handling of the situation once the marriage was over. Jobs says, "Larry's my best friend, and I have a lot of feelings for him. But I'm proudest of him for the way that he has worked at the relationship with his children. I know that situation from my own life; it's really easy not to have a relationship with the child when you're not close to the mother or don't want to be. But Larry has put a lot of energy into being a father, and he's done a really good job."

• • •

While Ellison didn't lose his taste for dating young, pretty Stanford graduates who were doing a stint on Oracle's reception desk, the idea of trying his hand at marriage again had lost all attraction. Although Ellison preferred serial monogamy (or something like it) to multiple casual relationships, he thought he knew enough about himself by now to know that he would always find fidelity a struggle over the long term. "I was never happy with what I had. If I had a stable family life, I'd miss the adventure of dating. If I was dating, I'd miss the love and comfort of a family. I was always afraid I was missing something."

By the time Ellison started seeing Kathleen O'Rourke in 1989, he was in his midforties, Oracle was riding high, and he was well on his way to his first billion dollars. He remembers, "I was walking into our new headquarters building and there behind the reception desk was the most angelically beautiful smiling face I'd ever seen. I walked up to her and said, 'Hi, I'm Larry Ellison.' She said, 'Hi, Larry Ellison, I'm Kathleen O'Rourke, and this is my first day at work.' . . . About five minutes later, John Luongo, the head of our international sales organization, came bursting into my office and blurted out, 'Who the hell is that girl at the—' Before he could finish his sentence, I answered, 'Kathleen O'Rourke.' Kathleen was hard to miss."

Ellison quickly found out that Kathleen had recently graduated from Stanford and rode her bicycle to work from her home in Palo Alto. An avid cyclist himself, Ellison suggested that if he brought his bike in the next day, they could ride home together. Just two days after starting at Oracle, Kathleen was leaving work with the guy who ran the company. Catching sight of them about to ride off together, John Luongo drove up to them, lowered his car window, looked first at Kathleen, then at Ellison, and observed amicably, "You'll burn in Hell for this." To which Ellison replied, "I think that's a fair trade."

Kathleen had only a hazy idea about how rich her new boyfriend was. "Soon after we started dating, Kathleen became very concerned about how much money I was spending. When she found out how much the new house in Atherton cost, she got upset and told me I was crazy for spending so much of my money on a house. So I asked her, 'Kathleen, how much money do you think I have?' She said, 'Well, I looked in the annual report, and it says you have twenty million dollars.' I said, 'No, I've got twenty million *shares,* not twenty million dollars.' Her eyes got wide as she did the multiplication in her head, 'Oh my God, you're really rich.' Kathleen majored in biology, not economics."

Although Ellison had strong feelings about Kathleen, they were not so overwhelming that he thought they should get married or that he should stop seeing other women. Ellison says, "I was madly in love with Kathleen, more in love than I had ever been up to that point in my life. She wanted to get married. I loved her dearly, but marriage scared the hell out of me. And our relationship was not one hundred percent perfect. Kathleen had this incendiary Irish temperament. When she couldn't make her point by yelling, she started swinging. She looked like an angel, but she punched like Tommy 'The Hitman' Hearns. Kathleen just loved to fight.* It was her favorite sport. She found it cathartic. Not me. I can't sleep after a fight. I hate confrontations. All the fighting eventually caused me to start dating other people—which led to still more fighting."

What made things even more difficult for Kathleen was Ellison's propensity to find most of his girlfriends at Oracle. While some companies (usually with little success) try to maintain strict rules designed to discourage sexual relationships between employees, unsurprisingly, that was never part of the culture at Oracle. Ellison explains, "Oracle was filled with bright, good-looking, single young men and women spending most of their waking hours at work. It never occurred to me to have a policy restricting dating among our employees. Meeting interesting, eligi-

---

*LE writes: Kathleen was slam dancing at the Hookers' Ball—a big charity event in San Francisco—when she accidentally bumped into a six-foot-tall lady of the night. Kathleen said excuse me, but the lady was unforgiving. She retaliated by intentionally slamming right back into Kathleen. Big mistake. Kathleen bangs into her again, this time really hard. The lady goes nuts. She spins around, opens both of her hands like claws, and starts screaming wildly while charging right at Kathleen. Bigger mistake. Kathleen instantly adopts the perfect boxer's stance, knees slightly bent, both fists raised on either side of her face, and then she fires off a beautiful right hand at the charging six-footer. It was a devastating one-punch knockout, quite similar to the punch Lennox Lewis threw at a charging Michael Grant in the first round of their recent championship fight. I have other great Kathleen stories, but I'm afraid to tell them.

ble people was one the benefits of working at Oracle. We had dozens of Oracle marriages and Oracle babies every year."

By now Ellison was beginning to get the playboy reputation that has stuck with him ever since. He's honest enough to recognize that he did nothing to discourage it. "I admit, at first I kind of liked it. It's a guy thing—an immature guy thing, to be precise. But it got way out of control. Journalists started reporting on rumors that I was dating this woman or that woman—women I had never even met. But the stories got repeated over and over again anyway. The press operates like an echo chamber. The story doesn't need to be true, necessarily; it just needs to be interesting. It didn't take long for my public image to get morphed from outrageously outspoken CEO to frivolous playboy." The freewheeling culture at Oracle and the sheer amount of opportunity it offered its CEO was to land Ellison in very serious trouble—trouble bad enough to almost finish him.

Having emerged in 1992 from the long struggle to put Oracle back together again after its near death, and tiring of the fights with Kathleen, Ellison was on the lookout for sexual adventure. He soon found rather more than he'd bargained for. His relationship with Adelyn Lee, a twenty-something Chinese American who was a marketing coordinator, began in an elevator at Oracle. Ellison had ridden up in the elevator with her a few times before, but this time, she brashly asked him if he would take her for a spin in his new Ferrari. It seemed like a joke, but she quickly followed it up with an e-mail, apologizing for her forwardness. Ellison knew that he was being pursued—unattached, enormously rich, and looking younger than his forty-eight years, he was becoming relatively accustomed to predatory females—but Adelyn Lee interested him. "A lot of women approached me, but most of the time I wasn't interested. But there was something different about Adelyn, something incredibly intriguing. I just couldn't figure out what it was that made her so different." *

After taking Lee for a ride in his Honda NSX (Ellison had owned two Ferraris, but both had managed to catch fire without any outside help), they started dating a couple of times a month—all that Ellison could fit into a complicated private life that still included O'Rourke and another Oracle employee, an Argentinean named Andrea Zeman. In an effort to

---

*LE writes: It took me a while, but I finally figured out what it was: the woman was pure evil.

try to work things through with O'Rourke, Ellison called time on his relationship with Lee, a decision she seemed to accept with good grace and an apparent desire to stay in touch "on a platonic level." The good intentions didn't last long, however, and fairly soon things were going on much as before.

But there was one difference: Lee seemed to be increasingly intent on tapping Ellison for money and expensive gifts, sending a series of e-mails to him from early 1993 asking him respectively for a $150,000 loan; inside information about the timing of a possible flotation of nCUBE (the massively parallel computing business that Ellison had bought to further his video-on-demand vision); a ritzy watch and ultimately a Honda NSX just like Ellison's. Faced with such a barrage of demands, some people might question what it was that was driving the relationship. But while Ellison largely ignored Lee's badgering, he was quite happy to go on seeing her.

It turned out that Lee was exploiting the relationship in other ways as well. Ellison says, "Craig Ramsey, our VP of sales, was Lee's boss. He called Jenny [Overstreet, Ellison's assistant] and said that he wanted to fire Lee, but he was concerned about how I'd react because of my relationship with Lee." Lee was unpunctual, rude, and generally gave herself airs, said Ramsey. Overstreet discreetly checked with Ellison. Ellison says, "I told Jenny that Craig could do whatever he wanted. The fact that she's going out with me shouldn't influence him at all. That Friday, Adelyn and I went to a movie. The following Monday, she was fired. Shortly thereafter, she sued Oracle for wrongful termination."

Ellison had thought that he could somehow manage to stay out of the whole business, punctiliously not only maintaining the "separation of church and state" but, just as important from his point of view, avoiding any confrontation with Lee. "I wouldn't have anything to do with her job. I wanted to stay out of that entirely. I guess I was stupid and naive enough to think I could keep the two things separate. I refused to accept that two consenting adults were not free to date if they wanted to. I couldn't imagine that she'd just make up a crazy series of stories about what happened on that Friday night." That Friday in April 1993, Lee had gone to Ellison's home in Atherton. After spending some time there together, they had gone out to a movie. When Lee's case came to court six months later, that was about all they did agree on.

A day after Lee's dismissal—she had to be escorted from the Oracle building by security guards after locking herself in a room and trying to phone her lover—Ellison had a nasty surprise while going through his e-mail. "I get this e-mail from Craig Ramsey saying: 'Larry, I've terminated Adelyn per your request. cdr.' I'm stunned and furious. I start pounding the keyboard: 'Craig, you fucking idiot, what the hell are you talking about? I never told you to fire Adelyn. Are you out of your fucking mind?' Then I freeze. . . . I realize. . . . Oh my God, it's a setup. . . . Oh shit, here we go. So I erase what I had typed and send Craig a very carefully worded reply."

Ellison's reply, which was copied to Oracle's legal counsel Ray Ocampo and Jenny Overstreet, read, "craig, are you out of your mind! I did not 'request' that you terminate adelyn. I decided not to veto your decision. I did not want to get involved in the decision for obvious reasons. this is the most amazing note. wait a second. . . . craig, did you send this note? larry."

Although Ellison had been smart enough to guess what was going on and how anything he said or wrote from that point on was likely to be used in evidence, things would soon get worse than he could possibly have imagined. "Lee's lawsuit claimed that I dragged her into my bedroom and forced her to have sex with me, after which we went out to see a movie, *Benny & Joon*. That's the story that appeared in the press—except they left out the part about the movie. The day the story broke, I was riding the elevator to my office with this woman I'd never seen before. She gave me this look, like I'd slithered out from underneath a rock. It was a really bad day."

Not surprisingly, it was a media circus as first Lee's allegations and then Oracle's counterallegations were splattered all over the local press. With Ellison's fame as a businessman also rising thanks to his first appearance on the cover of *Fortune* magazine, *The Wall Street Journal* and *The New York Times* also covered the story. Apart from demolishing Lee's account of events, Oracle was determined to show that Lee had forged the e-mail purportedly from Ramsey (which Lee, suspiciously, had a printout of). It had technical evidence that the e-mail had been sent by modem near where Lee lived, but the clincher was that Ramsey had been talking on his car cell phone at precisely the time the e-mail had been sent. Oracle could also show that the procedures to sack Lee had been well under way before Ellison and Lee's last date. The police also thought Lee's story was a little flaky—rape followed by a trip to the movies was something they hadn't encountered before. Under pressure, Lee now claimed that she had refused to have sex with Ellison, suggesting instead that she had reluctantly masturbated him after he had threatened her. Ellison says, "Lee completely changed her story during her deposition—her pretrial testimony given under oath. Her new story was that she refused to have sex with me that Friday and that's why she was fired. The fact that her story had changed totally didn't seem to bother the press at all. While the district attorney and the police were interested in the credibility of her claims, the press focused their reporting on the lurid details of the sex. It was a good story, and they ran with it."

Just before the case was due to come to court, on St. Valentine's Day 1995, the two sides settled. Oracle agreed to pay Lee $100,000 (somewhat less than the $1 billion she was after) "as consideration for particular elements in the law suit" and all parties agreed to drop any intention of suing each other again. It's easy to see that Lee's lawyer, Lawrence Viola, had concluded that it wasn't in his client's interests to go to court, but why were Ellison and Oracle willing to settle when doing so would leave a stain on his reputation?

Part of the answer is that in the aftermath of the O. J. Simpson case, Ellison was ready to believe that courts come up with spectacularly perverse verdicts. It would not be difficult to present him to a jury as a sexually predatory billionaire who was known for ruthless business practices and a determination to get his way. In the climate of the times, who knew what might happen? Ellison also heard from his nephew, Jimmy Linn, now a Chicago judge, just how bad the experience could be. Ellison says, "The judge told me that trials like this were totally unpredictable. It's one great big scary roll of the dice. If it came down to a matter of 'He said, she said,' juries don't always get it right. The downside was too great. Losing the case would ruin my life. He urged me to settle." *

Despite that, Ellison claims that he was still inclined to press ahead—"Risky or not, I felt I had to go to trial. Lee was a con artist. It was unbearable to think she was going to get away with this." Until he realized that maybe there was a better way after all. He says, "Then I got this interesting idea: What if we settled the civil case—Lee's wrongful termination lawsuit—and then we provided the district attorney with all the evidence we had about Lee's criminal behavior. I thought that the D.A.

---

*LE writes: It is no longer considered an acceptable legal risk for a male doctor to examine a female patient without a female nurse being present. If the doctor gets accused of inappropriate behavior, it's the nurse's testimony that keeps it from being a case of his word against hers. That's what Judge Linn was most afraid of—that this case was going to come down to my word against Lee's. Fortunately, we had hard evidence that Lee was lying.

would have no choice but to file a criminal complaint against Lee. We were the defendant in Lee v. Oracle. Now it was her turn to be the defendant in the State of California v. Lee. She had violated several criminal statutes in her little billion-dollar shakedown scheme. And we could prove it."

It turned out to be uphill work. When Oracle's lawyers went to see the district attorney of San Mateo County, James Fox, he told them that he had no interest in pursuing the case. Finally Ellison himself saw Fox. "I was not happy. Fox seemed to be unwilling to even look at the case? He's the D.A. It's his *job* to look at the evidence and then decide whether or not to prosecute. After a rather heated discussion, he finally agreed to have an assistant D.A. review the case. A couple of days later, into my office walks Paul Wasserman, San Mateo County's smartest, toughest assistant district attorney. Wasserman immediately starts asking me a series of prepared questions carefully designed to trip me up if I was lying. As I answer question after question, I watch the expression on Wasserman's face slowly change from disdainful skepticism to mild amusement. Then he gets this big grin on his face, he starts shaking his head from side to side, and then he start laughing. I'm just staring at him, unable to figure out what the hell is going on. He stops laughing for a moment and says, 'I didn't expect this, but I believe what you're telling me. Boy, did you get fucked. God, are you stupid. Why did you go out with her?' Then he starts laughing again. He just thinks it's hilarious. Then I tell him that I wasn't a defendant; I was really just a witness. 'Witness?' he says, 'man, you're not a witness, you're the victim. Who would believe it? Larry Ellison the victim? This is funny!' I didn't think it was funny, but I was glad he believed me."

Not only was Wasserman prepared to take the case, another powerful piece of evidence came to light that further undermined Lee. Andrea Zeman, the Argentinean woman Ellison had been going out with at the same time as he was seeing Lee, had read about the case in the newspapers. After several fruitless attempts to call Ellison, she finally got through with some very interesting information. It turned out that Lee had once telephoned her and had said, "I understand we're both dating Larry Ellison. You know, if we play our cards right, we can each get a million dollars out of this." Zeman replied, "Really? I was just hoping for dinner." Ellison asked her if she was willing to testify to that in court. "That's why I called," she said. Zeman had broken off with Ellison a couple of years earlier and had left Oracle. Before doing so she had written Ellison a letter explaining her reasons. Ellison says, "It was one of the most thought-provoking letters I've ever received. It was a brilliantly written explanation of my unwillingness to take emotional risks. It was so insightful that it made me want to date her again. But she was too smart to fall into that trap a second time." But luckily for Ellison, the sincere and serious Zeman was a perfect witness.

Ellison also turned out to be a pretty good witness when the case eventually came to court almost four years after Lee's departure from Oracle and the technical evidence relating to Lee's forgery was conclusive. She was convicted of two counts of perjury and one of creating false evidence. She was sentenced to spend a year in jail without parole and to give back the $100,000 she had earlier received in settlement from Oracle. To make matters worse for Lee, she was also sentenced to an additional three years in prison for a bizarre incident in which she had burst into a next-door neighbors' home brandishing a gun and told them that if they didn't turn off the music that was disturbing her, she would blow them away. Lee claimed she had been holding a comb rather than a gun. But nobody believed her.

Ellison still feels bitter about the effect of the Lee case on his reputation. He complains that her allegations received infinitely more media coverage than the fact that they were eventually disproved in court. A *Washington Post* writer, putting together a big profile on Ellison in late 2000, assured him that he wouldn't be writing about the Lee affair, as if it were something that Ellison should be ashamed of. "The article was a hatchet job," says Ellison. "And me being a victim just didn't fit with the rest of his story." *

• • •

In the years after the break-up with Kathleen O'Rourke, Ellison's life was quite lonely. Steve Jobs could see that his friend's personal life was less than satisfactory: "Larry had been married a few times, and he was working really hard, and he just ended up doing some of the things in his forties that most people do in their twenties, except that Larry had more

---

*LE writes: The accusation of my wrongdoing was a sensational story, so it got front-page coverage. Me being proven innocent was a much less interesting story, so it got a lot less coverage. Besides, it contradicted all the earlier stories. That's just how the news business works: the sensational stuff goes on page one. To be fair, one publication, Elle magazine, did run a cover story called "Sex, Lies and Email in Silicon Valley" after the trial was over.

resources than most people in their twenties, so he did it on a rather grander scale. After breaking up with Kathleen, he went out with a lot of people, but I think that after a certain amount of time he realized that it wasn't very fulfilling." Another friend, the Nobel Prize–winning scientist Dr. Joshua Lederberg, recalls, "At that time, he had almost no one staffing the house, maybe just a housekeeper and one other. There was no one else there. I would sometimes have to enrich his pantry. I thought he was leading a very lonely life." *

Whether or not Ellison was searching for a more serious relationship when he met Melanie Craft while departing a crowded San Francisco restaurant in 1996, it's hard to argue with him when he claims that it was love at first sight: "I took one look at her, and I was finished." There was something about the striking twenty-six-year-old with the high cheekbones and flowing dark blond hair that made him go over and start talking to her. Craft, who was at Bix with a girlfriend, says, "He just sauntered up and introduced himself. He told me who he was in the first few minutes, but I'd never heard of Oracle. I guess he sort of chatted me up—I don't know what else you could call it."

When Craft told him that she was a writer working on a romantic novel, Ellison bragged that he knew people whom she might find interesting and told her that he might be able to find her an agent. Pushing his luck, he suggested that maybe they should get together sometime. Politely, but firmly, Craft informed him that she was engaged and very definitely not on the market.

Unabashed, Ellison's next move was to send his driver, Carl Olsen, back to the restaurant with a note. The letter said a little more about himself, including the information that he too was in a serious relationship, by coincidence, with another writer. Craft says, "He was trying to defuse the tension in the situation. I thought, well, this is interesting. He knows that I'm not available for dating, but he's not going away. He's smart and funny, and there's no reason why I can't get to know him. To be honest, I thought he'd be great material for me. I was writing romance novels with larger-than-life heroes. But how often does someone like me meet someone like that?" In fact, the relationship that Ellison alluded to and that put Craft at her ease wasn't quite as serious as he'd made out: "I'd been

---

*LE writes: Josh would usually stay at my house when he was in town. I always looked forward to these visits. We'd spend the late evenings eating oatmeal cookies and discussing politics, molecular biology, and the Internet.

out with this other writer a few times—but I was stretching it a bit to call it a 'relationship.' "

Craft was engaged to and living with a young man she had met seven years earlier at Oberlin College, who was her first and, until then, her only boyfriend. After college, they had spent time together in Kenya and then had moved to San Francisco when Palmer had begun a Ph.D. at the University of California. The couple were broke: he was doing a little teaching while Craft did odd jobs—cleaning houses, working as a bartender, making pastries at a bakery—to support her writing. Ellison decided that the best approach was patience. "Whenever I was going to a particularly great event, I'd invite Melanie." One such was the premiere of the movie *Toy Story*, made by Steve Jobs's "other company," the computer animation firm Pixar Animation Studios. If meeting Jobs at a film premiere wasn't enough to impress Craft, Ellison was soon able to top that.

Invited to a dinner in honor of President Bill Clinton by California senator Dianne Feinstein, Ellison insisted that Craft go with him. Ellison says, "We're in this room with the senator and about forty other people. Suddenly, without any announcement, the president appears in the entryway. All heads turn toward 'the man,' and everyone stops talking. Then, in this dead silent room, the president looks right at me and says, 'Hi, Larry.' Melanie's eyes widen as the president walks over and starts talking to us. It was perfect. Thank you, Mr. President. So, here I am, pulling out all the stops, introducing her to the most fascinating people I know— Steve Jobs, Josh Lederberg, the president—desperately trying to make some progress with this woman. But it's not working. I mean, she's having a good time when we get together. She thinks my friends are interesting. She thinks I'm interesting. But she didn't want to date me."

Inexperienced though Craft was, it didn't take a genius to realize that Ellison's interest in her went further than having someone cute on his arm to accompany him to glitzy events. But she enjoyed his company and reckoned that if she didn't respond, he would get over it. She was also well aware that his persistent courtship didn't mean that he wasn't seeing other women. She says: "I looked him up on the Internet, and there was all of this awful, tabloid-style press about him. It was obvious that he wasn't living as a monk, but he never made a move on me. I think he knew that it would be the surest way to make me disappear. I liked him, liked spending time with him, and I was trying hard to keep us out of the kind of confrontational situation that would force an end to the friendship. It's funny, in retrospect. Knowing him now, I'd guess that my unavailability was part of what kept him interested in me. It's just like they tell you to behave in *The Rules,* but I meant it."

Not only did Ellison continue to ask Craft out, he would even ask her fiancé as well, on one occasion inviting both Melanie and her fiancé to his annual garden party at Atherton to celebrate the cherry blossoms. At the party, Ellison introduced him to Steve Jobs. Afterwards Jobs asked, "Larry, did you say that guy was Melanie's fiancé? What's going on? What do you think you're doing?" "It's all part of the strategy," explained Ellison. "Strategy?" said Jobs. "You call this a strategy?" Ellison says, "It became sort of a long-running joke. Every time Steve saw me, he'd ask, 'How's the Melanie strategy going?' Then he'd laugh at me. He never missed an opportunity to tell someone we both knew all about it. One day I heard this raucous laughter coming from Ray Lane's office. It sounded like there was a fraternity party going on in there. So I walk in, and there's Steve with Ray. They take one look at me, and they both start laughing again. They had been discussing the 'Melanie strategy.' Steve thought it was one of the stupidest things he'd ever seen, me having a mad crush on this young girl."

In fact, even without Ellison's genteel pursuit, Craft's relationship was already breaking down. When the couple broke up, Ellison was there to pick up the pieces. Ellison says, "A year and a half after I met Melanie, I kissed her for the first time. We were both sitting on the couch in my living room. Right after I kissed her I told her, 'Don't move, I've got to do something.' " Ellison picked up the phone and Melanie watched him dial. "Steve, you know the Melanie strategy? Yeah, well—it worked." Then he hung up.*

Not long after, Craft moved into Ellison's house on Isabella Avenue. Craft says, "When I first met him, I thought he was a 'suit.' In my value system at the time, a businessman was a big step down from an academic or an artistic type. But Larry surprised me. He's the smartest guy I've ever known. The suit, I learned, is his way of giving the finger to that conformist casual dress code in Silicon Valley. Larry isn't one for following the crowd." One of the things about Ellison that most impressed Craft, which may surprise some people, was his honesty: "He's very truthful. He says the things that other people are afraid to say. As a woman, I've

---

*LE writes: I can't believe I immediately called Steve. But I did. I felt like I had been drafted in the first round by the Lakers, and I wanted to tell my best friend.

learned to dissemble, but I get pretty damn tired of it sometimes. In him, I saw the personification of that quote from Shakespeare: 'While you live, tell truth and shame the Devil.' "

Six years later, the relationship is still going strong, which means that it has already outlasted all previous ones other than his first marriage. It seems to work mainly because each has found a way of allowing the other space. Ellison says of Craft, "She writes, and writing is an all-consuming, solitary task. If she's not writing, she's not happy. So she spends a lot of her time alone. She does, however, come out of her room for meals." She says of him, "He needs freedom within a stable framework, but I haven't always been able to offer him—or anyone else—either of those things. I was really young when we met, and Larry has had to push me toward adulthood at times. I didn't always go willingly, but the end result is that our relationship has gotten stronger as I've gotten older and become more focused on doing a good job with my own life. It took a lot of hard work on both of our parts. It could easily have gone the other way."

During what she sees as that period of dependency, Craft was desperate for Ellison to marry her. She says now, "I pushed much harder than I should have. I mean, I hardly even knew Larry when I was demanding that I become his wife. It was childish of me, and quite rightly, it scared the hell out of him. At the time, I didn't understand his history with this issue, and I was angry with him for being so cautious. He had to do a careful balancing act with me. He never said, 'No, I don't want to marry you.' He'd say, 'Yes, let's do it in the spring, when the cherry trees are blooming.' And then spring would come closer and closer, and I'd feel his reluctance. It was painful, because I read it as a lack of love, rather than a lack of confidence.

"I don't feel that reluctance in him anymore, but I know things now that I didn't know then. I learned—the hard way—that outside of our friends and family, the world doesn't give a fig about me, other than as Larry's partner. When I was working lousy jobs, dreaming of someday hitting *The New York Times*'s best-seller list, I sure didn't foresee that the first mention of my name in print would be in *Vanity Fair* as Larry Ellison's latest girlfriend, a 'blond twenty-something in tight jeans.' But that's the way things work. My second book comes out in the fall, and I want to have accomplished at least that much before Larry and I go on to the next stage. I know now how easy it is to get subsumed. I don't think that it would happen again, but I'm not as sure as I'd like to be."

Craft's writing may be the savior of their relationship. Now finishing her third book, Craft rarely goes anywhere without her Apple laptop, frequently tapping away in the back of a limo or on the plane when accompanying Ellison on business. Hunched over her Mac, she seems to be proclaiming that although she's with Ellison, she has a life and identity that are separate and distinct from his. Ellison says, "She once read to me from a book about the temperament of writers. It said that writers should never get married because they are so obsessive, self-possessed, and narcissistic. I thought, 'Really? Me too. This just might work.'" Ellison dreads the kind of relationship in which two people almost merge into one: "The happier you are with your separate and independent life, the better your relationship is likely to be. Our relationship is best when her writing is going well and things are good at Oracle."

For all that and the age difference—of which Ellison is more aware than Craft—they are comfortable with each other. Returning with Ellison from a business trip to Washington, D.C., on board the GV, Ellison suddenly said to me, "A child is irreplaceable. You'd never trade your child for a smarter, more beautiful child. Your child is part of your family. Melanie's part of my family now. Maybe there's a woman out there who's smarter or better-looking or whatever, but it doesn't matter. I'm not looking for something better. I'm happy with what I have." He went on to say that he had even been thinking of having children with Melanie, if that was something that she also wanted to do: "I'd love to have more children, but it's completely her call." Although the pressures at Oracle were building, he seemed very happy.

Those closest to Ellison, such as Jimmy Linn and Steve Jobs, agree that Craft has been good for him, bringing a stability and constancy to his life that was alarmingly lacking before. Jobs says, "Guys can get an illness in which they believe there can always be a better girl around the next corner. Nick Hornby, in the book *High Fidelity,* calls it 'death by small increments.' It's a disease that can get worse if you're very successful and you have a great many options. But time takes options away. I remember chatting with Larry when he was in his dating phase and saying, 'You're fifty now, imagine yourself when you're sixty doing this. Imagine yourself when you're seventy doing this; it's going to get really fucking weird.' I think he gets that now, and the relationship with Melanie is what's finally got him there."

But positive though friends are about Ellison's relationship with Craft, there's a lurking fear that marriage and children could alter something that works on its own terms. One said, "He loves Melanie, but Larry's a very fluid guy." Others expressed skepticism about Craft's apparent uncertainty about whether to go to "the next stage," as she puts it, suggesting that she might "only want to have children to solidify her standing with Larry."* Others, less uncharitably, are just worried about the damage that failing to sustain a fourth marriage might do to their friend.

Ellison and Craft both know that children would change the dynamics of a successful relationship fundamentally—and that's always scary. They wouldn't be the first couple to decide that the risk is simply too great. That they love each other is not in doubt. But most crucially, and despite everything they both say about the need to give each other space, I think they have come to depend upon each other. There is much about the relationship that is difficult for Craft: the age difference alone is a challenge; Ellison dominates even when he doesn't intend to, and he comes with quite a lot of personal baggage. The main reason, however, why this relationship is more likely to endure than the others is the change that has taken place within Ellison himself. As he says, "I can divide my life into two phases: the first, where I was desperately trying to be the person I thought I should be, and the second, where I finally accepted the person that I really am. The second phase has been much happier than the first." In other words, to be capable of accepting the love of others, you first have to love yourself.

---

*LE writes: Clearly this anonymous critic has Melanie confused with a character in a Tom Wolfe novel.

21

LARRYLAND

"Hey, Ellison! You're out of fucking control!" The familiar voice of Scott McNealy, the feisty, *faux*-blue-collar boss of Sun Microsystems, rang out across the lake. It was April 13, 2002, and Larry Ellison was holding his annual cherry blossom party for about fifty of his closest friends. Although the parties were famous in Silicon Valley for the exclusiveness of the guest list and their restrained elegance, this year's was something special. Instead of holding it in the pretty grounds of his house in Atherton, Ellison had decided to throw open Sanbashi (Three Bridges), his lakeside Japanese village inspired by the houses and gardens of imperial Kyoto, to his friends for the first time. He had been building this home, at first in his imagination and then in the Woodside hills, for more than ten years.

I was the first to arrive because Ellison had promised me a tour of the six houses, based on originals built between the fifteenth and eighteenth centuries. I'd been over the place several times in the previous eighteen months, but this was the first time I'd been there since the water had gone into the five-acre lake that lay at the heart of the forty-acre site. As Ellison had promised, the water didn't just provide a focal point, it seemed almost magically to shrink the houses. When I had first seen them, protected by scaffolding and cladding, standing proud above the twelve-foot-deep concrete lakebed, they had seemed substantial, even imposing, structures. But now they withdrew into the artfully designed landscape scenery, dwarfed by the giant redwoods behind them.

From a distance, they seemed so polite and unassuming that it was difficult to comprehend either the ambition or the expense—at well over $100 million, probably the costliest American home built for a private individual since William Randolph Hearst's grandiloquent San Simeon. Although far more human in scale than San Simeon or Cornelius Vanderbilt's great house at Newport, Rhode Island, The Breakers, it was just as fantastic.

Yet McNealy's idea that Ellison was out of control was precisely wrong. Just as Ellison at times appeared determined to use the centralizing power of Oracle's computer technology to control every lever of a giant company, it seemed that the beautiful park he had created was all about control, too. Ellison had spent years learning about the Japanese aesthetic and thinking about the kind of environment that would most soothe his senses and calm his soul. Nothing was more controlling than the Japanese approach to landscape design in which nature was distilled to its sublime essence. At its heart was a supreme paradox: heightened naturalness is the result of hugely disciplined contrivance.

• • •

As the party guests arrived, their cars were valet-parked in a concealed compound and they were ushered toward the elegantly curving boathouse, where an electrically powered replica of a traditional Japanese lake boat was waiting to transport them silently past the large waterfall (courtesy of the giant engineering firm Bechtel) to the landing stage of the main house. From there they wandered from house to house, stopping to take in the vistas and to marvel at the craftsmanship of the little wooden buildings. People would stroke the satin-smooth surface—achieved by planing and neither painted nor varnished—of the cedar wood and pine.

With the exception of McNealy, whom Ellison had once identified as a possible successor at Oracle, there were relatively few Silicon Valley movers and shakers on the invitation list and only two from Oracle— Sohaib Abbasi and Safra Catz—apart from board members such as Don Lucas, Jeff Berg (the Hollywood *über*-agent), and Michael Boskin (a professor of economics at nearby Stanford). Among those present were admired friends such as Tom Lantos, the distinguished California congressman and campaigner for human rights, and Joshua Lederberg, the Nobel Prize–winning geneticist.

But for the most part, the guests were people Ellison had known for a long time. If there was a dress code, it spanned from woolly sweaters and jeans to one or two full-length ball gowns. He had even sent his plane to Chicago to make sure that his family would be there. Despite the grandeur of the setting, a Japanese banquet of considerable sophistication, and after-dinner music courtesy of one of the world's greatest classical guitarists, Pepe Romero, it wasn't a show-off's party. In some ways, it felt more like a christening or a wedding. Ellison, with Melanie affectionately at his side, radiated pride and happiness. For a time, Oracle's problems seemed a long way away.

• • •

Ellison's preoccupation with the Japanese aesthetic had been triggered during a business trip to Japan in his late twenties, when he had been working for Amdahl, a junior rival of IBM. While there, he managed to squeeze in what turned out to be a life-changing excursion to Kyoto, where he visited the Heian shrine. "By Japanese standards it's not a spectacular garden, but it was the first authentic Japanese garden I'd ever seen, and it had a profound effect on me. I spent five hours there, sitting on a bench, taking it all in.

"I like all gardens, but Japanese gardens seem to have been painted by God. The controlling hand of man is hidden from view. It's as if you were wandering through a forest and just happened upon a beautiful mountain meadow and lake. The sights, sounds, and scents of a Japanese garden trigger something deep inside of us. There's this primal connection to the sound of the water, the moisture in the air, the rich smell of pine needles, and the damp soil. Early man would always build his villages near water. Japanese gardens re-create our evolutionary environment. When we visit a Japanese garden, we recall our ancient home. The memory fills us with a reassuring sense of safety and peace. It's a sublime experience."

Other qualities of the Japanese aesthetic also appealed to Ellison. The relatively small scale of even the houses built for princes was another aspect of its determination to achieve a harmonious relationship with nature—very different from great European palaces and the imitations erected by bombastic American tycoons that were designed to dominate the landscape and encourage a feeling of awe. Ellison also liked the way the minimal interiors reflected the simplicity of the gardens outside; he's fond of saying, "Your garden is not complete until there is nothing more you can take out of it." Above all, he prizes the deliberate ambiguity between outdoors and indoors. "Japanese houses," he says, "are so low to the ground that when you open the *shoji* [paper wall], you can put your hand out and touch the ground."

Further inspiration came from Kona Village, an exclusive resort in Hawaii made up of grass huts strung around a lake, where Ellison had spent family holidays with Steve Jobs. He says, "Gradually the design took shape. I wanted to have a lake surrounded by a village of small wooden buildings. An upper pond was to be connected to the lower lake by a pair of streams, so that the garden would be filled with the sound of running water."

Ellison began to make sketches and build a series of scale models. His collaborators were Ron Herman, who had landscaped the Japanese-style garden at Atherton; Paul Discoe, an eccentric perfectionist who, in his zeal to become a Zen priest, had wandered around Japan, often barefoot in the snow; and Isuke Shigeru, who spoke almost no English but knew all about the placing of rocks and boulders.* Discoe was a largely self-taught architect who had no engineering background, but what Ellison liked about him was his passionate dedication to authenticity. After he constructed a perfect small teahouse in the grounds of Ellison's home in Atherton, Ellison had no hesitation in entrusting the project to him.

At times, even Ellison has been startled by Discoe's intensity. He says, "I learned to be a little wary of Paul's zealous quest for authenticity. Authenticity has its limits. Paul wanted little itty-bitty lavatories—holes in the ground, basically. I prefer toilets with running water." More recently, Discoe refused to sink lighting into the cedar ceiling of the houses. After nearly a year of pressure from Ellison—"Hey, guys, gimme a break, I gotta live here. It gets dark at night. I want lights"—Discoe relented, but not until he and the carpenters held a small ceremony during which they begged the forgiveness of the wood gods for the brutalities that Ellison had ordered to be inflicted upon them. Ellison says, "It was quite traumatic for them."

After Ellison had bought the land, removed several existing houses in the process, and satisfied the local planning authorities that the lake and the houses would comply with stringent earthquake regulations, the work could finally begin. Ellison went to Japan to recruit master carpenters and plasterers. "The best craftsmen in Japan are considered national treasures. That's who we hired." The rest of the team included an army of aging hippie craftsmen, most of whom came over from Berkeley each day, and hard-hatted civil engineers from the likes of Bechtel.

The first projects were the landscaping and the lake. To ensure that in an earthquake the water wouldn't carry half of Woodside down to Highway 280, the lake had to be built with three layers of concrete with a

---

*LE writes: Shigeru is a genius. He's the master sculptor who turned the garden into art.

water membrane between each two layers—a major feat of engineering over such a large area. In all, seven houses ring the lake: the bridge house, the two parts of the main house, the Katsura house, the waterfall house, the guest house, and the boathouse. Each of them is different in size and character, the architectural styles spanning from the fifteenth to the eighteenth centuries. The idea, says Ellison, is that it should look like a village that has grown up over time. Beneath the houses, hidden from view, are mighty concrete foundations, the filtration system that drives the waterfall and replenishes the lake with drinking-quality water, a cinema, offices for staff, and parking for cars.

Although the overall effect is startlingly beautiful and the houses look, smell, and feel gorgeous, I still find myself wondering whether Ellison and Craft will enjoy living here. Will the carefully contrived perfection of the place turn out to be stifling? Will those "human-scale" houses actually seem too small once they are occupied? Will the rigorous asceticism of Discoe deny them too many creature comforts and technological conveniences? Ellison says simply that if he doesn't like it he won't live there, but that he can't imagine that happening.

• • •

If Sanbashi seems like an extravagant fantasy, Ellison's other "grand project" is just as ambitious: nothing less than one of the biggest and most beautiful private yachts in the world.

Ellison's first "proper" yacht was *October Rose,* which he had bought in 1996 from Kirk Kerkorian for $10 million. The 192-foot *October Rose* was a gorgeous boat but a little too slow and staid for Ellison's tastes. A couple of years later, he paid the widow of the Mexican media tycoon Emilio Azcarraga $25 million for one of the fastest megayachts ever built, the 244-foot Francis design *Eco.* With two 5,000-horsepower diesels flanking an 18,500-horsepower GE turbine like the ones that power an F-18 fighter jet, *Eco* could do more than thirty-five knots.

But for Ellison, that was only the starting point. He renamed her *Katana* and poured another $35 million into her. He stripped out her garish interior and replaced it with the light woods and cream-colored furnishings he loves. Out went the seaplane that hogged the afterdeck and in went a basketball court, a giant plasma-screen viewing system, a two-tier owner's "apartment" complete with wing station–mounted outdoor hot tub, six spacious guest staterooms, and more than twenty full-time crew to sail the boat and cosset Ellison and his friends.

Along with the 192-foot Norman Foster–designed *Ronin* (picked up for a bargain $15 million and "fixed up" for a mere $20 million) based at Sausalito and ready to cruise anywhere in the Pacific with its crew of fifteen, most people might have thought that Ellison had as much boat as any human being could reasonably want. But just as living in the pastiche Japanese villa at Atherton had driven Ellison to attempt a more perfect realization of the Japanese aesthetic, so the almost perfect *Katana* drove him to contemplate what the perfect boat would be like.

Ellison had a clear idea of what he wanted. He and Craft had decided that the new boat would be their second home—a place where they would spend an increasing amount of time, eventually as much as three or four months each year. For several reasons, a much bigger boat than *Katana* was dictated. The first was that Ellison wanted to have space and privacy in which to live and work even when he had guests aboard, yet he insisted on a shape that was low and sleek. She had to be beautiful and ultramodern, but she must look like a proper ship, not some ghastly floating palace. He says, "This project will result in the creation of a wonderful piece of kinetic sculpture. Modern yachts pack as much structure as possible on top of the hull. I wanted just the opposite. Our design wastes space, but it has the long, low, graceful lines of those beautiful old Atlantic steamers."

Second, he demanded both enormous cruising range and high speed. *Katana* achieved her speed thanks to her thirsty turbine, whereas *Ronin* had a semiplaning hull. As a consequence, both were compromised. The only way to get what he wanted was by conventional diesel propulsion and sheer length along the waterline.

But who would be the equivalent of Discoe and Shigeru, a driven obsessive who would share and articulate Ellison's vision? Ellison interviewed just about every major boat designer in the world. Finally, in late 1999, he called on Jon Bannenberg, an Englishman in his early seventies who worked from a studio just off London's Kings Road. More than thirty years earlier, he had designed one of the most elegant yachts ever built, the sublime *Carinthia VI*. Coincidentally, like Discoe (or maybe not), Bannenberg had no formal training. He was known for being headstrong and difficult to deal with. Ellison recalls, "Everyone told me it was a waste of time to talk to Jon. They said he never designs what the client wants, just what he wants. Well, I wasn't happy with any of the other designers, and I tried them all, so Jon was my last resort. Within five minutes I knew I had found the right guy."

Bannenberg was just what Ellison had been looking for: another crazy perfectionist to work with. He says, "People who set incredibly high standards for their work find it difficult to collaborate with people who don't understand and appreciate their reckless pursuit of perfection. But I love working with these brilliant people with their compulsive personalities. I find them interesting, and I think I understand what drives them. I was very lucky to find Jon. Without him I never would have gone ahead with the project."

Bannenberg, at an age when most men are well into retirement, had found the perfect client: somebody who shared his aesthetic sense and who had the wealth and ambition to inspire him to do his very best work, to create a masterpiece that might surpass even *Carinthia*. Right from the beginning, Bannenberg realized that Ellison would be an exceptional client. "I had an instant connection with Larry through all kinds of philosophical things and interests . . . : his interest in architecture, the combination of being a radical thinker yet a disciplined one, his willingness to take on establishment ideas and win. He was fascinating, amusing, opinionated, and very attractive."

Bannenberg, on principle, had earlier refused to pitch for Ellison's business by taking part in a beauty contest with rival designers. But immediately after the meeting in London, he contacted Ellison's yacht broker, Mel Wood, and told him that he would do a drawing and make a model because he was absolutely sure that he could make Ellison what he wanted. "I didn't see it as a beauty contest anymore. He had been inundated by designs from all these people who thought that because Larry was so rich he must want something very elaborate, whereas what he wanted was a no-nonsense, stripped-down, shipshape, powerful vessel. I knew that I could do it and that nobody else could. Arrogance. So that's what I did, and of course he went crazy over it. It was what he had in his mind, but no one else had been able to release it."

Once news got out that the great boat was going to be built, there was the inevitable feeding frenzy among the major shipyards and the committees of consultants who make a fat living from appearing to manage such projects. Right from the outset, Bannenberg and Ellison agreed that they would work differently. Bannenberg believed there was only one yard capable of the work—Lürssens in Bremen, Germany, which had built *Carinthia*—and that consultants would only get in the way. Bannenberg pointed out that Lüssens had been going for 125 years. He said, "This business is crazy enough as it is: it's as if we're building one-off, handmade 747s with no R and D. It helps that Larry and I have a hugely simple and powerful association. Larry doesn't demand endless work reports as long as you're doing the job and you don't fuck it up. . . .

"One of the greatest pleasures in my life is that through this work I have met Larry. As for where this yacht stands in my life, it's not only the greatest yacht that I have ever built but *the* greatest that has ever been built in the tradition of great yachts going back to 1810 because of its absolute purity of purpose. There is no question about that."

Although *Sayonara*, as she is likely to be called in honor of Ellison's world championship–winning maxi,* would not be radical for the sake of it, the design still called for considerable innovation. The deck was being built completely flush, like a sailboat's, with all the fittings hidden to ensure that nothing extraneous interfered with the elegant silhouette. The swept-back funnel would be constructed from titanium and carbon fiber. But perhaps the most eye-catching and technically demanding feature would be the glass walls around the top two decks. With the yacht likely to tip the scales at around 70,000 tons, the glass alone will weigh more than 40 tons. Inside, Bannenberg has included a glassed-in walkway across the engine room from which to observe the massive diesels hard at work.

I asked Bannenberg what he would say to people who might well regard a 450-foot yacht for personal enjoyment as an obscene self-indulgence. "If you start on that road, where does it lead? Nobody needs a yacht, nobody needs a racehorse, nobody needs art or music or opera houses. You don't have to have any of these things—so what's left? People aren't motivated, thank God, just by need. If humans didn't create things they didn't need, there'd be no art of any sort. Larry is often portrayed by ignorant philistines as just a rich git who likes showing off. There are people building big yachts who just want to show off, but Larry's not one of them. I encourage Larry to think about the worth of what he's doing."

If a fine building could be considered art, why not a boat? It was clear that Bannenberg thought of Ellison as a brave and enlightened patron. And part of Ellison saw himself as an impresario creating the conditions in which gifted and driven people could do their very best work. After all, he had often said that he thought it quite likely that he would be remembered as the man who built Sanbashi rather than as the founder of Oracle. But that's not why he did it. He built it because he wanted it. Just as with the Woodside project, it seemed far more important to make the

---

LE writes: I've finally decided to call the new motor yacht Rising Sun. *Sayonara will be reserved for a racing sailboat—if I ever build another one.*

boat perfect than to make the boat fit within a specific budget. Is it a form of madness? Probably. No wonder Bannenberg was such a happy man.

• • •

A few months after I met Jon Bannenberg, he was diagnosed with a brain tumor. He died in May 2002. Although he never saw his creation become a physical reality, his work was largely complete, and, as Ellison said, he saw it as clearly in his mind as if she had been floating at anchor outside his cramped studio.

When he received the news of Bannenberg's death, Ellison e-mailed me: "Jon was one of a handful of people I liked and admired so much that I made him a role model along with Tom Lantos and Josh Lederberg. He was more fit and vital in his seventies than most people are at thirty. Age failed to slow him down until it conspired with cancer. Even then Jon worked on the project right until the end. He never accepted there was a problem he could not solve or a fight he could not win. I'll miss our dinner conversations about history and human nature. I'll miss listening to him play the piano. I'll miss watching him charm Melanie. What do you think the creator had in mind when he let this happen?"

• • •

In Paul Discoe and Jon Bannenberg, Ellison had found uncompromising, driven perfectionists who shared his appetite to create something extraordinary. But the person he depended upon to make it all work was a San Francisco–based designer, Laura Seccombe. He had first used Seccombe in 1985 for corporate work. Even on that first project some things were already apparent about Ellison. One was that green was his favorite color and "he wanted a lot of green in the building." The second was that he had a strong sense of visualization. Seccombe says, "A lot of clients can't see three-dimensionally, but Larry can. It means that when you're explaining something to him that you want to do, he gets it and remembers it."

After that came a helter-skelter of both corporate and personal commissions. Although Seccombe had never worked on a private house, she was intrigued enough by what Ellison wanted to achieve with his newly purchased Japanese-style villa in Atherton to leave her architectural practice and set up her own firm. When Oracle moved from Davis Drive to Redwood Shores in 1988, it was Seccombe and Ellison who between them created the look of the new campus whose gleaming cylindrical towers today dominate the flat Bay Area landscape, and as she says, "make a very powerful and sophisticated statement." Of the interior she says, "Larry wanted an environment that would boost morale, so he was adamant that everything had to be done to a certain level of quality." During Oracle's crisis in the early 1990s, the extravagance of the campus, with its 35,000-square-foot gym, manicured gardens, and ornamental lake was used as a stick to beat Ellison with, but Seccombe believes that his commitment to quality has contributed to Oracle's subsequent success. She says, "He's unique in the industry both for his involvement and concern for aesthetics."*

A very different domestic project from Ellison's home at Atherton was the house he bought in 1991 in San Francisco's Pacific Heights. Designed by the celebrated architect Bill Wurster toward the end of his life for heirs of the Spreckels sugar dynasty, the house occupies a spectacular position on Broadway, looking out across the bay toward Sausalito with the Golden Gate Bridge to the left, Alcatraz to the right.

After much negotiation with the city authorities, who considered it a historic building, Ellison won permission to open up the whole of the back facade, essentially creating a single glass wall extending over four floors. Inside, Ellison wanted a highly modern, ultraminimalist look. Although conceptually far removed from his home in Atherton, according to Seccombe the houses have one thing in common: in both, what lay outside was what mattered most—in one the garden, in the other, the extraordinary views.

Seccombe has also redesigned the interiors of both *Ronin* and *Katana*, so it was natural for her to work with Jon Bannenberg from the outset, visualizing and designing interior spaces that would match the drama of Bannenberg's naval architecture. However, Ellison deliberately kept her away from Paul Discoe and Sanbashi until the project was nearing completion. But with about eighteen months to go before he was due to move in, he asked her to get involved: any earlier, and she would inevitably have clashed with Discoe, demanding compromises that would have diluted the purity of his approach; any later, and it might have been impossible to make the compromises required for Ellison actually to be able to live there.

I sensed that Seccombe was troubled by Sanbashi, although that may just have been the understandable tension that existed between her and

---

LE writes: Steve Jobs cares just as much about aesthetics as I do—maybe more.

Discoe and the fact that she felt she had been brought in to "fix some-thing" that was not her creation. She was much more enthusiastic about the collaboration with Bannenberg. "When Larry first talked to me about it, he said he wanted it to be like a floating Broadway. It will have the same discipline as Broadway. Things will only be there because they are functional or beautiful and absolutely correct. It's what you take away that makes it perfect."

• • •

In June 2002, Ellison flew to London from Bremen in his brand-new Bombardier Global Express (a $35 million replacement for the narrower-bodied GV). Because of work pressures and Bannenberg's death, it was his first visit to the Lürssen yard since work on the new yacht had begun. The hull had recently been launched, but problems with cutting-edge glass-bonding technology had delayed the project, and delivery was now unlikely until 2004. What's she like? I asked him. "Big," said Ellison. "She's very big." It seemed like a curiously flat answer, and I said so.

Ellison sighed and said, "Yes. The boat is very beautiful—a kinetic sculpture made of metal and glass. But in a post–September eleventh world it seems excessive. Now everything that's not essential seems ex-cessive. Building beautiful gardens and beautiful boats have lost their place in the dangerous new world we live in. They no longer promise an escape from the world. There is no escape anymore."

Ellison, in common with more than a few other high-profile CEOs, was also feeling the kickback against corporate greed following the Enron and Global Crossing scandals (WorldCom was still to come). While nobody suggested that there had been any cooking of the books at Oracle or that the company was anything other than immensely prof-itable, its stock was still bumping along the bottom and Ellison had been through a torrid couple of months during a pitched political battle in Cal-ifornia over an Oracle software-licensing deal. He said, "Everyone's so angry about all the money they lost. People feel they were cheated, and some were. But we need to be careful about separating the guilty from the innocent before we start marching people off to the guillotine."

In other words, the great projects that Ellison had embarked upon with such confidence and optimism during tech's "roaring nineties" now struck him as excessive and out of time. Ellison had been through a rough couple months, but somehow I didn't think his gloom would last too long. It was more worrying that for the first time he seemed to be bending his knee to political correctness. That probably wouldn't last, either.

22

A LIFE BEYOND ORACLE

When Joshua Lederberg addressed a Stanford University symposium in 1990, he didn't notice Larry Ellison; nor is it likely that he would have known who he was.

The molecular biologist had left Stanford in 1978 after running the genetics department for some nineteen years but often returned to see old friends and engage in seminars and workshops. He had also had a fruitful collaboration with the university's renowned computer science department, pioneering the development of artificial intelligence. Lederberg had long been interested in the ways in which computers could help in the planning of experiments. After giving his talk, Lederberg received a note from Ellison, explaining who he was and suggesting that they meet up sometime, as they had some shared interests.*

In the event, it was nearly two years before they got together; Lederberg lived in New York, where he was president of Rockefeller University, and Ellison had been fighting for his business life. When finally they met, at Ellison's home on Isabella Avenue, the friendship that developed

---

*LE writes: I was attending a weekend seminar on the Human Genome Project at Stanford. When it was Josh's turn to talk, he used his first five or ten minutes to summarize and integrate the ideas of the speakers who had preceded him. The crystalline clarity and lyric eloquence of his speech were mesmerizing. I had never experienced anything like it. I wasn't alone. Paul Berg (Nobel laureate and father of molecular engineering) told me the same thing happened to him when he talked to Josh.

changed the lives of both men—the Nobel Prize–winning scientist and the brash Silicon Valley entrepreneur.

Today, approaching eighty, Lederberg conforms perfectly to the popular idea of the distinguished polymath. Sartorially disheveled, with a great grizzled head, he speaks softly but with great precision and deliberation. You sense not just intellectual power but considerable moral force. There is something almost prophetic about him.

What were Lederberg's first impressions of Ellison? "I knew nothing about the difficulties that Oracle had been through. He just seemed to me to be one of the smartest people I'd ever met,* someone who was really fired up about what I considered to be a revolution in human communications as important as the printing press." After a couple of meetings, Ellison said to Lederberg, "Here's the key to my house. If you stay anywhere else when you're out here, I'll be very annoyed." Though taking him up on his offer, Lederberg was struck by the contrast between Ellison's beautiful house and the relatively frugal and even rather lonely life he seemed to live there. And while Ellison would frequently return late in the evening, ostensibly from Oracle, their wide-ranging discussions almost never touched on anything that was going on at Redwood Shores. Oracle and girlfriends had compartments in Ellison's life, and so did Nobel Prize winners.

As far as Lederberg could see, Ellison's interest in molecular biology was purely intellectual. He says, "I didn't see him investing or getting practically involved. I had any number of connections with biotech companies, and I thought I'd be doing him a favor to mention some, but he didn't seem to bite on any of those suggestions." Lederberg and Ellison didn't talk only about computers and genes. Lederberg was deeply involved in foreign and domestic policy, and he found some of Ellison's views about the ability of technology and military force to solve problems "somewhat simplistic." Gently he would suggest that maybe things were a little more complicated than Ellison had assumed: force some-

---

*LE writes: Josh is the very smartest person I know. Josh invented computer artificial intelligence just because he needed a tool to solve the structure of large organic molecules. He just dropped by the computer science department and invented AI. Unbelievable. Who else does stuff like that? Of course, Isaac Newton invented the calculus because he needed a tool to solve a few physics problems he was working on. But Newton did most of his work in England, so I never met him.

times had to be used sparingly, and technology would not automatically benefit the poor unless capitalism were tempered with some humanity.* Lederberg observes dryly, "Larry is usually ready for some modulation when we get into the detail."

Ellison's willingness to learn from Lederberg wasn't just confined to late-night intellectual schmoozing. In the summer of 1994, Ellison spent a fortnight's "vacation" in Lederberg's lab working as a humble technician. "He got his hands dirty and enjoyed it very much. He participated in our day-to-day discussions about how the experiments were being planned and the significance of the information we were getting from them. Within two or three days, he'd caught up enough to be able to play a real part—he has a very avid, quick mind. I think the experience helped to confirm his interest in this field, and I began to hear more and more from him about what was going on in other areas." †

Soon afterward, Lederberg felt confident enough of Ellison's seriousness and his friendship to ask him what he wanted to do with his money from a philanthropic point of view. He had just retired from Rockefeller University, so there was no question of putting the bite on Ellison for his own institution. He was convinced, however, that Ellison was ready to listen to some ideas. Lederberg says, "I knew something about philanthropic investment: what works and what doesn't; what can really produce some serious returns; and how to organize it."

Lederberg was careful not to put Ellison under any pressure. But after a series of conversations, the idea formed for Ellison to endow a medical research foundation. For years Ellison had been preoccupied with gaining a better understanding of cancer, the disease that had claimed the lives of his "two mothers" and his Oracle cofounder, Bob Miner. Given the speed at which medical science had been moving in other areas, Ellison thought that real progress in combating cancer had been "pretty dismal."

Lederberg's prompting could not have come at a better time. Having survived Oracle's recent trauma and crushed most of its database competition with Oracle 7, Ellison was convinced that his company would now

---

*LE writes: When capitalism is tempered by democracy there is the hope of combining prosperity with humanity.

†LE writes: I learned a lot by working in Josh's lab. And I had a great time. During lunch breaks a bunch of the postdocs and I would go out and play basketball in the park. It was the perfect way to spend my fiftieth birthday.

be able to handle whatever commercial rivals or the economy threw at it. For Ellison personally, there were two consequences. The first was that he was starting to get accustomed to the idea that he was not only extremely wealthy but highly likely to stay that way. The second was that he was ready for new challenges. Ellison says, "I'd always been curious about the fundamental mechanisms of molecular biology, and now I had this big lever—lots of money—that enabled me to influence the direction the research was going."

For Ellison, simply writing checks to good causes was never an attractive option. Always distrustful of conventional altruism, Ellison needed to develop a version of philanthropy that would work for him. He says, "I really can't distinguish my approach to philanthropy from my approach to anything else I take seriously. It's about discovering my own limits and learning about what it means to be alive. I set goals and live my life in hot pursuit of them: I want to win the America's Cup; I want Oracle to be number one in software; I want to help find cures for cancers. The America's Cup is just a silly game; nevertheless, I work at it. Oracle's an important business, so I work much harder at that. But you know, pursuing cures for cancer is incomparably more interesting and much more important than any of my other goals. So maybe that's what I should focus the rest of my life on. As far as I can tell, 'living large' means working on the most interesting and important problems." And there was another thing: Ellison's lack of religious belief contributed strongly to his sense of waste when a life was cut short by premature death or debilitating illness. "Fundamentally," he says, "life is the only miracle, and understanding how life works is the most interesting mystery remaining to be solved."

It's typically quixotic of Ellison to characterize his philanthropy as a dramatic personal quest to discover a cure for cancer. In an interview with *Fortune* magazine published in August 2001 (the first in which he drew public attention to his philanthropic activities), Ellison was careful to distinguish between the work of his medical foundation, which is primarily concerned with diseases related to aging, and his investment in the privately held Quark Biotech, a commercial company whose research may revolutionize the treatment of various cancers. But Ellison went on, "Someone asked me once how much I would pay to cure cancer if I could. And I replied, 'Everything I've got.' What do you think is cooler: being the richest guy on earth or helping find the cure for cancer? What would you want to do? That's a pretty easy question. Let me nail the Big

C." It left the reader with the rather misleading impression that cancer research was the primary recipient of his philanthropy.

Ellison adds another rider to his definition of philanthropy that he suggests differentiates it from—not coincidentally—the work of the Bill & Melinda Gates Foundation. He argues that the only thing that matters is results—whether any lives are saved. Until you can say that a certain proven lifesaving drug exists only because of research that would not have been funded without your money, it's best not to say anything at all. Ellison says, "We measure philanthropy and philanthropists with the wrong yardstick. It's not the size of the investment as measured in dollars contributed; it's the size of the return as measured in lives saved. That's what we should measure. What good it is to write a check for $100 million if the money is wasted? It may make you feel good, but you didn't help anybody. Money and motives grab a lot of attention, but I don't think you can climb into a person's soul and understand their motives. The correct measure is how much good you did for how many people: how many lives did you save; how many children did you educate; how many jobs did you provide?"

It's hard to say how much of this Joshua Lederberg (or deep down, Ellison himself) agrees with. It does, however, provide Ellison with a kind of shield against questions of motive and comparisons between him and Gates, who has undoubtedly committed greater sums of money to medical research than Ellison. For the record, Ellison has committed $250 million to his own foundation since it began in 1998, and he's made it clear to Lederberg that as the number of sponsored research projects grows, the funding will expand to meet the demand. But it goes deeper than the slightly absurd rivalry with Gates. Ellison can't bear the idea of being categorized as simply a rich man with a simple desire to do some good in the world. Even his philanthropy has to be judged by rules that don't apply to others. It also comes back to his suspicion of altruism and the baggage of political correctness that, these days, often accompanies it. "God won't grant you absolution just because you wrote a few checks," he says.

Whatever Ellison's eccentricities as a philanthropist, Lederberg's influence as chairman of the Ellison Medical Foundation has been powerfully present in setting its goals. Lederberg has a strong sense of how philanthropic funds should be used, in contrast to investment, which expects an economic return, or the aid that governments should give on behalf of taxpayers. For example, if the only concern is a straightforward cost/benefit analysis of the best way to save lives, there's not much doubt that putting money into better sanitation and clean drinking water in the Third World would be the way to go. But both Lederberg and Ellison believe that such uncontroversial projects, which simply require money and management, are the role of governments and aid agencies rather than individuals, however wealthy. Ellison, who unlike many rich men has no objection to paying higher taxes, says, "Higher taxes don't bother me at all so long as governments spend the money efficiently on projects that make the world a better, safer place. Unfortunately most government agencies are quite inefficient, so an awful lot of the money they spend is wasted."

From the outset, Lederberg counseled Ellison against seeing the EMF as a vehicle for waging a personal war against the Big C. He says, "Finding a cure to cancer is not going to happen in any one step. Cancer is a lot of diseases, although there may be conceptual approaches that are shared in a number of areas. I think there will be incremental successes from time to time; however, in twenty years' time there will still be a lot of cancers, albeit not the same ones that we see today. But the main thing is that cancer is probably the most heavily invested area in biomedicine—it's actually very hard to find new niches for an investment in cancer. Which isn't to say that if an idea was presented to us that we were convinced was hot and for some reason wasn't acceptable to other funding sources, we wouldn't support it. But we decided against actively soliciting in cancer." The same was true of AIDS, another illness that doesn't lack for private sector funds.

The decision was made to focus the EMF on diseases that were related to aging—an oddly unfashionable area of research despite the fact that we are all living longer and increasingly susceptible to such illnesses. Our golden years may turn out to be more of a curse than a blessing, and the cost of caring for the sick elderly is in danger of bankrupting social security systems.

Ellison says, "The longer you live, the more likely it is that you'll get one of the common diseases of aging: Alzheimer's, osteoporosis, Parkinson's, and so on. But because health care has improved, these diseases no longer kill you right away. That's the good news. But a longer life span comes at a very high price: higher health care costs and extended periods of human suffering. The only way to avoid paying this price is to find cures for these diseases. Cures are vastly more humane and much more economical than care. Caring for a family member with Alzheimer's, osteoporosis, or Parkinson's can be financially and emotionally exhausting. Unless we cure these diseases, they'll devastate our families and destroy our health care system." *

One of things that has riled Ellison is the perception, stimulated by speculative newspaper articles, that the real purpose of the EMF is to give its benefactor early access to treatments that will extend his own life. A typical example appeared recently in the *San Jose Mercury News*. It suggested that because Ellison was known for reacting badly to the death of loved ones, appeared in good shape for his age, and was an active sportsman, it followed that he was pouring his billions into seeking the "fountain of youth." The piece even managed to chuck in a reference to the age discrimination case brought against Oracle by Randy Baker as further evidence that Ellison had a horror of old age.

Ellison says, "Our medical foundation has marshaled so many magnificent minds and committed hundreds of millions of dollars in an attempt to better understand the fundamental biology underlying the diseases of aging, and somehow the *San Jose Mercury* found a way to write a negative story about it. I think that says a lot more about the *Mercury* than my medical foundation." He does, however, agree that humanitarian issues as well as economic ones are at stake and that his own experiences have affected him: "Diseases of aging—and I consider many cancers to be diseases of aging—hit hard at most of our families. My mother died of leukemia. My brother-in-law got Parkinson's. It was awful to watch his body tremble and the personality I knew so well just slowly disappear." Lederberg simply observes that the time scale involved in bringing primary research from the lab even to the product-testing stage is unlikely to be of much personal benefit to someone of Ellison's age.

If there is a criticism, it is that the diseases that the EMF is focused on are predominantly those of the rich. In poor countries with lower life expectancy, they are simply far less prevalent than other killers. Lederberg

---

*LE writes: Several years ago, I gave a commencement address at Carnegie Mellon University called "Care Less and Cure More." It was my attempt to highlight the high cost of caring for, rather than curing, society's most pressing problems. Diseases of aging affect one segment of our population, while illiteracy affects another. Caring for people who are illiterate is much more expensive than teaching them to read and write. Curing our problems upstream is always better than caring for them downstream.

and Ellison answer the question in different ways. Lederberg argues that once people in the Third World have surmounted the perils of early childhood, and assuming they don't fall victim to violence or AIDS, life expectancy is not as different as the statistics suggest: "This is something that's shared by the whole of mankind, not just the rich." Ellison points out that one of the results of lavishing expensive care on an aging population that votes is that there's less money available for programs for the poor. In the intensifying competition for resources, the education of inner-city children drops to the bottom of the list.

That said, the Ellison Medical Foundation has now added research into infectious diseases of the Third World to its dossier. One of Lederberg's preoccupations is that too many treatments for many diseases, above all AIDS, are simply too expensive for people in poor countries and that drug companies are unwilling to invest in those markets. "Because the people are too poor to buy the medicine, you have to find another approach—it's not intrinsically necessary that a treatment for HIV has to cost $10,000 a year. We should be making long-term gambles in the direction of producing treatments for tuberculosis and malaria and so on that are, above all, affordable."

One thing that may have held the EMF back a little is the relative lack of publicity it has received because of Ellison's uncharacteristic decision not to brag about the work it is funding until something concrete has been achieved—an approach he contrasts with the publicity machine that broadcasts the beneficence of the Gates foundation. But as word has gotten out, so has the number of research projects, now running into hundreds each year, being submitted for sponsorship to Lederberg, Richard Sprott (the former director of the Biology of Aging program at the National Institute of Aging, who was hired to run the foundation), and its superdistinguished Science Advisory Board (SAB). For Lederberg, the only disappointment has been the difficulty of getting Ellison involved in a more hands-on role. Lederberg says, "I've tried very hard to get Larry to engage in SAB meetings, but his time commitments have made it impossible."* Although Ellison has talked about making up to $2 billion available over time, you sense that Lederberg would be more confident

---

*LE writes: At this point in my career, I think I should spend most of my time making money, while the foundation figures out how best to spend it. When I leave Oracle, I'll be able to devote much more of my time to working with the foundation. I'm looking forward to it.

about the future if Ellison were just a little more engaged. "We'll have other options to present to him [to add to aging and infectious diseases] in a couple of years. But these are all open questions. If I could count on his interest in doubling the foundation every three or four years, Larry will become the country's major philanthropist in the biomedical area." Ellison says simply that if Lederberg believes that there are projects that should be funded, they will be.

Two other schemes may compete with the medical foundation for resources. The first is a $100 million project to found a school to study the impact of technology on politics and economics. Ellison would like to see the PET (Politics, Economics, Technology) school investigate the interactions between technologically extended life expectancy, social security spending, and the competition between social groups for scarce public-sector resources. Ellison has approached Stanford, Harvard, and MIT, but he has discovered that trying to do anything genuinely interdisciplinary is hellishly difficult at institutions that aren't set up to run that way. One possibility is to make it a freestanding institution, but it currently seems more likely that if the PET school happens at all, it will be on a much more modest scale than originally contemplated.*

The second idea, a research university focused on biology, which has Lederberg's fingerprints all over it, reflects some of Ellison's suspicion of conventional academic institutions. Ellison believes that one of the major problems in getting potentially lifesaving ideas to market is the squabbling between researchers and their sponsoring universities when there is money to be made from the exploitation of a patent.

Ellison says, "Within a traditional university there's a lot of ambiguity about the ownership of intellectual property. Who owns the patent: the researcher or the university? Who gets the royalties? So I'm thinking of starting a research university that enables scientists to pursue their ideas, patent them, and even create companies on the outside to commercialize their ideas, if that's what they want to do. I want to break down the remaining walls between university research departments and commercial biotechnology companies. Hopefully that will allow new drugs to come to market more quickly. Lives will be saved, and fortunes will be made. Patients will get healthy, and professors will get rich. A perfect marriage of humanitarian ideals and market incentives: human nature at its very best."

---

*LE writes: I've pretty much given up on this idea. Interdepartmental cooperation within a university is near impossible.

What Ellison is now thinking of is something like a "Rockefeller West"—something akin to the university in New York that Lederberg used to run but based in or around San Francisco and dedicated to biotech research. Combining a standard 80/20 "no-haggle" split of royalties* between researchers and the school with Silicon Valley's genius for encouraging entrepreneurs and its established infrastructure for bringing new businesses into existence seems to him the best way to ensure that the crossover from lab to market would happen faster there than anywhere else. Ellison quips, "The medical foundation and the research university will get ninety-five percent of what I earn in my lifetime. I don't think they'll have any problems spending it, either." They'll also get most of his time. He says, "Once I've completed the earning portion of my life, I'll have the time to get deeply involved in the operation of both of these institutions. That should begin to happen three to five years from now as I start to disengage from Oracle."

His impatience with academia and his own ambivalence toward the philanthropic ethic may also help explain why Ellison talks about Quark Biotech Inc. (QBI) with greater excitement than he does about his medical foundation despite "the dazzling work" being done there. Although it is incorporated in California, QBI is an Israeli company, and Ellison, although not a practicing Jew, has something of a love affair with Israel, admiring its steely pragmatism, respect for intellect, and ingrained entrepreneurialism. Having owned 70 percent of the company since 1996, representing an investment of about $100 million, he feels even more responsible for it than for the medical foundation. Finally, the fact that QBI is working on drugs that have the potential to produce dramatic improvements in cancer treatment provides a different order of excitement for Ellison.

And while Quark's long-term projections are daunting for ordinary investors and the odds against hitting the jackpot are long, the possibility that Quark could win big only adds spice to the game. Ellison doesn't disagree but adds, "The time frame is pretty long at QBI [because the whole drug approval process is such a drawn-out business], but they'll deliver lifesaving drugs sooner than the research being done by the medical foundation. That's why I'm so excited about QBI. If I judge myself on the number of lives saved, most likely they'll be the first to deliver. I guess it's just another example of my own impatience and immaturity.

---

*LE writes: I've now decided to give one hundred percent of the patent property to the researcher. It's much simpler that way.

"QBI is developing both therapeutic drugs and diagnostic tests. One test screens a patient's DNA to see if that person is especially sensitive to radiation. There's a small percentage of the population that should not be exposed to radiation of any type—not even dental X rays. Unfortunately, there's no simple test to identify these people. So QBI is developing one. Well, if you can identify people who should avoid radiation, you should also be able to identify people who should avoid taking a particular drug that would be harmful to them. It turns out that there are numerous drugs that have been proven to be very effective at treating a disease, but the drug fails the clinical trial because it's toxic to some people. Now, by looking at the DNA and the clinical outcomes of everyone who took the drug—it cured you, it killed you, it did nothing—we should be able to identify the people this drug is likely help and screen out the people the drug is likely to hurt. It's called drug personalization. It's sort of like how Amazon.com can look at all the books you've previously read to recommend a new one for you—except we look at your genes and recommend the right drug for you. It's a monumental breakthrough because it enables not just one new treatment but thousands of new treatments that previously failed their clinical trials."

Another technology, known as the PFT (Pifithrin) Compound, being pioneered by QBI, is designed to make existing cancer treatments exponentially more effective while reducing their damaging side effects. Ellison says, "The most common forms of cancer therapy are radiation and chemotherapy. Unfortunately, when you use either one of these to kill cancer cells, there is a tremendous amount of collateral damage to healthy cells. That is, large numbers of healthy cells die along with the targeted cancer cells. It's the death of these healthy cells that causes the terrible 'side effects' that accompany most forms of cancer therapy. The healthy cells die because the radiation or chemotherapy damages their DNA, which in turn causes the cell to 'commit suicide' through a process called apoptosis, or programmed cell death. When healthy cells detect that they have DNA damage, they increase the production of their p53 gene. The p53 gene is the primary molecular mechanism that induces programmed cell death in normal, healthy cells. Interestingly, the p53 gene is 'broken' in most cancer cells, so cancer cells will not commit suicide. That makes cancer therapy very difficult. Cancer cells are much harder to kill than healthy cells, because healthy cells have a working suicide mechanism and cancer cells don't.

"QBI solved this problem by developing a drug that turns off the p53 gene in *all* cells for a few hours during and after radiation or chemotherapy. That eliminates most of the collateral damage to healthy cells, thus eliminating most of the side effects. Even better, this enables the physician to go after the cancer more aggressively by increasing the dosage of radiation and chemotherapy without damaging too many healthy cells. We've tested up to ten times the lethal dosage of radiation with minimum ill effects on healthy cells. So the Quark compound flips off the p53 gene for a couple of hours and death takes a holiday. It's a very big deal."

A big deal indeed, but unfortunately Quark has itself fallen foul of the Food and Drug Administration's (FDA's) approval process with PFT. Ellison admits that QBI wasn't sufficiently rigorous in its preclinical trials, with the result that almost two years may have been lost, but he's perplexed by an approval process that is so ultracautious that it can allow many people to die by denying them a new wonder drug because a handful of patients may suffer an adverse reaction. "The FDA and our legal system work hand-in-hand to virtually eliminate errors of commission; unfortunately, this leads to a dramatic increase in errors of omission. Here's why: If a drug saves a thousand lives for every one person it kills, the drug is not likely to be approved. You can't get sued for not releasing a drug that would have saved a thousand people; you can and will get sued for releasing a drug that killed one person. It's pretty bad math and worse ethics, if you ask me."

Quark may have fewer than 300 people on its payroll, but about 130 of its employees have a Ph.D. in molecular and cell biology, gene discovery, signal transduction, pathology, chemistry, or medicinal chemistry. In addition, it employs more than 50 specialists in DNA and protein analysis, algorithm development, programming, and statistics in what it calls its Bioinformatics Group. Lederberg, who sits on the board, says, "They're brilliant. That's the only word to describe them. Whether QBI will add up to a single coherent business is a little less obvious to me. But some of the things they're working on could turn out to be real blockbusters."

Ellison has constantly reiterated that biomedicine will be his second career. It's consistent with his belief that the computer industry is maturing and consolidating; that the great platform shifts that required technology visionaries are now, thanks to the Internet, a thing of the past; that the few surviving computer companies (including Oracle) will increasingly take on the character of business utilities. In short, Ellison thinks that biotech not only is the area that will best leverage his money for the good of mankind—although he'd never put it quite so portentously—but is also where he's likely to get the most intellectual stimulation and the most fun.

Don Lucas, who knows as well as anyone what makes Ellison tick, hopes more than anything that he won't leave it too late. Until his philanthropic interests absorb more of his time, he says, Ellison will never understand just how much pleasure and sense of worth they can give him. Jobs says something similar, albeit from the perspective of a younger man. He says, "My sense of it is that he's not quite ready for the next stage of his life. I don't think Oracle allows him enough time for much of anything but his family and a little bit for himself. This is a hobby now, but it's not yet a passion. However, I think it will become a passion in coming years that will be both fun and tremendously fulfilling for him."

• • •

Besides biotech and finding interesting ways to apply his wealth for the public good, Ellison is dabbling with the idea of going into politics. At a time when high-profile CEOs are not exactly topping the "Who do you most admire?" polls and when the memory of Oracle's wounding spat with the State of California is only just beginning to fade, it seems like a pretty crazy notion. And with the possible exception of Michael Bloomberg in New York—though the jury is still out on him—successful businessmen rarely make good politicians. They tend to share an autocratic style, a dislike of compromise, and a desire to quantify and analyze problems and set goals that they expect to be met. Most CEOs are also pretty useless when it comes to the arts of schmoozing and small talk that lubricate political wheels and flatter voters. Given that most of the above applies to Ellison in spades and is compounded by his hatred of pompous authority and determination never to do anything he doesn't want to, one might ask if he's taken leave of his senses.

It's partly Ellison's curiosity and constant challenge seeking, partly vanity—he has to believe that he would do a better job than some of the office-clinging nonentities with whom he is forced to do business—and partly idealism. He is genuinely passionate about improving the low standards in America's public schools and applying information technology to solve some of their problems (Oracle has given away thousands of network computers, and Ellison is thinking of using his own money to put expensive textbooks online).

His close friend Tom Lantos, the human-rights-campaigning California congressman, has urged him to make a run for the Senate. But Ellison admits, "I think I'd be a terrible freshman senator. I'm too impatient and uncompromising."

What does appeal to him is taking a pop at becoming governor of California. Since his bruising encounter with Governor Gray Davis—"the master of expediency"—over the alleged misselling of database licenses (see Chapter 25), the idea of running in 2006 as an independent has become even more interesting; one thing that Ellison would not have to worry about is money to fight an effective campaign. And it's probably as much the idea of the campaign that attracts him as the possibility of winning. As Joshua Lederberg said to him, "So you win. It's the day after that your problems begin."

So what exactly are Ellison's politics? He says that politics were always talked about at home. His adopted father, Lou, once ran unsuccessfully for the state legislature (Ellison thinks, but doesn't seem totally sure), while his brother-in-law, David Linn, was politically active and served on the Illinois Constitutional Convention. Ellison says, "In my family, you were either a liberal Democrat or a very liberal Democrat. Those were the only two political ideologies represented around our dinner table." In what he describes as the "Jewish ghetto" in Chicago where he was raised, the politics of the Ellisons and Linns were fairly typical. The big issue during Ellison's teen years was civil rights, which, naturally enough, everyone he knew was passionate about.

Perhaps as a result, Ellison's first foray into political activism was working for Robert Kennedy's presidential campaign. Ellison's political heroes are all of the "man of destiny" type—Winston Churchill, Napoleon, Douglas MacArthur—and, like them, Kennedy was a contradictory character, tough but complex. Ellison says of Churchill and MacArthur, "They had great intellectual and moral integrity. They had the courage to do what they believed to be right rather than what was popular or politically expedient at the time. I admire people with the strength to take a stand against the majority, when they believe the majority is wrong. Churchill took a strong stand against Hitler in the mid-1930s, and he was ridiculed and ostracized from his own party for doing so. But he did it anyway. That's courage. That's integrity. I admire risk takers. I like leaders: people who do things before they become fashionable or popular. I find that kind of integrity is inspirational." *

---

*LE writes: There are inspirational leaders in all walks of life. Johnny Cash, for example, wrote songs and did concerts supporting Native American causes long before it became fashionable or popular to do so. He was way out in front of everybody else. These days most artists will do concerts to raise money for good causes. I think that's great, but it's not the same.

After Robert Kennedy's assassination in June 1968, Ellison's interest in politics waned—"I kind of gave up after they shot Bobby. I just didn't care anymore. There was nobody left that I liked." * It was Ellison's growing business success in the late 1980s that helped to reengage him. As a wealthy individual who was making his money in the glamorous world of high tech, Ellison was a perfect target for fund-raisers. However, few of the politicians who approached him for money made any impact on him.

Al Gore, with his carefully cultivated contacts in the tech business and high-profile support for the Internet, might have seemed a natural home for some of Ellison's money. But Ellison despised Gore. After buying the parallel processing computer firm nCUBE, Ellison went to see then Senator Gore to complain about the preferential treatment that a rival, Thinking Machines, seemed to be getting. Not only was Thinking Machines winning government contracts at nCUBE's expense, but it was also being directly supported with tax dollars that Gore had been instrumental in steering its way. Ellison says that when he complained to Gore about this double whammy, the future vice president smiled and said to him, "What you've got to understand, Larry, is that Thinking Machines has been very good to me." Ellison exploded. "What do you mean, they've been good to you? Just how good have they been, Senator? What units of goodness are we talking about here?" Ellison says simply, "I guess he just wanted me to offer him a campaign contribution similar to the one he was getting from Thinking Machines, but back then I didn't know how the game was played, so I just kind of lost it." †

Ellison met plenty of other pols but says, "I was profoundly unimpressed by nearly all of them." Until Bill Clinton. "I met him when he was governor of Arkansas. We spent a few hours together discussing a variety of issues. He's incredibly smart and just plain interesting. I ended up being the second largest contributor to his first presidential campaign

---

*LE writes: I didn't really re-engage in politics until I met Tom Lantos, the only Holocaust survivor who is a member of Congress. Tom and his brilliant wife, Annette, restored my hope in the potential of human beings to govern themselves.

†LE writes: Now I know how the game is played, but I don't want to play it. We need some kind of campaign finance reform that doesn't clash with the Constitution. Not an easy problem to solve, though.

in 1992. I gave him about half a million dollars. That was before he picked Gore as his vice president. After that I didn't contribute a dime." *

It's curious that he was so drawn to someone whom many people would consider the very antithesis of Ellison's heroes—an infinitely flexible political pragmatist rather than a man of unbending principle and conviction. Nor did Clinton when in office pursue the kind of agenda that Ellison particularly supported: his halfhearted use of American military power; his tedious political correctness on issues such as recruiting homosexuals to the military; his being in thrall to his ideological wife over her disastrous attempt to reform health care; and his lack of conviction on the subject closest to Ellison's heart—the appalling state of the nation's secondary schools—because of his timidity in the face of the teachers' unions.†

The most probable explanation is that Ellison, like many other people, was bowled over by Clinton's extraordinary charisma and his intellectual quickness. Ellison doesn't demur: "I just like the guy. He is so interesting: brilliant, complex, ambitious, troubled, talented. I've never met anyone quite like him. Nobody loves being alive more than Bill Clinton. And you can't help feeling the same passion for life when you're with him. Melanie and I had an unforgettable time jazz-clubbing with him in New Orleans. The man heightens your senses and teaches you what it means to be alive."

Roughly the same age, both illegitimate, both extremely successful, both risk takers in their professional and personal lives, and both a little bit in love with their own wit and intelligence, it's not surprising that the two men hit it off and have remained good friends. Nonetheless, Clinton in office was a disappointment to Ellison.

Ellison's anger about the quality of secondary education may have been influenced by his own experience at school. As an employer of some forty thousand people, a good many of them not only superbright but also the products of the education systems of much poorer countries, Ellison knows something about American secondary education. As he puts it, whatever the failings of America's health care system (mainly that it costs

---

*LE writes: Needless to say, I didn't support Gore for president. Thank God for the butterfly ballot.

†LE writes: All true, but you have to give President Clinton credit for NAFTA. He stood against his own party and the unions to create a more prosperous Mexico on our border. That's Bill Clinton's profile in courage in my book.

a lot and is socially divisive), people still get on planes to come and get treated in America, but it's a long time since he's heard of anybody coming because of the excellence of America's publicly funded high schools.

He's most incensed by the nexus between the teaching unions and the Democratic Party—"The teachers' union is one of the anchor tenants of the party," he grumbles—and the obstacle that places in the path of worthwhile reform. He's particularly fond of the idea of education vouchers to give some economic clout to poor families. He says, "The California public schools are a disgrace. Too many poor minority children are condemned to go to schools that fail to teach. African-American and Hispanic children should have a choice of schools. Any mechanism that gives them that choice—magnet schools, open enrollment, vouchers—I'm for. I'm prochoice on schools." *

If he ran for the governorship, he would concentrate on introducing vouchers, improving health care, and "keeping the lights on." He says, "California is a huge economy, and there's plenty of money available to solve our educational and health care problems if we can get rid of some of the unconscionable waste. Apart from that, I'd concentrate on not doing anything monumentally stupid like losing billions speculating in the energy market. I'm a pretty good problem solver, so I might be a good governor." Another thing he points out as being in his favor is that no special-interest group could buy him.†

How serious is he? He's definitely drawn to the idea of running and the opportunity it would give him to put issues that he cares about on the agenda. And compared with the well-named Gray Davis or his equally drab Republican rival in 2002, Bill Simon, Ellison would have presence and charisma to burn. But Ellison's flamboyance may also have made him too many enemies in business to survive a tough campaign against embattled party machines. And there's no escaping the fact that he has enough personal history to give a prurient press a field day. Is that what he really needs?

Ellison says that it all depends on how fed up people are with the traditional politicians by the time he's ready to run—fed up with their in-

---

*LE writes: I do not favor giving school vouchers to the rich. Only poor families need vouchers, and then only when their local school is failing.

†LE writes: My family has threatened to stop talking to me if I run for office. If I don't run I'll probably support Arnie [Schwarzenegger], but only if he invites me to the opening of Terminator 3.

competence, their pandering to special-interest groups, their "news-speak," and their dreary political correctness. If Jesse Ventura can make it, he says, why not Larry Ellison? But Ventura could more easily present himself as being on the side of the little guy than California's wealthiest citizen can. The only thing that can be said with certainty is that if Ellison does decide to run, it won't be dull.

• • •

What's also certain is that Ellison wants to stay busy. One thing that he is acutely conscious of, despite rumors to the contrary, is his own mortality. "Life is the only miracle," he often says. With sixty fast approaching, he thinks increasingly about how to extract the most from what is left to him: "I don't waste a lot of time. I work intensely on things I care about, and I spend my time with people that I care about. I do what I want to with my time, because I know there's not much of it left."

Some of this urgency may be the consequence of Ellison's lack of any religious belief. Although he was brought up in Reform Judaism, his family was not particularly religious and the teachings at Hebrew school never stuck. The closest that Ellison is prepared to get to God or anything that might be termed spiritual is nature: a sunrise in Yosemite Valley or the cherry blossoms blowing in the wind at sunset in Kyoto. "That is where I find God," he says, "in this glorious accident of being alive."

What may also have concentrated Ellison's mind on the fragile glory of life are his still recent brushes with death. Although he has never had any serious illness, he nearly killed himself twice in 1992—when he broke his neck while bodysurfing in Hawaii and, soon after, smashed himself up in a serious bicycle accident. Careering down a mountain in Napa, he managed to stick the front wheel of his bike into a section of disused railroad track. The impact as he hit the ground was traumatic, smashing his arm in twenty-eight places and blowing the bone through the skin. It took four operations to rebuild the arm, using bone from Ellison's hip, and more than two years of rehab in the gym, where he trained with Joe Montana, before he regained his strength. Typically, Ellison boasts that at the end of this period he managed to beat a champion triathlete at dips (although he does admit that the lighter triathlete was handicapped by wearing a thirty-five-pound weight vest).*

---

*LE writes: When I told Joe that my elbow injury was worse than his, he said, "True, but you don't earn your living with your arm."

If the feelings of power and well-being that come from physical fitness are a critical part of "the glory of being alive" for Ellison, so too is constant mental stimulation. He says, "As long as you're learning, as long as you're solving problems, as long as you are working with your mind, then you're alive. Problems intrigue, excite, and energize me."

Although Ellison jokes about his dislike of drinking alcohol, saying that it makes him even more unbearably over the top than he already is, the real reason is that he has what amounts almost to a terror of anything that might interfere with the working of his brain. He says, "I can't stand anything that clouds my mind. I couldn't take the painkiller they prescribed for me when I was in the hospital with my arm broken in twenty-eight places. I took Tylenol instead. I'd rather deal with the pain than lose my mind to the medication. I have no problem with people drinking; I have no problem with other people smoking dope. If that's what they want to do, God bless them, that's their business. But I can't do those things."

Ellison, I think, will find coping with the debilities of old age even more difficult than most of us will. What would he prefer, I wondered, a relatively shorter life and going out with a bang or dealing with the feebleness of advanced age? "Would I rather die at eighty or be feeble between eighty and ninety? I'll take feeble if that's okay with you. I'd never accept being feeble, though. I'd work out by competing in walker races against the seventy-year-olds." He admitted that much of what the medical foundation was working on are ways to help people live the last years of their life "in a healthy and robust fashion."

In the absence of any near-term breakthroughs from the EMF, I couldn't help asking Ellison whether he was taking anything to help him stay youthful. The answer was disappointingly prosaic: just a few over-the-counter dietary supplements available for a few dollars, such as DHEA (a steroidal precursor that encourages the production of testosterone in older men) and melatonin (a natural sleep enhancer that compensates for the declining efficiency of the pituitary gland). So no fountain of youth and (hand on heart) no cosmetic surgery since his broken nose was fixed nearly thirty years ago.

If Ellison was so certain that there was no life after death, was he, like many rich men, trying to secure a kind of immortality with his money? "Well," he said, "I hope my children will be proud of me after I've gone. But I think it's a big mistake for people to die very wealthy and leave it to their spouse or their children to give their money away. Why should they have all the fun? I want to give it away myself and see some of the results before I die."

Surprisingly, perhaps, Steve Jobs believes that for all his emotional difficulties in dealing with the deaths of others, Ellison has succeeded in coming to terms with his own mortality. Jobs says, "What makes some people very effective in the way they use the time left to them is that they frequently remember that they're going to die soon. A lot of people get to the end of their lives and only then realize that they're going to die and that they should have made a lot of decisions differently. Larry thinks about death often, and I think a person like that has a much better chance of growing old gracefully."

I think that one day Ellison will be able to disengage from Oracle, but as long as he thinks Oracle needs him, it will continue to have a prior claim over anything else. However, assuming he does create a few degrees of separation between himself and Oracle, he will plunge more deeply into those other areas of interest. He probably won't find the cure for cancer—as Josh Lederberg says, that's going to be a long haul—but through his medical foundation, Quark, and his proposed "Rockefeller West" research university, he has a wonderful opportunity to have fun and do a lot of good at the same time. But he should forget about the politics. Even in winning he would be bound to fail. If you're Larry Ellison, why choose to be unhappy?

23

"A SCRAP OF INFORMATION"

On the morning of September 11, 2001, Larry Ellison was up before dawn, getting ready to do some work on his e-mails, when one of his household staff burst into his study. "Mr. Ellison, turn on the TV right away. An airplane just hit the World Trade Center in New York." He was just in time to see United Airlines Flight 175 smash into the South Tower. As he watched the unfolding horror, two thoughts crowded his mind: how to keep the businesses running for the many Oracle customers based in the Twin Towers, and whether there had been any Oracle people in the buildings.

That morning Oracle lost eight employees. Six were consultants working with clients in the Towers, and two were among the many heroes created on that awful day. One who had some emergency medical training had gone inside one of the towers to see if he could help the injured. He was never seen again. Finally, there was Todd Beamer, a thirty-two-year-old account executive on his way home to San Francisco on United Airlines Flight 93 from Newark. It is Beamer who appears to have led the fight against the terrorists on the doomed plane that crashed near Shanksville, Pennsylvania.

Ellison says that making the calls to the families of the Oracle men who died on September 11 was the hardest thing he's ever done. Two days later, he sent out an emotional e-mail to the victims' colleagues at Oracle:

Everyone,
It is with indescribable sadness that I inform you that several of our people lost their lives in the terrorist attack on the United States. Todd

Beamer lost his life when United Flight 93 crashed in Western Pennsylvania. Seven more are missing in the rubble that was the World Trade Center. We pray that some may be found alive.

We know that Todd Beamer is dead. We believe he died when he and other passengers aboard Flight 93 tried to recover the hijacked airplane from the terrorists. In the struggle, the plane crashed. Todd's courageous actions may not have saved the lives of his fellow passengers, but he helped prevent the airplane reaching its target—our nation's Capitol. Considering the devastation wrought by the other aircraft, it is unquestionable that Todd's brave actions, and that of his fellow passengers, saved countless lives on the ground. We are very proud of Todd. We will miss him. Our heart goes out to Todd's wife, and his two young children.

Seven other Oracle people are missing. Six of them are consultants that were working on the 97th floor of the South Tower of the World Trade Center. We have not given up hope. Rescue workers are still searching, so we will not reveal their names at this time. I will tell you that two of the missing consultants were from the United States, three were from India, and one from the United Kingdom. This terror and tragedy is reaching families around the globe. The entire civilized world is in mourning.

The last Oracle person missing was trained as an emergency medical technician. He was near the World Trade Center when the first airplane hit. When everyone else was running out of the building, he ran in. Like the police and fire fighters, he risked his own life trying to save others. We will never know how many people he helped, or if he was able to save any lives. We do know he ran into the building and tried. In trying, he risked—and perhaps lost—his own life. Nothing is more heroic than giving your own life in an attempt to save another.

Several Oracle people are lost. Some we knew. Some we didn't. Some were heroes. All were family.

Larry

I talked to Ellison on September 12. He was deeply distressed, but he was clear that Oracle had to go on working. Oracle's first-quarter earnings call was due later in the week, and he didn't want to postpone it unless the markets remained closed: "Our people were in a state of shock. It was really hard to focus on work. But there was no time for a break. Most emergency services—police, fire departments, hospitals—depend on our systems working twenty-four hours a day, every day." What effect the atrocity would have on the economy or Oracle's fortunes, he had no idea. "I really can't think about the stock market at a time like this—except to say that eventually it will recover. And our economy will recover. We always recover. The American people are very resilient. We'll recover from this attack. We'll learn from it, and we'll be stronger because of it."

Apart from anything else, all the government agencies and departments that dealt with the aftermath of the attacks and hunted for the terrorists depended on Oracle databases. He had already made arrangements with the army for more than two hundred technical staff from the damaged Pentagon to be accommodated in Oracle's Washington offices. A secure Special Response Center had been quickly established to provide support for government agencies needing security-cleared communications channels. Ellison said that in New York a similar effort was under way, including the creation of an "emergency office locator" to help identify the temporary office locations of thousands of displaced workers.

As the provider of the software that powered nearly all their databases, Ellison knew better than almost anyone that the U.S. security agencies were technologically ill prepared to protect the United States from further terrorist outrages. There were two major deficiencies. The first was the ease with which potential terrorists could enter the United States and disappear, thanks to a combination of lax rules for the issuing of visas and the lack of a standardized ID card system. Most of the hijackers had multiple stolen identities. The second was the difficulty of creating an effective and cross-checkable watch list, without which monitoring suspicious behavior was impossible. And just as the root cause of poor information management in the private sector almost always turned out to be fragmented data caused by information being dumped into too many small databases that couldn't easily communicate with one another, the same was true in spades of government in general and the security services in particular. Making the problem even worse were long-standing interagency rivalries, especially between the FBI and the CIA, which reinforced the chronic data fragmentation with a cultural bias against sharing intelligence.

Ellison's remedy was the introduction of a national standard for government ID cards using biometric authorization technology linked to a single, consolidated national security database. He knew that while what he was proposing was technically not difficult for Oracle to do, both ideas would be deeply controversial on both civil libertarian and political grounds. But he had been impressed when the secretary of defense, Donald Rumsfeld,* had remarked that the difference between the war against terrorism and more conventional conflicts was that this was a war that would be won not by cruise missiles or bombers but by some scrap of vital information. Within a few days of the terror attacks, Ellison had decided that it was his public duty to campaign for both national standards for government ID cards and a national security database and that Oracle would donate the software to make it possible.

The first stage of the campaign was to start talking and writing about it. Ellison spent several days sweating over an op-ed piece that he hoped to place in *The New York Times*. The *Times* declined to take the article,[†] but *The Wall Street Journal* offered it a home, albeit in greatly shortened form. This is what Ellison wrote:

DIGITAL IDS CAN HELP PREVENT TERRORISM
by Larry Ellison
10/08/2001

Since the September 11 attacks, our country has been thrust into a debate over how to root out terrorists while also maintaining our civil liberties. One of the suggestions proposed, though not yet fully debated, is that of national identification cards.

Many Americans instinctively fear that a **national ID card** would sacrifice basic freedoms and compromise personal privacy. They suspect our government would build Big Brother databases that would be better at snooping on law-abiding citizens than catching terrorists. They rightly agree that if we lose our liberty, the terrorists will have won.

On the face of it, issuing ID cards does seem a significant step. Trust-

---

*LE writes: I like Donald Rumsfeld, but not as much as Melanie does. She has a Donald Rumsfeld screen saver on her Macintosh laptop.

[†]LE writes: I submitted my op-ed piece to The New York Times, *but they rejected it. I suppose they thought my position on ID cards was a bit too far to the right. However, shortly after my article appeared in the* Journal, *the* Times *ran a piece by the Harvard constitutional law professor Alan Dershowitz that called for a mandatory national ID card. All I wanted was a national standard for our existing voluntary government ID cards. So for the first time, I found myself standing slightly to the left of Alan Dershowitz on a civil liberties issue. Things had changed. September 11 convinced Alan and a lot of other people that we live in a very dangerous world.*

ing government to maintain a database with our names, addresses, places of work, amounts and sources of income, assets, purchases, travel destinations, and more, seems a huge leap of faith. But we should remember that these databases already exist, and that we willingly helped in their creation. For years, companies like American Express and Visa have been issuing cards and building up information on millions of Americans. The databases they maintain are searched and sold on a daily basis.

We should remember, too, that the government already tracks things—lots of things. Federal, state and local agencies issue Social Security cards, driver's licenses, pilot's licenses, passports and visas. They maintain thousands of databases to keep track of everyone from taxpayers and voters to suspected terrorists.

And so the question is not whether the government should issue ID cards and maintain databases; they already do. The question is whether the ones we have can be made more effective, especially when it comes to finding criminals.

Do we need one national ID card? No. But the IDs that the government issues—such as Social Security cards—should use modern credit card technology. Do we need more databases? No, just the opposite. The biggest problem today is that we have too many. The single thing we could do to make life tougher for terrorists would be to ensure that all the information in myriad government databases was integrated into a single, comprehensive national security file.

Today, every federal intelligence and law enforcement agency— the Central Intelligence Agency, the Federal Bureau of Investigation, the Immigration and Naturalization Service, the National Security Agency—and all manner of state and local bodies maintain their own separate databases on suspected criminals. All these separate databases make it difficult for one agency to know about and apprehend someone wanted by another agency.

That's why one of the September 11 hijackers made it through U.S. passport control, even though he had an outstanding arrest warrant in Broward County, Florida. The FBI was searching for several other of the terrorists, because CIA intelligence revealed they had ties to Osama bin Laden. Four more were sought by the Immigration and Naturalization Service because they were in the country illegally.

Such a national database, though a large undertaking, is possible. My company, for example, has already offered to provide the necessary software for free, and I'm sure other companies would pitch in with hardware and support. It's important these donations be made with no strings attached: The database would be maintained and run by the government alone, with no question of corporations benefiting.

The uses of such a database would be significant. Airlines, for example, could cross-check the names of passengers with names on a watch list. If this had been done, many of the September 11 terrorists would have been caught before they boarded their flights. Mandatory checks could be supplemented with voluntary checks. Companies, for example, might elect to submit the names of [job] applicants as a part of their reference-checking process. If the submitted name were on the watch list, the FBI (not the company) would be notified.

Another challenge is tracking people with multiple or stolen identities. The good news is that a national database combined with biometrics, thumb prints, hand prints, iris scans, or other new technology could detect false identities. Gaining entry to an airport or other secure location would require people to present a photo ID, put their thumb on a fingerprint scanner and tell the guard their Social Security number. This information would be cross-checked with the database.

The government could phase in digital ID cards to replace existing Social Security cards and driver's licenses. These new IDs should be based on a uniform standard such as credit card technology, which is harder to counterfeit than existing government IDs, or on smart-card technology, which is better but more expensive.

There is no need to compel any American to have a digital ID. Some Americans may choose to apply for a digital ID card to speed the airport security check-in process. Some states might use digital IDs for their next generation of driver's licenses. Companies might want to replace their current hodgepodge of IDs with the new system. In fact, a voluntary system of standardized IDs issued by government agencies and private companies could prove more effective than a mandatory system.

We don't need to trade our liberties for our lives. By law, Fourth Amendment protections against unreasonable search and seizure would govern access to the national security database. The "probable cause" standard will still have to be met.

Two hundred years ago, Thomas Jefferson warned us that our liberties were at risk unless we exercised "eternal vigilance." Jefferson lived in an age of aristocrats and monarchs. We live with the threat of terrorists getting their hands on weapons with the capacity to destroy entire cities. Only by giving our intelligence and law enforcement agencies better tools can we expect to save life and liberty together.

As well as writing the article, Ellison was preparing for a visit to Washington, D.C. Meetings had been scheduled with the heads of the NSA, the CIA, and the FBI. He was also hoping to see the attorney general, John Ashcroft, and Vice President Dick Cheney. While finding out what the law-and-order agencies needed in order to do a better job of analyzing the huge quantities of information they were now feverishly gathering on the bin Laden global terrorist network, it would be an opportunity to evangelize the proposals in his article to the people who could actually make it happen. Afterward, he would fly to New York for TV interviews to publicize his ideas and, more prosaically, a CEO roundtable to sell software.

Arriving late in the evening of October 9 at the Ritz-Carlton in Tysons Corner, Virginia (an unattractive hotel catering for conferences some twelve miles from Washington, supposedly chosen by Jay Nussbaum because of its closeness to the CIA) Ellison's first meeting the following day is one that he would rather not have been having at such a time. The "digital hospital" project that had been launched with such fanfare at HealthSouth's Birmingham campus some six months earlier is in trouble, and HealthSouth's CEO, Richard Scrushy, is determined to grab Ellison while he's relatively nearby.

HealthSouth personnel have turned up in force, but so have Oracle's, with key members from Nussbaum's team (known within Oracle as "Jay Inc.") and John Wookey, a high-ranking developer who built large parts of the services version of Oracle's ERP suite. Although Ellison is more than half an hour late, he and Scrushy seem quite happy to waste the first five minutes chatting about airplanes. But when Scrushy gets going, it's clear he's livid, accusing Oracle of falling down on the undertakings it made when the project was announced. Ellison starts off by recapping what his understanding of Oracle's commitment is. Oracle, he says, is responsible for creating an architecture, an "information heart," for the hospital's clinical and administrative systems—a central repository for applications to place and retrieve information. The idea is for Oracle to establish a common data model that all the other vendors involved in the project can easily write to. "We want to make the integration trivial," says Ellison. "Has anything changed?" He implies that if there is a problem, it must be because other vendors are not cooperating.

After protracted attempts at negotiating the HealthSouth contract, Ellison decides he's had enough of the whole sorry mess.* The health care initiative that means so much to Oracle now has its own momentum thanks to the relationships that John Wookey has built with other partners. And Ellison will be very happy not to spend any more time with his fellow flying enthusiast Richard Scrushy. Even when the digital hospital project was in its promising infancy, there was something about Scrushy that troubled him, but now he can't stand the sight of the man.

• • •

The postmaster general's large office faces south with views across the Potomac and to the Pentagon beyond. From where we're sitting, it's not difficult to see where the American Airlines Boeing 757 plowed into Washington's most formidable building. Although Ellison, Jay Nussbaum, and Kevin Fitzgerald (the sales executive Oracle recently poached from archrival Siebel) have come to sell software, everyone seems uncomfortable about raising the subject. Ellison asks Jack Potter, a large, rather shambling veteran of the postal service who has been in the top job for five months, how September 11 has affected his business. Potter reckons that he's already suffered a $500 million loss of revenue, but he's relieved that, miraculously, given the number of postal workers in lower Manhattan, he didn't lose any people. Now he's worried about the envelopes containing anthrax powder that have turned up in Washington, D.C., and New York. (He could not know that the next fatality in the terror campaign would be a worker in a Washington, D.C., sorting office.)

Ellison's pitch is the best and simplest there is: Your biggest commercial rival is UPS, and we've transformed its business with software called Advanced Planning and Scheduling. UPS, says Ellison, has achieved huge cost savings. With more than 250,000 vehicles to manage and dispatch, making the postal service the biggest logistics business in the United States, the potential for efficiencies is staggering, but only as long as there

---

*LE writes: During a long negotiation with HealthSouth, we became more and more uncomfortable with their senior management team. In the end, we decided that they were not people we wanted to work with, so we walked away from the deal. Eighteen months later, when Richard Scrushy was charged by the SEC with what it described as "massive accounting fraud," John Wookey sent me an e-mail saying how thankful he was that we were watching this from the sidelines.

is enough flexibility within the organization to allow the new systems to work. Although the issues facing Potter are very different from those of the security agencies, Potter says that because of the crisis the time for doing something ambitious is right. It's not the only time we'll hear that sentiment while we're in Washington.

In a recent interview in *Catalyst* magazine, Health and Human Services Secretary Tommy Thompson painted a picture of IT chaos within the department with the biggest budget—$436 billion—in the federal government: "We have over 3,000 different servers and 2,900 IT staff. We have 1,200 different computer systems with different e-mail capabilities, some of which do not communicate with each other. We have 63,000 employees but 83,000 workstations. We have 12 operating divisions, all of which set their own IT systems, their own bookkeeping systems, their own budget, their own lobbying and PR systems. They go their own ways on human resources, grants management, acquisitions, and logistics. We have 2,000 Web sites with 800,000 pages and 981 toll-free numbers. In one division, I found we had 5 financial systems, 13 grant management systems, 6 acquisition systems, 6 personnel systems, and 13 separate e-mail systems. Now, how do you run a department like that?" It will be interesting to see whether Thompson's appetite for radical reform has survived the journey from the governor's mansion in Madison, Wisconsin, to HHS's vast neo-Stalinist fortress at 200 Independence Avenue. It's also Ellison's chance to float his Other Big Idea, the one about a single national medical records database.

Jack Kemp, onetime Republican vice presidential candidate and an Oracle board member, has helped to fix the meeting with Thompson and is there to meet us under a bust of Hubert Humphrey, a politician of a very different stripe. Kemp is an affable man with a disconcertingly loud voice and a mop of carefully sculpted white hair.

When we arrive in Thompson's office, he seems genuinely thrilled to meet Ellison and insists on going through a rather ridiculous performance, seating a slightly embarrassed Ellison at his desk and having him pose for a photographer as "acting secretary." With these jollities out of the way, Thompson, a small man with rather florid features, opens the conversation with a statistic that could have come straight from Ellison's own mouth: "As many as ninety-eight thousand individuals allegedly died last year from medical mistakes. Most of those deaths were caused by the administration of drugs and drug interactions." The cause, says Thompson, is the antiquated way in which prescriptions are made out and drugs distributed. "The lack of technology in our hospitals," he says, "is an absolute disgrace."

Ellison can hardly contain himself. With an almost beatific smile he embarks on a well-practiced riff: "A single national medical records database would save thousands of lives every year by preventing dangerous combinations of drugs from being prescribed. And a national health records database would save billions of dollars because it is so much cheaper to run than all those separate medical records systems we currently use. You have to be willing to save money if you want to save lives." For example, Walgreen and Rite Aid, two of the biggest pharmacy chains, have built database systems to record patients' prescriptions and to issue alerts about possibly dangerous drug interactions. But they're entirely separate systems that can't communicate with each other, so if you don't always buy your medicine from the same chain, they won't be able to help you. Ellison asks, "How much are we spending on medical record keeping out of the $1.3 trillion we spend on health care each year? I've heard estimates as high as thirty cents on the dollar, or nearly $400 billion. We'd save half of that—$200 billion—if we had a national medical records database. And with one medical records database we'd get better privacy and better accuracy. But most important, we'd save lives. The opportunity is extraordinary." Thompson thinks that record keeping may be costing "only" eighteen cents on the dollar, but he gets the point. "It's so shameful," he says, "but how do we do it?"

As Ellison expands his thoughts, explaining how it would be possible for all parties to keep their existing databases if they wanted to, as long as they agreed to copy everything that went into them into one central database, Thompson again asks, "How do I accomplish this?" Thompson's problem is that, understandably, he feels overwhelmed by the scale of the task before him. He's already encountering bureaucratic inertia and special-interest-group pushback of a kind that fourteen years as governor of Wisconsin haven't prepared him for. It's even possible that he's beginning to fear that in the three and a half years left to him in the job, he may end up achieving little of what he wants to do. And here comes Ellison, not just singing from the same hymn sheet, not just telling him what the problems are, but offering solutions.

Ellison has two suggestions. The first is that Thompson, who says he wants to introduce "paperless" hospitals and self-service check-in for patients, should meet with the Oracle/HealthSouth team. The second is that Thompson should follow the same path as Ellison when he started turning Oracle into an e-business—start with some "cheap thrills" that will demonstrate to skeptics what's possible and use the cost savings they generate to fund more ambitious projects. "Start with e-mail," says Ellison. "We could replace all your e-mail systems with just one unified system in ninety days. If we don't eliminate seventy-five percent of your e-mail costs, I'll personally pay for it." Thompson is so impressed that he wants to know from his advisers whether he can start on it right away without putting out a Request for Proposal (RFP) to allow other vendors to bid. Ellison's story about how Oracle succeeded in halving its IT budget and getting "dramatically better information" in the process has gotten him hooked.

On the way out, Ellison asks me, "Could we have had a meeting like that before September eleventh? I don't think so." Nussbaum adds, "You're not kidding. Something really changed in this town. People want to do things they would never have dared before." Next stop for Ellison is a helicopter ride to the National Security Agency at Fort Meade in Maryland to have dinner with its director, Lieutenant General Michael Hayden. On September 13, the NSA asked Oracle for assistance at the "premier technical level" and Oracle offered to give any help that was needed. Oracle's chief corporate architect, a very bright, very laid back young engineer named Ed Screven who oversees all the company's development work, is taking a polygraph test this week to get full security clearance. The following morning Ellison will be seeing the directors of both the FBI (Robert Mueller) and the CIA (George Tenet) who, in a sign of the times, will be together with their respective senior teams at the CIA's headquarters in Langley, Virginia. Lunch is scheduled to be with Attorney General John Ashcroft.

For security reasons, I'm not able to be present at any of these meetings, but Ellison has promised to tell me as much as he prudently can when we fly to New York on Thursday evening. Late on Wednesday, when Ellison returns from the NSA, I meet him for a drink in his suite at the Ritz-Carlton. He says, "The good news is that we're making real progress on gathering information about the bad guys. The bad news is that the bad guys are very bad—pure evil. There is no limit on what they're willing to do to harm us. If they could kill us all, they would."

The next day I meet Ellison outside the Department of Justice on Pennsylvania Avenue after his lunch with Attorney General Ashcroft. Our next appointment is at the Pentagon with the Comptroller at the Defense Department, and after that we're going to the Hill to see an old friend of Ellison, the former mayor of San Francisco and now the senior California senator, Dianne Feinstein. Senator Feinstein has asked to see Ellison after reading his article in *The Wall Street Journal,* as she will be chairing a hearing of the terrorism subcommittee on Friday. But I'm eager for news of the morning. The time spent at Langley was impressively productive, but although Ellison is slightly reluctant to admit it, his encounter with Ashcroft was something of a disappointment. He says that Ashcroft seemed to be rather remote and unwilling to talk about anything substantive. His main preoccupation was privacy legislation, which makes the job of law enforcement more difficult—how can we be expected to catch terrorists when the law forbids a parent to have access to her own child's exam results?

On the way to the Pentagon, Kevin Fitzgerald explains that the Defense Department has put out an RFP for a commercial financial system that would be used servicewide. It's likely to be a bake-off between SAP and Oracle. Fitzgerald says it could be one of the biggest financial applications deals ever, with the opportunity to sell other E-Business Suite applications that need to be integrated into the financials package. Although Oracle is not heavy-handedly making the point that it would be odd for the Pentagon to buy German, Fitzgerald wants to hire the lobbying company of the previous defense secretary, William Cohen.

We then head back across town to the Hart Senate Office Building for a meeting with Senator Feinstein. When Feinstein joins us in her conference room, she embraces Ellison tenderly and starts pumping him for views and information she can use at the next day's hearing. She's particularly exercised about the lax oversight of the 30 million or so temporary visitors to the United States each year. Without an adequate tracking system, she says, our country has become a sieve, creating ample opportunities for terrorists to enter and establish their operations without detection. Ellison talks about his national ID plan and how he would make it mandatory for anyone entering the country to have a visa and a card with biometric information on it.* Whipping out his wallet, he asks her to compare the sophistication of his credit card—a black Centurion American Express card—with the shoddy and easily forgeable little piece of cardboard that is his commercial pilot's license. Feinstein is so ap-

---

*LE writes: I don't believe that American citizens should be required to carry digital ID cards; I do believe that all foreign visitors should be issued a digital ID card before they can get into our country.

palled that she immediately gets an aide to fire off a letter to the secretary of transportation.

For much of her legislative career, Feinstein has been promoting precisely the kind of privacy measures that are now making the job of the security agencies so difficult. She rather limply suggests that Ellison's plan would provoke a huge uproar, but she doesn't protest much when Ellison points out that we've already lost our privacy thanks to the easily available information on nearly all of us that the credit card firms are prepared to hawk. He says, "I'm for privacy; I'm against secrecy. The Constitution doesn't give anyone the right to have multiple stolen identities." Feinstein is even prepared to admit that the existing privacy laws have gone too far. "We'll pay the piper for it," she says. Feinstein also wants to hear more about Ellison's offer to donate the software for the national security database. Ellison confirms it while explaining that he's talking about just the software, not the labor or network or hardware. Whether Feinstein understands exactly what he is proposing is uncertain, but she calls it "the best offer we've had all day" and asks Ellison if he'll put his offer in a letter that she can brandish at her committee's hearing next day.

Descending the steps of Congress into the warm autumn sunshine, Ellison seems suddenly overwhelmed by emotion. "I can't help thinking about how close we came to losing this building . . . how the Capitol dome could have come crashing down on top of all those people we picked to represent us. I look at that dome now, and I see something quite fragile, something that needs to be protected."

Jay Nussbaum is there to meet us at the Dulles Jet Center, where the G5 is waiting to take us up to New York. Bustling toward us, he can't wait to tell Ellison that not only has Tommy Thompson's office been in touch to get things moving on Ellison's e-mail offer (though there's some nervousness about their boss's determination to cut through red tape and give Oracle "sole vendor" status without an RFP), but the FBI has been on the phone seven times in the course of the afternoon. "Jeez," says Nussbaum, "I've never known anything like it. This is something completely different. I'm just stunned."

• • •

On the plane, Ellison and I settle down to discuss the last forty-eight hours and the way that Oracle is finding itself in the front line of the administration's war against terrorism. Ellison reflects, "Our first customer was the Central Intelligence Agency, our second customer was the Defense Intelligence Agency, and our third customer was the National Security Agency. At the very beginning of my career, I was building information systems for these intelligence agencies, and here I am, at the end of my career, building information systems for the same intelligence agencies. What's different is their sense of urgency. Since the attack of September eleventh, this town's been on a war footing. The last time things moved this fast was World War II."

Since his *Wall Street Journal* article, Ellison has noted how ironic it is that credit databases for managing financial risk do a much better job of tracking people around the world than the intelligence databases do. What sort of conversation was Oracle having with the intelligence agencies to improve the situation? "The intelligence that's gathered has to be analyzed efficiently and shared appropriately among the different agencies. We need to provide the analysts with the appropriate data-mining and analysis tools so they're not overwhelmed by the sheer amount of data that's being gathered. That's what we focused on today."

I knew that Ellison had been pretty appalled by the neglected state of the FBI's systems after the chronic underinvestment during the Clinton years—the agency wasn't even using the Internet to connect its people. How bad was it? "They're like most large companies: they have lots of separate automation systems, which means their data is badly fragmented. Their procedures are inconsistent from department to department: some of their procedures are automated, others are still manual. Their internal network needs to be upgraded. The FBI has tremendous human resources—great people—but their computer systems are in desperate need of modernization.

"The question is, how quickly can the FBI's information management and communication systems be upgraded? That depends on who does the work. I think we can do it fast. We can install a secure e-mail and document-sharing system within ninety days, guaranteed. That's easy. We can also get version one of the national security database up and running in ninety days. That's much harder. We'd have to use the Oracle database development team to do the work. And we'd have to work in shifts, seven days a week, twenty-four hours a day. But it could be done."

How much could Ellison tell me about the meeting at the CIA? "Just like at the NSA last night, the primary focus was on the analyst. We have to get better at filtering out the irrelevant information. It really is the needle-in-the-haystack problem, except it's a really big haystack called the planet earth. We're very good at collecting information using satellites and computers, but you have to organize the information properly, and you have to provide the right tools so the analysts can do their jobs. You've got to store vast amounts of data very efficiently, or your data-mining, pattern-matching and predictive modeling software will run too slowly to be of any use. And there has to be a single standard for exchanging information between intelligence agencies. When the CIA provides information to the FBI about a bad guy, both agencies' computer systems need to be speaking the same language. The data model for tracking people in both agencies must be the same." *

Given the traditional degree of interagency rivalry and distrust, are the CIA and FBI really prepared to go down the shared-data-model path that Ellison is advocating? "I think so. We talked about it at length in the meeting at Langley. Everyone agreed, and I expect the FBI to move very quickly now. The FBI has a greatly expanded mission, so they need new systems. I think Bob Mueller understands the size of the job in front of him. Before September eleventh, you couldn't get the first draft of a Request for Proposal out in ninety days. Now the FBI is talking about building a complete new computer system in ninety days. I've been working with these agencies the whole of my professional life, and I've never seen anything like it. These days, everyone in Washington is extremely focused and working hard. They have a new sense of urgency, motivated by a great and deep concern about the security of our country. They want to make sure that the events of September eleventh aren't repeated. We're at war—you can feel it."

• • •

Ellison's first appointment in New York is to record an interview about his ID card proposals for the *CBS Evening News*. However, when we arrive at the studios on West Fifty-seventh Street, the place is in an uproar. The news has just broken that an employee across the way at NBC has contracted anthrax poisoning from a letter sent to the studio. There's

---

*LE writes: Of course there is some information in certain intelligence databases that is so sensitive that there should be no automated sharing system. These databases are on computers located in underground vaults, with two marine guards stationed outside the vault door. If you're trying to log on to one of these databases and you don't "remember" your password, the marine guards shoot you.

great anxiety, subsequently confirmed, that Dan Rather, the CBS News star anchorman, and an assistant may have come into contact with a similarly booby-trapped letter. Ellison's interview with Anthony Mason has to take place in what looks like a storeroom because the studio we have been sitting in has to be swept for possible contamination.

Despite all the turmoil, the planned CEO roundtable is scheduled to go ahead. Among the guests are the home goddess Martha Stewart and the CEOs of ADP (a big provider of payroll services), UBS PaineWebber, and 1-800-Flowers.com. Also present are Ross Perot, Jr., the son of the former presidential candidate and now the CEO of Perot Systems, and Lex Fenwick, an Englishman who is running the financial news agency Bloomberg while his boss is campaigning to succeed Rudy Giuliani as mayor of New York. But the person who is likely to get Ellison's closest personal attention is Andrew Benton, the president of Pepperdine University in Malibu, where Ellison's son, David, has just started his freshman year.

Inevitably, they all want Ellison to talk about his ID card plan and the national security database that goes with it, and what sort of reception Ellison's ideas received in Washington. He's happy to oblige, and, of course, it all neatly segues into the perennial theme of the urgent need to consolidate data if you want to know what's going on, whether you're running a federal agency or a business. But when Ellison gets on to telling them about the E-Business Suite and how it can help them both save money and get better information, he senses that he's lost their full attention. Maybe some of them have heard the pitch, while others find the idea of spending a lot of money to upgrade their systems with fancy new software just plain inappropriate for the times. He decides to try something new, even though Jay Nussbaum has advised him against it because it hasn't yet been fully thought through.

The night before, in Washington, during a meeting with Diebold, a systems integrator specializing in security and servicing ATMs, Ellison came up with a new customer offer. Diebold's boss, Wally O'Dell, told Ellison that while he didn't need convincing about 11i conceptually, he wasn't in a mood to take any risks when it came to uncertain returns from investing in new software. If Ellison really believed what he was saying about the suite, what about shifting some of the risk to Oracle? Ellison told O'Dell that if he gave him his existing IT budget, he'd reduce it by 5 percent each year for the next five years and provide him with completely new systems, everything that Diebold needs to run its business. As a company in the IT business, Diebold might be expected to have little enthusiasm for such an innovative outsourcing deal. But the opposite is true: O'Dell is very interested indeed.

And so are the CEOs in New York. Ellison says, "We'll give you all our E-Business Suite software for free; we'll give you the computer hardware for free; we'll give you the network for free. Our consultants will upgrade your entire company to the E-Business Suite for free. We'll pay for everything. In return, you pay us your existing IT budget, and we'll guarantee to reduce it by five percent per year for the next five years. We'll sign a contract and guarantee it. And we have $7 billion in cash in the bank to back it up. You'll get a single global customer database. You'll get secure e-mail. You'll get the whole E-Business Suite. And you'll get it all for a lot less than you're spending now. There's no up-front cost. Your IT expenses go down immediately. We make the investment, we take the risk— you get a fixed, predictable bill."

The reaction in the room is silence. Surely it is too good to be true. The devil would be in the details. James McCann of 1-800-Flowers nervously asks whether this is "a new pricing paradigm." "Totally," says Ellison, and just before he has to start explaining what he meant, Art Weinbach, the tech-savvy CEO of ADP, comes to the rescue: "This concept works. It's a strategy that would work over a long period of time. The pricing is fascinating."

Ellison relaxes. "It just kind of slowly dawned on me. I have complete confidence in the suite approach. I know it saves money. I know it provides better information. But how do I convince people? Simple: move the risk from the customer to us; guarantee the price, and guarantee the savings. IBM can't do that. IBM's telling them to go best-of-breed, because IBM makes a bundle gluing it all together. But the IBM approach costs a fortune. They can never compete with us on price. Everything they do is one-off custom. So with our new E-Business Suite outsourcing offer, we take the risk and we share in the reward. I'm very confident that we'll make plenty of money, because we can lower IT costs at a much faster rate than five percent per year. We cut our own IT costs by more than half when we put in the E-Business Suite."

Martha Stewart, whose fast-growing company, Martha Stewart Living Omnimedia, is upgrading from a Microsoft to an Oracle technology platform, is impressed. She says to Ellison flirtatiously, "Do I call you? Can I have your home phone number?" The innuendo, however, seems to pass Ellison by. "Sure," he says. "Find out how much you're paying for IT, and then think about five percent savings each year and no capital costs. If twenty percent less after five years is interesting—let's talk."

Elsewhere in New York, Mayor Giuliani is speaking to a packed news conference about the anthrax attacks on the television companies and calming panicky New Yorkers. Selling software doesn't seem quite as important as it once did.

24

THE GOLDEN NUGGET

Amsterdam
January 2002
About fifteen thousand of the Oracle faithful have gathered at the RAI
Center in Amsterdam for the European leg of AppsWorld, the annual
jamboree to evangelize Oracle's application products to its customers, its
partners, and the technology media. Although Europe is SAP's backyard,
Oracle is the strong number two in most of the major European markets
other than Germany, where the firm from Walldorf has things pretty well
locked up.

The big announcement in product terms at the RAI is something that
Ellison calls Daily Business Intelligence. His big complaint with business
applications is that although they have become quite good at automating
key processes, it's still extremely difficult to get any useful information
about your business out of them. As a result, on top of the huge sums of
money big companies spend on applications, they also have to shell out
for separate data-mining tools and data warehousing. Unfortunately,
these so-called business intelligence products have some serious flaws:
not only are they expensive, but they're difficult to use and the information they throw up is a snapshot of the past, not of the present. That's
okay if you want to know everything about your sales of, say, driveshafts
in Brazil over the last three years. But it's next to useless if you want important metrics at your fingertips about how every aspect of the business
is operating in real time.

Ellison has believed for a while that one of the overwhelming advantages of a complete and integrated suite of applications sharing one set of

data schema and running on top of a single database is that it would make it possible to create an "executive dashboard" that constantly updates every key performance indicator. But what in theory should be perfectly doable, has turned out to be very hard. Nonetheless, Ellison still wants to demonstrate a working product here in Amsterdam that, he's assured me, "will blow your mind."

There are a couple of other themes at Amsterdam of at least equal importance, both aimed at repairing some of the largely self-inflicted damage of the previous eighteen months. The first is to stress that although "completeness" is still a unique selling point of the E-Business Suite, what's really vital is the underlying information architecture. Markedly changing its tune from the ill-tempered AppsWorld in Paris a year ago, Oracle is now making a point of saying that legacy applications can successfully be integrated with its suite as long as they can be hooked into the shared architecture. The same goes for "extension" applications made by specialist third-party software vendors, such as those in the health care business. By publishing its data schema and application program interfaces, Oracle is trying to show that it has created an open, flexible platform. Ellison says, "We've always been able to connect the E-Business Suite to your existing legacy applications or to other vendors' applications. Now we use the very latest technologies to make systems integration as rapid and painless as possible. But understand, even though the tools have improved, integrating several separate software systems remains a complex and expensive process."

The second message—and maybe the most vital one—is that the suite, whatever users may have heard before, is now fully stable and delivering real-world efficiency gains and huge cost savings to an ever-increasing number of customers. The trouble is that for the best part of a year, Oracle has been saying with each new 11i release (and there's been one just about every three months) that pretty much all the issues have been dealt with. Even if what's being said is now completely true, there's a big credibility problem, one that Oracle itself tacitly acknowledges. Since the summer, Ellison has been saying that the only way to sell the suite going forward will be with a wide range of customer references. But Oracle has been hit by the double whammy of still sluggish corporate technology spending and the "wait-and-see" * approach within much of the installed

---

*LE writes: They waited, and they liked what they saw. Today, most of our fifteen thousand applications customers have very happily upgraded to the

base, which the press reports about the difficulties encountered by enthusiastic early adopters have contributed to.

This means that those references that Oracle does have—and there are now well over a thousand mostly satisfied E-Business Suite users—are being milked in Amsterdam for all their worth. For several months, the reference poster child has been POSCO, the Korean steel firm that is also the world's biggest and most efficient. Although the "go-live" on 11i was back in July, it's still one of the biggest "big-bang" installations to date. But what's really making the Oracle execs purr is that just in time for Amsterdam, POSCO's CIO has told them that the efficiency gains have been so spectacular that his team is doubling its already aggressive forecast of $4 billion savings over ten years—in other words, about $600 million in savings a year directly attributable to the E-Business Suite. You might never have heard of POSCO, but Oracle is doing its damnedest to rectify that.*

Much of Ron Wohl's presentation is devoted to the superiority of Oracle's information architecture, and as the point man on the POSCO implementation, he also has plenty to say about that. It's a confident and convincing performance from somebody who lacks a natural stage presence. Backstage after his presentation, I ask Wohl about the twelve-month struggle to bring 11i to maturity after it became clear that Oracle had launched a product that, though conceptually brilliant, just wasn't ready for prime time. He sucks in his breath and begins, "Looking back at the release, you always have the wisdom of hindsight. Fundamentally, we tried to do something that I think was much larger in scope than even we realized and was much larger than the scope of any software we had released beforehand. In retrospect, we didn't do a good

---

E-Business Suite. It wasn't easy, and it wasn't on time, but for our customers 11i was worth the wait.

LE writes: POSCO is the best-run—most profitable—steel company in the world. When they told us they were getting $600 million a year in savings because of our E-Business Suite software, we got very excited. Many companies spend a fortune on enterprise software and get no measurable return on their investment. Now we had a large and respected company saying that huge savings were possible if you used an integrated suite. We saved a billion dollars a year at Oracle using our applications, and now we had a key customer confirming that the savings were real.

enough job up front—our QA [quality assurance] procedures didn't work because they had outgrown our scale. In retrospect, I would have liked to have done two things differently: we should have changed a number of processes within development to deal with the scale of the release, which we have now done; and two, knowing what we know now, we would have been wiser to withhold the release a little bit. We would have been better off as a company if we had deferred the release by three or four months."

Wohl was ready to concede that the heart of the problem was the gamble he and Ellison had taken with the order management system. "It was one of the last parts of the 11i software to be completed, and as a result we had more stability issues in order management than in other parts of the ERP code. But the stability improved at a very rapid pace. You could see it in the bug numbers, and you could see it in the customer satisfaction levels. Customers who had started on a later version—11.5.3 and above—were extremely happy. If you talked to customers who started on one of the early versions, they weren't happy, and they had a right to be upset with us. But we made it up to them by really going out of our way to help them through their difficulties.

"Take a look at where we are now, about a year and a half after the release of 11i. We have more than one thousand customers live, achieving billions of dollars of benefit. You have to compare the problems to the accomplishments, and the accomplishments, by any measure, have been profound. In this business, there's always a three- to six-month lag between perception and reality. We benefited from that in the beginning, but now it's hurting us. If we talk in three or four months, the reputation of our E-Business Suite will be much improved. Reputations change very quickly in our business. Right now, the reality is that our software is extraordinarily good, our references are extraordinarily good, and the demos are fabulous. Coming out of this, nobody will be able to stop us, I honestly believe that. No one can match our software. Before, there was a lot of doubt, and frankly some of the ongoing skepticism is because we didn't do a good enough job initially. But now we've got it right, and we've proved it works. No one can argue with our live-customer stories; those are real."

Wohl's other point was the same one that George Roberts, Oracle's top salesman, had made to me some months earlier: the suite concept was winning acceptance in the market. Wohl says, "Some people thought we were crazy; they said that no one company can do all that. But look at what's happened to all the best-of-breed vendors, except maybe Siebel, they've dived and hit the dust.* They'll stick around for a while, but they are just not going to grow, they are not going to evolve and succeed, because the integration costs are too high. Also, notice that SAP is now calling itself an integrated business suite company, and so is PeopleSoft. They've both copied our marketing message, but they can't copy our software. The integrated application suite marketing message is what the applications vendors with a future have in common. But we're the only suite with an information architecture based on this single-data model in one database, and our competitors know it. The value of the simplicity . . . can't be overestimated. This is what will allow us to beat SAP and put PeopleSoft to bed."

Although in his quiet way, Wohl is as intellectually arrogant as anyone I've ever met, he is not normally given to making such bombastic statements. He has the air of somebody who has been through a great deal and now feels vindicated. It isn't just the experience of the previous torrid twelve months that has created this battle-hardened certainty, but the last decade, when Wohl was held up for ridicule within Oracle (especially by Ray Lane) and time and time again depended on Ellison's (to many people, quite baffling) faith in his ability, for his survival. He has the air of a man whose moment has come.†

If Ron Wohl had the scent of ultimate victory in his nostrils, I expected more of the same from the naturally cocky Mark Barrenechea. But he turns out to be far from happy. He starts by saying that in the last year and a half "we've done some brand damage." He puts the blame squarely on the order management system (and by implication on Ron Wohl): "We've been in order management for fifteen years, and we still didn't get it right. We've had quality issues with many of the underlying ERP components [Wohl's side of the suite], and in many cases we didn't even do damage limitation well." He even expresses some doubts as to whether the latest release to ship—11i 5.5—has dealt with all the problems. "Some of the

---

*LE writes: Now Siebel's "hit the dust" too. Best-of-breed is dead—except for dog shows.

†LE writes: Most people don't realize just how hard it is to build software as complex as the E-Business Suite. But I know. I'd been through it before with Version 6 of our database. Software megaprojects are very late—or they never finish. Ron and his team can be proud of finishing what they started. It was a major feat of engineering.

early indicators suggest that many of the issues are behind us, but if history repeats itself it's still going to take a lot to flush them out."

When I ask Barrenechea how the CRM modules, the part of the suite that he's responsible for, are performing, he vents his frustration. He claims that because most of Oracle's fourteen thousand existing applications customers inevitably begin their 11i implementation by upgrading their ERP systems, the quality problems they've hit have often meant that the money runs out before they even get to installing "his" CRM software. "By no means has our CRM execution faltered, not at all. But in many cases we don't even get to the starting gate because all the implementation dollars have already been used up. It may take three years now before they get to try them. It makes me very impatient." *

Barrenechea accuses Wohl's team not only of mishandling the major rewrite of the crucial order management module, but also of not writing all its software to conform to the new Trading Community Architecture (TCA), or "customer master," that is meant to be the basis of the 11i platform. He says, "We've all been told to standardize on TCA, and yet we find the other organization somehow missed it along the way. So we had quite a bit of cobbling to do to get the new customer master and the new order management working across CRM. It kind of comes down to bad management in the other organization."

This is a pretty serious accusation from one of Oracle's most senior executives. I point out to Barrenechea that Ellison argues that the most important single contribution he has made since becoming involved in apps development in 1998 is to get the various parts of the development organization working together cooperatively. Barrenechea laughs and nearly chokes on the cake he's eating. "Oh, sure—it's a *lot* better than it used to be. At least we're not spitting at each other anymore. . . . Look, Larry has a brilliance, and he's certainly a virtuoso when it comes to understanding organizational structures. But he likes seeing two organizations compete so facts arise. Part of the difficulty for me in understanding this is that it translates into nonconsolidation of responsibility. Most companies would consolidate responsibility onto one sales guy, one consulting guy, one chief product developer. Right? This is either one of the most wonderful characteristics of Oracle, or it's one of the greatest flaws. And I can't work it out yet. It's so Larry."

---

*LE writes: Maybe I'm mistaken, but I think Mark was frustrated because the ERP products were outselling the CRM products.

I can see where this is leading, and sure enough Barrenechea says, "We need one applications organization.* And we need one product development organization that, over time, does not consolidate to Larry. And we have to envisage an Oracle, someday, without Larry. And be working toward that."

As if realizing that he may be overdoing the criticism, Barrenechea returns to his usual optimism. Despite all the problems, which come from doing something that is intrinsically very hard, he is convinced that Oracle's approach is "absolutely right" and that no one else can match what's been achieved. He says that the release that's about to ship—11i 5.6—is working really well within Oracle, smoothly integrating both the ERP and CRM sides of the suite, an indication that it's now ready for very wide scale deployment.

He takes particular heart from what looks like a major win over Siebel with AT&T's business services division. The deal has had to withstand a raft of executive departures at the crisis-torn telco as well as the departure of Jay Nussbaum on the Oracle sales side. What has won the deal for Oracle, says Barrenechea, is its ability to automate an entire business flow (from lead to opportunity to configured quote to order to contract to billing) involving twenty thousand sales representatives, thus reducing the process cycle from five months to thirty days. Coming on top of the BellSouth deal, it will make Oracle's CRM product very hard to beat in the telco market. He's also excited about winning business from Dell Computer, which has decided to standardize all its applications—a mix of bespoke apps and Oracle's products—on Oracle's information architecture. Given that Dell has few peers as a business process innovator, it's a major validation of Oracle's approach.

Mark Jarvis, the Englishman who spears Oracle's always aggressive marketing effort, readily admitted that after "eighteen months of Hell" he hoped Amsterdam would mark a turning point. He said, "I'd never previously thought that I might be fired. But in the last six months I have thought about it several times. I'm used to getting occasional notes from Larry, but I'd never had one like the one I got from him a few months ago, saying that the marketing is the worst it has ever been and our press cov-

---

*LE writes: I agree. We have in fact moved to a more conventional consolidated management structure in development. We now have one person responsible for all of applications development and another person responsible for all of technology development.

erage is the worst it has been in the history of the company." (I asked Ellison later whether Jarvis was in danger of getting the sack. He said, far from it. He'd "weep" if Jarvis ever left, but Jarvis needed better-quality managers at the level just below him, especially for dealing with the media.) *

In talking about turning points, was Jarvis just whistling to keep his courage up? He honestly seemed to believe otherwise. In the course of the last few months, Oracle had made its peace with the systems integrators, with the possible exception of the usually hostile Accenture. In particular, both Ernst & Young and PricewaterhouseCoopers agreed that they should be making most of their money from business process re-engineering rather than customizing other people's software.† (In fact, I'd recently attended a very positive meeting between Oracle and PWC's top team in Washington, D.C., and PWC had been the lead consultant on the POSCO implementation. And in Amsterdam, I'd talked to a senior partner from Cap Gemini who was also singing from the same song sheet.) Just as important, Jarvis claimed that most of the financial analysts, if not yet the software industry analysts, had now come out in favor of the suite as the right approach over best-of-breed.

The Daily Business Intelligence, which Jarvis and Ellison were demonstrating in Amsterdam, was a dramatic illustration of what became possible with a single data model. It was one thing to show slides illustrating how SAP's applications ran across five separate databases linked by clunky messaging compared with the Oracle suite's tight integration with a single database. It was rather more impressive to be able to offer something that was both spectacularly useful and beyond SAP's capabilities because of the inferiority of its information architecture. The same could also be said of business flows, but Daily Business Intelligence was a much easier concept for most people to grasp and thus to sell to them.

Jarvis admitted that while his people used Oracle's CRM software to gather information on customers and target marketing campaigns, like

---

*LE writes: After we hired Jim Finn, our media relations improved markedly.

†LE writes: This was a huge philosophical victory for us. When I first started telling customers and consultants not to change our code, it was considered a radical idea. Now everyone was beginning to understand the risks and costs associated with too much customization. Plain vanilla was becoming the favorite flavor for applications software. Suites were literally killing best-of-breed. We had gotten a few things right after all.

most senior executives, he'd never used it personally: "I had never used any of this stuff until about two weeks ago. I'm a total convert. That . . . made me realize that it was all worth it. We'd been through hell, but wow! Look at this—a golden nugget. We've been searching for a long time, but we finally found the gold mine."

Later the same day, Ellison used his keynote to explain why the Daily Business Intelligence was not just another nice feature but was pretty close to being the Holy Grail of business IT. As usual, he blamed most of the problems afflicting business computing on the fatal combination of fragmented information and incomplete automation: "Most business processes are not completely automated; they're a combination of online and offline activity. For example, in the sales process called 'opportunity to order' each line of the sales order is always entered into the application system, but the price quote and sales contract might be stored separately in an Excel file or a document image file. If you store your price quotes in Excel files, that means your applications database is incomplete, so you can't ask the system questions like 'What is the total value of all my outstanding quotes?' Similarly, if you use a document image file to store contracts, you cannot ask the system, 'How many of my contracts have nonstandard limitation-of-liability clauses?,' because that information is not stored in the applications database. In other words, if your process automation system is incomplete—and most are—then your applications database will be incomplete as a consequence. And an incomplete database makes building a business intelligence system virtually impossible."

It's the "completeness" of the E-Business Suite's process automation and the single-data model, which allows you to keep all your information in one database, that makes Daily Business Intelligence possible. "Every day, Oracle sales managers see updated sales figures and sales forecasts. Every day, salespeople see how much they sold and how much they spent so far this month, this quarter, this year. They see exactly where they rank among their peers in sales and expenses. If they're in the lower ten percent in sales and the upper ten percent in expenses, that fact greets them every day on their home page. If you're an Oracle engineering manager, you see how well your product is selling, and you see how many service requests your product is generating. If your product is in the bottom ten percent in sales and the top ten percent in service requests, you know you have a serious quality problem that needs to be fixed. The Daily Business Intelligence system not only provides managers with up-to-date data to make better decisions, it provides every individual in

Oracle with better information—so they know what to do and how well they're doing it."

As well as providing detailed, almost instantaneous information about every aspect of Oracle's business, it also has a dramatic impact on the behavior of individuals: "Perhaps the most interesting aspect of Daily Business Intelligence is the comparison of your job performance with that of your peers. The reaction to these rankings is fascinating. People not only work harder to move up in the rankings, they work smarter. They study the people with the best performance and learn from them. And everyone gets daily feedback that lets them know if their job performance is improving. This makes a manager's job much easier. The manager doesn't have to constantly tell people that they're doing a good job or a bad job; the system does that. When Sally arrives at work and logs on to the system, her home page pops us and says: 'Hi, Sally, you rank in the top twenty-five percent in sales, congratulations, but you're in the top five percent in entertainment expenses—knock it off; stop eating at all those fancy French restaurants.' But you know what, the second that Sally realizes we can see how much she's spending on expensive dinners, her behavior changes . . . she stops ordering the expensive wine with dinner. Constant feedback, whether it's from a boss, a parent, a teacher, or the E-Business Suite's Daily Business Intelligence system, encourages people to improve their behavior. Hard facts about how well you're doing your job in comparison with other people in your company takes most of the human bias out of performance assessment. It doesn't matter much if your boss likes you or dislikes you, it's all about your numbers." *

• • •

Backed up by an onstage demonstration of how the "executive dashboard" works and how easy the user interface makes it to drill down for extraordinarily fine grained data, Ellison's presentation makes a power-

---

*LE writes: Of course Daily Business Intelligence cannot take the place of good management judgment; it simply provides better data so managers can base their decisions on hard facts rather than gut feelings. Those "hard facts" are very difficult to come by in most companies, because current computer systems are a bunch of loosely connected process automation systems that are terrible at providing useful information about the business to management. A single, unified process automation database with integrated Daily Business Intelligence moves a company out of the dark and into the information age.

ful impact on the packed hall. But maybe because this is Europe rather than America, I detect a slight uneasiness in the nervous laughter that greets some of Ellison's jokes. Impressive proof though Daily Business Intelligence is of the computing philosophy behind the E-Business Suite, how many people would really welcome the introduction of such brutal transparency into their working lives? If Ellison has his way, it's something they'll just have to get over.*

Before going onstage, Sergio Giacoletto, Oracle's Italian head of European sales, has asked Ellison not to mention two things that are in the pipeline. The first is the "outsourcing with a twist" offer, which first broke cover at the New York CEO roundtable back in October. This is the deal in which Oracle proposes to take over a customer's entire IT budget and provide all the software (suite, apps server, database), hardware, and networking gear that's needed for a state-of-the-art computer system. Each year for the five-year term of the contract, Ellison commits to reducing that IT budget by 5 percent. Giacoletto reckons that it will give Oracle a formidable weapon to fight SAP in the European midmarket, which neither of the two rivals has penetrated much. But he wants to announce it when he's good and ready. However, when someone asks about Oracle's ASP (application service provider) strategy, Ellison can't resist the opportunity to pitch his new deal.

The second thing that the Oracle execs want kept under wraps is a radical new pricing plan for the E-Business Suite, which has barely been signed off on back at Redwood Shores. But at the press conference after his keynote speech, once again, Ellison can't help himself. From now on, he declares, the E-Business Suite will be sold to every customer in its entirety, and there will be just two license prices: $4,000 a year for power users and $400 for occasional users. What it means for the customer is that it will no longer be necessary to work out minutely in advance what modules in the suite are likely to be needed and how many licenses should be purchased, say, for financial users or sales-force users. As Ellison says, "Our pricing didn't match our product. Our product was an integrated suite, but our pricing was component by component. That meant when you were buying the suite you had to decide in advance how many users to buy for each application component: marketing, sales, service, financial, manufacturing, and so on. If you guessed wrong, you had

---

*LE writes: Your best people want management to know how well they're doing their job. Keeping relative performance a secret is not fair to them.

to come back and negotiate a new license." In other words, customers had to predict their future business needs and processes in a way that was inherently spurious. From now on, they would be able to turn on whatever parts of the suite their evolving requirements justified, and users would be allowed access to any applications they wanted to work with.

From Oracle's perspective, the new pricing model made even better sense. The bundling of features into the database and the apps server that customers could either use or not use was a neat way of locking competitors out of profitable niche markets—as Microsoft had proved over and over again (the legal difference was that, sadly for Ellison, Oracle was not a monopoly). If an ERP customer had already installed the whole suite and was thinking about deploying CRM, why not just switch on the Oracle stuff it already had rather than go to all the bother of buying and implementing a system from Siebel? The new pricing model leveraged the completeness of the suite without imposing it.

There were two further advantages from Ellison's point of view: first, it would no longer be a stretch to claim every 11i customer as a suite customer;* second, it might help to diminish some of the internal sniping between the Wohl and Barrenechea teams. Ellison told me later, "We'll now be measuring Suite sales in total, rather than ERP and CRM sales separately. That should take some of the edge off the intramural competition that's been going on between the different applications development groups. When a customer buys the entire suite, our sales system will record it as a Suite sale, but our support system will tell us exactly which applications in the Suite are actually being used."

Ellison's premature announcement at the press conference had two effects, one predictable, the other less so. The first was to send Oracle's marketing machine into a spin. When Ellison started to reveal the new pricing plan, Mark Jarvis exclaimed, "Oh my God. He said he wasn't going to do it. He always does this. This will be running on the wires, and the press will start calling Safra in a couple of hours [it was still 7 A.M. in California], and she won't know what the hell's going on." Jarvis had to prepare a detailed press statement in a couple of hours. The second, more positive, was that for the first time in a large gathering of skeptical journalists, not a single question about the value of the suite versus best-of-breed had been asked. A corner turned.

---

*LE writes: Not quite. Customers still have the option of buying the applications à la carte, which they do about half the time.

On the plane from Amsterdam to London, I discussed the last few days with Ellison, including an edited version of Barrenechea's attack on Ron Wohl. As to the latter, his reply is terse: "You know, Mark Barrenechea is a very smart guy, and he has some interesting theories that explain our CRM sales results. Indeed, our CRM sales are influenced by lots of things beyond Mark's control: the quality of our ERP software, the size and experience of our CRM sales force, the state of the economy, and the relative strength of the CRM competition." I asked him whether he agreed with Jarvis that Oracle had suffered real brand damage during the last twelve months.

He sighed; the expression "brand damage" had come from him a few months earlier, when he had wanted to draw attention to the fact that the quality issues affecting some 11i customers were the overriding priority for development. "We were all very pleased with the progress being made on our applications product quality issues, but I didn't want to let up. I wanted our developers to stay intensely focused on quality, quality, quality. So I casually said that the early versions of 11i had done some 'brand damage' to Oracle, and to repair that damage we'd have to constantly improve quality. I'm sorry I ever used the expression 'brand damage.' The phrase 'brand damage' caught on, and everyone started using it. A negative article in the press caused 'brand damage.' A sale didn't close because of 'brand damage.' I've been plagued by the expression 'brand damage' ever since I first used it. Never use catchy phrases to describe something negative about your own company. Aim the dark marketing at the competition, not yourself." Interestingly, Ellison added that the roll-out of Daily Business Intelligence within Oracle had made it much easier to dig down into finding where the problems were and who should be responsible for fixing them: the transparency ended what had been a blame game between support and development.*

For all that, I suggested that from what I had seen over the last few

---

*LE writes: As we started to put in Daily Business Intelligence, I realized that Oracle had the wrong product-quality metrics; we had been measuring the wrong things for years. Oracle had held engineering accountable for product defects—bugs—rather than service requests. A product can be bug-free and still generate too many service requests because it's difficult to install or difficult to use. We decided that our primary measure of product quality would be the number of service requests, not the number of defects or bugs. Once we got the metrics right, the squabbling between support and development ended, the number of service requests started trending downward, and customer satisfaction went

days of Oracle's customers and integration partners, the technology press, and even some of the analysts, the idea that a corner had been turned in Amsterdam didn't seem far-fetched. Ellison wants to agree, but he also wants to put things into context: "A big technology transition—a massive rewrite of one of our major products—happens infrequently, once every ten or fifteen years. When it does happen, it puts a huge strain on us and our customers. It's a little bit like childbirth. It's painful for what seems like a very long time, but the pain is suddenly forgotten when you see the beautiful baby. When Oracle 7 came out, nobody remembered the pain of Oracle 6. Rewriting the applications was a much easier transition than rewriting the database. But nobody remembers the extent of the problems we had with Version 6 of the database. Everyone's repressed it. It's just fascinating. Somebody said to Jeff Henley, 'Oh my God, this is as bad as the database rewrite back in 1991.' Jeff and I had to laugh. During the database rewrite we almost went bankrupt. Today we have $6 billion in cash and profit margins of around thirty-five percent. But more important, we now have the only suite of applications integrated around a single applications database. We have the only applications database with built-in business intelligence. In other words, we have the smartest, best-looking baby in town."

Maybe the only thing that mattered was a return to sales growth? Ellison had said to me more than once that the one thing that would make a difference was a quarter that beat expectations. "Analysts don't try to foretell the future; they try to explain the recent past. If you have a series of bad quarters, they explain that it must be because you have product problems. If you then have a series of good quarters, they explain that it's because you've overcome your product problems. They'll conclude that our E-Business Suite product problems are over when we start growing faster than our applications competitors. It's that simple—they just look at the numbers." *

• • •

The tension in Amsterdam between Ron Wohl and Mark Barrenechea would soon be resolved. Getting Daily Business Intelligence to perform

---

up dramatically. *Daily Business Intelligence is a powerful tool for changing behavior, but be careful of what you measure. If you measure the wrong things, behavior will change the wrong way.*

LE writes: Not all the analysts. A few good ones actually survey customers.

all its tricks proved to be difficult, and as a consequence, soon after returning to Redwood Shores, Ellison, threw himself into the effort to get the product finished: "We were getting most of the data we wanted out of Daily Business Intelligence, but not everything. There was some data that I considered very important that we were unable to track for some reason. I wanted to understand why." As usual when an engineering problem struck, he insisted on embarking on a process of highly detailed reviews of every product element to try to identify the issues.

The urgent need to make Daily Business Intelligence a reality had an unforeseen effect: it exposed weaknesses in the integration between the ERP and CRM sides of the suite that neither Ellison nor anyone else had been fully aware of. The more Ellison drilled down into the code, the more alarmed he became: "By March, I had found a couple of database schema errors that seemed to be the source of the Daily Business Intelligence problems I was working on. But schema errors were only a symptom of the real underlying problem: the ERP and CRM components of the suite were not as tightly integrated as they should have been, because our two development teams were not working as closely together as I thought they were. I discovered I had a serious organizational problem in applications engineering. I should have seen it and fixed it a while ago. I totally screwed up."

It may have taken Ellison longer than it should have to discover the defects in his applications development organization, but once he did, he acted decisively. Ellison says, "Once it's clear to me that I've made a mistake, I move pretty quickly to fix it." He determined that CRM would, in effect, be merged into Wohl's side of the house, with John Wookey, the senior development manager who had delivered Oracle's financials application and was currently working on health care, becoming responsible for the CRM sales and marketing modules; Don Klaiss, who was responsible for Oracle manufacturing products, would take over the CRM service modules. If there ever had been an argument for nurturing a "creative tension" between the two sides of Oracle's applications business, by now there was none. While CRM was newer and sexier than ERP, Ellison reckoned that it was nonetheless a lot easier to do: "I believe that CRM is a layer or feature set on top of your ERP customer database. CRM is pretty easy to build if and only if you have a unified customer database, but near-impossible to build if you don't. Once again, a single database and integration is the key. CRM applications should not be separated from the ERP applications, and we got ourselves into trouble when we tried to build them separately. The organizational structure I set up was wrong; it was my fault, my mistake—*mea culpa*."

25

A PERFECT STORM

For Larry Ellison, Thursday, May 2, 2002, was meant to be a routine working day. Through the morning he had worked on the deck of his home in Atherton, taking the usual mix of calls from his senior executives, business partners, and customers. Much of the rest of the day, as had been the pattern for several months, was scheduled to be spent in the eleventh-floor boardroom at 500 Oracle Parkway hammering out problems with the newly unified applications development team. But by late afternoon, Ellison found himself engulfed in what soon became known within Oracle as the "perfect storm"—a vicious combination of political feuding driven by large egos and the impending gubernatorial election, a fashionable post-Enron obsession with "corporate wrongdoing," and a hyperaggressive media that had worked itself into a feeding frenzy. It was the worst crisis the company had faced in more than a decade.

The telephone call announcing the storm's arrival was from Ken Glueck, Oracle's Washington-based senior political operative. Glueck is a big, unflappable man whose calm and geniality were never threatened even at the height of the "Dumpster diving" brouhaha (when Glueck had helped to expose Microsoft's secret bankrolling of purportedly independent industry lobbying groups that just happened to take the software giant's side during the epic antitrust case). But now Glueck was agitated.

Alerted by an Oracle lobbyist in Sacramento, Glueck had been watching live TV coverage of the California Highway Patrol raiding the state's own Department of Information Technology (DOIT) "to secure all shredders and trash." The news bulletins were also carrying reports that DOIT's director, Elias Cortez, had been suspended by Governor Gray

Davis pending a criminal investigation and that the governor's e-government adviser, a longtime political aide named Arun Baheti, had been fired. Baheti had accepted a $25,000 campaign check from an Oracle lobbyist just as the state was completing a big software contract (worth between $95 million and $122 million depending on whether it ran for five or ten years) with Oracle. Although there was nothing wrong with Oracle's making a political contribution, Davis had issued orders to his administration staffers not to accept money personally. It was clear to Glueck, Ellison, and Safra Catz that Oracle was now embroiled in a major political scandal. Ellison told me later, "I could see a headline with words like 'police raid' and 'shredders and trash' with 'Oracle' right in between. I didn't look forward to being served up as the tasty part of that media sandwich."

Increasingly ominous looking clouds had been gathering for some time, but Ellison hadn't noticed them—it had never occurred to him that Oracle had done anything wrong.* The origins of the crisis had been more than a year earlier. California's DOIT had hired Logicon, a consultancy and systems integrator that was a subsidiary of Northrop Grumman, to look into the state's future IT requirements and propose a cost-effective solution. Logicon had recommended a six-year so-called enterprise license agreement (ELA: a kind of heavily discounted "all-you-can-eat" licensing arrangement sometimes favored by big corporate and public sector customers, in which they pay a lump sum for an unlimited number of database seats combined with long-term maintenance and support) with Oracle, with a further four years' option. The state and its 104 agencies were already big Oracle users, and Logicon reckoned that it could leverage their combined buying power to get a very good deal out of Oracle for both California and itself. Which is exactly what Logicon and the DOIT believed they had gotten. If the deal was allowed to run its full ten-year term, they calculated that the savings compared with buying Oracle database licenses on a piecemeal basis were likely to be around $110 million. It also meant that agencies could bring as many users online as they wanted, when they wanted—a big incentive to developing innovative and cost-saving e-government initiatives.

---

*LE writes: It never occurred to me that Oracle had done anything wrong, for the simple reason that Oracle hadn't done anything wrong. Unfortunately, it took a while for that fact to come out. In the meantime, the media simply presumed us guilty of something—without ever saying exactly what.

Why Oracle was willing to do the deal is another matter. It was getting paid only $30 million to allow up to 270,000 people to use its software for ten years, while support and maintenance, which included free upgrades to the latest versions of Oracle's technology, were pegged to a flat rate that worked out at $5.2 million a year for the life of the contract. Unknown to Oracle, there was an escalator clause in the maintenance part of the contract that would give Logicon $12 million for doing little more than man a help desk. Logicon was also doing well out of the transaction: from the $52 million the State of California was paying for licenses, Logicon was getting a $10.7 million sales commission, while the remainder was accounted for by sales tax and the charges of the leasing firm that had been brought in by Logicon to finance the deal. But from Oracle's point of view it made little financial sense. Ellison later complained to me, "It was a spectacular deal for Logicon and a good deal for the state, but it was not a good deal for Oracle."

Even at the time, plenty of people at Oracle, including Ellison, thought the contract was far too generous and an example of precisely the kind of "scorched earth" deal in which future earnings were sacrificed for the sake of making a quick buck in the present, which Ellison and Catz had actively campaigned against. If Oracle itself had negotiated the contract, the terms would have been very different. However, Jay Nussbaum, still the head of Oracle Service Industries, reasoned that although the State of California had been give very substantial discounts on Oracle products, there was something to be said for an arrangement that would help lock in a big customer for the foreseeable future.

But if the deal was controversial at Redwood Shores, it was rapidly becoming political dynamite a hundred miles away in Sacramento. The DOIT had a good many enemies among Sacramento legislators and, facing a reauthorization that many thought it would fail to get, Cortez was desperate for a big IT win to prove its worth; Barry Keene, the director of General Services, whose department was responsible for negotiating the contract, was eager to get the publicity that a deal of this size would bring. Sure enough, Cortez, Keene, and Arun Baheti had all appeared, grinning from ear to ear, on the pages of InfoWeek. Predictably, the pictures, and others like it in a host of publications that exist to massage the egos of senior government employees, were, to the DOIT's many critics, like a red rag to a bull. At the same time, issues began surfacing that were troubling to even neutral observers.

The Department of Finance suggested that neither it nor the other offices involved had exercised proper diligence in determining whether the cost savings that the ELA was meant to bring were probable or were based on spurious estimates provided by Logicon after it had been hired as a consultant. The accusation was supported by the haste with which the deal had been put to bed and the ambiguity of Logicon's status, which stemmed from changes in its commercial relationship with the state. Logicon was now receiving all its remuneration from commission both as a distributor for Oracle and for arranging financing with a leasing firm. Consequently, there were legitimate doubts about how disinterested its advice had been while in its original consulting role.*

And that wasn't all. Suspicions were further raised because the contract had not been put out to tender. At the last moment, Cortez, determined to wrap things up as quickly as possible, had insisted that Oracle, rather than Logicon, be the prime contractor. Oracle was one of a select group of companies on a General Services Administration list that qualified it as a sole-source vendor. Ellison says, "The best place to buy Oracle software is from Oracle Corporation." Up to a point. The problem was the suddenness of the switch from Logicon to Oracle and, once again, uncertainty about what Logicon was bringing to the table and how much it was being paid. Finally, there was the nasty little kicker of the $25,000 check that Ravi Mehta, a political consultant on Oracle's books, had handed over to Arun Baheti while the two men were having a drink in a Sacramento restaurant. At the very least, the timing of the payment, the details of which had only just emerged, was unfortunate.

For Dean Florez, the Democratic chairman of the state Joint Legislative Audit Committee (JLAC), the target was too big and too tempting to ignore. Florez, a political maverick who saw himself as California's answer to John McCain, had a burning desire to make life as unpleasant as possible for Governor Davis and his administration. What Florez wanted and what Florez got was a full review "of the State's contracting practices in entering into an enterprise licensing agreement with the Oracle Corporation." The surprising thing is that nobody at Oracle seemed to realize that this was a portent of serious trouble.†

It was months later, toward the end of 2001, before even muffled

---

*LE writes: Logicon, not Oracle, recommended the deal to the state; Logicon, not Oracle, negotiated the terms of the deal with the state; Oracle, not Logicon, got all the headlines.

†LE writes: We naively believed that because we hadn't done anything wrong we had nothing to worry about.

alarm bells at Redwood Shores started ringing. State Auditor Elaine Howle was a long way from completing her report, but Oracle executives were beginning to worry about the kind of questions they were being asked. Belatedly, it occurred to them that Howle might be set on reaching a hostile conclusion. In January, fearing the worst but still convinced that the state had no grounds for complaint, Oracle took the precaution of asking Howle's vastly experienced predecessor, Kurt Sjoberg, who was now in private practice, to carry out his own "independent" report on the deal to see if, in his view, California would, as Logicon had claimed, save a lot of money. On April 10, Sjoberg Evashenk Consulting reported that over the full ten-year life of the contract the state stood to save between $110 and $163 million. In other words, Logicon's estimate of the contract's value had been respectably at the low end of the range. Surely even a skeptical Elaine Howle would have to admit that California was getting a pretty good deal after all.

Just six days later, Howle reached a very different conclusion. In a stinging report, the bureau argued that over six years the state would *lose* $40.6 million (although it admitted that this would be reduced to $5.6 million if the contract ran the full ten years). The state auditor made no mention of the campaign check from Oracle, but in just about every other respect, it was as bad as it could be. She accused DOIT of ignoring the results of its own survey of 127 state departments, undertaken prior to signing the contract, which had provided evidence that "few state workers might need or want any new Oracle Corporation products." All three departments responsible for overseeing large IT projects were lambasted for failing to assess the state's actual need for the contract. She further inveighed against "General Services' unprepared and inexperienced negotiating team" for agreeing to a contract "that left the state unprotected against numerous risks." "Lacking an in-depth understanding of whether the ELA might fill a legitimate need for state departments, and without knowing the true costs and benefits of the contract, the state committed millions of taxpayer dollars to a questionable technology purchase."

It got worse. Howle argued that because of Logicon's "undisclosed role, actions and compensation," questions had been raised about the validity of the contract. Howle calculated that Logicon stood to make no less than $28 million out of the $95 million the state would be paying for the first six years of the contract. Legal advice to the audit bureau suggested that despite Oracle's status as a vendor that could be exempted from competitive bidding requirements, the same didn't apply to Logicon. Given that it was taking 30 percent of the contract's value, a court might judge the contract to be void. But for Oracle, it was the second half of Howle's report that was most damaging; it read like a sustained attack on the software firm's business practices. The report claimed that Oracle was well known for:

- Aggressively selling to the highest levels of an organization by basing its arguments on the "positive impact on the customer's business" rather than the technical details of the database and the competition;
- Using high-pressure sales tactics to close long-term, high-value deals quickly—saying, for example, "If you buy databases for ten computers this year and promise to buy databases for fifty computers over the next five years, we'll give them to you at the special rate we have now. Prices are going up; it's the fourth quarter, and we're ready to deal."
- Practicing the Oracle maxim, "Lock customers in, lock competitors out," by getting from customers a long-term commitment that encourages migration to Oracle products and helps establish Oracle as an organizational standard. The high cost of future transition away from Oracle products to those of competitors discourages future competition.
- Changing the way it licenses its products, making long-term commitments problematic. For example, the most recent version of the Oracle enterprise database software, Version 9i—released two weeks after the state executed the ELA—has certain features that are separately licensed. If the state wanted to upgrade from 8i to the 9i version and also wanted these special features, it would have to pay a separate license and maintenance fee for them.

The analysis continued, "According to our technical consultant [who had also provided the insights above], other Oracle business developments that were occurring shortly before the contract was finalized included pricing pressure from its customers. In 2000 and the first half of 2001, Oracle's users and prospective clients were putting tremendous pressure on the company to lower prices. Oracle's database market share was being threatened at the high-end (large, complex systems) by IBM and at the low-end (small, departmental systems) by Microsoft." The findings of Howle's "technical consultant," it emerged, were being assisted by none other than Ellison's old enemy—the Gartner Group, probably the technology consulting firm most consistently hostile to Oracle. Not surprisingly, Gartner "questioned the wisdom of establishing Oracle as a standard for the entire state."

The auditor's report was a nasty shock to Oracle. Ken Glueck said to me later, "The section of the report about our business practices simply couldn't be reconciled with what had happened. Our salespeople were not engaged at all in the negotiation of the deal, and the four guys from our side who were involved in it, you would instantly realize if you saw them, are just not capable of aggressive tactics. And besides, Kevin Fitzgerald, who had succeeded Nussbaum, kept telling us that the terms of the contract were the most favorable he'd seen during the twenty years he'd worked with the public sector. But the way Howle's report was written provided a lens for looking at the contract that was intended to make us look bad."

From that moment on, no reporting piece on the contract wrangle—and there was a never-ending stream of them—was complete without the words "Critics of the contract have noted that Oracle has long been known for sales tactics considered aggressive even in the high-stakes, high-pressure world of corporate software sales." According to Ellison, Oracle's sales team "simply agreed to take over a contract that had been fully negotiated and agreed to by both Logicon and the state. The state asked us to take over the contract, and that's what we did. I don't think that our sales team met with the state for more than a couple of hours. Yet they were accused of using such 'aggressive, high-pressure tactics' that they had 'forced the state to buy more software than the state needed.' Just how did they manage to do that in a couple of hours?"

Horrified by the likely impact of Howle's report, Ellison claims that he immediately told General Services' Barry Keene that he was prepared to scrap the deal. "I said we'd be happy to undo the deal if they want to undo it. But they said, 'No, we love the deal. We don't want to undo it. We'll stick by it.' " That is consistent with Keene's official response to the auditor. While agreeing that there were some steps that needed to be taken to ensure that the state received full value, he continued to maintain that the savings would be very substantial.*

The auditor's report was all Florez needed for his committee to em-

---

*LE writes: The state was saying it was a very bad deal, and at the same time, the state was refusing to undo the deal. It was a bit hard to understand—like the conversation between Alice and the Red Queen.

bark upon lengthy and politically charged hearings that would last more than two months. Of course, Oracle wasn't the primary target; that was Governor Davis. Florez made no bones about his belief that Davis ran an incompetent and greedy administration. The fact that he was handing ammunition to Davis's Republican rival, Bill Simon, in an election year troubled him not at all. If he could use Oracle to damage and embarrass Davis, he would be happy to do so. Ellison said, "It was like a drive-by shooting. Florez was aiming at Davis, but he hit us. We were in the wrong place at the wrong time." The first casualty, however, was Keene. One of the committee's early witnesses, he was forced to concede that his decision to proceed with the deal had been "an error of judgment." A few days later, Davis pushed Keene, a sixty-two-year-old former State Senate majority leader, out of his job.

From the governor's point of view, one of the most dangerous developments was the connection Florez was making between Oracle's $25,000 campaign check and what was now officially a profligate misuse of taxpayers' money. While trying to push through a $2 billion tax hike during the state's energy crisis, Davis had also managed to accumulate a $40 million reelection war chest. Davis now felt highly exposed. Ellison said, "Bill Simon accused Governor Davis of running a coin-operated government. The Republicans and some Democrats in Sacramento were jumping up and down saying the governor was selling contracts for campaign contributions. First the governor wastes the taxpayers' money on energy, now on software. We found ourselves in the middle of a no-holds-barred political battle. I couldn't believe it. How the hell did we get to be a part of the campaign to defeat Governor Davis in the upcoming election?"

Davis had to show that he was just as mad as anybody about what had happened and that he was going to make things right. By firing or suspending underlings, demanding that the state should get its money back from the rapacious Oracle, raiding the offices of DOIT, and endorsing an investigation by the state attorney general, Bill Lockyer, Davis was able to present himself as being both valiant for truth and the victim of his subordinates' wrongdoing. When Oracle's press spokesman, Jim Finn, said that not only was his company ready to rescind the contract but it had made the offer several weeks earlier, nobody in Davis's office could recollect such an offer being made.

Another interpretation of Davis's actions is that he panicked. From Oracle's point of view, Davis had helped stir in a further dash of toxicity to the already seething cauldron by lending his weight to the idea that some kind of crime had been committed. By talking about "shredding" because of the "need to preserve evidence in our investigation" at the doomed DOIT, Barry Goode, the governor's chief counsel, was throwing fuel on the flames.

As far as the $25,000 check from Oracle was concerned, although it was made to look bad, it's doubtful whether anyone really believed that there was a connection between it and the ELA. In the first place, compared with the size of the contract, not to mention Oracle's size and profitability, it was a piddling amount. Second, the check had been promised at a fund-raising dinner organized by EDS, the big systems integrator. It was neither the biggest nor the smallest amount pledged that night by thirty tech firms. Ken Glueck points out that as well as being a rather small scale political contributor, the only states where Oracle made any contributions at all were California and Virginia, where, in both cases, it was a substantial employer. If Oracle was in the business of buying contracts, surely it would be politically active everywhere it sold software?

But for a number of reasons, the check still didn't look good. Although it had been issued in March, the fact that it had been handed over just as a major deal was closing was enough to raise suspicions. Glueck says, "Ravi Mehta did nothing illegal, but he showed bad judgment: first, by holding on to the check when he shouldn't have; second, by giving it to Baheti in a restaurant—which of course became a bar in the newspaper reports."

Meanwhile, the circus in Sacramento, with Dean Florez as ringmaster, dragged on, working its way through a mass of evidence and witnesses, all calculated to denigrate the Davis administration and to add further to Oracle's misery. Not all of it went Florez's way: he had boasted that Ohio, North Dakota, and Montana, as well as the city of Toronto, would testify damningly about their experiences of working with Oracle. But having seen what was going on in Sacramento, those states elected to put their relationship with Oracle ahead of participating in the JLAC inquisition. Ben Piscitelli, a spokesman for the Ohio Department of Administrative Services, said, "We continue to have a normal business relationship with Oracle. This really is a California-versus-Oracle issue, and we're leaving it at that."

But Florez was winning some rounds. Committee investigators dug up some incriminating e-mails from the unfortunate Mehta. Dated January 5, Mehta's e-mail to Robert Hoffman, Oracle's director of legislative affairs, listed nine state politicians who, in Mehta's view, were important to Oracle and should be given money. Oracle's response was to say that

Mehta's suggestions had, at the time, been ignored. But when Mehta, appearing under subpoena, took the Fifth Amendment, it made it look as if there had been some kind of cover-up. Glueck suspected that Mehta refused to testify because of irregularities in his reporting of invoices. Glueck reckoned that he must have been ripping off Oracle by claiming expenses that he hadn't incurred, or that he had failed to report them and was guilty of noncompliance. Glueck didn't think (and certainly hoped) that Mehta's reticence had anything to do with the ELA contract. On May 31, Glueck terminated Mehta's contract with Oracle. He said, "In hindsight, Ravi working for us was probably a mistake."

If Mehta was an embarrassment, everyone at Oracle was furious that the committee attacked their company mercilessly but gave it no opportunity to defend itself. There were two particular bones of contention. The first was Florez's intention to call only five relatively junior Oracle salesmen who had been involved in the deal to testify and his refusal to allow them to make any opening statement. Oracle insisted that a senior sales executive, Kevin Fitzgerald, accompany them and be allowed at least fifteen minutes to state Oracle's position. Oracle was also adamant that information that Florez was demanding about the salesmen's personal remuneration on the deal was a breach of confidentiality that would leave it open to legal action by its own employees. The second spat was over Florez's lack of interest in hearing former state auditor Kurt Sjoberg's very different analysis of the value of the deal to the state. At the end of May, the usually mild-mannered Jeff Henley fired off a splenetic letter to Florez.

Dear Chairman Florez and Members of the Committee:
This letter is a formal complaint regarding the manner in which the Joint Legislative Audit Committee ("JLAC" or "Committee") has conducted its inquiry into the May 31, 2001 Enterprise License Agreement between Oracle Corporation and the State of California ("ELA") and the Bureau of State Audits Report regarding the ELA ("BSA Report").

For nearly six weeks, the JLAC has conducted numerous hearings that have been severely critical of Oracle and the ELA. Despite repeated attempts by Oracle to be heard by the JLAC, the Committee has yet to hear directly from Oracle, and Oracle has not been given a single opportunity to defend itself against the baseless allegations in the BSA Report relating to the value of the ELA.

For the reasons listed below, we respectfully request that the Committee immediately give Oracle an opportunity to have a senior company executive, Mr. Kevin Fitzgerald, Senior Vice President, Oracle Government, Education and Healthcare Sales, testify before the JLAC as to why the ELA is an extraordinary value for the State of California.

- As the Committee is aware, Oracle has *voluntarily* produced thousands of pages of documents pursuant to the Committee's requests, *voluntarily* agreed to have five Oracle employees testify at the previously scheduled hearings on June 4th and 5th, and *voluntarily* agreed to make these five individuals available for interviews with Committee staff prior to the hearings. Oracle's cooperation with this Committee cannot be placed in question. Despite that cooperation, we have been told repeatedly by members of the media that you, as Chairman of the JLAC, have characterized Oracle as uncooperative. Nothing could be further from the truth.

- On April 18, 2002, just two days after the BSA Report was released, Oracle wrote to the State Auditor and the JLAC pointing out a specific material error in the BSA Report. *This single error changes the value of the ELA* from the State Auditor's estimate of a net loss for California taxpayers to a net benefit. The Auditor has not answered our letter, has refused to meet with Oracle, and has referred us to the JLAC to discuss questions related to the value proposition of the ELA. We have asked the JLAC for the opportunity to discuss this material error in public at the Committee's hearings, and we have been told by your staff that the Committee has no interest in having that discussion. Moreover, we have requested numerous meetings with the JLAC and have been told that you, as Chairman, will not meet with Oracle. It is unheard of—perhaps unprecedented—that the subject of an audit report is not given a single opportunity to engage in a thoughtful discussion about the report. We believe that the material error identified in our letter of April 18th is only one of many such issues that deserve serious and thoughtful attention from the JLAC.

- During the process of these hearings, you, as Chairman, have unjustly accused Oracle of many things and have permitted the hearing record to be filled with reams of undocumented innuendo and speculation. Oracle has repeatedly asked you, as Chairman, for the opportunity to have a senior Oracle executive address the Committee. It is inconceivable to Oracle that after nearly 75 hours of Committee hearings in six weeks, the Committee cannot find the time to give the subject of those hearings a single opportunity to present its views. We believe that as a historical matter of legislative investigations—in Sacramento and nationally—this position is unprecedented. Your refusal to schedule this hearing reflects poorly on the entire legislature and calls directly into question your motives for holding these hearings.

- Oracle has been informed by the Committee that when Oracle's sales staff do testify, they will not be allowed to address the Committee with even a brief opening statement. Again, this is unprecedented. Even the most notoriously unfair legislative investigations in the history of our country, such as the House Un-American Activities Committee or its Senate counterparts, allowed its witnesses to make opening statements. A fifteen minute opening statement by the witness would permit Oracle to at least frame those issues it believes the Committee should review in any search for the truth about the ELA.

- Oracle has formally asked you, as Chairman, if Oracle's sales staff will be permitted to address the value proposition of the ELA during the hearings, as this is *the central issue* in the BSA Report. As we have sought to explain to the Committee, Oracle firmly believes that the ELA will save California taxpayers in excess of $100 million. This request was rejected by your staff.

- Oracle asked former State Auditor, Mr. Kurt Sjoburg, to perform an independent analysis of the ELA. That analysis *confirms the value proposition* presented to the Department of Information Technology, the Department of General Services, and the Department of Finance last year. Again, we have asked you, as Chairman, for the opportunity to address this report, and that request was also rejected.

- On May 20, 2002, Oracle sent you, as Chairman, and JLAC a very clear letter requesting that Oracle's Senior Vice President, Mr. Kevin Fitzgerald, be permitted to testify at the June 4th hearing. In addition, we were very clear in that letter that *Oracle was not refusing to provide other witnesses* that the Committee was requesting. Rather than work with us to come to a mutually acceptable resolution, you, as Chairman of the JLAC, misstated and misrepresented Oracle's position before the Joint Rules Committee. As a result, in our view, you, as Chairman, sought to seek subpoenas for no substantive cause; other than to create a media opportunity for the Chair.

Last, let me turn to the Committee's most recent document request dated May 23, 2002, which continues the pattern of trying to create issues rather than address facts. The JLAC letter requests:

" . . . communications and documents related to the retained services by Oracle through Manatt, Phelps & Phillips or the consulting firm of Sjoberg Evanshank. The requested documents include, but are not limited to, requests for proposals, letters of engagement, contracts for services, and all analyses prepared by Sjoberg Evanshank in relation to the Oracle ELA and State Audit Report #2001-128."

As you know, the Sjoberg firm was retained by Oracle's outside counsel to provide expert advice to Oracle. Oracle has delivered to the JLAC copies of the report prepared by that firm, which confirms that the State's savings from the ELA are $110–163 million, and a further $33 million in savings to local governments. In addition, Oracle has provided you with a copy of Mr. Sjoberg's letter of April 29, 2002, confirming his analysis of the savings despite the contrary findings of the BSA Report.

As we indicated above, you, as Chairman, have told us that you will not permit any discussion of Mr. Sjoberg's report or his analysis of the savings to the State to be achieved under the ELA. However, you are well aware that you are seeking to invade the attorney/client privilege and attorney work product doctrine to obtain attorney communications and other materials that are plainly protected by the law. By making this request for information, which is clearly beyond the limits of permissible legal discovery, it is clear to us that you, as Chairman, are *seeking a subpoena confrontation* with Oracle (and its more than 10,000 California-based employees).

You, as Chairman, also requested:

"records of all commissions recorded, promised or paid to any individuals related to the Enterprise License Agreement entered into on May 31, 2001, between the State of California and the Oracle Corporation."

This material pertains to intensely private personal financial information of four individual salesmen of the company that the company is not free to disclose without the employees' consent. In fact, a private attorney representing one of those individuals has advised Oracle that he wishes to invoke the salesman's right under the California Constitution's right to privacy not to have his client's personal financial records produced by the corporation. Your request and the employees' rights cannot both be met.

There is a significant body of California case law that specifically prohibits employers from violating the privacy rights of their employees. In addition, Oracle Corporation's sales commissions structure and compensation programs are proprietary trade secrets of Oracle.

Again, you, as Chairman, are well aware of these rights and privileges. As there is clearly no reasonable basis for the request, we can only view this as a punitive attempt to seek an unnecessary confrontation with Oracle in order to further the Chair's media strategy. It appears that no amount of cooperation, including voluntarily producing documents, witnesses for interviews, or witnesses for hearings will satisfy the ever increasing demands placed upon Oracle in this matter.

•

It is now very clear to Oracle that the merits of the ELA do not matter to the JLAC. For the reasons stated above, Oracle formally requests the right to be heard immediately, before the Committee continues its punitive abuse of one of California's most successful companies and employers.

Very truly yours,

Jeffrey O. Henley

Executive Vice President and Chief Financial Officer

cc: Senator Alarcon, Vice Chair, Joint Legislative Audit Committee

Members, Joint Legislative Audit Committee

Members, Joint Rules Committee

Although Florez described Henley's charge (in a letter to Ellison) that Oracle had not received a fair shake from his committee as "utter nonsense" and said that the overall tone of his complaint was one of "harsh and inaccurate criticism" of both him and the JLAC, for the first time he admitted on the record that it was state officials who were in the dock, not Oracle. And, albeit very late in the day, Oracle did get a hearing for its side of the story. On June 5, after Elaine Howle had testified that she was standing by her numbers, her former boss, Kurt Sjoberg, finally took the stand for Oracle. Sjoberg walked the committee through his rigorously conducted twenty-five-page audit on the deal, patiently trying to explain the difference between his conclusions and Howle's. He pointed out that Howle had not actually attempted to analyze the value of the contract but instead had simply tried to check the accuracy of the projections originally made at the time the state first considered the contract. Not only did the audit bureau have far less complete information than his team had been able to extract from Oracle, but its whole methodology had been fundamentally different and, in his view, consequently flawed.

In an article for the *San Francisco Chronicle* three weeks earlier, Sjoberg had spelled out those differences and why Howle's calculations made little sense. Among Howle's mistakes, she had chosen fiscal 2000 as the baseline year—a period covering nine months of calendar 1999, a time when public sector IT budgets had been almost wholly dedicated to preventing millennium bug meltdown. Ellison says, "The two audit reports came to diametrically opposite conclusions; therefore, one of the two auditors must have been wildly mistaken in their analysis and calculation of savings. Sjoberg had about twenty years' experience as state auditor, while Howle was brand new to the job. It was obvious to anyone who bothered to read both reports which one was right." Sjoberg's report was casually and rather disgracefully dismissed by Florez ("After sitting through nine hours of testimony, my conclusion is that we stand by the state auditor's report. You get the numbers you pay for, and Oracle got those numbers."), and he was equally unimpressed by the evidence from Kevin Fitzgerald about Oracle's minimal involvement in drawing up the contract. Other members of the committee, however, had the decency to look a little uncomfortable. Ellison observed, "When the facts finally came out, Florez found it hard to completely ignore them—but he tried."

When Dean Florez finally called it a day on June 17 after two months, thirty witnesses, and more than 2,500 pages of documents, there was still no smoking gun. Most critically, nobody had been able to make any connection between the contract and "the buying of lawmaker influence," as one headline had optimistically put it. Florez concluded, "I think we got taken to the cleaners. If we have accomplished anything, I hope it is to warn state officials that the next time a smelly deal crosses your desk at the eleventh hour, you'd better do what's right instead of what's politically convenient." But he tacitly admitted failure when he decided to close the investigation without producing a report. John Borland of

CNET, the San Francisco–based technology news Web site, wrote: "Contradictory testimony throughout the trial has failed to provide an accurate picture of how the deal was finalized or structured. It's also unclear whether Oracle or Logicon is to blame for the convoluted contract—or whether state officials were too trusting of the promised cost savings and license estimates in the first place." Or if Elaine Howle had simply gotten her sums wrong, he could also have added.

In the aftermath, there was a conspicuous attempt to mend fences. On July 23, Oracle's offer to rescind the contract was gratefully accepted by the state's attorney general, Bill Lockyer: "Today's agreement serves California taxpayers and successfully meets the state's objectives by rescinding a $95 million contract that had become controversial. Oracle and Northrop Grumman [the parent company of Logicon] were under no obligation to help California by rescinding this contract, and we appreciate their cooperation and willingness to rescind the ELA."

Three weeks after the closure of his committee's hearings, Dean Florez was stripped of his chairmanship. It was, of course, an act of vengeance by supporters of Governor Davis, but Florez had won few admirers by his relentlessly egotistical behavior. The *Sacramento News and Review* editorialized, "Let's talk about what a legislator ought not to be: more about self-interest than public interest, arrogant, grandstanding, difficult for both friends and enemies to deal with. This describes Dean Florez to a T. There are few people in the Capitol with anything nice to say about the Democrat from Shafter, except maybe for Republicans who cheered his over-the-top investigation of the Oracle scandal, and even they grumbled about his autocratic tendencies during the hearings."

• • •

How much real damage had the whole messy business done to Oracle? It wasn't as if its "perfect storm" had come out of a cloudless sky. The company was only just beginning to recover from the damage caused by the birth pangs of the E-Business Suite and was continuing to suffer slack demand for enterprise software. Also, more or less coincident with the California imbroglio, the market research arm of Gartner delivered what looked like another hammer blow: survey numbers suggesting that IBM's DB2 had pushed Oracle into second place in the high-end database market for the first time in years—a finding gleefully leapt upon by the tech press and a good many analysts who ought to have known better.

Morgan Stanley's Chuck Phillips was pretty much a lone voice in putting the apparently sensational news into context. He wrote, "Gartner

Dataquest's numbers largely reflect whatever Microsoft and IBM provide to the market analysts as revenue for the past year's performance. There is no way to verify the numbers since they aren't audited and aren't provided to financial analysts. IBM allocates database revenue out of deals that include services, hardware, and even mainframe maintenance. We don't think IBM gained in the last year although they did in the previous year when Oracle was too focused on dotcoms and raised prices too aggressively but even then it was a small gain. We tend to look to actual usage since that's a more realistic measure of what customers believe they are buying in; by that measure Oracle is still around 50% share, Microsoft 25%, and IBM 34%. [The numbers total more than 100 percent because some companies use more than one database.] This is a numbers and marketing game between Microsoft, IBM, and Oracle that has gone on for years. Oracle has no flexibility since its numbers must be reported externally and audited. It has two large competitors that can allocate from other product areas. The game helps Microsoft and IBM, which is why they keep playing it and there is no downside for them since journalists and market analysts pretty much print the numbers they are provided." *

However, just as more analytical reporting of the "Oracle scandal" in California would have "spoiled the story," so would listening to the punctilious and experienced Phillips. But for all the media's pleasure in using these misfortunes to paint a picture of a company in deep trouble, apart from the flagging stock price, the actual harm to the business was probably far less than met the eye. Real-world customers were largely uninfluenced by dubious market-share figures—most of the growth in Oracle's database business is founded on selling more licenses to its installed base. For the same reason, although some analysts speculated that the adverse publicity in California would hurt Oracle's vital public-sector sales, there was subsequently no evidence of it. Ellison said, "Several large deals in the quarter got slowed down; they were delayed, but they didn't disappear. In the end, if you need the software, you buy the software." That would also apply to California: Ellison had no doubt at all that the state would end up paying more for less software because of canceling the ELA. In principle, he never wanted to do another deal like that

---

*LE writes: To this day, Gartner calculates market share numbers using unaudited sales figures provided by IBM and Microsoft, rather than taking the trouble to survey customers.

one: "These big up-front all-you-can-eat deals are just not as profitable for us as selling software on an as-needed basis."

The whole episode, however, made Ellison deeply miserable. For somebody not temperamentally given to depression, he came close to it. Above all, the sheer capriciousness of events combined with the mounting hostility toward big business had shaken him. When we met in London late in June, I was struck by how gloomy he seemed. He told me, "I'm not depressed, exactly. I'm just tired, and I feel vulnerable—like a zebra on the savanna at night. There are a lot of hungry animals out there hunting. They'd like to eat me and my family. I have to be alert, and I have to stay alert all night. And this is going to be a very, very long night. When the sun rises, a lot of zebras are going to be gone."

• • •

The California brouhaha had upset Ellison deeply. Oracle had finished its fiscal year quite strongly, beating analysts' expectations with fourth-quarter revenues of $2.774 billion combined with profits and margins exceeded in the software industry only by Microsoft. But the solid showing was rather undermined by Jeff Henley's downbeat forecast. The market took fright at his view that first-quarter license revenue could be anything between 15 and 25 percent down, sending the company's already sagging stock price to little more than $8. Even prompting Ellison to talk about his prospects in the America's Cup—just three months away—didn't seem to lighten his mood.

Yet only a few weeks later Ellison gave what Carolyn Balkenhol, among others, thought was one of his feistiest and most compelling performances at Oracle's Analyst Day. Nearly three hundred analysts and reporters had shown up at Oracle's conference center expecting to put Ellison on the rack. Typically, he came out fighting with plenty of jokes and a major product announcement. The big news was the launch of what Oracle was calling its Collaboration Suite—a software package that combined e-mail, voice mail, calendaring, scheduling, file sharing, and an enterprisewide search engine—all accessible by wireless. But this wasn't just any old product announcement. What really juiced it up was that the Collaboration Suite was targeted at a major Microsoft business. For all the rivalry between the world's two biggest software firms over architectural issues (the Internet versus client/server and, more recently, .NET versus the J2EE Java standard) and Microsoft's persistent harrying of the low end of Oracle's business with its SQL Server database, this was the first time that Oracle had gone directly after a big chunk of Redmond's revenues.

Since the previous summer, Ellison had been touting the advantages of running e-mail on top of Oracle's database rather than employing the hundreds of Microsoft Exchange servers that were common in most big companies. Keep Microsoft's Outlook as your desktop e-mail interface, he'd been saying, but replace Microsoft Exchange with Oracle's e-mail server and get the virus protection, security, reliability, and ease of administration that come with our database. In addition to e-mail, Collaboration Suite included a new technology called the Database File System: an extensible file system for storing, sharing, and searching all your PC files regardless of format. In other words, Oracle's Collaboration Suite wasn't just a replacement for Microsoft's Exchange servers; it was a replacement for Microsoft's file servers as well.

A year earlier I'd been with Ellison in a meeting with Ned Johnson, the chairman of America's biggest mutual fund, Fidelity Investments. Ellison had dubbed Microsoft's e-mail server software the "Virus Exchange" and had asked Johnson if he knew how much he was paying for this truly terrible system. Johnson's CIO had figured maybe as much as $300 million a year.* Ellison had immediately offered to write Johnson out a personal check for that amount if he couldn't save him at least 85 percent of the cost while replacing it with something much better. It was the same pitch he'd made a few months later to Tommy Thompson in Washington, D.C. It was a pretty good way of getting the customer's attention.

Unfortunately, at that stage Oracle didn't have a complete product. Although it had the e-mail and the file system, it lacked a calendar—critical for coordinating meetings, travel, and appointments. Oracle's developers had discovered that although Microsoft's Outlook e-mail interface supported e-mail servers using either the standard IMAP4 Internet messaging protocol or Microsoft's proprietary MAPI protocol, the moment you put an IMAP4 e-mail server such as Oracle's underneath Outlook, Microsoft's Calendar server automatically turns off. The result was that Oracle's e-mail server and Microsoft's calendar server wouldn't work together. Ellison observed, "Microsoft is incapable of competing fairly.

---

*LE writes: Microsoft's e-mail and file servers are astonishingly expensive to run. Most companies can't even calculate their total cost of ownership, which includes hardware, software, network, and labor costs. Then there are the huge additional costs related to e-mail viruses and lost files. Microsoft Exchange has probably lost business more money than any product in the history of the software industry.

First they bundle their Outlook e-mail interface with Windows so everyone gets Outlook for 'free.' Then, if you use the 'free' Outlook as your e-mail interface, Microsoft makes it as difficult as possible to use any e-mail server other than theirs. Microsoft may claim that Outlook works with industry-standard IMAP4 e-mail servers like Oracle, but if actually you try to use one, everything else breaks. This isn't bundling 101; this is graduate-level bundling. They're the world's experts. They should host a symposium on bundling theory. They have loads of land mines buried in their software to blow up the competition. It's illegal, but they'd gotten away with it for years, so we had to figure out a way around the problem." The solution, in June 2002, was to buy a little Canadian company named Steltor that claimed to make "the best open-system time management communication solution on the market" and had a formidable customer base that included BMW, Verizon, Texas Instruments, and Kellogg. Best of all, Steltor's software fully supported every one of Outlook's features. It was Oracle's key to Microsoft's door. Suddenly, all the pieces worked together.

The Collaboration Suite wasn't just a welcome stick to beat Microsoft with. For years, Ellison had been arguing that Microsoft's low-price, high-volume model wasn't all it seemed because it brought with it so much complexity that had to be expensively managed. But now he was explicitly trying to beat Microsoft at its own game, and he was determined to enjoy himself in front of the assembled analysts. "Okay, here's where we have some fun. Just for the heck of it, we decided to price Collaboration Suite, with all its features, at one third of what Microsoft charges just for its e-mail server alone. Bill says that Microsoft's the place to go for low-priced software. Really? Not anymore. Collaboration Suite includes a secure, reliable database e-mail server, plus the best calendar/scheduler in the world, integrated voice mail, and a powerful database file-sharing system. Microsoft Exchange includes an e-mail server, plus a never-ending plague of viruses. Keep using Outlook; say good-bye to viruses with Oracle Collaboration Suite." To cap even that, Ellison had a further offer: for $10 a user per month, Oracle would supply a completely outsourced service.

Launching the Collaboration Suite had allowed Ellison to do one of the things that in front of an audience he was great at: making jokes about Gates. But it also helped him make a much more serious point: Oracle might think that it didn't need lessons from Microsoft about building software, but it could learn a great deal from the business strategies that had made Gates's firm one of the world's most fearsome competitors. From now on, Ellison was saying, Microsoft would be the model for the way Oracle would do business. It had started with the E-Business Suite, but now in everything that Oracle did it would emphasize the same tight integration that Microsoft understood so well, the same determination to throw in a bewildering array of features that smaller rivals had to charge for, the same aggressive pricing and ruthless pursuit of volume.

Ellison told the analysts, "Our strategy in enterprise software is integrated suites with a low total cost of ownership. The only software company we worry about, watch, and try to learn from is Microsoft. We think their basic model—integrated suites, low price, high volume—is the winner. Nothing else works, and that's where we're going. In the end, there will be just three software infrastructure companies: Microsoft and their proprietary Windows and .NET stuff; and IBM and Oracle supporting Linux, Java, and open systems. That's it. Nobody else."

If anyone in the audience disagreed, they weren't saying so. The toughest question Ellison faced was about the impact on Oracle of competing in the America's Cup. After "getting a pass" on winning four world maxi-yacht titles in recent years, Ellison said he'd been hoping for the same on the America's Cup, "but it's just much more visible." However, he didn't think it would be that bad: "eight weeks of driving and racing max over this year and next year—and that's only if we win." Most years, Ellison said, he took five weeks out of the office on vacation. As he'd be working through August, he didn't think he'd have more time away from the office than usual. However, if Oracle BMW Racing went all the way, Ellison would be in Auckland for around eight weeks in 2002 and another four weeks in 2003. Luckily, none of the analysts seemed to have consulted the official race calendar.

And the dog that didn't bark? Throughout the entire day there was just one question about the effect on Oracle's business of the state of California contract "scandal": Would Oracle find itself in the "penalty box" with some states and agencies? Not at all, replied Kevin Fitzgerald smoothly. Even in California itself, he expected to see new revenues in the current quarter. As for other public-sector customers, Fitzgerald said, "Most agencies and government entities recognize it for what it was. They ask you what lessons you learned. You say, don't get in the way of an ambitious politician, and don't become an issue in a gubernatorial election year."

26

"THE FIRST LOSER"

Hauraki Gulf, Auckland
December 2003

I've flown in with Ellison from San Jose for the semifinals of the Louis Vuitton Cup, the winner of which will go on to challenge Team New Zealand for the America's Cup in February. When we arrive, we find that *Katana,* which has been Ellison's base in New Zealand for the past year, has been moved out of Auckland's pretty, but crowded, inner harbor to a pier just outside that both affords more privacy and allows the big boat to make a quicker getaway each morning before the day's racing begins. At the landward end of the pier is sailing's equivalent of gasoline alley, known as Syndicate Row, along which are lined the high-tech boat garages of the nine teams that arrived here many months ago in their quest for the "auld mug." There's a constant sound of banging, grinding, and drilling, signaling the unremitting effort to hone and fettle the boats.

After a patchy start during the first round-robin races in October (when every team races every other team), Ellison is buoyantly confident. Since he brought his favorite sailor, Chris Dickson, back from exile on his farm near Auckland to skipper the team, Oracle BMW has been literally unbeatable, scoring eleven victories in succession—a run of wins that has now taken it through to the semifinals. Most satisfyingly, in the quarter final, Dickson trounced OneWorld, the team from Seattle that's owned by the cell phone pioneer, Craig McCaw, and backed by Microsoft co-founder Paul Allen. Quite apart from the Microsoft connection, there's not much love lost between them and Oracle. OneWorld has been dogged by accusations that it had stolen design secrets from Team New

Zealand, and Ellison refers to them in private as the "cheaters from Seattle." A little too cheerfully, on the morning of arrival, he tells reporters in the regatta press center how distressed he is "as an American" that this team, financed by billionaires, might have stolen from the impecunious Kiwis, who have had to raise money by public subscription. "If it can be proved that OneWorld is guilty," he intones solemnly, "they should be thrown out of the regatta." He might almost be talking about Microsoft during the antitrust case.*

Ellison is also openly scornful of McCaw and Allen's sentimental environmentalism: "OneWorld issued this press release saying that they were racing in the America's Cup for a 'higher purpose'; they said they were racing 'in the name of the health of the oceans.' Can you believe those guys? I mean, how does spending tens of millions of dollars on a sailboat race improve the health of the oceans? They travel to New Zealand in private jets and drive around the gulf in a boat that's twice as big mine [Allen's 302-foot *Tatoosh*, purchased from McCaw, is moored on the opposite shore]. You can't be a world-record consumer of fossil fuels and still claim to be a conservationist. Their crew was planting trees for the benefit of the TV cameras, not the environment." The stunt that Ellison is referring to was indeed pretty nauseating. Somebody from OneWorld calculated the amount of emissions caused by the team's armada of chase boats and further worked out that the precise remedy would be to plant ten thousand trees on the slopes of a nearby island volcano. Just how many trees you'd need to stick in the ground to clean up the atmosphere every time Allen fires up the twin 4,500-horsepower engines of his megayacht, nobody's saying.

One half of the draw will be contested between the two most successful boats so far, Oracle's USA-76 and Alinghi's (the Swiss challenger) SUI-64, while the bottom half is between the winners of the "repechage" quarterfinals, Prada from Italy (the winner of the Louis Vuitton three years ago) and OneWorld—if it's not chucked out. Under the complicated rules, the winner between Oracle and Alinghi, owned by billionaire biotech tycoon Ernesto Bertarelli, will progress directly to the finals, while the loser will have a second chance to qualify by racing against the winner of the best-of-seven series between Prada and OneWorld.

---

*LE writes: OneWorld eventually confessed to having design data from Team New Zealand in its possession. It was penalized one point for violating the rules, but it was allowed to go on racing.

With racing due to start on Monday if the unpredictable Hauraki Gulf winds are not too strong—Alinghi has just had a narrow escape, losing the top of its mast during its Sunday-morning practice session—everyone's expecting a close and hard-fought battle between the two favorites. After the press conference, at which Ellison unassumingly sits in the audience, Dickson comes over to *Katana* to brief his boss on how things have gone in Ellison's absence during the fortnight's lull in the racing. Although Dickson never loses his intensity, by his standards he seems pretty relaxed and brimming with confidence. He says that the team has been working well together and has extracted some useful extra speed from the boat. Although he has a huge amount of respect for Alinghi (the Swiss boat is actually dominated by the Kiwis, who won the last America's Cup, in particular through the partnership of skipper Russell Coutts and tactician Brad Butterworth, controversially lured by Bertarelli with a check for $5 million), his body language suggests that he expects to win.

In terms of sheer boat speed, all the evidence suggests that unless one or the other side has hit on an especially effective "tweak," Alinghi and Oracle BMW should be pretty evenly matched. Bruce Farr has delivered a more than competitive design, but USA-76 is not quite, as Ellison earlier bragged, a "take-your-blazer-to-the-cleaners" boat, meaning one that is so far out ahead that all you have to worry about is looking your best when receiving the cup. Both are optimized for sailing upwind to try to grab crucial advantage between the start and rounding the first mark, where races are frequently won and lost. But after Oracle lost four out of five races between the end of the first round-robin and the beginning of the second, its sails have gotten bigger and the massive bulb on its keel lighter in a bid to improve its light-air and downwind performance.*

But the real worries are more to do with the crew than the boat. Ellison summed it up: "Alinghi runs like a fine Swiss watch; we're more like an American daytime TV soap opera." The problems had been there since the very beginning. The decision to buy the two boats from the AmericaOne syndicate, which had lost in 2000, had turned out to be a double-edged sword. It meant that Ellison's team had gotten onto the water early, giving them a head start in training and development, but the

---

*LE writes: After a disappointing round-robin one, we increased the size of our mainsail from 188 square meters to 200 square meters. Our results in round-robin two were much improved, but that had more to do with crew changes than the increased sail area.

boats had brought with them their skipper, Paul Cayard, and most of his losing crew. Right from the get-go, Cayard's Americans and the New Zealanders who had come from *Sayonara* didn't get along. But the biggest point of friction was between Dickson and Cayard, whose different styles and rivalries proved an impossible combination. Even Ellison's removal of Cayard, a man he'd never much liked, by locking him in "golden handcuffs" and pushing him off the team, had failed to bring harmony.*

Ellison told me, "There was a lot of infighting between the AmericaOne guys and the *Sayonara* guys. In hindsight, it should have been a very easy problem to solve; all we had to do was pick the right people and get on with it. But that's not what we did, because we couldn't agree on who the right people were. I wanted Chris. Others wanted Paul. So I made the worst decision possible: no decision. I just didn't have the time to gather the facts and figure out what was really going on down in New Zealand. Silicon Valley was in the middle of a severe recession, and I was 110 percent consumed by my job at Oracle. But I couldn't delay forever, so I made the second worst decision possible: I delegated the decision to somebody else. A few days later, I was informed that as a result of Chris's being too hard on the crew, he had been 'voted off the team.' I was told that Chris had a 'dark side.' Well, I'd never seen this 'dark side' of Chris's

---

LE writes: Paul Cayard is a formidable competitor. I found out just how formidable when he was skippering Boomerang *in the maxi world championships in Sardinia. I thought that* Sayonara *would easily defend her title that year, but Paul had other ideas. The racing had turned out to be very close, and the championship was decided on the very last race on the very last day of the regatta. If* Boomerang *beat us in that race, it would take the title. The start was critical, and I lost it.* Boomerang *got out ahead early. We were both on starboard tack, with* Sayonara *to weather a couple of boat lengths behind. It looked pretty grim. But very gradually, I was able to creep up and close the gap—meter by meter—until* Sayonara *got to the point where* Boomerang *couldn't tack and safely cross in front of us. If she tried, she might be penalized or have to tack on our lee bow to avoid us. She didn't tack, so from that point on, it became a drag race out toward the port lay line. We got there first, tacked in front, and led them to the weather mark. We rounded the buoy more than three boat lengths ahead and held on the rest of the way home.* Boomerang *had never come close to beating* Sayonara *in a regatta. But somehow Paul Cayard found a way to make her competitive. He is America's best big-boat sailor.*

personality that people were telling me about. All I saw was a guy who pushes himself and others because he wants to win. I'd been sailing with Chris for years. I couldn't imagine being on the boat without him. He's incredibly smart, organized, disciplined, hardworking, and intense. From what I can tell, he's the best sailor in the world. How can we fire the best sailor in the world? *

"It was a monumentally stupid mistake! When I finally got to New Zealand and started practicing with the sailing team, I discovered that the guys were pretty evenly divided between the pro- and anti-Chris factions. Several of the people I had sailed with on *Sayonara* told me that they were absolutely furious about how badly Chris had been treated. I felt terrible. How could I have let this happen? Chris is my friend. He trusted me. How could I let him down like that? Some of the key guys on the race boat didn't like Chris and didn't think we needed him; they were wrong. I was on the boat for all the races of the first round-robin of the Louis Vuitton Cup. It was painfully obvious that we were lacking leadership on the water.

"We had started our America's Cup campaign with three top-rated America's Cup drivers: Chris Dickson, Paul Cayard, and Gavin Brady. But somehow we managed to lose all three of them. We lost Gavin Brady early on, because he thought Chris and Paul would be driving our two boats and he wouldn't get a chance to drive at all. As it turns out, if he had stayed, he would have driven our race boat, but instead he went to Prada to drive their warm-up boat. That meant that Peter Holmberg, who started as our number four driver, was now our number one driver and skipper. Peter was ranked number one in the world in small-boat match racing, but he had done very little big-boat racing and he had virtually no America's Cup experience. As the Cup racing began and the pressure built, the team started making mistakes. We hit a stretch where we lost four out of five races."

---

*LE writes: The Apple board replaced Steve Jobs with John Scully, didn't it? How stupid was that? Brilliant, disciplined, intensely goal-oriented leaders routinely alienate the people they work with because they push too hard. They make the mistake of thinking everyone else on the team wants to win as much as they do. Michael Jordan was not popular with many of his teammates because he'd get in their face for not playing hard enough. Vince Lombardi "Winning is everything" types have a hard time coexisting with Rodney King "Why can't we all just get along?" types.

What made it possible to bring Dickson back was that losing streak. Although Oracle BMW's skipper, Peter Holmberg, had proved a fiercely competitive starter, according to Ellison, he was prone to errors while driving the rest of the race, which, in turn, was putting pressure on lead tactician John Cutler that he couldn't handle.* The result was that twice USA-76 lost the lead and the race against clearly weaker opposition. After losing one race against the unimpressive GBR from Britain, Ellison told me that, riding back to base in the tender, he had been closer to losing his temper than he could remember for a very long time.

Demoting Holmberg and restoring Dickson provoked a near mutiny, with four crew members threatening to quit (although only one, Stuart Argo, a headsail trimmer, actually did). It also put Bill Erkelens, Ellison's inexperienced team manager, in an awkward position, having had his earlier judgment so comprehensively overruled. Ellison is unimpressed: "This time I didn't have to rely on someone telling me what was going on. I was on the boat for every race. I saw firsthand how people performed under pressure. I had all the facts I needed. During the GBR race the British boat jibed and our tactician, John Cutler, said, 'GBR jibes, do we go with him?' You can't do that. It's too slow to take a vote *after* the other boat jibes; you have to decide in advance what you'll do *if* they jibe. The tactical situation needs to be evaluated in advance, the decision has to be made in advance, and then the decision has to be clearly communicated to everyone in the crew so we all know what we are going to do well in advance of actually doing it. It takes several seconds to get set up for a jibe on an America's Cup boat; those seconds can be the difference between winning and losing the race. The command should have been 'If GBR jibes, we go with them' or 'If GBR jibes we let them go.' We were in desperate need of an experienced, decisive leader, so I asked Chris to come back.

"I held a team meeting to announce and explain my decision. It got

*LE writes: It's not fair to blame Peter for the mistakes. Everyone in our after guard, including our tactician, strategist, and navigator, contributed. We made so many errors during the GBR race that it's hard for me to remember them all: we called the wind shift wrong on the first two beats; we did a bear-away set when we should have done a jibe set at the second weather mark and got passed as a result; we set the wrong spinnaker on the second run; and so on and so on. It was a fiasco. Before the race I had told Melanie that the only way we could lose to GBR was if we sank. It would have been less embarrassing if we had.

ugly. Some of the crew complained bitterly, saying they didn't like Chris and they didn't want him to come back. I said they didn't have to like him—I wasn't asking them to date him, I was asking them to sail for him. Some threatened to quit. They said they voted him off the team twice. Interesting. I'm voting him back on the team. They said Chris being on the boat put too much pressure on the crew to perform. What? If the crew can't take the pressure of Chris being on our boat, how are they going to handle the pressure of racing against Russell and Brad on the Swiss boat? One of the guys said, 'I thought we were here to have fun.' Do you think losing is fun? I don't. This is professional sports, not high school. We're here for one and only one reason—we're here to win. You're paid to win. But we're not winning, so you've got a new boss. I said it as clearly as I could: 'Chris Dickson is skipper of Oracle BMW Racing until we win the cup, or we're beaten on the water.' By the end of the meeting I had achieved two things: the best sailor in the world was back on board, and he was no longer the most hated guy on our sailing team—I was."

Dickson's resurrection had another consequence. After driving and winning his first race out, the intensely self-critical New Zealander had concluded that he couldn't make up for the months of practice lost while kicking his heels on land; he also knew he had to do something to try to bind the feuding team together. He therefore made it a priority to persuade Holmberg to continue to start the boat and do most of the driving, while he made the tactical calls. But that meant there was no longer room for Ellison on board—no team could afford to race with three drivers. It was a tough call for Ellison, as he had been pleased with his performance against the world's best professionals. "Every time I drove, we increased our lead over the other boat. I'm proud of that. But, at the same time, I know I wasn't making the difference between winning and losing because I was only driving when we were already in front. And I wasn't enjoying myself. I hadn't had much time to practice with the team, and I hardly knew most of them. The only enjoyable race for me during the entire Louis Vuitton Cup was Chris's first day back on the race boat. Several members of our sailing team went on strike to protest Chris's return, so we had to replace them with a bunch of our old *Sayonara* guys. It was great to be with the guys I had sailed with for years. It was just like the old days, except we were in USA-76 racing our way toward the America's Cup. Chris easily won the start, drove for a while, and then I took over. It was a clear sunny day on the gulf with the wind out of the northeast at fourteen knots. We led from start to finish. That was my last turn at the wheel. Once it became clear to everyone that Chris was here to stay and we'd race with or without the striking crew members, the strike was broken. All but one of the sailing team members returned and agreed to sail under Chris's leadership. Their return meant there was no room for me on the race boat. Being on the boat hadn't been great for me, but still, I really hated getting off." He also knew that if he had insisted on staying, Dickson's job would have been even harder than it was already: "The same people who didn't want Chris on the boat didn't want me there either."

The transformation of the team's performance since Dickson's return had triumphantly vindicated Ellison's decision. But winning races had suppressed rather than ended the grumbling and the personal animosities in the camp. The chances were that any reversal of fortune would quickly bring them bubbling to the surface again.

• • •

The first scheduled semifinal race day is canceled because the wind is averaging about twenty-four knots—according to the rules, too much for the highly tuned boats to sail in safely. The following day, however, is set fair, although the wind is expected to get up later. This should suit Oracle BMW, which is thought to have an advantage in strong breezes. Soon after 9 A.M. the teams begin the exodus from the harbor. They leave in pairs, towed by the powerful launches that carry spare parts, additional sails, and nonsailing team members. It takes about an hour and a half to reach the course, which is well out in the gulf. When they get there, the first- and second-string boats from each of the four teams still in the regatta will sail against each other for a couple of hours of warmup and shakedown. Soon after the racing boats set off, the rest of the flotilla, bearing officials and spectators, starts streaming out of Auckland. Among them are Bertarelli's 150-foot *Vava* and *Katana*.

To get closer to the action than I can on *Katana*, I decide to watch the race from one of the Oracle BMW chase boats—forty-foot RIBs (rigid inflatable boats) with powerful diesel engines. The previous day, I'd been on board a boat crewed by a couple of New Zealanders. They had been friendly and open, but it hadn't been long before they had started telling me about how fed up they were with the feuding in the camp. Supporters of Dickson, they said that too many of the crew on the race boat were there for political rather than sailing reasons. The atmospherics aboard the boat I'm on today are very different. There's almost no banter among the seven or eight team members on board, and while that may be due to tension, I get the distinct impression that because I'm associated with Ellison, I'm not a welcome presence.

The race itself goes badly. Although the weather conditions are poor—it's overcast and squally with quite heavy seas—they should suit USA-76. Holmberg is driving, while Dickson is calling the tactical shots. But despite what looks like a slight advantage at the start line, it quickly becomes clear that Alinghi has found more breeze by going out to the right-hand side of the course. By the time the boats reach the first mark, SUI-64 has opened out a lead of nearly fifteen seconds. Thereafter, Coutts and Butterworth continue to stay in phase with the wind shifts, finally crossing the line more than a minute ahead of a well-beaten USA-76. On the chase boat, there's no display of emotion. The truth is that the race was over within the first ten minutes and that Alinghi has given Oracle BMW a lesson in match sailing. After those eleven wins on the bounce, it's desperately disappointing, but Ellison doesn't seem too down when I find him back on *Katana*. "They won the right side, got the first shift, and it was over," he says.*

But the next day, things don't go any better. Although Holmberg manages to get to the far right of the course where the wind is once again, Coutts somehow manages not only to stay in contention but to get to the first weather mark a little ahead. It's enough to lock Oracle BMW out for the rest of the race. This time, Ellison is not inclined to make excuses for the team. He says, "We had a pretty even start with Alinghi, so it became a drag race to the lay line. When both boats are side-by-side racing in a straight line like that, you have to drive very smoothly inside a narrow performance envelope of wind angles and boat speed. It's a combination of driving by feel and driving by the instruments. Most of Peter's experience is in small boats, so he relies more on what he feels than what the instruments are telling him. I don't think you can beat Russell Coutts in a

---

*LE writes: Alinghi won the first race because Russell Coutts won the start. The start is critical in match racing. Winning the start does not necessarily mean that they started in front of us; it means that they got the side of the race course that they wanted. Five minutes before the race begins, both boats decide which side of the race course has the better wind conditions: more wind and/or a favorable wind shift up the course. If both boats pick the same side of the course, they fight for it by executing a complex set of maneuvers with each boat trying to gain a right-of-way advantage against the other. This five-minute maneuvering period before the start is called the prestart. It's the most exciting part of match racing. Peter's good at starting, but not as good as Russell Coutts. Russell won the start ten of the twelve times we raced Alinghi.

drag race if you drive that way." Consequently, Ellison decides to make another throw of the dice, taking Holmberg off the boat and persuading Dickson—"the best straight-line driver I've ever seen"—to replace him at the helm.

It really is a gamble. Dickson has been able to get some practice in since he came back on the water, but not enough to make up for the eight months spent on gardening leave. But that's not the only problem: it's impossible to drive and plot race tactics at the same time—you don't see the whole picture when you're at the wheel. Even if Dickson matches Coutts, he doesn't have anyone of the caliber of Brad Butterworth to help him. He also knows that some of the guys on the boat who are close to Holmberg may even be hoping he fails.

I ask Ellison whether, for the sake of harmony, this might be the moment to sling some of the troublemakers out of the team and bring some of the talented sailors from USA-71 on board the race boat. The following day, Ellison does decide to fire a couple of the worst agitators from the shore-based team, but tempting though it is to root out the factionalism, he thinks it's too late to make wholesale changes. Even if the first semi-final goes to Alinghi, Ellison is confident that Oracle can reach the Louis Vuitton final by again beating OneWorld (the likely winner against Prada). With some speed tweaks to the boat, he still thinks there's a chance of going on to the America's Cup itself. "To take the team apart and reassemble it at this stage might be emotionally satisfying, but it's not the way to maximize our chances of winning."

When the local press realizes that the next day the two biggest names in New Zealand's yachting history are going head-to-head, there's a frenzy of excitement. Sailing journalist Ivor Wilkins writes, "*Fire and Ice* might be the putative title of this drama, with Dickson representing fire and Coutts ice. Dickson, mercurial, solitary, unpredictable is willing to make the high risk plays—using cunning, a lawyer's instinct for loopholes in the law, and a fabulous intuitive talent. In the nature of high risk moves, some don't succeed, but when they do, the results are usually spectacular. Iceman Coutts is more methodical and analytical. In the great match-racing chess game, he always plays the percentages, making his moves with patience and planning his strategies long in advance."

After the frostiness on the chase boat the day before, I decide to watch the race from *Katana* after a short spell as the seventeenth man on the warmup boat. On board *Katana* there's live satellite television coverage from the circling helicopters and a neat software package known as Virtual Spectator that shows not only the exact position of the boats in real time but also the strength and direction of the wind in different areas of the racecourse. As usual, Ellison has holed up in his stateroom for the duration. He gets so sick with the tension that he literally finds it hard to speak until the race is over.*

At the start, it's Coutts who uses all his experience to get the upper hand over Dickson, Alinghi managing to sail right over the face of USA-76, "locking out" the American boat to windward. But Dickson responds brilliantly. Tacking twice, he succeeds in wriggling clear of the Swiss team's close cover and finding a nice little puff of wind out on the right-hand side of the course that's enough for him to pass ahead when the boats converge on the next tack. From that point on, Dickson, his face screwed up in what looks like concentration but is actually a searing migraine, seems to have control of the race, keeping Coutts comfortably at bay for well over an hour until the final beat. Then disaster strikes. Inexplicably, instead of covering Coutts when he strikes out to pick up a small wind shift on the left side of the course, Dickson holds course. The result is that with the finish line in sight, Oracle BMW suddenly finds itself three boat lengths behind. Instead of gaining a morale-boosting win to go 2–1, USA-76 now trails SUI-64 3–0—it's a crushing blow. Emerging from his cabin, a downcast Ellison says, "The problem with having Chris on the wheel is that it means we don't have Chris as tactician. Nobody can do both jobs at once. He drove the drag race brilliantly and beat Coutts to the lay line. We had the race won until we made that tactical blunder."

Although Alinghi still needs to win one more race to reach the final, realistically, the chances of pegging back Coutts and Butterworth are now slim, and while Dickson has promised to make a fight of it, the focus of attention is already shifting beyond the next race. Ellison and Dickson have decided to move things around again. Holmberg is to return as the starting helmsman but will immediately hand over to Dickson once the balletic duel of the start gives way to the race proper. When and if Dickson establishes a decent fifty- to seventy-five-meter lead, the plan is for them to switch places again, allowing Dickson to "have his head out of the boat," fully focused on keeping race-losing tactical errors down to a minimum. Ellison says that whatever happens, this will be the final configuration. Holmberg, he says, has been "very professional about all the

---

LE writes: I spoke, but it's a good thing that nobody was around to hear what I said.

different things we tried," but Ellison knows that compared with the so-lidity and consistency of the Coutts/Butterworth partnership, they are making it up as they go along.

The next day, the racing is close, but Alinghi books itself into the Louis Vuitton final with another impressively error-free performance. If Oracle BMW is to have another shot at the Swiss team, OneWorld, which has knocked out Prada, will have to be beaten again in the repechage (second-chance) semifinal. Unfortunately for me, before the racing starts again, I have to leave New Zealand. When I arrived, Oracle BMW had won eleven races in succession, but while I've been there the team has lost four in a row. Inescapably, I've come to identify with Ellison's black boat and it's bitterly disappointing: I feel like some kind of Jonah.

Before I head back to London, I ask Ellison how he rates his chances now. Despite Alinghi's apparent superiority, he's typically optimistic: "I know we can beat them. We have several engineering changes scheduled that should speed the boat up before we have to race them again. We'll put some of them on for the repechage. The new keel bulb we used this week actually made us a second a mile slower. We'll replace that right away. But I'm not concerned about beating OneWorld, so we'll hold back most of the changes for the final." Ellison is hopeful because he thinks that SUI-64 is further up its development curve than is the newer USA-76, and for most of America's Cup history it has been the quicker boat rather than the best sailing team that has usually won. It's similar to For-mula One car racing: put a middling driver into the fastest car, and nine times out of ten, he'll beat the fastest driver in a middling car.

• • •

Ellison is right about one thing. Once again, Oracle BMW turns out to be too powerful for the team from Seattle, USA-76 claiming its place in the finals against Alinghi with a 4–0 walkover concluded inside a week. With OneWorld safely disposed of, the sailing team will have a short break over Christmas while major changes are made to the boat that El-lison is gambling will provide an edge against Alinghi. He has more or less conceded that preventing Coutts from dominating the starts and the first upwind leg is unrealistic. But to even the score, the plan he's come up with requires standing America's Cup racing conventional wisdom on its head: "The first boat to the first weather mark wins the race eighty-five percent of the time. That's why most America's Cup boats have an up-wind design bias; that is, the boats trade away a lot of downwind speed for a little more upwind speed. But to take advantage of your upwind speed, you have to win your fair share of the starts so you can get onto the favored side of the racecourse. That's not happening for us. Russell's killing us in the starts, so Alinghi is beating us to the first weather mark almost every time. I don't think that's going to change. So the question is: How do we win the race even though they beat us to the first weather mark?"

Ellison had decided to transform the boat from being heavily biased for sailing upwind to being biased for sailing downwind. Because USA-76 is very narrow, the theory is that with the bigger sail area [the mainsail had gone from 188 to 214 square meters] that's allowed if you lighten the keel bulb, it should be a downwind flyer, making it possible for Oracle BMW to roll past Alinghi on a downwind leg and then sail defensively for the rest of the race. What makes Ellison hopeful is that with the other tweaks, USA-76 appears to have lost very little of its upwind pace.*

The first race of the best-of-nine series goes Alinghi's way. But in the second race, USA-76's speed on the run is confirmed, a lead of twenty-six-seconds at the first mark for Alinghi being cut to little more than a boat's length by the leeward mark. However, when Oracle BMW runs over its spinnaker and breaks its spinnaker pole, the chance to peg Alinghi back is lost. If that's frustrating, there's worse to come. In the third race, although SUI-64 once again takes the lead, on the second downwind leg, the two boats engage in a furious duel in which Alinghi could have been penalized but in fact Oracle BMW is, for ramming its rival's stern scoop. Although the American boat manages to stretch out a twenty-eight-second lead at the final weather mark, in the end it's not quite enough to unwind the penalty (a mandatory 360-degree turn) and still beat SUI-64 to the line: both psychologically and practically, 3–0 is very different from 2–1.†

———————————————————

*LE writes: With the larger sail area, USA-76 was faster downwind in all wind conditions and faster upwind in wind speeds of less than ten knots. We had gone from being a heavy-air upwind boat to being a light-air downwind boat. If the weather cooperated and we sailed well, we had a good chance of beating Alinghi in the finals.

†LE writes: The engineering changes worked perfectly. As expected, Coutts kept winning all the starts and getting to the weather mark ahead of us, but we had enough boat speed to catch up on the downwind leg. Unfortunately, we kept making mistake after mistake out on the water. A bad approach to the first leeward mark caused a cascading series of disasters that took us out of the

The next race provides conclusive proof that if only Ellison's team can avoid mistakes, beating Alinghi is possible. Even though it's the Swiss boat that again takes the early lead, this time the combination of a good weather call and the sheer downwind velocity of USA-76 proves decisive, resulting in a winning delta of more than two minutes. Race five is tantalizingly close, the two boats swapping the lead several times and matching each other for both sailing skill and speed through the water. Unfortunately for Ellison, it's the nerve of Coutts and Butterworth that holds the steadier to deliver a fourth win, but by a little more than a boat's length at the line after more than two hours of the most intense racing. With Oracle BMW faced with elimination if it loses the next race, it's not surprising that the heat is on Holmberg to gain an advantage at the start. Perhaps he's trying too hard, but the upshot is that he's penalized at the start. Knowing that USA-76 will have to complete a penalty turn at some point in the race allows SUI-64 to sail a conservative race. Despite Oracle BMW's taking the lead on the final run, the outcome is never much in doubt.

It's a sad ending to the campaign, but the 5–1 margin of defeat doesn't do Ellison's still bickering team justice. Two-time America's Cup winner Peter Isler concluded, "It was a close series. Look at the number of lead changes compared with other rounds—that's an indication of the closeness." In fact, there were eight lead changes in the last four races, including two in the last half mile of the final race alone. However, Isler also pointed a finger at where he thought the weakness was: after going 2–0, Dickson had handed the helm back to Holmberg, but they had never managed to work together in the manner of Coutts and Butterworth. Isler, who used to navigate for the legendary Dennis Connor, commented, "Dickson calling the shots for Holmberg created a micromanaging afterguard structure that maybe wasn't a good way to play it. In a match race, the helmsman has to be able to take control. In some ways it would have been better to have Chris driving." *

The truth was that there was no ideal way for Holmberg and Dickson to work together. The penalties told a story of mistakes being made under

---

second race. In the third race we actually crossed the finish line well ahead of Alinghi, but we lost because of a penalty. We had no one to blame but ourselves. We just sailed badly.

*LE writes: When we tried that, we missed Chris as tactician. We needed a second Chris.

pressure. But how much of that pressure came from within the team? And, as Ellison summed it up in an e-mail to me, "The two penalties just killed us. Without the penalties the score would have been 3 to 3 and the racing would have continued. But you have to give Alinghi credit. Brad and Russell sailed brilliantly. We gave them a lot and they gave us absolutely nothing in return. It was a brutal experience."*

For Ellison, defeat was hard to take on many counts. It was bad enough realizing that they could have beaten Alinghi. A sympathetic e-mail from Dennis Connor provided scant comfort: "I am sure you have had better days but you did a terrific job and have every reason to be proud of your effort. I thought the boat was very good and the guys just let you down, nothing you could control. I hope you enjoyed the experience and will continue to be involved. All the best!! warm regards dennis" Unintentionally, Connor rubbed salt in the wound when he e-mailed again a couple of days later: "I thought you would like to know that last night Russell said your boat was definitely faster in the last three races. My feeling was that when the boats sailed straight for any length of time you were quicker but may have suffered in the tacking duels. Cheers! dc." But when the Swiss team went on to trounce Team New Zealand 5–0, Ellison also knew just how close he had come to the greatest prize in yachting.

When asked if he would make another attempt to win the cup, Ellison's answer was "Absolutely." But until Alinghi's triumph against the holders—something he, along with most people, had thought highly unlikely because of Team New Zealand's innovation-packed boat—Ellison was far from certain that he would carry on. He told me, "Yeah, I said 'absolutely,' but the answer that kept flashing through my mind was 'On Monday I start tennis lessons.' Tennis is much less expensive than America's Cup racing, and it's a lot more fun." Almost needless to say, it was the latter that mattered more than the former. When I was with him in New Zealand, it had seemed as though he hadn't been getting much

---

*LE writes: The finality of the defeat is hard to describe. All the time and effort you spent wasn't enough. You weren't smart enough. You weren't good enough. You lost. It's over. Go home. It's a vacant, numb feeling. You congratulate the winners and slip away as quickly and as quietly as you can. As you leave you can hear the cheering—but they're not cheering for you. You just don't matter anymore. Your race is over. I hate that feeling. I hate being beaten. Especially when I know it was because of mistakes I made.

fun out of it. Ellison had said, "Fun? Fuck no, it wasn't fun. I got kicked off my own boat, and then we lost. All I wanted to do was come down here and drive a sailboat. What I ended up doing was running a screwed-up sailing team. It wasn't fun. It was just another job, a job I didn't want. I didn't do the job very well either, because we lost. Yeah, I know we came in second. Big deal. Second place is just the first loser."

To mount another challenge, Ellison said that he would need two things: a united team composed not only of very good sailors but of people he liked and trusted; and a radically different format for America's Cup racing. "The whole idea of practicing for three years, then sailing for three months, is idiotic." The first part is relatively easy: "This time we'll build the sailing team around Chris Dickson. There are plenty of talented guys who would love the chance to sail on an America's Cup boat with Chris." Practically the first signing Ellison intends to make is the young New Zealander Gavin Brady, who sat out most of this Louis Vuitton after falling out with his Prada team. Brady has a reputation for being a tad hotheaded, but he may be the best racing helmsman in New Zealand. He reminds Dickson a little of himself when he was younger.*

The second part was dependent on Alinghi's winning the America's Cup. The winners, in concert with the team they accept as "challenger of record" (usually the next most successful competitor) have a huge power to decide the rules for the next series. During their time in Auckland, Bertarelli and Ellison had developed a mutual liking and respect. Ellison says, "One of the good things that's come out of all this is that Ernesto and I have become friends. It was a historic moment in sailing when he and Brad and Russell won the Cup and took it to Europe for the first time since 1861. They're a great team. They certainly kicked our butts. They deserved to win." Between them, the two men have hit upon the idea of turning America's Cup racing into something much more like the Formula One car-racing circus. With Alinghi installed as holder and Oracle BMW Racing as challenger of record, Bertarelli and Ellison can drive through the rule changes they want. Of these, the most important is that there will now be at least four International America's Cup Class regattas a year. They will be held in different parts of the world and will count as qualifying rounds for the next Louis Vuitton Cup challenger series. The

---

*LE writes: If we hadn't lost Gavin Brady to Prada, we just might have won the Cup. It was that close. We were just one person away from giving Brad and Russell a real race for it.

holders will also race, and some races will be specifically for "owner-drivers." It means not only plenty of sailing for the likes of Bertarelli and Ellison but a much more attractive and consistent package for television and sponsors.

The first regatta, in recognition of Ellison's official challenger status, is to take place in September 2003 in—where else?—San Francisco Bay. This time, naturally, Ellison is quite certain that his Oracle BMW team will beat the Swiss. And this time, he really will get to drive.

27

THE BIGGEST WATER BOTTLE

In the weeks after his return to California from New Zealand, as well as reimmersing himself in Oracle's affairs Ellison worked on his "dialogue" with this book—the commentary that runs through these pages. We had agreed to meet up in California in early April to review and complete the work; partly because of the emotional roller coaster of the America's Cup, an earlier deadline had already been missed. For me, it would also be a chance to talk not only to Ellison, which I had continued to do regularly, but also to some of the other Oracle executives I had come to know during the two years or so I had been involved in the life of their company. As well as catching up, it would help to put all that had happened into some kind of rough perspective.

Neither of the two Ellison campaigns I had intended to chronicle had exactly gone smoothly. The E-Business Suite was still some way from realizing Ellison's prediction that it would become the default choice for any firm wanting to use the Internet to change its way of doing business, while the America's Cup was sitting proudly in the trophy room of the Société Nautique de Genève rather than that of the Golden Gate Yacht Club. In fact, there were similarities between the two. Ellison's USA-76 was almost certainly the fastest boat in the regatta and could have won had it not been for some silly mistakes on the water. So too, the extraordinary technical ambition of the E-Business Suite had been temporarily set back by what, with hindsight, seemed frustratingly avoidable execution errors. The difference was that the failure to win the America's Cup was brutal and definitive, while it is clear that the campaign to establish the dominance of the E-Business Suite is only now getting into its stride.

The E-Business Suite challenges conventional software industry thinking on so many different levels that the arguments have to be won one at a time. It's a process of attrition: a war, not a battle.

The inescapable background to the writing of this book has been the aftermath of the "tech smash." Oracle's stock had defied gravity longer than just about anybody else's save those of Microsoft and IBM, neither of which had enjoyed the same run-up during the years of Internet fever. But coincidentally, the crack had come just weeks before I started work, when Jeff Henley issued his first earnings warning since 1997. Like other big Internet infrastructure players, such as Cisco and Sun, Oracle had been unable to escape the fallout from disappearing dot coms and the imploding telecom sector. The vision of Oracle's coming world domination (at least in terms of the software business) that Ellison had sketched out in his garden at Atherton with such certainty only a few months earlier suddenly seemed a long way off.

Some of the damage done to Oracle's prospects was undeniably self-inflicted. As Ellison subsequently acknowledged, the supposedly all-conquering E-Business Suite had been hit by lapses in quality control, an overaggressive rollout, and a marketing message that rivals and analysts found all too easy to hijack and distort. Oracle had also managed to make enemies unnecessarily: by initially attempting to impose pricing models that only confused the market; by allowing a minor spat with the application users' group to escalate into full-scale hostilities; and by appearing to declare war on the systems integrators. But while a little application market share was temporarily lost as the bugs infecting 11i's stability were being hunted down, the overwhelming cause of Oracle's slowing license revenues was the collapse in IT spending by companies that had gorged themselves on new technology during the Internet boom years and were now sitting on more hardware and software than they knew what to do with. For much of Oracle's installed base, waiting a year or two for the E-Business Suite to overcome its well-publicized teething problems was just common sense.

That said, the extent of Oracle's difficulties during the IT spending slump needs some context. Unlike both Cisco and Sun, far from plunging into big losses and write-offs, Oracle has remained steadfastly profitable, with its operating margins staying in the mid-thirties—a level barely contemplated, let alone seen, in the previous decade. As it has kept up the momentum of its internal e-business revolution, it has shed small pockets of labor, but Oracle has completely avoided the large-scale layoffs that have scarred the rest of Silicon Valley. And while others have pared research and development to the bone, Oracle continues to spend more than a billion dollars a year. Meanwhile, its cash mountain of nearly $6 billion has remained untouched and unchanged.*

Although Oracle's market cap was "only" about $60 billion in April 2003 thanks to one of the lowest multiples in its history, it is still worth nearly two and a half times as much as the third biggest software firm in the world, SAP. Microsoft, it is true, has weathered the storm still better. But Microsoft is not as dependent on corporate spending and, crucially, has been able to exploit its monopoly by raising its prices as sales have slowed. Ellison says, "What do you do when there's a recession? Raise prices, of course. Bill's a genius. Why didn't I think of that?"

As for the specialized business application vendors that achieved spectacular valuations during the B2B phase of Internet hysteria, e-procurement specialists Ariba and Commerce One have almost disappeared beneath the waves, while the onetime supply-chain leader, i2, whose shares once reached $110, is now almost worthless, its stock having been delisted from the Nasdaq in May 2003 because of "accounting irregularities."

In a way, even more dramatic is Siebel's fall from grace. Two years ago, Siebel, the sales automation pioneer, had a claim to being the hottest software company on the planet. But in 2002 it plunged into loss as software sales evaporated, and a huge restructuring charge took an additional toll. Siebel was further tarnished as a result of doing too many of the now-discredited swap transactions that created such accounting havoc in the telecom sector. Siebel earned $30.7 million in the three months before June 2002 from deals in which the company had purchased goods or services from vendors within six months of having licensed software to them. Strip out Siebel's cash pile of $1.6 billion, and the firm that Tom built is these days worth only a bit more than Oracle will spend on R and D this year. Unlike most of the others, it's too early to write Siebel out of the game. But analysts for whom Siebel could previously do no wrong are predicting that it will find it hard to survive as an independent entity—SAP, Oracle, and even little PeopleSoft, once worth only a fraction of Siebel's towering market cap, have all been touted as potential preda-

---

*LE writes: We could have accumulated a lot more cash, but we bought back $16 billion of our stock.

tors/suitors. Ellison, who bitterly regrets not buying PeopleSoft a few years ago, admits to having been tempted—not because he wants Siebel's software but because he wouldn't mind buying its installed base.

But Siebel's problems go much deeper than some sloppy accounting and a nasty downturn in the economy. As Ron Wohl puts it, "Siebel had a near monopoly in CRM, but it turned out that Tom's business model was flawed. It is now clear to nearly everyone that CRM is not the integration point. In a sense, there is no such thing as CRM, only sales and service automation that has to integrate with all the other ERP modules." Many of Siebel's customers had found, to their cost, that implementing the software they had bought was expensive and difficult. Nucleus Research, an East Coast consultancy, issued a damning report on Siebel during the summer of 2002. Based on interviews with sixty-six reference customers that Siebel had profiled on its Web site, Nucleus found that 61 percent believed they had achieved no positive return on investment (ROI) from their deployment and that nearly 80 percent claimed a major reason was because the software was much too difficult to use. Ellison's charge a year earlier that Siebel often ended up as "shelfware" seemed proven.

But the main threat to Siebel is the growing credibility of the main suite vendors' CRM offerings. It had taken Oracle and SAP a long time even to create "good-enough" CRM. And Ellison still wasn't convinced that the CRM components in the E-Business Suite were capable of the sophisticated sales "choreography" that he was looking for.* But in a "down" market that was risk-averse toward both complex implementations and software companies that might not be around long enough to maintain and upgrade their products, integrated suites from mature vendors with both a history and a future had become mighty attractive. Ellison says: "Best-of-breed products are just transitional technologies;

---

*LE writes: CRM systems automate only a part of the lead-to-order sales process: opportunity management, forecasting, and proposals. CRM systems don't automate contracting, quoting, and ordering. It is a classic example of incomplete automation. In contrast, the E-Business Suite automates the entire selling process end to end because it's complete. That makes it possible to engineer, implement, and enforce standard sales processes within your company. The days of the ad hoc, make-it-up-as-you-go-along sales force are coming to an end. It won't be long before all processes within a company will be carefully engineered—even selling.

suites always win in the end. Every six months Oracle and SAP come out with improved CRM products, and we eat another slice of Tom's pie. I don't see how he can survive. Siebel is the largest best-of-breed vendor and the last one standing. The second largest, i2, is dead and buried. Best-of-breed is too complex, too labor-intensive, too expensive to survive the stress of a long-lasting technology recession." Ellison is more convinced than ever about the pace of consolidation in the application business: PeopleSoft had a chance of hanging in as a viable midmarket competitor in the United States, but the future belonged to the big battalions from SAP and Oracle.

Before he was replaced as head of North American sales by Keith Block, George Roberts had said to me, "There are three street rules if you're going to survive in technology. First of all, don't screw up so bad you knock yourself out of the market. Second, it's a marathon, not a sprint. Lastly, when you get up in the morning you better be running. This is like the world championship of poker. Every year you've got to ante up more and more just to stay in the game. I don't see any way that these smaller software companies can continue the level of investment they need, based on their profitability level versus the profitability and assets of companies like Oracle. I think you're going to see them one by one all drop by the wayside. We're all in the middle of the desert. We'll see who gets out the other side." It was similar to a metaphor coined by Mark Jarvis: in the world of business software, Oracle had the largest water bottle.

As for screwups, Oracle had certainly made a few with the E-Business Suite, but none had been bad enough to take it out of the race, a race made longer still by the downturn. It seemed to me this was Ellison's single biggest mistake. Despite his almost matchless experience of the software business, he had expected success for the E-Business Suite to come much more quickly and more easily than it could ever realistically have done—even without the screwups.*

But although Ellison had been hopelessly wrong about timing and crazily overconfident about the true state of the E-Business Suite in the

---

*LE writes: Megasoftware projects, those scheduled to take two to three years or longer, are almost always late. The longer the project, the more likely it is that new ideas and technologies will emerge that you want to incorporate into your new product so it isn't obsolete the day you deliver it. It's hard to resist the temptation to make it better, even when making it better also makes it later.

months immediately after its launch, about the really big things he'd been vindicated: the superiority of suites over best-of-breed; the importance of reengineering business practices to fit the software instead of rewriting code to produce customized systems that were unreliable and impossible to upgrade; the need for the automation of whole business flows to be complete and seamless; the understanding that the key to getting useful information out of complex computer systems was for applications to share consistent database schemata.

But despite the rightness of Ellison's architectural vision, there were still many doubters. In April 2003, Ron Wohl said to me, "At the outset, people said that it was impossible for the E-Business Suite to do just about everything. Then they said, maybe it was possible after all, but you messed up the execution. Next they said, okay, it works, but it's not for us. How do we persuade people finally to accept the superiority of the E-Business Suite? References and proven cost reduction. If you save time and dollars, nobody can debate it." *

Within Oracle, there continued to be worries, as Mark Jarvis put it, that "Larry was too much the visionary purist—to some people he seems to be describing a perfect enterprise that in reality doesn't exist." Jeff Henley adds, "Larry still hurts himself by being too pure. Large companies get confused by the message—we have to do more to show that we live in a complicated world." Keith Block had a slightly different perspective. He says, "CEOs like the architectural sell, and they really get the idea of the single data model. But the truth is that procurement tends to be driven further down the organization. If a CIO has invested $100 million in an SAP implementation, he's not going to want to admit that he's made a mistake."

Although Oracle had taken major steps nearly two years earlier to ensure that integrating the E-Business Suite with legacy systems was perfectly feasible, you would not have gotten that impression from the firm's advertising. Whereas SAP was forever banging the drum for its NetWeaver integration platform and talking up how its Web services and messaging software could make all kinds of applications work together without the pain of customization, Ellison was steadfastly dismissive of that approach: "Web services makes it easy for one application program

---

LE writes: Today, we have thousands of E-Business Suite references attesting to savings of up to $600 million per year and reduced IT costs of more than 60 percent.

to connect and pass data to another application—even if the applications are running on different computers. That's great. But the data passed by one application has to be structured in a way that's understandable by the other applications. Web services are analogous to the global telephone network, which makes it easy to call and connect to any telephone in the world. But if the guy you call only speaks French and you only speak English, you still can't communicate even though you're connected. Web services give us easy connectivity but not a common language. Web services on their own don't enable Siebel applications to talk to SAP applications." Both SAP and Ellison were exaggerating. Web services were by no means the silver bullet that the German firm claimed, but they could help deliver some functionality across a heterodox collection of applications, more anyway than Ellison was prepared to admit.*

The irony of this was twofold: Oracle was itself a big player in Web services, and the company's entire tradition was based on working with open standards. Nothing had changed, but it sounded as if Oracle had gone "proprietary." While SAP was delivering a message of comfort for customers who feared being locked into a single vendor, Oracle seemed to be saying, "it's all or nothing." It was a real dilemma for Oracle's marketing. On the one hand, Ellison didn't want to muddy the differences between what he believed was the hopelessly compromised SAP philosophy and the much more elegant Oracle way of doing things. On the other, Mark Jarvis had a point in saying, "Oracle needs to bend a bit with the market. We have all the interfaces to link to other systems, but what we don't have is a strong integration marketing message."

The "purity" of Ellison's vision was, however, unambiguously an advantage when it came to delivering what he and others were increasingly

---

*LE writes: I was just trying to keep our applications marketing message simple: We have a complete and integrated suite of applications built on top of a single database. They don't. A single database is the key to providing everyone with the information they need to do their job better—aka Daily Business Intelligence. End of message. I hate complex technobabble marketing messages. It so happens that we use Java and Web services in our applications much more than SAP, but the only people who really understand how Java Web services work are programmers. I find it all very strange. Almost no one understands it, but everybody wants it. Okay, I give up. It's futile to fight fashion. We now chant "Web services, Web services" in supplication to the marketing gods. We hope our prayers will be heard and rewarded with sales.

calling the "utility model" of delivering IT services. In Ellison's view, the "information utility" was something much more than a fancy new name for the old-style outsourcing of data center management, practiced very profitably by the likes of IBM and EDS. If the utility concept meant anything, it had to deliver a quality service at very low cost and with complete reliability. That meant using only software that was preintegrated and designed to work out of the box on certified hardware. Ellison's point was that computer systems didn't need to be different. The "Oracle guarantee," in which Oracle promised to fulfill all a firm's computing needs for a guaranteed, fixed price—something quite revolutionary in an industry that has trained its customers to write blank checks—was rapidly winning converts, and not just in the midmarket, as had been expected. Big firms, such as the networking giant JDS Uniphase, were going down that road, and even the federal government was showing signs of interest.*

The future prospects of the E-Business Suite are good, but how good? As even Gartner has acknowledged, it is stable, mature, and comprehensive. Over time, Oracle should be able to prove that architectural purity brings with it a host of real-world benefits—the promise of being able to do more with less. As customers turn on more and more of the modules in the suite, they should increasingly leverage its power. The Daily Business Intelligence will also be a proof point for Ellison's approach: the "golden nugget," as Mark Jarvis described it. But as with almost everything to do with the E-Business Suite, that has proved much harder than expected to do. It is now expected to debut at the end of 2003, almost two years since the product announcement in Amsterdam.

A more unambiguous and, in some ways, unexpected triumph has come in the shape of Linux. When Oracle 9i was launched just after the E-Business Suite's problems had started to surface in the press, Ellison had been certain that it would be "the last database"—RAC (Real Application Clusters) was even capable of making Windows unbreakable. But if it could do that for Microsoft, it could also do it for the free open-source operating system. Thanks in good measure to the campaigning of IBM and the cooperation between Intel and the PC server makers such as Dell and Hewlett-Packard, determined to reduce their dependence on Microsoft, Linux had acquired credibility as an operating system for the

---

*LE writes: Our low-cost outsourcing service has attracted some very large clients, including Merrill Lynch, J. P. Morgan, Qantas, JDS Uniphase, and Agilent.

enterprise. With Oracle's RAC, Linux could make a huge additional step. Corporate data centers could now be filled with racks of cheap two-processor Intel boxes. What's more, they could provide availability and speed superior to those of million-dollar multiprocessor computers or giant mainframes.

The next version of the Oracle database—10g (the "g" stands for "grid")—which is likely to be released toward the end of 2003, will have an extension of clustering that will make it the computing equivalent of the electricity grid, automatically balancing loads, allocating resources, and scheduling jobs. Ellison says, "Oracle 10g is designed to run on a grid of 8 to 128 cheap Linux computers. Any application that runs on the Oracle database—SAP, PeopleSoft, Siebel—will run much faster and more reliably on the grid. The grid is Oracle's answer to high-performance, low-cost, fault-tolerant computing. Our Linux grid approach is the opposite of the 'one big computer' approach to high-performance computing invented by IBM a long time ago. Since neither IBM nor Microsoft can run a standard application like SAP on more than one database server computer, their only approach to high performance is to make that single-database computer as big as possible. IBM is very good at building software for big computers because they've been doing it since they invented the mainframe way back in 1964. What's mind-boggling is that Microsoft has just introduced software for their first mainframe—a very expensive thirty-two-processor Windows mainframe. Can you believe it? Microsoft reinvents the mainframe forty years after IBM. Bill is the king of 'innovation,' but this is something truly special. The master copiers are copying the wrong stuff. I think they meant to break into the IBM research lab, but they broke into the IBM museum by mistake." *

And from Oracle's point of view, Linux provided something else. For years, its nightmare had been that Windows would eventually be strong enough to inflict a slow death on UNIX. Although UNIX would continue, new database business would depend on running Oracle on top of the operating system of its most hated and dangerous rival. While Linux may never displace Windows from the desktop, there is now every chance it will stymie its assault on the corporate server market, considered crucial by Microsoft for both growth and computing influence.

---

*LE writes: Oracle is promoting grids of small, low-cost Linux servers while Microsoft is pushing expensive Windows mainframes. What a turn of events. It's like the plot in the Eddie Murphy movie Trading Places.

Chuck Rowzat, who runs Oracle's platform business, says that Microsoft has no good arguments to range against the cost and flexibility of Linux, and what's more, it is trying to argue against fashion, which, as Ellison concedes, is a very hard thing to do. "Linux," he says, "is the first thing that customers always ask about. They love it." Mark Jarvis says that Microsoft has no idea what to do because it has been caught up in a form of asymmetric warfare: "When they felt threatened by Netscape, it was just another company with a known HQ they could go out and bomb. But that won't work with Linux, just as it didn't work with Apache [the open-source Web server]. Apache creamed them, and so will Linux. Microsoft has lost the server war."

When Ellison announced RAC, there was widespread skepticism about his claims for it. But now it has impressive traction—in less than nine months to March 2003, the number of RAC users went from 210 to 1,864. Jeff Henley expects that very soon, more than half of the installed base will be running the clustering software. Henley says that customers now believe that even compared with Microsoft's SQL Server database, Oracle on Linux is now the low-cost option, as well as working much better. The Collaboration Suite has done something similar, giving Oracle a direct play against Microsoft with something that is not only far more capable but also a great deal cheaper. Keith Block says that more than twenty Fortune 500 companies are piloting the Collaboration Suite and that some large installations, such as 100,000 seats at Credit Suisse First Boston, are under way. Partly as a result of new regulatory requirements, firms are beginning to realize that their e-mails are as important a source of data as their accounts and that the right place to keep and manage them is inside the database.

If Oracle's strategy for taking on Microsoft is increasingly to win market share by imitating its rival's volume pricing model, it is also taking a leaf out of IBM's book with its outsourcing strategy. Ellison doesn't think much of Big Blue's software, but he has been forced to admit the power of its services organization: "I want us to imitate the one brilliant thing IBM has done over the last decade. They got more money from their huge installed base of mainframe customers by selling them a much broader range of services, including taking over and running their customers' data centers. We would like to sell outsourcing services to our fourteen thousand applications customers. We have hundreds of applications customers who are saving money using our outsourcing. We need to grow to thousands of outsourcing customers. It's a great new business for us, and the customer saves a lot of money. We buy the computers, back up their data, run their applications, and upgrade their software much more cheaply than they could ever do it themselves. It is simply a matter of finally applying specialization of labor and economies of scale to the running of computer systems." In other words: the information utility, Oracle style.

What excited Ellison was his conviction that the utility model played to all of Oracle's strengths. Although IBM was spending a fortune on a typically well crafted advertising campaign to popularize and get people thinking about the information utility, Ellison argued that IBM could never achieve the same-scale economies as Oracle because its model meant never building exactly the same data center twice. "IBM's approach to outsourcing is highly customized on a customer by customer basis. In comparison, our outsourcing has little to no software customization. We have a true low-cost, high-volume utility model. So once again, IBM has a great marketing campaign around something they don't do."

SAP would also be at a disadvantage: its software was less flexible than Oracle's; it was present in only one part of the "stack," whereas Oracle had all the pieces; and, compared with Oracle, it had only a tiny service organization. Both Oracle and SAP had targeted the relatively unpenetrated midmarket as the main driver of applications sales growth in coming years, but Ellison was now convinced that 99 percent of that market would opt for the utility approach that Oracle was best placed to deliver. With the "Oracle guarantee," Oracle would provide all a firm's computing needs for a fixed price. Keith Block reckoned that already 25 percent of new applications business was based around the "software as service" model. And what was Ellison's answer to the worried CIO who feared being put out of a job? "CIO stands for Chief *Information* Officer. CIOs should focus on providing people in their companies with the *information* they need to do their jobs better. Currently CIOs spend most of their time evaluating, buying, and assembling cool little technology components into expensive computer systems that don't work very well and provide precious little useful information to the people running the business."

So did Ellison believe that the race to be the dominant software firm of the twenty-first century was still Oracle's to lose? "Yes. We've had some significant screwups, but we've still managed to move far ahead of our competition in both database and applications. You don't have to be perfect, you just have to be better than the other guy. We're now far enough ahead to win. The Internet model of computing has given birth to the utility model of computing and software as a service. We couldn't be better positioned. Our fault-tolerant grids of Linux database servers provide the ideal low-cost, high-performance infrastructure for utility computing. Our applications outsourcing is one of the largest examples of software as a service in the industry. I know it won't be easy to catch Microsoft. They're more than three times bigger than we are, but they make their money on desktop computing—Windows and Office. They're nowhere in utility computing. SAP is nowhere in utility computing. IBM is advertising utility computing but delivering labor-intensive custom systems. So if utility computing is the future, then the future is ours. It took longer than I thought: Real Application Clusters and Database Grids; the E-Business Suite and Daily Business Intelligence. It always does. But it was worth the wait. Much longer road, much bigger payoff." In other words: victory not lost but postponed.

• • •

One consequence of stretching time horizons was that Ellison's idea that he might start to disengage himself little by little, devoting himself to biotech research, was very definitely on ice. Although he liked to think that he could do whatever in the world he wanted, the one thing he knew he couldn't do was walk away from Oracle until the last battle had been won or he no longer had anything left to contribute. Like most people who knew the company and the man, I found it almost impossible to imagine Oracle without Ellison or Ellison without Oracle.

Which was just as well, given that any arrangements for an orderly succession seemed to be as far in the future as ever. I agreed with Ellison that the "strong number two" and heir apparent whom everyone outside Oracle appeared to think so vital was irrelevant. Ellison was also right in saying that there was no shortage of management talent at Oracle. The ten or twelve most senior managers who made the place work would have had far less opportunity to develop if a "strong number two" had constantly been pressing down on them. And Ellison was lucky in having both Jeff Henley and Safra Catz to complement him in the leading "outside" and "inside" roles at Oracle. Catz, like some other fiercely intelligent women I have known, and quite unlike most men, had a degree of loyalty to her boss that transcended any personal agenda of her own. Henley was a straight arrow who was rich enough, old enough, and wise enough to tell Ellison the truth when he needed to hear it. He was also responsible for Oracle's having, without a doubt, the cleanest books in the high-technology business*—something Oracle gets insufficient credit for among the financial analyst community. He and Ellison were among the first corporate executives in America in the wake of the Enron scandal to file sworn statements with the Securities and Exchange Commission about the accuracy of their company accounts.

Ellison was very specific about the qualities his "dream candidate" would need to lead Oracle after him: "That person must be an engineering manager who's not only very good at building products; he or she must be very good at marketing and selling the products as well. But first and foremost, the person must be a good engineer. At its core, Oracle is a software engineering company, and we need to be run by a software engineer." What would be less important in the future was "visionary" leadership. Ellison continued to be certain that there would be no more major platform shifts in software that you either called right or died. "It's mainly going to be about execution—there aren't any more life-threatening technology revolutions ahead."

When pressed, Ellison was prepared to talk about only two of his managers who might turn out to have the necessary qualities. One was Thomas Kurian, an Indian in his mid-thirties who had arrived at Oracle in 1996 via Princeton, McKinsey, and Stanford. Kurian was intense and serious—a little dour, even, although Ellison assured me that he'd managed to make him laugh at least once. But Kurian, in only a few years, had achieved something remarkable and of incalculable strategic importance to Oracle: after its successive failures in building a competitive application server and the departure of those who had been responsible, Kurian had made Oracle, according to its own numbers, second only to the incumbent BEA in the application server market. As well as being a fast-growing and, in time, juicy new revenue earner, the application server was critical to Oracle's ambition to be the dominant enterprise software infrastructure provider committed to using open standards. Kurian had created a strong engineering team, driven it with a combination of discipline and pragmatism, produced a quality product, and then sold it with passion and energy to the outside world. When Ellison mentions Kurian, he can't help beaming. "Thomas has done a brilliant job, absolutely extraordinary," he says.

---

*LE writes: No question about it. Jeff Henley is the best CFO in the computer industry. The shareholders can rely on him, and so can I.

The other was forty-three-year-old John Wookey. Although Wookey had joined Oracle only in 1995, he had written much of Oracle's highly rated financial application. For the last three years he had been in charge of extending the capability of the E-Business Suite into a complete "solution" for the higher education and health care industries. After Ellison's welding of the two applications division into one organization, it was Wookey who had been given the tasks of fixing the defects in CRM and pushing the Daily Business Intelligence toward release (it is finally due to make its debut in November 2003 as part of 11i8). There was a lot riding on Wookey. Ellison said, "John was already managing all our medical applications and our student records systems, but Ron thought that we should give him the marketing and sales automation systems as well. That's quite a load, but John jumped right in and the progress has been amazing. John's an excellent engineering manager and leader; he's well respected throughout the company."

If either Kurian or Wookey turns out to have what it takes to do the top job at Oracle—and for all their ability, I'm not sure that either has a large enough personality even to begin to fill Ellison's boots—the second in command could well be Keith Block. In October 2002, Ellison promoted Block to be head of all of Oracle's sales and consulting operations in North America. Block came to Oracle in 1986 from Booz Allen Hamilton, Ray Lane's old firm. That is not something that Ellison holds against him. Block is now charged with finally delivering what Ellison hopes will be the death blow to the infamous cowboy sales culture that he has for so long despised. That was the job Lane was himself brought in to do more than a decade ago. But as Ellison put it to me, "I've thought a lot about what happened to Ray while he was at Oracle. I know he set out to change the Oracle sales force, but in the end, the Oracle sales force changed him. He began as their leader, but with the passage of time he became their spokesman, their advocate, and their defender." Block is hiring naturally service-oriented people from what used to be the Big Five consultancies to help drive cultural change through the sales organization. Ellison says, "All we need are highly intelligent people who have a deep understanding of how our products can solve our customers' automation and information management problems. That's it. The 'Go for the gold' culture of greed is distant history."

As ever, when it comes to sales, Ellison tends to oversimplification. The truth is that Oracle lost a lot of sales talent during the dot-com boom years, and it is only now being replaced. And while the days of the cowboy deal makers and their scorched-earth approach to selling have gone,

Oracle still needs more of the kind of salespeople who can call high in organizations and be listened to with respect. One reform that Block has introduced is to divide the sales force into technology and applications specialists. The spread of Oracle's technology offerings and the sweep of the E-Business Suite made it impossible for anyone to sell both with credibility. Block also points out that while technology requires what he calls a "transactional culture"—selling on features and performance—applications require a "consultative culture" in which, over time, you learn to match your products against a customer's business needs. The amazing thing is that it has taken Oracle so long to work this out.*

• • •

And what of Larry Ellison the man? Although much of my time with him coincided with a period of adversity for Oracle, other than during Oracle's two months of purgatory in Sacramento, I never once saw Ellison downcast. His unquenchable optimism and almost messianic self-belief never faltered, even when events occasionally conspired to make a fool of him. It is, of course, this aspect of Ellison that many people who either don't know him or know him only a little find most objectionable. For them, he is at best a bombastic showman; at worst, a false prophet and even a self-serving liar. Yet I am more convinced than I was at the beginning of my journey with him that Ellison is an extraordinary person, quite different from and infinitely more interesting than the caricature beloved of the media and even much of the analyst community. He's funny and entertaining but also highly serious, always interested in ideas and eager for new ones. Above all, Ellison is intense. Even when he's meant to be relaxing on one of his huge boats, there's a restlessness about him.

Much about Ellison is paradoxical, even contradictory. He's enormously vain, intellectually dominating, and irrepressibly extrovert. But he's also shy, has relatively few close friends, and is in constant need of the emotional reassurance that for much of his life has been lacking. He is determinedly youthful. But he is never far from thoughts of mortality. He detests vulgarity and yearns for simplicity and naturalness. But he also derives straightforward pleasure from owning hugely expensive ma-

---

*LE writes: For years I've pushed for separate specialized applications and technology sales forces. But until Keith, I couldn't convince a single one of our field sales executives to give it a try. My biggest mistakes don't result from pushing too hard; they result from not pushing hard enough.

terial status symbols. He desperately wants his wealth to do some good in the world. But such is his terror of being found a hypocrite that he recoils at the very idea of altruism. He lavishes praise on sometimes overpromoted subordinates in whom he places huge—at times excessive—trust. But he acts with ruthless dispatch toward anyone he feels has let him down professionally. He combines great sensitivity and empathy to the feelings of those around him with a capacity for sometimes childlike selfishness. He is ultraconfrontational in business. But he goes to almost any lengths to avoid confrontation at a personal level. He either delegates to the point of detachment or is obsessively controlling down to the last detail. He prides himself on never losing his temper. But he is manifestly driven by overwhelming passions. Ellison is nothing if not complicated.

About one thing, however, Ellison is relentlessly consistent: he sees life as a constant series of tests through which he can discover his limits. And when it fails to throw up enough of them, he goes looking for more.

AFTERWORD

On June 2, 2003, Larry Ellison rose to the news that PeopleSoft, the number three player in the business applications market, was buying J. D. Edwards, a smaller rival, for $1.7 billion. It wasn't entirely a shock. Oracle had itself been toying with the idea of buying J. D. Edwards for some time, and after declaring a loss in the previous quarter, the Denver-based company was now going cheap. Eager to get talks moving again, Safra Catz had left a long voice mail the previous week for J. D. Edwards's CFO, Rick Allen. But Allen hadn't returned her call. Ellison and Catz had always thought that PeopleSoft might try to snatch J. D. Edwards's from Oracle and they had already "gamed out" their response. At 7:40 A.M., Catz e-mailed her boss: "Time to move on psft." A minute later, Ellison replied: "Just what I was thinking."

Within 48 hours, Oracle had held two board meetings and hired Credit Suisse First Boston both to advise it and provide a $5 billion revolving credit facility. Two days later, Craig Conway, PeopleSoft's chief executive and a former Oracle salesman, was in Paris meeting customers when the news came through from New York that Larry Ellison had just announced a $5.1 billion all-cash bid for his company. Playing on the tradition that hostile bids in the software industry are almost unknown, an appalled Conway condemned the move as "atrociously bad behavior from a company with a history of atrociously bad behavior." According to Conway, his first thought—influenced by the stingy 6 percent premium Ellison was offering over the previous day's close—had been that it was a ploy to wreck his deal with J. D. Edwards. But Ellison wasn't just playing the spoilsport. He couldn't have been more serious.

Since the collapse of the tech boom Ellison had been talking about the need for consolidation in a maturing industry that had been left with an overhang of excess capacity. During those first conversations at the beginning of my journey with him more than two years earlier, he had forecast the imminent demise of the best-of-breed firms. The future, he had argued repeatedly, would belong to the suite vendors, and only Oracle and SAP were big and rich enough to survive in the harsh new climate for software. PeopleSoft claimed to be a suite player too, but, according to Ellison, it didn't have the scale or the development resources needed to match Oracle or SAP. What residual strength it had lay in the installed base of loyal customers using its market-leading human resources application. But with or without J. D. Edwards, which had more than enough problems of its own, PeopleSoft's prospects were poor. They were both, in Ellison's words, companies "in distress." By hastening an end to their misery, Ellison was simply putting his money where his always energetic mouth had been for quite some time.

Crucially, Ellison's bid for PeopleSoft didn't rely on winning over the firm's management or trying to integrate its product line with Oracle's. With characteristic disdain for the normal conventions, Ellison made it clear that what he had in mind for the well-liked Pleasanton-based company and its 13,000 staff was the corporate equivalent of euthanasia.* Oracle would provide enhanced maintenance to PeopleSoft's 11,000 customers, even keeping going older software that Conway had declared he would no longer support. If they wanted to move from their client/server systems, they could choose between the web-based People-Soft 8 or Oracle's E-Business Suite. Whichever they opted for, Ellison promised that the upgrade would be both "free" and "graceful." Over time, he expected that most PeopleSoft customers would either switch to Oracle or, if they were running SAP's financial application, to the German firm's suite. There would be jobs at Oracle for PeopleSoft's best developers, service engineers, and salespeople. A few years ago the talent would unquestionably have walked, but Ellison reckoned that in Silicon Valley's depressed labor market, few would turn down the offer to work for Oracle. Over time, PeopleSoft as a brand and an entity would wither away. Ellison observed: "I guess you could say I've become a corporate raider."

---

*LE writes: Actually, we'd be saving PeopleSoft and their customers. I don't think they can survive on their own.

From Oracle's point of view the deal made a lot of financial sense. Just taking over PeopleSoft's maintenance contracts would bring in additional revenues of $800 million a year. It was more difficult to calculate the value of migrating PeopleSoft's customers, most of whom already ran on Oracle's database, to the E-Business Suite, but there was no doubting the size of the opportunity. Ellison told me: "It's so fabulously accretive from the outset that I'm almost embarrassed to say." The same thought had also occurred to most Wall Street analysts, who were quick to pronounce that Ellison would have to raise his "low-ball" offer by at least 25 percent to win over PeopleSoft's mainly institutional stockholders.

As this book was going to press, that seemed the most likely outcome, and there was no doubt that Oracle could afford to pay more if necessary. But Ellison reckoned that people were overestimating the size of the premium needed to carry the day: "First of all, I don't think there are going to be any other bidders to push the price up. SAP benefits by doing nothing. IBM is like Switzerland—its business model is based on strict neutrality between vendors. Microsoft's strategy is to come into this market from the bottom up. There's nobody else. PeopleSoft's shareholders have got to decide whether they prefer our cash or Conway's very risky strategy of trying to put together two failing companies." He also argued that time was on Oracle's side. While Ellison was confident of announcing a great quarter later in June, PeopleSoft, having already seen software license sales fall by 39 percent in the previous three months, would be weakened further just because it was in play. Who would buy software from a company that probably wouldn't exist in a few months' time? Ellison e-mailed me: "We carefully thought this through and they didn't. Conway made a series of mistakes and now finds himself in an impossible position. Checkmate!"

Even with Oracle's bid for PeopleSoft still far from a done deal, its impact was already being felt: it was as if Ellison had lobbed a grenade into tech's stagnating pool. Suddenly, "consolidation" was an idea whose time had come. The crazy notion that soon there would be only the suites of Oracle and SAP fighting it out in the enterprise applications market now looked convincing enough to become almost the conventional wisdom of the industry analysts. Some predicted that Siebel might be next on Oracle's shopping list—a theory fueled by Ellison's mischievous revelation that Tom Siebel had visited him at home some months earlier to discuss a deal. A few analysts were even beginning to wonder how long IBM's love affair with the best-of-breed could be sustained. Most tellingly,

Accenture (the giant systems integration and consulting house that had always given Ellison the cold shoulder) had phoned to say how nice it would be to have a chat about forging closer relationships with Oracle. Two and a half years before, Ellison had told me that the prize was his to lose. That now seemed truer than ever.

INDEX

ABOUT THE AUTHOR

Matthew Symonds is currently political editor of *The Economist* and writer of the "Bagehot" column, but before that he was the magazine's technology and communications editor for nearly four years. He was also a founding editorial director of *The Independent* and has been strategy director of BBC Worldwide Television. Symonds lives in London with his wife and three children.